Subjectivity

ETHNOGRAPHIC STUDIES IN SUBJECTIVITY

Tanya Luhrmann and Steven Parish, Editors

Subjectivity

Ethnographic Investigations

Edited by

JOÃO BIEHL, BYRON GOOD, AND ARTHUR KLEINMAN

University of California Press

BERKELEY   LOS ANGELES   LONDON

University of California Press, one of the most distinguished university presses in the United States, enriches lives around the world by advancing scholarship in the humanities, social sciences, and natural sciences. Its activities are supported by the UC Press Foundation and by philanthropic contributions from individuals and institutions. For more information, visit www.ucpress.edu.

University of California Press
Berkeley and Los Angeles, California

University of California Press, Ltd.
London, England

Library of Congress Cataloging-in-Publication Data

Subjectivity : ethnographic investigations / edited by João Biehl, Byron Good, Arthur Kleinman.
    p.   cm. — (Ethnographic studies in subjectivity ; 7)
    Includes bibliographical references and index.
    ISBN 978-0-520-24792-5 (cloth : alk. paper) — ISBN 978-0-520-24793-2 (pbk. : alk. paper)
    1. Ethnology—Research.   2. Ethnology—Philosophy.   3. Subjectivity.   4. Ethnopsychology.   5. Medical anthropology.   I. Biehl, João Guilherme.   II. Good, Byron.   III. Kleinman, Arthur.

GN345.S83   2007
306—dc22   2006037482

Manufactured in the United States of America

16 15 14 13 12 11 10 09 08 07
10 9 8 7 6 5 4 3 2 1

This book is printed on Natures Book, which contains 50% postconsumer waste and meets the minimum requirements of ANSI/NISO Z39.48–1992 (R 1997) (Permanence of Paper).

Contents

Acknowledgments

This volume grew out of papers and discussions produced in the Harvard Medical Anthropology Program's Friday Morning Seminar. The Friday Morning Seminar is generously supported by a National Research Scientist Award from the National Institute of Mental Health (MH 18006). The coeditors thank the other faculty and fellows who helped organize the 1999–2001 seminars—Mary-Jo DelVecchio Good, Amaro Laria, and Sandra T. Hyde—and the presenters and participants in the seminars for their insightful contributions. We also thank members of Harvard's Departments of Anthropology and Social Medicine and members of the Program in Science, Technology, and Society at the Massachusetts Institute of Technology. We are grateful to Ian Whitmarsh, William Garriott, and Peter Locke for their invaluable help with research and writing, and to Margaret L. McCool, Linda Forman, Lindsay Smith, and Marilyn Goodrich for their assistance. Harvard's Michael Crichton Fund and Princeton's Committee on Research in the Humanities and Social Sciences supported the preparation of this volume. João Biehl is thankful for the support of the School of Historical Studies of the Institute for Advanced Study. We also thank the reviewers for the University of California Press for their constructive comments and Stan Holwitz and Tanya Luhrman for supporting this project.

Contributors

JOÃO BIEHL is Associate Professor in the Department of Anthropology at Princeton University. He is the author of *Vita: Life in a Zone of Social Abandonment* and *Will to Live: AIDS Therapies and the Politics of Survival.*

ELLEN CORIN is a Researcher at the Douglas Hospital Research Centre and Associate Professor in the Departments of Psychiatry and Anthropology at McGill University. She is also a practicing psychoanalyst. She is the coeditor of *Beyond Textuality: Asceticism and Violence in Anthropological Interpretation* and has edited several issues of *Anthropologie et Société.* Her work has appeared in several edited volumes and in journals like *Culture, Medicine and Psychiatry; Psychiatry; Transcultural Psychiatry;* and *Journal of Phenomenological Psychology.*

RANENDRA K. DAS is Associate Research Scientist at Johns Hopkins University and a retired Professor of Economics at the Delhi School of Economics. He is the author of *Optimal Economic Planning* and coauthor of *Basic Statistics.*

VEENA DAS is Krieger-Eisenhower Professor of Anthropology and Professor of Humanities at Johns Hopkins University. She is the author of *Structure and Cognition: Aspects of Hindu Caste and Ritual; Mirrors of Violence: Communities, Riots, and Survivors in South Asia; Critical Events: An Anthropological Perspective on Contemporary India;* and *Life and Words: Violence and the Descent into the Ordinary.* She is the editor of *The Word and the World: Fantasy Symbol and Record,* and coeditor of *Social Suffering; Violence and Subjectivity; Remaking a World; Social Science and Immunization;* and *Anthropology in the Margins of the State.*

MICHAEL M. J. FISCHER is Professor in the Graduate Program in History, Anthropology and Science, Technology and Society (HASTS), the Program in Science, Technology and Society (STS) and the Program in Anthropology at MIT, and Lecturer in the Department of Social Medicine at the Harvard Medical School. He is the author of *Iran: From Religious Dispute to Revolution; An-*

thropology as Cultural Critique (with George Marcus); Debating Muslims (with Mehdi Abedi); Emergent Forms of Life and the Anthropological Voice; and Mute Dreams, Blind Owls, and Dispersed Knowledges: Persian Poesis in the Transnational Circuitry.

ERIN FITZ-HENRY is a graduate student in the Department of Anthropology at Princeton University. She is doing fieldwork in Ecuador.

BYRON GOOD is Professor of Medical Anthropology in the Department of Social Medicine of the Harvard Medical School and in the Department of Anthropology at Harvard University. He is the author of Medicine, Rationality, and Experience: An Anthropological Perspective, and coeditor of Culture and Depression, Pain as Human Experience; Clifford Geertz by His Colleagues; Clinical Hermeneutics (in Italian); and Postcolonial Disorders. He was co–Editor in Chief of Culture, Medicine and Psychiatry from 1986 to 2004.

MARY-JO DELVECCHIO GOOD is Professor of Social Medicine in the Department of Social Medicine at the Harvard Medical School and in the Department of Sociology at Harvard University. She is the author of American Medicine: The Quest for Competence and coeditor of Pain as Human Experience, The Politics of Science: Culture, Race, Ethnicity and the Surgeon General's Supplement on Mental Health; Clinical Hermeneutics (in Italian), Postcolonial Disorders. She was co–Editor in Chief of Culture, Medicine and Psychiatry from 1986 to 2005.

STEPHEN GREENBLATT is Cogan University Professor of the Humanities at Harvard University. He is the author of Marvelous Possessions; Learning to Curse; Shakespearean Negotiations; Renaissance Self-Fashioning; Hamlet in Purgatory; Practicing New Historicism (with Catherine Gallagher); and Will in the World: How Shakespeare Became Shakespeare. He is also coeditor of The Touch of the Real and The Greenblatt Reader.

EVELYN FOX KELLER is Professor of the History and Philosophy of Science in the Program in Science, Technology, and Society at MIT. She is the author of A Feeling for the Organism: The Life and Work of Barbara McClintock; Reflections on Gender and Science; Secrets of Life, Secrets of Death: Essays on Language, Gender and Science; Refiguring Life; Keywords in Evolutionary Biology (with Elisabeth A. Lloyd); The Century of the Gene; and Making Sense of Life: Explaining Biological Development with Models, Metaphors, and Machines.

ARTHUR KLEINMAN is Esther and Sidney Rabb Professor of Anthropology and Chair of the Department of Anthropology at Harvard University. He is also Professor of Psychiatry and Medical Anthropology at the Harvard Medical School. He is the author of Patients and Healers in the Context of Culture; The Illness Narratives; Rethinking Psychiatry; Social Origins of Distress and Disease; Writing at the Margin: Discourse between Anthropology and Medicine; and What Really Matters: Living a Moral Life amidst Uncertainty and Danger. Among his coedited volumes are Culture and Depression; Pain as Human Experience; Advancing Health in Developing Countries; Social Suffering; Violence *and Subjectivity; Remaking a World; SARS in China;* and *Global Pharmaceuticals.*

ERIC L. KRAKAUER is a physician in the Palliative Care Service at Massachusetts General Hospital and an Instructor in the Departments of Social Medicine and Medicine at Harvard Medical School. He is the author of *The Disposition of the Subject: Reading Adorno's Dialectic of Technology.*

ANNE M. LOVELL is a medical anthropologist and Senior Research Scientist at the French National Institute of Health and Medical Research (INSERM). She is the coauthor of *The Psychiatric Society.* She is also the editor of *Santé Mentale et Société,* and coeditor of *La santé mentale en mutation,* and *Psychiatry Inside Out: Selected Writings of Franco Basaglia.*

PAUL RABINOW is Professor of Anthropology at the University of California, Berkeley. He is the author of *Symbolic Domination: Cultural Form and Historical Change in Morocco; Reflections on Fieldwork in Morocco;* French Modern: Norms and Forms of the Social Environment; Michel Foucault: Beyond Structuralism and Hermeneutics (with Hubert L. Dreyfus); *Making PCR: A Story of Biotechnology; Essays on the Anthropology of Reason; French DNA: Trouble in Purgatory; Anthropos Today: Reflections on Modern Equipment;* and *A Machine to Make a Future: Biotech Chronicles* (with Talia Dan-Cohen). Among his edited volumes are *The Foucault Reader* and *The Essential Works of Michel Foucault.*

AMÉLIE OKSENBERG RORTY is Visiting Professor in the Committee for Degrees in Social Studies of Harvard University and Honorary Lecturer on Social Medicine at the Harvard Medical School. She is the author of *Mind in Action.* Among her edited volumes are *The Many Faces of Evil; The Many Faces of Philosophy: Meditations and Reflections; Philosophers on Education: Historical Perspectives; Essays on Aristotle's Ethics; Essays on Descartes' Meditations; The Identities of Persons; Perspectives on Self-Deception;* and *Explaining Emotions.*

NANCY SCHEPER-HUGHES is Professor of Anthropology at the University of California, Berkeley. She is the author of *Saints, Scholars, and Schizophrenics: Mental Illness in Rural Ireland* and *Death without Weeping: The Violence of Everyday Life in Brazil.* She is the coeditor of *Psychiatry Inside Out: Selected Writings of Franco Basaglia; Small Wars: The Cultural Politics of Childhood; Commodifying Bodies;* and *Violence in War and Peace.* Her next book is *Parts Unknown: The Global Traffic in Organs.* She is the founding director of Organs Watch.

SUBANDI is a Lecturer in the Faculty of Psychology of the University of Gadjah Mada, Indonesia.

ALLAN YOUNG is Professor of Anthropology in the Departments of Social Studies of Medicine, Anthropology, and Psychiatry at McGill University. He is the author of *The Harmony of Illusions: Inventing Posttraumatic Stress Disorder* and co-editor of *Paths to Asian Medical Knowledge*

Introduction:
Rethinking Subjectivity

JOÃO BIEHL, BYRON GOOD, AND ARTHUR KLEINMAN

This book is an extended conversation about contemporary forms of human experience and subjectivity. It examines the genealogy of what we consider to be the modern subject, and it inquires into the continuity and diversity of personhood across greatly diverse societies, including the ways in which inner processes are reshaped amid economic and political reforms, violence, and social suffering. It is an ethnographic conversation, with authors confronting specific forms of social life in particular settings, and it is a theoretical conversation, exploring the debates and disciplinary disagreements about how we think and write about human agency today.

The writings in this book suggest that contemporary social formations, with their particular ways of being and the theoretical frames available for analyzing them, have destabilized our observation, thinking, and writing about subjectivity. In editing this collection, we have sought to show the multiple ways in which scholars address the diverse phenomena we call *subject* and *subjectivity*. Striving for a single analytic strategy would have been limiting and premature at best. This volume is thus exploratory, aiming to provide new directions for studies of subjectivity and intersubjectivity in today's distinctive conditions.

In the many settings in which anthropologists now work, the vagaries of modern life are undoing and remaking people's lives in new and ominous ways. The subjects of our study struggle with the possibilities and dangers of economic globalization, the threat of endless violence and insecurity, and the new infrastructures and forms of political domination and resistance that lie in the shadows of grand claims of democratization and reform. Once the door to the study of subjectivity is open, anthropology and its practitioners must find new ways to engage particularities of affect, cognition, moral responsibility, and action.

1

REGARDING OTHERS

Examples of remaking subjectivity are everywhere. "Amid China's Boom, No Helping Hand for Young Qingming," reads the front page of the *New York Times* of August 1, 2004. Fearful of being left behind in China's fast-paced but deeply uneven economic boom, Zheng Qingming threw himself under an approaching train in his rural village on June 4. That day, Qingming had learned from a school administrator that he would not be allowed to take the annual college-entrance examination. "I don't have the money," he had said. "I don't care if you sell a life," the supervisor had replied. One of Qingming's friends reportedly offered to sell blood to help him out.

Without the needed eighty dollars and with his hopes of a college education and mobility cut short, Qingming fled the school and spent the day wandering through the village. Strangers who saw him that day said that Qingming had talked about working for Interpol—a fact the authorities used to justify their claim that the young man had "lost his mind." A mental condition (possibly traceable to the "mentally retarded" relatives who adopted and helped raise him) thus became the official explanation for this young man's profoundly willful act of ending his life.

To the grandfather who is now suing the school, the boy he had raised to be a healthy and hard-working man was "upset, not insane." A scrapbook the grandfather now keeps as a memorial gives some insight into this young man's subjectivity and his response to the vanishing of familiar values. Qingming had pasted in a magazine article about a farm girl who had been raped and then abandoned by her relatives for the shame she inflicted on them. In the margins of the text, Qingming had scribbled, "We must extend our helping hand to any innocent underdog. Only by so doing can that person find a footing in society."

Chinese society is undergoing immense change. From a poor agricultural society beset with political chaos, China has, over a twenty-year period, become the world's third-largest economy with an established, if undemocratic, social order. But China's turn to capitalism has delegitimated the still-dominant Communist ideology just as radical Maoism undermined Chinese cultural traditions. The upshot is a culture of self-interest, rank materialism, and growing cynicism that has prompted widespread comment and criticism among the Chinese themselves. In the economy, health-care sector, social-welfare programs, and everyday lived experience of peasants and urbanites, the public emphasis on social solidarity and the righting of historical social inequalities to help the poor and the marginalized have given way to gated communities, deepening health inequalities, and a symbolic distance between rural and urban realities that harks back to the 1930s, if not the final decades of the Qing dynasty. A bitter joke is making the rounds in Beijing: "What is the definition of Communism?" Answer: "The longest and most painful road to capitalism."

In this setting, side by side with an improvement in infant mortality and adult mortality, China has seen the emergence or escalation of social-health and mental health problems, from substance abuse and sexually transmitted diseases to violence, AIDS, depression, and suicide. Suicide in Chinese society has always been associated with public and domestic injustice, so much so that many people at the margins see it as an acceptable way of coping with failure and hopelessness. Thus, to understand the suicide of Zheng Qingming, we need to see the act as rooted in a particular constellation that connects cultural representations and political economy with collective experience and the individual's subjectivity.

Suicide as social protest and resistance is a historical reality among Chinese. Only under the impress of the current phase of globalization is it beginning to be reinterpreted as the result of a mental disorder (usually depression but also any mental condition). That change comes from the infiltration of technical psychiatric categories from North America, biomedical practices, and the media into the daily affairs of the Chinese. A tragic irony exists, however, inasmuch as the mentally ill in China carry a deep stigma that marks them as not fully human and thus, among other things, not capable of rational suicide. Hence, in Zheng Qingming's suicide we see three aspects of subjectivity that illustrate differences across time and cultural spaces: historically situated differences in social sensibility and what it means to feel and regard oneself as human; cross-cultural differences in cognition, affect, and action; and the peculiarities of each individual.

For the purpose of this book, we need to see the increasing medicalization of depression and suicide not only as the state's response to a perceived new public-health crisis but potentially also as the spread of a form of diffused governance that substitutes everyday commonsense categories and practices for rational and technical ones so as to vitiate the moral and political meaning of subjective complaints and protests (chapters 2 and 6 in this volume). This form of self-governance—new to the modern Chinese state but well established in the West—is linked to the unmaking of time-honored value systems and occasions novel forms of control (Anagnost 1997; Lee 1999; Yan 2003). Subjectivity thus becomes the ground on which a long series of historical changes and moral apparatuses coalesce—in the emergence of new kinds of public-private involvements as well as a new kind of political authority. The unintended consequences of this process of societal and personal transformation may include the creation of hyper-individualism, which itself intensifies attention to human rights and, in turn, places new pressure on the nondemocratic state. Equally unintended may be the remaking of the habitual inner sense of endurance and the creation of new forms of desire that go beyond commercial interests to structure alternative ways of feeling and living, that change the world.

· · ·

In her essay "Regarding the Torture of Others" in the *New York Times Magazine* (May 23, 2004), the late Susan Sontag writes that the horror of the Abu Ghraib photographs "cannot be separated from the horror that the photographs were taken—with the perpetrators posing, gloating, over their helpless captives" (26). Sontag angrily condemns the Bush administration's attempts to displace the complex crimes of leadership and policy that the images reveal, first onto the photographs themselves—"as if the fault or horror lay in the images, not in what they depict" (25)—and then onto the individuals who carried them out, as if those actions were not representative of a reigning rationality and modus operandi. "The issue is not whether a majority or minority of Americans perform such acts but whether the nature of the policies prosecuted by this administration and the hierarchies deployed to carry them out makes such acts likely. Considered in this light, the photographs are us" (26).

Sontag compares the Abu Ghraib photographs to those of black victims of lynching during the 1880s and up through the 1930s—"souvenirs of a collective action whose participants felt perfectly justified in what they had done" (27). The Abu Ghraib photographs mark a shift in the use of pictures though: "less objects to be saved than messages to be disseminated, circulated. . . . There is more and more recording of what people do, by themselves" (27). For Sontag, this mass-type Internet-emulated subjectivity is captured by the statement, "If life isn't edited, why should its record be?"

These photographs, one could also argue, mark a shift in the ways people publicly organize their subjectivities vis-à-vis the suffering of others. The Abu Ghraib artifacts expose the range of moral sensibility operating in the interstices of political and legal domains. The images thus materialize a "culture of shamelessness" and the "reigning admiration for unapologetic brutality" (29). The pictures will not go away—but will be further covered-up by our "infinite digital self-reproduction and self-dissemination," writes Sontag (42). At stake here are no longer processes of memorialization or forgetfulness but rather the normalization of the Other's dehumanization and the creation of a moral complicity that destabilizes public discussion, making clarification and eventual resolution ever more unattainable.

• • •

This volume offers an interdisciplinary exploration of the inner lives of subjects. It also examines the interconnections among changing modes of subjectivation and transformations of social organization, modes of production, knowledge structures, and symbolic forms. The writers in this book treat subjectivity as both an empirical reality and an analytic category: the agonistic and practical activity of engaging identity and fate, patterned and felt in historically contingent settings and mediated by institutional processes and cultural forms. The book explores the ideas that subjectivity constitutes the material and the means of contemporary value systems and that capital accumulation and governance occur through the remaking of culture as well as the inner transformations of the human subject. The essays probe the nature and reach of these interior processes and new value systems.

The study of individual subjectivity as both a strategy of existence and a material and means of governance helps to recast assumptions about the workings of collectivities and institutions. Refracted through potent political, technological, psychological, and linguistic registers, inner life processes capture the violence and dynamism of everyday life. By attending to subjectivity in ethnographic terms and in comparative social analysis, we encounter the concrete constellations in which people forge and foreclose their lives around what is most at stake. Examination of the complex ways in which people's inner states reflect lived experience within everyday worlds as well as within temporary spaces and transitions—moments of crisis and states of exception—can disturb and enlarge presumed understandings of what is socially possible and desirable. What is life for? What is an adequate life? Such study also helps us understand what psychological processes are about.

THE ANTHROPOLOGY OF SUBJECTIVITY

Even a cursory review of the etymology of the term *subjectivity* brings into view multiple historical processes and modifications of subjective form and sense. In the nineteenth century, *subjectivity* referred to an essential individuality, the consciousness of one's perceived states. This exclusive emphasis on the human mind or individual experience also implied a kind of affective domination, in which feelings, thoughts, concerns, and perceptions, all supposedly personal, overcome individuals and "cloud the eyes" (according to the *Oxford English Dictionary* of the day). One can argue that this modern quality of defining subjective facts or things existing only in the mind (experienced affectively or symptomatically) is the counterpart to the relentless encroachment of scientific worldviews and things, "the objective" and the objectification of reality (Daston and Galison 1992).

Modern subjectivity, however, also suggests the cultivation of a mode of being that finds its highest realization in art—"the individuality of an artist as expressed in his work." In contrast to objectivity, in this sense, subjectivity does not imply an error but connotes creativity, the possibility of a subject's adopting a distinctive symbolic relation to the world in order to understand lived experience, as in poetry (Milosz 2004):

> When will that shore appear from which at last we see
> How all this came to pass and for what reason?

The current understanding of subjectivity as a synonym for inner life processes and affective states is of relatively recent origin. Earlier etymologies of the subjective do not speak in such radically individual terms. The twelfth-century *suget* (subject) is "the one who is under the dominion of a monarch or reigning prince; one who owes allegiance to a government or ruling power, is subject to its laws, and enjoys its protection." The fifteenth-century Latin *subjectivus* (to be subjective) is first a characteristic of the political subject. Only a few centuries later would one speak of subjective alterations in persons, of subjective and thus peculiar sentiments, and of a subjective certainty of the truth, of knowledge as distinct from "beliefs" (B. Good 1994: ch. 1).

In classic Greek, the term *hupokeimenon* referred to the subject of attributes and the subject of predicates, but, for Aristotle, the subject was also "the very material out of which things are made" (see chapter 1 of this volume). These simple observations lead us to ask about the legal, religious, medicoscientific and social mechanisms, writ large, through which political domination has migrated into and become an invisible and constitutive part of modern subjectivity. What literally goes into making a human subject? What are the limits of the subject? And how do creative subjective leaps occur (Greenblatt 2004)?

. . .

In examining subjectivity today, we are forced to rethink older formulations and problematics associated with human nature, social control, agency— and culture. Clifford Geertz, in uniting psychological with cultural themes in the Harvard Social Relations Department's tradition in which he was trained, famously articulated a cultural approach to subjectivity and a subjectivity-oriented theory (Ortner 2004; Shweder and Good 2004). He did so at a time, from the 1950s to the 1970s, when the British tradition of social anthropology banished the subject and when French debates focused on subjectivity's dependence on language (Lévi-Strauss and Lacan), the materiality of discourses and epistemic thresholds (Foucault), or the innate dispositions governing social action (Bourdieu).

For Geertz (1973, 1983; Good and Good 2004), subjects embody culture, not in the simplistic fashion posited by the culture and personality school, but in the sense that people live in a distinct phenomenal world—spirits here, mystical powers there, particular categories of kin in each—and have access to that world through a set of embodied practices (Javanese meditation, Balinese dance, or simply activities associated with growing up in a Balinese household). They encounter realities that "clothe those conceptions with . . . an aura of factuality." Culture shapes "the behavioral environment," as well as the selves who inhabit that environment; the moods and motivations that are part of these selves are not limited to the religious perspective but carry over into the everyday, commonsense world. Anthropology, from this perspective, understands subjective life by analyzing the symbolic forms—words, images, institutions, behaviors—through which people actually represent themselves to themselves and to one another.

But critical appraisals of the Geertzian legacy of cultural analysis—even by Geertz himself (2000, 2005)—have produced a growing consensus within anthropology that conceiving culture as a sui generis symbolic domain is hazardous. Whereas some anthropologists have called for the outright elimination of culture from the analytic lexicon (Lutz and Abu-Lughod 1990), others have insisted on its continued relevance.[1] Maintaining the importance of subjectivity in social life, these anthropologists have rethought culture, seeing it as emerging from institutional and intersubjective interactions and as an evolving phenomenon, constantly remade through social encounters, ethical deliberations, political processes—and writing (Boon 1982; Clifford and Marcus 1986; Fischer 2003; B. Good 1994; Marcus and Fischer 1985; Ortner 1999; Rabinow 1978; Rosaldo 1989; Stoler 1995; Taussig 1986; Tsing 1993).

There is no culture, and all we do is cultural, writes Michael M. J. Fischer: "Culture is not a variable; culture is relational, it is elsewhere, it is in passage, it is where meaning is woven and renewed often through gaps and silences, and forces beyond the conscious control of individuals, and yet the space where individual and institutional social responsibility and ethical struggle take place" (2003: 7). This formulation suggests the need for cultural analyses that make visible differences of interests, access, power, needs, desires, and philosophical perspectives. The writers in this book suggest that ethnographic practices and theories that link investigations of symbolic forms with studies of the lives of individuals can provide such analyses.

Who empirically is the agent of this making and remaking of culture? How is this process mediated by individual lives? What do psychological structures and modes of experience contribute to the work of culture? And how do modes of subjectivity intertwine with particular configurations of political, economic, and medical institutions? In other words, how, under quite new conditions, do people value life and relationships and "enact the possibilities they envision" (Rosen 2003: x) for themselves and for others?

EVERYDAY REFLEXIVITY

In a "world in pieces" (Geertz 2000), older notions of the subject who is cultural "all the way down" seem inadequate. Moreover, "the body" has reemerged in anthropological analysis much as Mauss and, later, Bourdieu conceived it, as a privileged heuristic to historical and social processes, thus extending cultural phenomenology to political subjectivity. The presumed subject of humanist theorizing has been deconstructed by poststructuralist, postcolonial, and feminist writers and shown to be a product of Enlightenment, colonial, and racialized and gendered discourses rather than a foundational reality for investigation. Ethnographic studies (such as Bourgois 2002; Comaroff 1985; Comaroff and Comaroff 1992; Csordas 1994; M-J Good 1998; Kleinman 1999; Lock 1993, 2002; Martin 1994; Scheper-Hughes 1992; Young 1995) have, using varying methodologies, shown how medico-scientific formations, political economy, and social networks are mediated by the body and the sense of psychological interiority. These studies go beyond mentalist reductionism and convey a key understanding of the self as corporeal, with the body as part and parcel of technical, political, and social processes. The "mindful body" (Hahn and Kleinman 1983; Scheper-Hughes and Lock 1987) has become an important part of our understanding of the person in diverse, but always specific, times and places.

By drawing attention to the importance of somatic processes for social life, anthropological studies of the body have cast light on some of the blind spots of a strictly symbolic approach. They have greatly helped to reveal human and institutional interconnectedness and to generalize ethnographic findings. Yet by treating the body as a privileged heuristic to reality, such studies have, at times, also produced a one-dimensional picture of individuals, as if they were a socially entrained physiology (that is, as if they were fundamentally determined, "all the way down," by traceable forms of control and discipline). Not surprisingly, debates on subjectivity that begin with this assumption often center on questions of domination, resistance, normalization, and social identity.

Essays in this volume build on the anthropology of the body literature and probe the extent to which market logics, institutional norms, and rational-technical interventions actually define the relationship between body and subjectivity. In chapter 3, for example, Das and Das chart the emergence of "local ecologies of care" by tracing the itineraries that the ill follow in their search for therapeutic attention in poor, urban contexts in India. Rather than looking for subjectivity in the embodied experience of illness or healing, Das and Das reveal the dynamic density of the interpersonal ties that become the contours of the sick person's local world and experience (see also chapter 7 in this volume). In this way, people come close to James Boon's "everyday reflexivity (regardless of culture)," disrupting the "comfortably consolidated transdisciplinary theme ('You-Name-It-Of-The-Body')" (1999: 263–65).

A "descent into the ordinary" (Das 1998) of often broken and fractured places has made necessary a rethinking of the terms of anthropological inquiry (see chapter 4 of this volume as well as Greenhouse, Mertz, and Warren 2002).[2] As Geertz has written, "In a splintered world, we must address the splinters" (2000: 221). Drawing from Michel Foucault's work on biopower, contemporary studies have turned attention to the centrality of error in (modern) life, charting the emergence of "mutant ecologies" (Masco 2004) and "biological forms of citizenship" (Petryna 2002), in the wake of technological disasters, for example. Studies of media and medical technologies have shown the truly prosthetic quality of such technologies as people deploy them to refigure capacities and value (Biehl 2001a; Cohen 1998; Rabinow and Dan-Cohen 2005; Rapp 1999; see also chapters 6, 12, and 13 in this volume). The body—real or imagined, living or dead, present or hypothetical—can mobilize scientific communities and patient populations in equal measure around quests for profits, knowledge, justice, or simply the will to live (see chapters 11 and 14).

In short, several anthropologists in this volume address the unfinished quality of the body, the surpluses and inadequacies that emerge through the demands made on it. Whether these demands come from institutions, discourses and disciplinary practices, or the subject's own desires and needs, the body, from the perspective of subjectivity, is always more and less than what it seems it should be. Thus, one continually learns and relearns to live *with* as much as *through* one's body, in its various states of health and illness, youth and old age, boredom and trauma, routine and instability.

EMERGENT VALUE SYSTEMS

By and large, contemporary anthropological writing considers the subject and subjectivity not as original forms but as dynamically formed and transformed entities (Borneman 1992, 2001; Cohen 1998, 1999; Collier 1997; Crapanzano 1980; Das 1997, 2000; Desjarlais 1997, 2003; Fischer 2003; Hammoudi 1997, 2006; Herzfeld 1996; Luhrman 2000; Pandolfo 1998, 2000; Turkle 1997). These insights reflect both altered theoretical sensibilities and changes in the world in which anthropologists do their research and in the personal lives of their informants. Awareness is growing that the kinds of social forms traditionally analyzed by anthropologists and thoroughly critiqued by Michel Foucault and Pierre Bourdieu—the family, village, school, sex and gender, labor and scientific practices, health-care systems—can no longer be the foundation for tracing and specifying delimited "identities" and "subject positions." Arjun Appadurai, for example, argued a decade ago that the twin engines of media and migration have so accelerated transnational processes of globalization that, under the aegis of the imagination, the "quickened beat of improvisation" stands to outrun the habitus's "glacial force" (1996: 6).

New information and life technologies enable new types of networks and allow people to imagine and articulate different destinies. Stable or imagined environments (such as nations and communities) are being transformed or displaced by ecological disasters, ethnic conflicts, free-trade economics, developments in the global pharmaceutical industry, terrorism, and war (Fassin 2005; Fassin and Vasquez 2005; Fortun 2001; Greenhouse, Mertz, and Warren 2002; Le Marcis 2004; Petryna 2002; Petryna, Lakoff, and Kleinman 2006; Redfield 2005; Tsing 2005). Anthropologists thus investigate subjectivity in contemporary settings of economic crisis, state violence, exploited migrant communities, massive displacements, hegemonic gender politics, and postcolonial states—settings increasingly familiar to them, though hardly new to the people under study. Research is showing that only through explicating the logic of key emotional and intersubjective constructs do major social dramas become intelligible; likewise, only amid such contemporary social enactments can we understand particular domains of affect and agency.

In the domain of health and medicine, not only are the raw effects of economic and social inequalities ever more devastating, but subtler and more hidden processes of reconstituting subjectivity are increasingly common-place. In their work on the global trade of human organs for transplantation, for example, Scheper-Hughes (2003) and Cohen (1999) reveal a new moral economy based on devastating global processes that revalue human beings as commodities and in so doing recast the self as market mechanism (as strategizer, broker, buyer). This economy normalizes selfishness and cyni-cism and pushes hyperindividuality to its autistic limits. At the same time, it recasts the real dangers of social life in the mode of a putative risk soci-ety, in which the person, supposedly in a state of anxiety, appraises and as-signs valuation to isolatable "risks" such as loss of employment, marriage, the death of a spouse, and other traumatic events that go to the very core of what it means to be human. Self is hollowed out, and society is reduced to a conventional middle-class vision in which individual threats are removed from local worlds, to be managed by drugs and other new technologies of the person.

Meanwhile, such a society denies systemic loss and normalizes insecu-rity, which becomes the basis for new states of exception, both social and personal. The rueful, the elegiac, that which is lamentably unchangeable in living—essentially, the moral core of experience—is replaced by the pro-gressivist myth that one can find magic bullets to solve life. Zones of aban-donment (Biehl 2005) absorb the people whose resources cannot sustain them, and the middle-class scene is sustained at the cost of loss, alienation, and deepening inequality that divides selves into separate classes of danger. In this scenario, we see the demoralization of everyday experience via sci-entific categories such as depression and post-traumatic stress disorder (see chapter 6) that remake people as objects of technological manipulation with-out allowing for the possibility of remorse, regret, or repentance.

An anthropology of illness and suffering confronts everyday settings of political violence, dislocation, and social trauma. Theorization of hegemonic states alternates with theorization of the dissolution of institutions—a world of "exceptions" and "camps" in Giorgio Agamben's terms (1998, 1999; see also Mbembe 2003)—and reflection of the forms of subjectivity emerging in underground economies and inhumane settings (Biehl 2005; Das and Poole 2004; Roitman 2005). Even when violence has lapsed, the memory of violence permeates the subjective experience of any number of people around the world. The work of memory and memorialization, as much as the work of repression and forgetting, has become central to an-thropology, requiring analytic stances that are at once personal and inter-subjective and that account for political processes and emergent, if fleeting, forms of care (Aretxaga 1997; Borneman 1997, 2002; Caruth, 1996; Daniel

1994, 1997; Das 1996, 1997; Povinelli 2002). Medical anthropology and an anthropology of social suffering are at the heart of this enterprise (Das and Kleinman 2000; Kleinman, Das, and Lock 1997) and are thus a critical part of anthropology.

Perhaps the "long littleness," to use Philip Larkin's (1983) term, of an individual's modernized self in the contemporary West also calls forth new ways of defining the projects of being human. Perhaps the very pretensions and formulations of the term *subjectivity* are pufferies that seek to disguise the anxiety of having to make meanings seem authoritative and convincing despite the fact that they have already lost their special forms of authority. Rather than soothing collective anxiety, the human sciences are challenged to reinstate the uncertainty and angst that life holds when it is actually lived rather than merely studied and theorized (Hammoudi 2006; Obeyesekere 1990; Rosaldo 1989). Perhaps this task is what ethnography, social history, and psychotherapy do best.

SELF-CRITICISM AND RENEWAL

This book grew out of papers and conversations in the Friday Morning Seminar of Harvard's Medical Anthropology Program. The program bridges the Departments of Social Medicine and Anthropology. Since 1984, faculty and fellows have organized this seminar, which focuses broadly on issues of culture and mental health. The 1999–2001 Seminar brought together anthropologists, historians, literary critics, and medical professionals to investigate subjectivity in the context of current political, economic, medical, and social developments. Our goal was to explore emergent patterns of self-formation and to comprehend how inner life and its relationship to values is changing; how will, thinking, and judgment are evolving in specific settings; how these transformations affect suffering and our responses to it; and what mental health and mental health care mean in this context.

The seminar started with the premise that after nearly three decades of research and writing in medical and psychiatric anthropology, little consensus exists about the relevance of diverse theories of subjectivity to our understanding of the transformative effects of illness experience, social suffering, and medical institutions and practices in the contemporary world. But if ethnographers often fail to engage relevant theorists, crucial ethnographic and cross-cultural studies have even more rarely been taken up by philosophers, literary critics, feminist scholars, and other theorists writing about subjectivity. The absence of serious engagements across these fields, we believe, has been to the detriment of theorizing subjectivity and studying it ethnographically.

For example, as Evelyn Fox Keller points out in chapter 11, poststructuralist analyses that have focused on the subject and subjectivity rather than on the self and experience have suggested that "subjects are epiphenomena, constructed by culturally specific discursive regimes (marked by race, gender, sexual orientation, and so on), and subjectivity itself is more properly viewed as the consequence of actions, behavior, or 'performativity' than as their source. . . . Selves are multiple and fractured rather than unitary, mobile rather than stable, porous rather than enclosed, externally constituted rather than internal or 'inner' natural essences." But this set of dichotomies is equally problematic, substituting a new set of images of the subject, opening space for certain analyses, and closing others. Framing analyses in these terms too often replaces studies of individual lives, diverse forms of intersubjectivity, and political consciousness and affects with studies of discourses and representations, generating not only oversocialized images of human life but also tending to make subjectivity less central than social structure.

Theories of subjectivity are too often overstated, obscure, and even dehumanizing. People who are subject to the most profound human experiences—suffering massive violence and incomprehensible cruelty, the routine degradation of poverty and despair, the terrors of madness and life-threatening disease, or even facing the impossible dilemmas of providing care, whether surrounded by the highest technologies or the near total absence of resources—have too often been transformed into remote abstractions, discursive forms, or subject positions. They become the objects of self-interested professional and disciplinary quarrels and abstractions. Agonistic and open-ended engagements with members of other societies are often largely absent from theorization of the subject, even in writings that address postcolonial subjects and cultural difference.

Writing about illness experience has often had a generalist quality, as though common humanity and cultural understanding, along with recognition of political oppression and global inequalities, are adequate bases for analysis. Social science and humanistic writing too often fails to account for central theoretical concerns about the fractured nature of subjectivity; the ways in which persons are constituted through social experience; the oft-invisible operation, in between institutions and within intimate relationships, of machineries that make people live and die; and the shaping of psychological processes through social encounters. The subjects of ethnography are rarely offered the depth of personhood as vulnerable, failing, and aspiring human beings—people who demonstrate the same qualities that we ourselves display in relationships.

Moreover, anthropology's overemphasis on cultural representation has had the unfortunate if unintended effect of downplaying the conceptual significance of lived experience, even when reports of experience are the major sources of anthropological data. For a discipline that focuses on "experience-near" analyses, the conceptualization of experience is by and large very thin. A more substantial conceptualization of cultural experience is in order, one in which the collective and the individual are intertwined and run together and in which power and meaning are not placed in theoretical opposition but are shown to be intimately linked in an intersubjective matrix.

· · ·

The need for developing more complex theories of the subject that are ethnographically grounded and that contemplate how individual singularity is retained and remade in local interactions has become ever more apparent. The subject is at once a product and agent of history; the site of experience, memory, storytelling and aesthetic judgment; an agent of knowing as much as of action; and the conflicted site for moral acts and gestures amid impossibly immoral societies and institutions. Modes of subjectivation are indeed determined by the vagaries of the state, family and community hierarchies, memories of colonial interventions and unresolvable traumas, and medicoscientific experiments and markets. Yet subjectivity is not just the outcome of social control or the unconscious; it also provides the ground for subjects to think through their circumstances and to feel through their contradictions, and in so doing, to inwardly endure experiences that would otherwise be outwardly unbearable. Subjectivity is the means of shaping sensibility. It is fear and optimism, anger and forgiveness, lamentation and pragmatism, chaos and order. It is the anticipation and articulation of self-criticism and renewal—what Albert O. Hirschman luminously calls "self-subversion" (1995).

While recollecting his own history, Hirschman describes the pleasure of discovering a different genealogy of his concepts as well as counterexamples to the generalizations he has worked hard to develop—"a moment of perplexity and concern" at the possibility of a "theory having been 'falsified'. . . . But past this moment, I feel genuinely more alive as I now have new interrelations and complexities to explore." And so our subjectivity orchestrates a field of defeats and achievements into value-feeling states of hope and hopelessness, robustness and demoralization, inefficacy and competence. Determining how this orchestration of the self actually takes place requires much more descriptive content, attention to processes, and perhaps entirely new forms of ethnographic research, such as projects that combine ethnography with epidemiology and aesthetics. Clearly, however, inasmuch as academic psychology and psychiatry have forsaken this project, anthropology and the humanities must summon the means and competence to take it on.

The seminar thus took on the task of bringing diverse theories of subjectivity and ethnographic data on illness, social suffering, and technologies of care into conversation with one another. We began, as we do in this introduction, with the recognition that no single analytic framework—whether from history, social relations, discourse analysis, political critique, phenomenology, psychoanalysis, economics, or biology—can fully account for the inner lives of people and the intersubjective relations in a local world. We did not begin with a genealogy or definition of the terms *subject* and *subjectivity*, though these terms were present in our discussions. Rather, we took as the objects of our inquiry the contingency of subjectivity and the openness of the term's meaning today. Cognitive theories, theories of affect and memory, diverse forms of psychoanalysis, models of pathology and normality and of rupture or continuity all make truth claims over the sense of psychological interiority. But this area of inquiry has as much uncertainty as does the study of modernity or postmodernity. Indeed, perhaps the ongoing trajectories of persons show us the existential elements in social and individual experience: subjects are themselves unfinished and unfinishable.

We do not seek to impose order in this conceptual disorder or to identify a unifying theory. Such a stance would be forced and false, and it would take us even further away from capturing the dynamic and unsolved tension between the bodily, self, and social/political processes that, we hold, is the core of subjectivity. This volume thus explores not a single point of view but multiple perspectives and ways of addressing phenomena related to the inner life of subjects. Of particular concern are the inward reworkings of the world and the consequences of people's actions toward themselves and toward others. In our understanding, this arena is precisely where the moral comes into view; through the ethnographic study of subjectivity, we attempt to explore what matters most in people's lives in the making and unmaking of meaning. Values and emotions are closely connected and are embodied and projected into domestic spaces, public life, and interpersonal struggles. We look through subjectivity to theorize not an intangible Subject but human conditions, to make sense of our ethical reflections on them, and to challenge anthropological work.

In the background of these observations and reflections lurk large questions: What constitutes modernity and modern subjectivity? Should we use modernity in the singular or plural? How did colonialism shape European and North American subjectivities? What cultural paths do emergent forms of subjectivity take in non-Western and postcolonial societies (Bhabha 1994; Mitchell 2000; Stoler 2002)? What does the anthropology of the contemporary world entail (Rabinow 2003)? Questions also arise about what methodologies we should use to address the diverse ways in which individuals actually interact with large-scale global processes and local symbolic forms, how to relate psychological constructs to analyses of political subjectivity, and how to make both these elements relevant to studies of everyday injury, violence, and mental illness. We hope that the papers in this collection will open these issues for deep intellectual and critical discussion that goes beyond conventional discourse in the popular media about the kinds of personality types emerging in our commercialized era and beyond formulations of human nature that rely on neurobiology and biologically based theories of psychopathology, now dominant in professional psychology and psychiatry. Reflections on contemporary forms of life, subjectivity, and ethics deserve much more.

· · ·

We organize the essays in this volume under four general headings. The first chapters (by Amélie O. Rorty; Arthur Kleinman and Erin Fitz-Henry; Veena Das and Ranendra Das; and Paul Rabinow)—in a section we call "Transformations in Social Experience and Subjectivity"—outline historical, philosophical, and cross-cultural frames of subjectivity. They also explore the relation of the individual to the collective and to powerful epistemological and political realities.

The second set of essays, organized under the overly simple rubric "Political Subjects," examines issues of trauma, memory, and therapies that have emerged in post–Vietnam War America (Allan Young) and in postapartheid South Africa (Nancy Scheper-Hughes). Stephen Greenblatt's work on the political dispute about the cult of the dead in early modern Europe and its migration into theatrical representation and into the phantasmagoria of psychological interiority helps illuminate the *longue durée* of sociopolitical workings of memory.

The third set of essays (by Byron Good, Subandi, and Mary-Jo DelVecchio Good; Ellen Corin; and Anne Lovell) appears under the heading "Madness and Social Suffering." These contributions include detailed analyses of the experience of psychosis in quite distinct settings (in Indonesia, in Canada and India, and among the homeless in New York). The essays find that the lives of persons with mental illness are entangled with social and symbolic violence and with religious activism and global psychiatric trends, as well as with the disruption of families and the dismembering of nations.

The final set of essays, under the heading "Life Technologies," examines how the life sciences and medical technologies are shaping distinctively contemporary forms of affect, identity, and personal ethics (Evelyn Fox Keller, Mary-Jo DelVecchio Good, Eric Krakauer, João Biehl). Michael M. J. Fischer provides a concluding overview of the chapters. Drawing from insights he gained during a journey into Israel and Palestine, Fischer suggests that the subjecthood of the citizen (or political agency), the self (or personhood), and discursive/enunciative positioning of the subject (or subject positions) are all required elements in present-day struggles to guarantee life chance for oneself and others. Differentiated cultural analyses can help articulate new social institutions for an evolving public sphere.

At the opening of each section, we briefly reflect on the central theme of each contribution, placing the essays in conversation with one another and suggesting some frames for reading them. Readers are invited either to use these introductory comments as an orientation to the papers that follow or to move directly to the papers and then return to our reflections on them.

NOTES

1. For a discussion of an anthropology that does not begin with the concept of culture, see Rabinow 2003 and his essay in chapter 4 of this volume. See Boon (1998) on "culture-as-paradox."
2. Veena Das's work on "the ordinary" draws from the work of Stanley Cavell. See, for instance, Cavell 1988, 1981, 1979. For Cavell's commentary on Das's work, see Cavell 1997.

SOURCES

Agamben, Giorgio. 1998. *Homo Sacer: Sovereign Power and Bare Life.* Stanford, CA: Stanford University Press.
———. 1999. *Remnants of Auschwitz: The Witness and the Archive.* New York: Zone Books.
Anagnost, Ann. 1997. *National Past-Times: Narrative, Representation, and Power in Modern China.* Durham, NC: Duke University Press.
Appadurai, Arjun. 1996. *Modernity at Large: Cultural Dimensions of Globalization.* Minneapolis: University of Minnesota Press.

18 / Introduction

Aretxaga, Begoña. 1997. *Shattering Silence: Women, Nationalism, and Political Subjectivity in Northern Ireland*. Princeton, NJ: Princeton University Press.
Bhabha, Homi K. 1994. *The Location of Culture*. New York: Routledge.
Biehl, João (with Denise Coutinho and Ana Luzia Outeiro). 2001a. "Technology and Affect: HIV/AIDS Testing in Brazil." *Culture, Medicine and Psychiatry* 25 (1): 87–129.
———. 2001b. "Vita: Life in a Zone of Social Abandonment." *Social Text* 19 (3): 131–49.
———. 2004. "Life of the Mind: The Interface of Psychopharmaceuticals, Domestic Economies, and Social Abandonment." *American Ethnologist* 31 (4): 475–96.
———. 2005. *Vita: Life in a Zone of Social Abandonment*. Berkeley: University of California Press.
Boon, James A. 1982. *Other Tribes, Other Scribes: Symbolic Anthropology in the Comparative Study of Cultures, Histories, Religions, and Texts*. Cambridge: Cambridge University Press.
———. 1998. "Accenting Hybridity: Postcolonial Cultural Studies, a Boasian Anthropologist, and I." In *Culture and the Problem of the Disciplines*, ed. John C. Rowe (New York: Columbia University Press), 141–69.
———. 1999. *Verging on Extra-Vagance: Anthropology, History, Religion, Literature, Arts . . . Showbiz*. Princeton: Princeton University Press.
Borneman, John. 1992. *Belonging in Two Berlins: Kin, State, Nation*. Cambridge: Cambridge University Press.
———. 1997. *Settling Accounts: Violence, Justice, and Accountability in Postsocialist Europe*. Princeton, NJ: Princeton University Press.
———. 2001. "Caring and Being Cared For: Displacing Marriage, Kinship, Gender, and Sexuality." In *The Ethics of Kinship: Ethnographic Inquiries*, ed. James Faubion (New York: Rowman and Littlefield), 29–45.
———. 2002. "On Money and the Memory of Loss." *Ethnografica* 6(2): 281–302.
Bourdieu, Pierre. 1977. *Outline of a Theory of Practice*. Cambridge: Cambridge University Press.
———. 1984. *Distinction: A Social Critique of the Judgement of Taste*. Cambridge, MA: Harvard University Press.
———. 2001. *Masculine Domination*. Cambridge: Polity Press.
Bourgois, Philippe. 2002. *In Search of Respect: Selling Crack in El Barrio*, 2nd ed. Cambridge: Cambridge University Press.
Caruth, C. 1996. *Unclaimed Experience: Trauma, Narrative, and History*. Baltimore: Johns Hopkins University Press.
Cavell, Stanley. 1979. *The Claim of Reason: Wittgenstein, Skepticism, Morality, and Tragedy*. Oxford: Clarendon Press.
———. 1981. *Pursuits of Happiness: The Hollywood Comedy of Remarriage*. Cambridge, MA: Harvard University Press.
———. 1988. *In Quest of the Ordinary: Lines of Skepticism and Romanticism*. Chicago: University of Chicago Press.
———. 1997. "Comments on Veena Das's Essay 'Language and Body: Transactions in the Construction of Pain.' " In *Social Suffering*, ed. Arthur Kleinman, Veena Das, and Margaret Lock (Berkeley: University of California Press), 93–98.
Clifford, James, and George E. Marcus, eds. 1986. *Writing Culture: The Poetics and Politics of Ethnography*. Berkeley: University of California Press.

Cohen, Lawrence. 1998. *No Aging in India: Alzheimer's, the Bad Family, and Other Modern Things.* Berkeley: University of California Press.

———. 1999. "Where It Hurts: Indian Material for an Ethics of Organ Transplantation." *Daedalus* 128 (4): 135–65.

Collier, Jane F. 1997. *From Duty to Desire: Remaking Families in a Spanish Village.* Princeton, NJ: Princeton University Press.

Comaroff, Jean. 1985. *Body of Power, Spirit of Resistance: The Culture and History of a South African People.* Chicago: University of Chicago Press.

Comaroff, John, and Jean Comaroff. 1992. *Ethnography and the Historical Imagination.* Boulder: Westview Press.

Crapanzano, Vincent. 1980. *Tuhami: Portrait of a Moroccan.* Chicago: University of Chicago Press.

Csordas, Thomas. 1994. *Embodiment and Experience: The Existential Ground of Culture and Self.* Cambridge: Cambridge University Press.

———. 2002. *Body/Meaning/Healing.* New York: Palgrave.

Daniel, E. Valentine. 1994. "The Individual in Terror." In *Embodiment and Experience: The Existential Ground of Culture and Self,* ed. Thomas J. Csordas (Cambridge: Cambridge University Press), 229–47.

———. 1997. *Charred Lullabies: Chapters in an Anthropography of Violence.* Princeton: Princeton University Press.

Das, Veena. 1996. *Critical Events.* New Delhi: Oxford University Press.

———. 1997. "Language and Body: Transactions in the Construction of Pain." In *Social Suffering,* ed. Arthur Kleinman, Veena Das, and Margaret Lock (Berkeley: University of California Press), 67–91.

———. 1998. "Foreword." In *Scarred Minds: The Psychological Impact of War on Sri Lankan Tamils,* by Daya Somasunderam (New Delhi: Sage).

———. 1999. "Public Good, Ethics, and Everyday Life: Beyond the Boundaries of Bioethics." Special issue, "Bioethics and Beyond," *Daedalus* 128 (4): 99–133.

———. 2000. "The Act of Witnessing: Violence, Poisonous Knowledge, and Subjectivity." In *Violence and Subjectivity,* ed. Veena Das, Arthur Kleinman, Mamphela Ramphele, and Pamela Reynolds (Berkeley: University of California Press), 205–25.

Das, Veena, and Arthur Kleinman. 2001. "Introduction." In *Remaking a World: Violence, Social Suffering, and Recovery,* ed. Veena Das, Arthur Kleinman, Margaret Lock, Mamphela Ramphele, and Pamela Reynolds (Berkeley: University of California Press), 1–30.

Das, Veena, and Deborah Poole, eds. 2004. *Anthropology in the Margins of the State.* Santa Fe: School of American Research Press.

Daston, Lorraine, and Peter Galison. 1992. "The Image of Objectivity." *Representations* 40: 81–128.

Deleuze, Gilles. 1995. *Negotiations.* New York: Columbia University Press.

Deleuze, Gilles, and Felix Guattari. 1983. *Anti-Oedipus: Capitalism and Schizophrenia.* Minneapolis: University of Minnesota Press.

Desjarlais, Robert. 1997. *Shelter Blues: Sanity and Selfhood among the Homeless.* Philadelphia: University of Pennsylvania Press.

———. 2003. *Sensory Biographies: Lives and Deaths among Nepal's Yolmo Buddhists.* Berkeley: University of California Press.

Fassin, Didier. 2005. "Compassion and Repression: The Moral Economy of Immigration Policies in France." *Cultural Anthropology* 20 (3): 362–87.

Fassin, Didier, and Paula Vasquez. 2005. "Humanitarian Exception As the Rule: The Political Theology of the 1999 Tragedia in Venezuela." *American Ethnologist* 32 (3): 389–405.

Fischer, Michael. 2003. *Emergent Forms of Life and the Anthropological Voice.* Durham, NC: Duke University Press.

Fortun, Kim. 2001. *Advocacy after Bhopal: Environmentalism, Disaster, New Global Orders.* Chicago: University of Chicago Press.

Foucault, Michel. 1980. *The History of Sexuality, Vol. 1: An Introduction.* New York: Vintage Books.

———. 2000. "The Subject and Power." In *Power—Essential Works of Foucault 1954–1984,* vol. 3, ed. James D. Faubion (New York: New Press), 326–48.

Geertz, Clifford. 1973. *The Interpretation of Cultures.* New York: Basic Books.

———. 1983. *Local Knowledge: Further Essays in Interpretive Anthropology.* New York: Basic Books.

———. 2000. *Available Light: Anthropological Reflections on Philosophical Topics.* Princeton: Princeton University Press.

———. 2005. "Shifting Aims, Moving Targets: On the Anthropology of Religion." *Journal of the Royal Anthropological Institute* 11: 1–15.

Good, Byron. 1994. *Medicine, Rationality, and Experience.* Cambridge: Cambridge University Press.

———. 2005. "Rethinking Emotions in Southeast Asia." *Ethnos* 69: 1–5.

Good, Byron, and Mary-Jo DelVecchio Good. 2004. "On the 'Subject' of Culture: Subjectivity and Cultural Phenomenology in the Work of Clifford Geertz." In *Clifford Geertz with His Colleagues,* ed. Richard Shweder and Byron Good (Chicago: University of Chicago Press).

Good, Byron (with Subandi and Mary-Jo DelVecchio Good). 2001. *Le sujet de la maladie mentale: Psychose, folie furieuse et subjectivite en Indonesia.* In *La pathologie mentale en mutation: Psychiatrie et societe,* ed. Alain Ehrenberg and Anne M. Lovell (Paris: Edition Odile Jacob), 163–95.

Good, Mary-Jo DelVecchio. 1998. *American Medicine: The Quest for Competence.* Berkeley: University of California Press.

Good, Mary-Jo DelVecchio, Paul Brodwin, Byron Good, and Arthur Kleinman, eds. 1992. *Pain as Human Experience.* Berkeley: University of California Press.

Greenblatt, Stephen. 2004 (September 12). "Shakespeare's Leap," *New York Times Magazine,* 50–55.

Greenhouse, C. J., E. Mertz, and K. B. Warren, eds. 2002. *Ethnography in Unstable Places: Everyday Lives in Contexts of Dramatic Political Change.* Durham, NC: Duke University Press.

Hahn, Robert, and Arthur Kleinman. 1983. "Belief as Pathogen, Belief as Medicine." *Medical Anthropology Quarterly* 14 (4): 16–19.

Hammoudi, Abdellah. 1993. *The Victim and Its Masks.* Chicago: University of Chicago Press.

———. 1997 *Master and Disciple: The Cultural Foundations of Moroccan Authoritarianism.* Chicago: University of Chicago Press.

———. 2006. *A Season in Mecca: Narrative of a Pilgrimage.* New York: Hill and Wang.

Herzfeld, Michael. 1996. *Cultural Intimacy: Social Poetics in the Nation-State.* New York: Routledge.

Hirschman, Albert O. 1995. *A Propensity to Self-Subversion*. Cambridge, MA: Harvard University Press.

Kleinman, Arthur. 1980. *Patients and Healers in the Context of Culture*. Berkeley: University of California Press.

———. 1988a. *The Illness Narratives: Suffering, Healing and the Human Condition*. New York: Basic Books.

———. 1988b. *Rethinking Psychiatry: From Cultural Category to Personal Experience*. New York: Free Press.

———. 1995. *Writing at the Margins: Discourse between Anthropology and Medicine*. Berkeley: University of California Press.

———. 1999. *Experience and Its Moral Modes: Culture, Human Conditions, and Disorder. The Tanner Lectures on Human Values*. Salt Lake City: University of Utah Press.

Kleinman, Arthur, and Byron Good, eds. 1985. *Culture and Depression: Studies in the Anthropology and Cross-Cultural Psychiatry of Affect and Disorder*. Berkeley: University of California Press.

Lacan, Jacques. 1978. *The Four Fundamental Concepts of Psychoanalysis*. New York: W. W. Norton.

Larkin, Philip. 1983. *Required Writing: Miscellaneous Pieces, 1955–1982*. Boston: Faber and Faber.

Lee, Sing. 1999. "Diagnosis Postponed: Shenjung Shuairuo and the Transformation of Psychiatry in Post-Mao China." *Culture, Medicine, and Psychiatry* 23 (3): 349–80.

Le Marcis, Frédéric. 2004. "The Suffering Body of the City." *Public Culture* 16 (3) 453–57.

Lock, Margaret. 1993. *Encounters with Aging: Mythologies of Menopause in Japan and North America*. Berkeley: University of California Press.

———. 2002. *Twice Dead: Organ Transplants and the Reinvention of Death*. Berkeley: University of California Press.

Luhrman, Tanya. 2000. *Of Two Minds: The Growing Disorder in American Psychiatry*. New York: Alfred A. Knopf.

Lutz, Catherine, and Lila Abu-Lughod. 1990. *Language and the Politics of Emotion*. Cambridge: Cambridge University Press.

Marcus, George, and Michael M. J. Fischer. 1986. *Anthropology as Cultural Critique: An Experimental Moment in the Human Sciences*. Chicago: University of Chicago Press.

Martin, Emily. 1994. *Flexible Bodies: Tracking Immunity in American Culture from the Days of Polio to the Age of AIDS*. Boston: Beacon Press.

Masco, Joseph. 2004. "Mutant Ecologies: Radioactive Life in Post–Cold War New Mexico." *Cultural Anthropology* 19 (4): 517–50.

Mbembe, Achille. 2003. "Necropolitics." *Public Culture* 15 (1): 11–40.

Milosz, Czeslav. 2004 (August 21). "Obituary," *Economist*, 72.

Mitchell, Timothy. 2000. *Questions of Modernity*. Minneapolis: University of Minnesota Press.

Obeyesekere, Gananath. 1990. *The Work of Culture: Symbolic Transformation in Psychoanalysis and Anthropology*. Chicago: University of Chicago Press.

Ortner, Sherry, ed. 1999. *The Fate of "Culture": Geertz and Beyond*. Berkeley: University of California Press.

———. 2004. "Geertz, Subjectivity, and Postmodern Consciousness." (Manuscript).

Pandolfo, Stefania. 1998. *Impasse of the Angels: Scenes from a Moroccan Space of Memory.* Chicago: University of Chicago Press.

———. 2000. "The Thin Line of Modernity: Some Moroccan Debates on Subjectivity." In *Questions of Modernity,* ed. Timothy Mitchell (Minneapolis: University of Minnesota Press), 115–47.

Petryna, Adriana. 2002. *Life Exposed: Biological Citizens after Chernobyl.* Princeton, NJ: Princeton University Press.

Petryna, Adriana, Andrew Lakoff, and Arthur Kleinman, eds. 2006. *Global Pharmaceuticals: Markets, Practices, Ethics.* Durham, NC: Duke University Press.

Povinelli, Elizabeth. 2002. *The Cunning of Recognition: Indigenous Alterity and the Making of Australian Multiculturalism.* Durham, NC: Duke University Press.

Rabinow, Paul. 1978. *Reflections on Fieldwork in Morocco.* Berkeley: University of California Press.

———. 1996. *Essays on the Anthropology of Reason.* Princeton, NJ: Princeton University Press.

———. 2003. *Anthropos Today: Reflections on Modern Equipment.* Princeton, NJ: Princeton University Press.

Rabinow, Paul, and Talia Dan-Cohen. 2005. *A Machine to Make a Future: Biotech Chronicles.* Princeton, NJ: Princeton University Press.

Redfield, Peter. 2005. "Doctors, Borders, and Life in Crisis." *Cultural Anthropology* 20 (3): 328–61.

Roitman, Janet. 2005. *Fiscal Disobedience: An Anthropology of Economic Regulation in Central Africa.* Princeton, NJ: Princeton University Press.

Rosaldo, Renato. 1989. *Culture and Truth: The Remaking of Social Analysis.* Boston: Beacon Press.

Rosen, Lawrence. 2003. *The Culture of Islam: Changing Aspects of Contemporary Muslim Life.* Chicago: University of Chicago Press.

Scheper-Hughes, Nancy. 1992. *Death without Weeping: The Violence of Everyday Life in Brazil.* Berkeley: University of California Press.

———. 2001. *Saints, Scholars, and Schizophrenics: Mental Illness in Rural Ireland.* Berkeley: University of California Press.

———. 2003. "Rotten Trade: Millennial Capitalism, Human Values and Global Justice in Organs Trafficking." *Journal of Human Rights* 2 (2): 197–226.

Scheper-Hughes, Nancy, and Phillipe Bourgois, eds. 2004. *Violence in War and Peace: An Anthology.* Oxford: Blackwell.

Scheper-Hughes, Nancy, and Margaret Lock. 1987. "The Mindful Body: A Prolegomenon to Future Work in Medical Anthropology." *Medical Anthropology Quarterly* 1(1): 6–41.

Shweder, Richard, and Byron Good, eds. 2004. *Clifford Geertz with His Colleagues.* Chicago: University of Chicago Press.

Stoler, Ann Laura. 1995. *Race and the Education of Desire.* Durham, NC: Duke University Press.

———. 2002. *Carnal Knowledge and Imperial Power: Race and the Intimate in Colonial Rule.* Berkeley: University of California Press.

Taussig, Michael. 1986. *Shamanism, Colonialism, and the Wild Man.* Chicago: University of Chicago Press.

Tsing, Anna L. 1993. *In the Realm of the Diamond Queen: Marginality in an Out-of-the-Way Place.* Princeton, NJ: Princeton University Press.

————. 2005. *Friction: An Ethnography of Global Connections.* Princeton, NJ: Princeton University Press.

Turkle, Sherry. 1997. *Life on the Screen: Identity in the Age of the Internet.* New York: Simon and Schuster.

Yan, Yunxiang. 2003. *Private Life under Socialism: Love, Intimacy, and Family Change in a Chinese Village, 1949–1999.* Stanford, CA: Stanford University Press.

Young, Allan. 1995. *The Harmony of Illusions: Inventing Post-Traumatic Stress Disorder.* Princeton, NJ: Princeton University Press.

PART I

Transformations in Social Experience and Subjectivity

．　　・　　・　　・　　・

Subjectivity is a "vanishing subject," writes Amélie Oksenberg Rorty in this book's opening chapter. As she traces the history of some of the philosophical insights that have shaped current understandings of subjectivity and the subject, Rorty finds not a progression but various contested movements and fragmentary meanings. Self-awareness has a different philosophical trajectory than individuated perception does; scholars have emphasized a diachronically unified persona and, at times, posed it against a synchronically unified persona; the meanings of emotions, the body, social interactions, and suffering as subjectivity have all been areas of contestation. For example, according to Rorty, "Where Aristotle finds self-recognition through the mutual mirroring of virtuous friends, Hume charts the construction of the idea of self in social practices that have associations with property and propriety." She suggests that current uses of subjectivity and the subject implicitly incorporate distinct meanings and associations that scholars have used differently and historically have posed against one another. Through different meanings of the first person, the mental state, and experience, concepts of morality, social responsibility, and intersubjectivity are thus being reworked.

Rorty applies her insights into the fragmented, recycling history of the idea of subjectivity to assess the contemporary focus on subjectivity in the anthropology of medicine and medical ethics. In different forms, anthropologists, physicians, and professional ethicists work through tensions between universal and individualized aspects of human experience. How can one articulate singularity in a language that aspires to universal reflection?

Though Rorty believes that the rhetoric of personal experience helps increase the sensitivity of medical practice, she finds that evoking "the subject" does not do the politically corrective work that critical social scientists and medics intend. Because the subject involves an archaeology of bodies, things, interests, practices, and meanings, people treat subjective knowledge in vastly different ways. According to Rorty, the problem with simply "listening to the subject" is that this approach does not tell you how to integrate what you have heard into therapeutic practice, for example. Can we produce an analytics that attends to what matters most to people, and how might such a language make a difference?

At the end of her essay, Rorty offers "respect" as an effective conceptual tool for exploring the differing power relations, desires, aims, and meanings of the subject. A focus on respect allows shared exploration of the parameters of mutuality—whether it be egalitarian or hierarchical, individualistic or collective, among contemporaries or between generations. As we open up philosophical and ideological issues in current uses of subjectivity for productive discussion, we can also open the door to "capturing the moment," the point in time between the subject and his or her sense of being alive.

The heterogeneities, conflicts, and contingencies of moral engagement, states Arthur Kleinman in his essay with coauthor Erin Fitz-Henry, create a local world where uncontrollability and the unknown define human qualities that are inadequately addressed by Western ethical discourse. By and large, this discourse assumes the existence of a unified human nature that is neurologically hardwired and historically unchanging. "Our subjectivities," says Kleinman, "certainly have a biology, but they also, and perhaps more critically, have an equally influential history, cultural specificity, political location, and economic position." As an antidote to the generalizations and abstractions that continue to define much mainstream ethical discourse, ethnography can help us ground and nuance our understanding of the processes by which people forge and negotiate moral predicaments at the dynamic interface of cultural representations, collective processes, and individual subjectivity. For example, in the summer of 1942, an intense ethos of group loyalty, an overwhelmingly anti-Semitic cultural orientation, and an "affectively open" context in which soldiers conceived of themselves as redeemers came together in a way that enabled the members of Police Battalion 101 in Poland to rationalize their participation in genocide.

As part of his effort to move away from biologically deterministic and philosophically atomistic conceptions of the self, Kleinman uses the term *human conditions* rather than *human nature* to describe the inherent malleability of lived experience as it shapes and is shaped by macrolevel social, political, and economic processes (1999, 2006). His notion of social (and moral) experience places the collective and individual in the same analytic space. Thus, whatever issue is at stake for people in a given moment—be it a religious identity, a political project, the preservation of a native language, or a set of relationships—is always embedded in the shifting exigencies of practical, everyday life as it unfolds in particular sociopolitical spaces. For Kleinman, to speak of the subjective is always to speak of the intersubjective; and to theorize the intersubjective is to decisively reject the notions of a universal human essence and autonomous subject that have historically underpinned ethics discourse.

Human conditions also create a space for analyzing change. Kleinman's analytical tools offer a way to connect the large-scale processes of market logic, global rationalities, and institutions that manage populations with the affect, meaning, and behaviors that convey individual subjectivity in everyday life. "As transnational trends . . . remake the condition of our lives and the parameters of our worlds," he concludes, "so, too, do they remake our most intimate inner processes: emotion, cognitive style, memory, our deepest sense of self."

"Institutional responses tend to fragment these problems into differentiated smaller pieces which then become the subject of highly particularized technical policies and programs, increasingly ones that last for short periods of time and then are replaced by yet others which further rearrange and fracture these problems," wrote Kleinman in his Tanner Lectures (1999: 30). The management of suffering via the practices of global rationality produces physical, institutional, and technical effects. As this logic particularizes and expands, a reciprocal process develops out of technical rationality, re-creating affect that in turn reshapes technical rationality; as moral processes are understood as sites to be managed via bureaucratic, market, legal, and medical logics, the use of these techniques and the perception of this rationality structure the moral process. Through this move, Kleinman importantly links the political economic and social processes by which populations are managed through affect. Thus, bodily affects and subjectivity become the media through which the collectivity is ordered and controlled.

Due to this organizing intersubjectivity, the techniques and institutions of global political economy reorder the landscape of local moral worlds. Personhood is unmade and remade. As suffering is increasingly managed through rationalities of efficacy and technologies of medical intervention, perceptions and experiences of suffering come to play a role in this remaking of lives and worlds. Maintaining these interrelated aspects in focus—the collective and the individual, economy and subjectivity, the bureaucratic and the affective—allows for a more enabling critique of the rationalities and ethical issues of policies and programs.

In her introduction to *Ethnography in Unstable Places,* Carol J. Green-house (2002) also calls for studies at the juncture of states, policies, and sub-jectivities that can demystify the conventions of scale (state as organization, for example) and address the individual, who, after all, cannot be subsumed under institutions, programs, and groups. The ethnographic challenge is to identify these empirical relations and linkages—technical, political, con-ceptual, affective—and to integrate them into critical analysis and public discussion.

In her anthropological work, Veena Das calls our attention to the con-tingencies and tensions of inner worlds that take shape amid the unfolding of critical events (1996). How can one reenter altered social realities and guarantee a new chance in life for oneself and others? What is the price one pays for making such life changes? How is inner change integral to local economies, and how does it become part of personal and public memory?

In the essay "Language and Body" (1997), Das observes that women who were greatly traumatized by the partition of Pakistan and India did not tran-scend this trauma, as, for example, Antigone did in classic Greek tragedy; in-stead, they incorporated it into their everyday experience. For Das, subjec-tivity is always a contested field. The self is a strategic means of belonging simultaneously to large-scale events and to familial and political-economic networks. Tradition, collective memory, and public spheres are organized as phantasmagoric-like scenes, for they thrive on the "energies of the dead" that remain unaccounted for in statistics and law. Das scrutinizes this bu-reaucratic and domestic machinery of inscription and invisibility that au-thorizes the real—a machinery with which people have to forcefully engage as they look for a place to inhabit in everyday life. Against violent world-historical trajectories, Das's subjects develop a will to live, even as the trauma they bear can do nothing but proclaim brutal violation.

In her work on violence and subjectivity, Das (2000) is less concerned with reality's structuring of psychological conditions than with the pro-duction of individual truths and the power of voice: What chance does speaking have of being heard? What power does it have to make truth or to become action? For her, inner and outer states are inescapably sutured. An ethnography of subjectivity illuminates the materials of this suturing and the language by which it is experienced: "language is not just a medium of communication or misunderstanding, but an experience which allows not only a message but also the subject to be projected outwards," writes Das with Kleinman (2001: 22).

In their essay for this volume, Veena Das and Ranendra K. Das explore how illness experiences are a relational testing ground and life experiment for the urban poor in New Delhi. Distinguishing differing medical practices, expertise, and practitioners, they chart the everyday ways in which illness categories emerge through medical interactions and local family dynamics. Das and Das look beyond governmental institutions to show the domestic and personal grounds of the state and medicine. Cosmologies are plastic, they argue, reworked for domestic and personal needs. Das and Das are particularly interested in relating interactions, representations, and practices to the materiality of everyday life for the poor, in which employment, health, and cash flow are precarious. They use the concept of illness experience to explore the way the poor live through and understand this precariousness. Out of illness experiences emerge interpretations that see temporality and the body as integral to the process of ordinary living.

Das and Das thereby connect the materiality of social conditions and the concrete experience of illness in the family and clinic to the symbolic side of sickness, in which people experience the normal and pathological in varied ways. Through that flow of experience, subjectivity emerges in family interactions, employment struggles, and efforts to obtain medical therapeutics for the poor. One's sense of being alive and of well-being forms amid the lack of money, the clash of law and illegibility, technology and affect, malfunctioning institutions, the danger of local life and individual vulnerability. Through symptoms and various forms of care (or nonresponse), a domestic form of citizenship crystallizes. The modern subject of the modern state comes into being. "The domestic sphere . . . is always on the verge of becoming the political" (Das and Addlakha 2001).[1]

Paul Rabinow also relentlessly grounds possibility in current practice. He explores the ways in which concepts, beliefs, and values change shape in the specificity of new assemblages, crucially including his own anthropological inquiries of the life-sciences industry. We must approximate the scientific places in which life forms emerge and examine how these forms catalyze actors, things, temporalities, or spatialities in a distinct mode of existence that makes things function differently in an altered public domain. And, he says, we must place all this activity in past and future perspectives, without adopting the pretense or illusion of an absolute view. Rabinow invites us to consider the contingency of motion as a more productive tool than progress for bringing into focus the specificity and contingency of assemblages, power arrangements, and the mediations of self-formation.

"What if we did not begin with the distinction of subject and object and its secondary assumption that it is the culture that is enunciated through speaking subjects? What if we did not begin with the distinction between a whole to be captured and an inquiring subject to be rendered transparent? What if we did not assume that our task is to write culture? And what if the search for another form of anthropological inquiry proceeded from a different set of distinctions precisely because its object of inquiry appeared to be composed of forces driving and articulating assemblages defined by accelerated creation, efficiency, and associated stress of and for subjects, objects, and the elements that mediate them? What, then, would observation consist in? And what operations would assist that new form of observation?" Rabinow asks.

Taking inspiration from Thucydides' account of the Peloponnesian War, Rabinow's methodology foregrounds the individual and collective processes that continually reconstitute subjectivity. He urges us, following Hegel, to let speak "not a borrowed consciousness but the speaker's own self-formation [*Bildung*]." Thucydides transcribed, in unabridged form, the political speeches delivered at each key turning point of the war. In so doing, argues Rabinow, he made public deliberation an object of analysis, identifying the immediacy of selves and relations as they form in the particularity of "discursive moments." This kind of observation does something to the world: the work of thought becomes social action in itself, obliging the reader to find his or her own ethical position vis-à-vis the "immediate history" that emerges.

Rabinow wants the anthropology of subjectivity to engage the new terms of the social scientific enterprise—to replace endless and sometimes paralyzing representational self-scrutiny with the imperative of an interventionist observation. Intervention is a cultural construction of our times that itself has great significance, but we ought to remain attentive to the larger implications of the idea that being becomes human and moral through social action: what happens to the work of thought in the process?

By forging a new relationship to emergent objects of knowledge and means of knowing, we once again come across the older imperative "dare to know," which we must understand in a new way today, savoring its complex bittersweetness. And we must find a way to live with what we find—that is, to integrate the quest for knowledge (of nature, of injustice and folly, and of the self) with a ceaseless search for ways to apply this knowledge to the care of the self and of others.

NOTE

1. Das and Addlakha (2001) argue that the domestic, "once displaced from its conventionally assumed reference to the private, becomes a sphere in which a differ-

ent kind of citizenship may be enacted—a citizenship based, not on the formation of associational communities, but on notions of publics constituted through voice."

REFERENCES

Das, Veena. 1996. *Critical Events.* New Delhi: Oxford University Press.

———. 1997. "Language and Body: Transactions in the Construction of Pain." In *Social Suffering,* ed. Arthur Kleinman, Veena Das, and Margaret Lock (Berkeley: University of California Press), 67–91.

———. 2000. "The Act of Witnessing: Violence, Poisonous Knowledge, and Subjectivity." In *Violence and Subjectivity,* ed. Veena Das, Arthur Kleinman, Mamphela Ramphele, and Pamela Reynolds (Berkeley: University of California Press), 205–25.

Das, Veena, and Renu Addlakha. 2001. "Disability and Domestic Citizenship: Voice, Gender, and the Making of the Subject." *Public Culture* 13 (13): 511–31.

Das, Veena, and Arthur Kleinman. 2001. "Introduction." In *Remaking a World: Violence, Social Suffering, and Recovery,* ed. Veena Das, Arthur Kleinman, Margaret Lock, Mamphela Ramphele, and Pamela Reynolds (Berkeley: University of California Press), 1–30.

Greenhouse, Carol J. 2002. "Introduction: Altered States, Altered Lives." In *Ethnography in Unstable Places: Everyday Lives in Contexts of Dramatic Political Change* (Durham, NC: Duke University Press), 1–34.

Greenhouse, Carol J., Elizabeth Mertz, Kay B. Warren, eds. 2002. *Ethnography in Unstable Places: Everyday Lives in Contexts of Dramatic Political Change.* Durham, NC: Duke University Press.

Kleinman, Arthur. 1999. Experience and Its Moral Modes: Culture, Human Conditions, and Disorder. The Tanner Lectures on Human Values. Salt Lake City: University of Utah Press.

———. 2006. *What Really Matters: Living a Moral Life amidst Uncertainty and Danger.* Oxford: Oxford University Press.

1   The Vanishing Subject

The Many Faces of Subjectivity

AMÉLIE OKSENBERG RORTY

Augustine says, "What then is time? If no one asks me, I know; if I want to explain it, I do not know. And yet I know" (*Confessions*, 11. 14). Augustine introduces his perplexity by noting that though the present is evanescent, and neither time past nor time future exists, he can nevertheless tell the time of day and correct himself if he finds he is mistaken. We can echo Augustine's dilemma in speaking about subjectivity. And indeed time and subjectivity are connected: if no one asks us, we are confident that our experience is ours. But the moment we try to define subjectivity, the sense of certainty vanishes. If subjectivity is an awareness of oneself, it seems to have no stable content: every moment brings a different "self" to light. As Montaigne says, "Anyone who turns his . . . attention to himself will hardly ever find himself in the same state twice."[1] If subjective reflection offers proof of the existence of the self, it does not necessarily deliver self-knowledge. Descartes says, "I know that I exist; the question is What is this 'I' that I know?" (*Meditations on First Philosophy*, II AT 27). Descartes is rightly puzzled: the greater part of the *Meditations* is a detective story that traces the momentary certainty of the momentary existence of the thinker through a labyrinth of arguments to discover that— grace à Dieu—the self is a particular compound unity of a section of two substances, Mind and Body (*Meditations* VI, AT 81). Reflecting on Augustine, Montaigne, and Descartes, we see that the concept—and perhaps the experience—of subjectivity is historically laden with philosophical presuppositions and controversies. In grammar and in fact, contemporary conceptions of subjectivity—and our experienced sense of ourselves— serve multiple functions and fuse distinctive archaeological layers of meaning.

THE SEMANTICS OF THE SUBJECT

Etymology and grammar help identify and distinguish the strata in the history of the conception of subjectivity. Contemporary English usage emerged as late as the sixteenth century, a crystallization of Old French *sougiet* and Spanish *sugeto*, both derived from the Latin *subjectum*. These words are relatively literal translations of the Greek *hupokeimenon*—literally, that which stands or is placed underneath, the material of which things are made. The *Oxford English Dictionary* sees the modern notion of subjectivity—"the condition of viewing things through the medium of one's own mind or individuality . . . dominated by personal feelings, thoughts, concerns"—emerging very late: Coleridge under the influence of Kant.

We can, for the time being, set aside the question of whether our contemporary usages of "subjectivity" designate a family of notions or a genus with distinctive species and varieties. In ordinary speech, "subjectivity" sometimes refers to first-person claims of incorrigible introspective authority. In this sense, it contrasts with objective, corrigible impersonal or neutral descriptions of states of affairs. But "merely" subjective claims of authority can be mistaken: they indicate a local, sometimes idiosyncratic perspective, a voice that requires hearing but that can be rightly overridden by other kinds of authority. Less dramatically, "the subject" is a grammatical term paired with "the predicate," designating the referent of attribution. More expansively, it denotes an area, a domain of investigation: "The subject of this essay is 'subjectivity.' " The ordinary verb usage of "subject" designates quite a different domain. The expressions "Tom subjected Tim to a tongue lashing" and "In his childhood, John was subjected to merciless teasing" and "The Midwest is subject to droughts and tornados" refer to conditions or events that mark some passivity in the face of external forces. This sense of *subject* encompasses the legal use, "falling under the jurisdiction of a law": "Jaywalking is subject to a fine." It is also allied to the political contrast between subjects of an authoritarian regime and consenting or self-legislating citizens. The *Oxford English Dictionary* chronicles all these senses without priority, distinguishing the logical, psychological, grammatical, metaphysical, and political senses without favor.

THE TRANSFORMATIVE HISTORY OF THE SUBJECT

Our philosophic history begins with Aristotle. Of course his Greek *hupokeimenon* isn't straightforwardly translatable as "subject." Grammatically, it is the subject of predication; metaphysically, it is the underlying entity in which attributes or qualities inhere; physically, it is the material of which things are made. None of these senses has a hint of awareness, still less of self-conscious awareness. Aristotle's account of the genesis of self-awareness locates it in perception *(aesthesis)*, which has no apparent connection with the subject *(hupokeimenon)* as the "grammatical/logical subject of predication or attribution, the material substratum of objects" *(Metaphysics* 1028B: 35ff.). In the first instance, the immediate direct objects of perception are specific qualities rather than the ego-self or its capacities. Perceptions have direct objects: the mind integrates the colors, sounds, and smells of objects presented by the sense organs. *Aesthesis* is always veridical *(De Anima* 427B: 10ff.): strictly speaking, neither a perceptual illusion of water on the horizon nor the dream of a red chamber is a *perception*. This feature of Aristotle's psychology may stand behind the later-transformed view that subjective reports are by definition authoritative and incorrigible: "If what I claim isn't there, I'm not actually seeing." This construal has the obvious unfortunate ironic consequence of being true at the expense of being empty.

Aristotle's leading idea is that the initial reflexive experience of the perceiving self occurs along with particular perceptions.[2] Aristotle remarks, "In perceiving, we perceive that we perceive" *(Nichomachean Ethics [NE]*1170a: 28ff.). This realization establishes only that every act of perception also involves reflective activity. It does not by itself deliver an immediate, continuous perception of the ego-self as a spatiotemporally unified entity. Recognizing that acts of perception are moments in the continuing life of a person involves a much more complicated reflection. The virtuous become aware of themselves—their lives—as well formed and unified through the reflective contemplative mirroring of true friendship *(NE* 1169b30–1170a4). Sharing their lives in deliberation and practical activity, such friends mirror one another's lives as "other selves" *(NE* 1170b6). Only by contemplating *(theorein)* the lives of their friends, their "other selves" do the virtuous come to realize that the sequence of their particular perceptions and actions constitutes *a life*, a well-formed whole.[3] For Aristotle, then, self-consciousness emerges from a special kind of intersubjectivity. But this view has a stringent condition: the content of (what we would call) a subjective sense of the self emerges from the mutual contemplation that occurs in friendship among the virtuous *(NE* 1170b1–14). Through friendship among the virtuous is revealed the role of subjectivity in forming genuine self-knowledge.[4] Aristotle's view may seem harsh and elitist to those of our contemporaries who link subjectivity to epistemic egalitarianism and who believe that—whatever the genuinely veridical objective truth may be—each person is the ultimate authority on the subjective character of his experience.

Augustine's *Confessions* marks a dramatic change in the conception of the subject. His acute introspective awareness, his questions and preoccupations, are quite different from those of Aristotle or even from those of the Stoics. Although the *Confessions* presents a brilliant example of the phenomenology of self-awareness, the book is not a philosophical analysis of subjectivity. It follows an errant mind's way to faith by reflecting on what that journey reveals about divine benevolence. Augustine's explicit account of self-knowledge emerges in the course of a philosophical argument against skepticism. He uses the capacity for unmediated self-reflection as a star example of something we know with certainty. "Without any illusion or fantasy, I am certain that I am, [and] that I know that I am" (*City of God[CG]* XI.26). We exist because if we doubted that we did, a doubter would exist. Moreover, we know that we know at least one thing, because—supposedly without depending on religious faith or philosophical assumptions—we just proved that we do. With similar certainty, Augustine adds with the same certainty: "I know that I love to exist and that I love to know" (*CG* XI.27). Although Augustine doesn't present an argument in this passage for this additional claim, we can speculate on its Platonic turn: we know that we love knowledge because we persisted in inquiring into whether we exist. And if we know we love knowledge, we know that we love; and if we persisted in inquiring about whether we exist, then we care that we exist. Although the defeat of skepticism brings a generalized epistemological assurance, it does not underwrite the truth of first-person psychological reports that go beyond the moment's proof for the ego's existence at that moment. Nothing follows about what else we know or what else we may be. Nor does Augustine's introspective argument by itself ensure that all moments of self-reflection refer to the same entity. An additional argument would be necessary to show that the self, whose existence is proven by its capacity to doubt, is identical to the person who admires Ambrose, loves his son Adeodatus, and is anguished about his inability to have faith in God's love.

Loyola's *Spiritual Exercises* provides a template practical regimen—a set of stages—to bring a person to his true self, to truthful self-knowledge.[5] For Loyola, the faith—and the transformation of the self—that Augustine thought could only be a gift of divine grace is the objective aim of a series of exercises that anyone can undertake for the sake of his immortal soul.

Loyola articulates ideas implicit in the views of some of the early church fathers: in man's fallen condition, his subjective self-perception, his reflective desires, his sense of self are false and corrupt.[6] To achieve genuine self-knowledge—true selfhood—a person must undergo a painful process of catharsis and reidentification. He must subjectively appropriate—subjectively internalize and experience—each sensory moment of Christ's passion.[7]

Loyola's ego psychology remains latent in some contemporary conceptions of subjectivity, such as the idea that an empathic identification that internalizes the psychological experience of an exemplary figure is necessary to develop a fully reflective ego. The empathic imagination in the service of developing an authentic self is fully sensory: Loyola's penitent must take on the burden, the weight of the cross; he is not only to imagine but to feel the pain of the crown of thorns. "Ask for grief with Christ suffering, a broken heart with Christ heartbroken, tears, and deep suffering . . . of the great suffering that Christ endured for me."[8] Moreover, the character of the empathic experience, which is physically and psychologically painful, is a mark of its transformative power, of the authenticity of the emergent spiritual self. As Ignatius's penitent experiences Christ's suffering as his own, Freud's therapeutic patient reexperiences his childhood traumatic sufferings and—by claiming them as his own—ideally achieves self-knowledge and selfhood. Like Loyola, Freud thinks that an intellectualized recognition of trauma is insufficient to achieve an authentic ego. The psychological-emotional expression of the recovered traumatic wound is also essential.

Despite apparently echoing Augustine's cogito and Loyola's meditative spiritual exercises, Descartes' introspective reflection delivers a radically different kind of subjectivity, a radically different ego-self. Instead of being a soul in quest of faith in God, the ego of the *Meditations* is a mind in quest of mathematical/scientific knowledge. The cogito reveals a thinking mind that is capable of unmediated introspective reflection. But no evidence is available that this self exists continuously or is individuated; and the self is unified only in containing—consisting in—a unified system of ideas. Like Augustine, Descartes offers the cogito as an answer to the radical skeptic. He has undergone the skeptical purgation: he has doubted he has a body, doubted he exists over time, and doubted whether any of his ideas are reliable, let alone true. He knows that as long as the mind is engaged in thinking, there is a thinking thing. So, he asks, in what does thinking consist? At this point in his analysis, thinking consists of episodes of perceiving, imagining, inferring, believing, and doubting. These activities supposedly tell us something about the powers and the faculties of a thinking being. Descartes' answer to the question "What is this thing which thinks?" depends on his memory: he must remember that he perceived, imagined, and so on. But the reliability of his memory is still in doubt, as is the trustworthiness, let alone the truth, of perceptual experience. Quite the contrary. All we know is that the thinker is a "perceiver," a believer.

When Descartes follows the rigorous model of demonstration set by the cogito, he recovers/discovers necessary, indubitable truths. Perceptions, memories, ideas of the imagination—contingent ideas that might have been different or illusory—are not a necessary part of the mind: the ego-mind would remain identical had these elements been different (*Meditations* VI. AT 73–74). The more Descartes holds fast to his existence as a reflective thinker, the less essential are perceptual experience and memory to his identity. The structure of the *Meditations* follows the Platonic ascent of the mind from the apparent contradictions of sensory claims to the light of intellectual insight.[9] The mind is contingently individuated only by its perceptions and memories. But if the ego's essential identity as a thinker consists of necessary truths, all minds providentially contain the same ideas. If all Cartesian thinking egos are, strictly speaking, identical, the mind whose existence was proven at one moment will be the same as that of all others. For necessary ideas—the clear and distinct ideas of mathematics—the problem of how to understand "other minds" vanishes.[10] The ideas that compose the essence of any mind are identical to those that compose all others. True self-knowledge cannot rely on the contingent and fallible perceptual ideas that are not essential to one's true self. The only place that Descartes provides anything like an individuated mind is *Meditation* VI, after God has been shown to guarantee/underwrite the truth of clear and distinct ideas. Only then do we tentatively trust the senses as highly fallible clues to the mathematically demonstrable truths of physics.

Descartes also tells a story that locates subjectivity in the passions of the soul. Like all that appears within the soul, the passions of wonder/amazement, sadness, joy, desire, love, hatred are *ideas* (*Passions of the Soul*, 1.27–29). The ego is aware of the conditions of "its" body only through the mediation of passion-ideas. These passion-ideas are functional but fallible indications of what endangers or sustains the compound union of mind and body (1.40). The insistence of the passions marks both their utility and their danger. The passions signal a need to correct an imbalance or discomfort. In a sense, such ideas are immediately and veridically accessible to the mind. (The angry mind has an unmediated awareness of its passion.) Yet passions can be highly misleading because they do not directly represent their causes or objects. (The angry mind may be mistaken about the sources and directions of its anger.) Considerable knowledge is required to understand—to decipher—the code messages of passion-ideas.[11]

For Descartes, the love of knowledge that Plato and Augustine considered the essence of the soul's experience of itself—its essential drive toward the Good—is an exogenous passion-idea. Like pain and hunger, wonder and desire prompt the mind-body to activities that can sustain that unity but that can also mislead the mind. They are by-products of the *embodied* mind's interactions with Extension (*Passions*, 1. 34–37). The reflective ego is individuated only as an embodied being, which is subject to unreliable passions. The subjective reflection that delivers certain knowledge delivers only mathematical science. The subjective reflections of passion-ideas deliver fallible indicators of the individuated mind-body; and these indicators are only as trustworthy as the individual's grasp of the scientific laws that seek to interpret the confusing information afforded by the passions.

Locke again dramatically and radically shifts the perspective on subjectivity. His analysis of personal identity is that of a physician and a legal theorist. His primary question is not "Who or what am I?" but rather "What are the origins and meaning of the idea of the person? What are the role and function of that idea in ordinary practice?" Locke, not Descartes, gives an account of a self whose individuated subjectivity is fixed by its consciousness, its memory of "its" sense experience. Distinguishing the criteria for the identity of the same *body*, the same *individual* human being, and the same *person*, he found the focus of the idea of the "same individual man" in the continuity of consciousness. "It [is] the same consciousness that makes a man be himself to himself. . . . It is by consciousness that . . . the personal self has of its present thoughts and actions, that it is self to itself now, and so will be the same self, as far as the same consciousness can extend to actions past or to come."[12] Consciousness ensures the continued identity of an individual only as long as the content of that consciousness remains the same. But because the contents of consciousness change with time, consciousness cannot by itself deliver the idea of a person responsible for any past actions of which "it" is not conscious. The forensic idea of *a person* responsible for its *own* past actions depends on the continuity of conscious memory. If memory is the criterion of continuing personal identity, a person can be responsible only for those actions that have left memory traces (*Essay Concerning Human Understanding*, II.27.26). There are two possible interpretations of Locke's criterion for the continued identity of a person. If the forensic identity of a person rests on *conscious* (and articulable) memory, his analysis of the conditions for moral and legal responsibility are dramatically stringent.[13] If Locke intends to analyze and preserve the common practices of liability, he must expand "conscious memory" to include experiences that leave unarticulated but in principle potentially recoverable psychological traces. On this interpretation of Locke's view, a combat veteran suffering from post-traumatic stress disorder (PTSD) is identical to the soldier who has experienced a battle trauma, even if he could in principle recover his memory or if his memory consists in the conscious experience of his PTSD symptoms.

In the name of common sense ("things are what they are, and not another thing"), Bishop Butler argues that Locke's criterion for personal identity presupposes—and thus cannot provide—what it seeks to establish. The person who reports—or evinces—his memories already has a conception of himself as the proper claimant of those memories. "Living and remembering can make no alternation in the truth of past matter of fact."[14] Butler argues that one might doubt whether an idea is a bona fide memory trace (rather than a fantasy); both the doubt and its resolution presuppose the establishment of a continuous personal identity.

Butler's critique of Locke brings us to their predecessor Montaigne and to their successor Hume. Montaigne, almost as if he were trying to follow Locke's dictum, attempts to find his constancy, his continued identity. Searingly honest man that he is, he confesses failure. Reflecting on himself, Montaigne finds no essence and no identity or continuity. Reflection brings constantly shifting ideas and moods: he is now merry, now serious, now bilious, now light-headed. Butler would ask, *Who* is remembering all this? In his skeptical mode, Montaigne responds, "There is no existence that is constant, either of our being or of objects. And we, in our judgment, and all mortal things go on flowing and rolling unceasingly. Thus nothing certain can be established about one thing by another, both the judging and the judged being in continual change and motion."[15] Arguing from a wealth of erudition, Montaigne ironically mocks the pretension to knowledge and to self-knowledge. "Whom shall we believe when he talks about himself?" (*Essays*, II.17–18). As Montaigne's *Essays* unfold, even his philosophical beliefs shift. Ironist throughout, he is now Stoic, now Skeptic, now Epicurean, just as in his early *Essays*, he was now complaisant, now suspicious, now calm.

Hume develops this reflective exchange further. Like Locke, he attempts to trace the source of the idea of personal identity in the content of experience—that is, in the sequence of impressions and ideas. Like Montaigne, he finds that introspection does not deliver a Self. There is only red here, loud here, discomfort here, pride here. "There is properly no simplicity in it at one time, nor identity in different. . . . The mind is nothing more than a bundle or collection of different perceptions, which succeed each other with an inconceivable rapidity." It is the imagination, rather than memory, that constructs the idea of the identity of a person, "The identity, which we ascribe to the mind of man, is only a fictitious one. . . . It proceed[s] from a[n] operation of the imagination."[16]

Hume faces a dilemma: if the self is nothing but a system or train of different perceptions, the idea of the self as a responsible agent is a nonsensical metaphysical fiction. But if the common ideas and practices of agency and responsible agency make sense, we must find their origins in the impressions of experience. Hume resolves his doubts: like Descartes, he projects *two* ideas of the self. Descartes' two egos are the self as mind and the self as the union of mind and body. Hume distinguishes the self "as regards imagination and the sequence of ideas" and the self "as regards the passions and the interest we take in ourselves": in short, the self as a thinker and the self who reflects—and acts—on his passions and preferences.[17] The self as a thinker has—*is*—only the habitual association of ideas. The thinker's reflections on the patterns of his passions—particularly those of pride and humility, love and hatred—reveal his idea of himself as an agent, who, in the nature of the case, projects the continuity of "his" preferences from the past to the future. Hume's agent-self remains a reflective thinker, whose agency consists in the associative and projective activities of the imagination.

The passions of pride and humility are natural and irreducible passions; both give rise to the idea of self as their object. "To this emotion [pride], . . . nature has assigned a certain idea, that of the self, which it never fails to produce." We feel pride or humility; those passions produce the idea of their object, which is the self of which we are proud or humble. Hume distinguishes the object or content of pride from its cause. "A hundred different things" can be the immediate cause of pride: ancestry and descendants, looks and bearing, property, achievements, and virtues. But these things produce the passion of pride only when they are related to the self, when they are thought of as *my* ancestors, *my* achievements. The idea of the self as an entity derives from the pleasurable pride of possession. Further, this pleasurable pride, the idea of what is properly *mine*—*my* ancestors, *my* son—is derived by comparison to others and by the social practices of respect and esteem. Pride requires comparison to others: we take pleasure in possessions that are relatively rare and that are "discernible and obvious, not only to myself, but to others also." Where Aristotle finds self-recognition through the mutual mirroring of virtuous friends, Hume charts the construction of the idea of self in social practices associated with property and propriety. Whereas Hume focuses on the role of pleasurable pride in producing the idea of self as admired for his property, the analysis can be extended to account for the origins of the idea of self as a moral person through the pleasurable pride of being recognized as just and virtuous.[18] With these arguments, Hume dramatically transforms sinful pride into the morally neutral source of all reflective motivation.[19]

Despite sometimes being advertised as the father of subjectivity, Rousseau delivers at least three distinct layers of the reflective self: the presumptive self, the self "in nature," the biological self as it might exist apart from the influence of family or society. This "natural man" has not yet become what nature intends him to become. He has *amour de soi*, the sentiment of his own existence, an instinctual nonreflective sense of his existence and his active well-being.[20] Free, self-reliant, prelinguistic, and preconceptual, natural man does not see himself as an object. He is neither social nor antisocial. A geological or geographical accident—an earthquake, a volcano—brings men into contact with one another. Also by accident, human beings discover the benefits of fire, the pleasures of expressive song, and the kind of minimal cooperation that prompts rudimentary communication. As they form families and societies, they become increasingly dependent on one another. But dependency changes the sense of self: men become self-conscious of themselves as objects, seeing themselves through the eyes of those on whose goodwill and esteem their survival and welfare depend (*Second Discourse* I.1–38). *Amour de soi* gives way to *amour propre:* prereflective subjectivity becomes conscious and is mediated by the judgment of others. The social self is a subject to others and a subject to himself only through others (II.1–30). To regain and fulfill its nature, the self must become rationally self-legislating. Experiencing himself as a citizen, man freely wills actions that accord with the general will. In nature, subjectivity is instinctual; in society, it is emotional; in political citizenship, it is rational and universal (II.31–58).

Fichte's version of transcendental idealism locates the unity of theoretical and practical reason in self-positing, self-constructing subjective reflection.[21] "What was I before I came to self-consciousness? . . . I did not exist at all, for I was not an 'I.' The 'I' exists only insofar as it is conscious of itself. . . . The self posits itself, and by virtue of this mere self-assertion it exists."[22] Through the subjective awareness of its own activity, the Ego comes to recognize others and to acknowledge their moral claims on him. Fichte argues that the subjectivity that pervades all conscious experience is coordinate with—and limited by—the realization of the freedom of others. A conception of justice is, he maintains, implicit in the activities of self-awareness: the recognition of a universally binding morality follows from the rational reflection of a free, self-positing, and self-constructing Ego, who recognizes that he is a subject to himself only because he is also a subject/object to others.[23]

Sartre sees the subjectivity of the ego-self as inescapably inauthentic.[24] "I am not what I am; I am what I am not."[25] What individuals regard as their core self is a projection of bad faith, fleeing the realization of its nonbeing. Like Montaigne and Hume, Sartre holds that the content of consciousness is always in flux. Indeed, like them, he thinks that consciousness has no essential structure or content. It is, so to speak, a mirror—a reflection—of whatever contingent content presents itself. Sartre's ego is a surprising combination of Hume's fictitious idea of the self and Fichte's self-positing "I." The content of subjective self-ascriptions ("I am a melancholy Albanian waitress") stands some distance from the ego that claims them. Even the ascription "I am an ego who chooses to describe herself as a melancholy Albanian waitress" does not capture the arbitrariness of the radical choice of self-identification. An indefinite regress of selves stands behind any choice or act of self-ascription. The denial of any contingent self-ascription—"I am not really an Albanian waitress because I could choose an indefinite number of other self-identifying ascriptions"—is equally inauthentic. After all, the person may, in fact, be an Albanian waitress. The claims and expressions of subjectivity are, and are not, trustworthy. Like Hume and Fichte, Sartre also sees the act of self-constitution as embedded in social recognition.[26] "The problem for me [in constituting myself] is to make myself be by acquiring the possibility of taking the Other's point of view on myself."[27] This stance generates a set of dialectical conflicts in which the mutual mirroring of self and Other construct a "we."[28]

Before turning to some contemporary uses of the concept of subjectivity, let us reconstruct and systematize its history. Our history reveals several distinctive strands in conceptions of subjectivity: it was constituted as a (1) first-person, (2) individuated, (3) self-referential, (4) authoritative veridical report (or expression) of an (5) occurrent (6) mental state (sensation, emotion, thought). These distinctive markers of subjectivity can occur independently of one another; indeed, they demarcate radically different conceptions. The "I" need not be individuated (Descartes and Fichte). The referent of the indexical "I" may have no specific determinate content that remains constant over an individual's biological life (Montaigne and Hume). The report/expression of an occurrent sensory experience need not be veridical (Descartes). Self-positing consciousness may be a condition for experience (Fichte). The choice of the content of self-awareness may be transformative or performatively constitutive (Loyola and Sartre). In some usages, subjective reports claim validity; in others, they are fallible. In some usages, subjectivity is contrasted with objectivity; in others, it is a self-constituting performance. In some usages, subjective reflection is individuated; in others, it reveals the structure of any and every mind's necessarily self-validating ideas. These radically distinctive conceptions of subjectivity have dramatically different roles in the phenomenology of reflective experience.

CULTURAL ANTHROPOLOGY
AND THE ETHICS OF METHODOLOGY

Although no consensus exists about the proper way to analyze subjectivity, there is a marked contemporary revival of interest in—and legitimation of—the deliverances of subjective reflection. Among those who have recently accorded authority to the first person are cultural anthropologists who consider themselves under a moral obligation to respect and preserve the voices of indigenous people.[29] Concerned that fieldwork in the third world is the continuation of colonialism by anthropological means, these activist anthropologists attempt to preserve the voices, the practices, and the economic integrity of second and third world societies by forming organizations like Cultural Survival.[30]

Other anthropologists—let's call them *methodological purists*—privilege the first-person viewpoint of their subjects, attempting to understand them in their own terms. While continuing to chart kinship structures and exchange systems, purists accord indigenous informants ethnographic authority on the meaning of these relations, without imposing or projecting the psychological categories or explanatory theories of their own cultures onto those of the Other. Instead of interpreting the subjective psychology of their informants in Western terms, they analyze the semantic patterns of indigenous self-representing discourse. Using only minimally interpretive translations, they distinguish and analyze the distinctive self-constituting discourse of men and women, elders, priests and warriors, the powerful and the marginalized.[31]

Philosophically minded anthropologists hold that semantic and pragmatic distinctions—between truth claims and expressive utterances, between literal and figurative expressions, and between beliefs and practices or rituals—do not designate or describe distinct psychological or linguistic categories. They argue that because such distinctions are philosophically theory bound, they distort explanations of indigenous practices.[32] Others join postmodern literary theorists in questioning the assumptions of essentialist "master narratives."[33] For didactic and expository reasons—because they are, after all, addressing culturally Anglophone readers—these anthropologists nevertheless freely speak of "subjectivity," recognizing that such a category may be incomprehensible to many indigenous peoples.[34]

Other anthropologists, influenced by philosophic analyses of problems of the indeterminacy of translation, criticize the purist quest as a hopeless project.[35] These anthropologists—let's call them *ironists*—see purist attempts to recover indigenous subjectivity as naive and exploitable.[36] Recognizing that their indigenous informants often engage in the power politics of self-transformation, they attempt to let their subjects—representative members of ethnicities, religions, genders, and classes—speak for themselves, according them the final authority of self-interpretation.[37] Sensitivity to the ways in which participant observers affect social practices and the dynamics of indigenous power struggles prompted research into the political ramifications of cultural intrusion.[38] Concerned about the deflections of the anthropological presence, many purists drift to the ironic view that there are no politically innocent ethnographies. Rather than taking indigenous self-identifying and self-ascribing characterizations at face value, they interpret these self-characterizations as rhetorically pragmatic and often political in intent.[39] Other ironists accuse purist ethnographers of either serving the ideology of their own cultures or using their ethnographies as thinly disguised criticism of their own cultures.[40] Ironically minded anthropologists chart the ways in which indigenous people actively become their own ethnographers, constructing "essentialist" cultural identities as a strategy in an internal power struggle or as artifacts for consumption in the politics of the global economy.[41] They argue that any vital sociopolitical group is internally subdivided, with no stable nonperspectival identity markers and with multiple group-specific linguistic practices that shift dynamically across subgroup associations.[42] Because individuals are members of cross-cutting and often conflicting associations, subjective identity characterizations shift widely between multiple perspectives.

While admiring the purism of clean hands and clear heads, ironists make a virtue of necessity: they see their anthropological intrusions as negligible in comparison to the mutually predatory raids of indigenous peoples, the dynamics of their internal power struggles, and the transformative effects of the global economy. Ironic autobioethnographies openly and frankly include reflective narratives of their personal and politically charged interactions and negotiations with indigenous peoples.[43] What started as a methodological respect for the subjectivity of indigenous peoples sometimes ends as a rhetorical trope in postcolonial and anticolonial politics and sometimes as a confessional moment in anthropological autobiographies. Attempting to bypass the politically charged dialectic of subjectivity, philosophers like Habermas analyze the "logical" preconditions for interpretation and communication, arguing that these preconditions establish the ethics as well as the method of intersubjective understanding.[44]

MEDICAL PRACTICE AND THE VOICE OF THE SUBJECT

The agenda of the recent focus on subjectivity and on "the subject" of medical practice focuses primarily on therapeutic and moral as well as epistemic and methodological concerns.[45] A number of distinctive strands conjoin to give authority to the testimony of subjective experience.

1) Diagnostic and therapeutic reasons exist for granting epistemic validity to patients' illness narratives without automatically overriding them with the presumed objective deliverances of medical authorities.[46] Patients' individual beliefs—sometimes culturally encoded, sometimes idiosyncratic—about their constitutions, diets, occupations, and family circumstances influence their medical conditions. Their interpretations of the sources and symptomatic expressions of illness are experientially as well as diagnostically relevant.[47] Fine-grain details of patients' medical conditions are affected by their perceptions of power, class, gender, family and occupational responsibilities, ethnoculture, and age. Medical practitioners increasingly depend on patients' subjective phenomenological reports, seeing these reports as an essential part of successful diagnosis and therapy.[48]

2) Sensitivity to the experience of pain and suffering conjoins diagnostic considerations in pressing for patients' active participation in the therapeutic process. Some medical ethicists argue that an "I-Thou" dialogic sensibility that responds to the voice of the subject evokes a constructive partnership in healing: it elicits attentiveness, engagement, and sensitivity from medical practitioners and active cooperation by patients.[49] Because patients benefit most from alert participation in their therapeutic regimen, they need to understand that process in their own terms. Uniting the methodological concerns of anthropologists with the practical concerns of physicians, medical anthropologists track the logic and logistics of treating patients as partners rather than as the subject-objects of the work of healing.[50]

3) Many medical ethicists base their arguments for legitimizing the authority of patient autonomy on a liberal political theory that accords individuals fundamental inalienable rights of rational self-determination, espe-

cially in matters of life and death.[51] Nevertheless, morally and politically committed to respecting patient subjectivity, these theorists typically also offer specific normative and regulative principles to guide "rational choice" in medical contexts. Minimally, and perhaps less nobly, the informed consent of the patient has become a pressing legal matter as well as a moral one.

Concern about preserving the authority of phenomenological patient-subjects in medical theory and practice surprisingly reproduces and echoes distinctive strands in the transformative history of the conception of subjectivity. Conceptions of subjectivity over time—the power that Augustine accords to confessional expression, the authenticity that Loyola accords to the unmediated experience of pain and suffering, the epistemic privilege that Descartes accords to introspective reflection, the role that Hume assigns to the social origins of the fictional idea of the self, the egalitarian direction of Rousseau's analysis of the rights of individual autonomy, the dialogical "we" that emerges from the Fichtean and Sartrean self-positing "I"—all reappear in the rationale of contemporary anthropological theory and medical practice. The distinctive moments in the history of subjectivity are still alive and well—and as multifaceted as ever. Despite the transformative history of conceptions of subjectivity—despite the fact that it appears to have no core meaning—the various themes of subjectivity continue to reappear: the repressed subject returns.

NOTES

I presented an ancestor of this paper at the Friday Morning Seminar in Medical Anthropology in the Department of Social Medicine and at Virginie Greene's seminar on medieval conceptions of subjectivity in the Department of Romance Languages, both at Harvard. I am grateful to the seminar participants and to MindaRae Amiran, João Biehl, David Glidden, Byron Good, Virginie Greene, Jocelyn Hoy, Arthur Kleinman, and William Ruddick for their constructive comments and bibliographical suggestions. A version of this essay appeared in the *History of Philosopy Quarterly* (July 2006).

1. Michel de Montaigne, "Of the Inconsistency of Our Actions," in *The Complete Essays of Montaigne,* ed. Donald Frame (Stanford, CA: Stanford University Press, 1966), II.1.

2. See Aryeh Kosman, "Perceiving that We Perceive: DA 3.2," *Philosophical Review,* 1975.

3. See Amélie Rorty, "The Place of Contemplation in Aristotle's Ethics," in *Essays on Aristotle's Ethics* (Berkeley: University of California Press, 1980), esp. 338–91.

4. See Aryeh Kosman, "Aristotle on the Desirability of Friends," *Ancient Philosophy,* 2004.

5. St. Ignatius Loyola, *The Spiritual Exercises if St. Ignatius,* ed. and trans. Louis Puhl (New York: Vintage, 2000).

6. Loyola, "First Week: The Examination of Conscience," *Spiritual Exercises*.

7. Loyola, "Third Week: The Events of the Passion," *Spiritual Exercises*.

8. Ibid.

9. See Stephen Menn, *Descartes and Augustine* (Cambridge, MA: Cambridge University Press, 1998), esp. II.6.A, 367–70.

10. See Amélie Rorty, "The Structure of Descartes' Meditations," in *Essays on Descartes' Meditations*, ed. A. O. Rorty (Berkeley: University of California Press, 1986).

11. See Amélie Rorty, "Descartes on Thinking with the Body," in *Descartes*, ed. John Cottingham (Cambridge: Cambridge University Press, 1992).

12. John Locke, *An Essay Concerning Human Understanding*, ed. Alexander Campbell Fraser (Oxford: Oxford University Press, 1844), II.27.10.

13. For an extended discussion of interpretations of Locke's criteria for personal identity see J. L. Mackie, *Problems from Locke* (Oxford: Oxford University Press, 1976), ch. 6.

14. Joseph Butler, "Of Personal Identity," *Dissertations*, Dissertation I.

15. Montaigne, "Apology for Raymond Sebond," *Complete Essays*, II. 12.

16. David Hume, *Treatise of Human Nature*, ed. David Fate Norton and Mary J. Norton (Oxford: Oxford University Press, 2000), 1.4.6.

17. Ibid.

18. Ibid., 2.1.5–6, 2.1.2, 2.1.5–6, 11, 1.6, III.3.1.

19. See A. O. Rorty, "The Structure of Hume's *Treatise*," in *Essays on Hume's 'Treatise,'* ed. Donald Ainslie (Cambridge: Cambridge University Press, 2006).

20. Jean-Jacques Rousseau, "Discourse on the Origins and Foundations of Inequality among Men," in *The Discourses and Other Early Political Writings*, ed. Victor Gourevitch (Cambridge: Cambridge University Press, 1997), n. 15.

21. J. G. Fichte, "Wissenschaftslehre, 1.1," *Introductions to Wissenschaftslehre and Other Writings*, ed. and trans. David Breazeale (Indianapolis: Hackett, 1994).

22. Fichte, "Second Introduction, 9," *Introductions to Wissenschaftslehre*.

23. See Stephen Darwall, "Fichte and the Second Person Standpoint," *International Yearbook for German Idealism*, 2005"; and "Respect and the Second Person Standpoint," *Proceedings and Addresses of the American Philosophical Association*, 2004.

24. Jean-Paul Sartre, *Being and Nothingness*, trans. Hazel Barnes (New York: Philosophical Library, 1956), II.1.1 and 5.

25. Ibid., III.3.3.

26. Ibid., II.1.2, III.3.3.

27. Ibid., III.1.1.

28. Ibid., III.3.3.

29. See Arthur Kleinman, *Patients and Healers in the Context of Culture* (Berkeley: University of California Press, 1980); and Arthur Kleinman, Veena Das, and Margaret Lock, eds., *Social Suffering* (Berkeley: University of California Press, 1997). See especially the papers by Paul Farmer, Allen Young, and Talal Asad.

30. See *Cultural Survival Quarterly*, a journal that has, for thirty years, covered issues of concern to indigenous peoples.

31. See, for example, Sherry Ortner, "Theory in Anthropology since the Sixties," *Comparative Studies in Society and History* 26, 1984; and N. B. Dirks, Geoff Eley, and Sherry Ortner, eds., *Culture/Power/History* (Princeton, NJ: Princeton University Press, 1994).

32. See Byron Good, *Medicine, Rationality and Experience: An Anthropological Perspective* (Cambridge: Cambridge University Press, 1994).

33. See, for example, Michel Foucault, *Language, Memory and Practice* (Ithaca, NY: Cornell University Press, 1980); Kevin Dwyer, *Moroccan Dialogues* (Baltimore: Johns Hopkins University Press, 1977); Dennis Tedlock, *The Spoken Word and the Work of Interpretation* (Philadelphia: University of Pennsylvania Press, 1983); Sherry Ortner, "Theory in Anthropology since the Sixties"; Michael Fischer with Mehdi Abedi, *Debating Muslims: Cultural Dialogue in Post-Modernity and Tradition* (Madison: University of Wisconsin Press, 1990); and James Boon, *Other Tribes, Other Scribes* (Cambridge: Cambridge University Press, 1982).

34. See, for example, Michelle Rosaldo, *Knowledge and Passion: Ilongot Notions of Self and Social Life* (Cambridge: Cambridge University Press, 1980); and Catherine Lutz and Lila Abu-Lughod, eds., *Language and the Politics of Emotion* (Cambridge: Cambridge University Press, 1990).

35. For the most influential formulation of the problem of indeterminacy in translations that led ironist anthropologists to become suspicious of purist ethnography, see W. V. Quine, "Ontological Relativity," *Journal of Philosophy*, 1968; and "On the Reason for Indeterminacy of Translation," *Journal of Philosophy*, 1970. See also Donald Davidson, *Inquiries into Truth and Interpretation* (Oxford: Oxford University Press, 1984); and Ernest Lepore, ed., *Truth and Interpretation* (Oxford: Oxford University Press, 1986).

36. I shall, for convenience, speak of *purists* and *ironists* as though they were committed to different anthropological methods and perspectives. Of course, most anthropologists attempt to combine these perspectives, sometimes self-consciously and sometimes apparently unaware of the shifts in their perspectives. See Clifford Geertz, *Works and Lives: The Anthropologist as Author* (Stanford, CA: Stanford University Press, 1988); Vincent Crapanzano, *Hermes' Dilemma and Hamlet's Desire: On the Epistemology of Interpretation* (Cambridge, MA: Harvard University Press, 1992); Renato Rosaldo, *Culture and Truth: The Remaking of Social Analysis* (Boston: Beacon Press, 1993); James Clifford and George Marcus, eds., *Writing Culture: The Poetics and Politics of Ethnography* (Berkeley: University of California Press, 1986). See especially the essays by George Marcus, Michael Fischer, Paul Rabinow, and James Clifford in this anthology.

37. See, for example, Marcel Griaule, *Conversations with Ogotemmeli* (Oxford: Oxford University Press, 1972); Leila Ahmed, *A Border Passage* (New York, 2000); Lila Abu-Lughod, *Writing Women's Worlds: Bedouin Stories* (Berkeley: University of California Press, 1993); Elizabeth Warnock Fernea, *Guests of the Sheik: An Ethnography of an Iraqi Village* (New York: Doubleday-Anchor, 1965).

38. See Clifford Geertz, "From the Native's Point of View: On the Nature of Anthropological Understanding," in *Culture Theory: Essays on Mind, Self and Emotion*, ed. Richard Shweder and Robert A. Levine (Cambridge: Cambridge University Press, 1984).

39. See, for example, Talal Asad, *Anthropology and the Colonial Encounter* (London, 1973); Ernest Gellner, *Anthropology and Politics: Revolutions in the Sacred Grove* (Oxford: Oxford University Press, 1995); John Hall and J. C. Jarvie, *Transition to Modernity: Essays on Power, Wealth and Belief* (Cambridge: Cambridge University Press, 1992); Sherry Ortner, *Making Gender: The Politics and Eros of Culture* (Boston: Beacon Press, 1996).

40. See George Marcus and Michael Fischer, *Anthropology as Cultural Critique*

(Chicago: University of Chicago Press, 1999); George Marcus, *Ethnography Through Thick and Thin* (Princeton, NJ: Princeton University Press, 1998).

41. For example, see Kay Warren and Jean Jackson, eds., *Indigenous Movements, Self-Representation and the State in Latin America* (Austin: University of Texas Press, 2002).

42. See, for example, Amélie Rorty, "The Hidden Politics of Multi-Culturalism," *Political Theory*, 1994.

43. See, for example, Clifford Geertz, *After the Fact: Two Countries, Four Decades, One Anthropologist* (Cambridge, MA: Harvard University Press, 1995); and *Available Light: Anthropological Reflections on Philosophical Topics* (Princeton, NJ: Princeton University Press, 2000). See also Paul Rabinow, *Reflections on Fieldwork in Morocco* (Berkeley: University of California Press, 1977).

44. See, for example, Jürgen Habermas, "The Hermeneutic Claim to Universality," in *Contemporary Hermeneutics*, ed. Josef Bleicher (Routledge, 1980).

45. See, for example, Dan Brock, *Life and Death: Philosophical Essays on Biomedical Ethics* (Cambridge: Cambridge University Press, 1993); Kleinman, *Patients and Healers*; Allen Buchanan and Dan Brock, *Deciding for Others* (Cambridge: Cambridge University Press, 1989); E. D. Pellegrino and D. C. Thomasma, *The Virtues in Medical Practice* (New York: Oxford University Press, 1993); T. L. Beauchamp and J. F. Childress, *Principles of Bio-Medical Ethics* (Oxford: Oxford University Press, 1989); Miles Little, *Humane Medicine* (Cambridge: Cambridge University Press, 1995); and Kleinman, Das, and Lock, *Social Suffering*. See especially the essays by Paul Farmer, Allan Young, and Talal Asad.

46. See, for example, Mary-Jo DelVecchio Good, Paul E. Brodwin, Byron J. Good, and Arthur Kleinman, eds., *Pain as Human Experience: An Anthropological Perspective* (Berkeley: University of California Press, 1994).

47. Alan Radley, ed., *Worlds of Illness: Biographical and Cultural Perspectives on Health and Disease* (London: Routledge, 1993); and his *Making Sense of Illness* (London: Sage, 1994).

48. Mark Zborowski, *People in Pain* (San Francisco: Jossey-Bass, 1969); Jay Katz, ed., *Experimentation with Human Beings: The Authority of the Investigator and Subject* (New York: Russell Sage, 1972); and his *Silent World of Doctor and Patient* (Baltimore: Johns Hopkins University Press, 2002); S. K. Toombs, *The Meaning of Illness: A Phenomenological Account of the Different Perspectives of Physician and Patient* (Dordrecht: Kluwer Academic Publishers, 1992).

49. See, for example, Jean Jackson, *Camp Pain: Talking with Chronic Pain Patients* (Berkeley: University of California Press, 2000); João Biehl, *Vita: Life in a Zone of Social Abandonment* (Berkeley: University of California Press, 2005); Thomas Csordas, *The Sacred Self: Cultural Phenomenology of Charismatic Healing* (Berkeley: University of California Press, 1994); and his *Body/Meaning/Healing* (New York: Palgrave Press, 2002).

50. See Kleinman, *Patients and Healers*.

51. Tom Beauchamp and Seymore Perlin, *Ethical Issues in Death and Dying* (Englewood, NJ: Prentice Hall, 1978); Brock, *Life and Death*; Buchanan and Brock, *Deciding for Others*.

2 The Experiential Basis of Subjectivity

How Individuals Change in the Context of Societal Transformation

ARTHUR KLEINMAN AND ERIN FITZ-HENRY

For years, the study of subjectivity has been dominated by theories of the self that interrogate cultural representations and performance. These studies have a certain richness in helping us understand how societies change because they are able to deal with collective transformations through major cultural meanings and practices. But they usually leave the intimate subjectivity of individuals unanalyzed, like a black box, or bring to it a decidedly sectarian view, such as Freudian psychoanalysis, which has long been overworked and overreached as an explanatory framework. However, anthropology has downplayed, at least since W. H. R. Rivers, the importance of theories of experience for understanding subjectivity. The study of the collective and individual poles of experience—and the insights it can give us into affect, memory, and other deeply subjective self processes—curiously has not been a major source of recent anthropological theory or research.

A problem in the study of subjectivity that troubles all anthropologists is the ongoing emphasis in philosophy, psychology, and other social science disciplines on a kind of universal human nature that is held to be neurobiologically hardwired and historically unchanging. Denis Diderot, for example, writing in the eighteenth century, asserted that "Human nature is the same everywhere," a sentiment echoed by twentieth-century structuralist anthropologists and even some contemporary cultural psychologists. Scholars have frequently invoked this notion of a unified human nature as the rationale for universals of all kinds, and it continues to be used as a justification for Western ethical discourse, which assumes a static, generalized subject that does not vary with changing historical circumstances, cultural contexts, or sociopolitical institutions.

Such formulations are problematic for anthropologists who, while respecting the neurobiological underpinnings of human behavior and cognition, as well as the urgent necessity of ethics discourse, recognize that human beings' complex commitments and moral challenges are far too intricate to explain by biological reductionism. Although infant and twin studies may offer important insights into the genetic bases of behavior, they still largely fail to account for the enormous complexity of human social experience—war, genocide, structural violence, poverty, and displacement—and the highly nuanced subjective states that those experiences engender. In dealing with the genocide in Rwanda; the civil wars in Cambodia, Liberia, and Sri Lanka; the repressive regimes in El Salvador and Guatemala; the street violence in Los Angeles; the suicide bombings in the Middle East; or even the more "routine" violences of social neglect and institutionalized racism, neurobiology simply cannot show itself to be immediately consequential. Our subjectivities certainly have a biology, but they also, and perhaps more critically, have an equally influential history, cultural specificity, political location, and economic position. In short, we are as responsive to biological blueprints as we are to alterations in political economy and social positioning, both of which, in turn, refashion the very biology of those blueprints.

To understand human subjectivity, then, we cannot simply resort to a biologically grounded universal human nature or take refuge in abstract, ahistorical ethical discourse; we need to affirm the variability, heterogeneity, and contingency of our subjectivities as they unfold within the realm of experience. Following Michael Oakeshott (1933) and many others, we define experience as the felt flow of interpersonal communication and engagements, or as William James says, "reality, life, experience, concreteness, immediacy, use what word you will . . . by reality here I mean where things *happen*" (1977: 96). Experience is intersubjective inasmuch as it involves practices, negotiations, and contestations with others with whom we are connected. It is also the medium within which collective and subjective processes fuse, enter into dialectical relationship, and mutually condition one another. We are born into the flow of palpable experience, where our senses are first patterned by the symbols and social interactions of our local worlds. But our emergent subjectivities also return to those symbols and interactions, reconfiguring, repatterning, and sometimes even completely reinterpreting them. Experience, then, has as much to do with collective realities as it does with individual translations and transformations of those realities. It is always simultaneously social and subjective, collective and individual. Thus, we can talk of moral experience as the fusion of affect and moral meanings in the interpersonal realm, where, for example, "loss of face" is simultaneously a personal and a collective process.

Most importantly, though, experience always takes place within particular social spaces and is inextricable from the shifting exigencies of practical, everyday life within those spaces. In villages, neighborhoods, families, and workplaces, people are aware that certain practical things matter greatly—status, relationships, resources, ultimate meanings, death, or transcendence—and they struggle to preserve and protect those things. This charged engagement with the things of a local world lends experience its intrinsically moral character: experience is the medium through which people engage with the things that matter most to them, both individually and collectively, whether a national identity, a collective memory of suffering, a personal aspiration, a health condition, or the preservation of a native language. And as the anthropological record has already extensively documented, what is at stake often varies radically from culture to culture and even within a given culture, where differences of class, ethnicity, political affiliation, gender, and individuality may further differentiate interests. People who are thrust to the outskirts of institutional power, regularly exposed to police violence, or battered by bureaucratic racism, will have an entirely different set of concerns, cultural representations, and collective processes than will people who live at the center of political and economic power and who are certain that their interests are being attended to by the state, their welfare is deemed valuable, and they have allies in the institutional structures that surround them.

Furthermore, the stakes for various communities and individuals are never static, because large-scale political and economic processes constantly alter the landscapes in which local worlds are anchored. Under the pressures of globalization, for example, traditional practices and economies often undergo dramatic shifts, as in China, where the transition from a centrally planned to a market economy has led to growing disparities between rich and poor, breakdowns in social networks, and entirely different ways of experiencing affect, now disconnected from the traditional sources of moral sentiment. Again, the effects of such changes are by no means uniform: alterations in macroinstitutions differentially affect various communities within a local world. For communities that have the natural and institutional resources to buffer their members from the potentially negative consequences of such changes, the effects on individual lives may be minimal, whereas for those lacking such resources, the effects may be, and often are, greatly influential, even at times lethal. Thus, the politics, resources, and institutional frameworks of local communities mediate between macrolevel social and political changes and microlevel individual transformations. The vector of change can also be reversed: individuals can and do change their contexts, and different persons exert different influences and are in turn influenced in different ways.

By focusing on the particularity of experience, we move further and further away from the idea of a universal human nature and toward an appreciation of the variety of human conditions within which often greatly different things are at stake. Recognizing the multiplicity of human conditions, we affirm that our subjectivities and the moral processes in which we engage are forever in flux—not static, abstract, biologically fixed, or divorced from political, social, and economic processes, but fluid, contingent, and open to transformation. As our worlds change, so do we. And as transnational trends, such as the latest phases of finance capitalism, remake the conditions of our lives and the parameters of our worlds, so, too, do they remake our most intimate inner processes: emotion, cognitive style, memory, our deepest sense of self.

Both historically and cross-culturally, the ethnographic record is rife with examples of such change, many of which testify to the inextricable interconnections between cultural representations, collective processes, and subjectivity. To narrow this huge and disorderly field, in this essay, we will focus primarily on these interconnections in settings of political violence. To be sure, extreme examples of political violence are so dramatically defining that one can see more clearly than usual how feeling and action are remade by social imagery and political strategies.

Psychosocial studies of participants in acts of genocide provide haunting reminders of how quickly and dramatically such changes restructure moral processes and redefine the stakes for local actors. Christopher Browning's 1992 *Ordinary Men: Reserve Police Battalion 101 and the Final Solution in Poland,* for example, is an attempt to understand how middle-aged reserve policemen from Hamburg came to participate in the deportation and slaughter of thousands of Polish Jews beginning in the summer of 1942. How were these "grassroots perpetrators," most of whom were working-class men between the ages of thirty-three and forty-eight, transformed, in the space of just a few months, into "professional killers"? On June 20, 1942, Browning tells us, Reserve Police Battalion 101 received orders for an unspecified "special action" in Poland, a euphemism for the massacre of more than 1,800 Jewish men, women, and children, the weakest of whom were simply shot on sight. Beginning at daybreak and continuing until early in the evening, the officers isolated the Jews in the central marketplace and then escorted them to a nearby forest, where the Jews were lined up, paired one-on-one with officers, and shot at close range, sometimes so violently that their skulls exploded. Perhaps the most disturbing aspect of Browning's account, however, is the fact that all these men were given the opportunity to refuse the action, but only a handful did. Why?

He suggests a number of reasons, both collective and individual. First, the members of this newly formed battalion experienced intense pressure to conform, along with an equally intense sense of loyalty and camaraderie. This close identification between the men in uniform proved stronger and more influential than their perceptions of the humanity of their victims. In this local world, where in-group affiliation was most at stake, "stepping out" meant "losing face," because it signaled that one was "weak," "cowardly," and willing to break rank (72). In addition, the standard cultural representations of Jews as those "outside the circle of human obligation and responsibility" played a role (73). Although few men in the battalion had consciously adopted the eliminationist anti-Semitic doctrines of the Nazi regime, they had certainly internalized the images of Jews so frequently invoked by their commanders, who did not hesitate to remind them that Jews were the enemy and that "the enemy [is] killing German women and children by bombing Germany" (73).

Also, however, the men rationalized the killings in substantially different ways. Some believed that regardless of whether they participated or not, the Jews would not "escape their fate," whereas others went so far as to see themselves in religious terms—as the "redeemers" of children who had lost their mothers. As one thirty-five-year-old metalworker explained, "I made the effort, and it was possible for me, to shoot only children. . . . I reasoned with myself that after all without its mother the child could not live any longer. It was supposed to be, so to speak, soothing to my conscience to release children unable to live without their mothers" (73). Thus, even within this local world, which had an intensely demanding ethos of loyalty and an anti-Semitic cultural orientation, psychological differences existed between the men—and even conflicts and contradictions, depending on the circumstance. Major Trapp, for example, the head commander of the battalion and the one responsible for conveying the orders to the troops, reportedly cried "like a child" on more than one occasion, whispering, simply, "everything is very terrible." On another, he confided to his driver, "If this Jewish business is ever avenged on earth, then have mercy on us Germans." And on yet another, with his hand over his heart, he lamented aloud, "Oh God, why did I have to be given these orders?" (58). Hence, the setting was not that of cold, ruthless brutality demanded of SS mass killers in the death camps, but of an affectively open context in which the killers and their leaders saw themselves as the true sufferers, men who often killed reluctantly and with pain and sorrow yet did their job to the bitter end. We see different ways, then, in which affect and personal identity come together with group norms, "orders," and mass murder. To understand the subjective transformations that culminated in the murder of more than six million Jews during World War II, we need to do more than simply trace changes in major cultural, political, and economic practices; we also need to describe the patterns by which cultural representations, collective processes, and distinct subjectivities came together in a particular local world—in this case, that of Police Battalion 101 in the Nazi state.

The 1994 genocide in Rwanda provides an equally unsettling portrait of the transformations of ordinary Rwandan peasants into citizens willing to murder between 800,000 and 1,000,000 of their neighbors and friends in the space of just one hundred days. To fully understand the Rwandan genocide, one must first delineate the historical trajectories along which the identities of Hutu and Tutsi were first constructed and later racialized by the Belgian colonial administration (Gourevitch 1999; Mamdani 2001). The colonial authorities justified their political and legal privileging of the Tutsis by institutionalizing the so-called Hamitic myth. Whereas initially the terms *Hutu* and *Tutsi* indicated little more than class or caste distinctions (Hutus were cultivators, and Tutsi were herdsmen), the Hamitic myth propagated by John Hamming Speke and other "race scientists" suggested that "all culture and civilization in central Africa had been introduced by the taller, sharper-featured people, . . . considered to be a Caucasoid tribe of Ethiopian origin, descended from the biblical King David, and therefore a superior race to the native Negroids" (Gourevitch 1999: 51). This absurd hypothesis became the cornerstone of the Belgian administration and was firmly fixed in law between 1933 and 1934, when the administration, much like that of South Africa, began to issue "ethnic identity cards" that virtually prevented Hutus from becoming Tutsis. Slowly, the Nilotic Tutsis became identified as an "alien minority" within Rwanda like the Europeans themselves and were allotted all the political and administrative privileges such a status afforded. In contrast, the Bantu Hutus, the "indigenous majority," were forced into communal labor on plantations, in forests, and along highways. This racialized distinction was the fuel that fired the social revolution of 1959, the rise of the Hutu Power movement, and the genocide of 1994.

But, again, to understand the transformations in subjectivity and moral sentiment that made possible the genocide that was carried out, village by village, in the early 1990s, we need to appreciate not just the "poisoned legacy of colonialism" but the contemporary intersections between changing representations of the Hutu and the Tutsi, the processes by which the Hutu Power movement was able to mobilize a "culture of fear," and the ways in which those processes and representations were appropriated by individuals with distinct motivations, in different socioeconomic positions, and in pursuit of disparate ends. As Mahmood Mamdani points out in his 2001 *When Victims Become Killers,* many Hutu farmers slaughtered their Tutsi neighbors and nonpolitical or dissident counterparts, not because of greed or hatred but because of a terrible fear propagated by Hutu extremists, who, beginning as early as 1957 with the publication of the *Hutu Manifesto,* convinced the farmers that the Tutsis were a *race* alien to Rwanda and that if they refused to kill, the RPF (Rwandan Patriotic Front) would confiscate their land and strip them of their rights. By November 1992, nightly radio broadcasts called on Hutu civilians to "wipe out this scum" and to destroy "these cockroaches." Kiruhara, an illiterate twenty-seven-year-old Hutu peasant, remembers, "[They] were always telling people that if the RPF comes, it will return Rwanda to feudalism, that it would bring oppression" (Mamdani 2001: 191). And as Benedicte Ndagijimana recalls of his fellow countrymen, "They hear over and over that the Tutsis are out to kill them, and that is reality. So they act not out of hate so much as fear. They think they have only the choice to kill or be killed" (191). Because of these manipulations of collective representations by Hutu extremists via the national radio and during "consciousness-raising" sessions, Hutu peasants came to believe that they were under attack and that if they did not kill, they would be subjugated by the armies of the RPF from neighboring Uganda. This state-sponsored fear and incitement of hatred, with its origins in the Belgian occupation, defined the local worlds of thousands of Rwandans.

In the context of "ordinary lives," however, people certainly had more than one motivation for participating in the genocide—and those motivations were rooted as much in the political history and cultural traditions of Rwanda as in the terrors and scarcities that defined individual lives. Some historians fault the Rwandese political tradition, which, both before and after colonialism, was "one of systematic, centralized, and unconditional obedience to authority" (199). From this perspective, this "culture of obedience" laid the groundwork for the collective assent to the genocide. As one Hutu lawyer explained, "conformity is deep, very developed here. In Rwandan culture, everyone obeys authority" (200).

Others, however, contend that the war is best understood against the backdrop of changing economic circumstances that culminated in land scarcity, declining food production, and intense rivalries for resources. Following the economic collapse of the late 1980s, thousands of young men had no prospects of employment, and these men formed the core of the Hutu militia groups, or *interahamwe,* in which they were trained not for agricultural or administrative work but in the use of machetes and the practices of disembowelment. Thus, the "culture of obedience," the "culture of fear," increasingly grim economic realities, and the collective representations of Tutsis as "horned devils" came together in a way that violently altered both collective and subjective processes. As one man said of his friend who had acquired Hutu identity papers, "He was a very nice person, . . . always trying to help people out, buying cigarettes, a place to sleep, blankets. . . . And then one night he changed completely. We couldn't talk anymore because I am Tutsi. This happened with so many people. They changed so quickly that you would say, 'Is this the same person?' " (Gourevitch, 92).

But how, specifically, were individuals changed? Working as a *New Yorker* journalist, Philip Gourevitch set out to understand this question in the spring of 1995, when he arrived in gutted, blood-strewn Rwanda to interview both perpetrators and victims. Among the former was Monsignor Augustin Misago, the bishop of Gikongoro. Like many of his colleagues in the church, Misago was divided about a "theological resolution" to the genocide, and although he denied that the apparition of the Virgin Mary on May 15 was a factor, this event, which the Rwandan media exalted as an iconic justification for the slaughter, may have proven decisive. Unlike others, however, Misago participated in the massacre of Tutsis in a particularly direct and gruesome way, abandoning more than ninety Tutsi schoolchildren to the police, who subsequently slaughtered eighty-two of them. When confronted about his role in the massacre, he responded, "What could I do? I don't have an army. What could I do by myself? . . . When men become like devils, and you don't have any army, what can you do?" (138–89). Again and again, he offered this line of defense: he had been powerless in the face of Hutu Power extremists. Furthermore, he said, not only did he lack sufficient resources to defend his parishioners, but he, too, was mired in the ignorance born of wartime propaganda, and he, too, just like the schoolchildren, had been abandoned. "We were badly informed," he continued. "The unfortunate thing was that among those policemen there were some accomplices of the *interahamwe*. I couldn't have known that." And later, in a more accusatory vein, "You—you Westerners—left and abandoned us all." Thus, Misago justified his desertion of the children at Kibeho by clutching at apparent alliances with them. By appropriating the images and affective motifs of powerlessness, ignorance, and abandonment, he sought, as Gourevitch says, "to be thought of as a victim of the same deception that had resulted in eighty-two children being slaughtered" (138). Misago made this sense of victimhood the centerpiece around which he defined his subjectivity.

But Misago's is not the only, nor, thankfully, the most representative story to come out of Rwanda. Faced with similar cultural, political, and economic circumstances, others, like Hutu dissident and hotel proprietor Paul Ruesabagina, acted quite differently—driven not by a sense of their own victimhood but by the imperative of procuring shelter and providing ongoing protection for the most vulnerable members of the community. Although Paul testified to feeling as "if he were already dead" and complained of a persistent lack of trust and diminished sense of freedom, he nonetheless managed to assume control of the Hotel des Milles Collines, besieged on all sides by *interahamwe*, and to oversee its functioning as a safe haven for Tutsi refugees. Unlike many of his counterparts, he did not opt only to "save his own skin" or to kill reluctantly; he chose to "save everybody he could, and if that meant negotiating with everybody who wanted to kill them—so be it" (127). Although Paul's ability to act in this manner was a product of his privileged economic position, simply being in an influential position, as the case of Misago demonstrates, no more consistently determines one's moral processes and responses than does any other social factor. Instead, as we have already argued, an ongoing exchange takes place between personal and collective processes, and the outcome of those processes at any given moment is determined by a unique and irreducible interpenetration of economic realities, political representations, collective dynamics, and temperamental proclivities.

During China's Cultural Revolution (1966–76), as Tony Saich and David Apter describe in their compelling analysis *Revolutionary Discourse in Mao's Republic*, a confluence of three historical changes fundamentally altered the relation between cultural meanings, collective experience, and personhood. First, political control extended to the level of the family—where it had never gone under China's imperial regimes. Second, Confucian norms were turned on their head: what formerly was highly valued now became objects of ridicule and hatred. Thus, intellectuals, the cynosures of the Confucian moral order, became "enemies of the people." Finally, intellectuals lost their legitimacy as an external source of moral criticism, a position that they had long held in Chinese society and that offered a check on imperial power and a model for ethical conduct that stood outside the ruling order. The result was starkly evident in student Red Guards' attacks on their teachers. The teacher-student relationship had been central to the Confucian moral code, but in the late 1960s, students beat, degraded, and even killed their teachers. Spouses turned on spouses; children, on parents. Afterward, erstwhile Red Guards often were at a loss to explain why they perpetrated their terrible acts. As one told the first author of this paper, "It was a tremendously exciting time. We thought we were changing the world. Beginning all over again. Some of us were destroying what we believed were feudal remnants—family loyalty, for example. Others took out old hatreds on easy targets. Me, I was excited by the destructiveness. I was really happy beating people. Until I began to see the wheel turn on my friends and family. Then I began to think. Something was wrong here. I dropped out."

Anne Thurston, a China scholar, offers the story of a former Red Guard who, after the first few chaotic years of the Cultural Revolution, by chance met a teacher whom he had assaulted and who was badly injured and disabled. Humiliated, feeling a deep need to repent, and wanting to be of practical assistance, the former Red Guard devoted much of his time to assisting his wounded teacher. In the aftermath of the Cultural Revolution, feelings of shame, repentance, and also revenge were widespread. Yet whether one actually acted on those public sentiments and private passions was uncertain and had multiple determinants. Yan Zhongshu, a Chinese physician who lived through this period and felt deeply the traumatic consequences of political violence that led to his wife's death and his own exile, had an opportunity to take revenge on a fellow physician in his work unit who had acted as his nemesis and seriously beaten Dr. Yan. But Yan Zhongshu found himself unable to carry out an act of vengeance that would have had the support of virtually everyone else in the hospital. He attributed his reluctance to his personality and the fact that he was simply not psychologically equipped to seek retribution. Dr. Yan pointed out that most members of his work unit, even in the most frenzied moments of criticism meetings, were able to control their aggression and limit their participation in violence. Thus, he rejected the ideas of crowd frenzy or the compulsion of the moment as explanations of the most violent acts and actors. Those actions, he believed, were motivated by past experiences, the particularities of relationships, or the special personality traits of individuals.

In writing compelling portraits of sectarian violence in India, Veena Das, Roma Chatterjee, and Deepak Mehta show that one can literally draw a block-by-block map of violence and trace how the past history of friendship ties and cycles of animosity determined why one block was able to avoid violence while another was consumed by it. Many factors come together to cause acts of violence or protection from them, but the quality of personal ties and participants' individual qualities can work with or against large-scale pressures to produce patterns of violence that require local explanations.

A different, though no less disturbing, case study of the interaction of cultural meaning, political reality, and emotion is that of "mother love" in the Brazilian *favelas*, as described by Nancy Scheper-Hughes in *Death without Weeping*. In Bom Jesus, in the Northeast of Brazil, where Scheper-Hughes conducted fieldwork, the local world is one of tremendous scarcity: little unpolluted water is available, hunger and thirst abound, health services are severely restricted, and employment prospects are grim. The community has been ravaged by colonial "greed, exploitation, and retaliation," and its fate has been determined by the development of a sugar monoculture controlled exclusively by wealthy landowners, whose modernization of farming techniques forced hundreds of peasant laborers into urban slums. The situation only worsened between 1964 and 1982, when the military dictatorship engaged in increasingly severe acts of political oppression, targeting poor communities like Bom Jesus as potential sites of social unrest.

How do such complete deprivation, violence, and state-sponsored oppression alter "maternal sentiments?" wonders Scheper-Hughes. "What . . . are the effects of chronic hunger, sickness, death, and loss on the ability to love, trust, [and] have faith . . . in the broadest sense of these terms?" (Scheper-Hughes 1992: 15). Bioevolutionary and developmental psychologists assert that a biological "naturalness" defines mother-child bonding practices and their accompanying affect. But, as her study illustrates, these practices and emotions are shaped by the political and economic contexts in which women must live and work and by the constellations of meaning, belief, and ritual that animate those contexts. In Bom Jesus, where people have a high expectancy of child death owing to thirst and malnutrition, mothers often delay attachment to infants who are considered "temporary visitors" in a household. They mortally neglect, "sacrifice," or treat with "holy indifference" those who seem to lack a "knack" for life, and they save others who exhibit a more pronounced vitality. In response to the death of their children, in this place mothers do not appear to feel the kind of maternal grief that psychoanalysts posit as universal, nor do they seem to repress their "natural maternal sentiments" in favor of a superficial stoicism that masks their numbness and shock. Instead, suggests Scheper-Hughes, they bury their children, often with indifference, because they exist in a "bad-faith economy" in which medical doctors, government officials, and even they themselves work together to misdiagnose their hunger and to systematically overlook the fact that it is state sponsored. The element that kills their children is not lack of medicine, as they believe, but a brutal, predatory environment in which hunger, thirst, scarcity, and the reality of unmet needs converge in a pattern of triage that forces male heads of households to desert their families, teenage girls to take refuge in cities as prostitutes, and mothers to systematically abandon those who cannot survive in such an environment. Quite simply, where resources are scarce, the women of Bom Jesus are forced to allocate the little they have to the family members most capable of being sustained by it.

But, as Scheper-Hughes repeatedly underscores, these women are not maternally deficient, psychoanalytically repressed, or worthy of moral blame; they are simply mothers who cannot grieve for their children in a local world that is predicated upon, and is entirely indifferent to, their children's deaths. They cannot, and indeed must not, be judged by the standards of universal ethics, which do not take into account the complexity of this bad-faith economy. Their experiences of mother-child bonding are understandable only against the backdrop of everyday military violence, the ongoing scarcity of natural resources, the exploitation of the patron-client social arrangement, and the pervasive silence of government officials. Thus, we can approximate the moral norms that govern their lives and the affect that accompanies (and is indistinguishable from) those norms only by recognizing the ways in which the social and the subjective interpenetrate—that is, how the mothers' pity and indifference are patterned by the economy in which they must live. Whereas a universal ethicist or a Lacanian psychoanalyst might be at pains to understand the subtle logic of their moral sentiments, Scheper-Hughes provides a framework for beginning to conceptualize the radical ways in which emotional processes can be altered, ritualistically transfigured, and embodied anew, albeit in different forms, in response to violence, scarcity, and eviscerating hunger.

Allan Young's *The Harmony of Illusions* takes this insight further. For Young, our subjectivities do not merely shift from one historical epoch (or cultural setting) to another; for him, the templates that scientists, psychologists, anthropologists, and other "experts" use to think about the processes that define subjectivity—memory, repression, dissociation, and so on—are themselves socially produced historical constructs. Detailing the emergence of post-traumatic stress disorder (PTSD) as a clinical reality, he traces the condition to the nineteenth-century discovery of "pathological memory," the new psychological language of "repression" and "dissociation" to which this discovery gave rise, and the subsequent transformations of that language by a new class of medical and moral authorities who rose to prominence during World War I. Although PTSD is indisputably real in the lives of its primary sufferers, we need to view it, he suggests, as an evolving conglomeration of political, moral, and medical processes, not a timeless neurophysiological reality. It is a "techno-phenomenon" generated and sustained by the official nosological practices of the American Psychiatric Association's *Diagnostic and Statistical Manual of Mental Disorders*, by changing clinical and research technologies, and by the social interests, political claims, and moral arguments of invested parties, such as diagnosticians, therapists, Vietnam War, Gulf War, and Iraq War veterans, and administrators of veterans' hospitals. Thus, even the ways in which we think about (and experience) ourselves and our memories are historically derived and socially constituted, and these self-reflections act on psychological and moral processes in the experienced self and the lived world to create new psycho-moral realities. He sees no distinguishing line between self and world, physical body and social body, subjectivity and intersubjectivity. Our affect is always both internal and external to us—located as much within the contours of our bodies as within the shifting parameters of our sociopolitical worlds.

Thus, proposing newer and more intricate conceptions of an autonomous self, the kind to which psychologists and others have for years granted primacy, no longer makes conceptual sense. Instead, we need a heightened recognition of the openness of the self to social experience—not its inner essence but its relations. When we delineate more clearly the porousness of the self, we shift away from notions of universal essences toward more contextual framings of moral experience, affect, and our deepest subjective processes. To talk about subjectivity, then, we must build our conversation around the fact, already amply documented by anthropological research, that the subjective is always social and the social, subjective. This dialectic of intersubjectivity, not just the dialectics internal to the self, needs to be taken up in subsequent framings of experience. Only then will we move decisively away from simplistic and misleading ethical discourse and unavailing conceptualizations of human nature. Indeed, we believe that such interpersonal processes will increasingly alter our conceptions of the self and self processes.

In such a short space, we cannot feasibly develop the ethnographic database to fully support our argument about the importance of experience or to work out a full theory of experience. The best we can do in this essay is to suggest how the ethnography and social theory of experience reshape the way we interpret subjectivity. One missing piece is a casebook of narratives of the self in its social contexts. These narratives will exemplify in detail the large claims we make here about the intersections between collective and individual processes (Kleinman 2006). That the moral, affective, and political sides of these processes are inseparable is our conclusion and the element that we take to be the prolegomenon for the anthropology of subjectivity.

REFERENCES

Browning, Christopher. 1992. *Ordinary Men: Reserve Police Battalion 101 & the Final Solution in Poland.* New York: HarperCollins.

Gourevitch, Phillip. 1999. *We Wish to Inform You that Tomorrow We Will Be Killed with Our Families.* New York: Picador USA.

James, William. 1977. *A Pluralistic Universe.* Cambridge, MA: Harvard University Press.

Kleinman, Arthur. 2006. *What Really Matters: Living a Moral Life Amidst Uncertainty and Danger.* Oxford: Oxford University Press.

Mamdani, Mahmood. 2001. *When Victims Become Killers.* Princeton, NJ: Princeton University Press.

Oakeshott, Michael. 1933. *Experience and Its Modes.* Cambridge: Cambridge University Press.

Scheper-Hughes, Nancy. 1992. *Death Without Weeping.* Berkeley: University of California Press.

3 How the Body Speaks

Illness and the Lifeworld
among the Urban Poor

VEENA DAS AND RANENDRA K. DAS

In this chapter, we reflect on the meaning and use of diagnostic categories to make illness knowable in the course of social transactions. The "illness narrative" has emerged as a classic genre in medical anthropology, and it offers a way of contrasting patient and physician perspectives on illness. The focus on the patient's construction of her experience is a powerful tool to contest and even reform the power that the expert exercises in clinical encounters. Thus, the emphasis on illness narratives and patients' "explanatory models" serves an important therapeutic purpose: Kleinman (1989) used it with stunning effect in his critique of psychiatric practice. The critical force of the concept lies in its potential to interrogate the dominant modes of biopower that Foucault (1991) identified as typical forms of governmentality under modernity.

Since its formulation, the concept of illness narratives has developed in different directions. For instance, Byron Good (1994) emphasizes the linguistic and narratological qualities of the narrative—not only pointing to genre and emplotment but also showing how the context of the telling may influence the way that the story is organized. Whereas this move opens the way for a subtle analysis of the complex relation between experience and representation in illness narratives, it also shifts the weight of analysis from the context of health seeking to that of storytelling, bracketing the important tension between the indexical and symbolic aspects of medical complaints.[1] Other scholars have analyzed illness narratives as part of the postmodern experience of illness, suggesting that modern and postmodern denote two different (even successive) styles of living with illness—"a modern style that accepts the authorized medico-scientific narrative and a postmodern style in which patients reclaim power as creators and narrators of their own distinctive stories" (Morris 1998: 25; see also Frank 1995). This account sees the subject as wresting the self from the representations of illness in the dominant expert discourses, yet it gives little importance to the materiality of the conditions within which people fall sick and seek therapeutic interventions. The emphasis on meaning completely eclipses the specificity of the conditions within which people experience health and illness; it is not even clear whether the voice of the patient is an embodied voice or whether it functions as a grammatical or literary voice.

Our paper has grown out of an engagement with illness experience among the urban poor: it looks at subjectivity as deeply enmeshed in the everyday life of the poor in a defined material and social space. Our concern is with the precariousness of everyday life in low-income neighborhoods in Delhi, India, the local ecology within which illness experiences take shape, and the way that medical practice mutates in the processes of giving treatment to the poor. The illness experience is the lens through which we try to give specificity to the political and economic circumstances within which the lives of the urban poor take shape, thus contesting any generic notions of "the poor."

MAKING ILLNESS KNOWABLE

Although every culture has recognizable lexical terms that point to the presence of an illness, these terms do not constitute a closed system within which the experience of bodily discomfort or a sense of ill being can be irrevocably placed. Rather, as Christopher Davis (2000) points out, diagnostic categories are the starting points or building blocks for constructing therapies. Thus, though common understandings may exist of the terms that make up a diagnosis within a shared culture, significant variations can exist in ideas about which of these categories *fit* together as individuals struggle to match therapies with illnesses. Further, there are no hermetically sealed cultures within which illness is experienced, diagnosis is made, and therapies are sought. Although biomedical categories and therapies have reached different parts of the world in very different ways, the condition of medical diversity or medical pluralism is now universal. This fact raises significant questions about how concepts of health and illness travel. How are these concepts translated, and how do people deal with different expert cultures in making intimate bodily experiences available for therapeutic intervention?

We begin with notions of complaint, symptom, and diagnosis as they arose in responses to simple questions such as "Were you sick this week?"

"If yes, what was the complaint?" "What do you think you had?" "Who diagnosed this?" These questions were posed as part of a weekly morbidity survey conducted in seven neighborhoods in Delhi over a two-year period (2000–02) by the Institute for Socio-Economic Research in Development and Democracy (ISERDD). The survey was part of a longitudinal study on urban health. Approximately three hundred households participated in the survey; the refusal rate in the recruitment phase was less than 1 percent.[2] Six households moved out of the localities in the first two years, complicating efforts to survey them on a regular basis. Morbidity surveys were conducted in two yearly cycles—a weekly survey lasting seventeen to eighteen weeks, followed by monthly surveys during the rest of the year.

We used three methods to elicit accounts of illness experiences, each of which captured different aspects of illness. All the interviews took place in the homes of the respondents. Although the ISERDD team also collected data on the interactions between the practitioners and patients through observations in the clinics of 291 practitioners, spending one day in each practitioner's clinic, these data enter this discussion only as background for patient accounts.[3] The first method of soliciting illness accounts was to ask questions in the course of the weekly morbidity surveys. This method helped identify the categories people used to express deviation from a state of health. Although we constructed our questionnaire to elicit a *sequence* of events—a story—the sequence resulted from the order in which the questions were asked: the story moved from reporting an experience of illness that week, to naming the practitioners consulted, the medications received, and the expenditure incurred.[4] Instead of adopting the usual survey method of eliciting information in a single interview (or in some cases in a follow-up interview some months later), field-workers from ISERDD contacted households every week for the duration of the survey. Thus, they were able to record the course of illness as it occurred, as well as the therapeutic regimes that patients undertook. This frequent contact was very useful in tracking the intersection between household decision making and the course of the illness, but it cut up the telling of illness-related events into weekly episodes.

The second method we used followed directly from our initial observations that, in the course of describing their illness experiences, people offered many other insights that called upon different realms of sociality and different ways of reckoning time.[5] For example, the story of the illness in many cases was also the story of kinship relations, of who helped and who betrayed; respondents often described how the episode of the moment related to earlier episodes of their own or others' illnesses, or they reflected on the social and economic conditions in which they lived. Not all illnesses invited such reflection, indicating that significant variations exist in illness experiences: some are passed over in a casual manner; others lead to more stories about engagement with different social and therapeutic contexts. Illness in the latter sense is profoundly social. To capture this aspect of illness experiences and to understand the relation of failures of the body to failures of one's social world (including the specific conditions that constitute poverty), our team of field-workers recorded such observations even when the accounts did not seem to have an apparent relation to illness and therapy, as defined in biomedicine. Field-workers who conducted weekly surveys kept diaries in which they recorded the conversations that occurred in the course of the interviews, even when these contributions did not seem strictly pertinent to the questions they had asked.[6] Over time, we found that stringing together these scattered observations gave us clues to unfinished stories, evolving tensions, and linguistic patterns, such as use of euphemisms or irony to express a range of affects through which illness was wedged between the self and others.

Finally, field-workers at ISERDD were trained to use the typical illness-narrative genre to conduct detailed interviews with at least one member of each household in the first year. Senior members of the ISERDD research team conducted these interviews. We made every attempt to see that different persons in each household had an opportunity to speak at some point during the year. Though the data are still being processed, we believe the survey results have acquired sufficient depth for us to be able to speak about these delicate issues. The weekly surveys permitted the survey population to speak about the ordinariness of many illnesses such as colds and coughs and mild, short-lived fevers. The ethnographic open-ended interviews, however, allowed respondents to address the dramatic nature of illness and to discuss what was at stake. Together, these interviews revealed the diversity of contexts in which survey participants experienced illness. At one end of the spectrum, illness was seen as a deviation from life that was easily absorbed into the normal; in these cases, it was part of the normal flow of life. At the other end of the spectrum, the story of the illness was haunted by the sense of a failure of the body and of social relations. How did people move between these registers of the normal and the pathological? In the eloquent formulation of Christopher Davis (2000), medical systems may be understood not only in terms of what they do as therapeutic interventions but also in terms of what they allow people to say.

THE LEXICAL TERMS

The lexical terms deployed to refer to illness or to abnormal bodily sensations are the linguistic means through which illness acquires a social existence. To respondents who answered in the affirmative to the question "Were you sick this week?" we first asked "What was the problem/discomfort?" *(kya taklif thi?)*. The answers revealed important overlaps between the notion of the symptom, the medical complaint, and the idea of discomfort because the term *taklif* could cover all three. Many of the answers to this question deployed terms that Davis calls "primary terms," those offered without elaboration. These terms rendered illness unproblematic and absorbed it within the normal ups and downs of life. The second kind of response offered elaboration on antecedent events, the physiological location of the discomfort, the attribution of illness to the specific economic conditions in respondents' lives, or a sense that the body itself was failing. In the third category were responses that viewed illnesses either as failures of social relations, especially of kinship and neighborhood, as the result of magical manipulations, attempts at divination, or other ways of accessing the sacred. Though we found that explanations of illness could be characterized in this way, none of the respondents' stories fit neatly into one category. Rather, their experiences of illness were ones of movement—with explanations, narratives, and therapies touching down in all these categories at one time or another. Thus, though we agree that illness is often talked about in the language of otherness—as the work of the other on the body—we also agree with Davis (2000) that experiences of illness move between the registers of the ordinary and the extraordinary, centered in one's social and material worlds yet carrying the power to propel one outside these worlds.

In this chapter, we build our argument on the discussions that took place in the ordinary give-and-take of life as recorded in the weekly diaries of the field-workers and in the long interviews that two of us (Veena Das and Rajan) conducted with members of the households. Yet we think that the dimensions of the problem require some appreciation of the quantitative data we collected. In the following discussion, the distinction between "sick weeks" and "full episode" (both are constructs for purposes of analysis) is important. Because field-workers recorded the data they collected through the weekly morbidity questionnaire on a weekly basis, initial information is coded in terms of the story of sickness *that week*. Obviously, many illnesses lasted more than one week. To capture this distinction, the data have been coded both in terms of *sickness weeks* and *illness episodes*.

For example, table 1 shows the entries for Ajay in one eight-week seg-

TABLE 1. Example of a Data Segment

Week	Were you sick this week?	What was the problem (taklif)?	Is this the same sickness as last week?[a]
1	No	Blank	Blank
2	No	Blank	Blank
3	Yes	Fever	Blank
4	Yes	Fever	Yes
5	Yes	Fever	Yes
6	No	Blank	Blank
7	Yes	Boils	Blank
8	No	Blank	Blank

[a]Field-workers asked this question only if a respondent reported an illness both in the previous week and in the survey week. They recorded chronic conditions, such as diabetes, separately.

ment of the data. The field-worker coded Ajay's information in different ways. First, the table records two *episodes*, based on the fact that Ajay reported he was ill with fever in weeks 3, 4, and 5; because he said that the fever was a continuing one, it counts as one episode of illness.[7] After reporting no illness in week 6, Ajay reported boils on his body in week 7, which counts as the second episode. However, we also record that in the total of the eight weeks, he reported illness for four weeks and hence had four *sick weeks*. Clearly, two measures of temporality operate here, and though these measures get entangled in the narratives, the distinction is useful for interpreting data on practitioner visits and on the extent of self-medication (Das and Das 2006; Das and Sanchez 2002). Table 2 gives the distribution of acute episodes in the sample population in the first year for one round of weekly surveys, and table 3 gives the duration of the episodes. We surveyed four localities for eighteen weeks (August 15, 2000, to the last week of December 2000) and surveyed three localities for seventeen weeks (January 2001 to first week of first week of May 2001).[8]

These tables illustrate two important points that will be of use when considering the narratives. First, about 52 percent of the sample population experienced one to three episodes in a four-month period, and second, a large proportion of illness episodes (nearly 70 percent) lasted less than one week. Only 24 percent of the population reported no illness. Of course, the illness burden was not equally distributed across localities, but no straightforward

TABLE 2. Number of Persons with X Number of Episodes

(Period: 17–18 Weeks)

Number of Episodes	Frequency	Percent	Cumulative Percent
0	384	23.69	23.69
1	352	21.71	45.40
2	282	17.40	62.80
3	209	12.89	75.69
4	136	8.39	84.08
5	105	6.48	90.56
6	62	3.82	94.39
7	51	3.15	97.53
8	24	1.48	99.01
9	7	0.43	99.44
10	7	0.43	99.88
11	1	0.06	99.94
12	1	0.06	100.00
Total	1,621	100.00	100.00

NOTE: Recording the number of episodes as 0 and the frequency as 384 means that 384 individuals reported no episodes of illness in the data set, and this number constitutes 23.69 percent of the total number of individuals.

relation is evident between income and illness burden. For instance, though the *jhuggi* cluster in Noida and the households in Bhagwanpur Kheda were next to each other in their average reported income, Noida had the lowest reported morbidity and Bhagwanpur Kheda reported the highest.[9] Although a nuanced analysis of the differences by locality and income must await another occasion, we can safely state that the poor and the rich tended to have different types of diseases. For instance, TB was found in all low-income localities, but not a single case was reported among the upper-income groups. Finally, the burden of chronic disease (as defined in biomedicine) was significantly higher among the upper-income groups, partly because the number of older people in that population was higher and partly because their access to better-quality practitioners led to easier recognition of chronic diseases such as diabetes and hypertension. This finding does not mean that *feelings of chronicity* were absent among the poor, simply that the symptoms they reported as chronic conditions were often a result of illnesses that were not diagnosed and hence kept recurring. With this back-

TABLE 3. Duration of Episodes

Week	Frequency	Percent	Cumulative Percent
1	2,566	69.65	69.65
2	669	16.16	87.81
3	196	5.32	93.13
4	85	2.31	95.44
5	53	1.44	96.88
6	38	1.03	97.91
7	19	0.52	98.43
8	8	0.22	98.64
9	10	0.27	98.91
10	4	0.11	99.02
11	8	0.22	99.24
12	5	0.14	99.38
13	3	0.08	99.46
14	4	0.11	99.57
15	2	0.05	99.62
16	3	0.08	99.70
17	3	0.08	99.78
18	8	0.22	100.00
Total	3,684		100.00

NOTE: This table records the number of weeks that each episode lasted. Recording the episode duration as 1 and the frequency as 2,566 means that 2,566 episodes (69.65 percent) lasted one week.

ground on the overall disease burden, we can consider how respondents deployed notions of complaints, symptoms, and diagnosis in the narratives and see what light these notions throw on the construction of the subject.

PRIMARY TERMS: ILLNESS AND NORMAL DEVIATION

When our informants described their illnesses using various lexical terms with little or no elaboration, we found that they attributed such disorders to the routine ups and downs of life—changes of season or changes in the body due to normal transitions in the life cycle.[10] For example, they described various kinds of colds and coughs—*sardi, zukam, nazla, cheenk, khansi, gala kharab*—cold, flowing nose, sneezing, coughing, and sore throat. They sometimes referred to fever as *bukhar* in Hindi or "viral" in English. Apart from attributing some ailments to seasonal variations, respondents could also absorb the changes in their life course within the idea of the normal. Examples included "diarrhea due to teething" in the case of a baby, menstrual cramps for young girls, and various pains and aches for old people—*budhape ka sharir*, "the body of aging." Certainly, contests still emerged over these definitions, but these contests centered on whether a condition was normal to the current season or phase of life or whether the evocation of normality was being used to mask a lack of care for the ill person.[11] We give two examples below.

M was washing clothes when Rajan went to interview her. She said that she had slight fever. "Viral fever," she said, "change of season, everyone is getting it." They then went on to talk about other things.

In contrast, B, an old (perhaps in her late sixties) widowed woman in Bhagwanpur Kheda, who lived with her son, his wife, and unmarried children, constantly complained of stomachache, feelings of weakness, and lack of appetite; she insisted that she had a "heart condition" or perhaps "TB"—*dil ki bimari, ya shayad TB*. B's husband had died a year before our survey began, and no one in the family was clear about the cause of his death. His son said he had been admitted to a referral hospital for TB, so the father could well have died of tuberculosis. However, the man's widow, B, said that her husband had had a heart condition and had been admitted for disease of the heart *(dil ki bimari)*. Such confusion of categories was not uncommon.

B was reported as "head of the household" when we collected demographic information at the initiation of the project: we noticed tensions over her status in the family that had a bearing on her illness. In the eighteen weeks of the survey, B was reported as sick for eleven weeks. Precise information on her illness was missing for seven weeks—one week because the households could not be surveyed and for six weeks intermittently because she went twice to visit her married daughter in a village on the outskirts of Delhi to "get treatment." There, she went to a local practitioner trained in biomedicine with an MBBS (bachelor of medicine and bachelor of surgery) degree. She showed us a couple of prescriptions that the practitioner had given her: the diagnosis was "old Koch." Throughout the survey period, her son bought medicines from the local chemist by showing him the old prescription. These medicines included Refka, a capsule for acute or chronic viral hepatitis—three capsules for three days; Liv 52 for improved liver function, intermittently during the period; and Pyrazinamide, a first-line anti-TB drug, for two weeks intermittently. Underlying the history of intermittent drug treatment, ranging from powerful anti-TB drugs to drugs for improving liver function, was her demand that she receive more attention from her son and daughter-in-law. However, whenever the daughter-in-law was interviewed, she would say, *"Budhape ka shrir hai aisa to hota hi hai par, amman mein sahan shakti kam hai* ("This is the body of old age; such things happen, but *amma* has no capacity to tolerate"). B's visit to her daughter's village was to show her displeasure with her son, and she stayed there for four weeks, pronouncing herself to be much better after she returned. Her daughter sent her some medicines from the practitioner in the village intermittently via a Delhi Transport Corporation bus driver who lived in that village and happened to be related. The entry in the last week against B's name records that she cited "mild TB" as diagnosed by the village practitioner. In this period, this family had spent 350 rupees, more than 1 percent of its annual income on medicine.

B's case shows another way in which the "normal" was positioned in the lives of the poor. Her representation of the illness is made up of complaints that she has picked up from the previous encounters with the medical system, especially during her husband's illness. Thus, while she represents her illness as "heart trouble" or *"thodi bahut TB"*—mild TB—her daughter-in-law represents her complaints as normal to the aging process and thus not signs of illness at all. Did the availability of categories such as "heart trouble" and "mild TB" allow B to reconfigure somatic changes that might have been considered "normal" for an aging person into categories of disease? In an influential paper on the cultural inflation of morbidity during decline in mortality, Johansson (1991) seems to suggest that such a process might indeed occur: "In general social scientists cannot or should not attempt to relate morbidity and mortality during the health transition because morbidity is made up of phenomena of several different kinds, each of which relates differently to sickness and death." He says further that "the more diseases there are, the more likely are individuals to think of themselves as sick or to be diagnosed by a professional as sick. In this way the incidence rate is a function of the culturally recognized stock of diseases, along with the *propensity of ordinary people* to classify biologically sub optimal states as sickness according to *culturally standardized breakpoint* on the health continuum" (44, emphasis added).

We agree with Johansson that the availability of categories may expand the possibilities of how to think of bodily discomfort, but we question the categories of "ordinary people" and of "culturally standardized breakpoint" on the health-sickness continuum. Instead, we suggest that the concrete experience of illness in the family and local community, along with the actual nature of the clinical encounter, makes up the stock of knowledge through which people represent illness categories and seek therapies. A tremendous struggle takes place as people try to determine how to authorize the "real": are these symptoms indicative of "mild TB" or of old age? The notions of normality or pathology take shape in this struggle within a set of family dynamics, as B's case shows.

ANOTHER IDEA OF THE NORMAL

A second way in which the notion of the normal emerged in the interviews was in the experience of the illness within the materiality of the lives of the poor: what was normal, they asked, for someone who was living in *those conditions* and doing *that kind of work?* The following entries by Shoyab Ahmad, a field assistant who conducted the survey in Noida, illustrate this point.[12]

> *September 3, 2001—household no. 9086.* When I reached R's house, I found her sitting outside washing vessels. On seeing me she put out a *charpai* [string cot] for me to sit on and asked me to be seated. I asked her about her husband's work, and she said that he goes out in search of work every day but until now, he has not been able to get anything. I asked, how are you managing? She said that they are managing by borrowing money from neighbors. The baby had loose motions, but there was no money to take him to the doctor; but he was probably teething—so he would get better—but if they had the money she would have taken the child to Khan (the practitioner visited most often in this locality, who has a degree in integrated medicine).[13] She said, "We are poor; our children have to get by with what we can give them."
>
> *September 4, 2001—household 9092.* As I was going to S's house, I met his son, who was sitting outside. I asked him how everyone was in the house. He said everyone was okay but that his papa was not well. As I was talking to him, S came back from taking a bath at the public pump and said his *nazla* [cold] was worse, and he had pain below his stomach. He said that he was getting it treated privately—"I don't mind spending four hundred or five hundred rupees—but when things become expensive—one has to consider the government hospital. I know that things won't go well in hospital *(durgati hoti hai),* but it is our helplessness. Now I have to go to hospital to get admitted." On the next visit, S had not gone to a hospital—he had obtained medicine from the local practitioner: "As long as my hands and feet are moving, I have to work. The pain has subsided."

The second example is from an encounter I (Veena) had with Z, a young man who was sitting outside his house and greeted me. I was not sure whether he was inebriated, but I asked him why he had not gone to work. He said, "My mind is not okay today—I get such disturbing thoughts, I am feeling so angry, I have pain in my head—I have to go and get some medicine." At this point, he held his head between the two palms of his hands and bent his head as if in despair. I joked, "Maybe you had too much to drink."[14] "No madam ji, people do not understand. Everyday, I have to lift such heavy weights. I feel my body collapsing. If I do not take some drink, I will collapse. Now I get these tensions, these terrible headaches. I have to do something. This doctor will give some medicine that will make it a bit better, and then again it will happen—but what can I do? I have to find some way of getting relief. Just as I have to drink some to make my body fit for work."

In such cases, the question of what is normal is mediated by the questions, what is illness? and what is treatment under conditions of poverty? I heard the expression "as long as my hands and feet are moving" as the trope through which Z represented the laboring body. Among the poor families in the ISERDD sample only 20 percent had jobs in the public or private sector; 30 percent worked informally as hawkers, rickshaw pullers, housemaids, or unskilled labor in factories and shops; and 44 percent were outside the labor force but sometimes engaged in domestic production, doing piecemeal jobs for minor industries in the area. Most people had only intermittent employment and thus had a constant sense that they were on a threshold, in danger of not finding work, or one step away from a serious illness that would throw them into debt. They also lived in fear that the nexus of relations through which they maintained their jobs, obtained loans, or found a doctor in a public hospital would somehow collapse. Households had some cash flow, but it was irregular. Though even the poorest households managed to have some disposable income, any large expenditure propelled them into debt.

The practitioner market as well as the therapeutic practices that practitioners offered in these localities show how attuned they are to the material conditions of the households in the neighborhood. Low- and middle-income neighborhoods are full of practitioners from alternative streams of healing (ayurvedic and *unani*) who have received some training in biomedicine as part of their curricula (Langford 2002). But regardless of the type of training and degree they have, their typical therapeutic strategy is to dispense medications for two or three days at a cost of twenty to thirty rupees and to ask patients to come back if they do not feel better. If a practitioner feels that a patient requires more expensive medication, he may write a prescription for purchase at the local pharmacy. Households often save such prescriptions and take them to the local pharmacist for refilling if they feel that the symptoms have recurred. In more than thirteen thousand interviews in the ISERDD survey, respondents reported visiting more than three hundred different doctors in twelve hundred practitioner visits. Less than 30 percent of all practitioner visits were to public hospitals or government-run dispensaries. The use of government facilities was much higher among the poor than among the rich, except in one area of upper-income households where many residents were employed in government service. Tables 4 and 5 show the distribution of various types of actions that respondents in Bhagwanpur Kheda and Noida took in response to reported acute illnesses during a typical week in the first year of the survey period.[15] Respondents in Bhagwanpur Kheda took no action in only 21.75 percent of cases. The figure is considerably higher for Noida, where respondents took no action in nearly 43 percent of cases. However, people typically consulted a practitioner rather than the chemist for treatment. Further, even in cases coded here as self-medication, patients often used earlier prescriptions or obtained refills.[16]

If we fill in this picture, we see that 70 percent of illness episodes lasted less than a week (see table 3) and people made high use of practitioners, even though households often reported such deviations from health as "normal." The typical mode of spending on illness was to get medication to meet the sufferer's immediate needs—to get relief, not a cure. Whether an illness could be treated even at this level depended upon the cash in hand. In most cases, the patient's need for relief combined with the practitioner's understanding of the pharmacopoeia carved out the therapeutic strategy.[17] We have an interesting assemblage here of biomedicine as embodied in the local strategies of care and the household as located in the materiality of the informal economy, which is characterized by precarious employment and small flows of cash. Through this assemblage, both biomedicine and households mutate to create a unique neighborhood ecology of care.[18] What kind of illness narrative do patients produce in this exchange and translation of illness categories in their lives? We offer low-blood-pressure (low-BP) syndrome as an example of this process.

In one of the first interviews I (Veena) conducted, P, a young woman with two daughters, told me that she suffered from low BP. She complained that she suffered from persistent body ache, blinding headaches, weakness, and sadness. "I have no life in my hands and feet. The world appears to bite me. I feel like leaving everything and running away." When I asked her if she knew what she suffered from, she said without hesitation that she had low BP. She went to a local practitioner, using the term "family doctor" in En-

TABLE 4. Actions Taken on Reported Illness in Bhagwanpur Kheda

Action	Frequency	Percent	Cumulative Percent
No action	319	21.75	21.75
Only practitioner	508	4.63	56.37
Only chemist as doctor	48	3.27	59.65
Only self-medication	389	26.52	86.16
Two or more actions	203	13.84	100.00
Total	1,467	100.00	

TABLE 5. Actions Taken on Reported Illness in Noida

Action	Freq.	Percent	Cum.
No action	319	42.25	42.25
Only practitioner	248	32.85	75.10
Only chemist as doctor	8	1.06	76.16
Only self-medication	123	16.29	92.45
Two or more actions	57	7.55	100.00
Total	755	100.00	

glish. The doctor did not measure her blood pressure, but whenever she felt that her symptoms were becoming difficult to bear, she went to the pharmacy and got a mixture of capsules and pills that she consumed for a couple of days. I found that others referred to their complaints as low BP also and that little difference existed in the way that practitioners and patients used the term. Weakness, giddiness, headaches, and sadness were often attributed to low BP, which was in turn often attributed to the "tensions" inherent in the conditions in which people lived. However, this category does not appear to belong to either the "folk" or the "expert" category; rather it carries the trace of the clinical encounters typical of low-income neighborhoods and their particular ecology of care. Practitioners in low-income categories do not seem to distinguish between diagnostic categories and symptoms. Thus, households in these neighborhoods tend to use what would be diagnostic categories as descriptive of symptoms. Members of higher-income households use the same terms in very different ways. Thus, when such households report that someone has a "BP problem," their meaning is much closer to the biomedical meaning, at least to the extent that they understand that BP reflects a particular measure, although this fact does not mean that they would fit the profile of compliant patients. We cannot endorse Johansson's very general claims about "the culturally recognized stock of diseases" or the "propensity of ordinary people to classify biologically sub optimal states as sickness according to culturally standardized breakpoint on the health continuum." None of these categories are transparent; instead, we must treat them as emergent categories that take analytical shape through the labor of ethnography.

Instead of thinking of symptoms and diagnostic categories as arising from culturally standardized practices of classification, we hope to shift the weight of explanation to the regimes of labor through which both body and temporality are produced and consumed in these local settings. As is widely recognized, analyses of the working day in the factory (Marx 1887) or work in the disciplined regime of the prison (Foucault 1977) objectified the experience of time into homogenous and equivalent units. The worker's or the prisoner's body is put to labor, and the question for the capitalist in the first case and the state in the second is how to ensure the reproduction of the laborer's/prisoner's body. Questions of a living wage or the minimum nutrition necessary for the prisoner arise out of this consideration. In contrast, temporality in our study is intimately tied to the experience of the precariousness of work and the irregular flows of cash in the household. The intersecting temporalities of work, cash flows, and the therapeutic practices of local practitioners have created certain ways of dealing with illness that emphasize immediacy and the short run rather than investment in cure. This situation in turn stems from the failure of the state to regulate practitioners and pharmacies so that categories such as "a little bit of TB" or "low BP" and the related modes of treatment—with intermittent and (from the biomedical perspective) inappropriate drug use—have come to dominate the health-seeking practices and health delivery in these localities.[19] The state does not act here to regulate irregular, peripatetic, and "unproductive" occupations. As a result, practitioners who cluster on the fringes of the city and give the local moral worlds their particular character become conduits for the distribution of pharmaceutical products that define their major therapeutic strategies.[20]

OUT OF THE LOCAL: OTHER SPACES

Though 70 percent of the illness episodes reported in our study lasted less than one week, more than 6 percent of episodes lasted three or more weeks. In such cases, families in low-income neighborhoods, despairing of the therapy available locally, begin to seek alternatives outside the regime of the local. One cannot describe this journey via a straightforward model of vertical or horizontal resort. The households were not consistent in their decisions about which illnesses were best treated through specific therapeutic systems (for example, they did not consistently seek allopathic solutions to acute diseases or homeopathic ones to chronic diseases); instead, they thought about which networks of information and influence they could activate.[21] The practitioners in these localities generally reported that when they could not manage a disease using the resources they had, they provided a service to patients by referring them to private, but more expensive medical facilities. We were intrigued by the fact that the billboards outside the office of some (but not all) practitioners displayed rates for various kinds of diagnostic tests, yet we could find no sign of such facilities in the offices of these practitioners. "How do you do these tests?" I (Veena) asked one practitioner. The practitioner, an active member of the National Association of Practitioners of Integrated Medicine, told me that he knew a good diagnostic laboratory in the area, and he received a small commission for referring patients there. Others did not display billboards but nonetheless acted as brokers between patients and providers of more sophisticated facilities or specialists. If the disease was seen to worsen and the practitioner began to fear that death might result, he advised households to take the patient there. Some households were able to borrow enough money to deal with emergencies; others accessed such facilities for a few days, decided they could not sustain the expense, and tried to find someone who could get the patient treated in a government hospital. The other route for patients was to access a public hospital: 30 percent of all visits to practitioners were to public hospitals. In such cases, the capital required to sustain treatment was often a "contact"—often a relative working in a hospital as an orderly or a janitor who could push the file ahead so that the patient could access the doctor without long delays. We found several variations in patients' reports about their treatment in the public hospitals. In the lower-middle-class area of Jahangirpuri, many households had effectively learned how to access the Jagjivan Ram Hospital in the area, but except in cases of TB, they could rarely sustain long-term treatment because of the demands on time. In other areas, such as Noida, the distance from a public hospital made access very difficult, whereas in Bhagwanpur Kheda, many patients claimed that they were told that the private medicines would work better even for TB, for which they received some but not all medications. Nevertheless, use of public health facilities was higher in Bhagwanpur Kheda than in Noida. To illustrate how patients come to use diverse pathways of care, we offer a detailed case study of a TB patient from Noida in the next section.[22]

Meena: Therapeutic Failure

Meena lived with her husband, their two sons, and her husband's father in one of the mud huts in the shanty settlement of Noida. Her husband held a job as a janitor in the U.P. Waterways Department. The family had a regular but small income. At the initiation of our survey (August 2000), Meena reported that she suffered from tuberculosis. She said that her first episode of TB had occurred three to four years ago and that she took medications for a long time—perhaps seven months, perhaps one year.

However, in a later interview she told one of the field-workers that she had had TB for the past eight years and had "never been cured." She described a complicated story about having a breast abscess after her child's birth, followed by a minor surgery as well as fever, cough, and weakness. This illness was when she lived in the village with her conjugal relatives while her husband searched for work in the city. Following is an extract from an interview done by our co-researcher Rajan.

RAJAN: *So, in your conjugal family did you know that you had TB?*

MEENA: In the beginning, I did not, and the doctor also did not say that.

RAJAN: *Then you were having cough and fever and weakness.*

MEENA: Yes, they gave me lots to eat, but still the weakness did not go. Then I became okay when they took me to Vrindavan.

RAJAN: *Government hospital or private?*

MEENA: Government hospital—but there the checkup and everything is free, but you had to buy medicines from outside.

RAJAN: *How long ago was this?*

MEENA: Eight years ago. I took medicines for three months. Then I became healthy.

RAJAN: *So did the doctor ask you to stop the medicine?*

MEENA: No, but there was no money. For three months, my husband's father bought medicines, but then the money got over and no one helped. (original text in Hindi, translated by Bhrigupati Singh)

From the village, Meena moved to Noida to join her husband. She said that she was healthy for a little while after moving to the city, but then her symptoms recurred after her one-year-old daughter died. When we began our survey, she reported that she had completed a course of TB medication recently but was still feeling very sick and weak. In the initial weekly survey period of four months in 2000, Meena reported that she was ill with various symptoms ranging from cough to fever during eight of the sixteen weeks. Because she had already completed a six-month course of TB medications recently from a government dispensary and had been reported cured after a sputum test, she did not return to this dispensary for treatment of her symptoms in these eight weeks. Instead, she intermittently sought treatment by a private practitioner in the area, who had a bachelor's degree in ayurvedic medicine and surgery, for relief of symptoms. He gave her a range of medicines, from analgesics to antibiotics. Her mode of accessing medical care was typical of many people in the area—that is, a mode in which practitioners treat symptoms by dispensing medications for a day or two for a consolidated fee of twenty to thirty rupees.[23] This period was difficult for her in another way because she suspected that her husband was having an affair with a married woman in the neighborhood. During conversations, Meena said she feared that her husband would send her to the village where his mother lived, on the pretext that he could not care for her adequately, and she worried that he might even marry the other woman. Meena wanted desperately to recover her strength so that she could attend to household chores effectively and keep her place within the family.

One of the field-workers made the following diary entries in the fourth week of the survey:

> Meena cried today. She had a small gash on the head. On probing, she said it is because her husband hit her. She is very weak and sad and told me with tears in her eyes that her husband was having an affair. The lady, Meena told me, lives opposite the house. . . . Mukesh (her son) has seen them walking hand in hand in Harola market. She was hit yesterday because she asked her husband "where are you going so early in the morning?" and he said, "I give you and your children food and shelter and it is none of your business to talk more." (original entries in English)

Toward the end of the first year of our survey in 2000, Meena's condition seemed to have worsened to the point of an emergency. She was beginning to cough blood-stained mucus and was constantly coughing. The neighbors reported to us that her husband had tried first to get her admitted to a private hospital in the neighborhood but did not have the money to make the advance payment demanded by the hospital. Eventually, a relative who was employed as a ward boy in a government hospital in South Delhi managed to get Meena admitted under another name on the pretext that she was his dependant relative.[24] Meena stayed in the hospital for six. months. Her son Mukesh described the event to Veena in the following way:

> VEENA: *Mukesh, why are you not going to school these days? You have lots of work at home?*
>
> MUKESH: No, it is not the work. But I feel very scared. I think Mummy is no more, and Papa is not telling us.
>
> VEENA: *But why should you think that?*
>
> MUKESH: Because that night when she had blood in the vomit, everyone had given up hope. The neighbors came, and they were preparing to lay her on the ground [in anticipation of imminent death]. So then someone said, take her to Kailash hospital, but Papa said that he did not have money for Kailash Hospital. So *where* did they take her?[25]

Frightened by this conversation, we found out the name of the TB hospital, and one of the members of the ISERDD research team visited Meena there. The entire story about the altered name and the help from the relative came out because her husband told us that she was admitted under a different name after a field researcher could not find her name among registered patients during an initial visit.

By the time Meena was discharged from the hospital, after a six-month stay, and returned home, the Pradhan (headman) of this cluster of *jhuggis* had acted decisively against the woman with whom her husband was having an affair as a result of complaints from the neighborhood. Consequently, the woman's husband was persuaded to send her to back to the village to live with the husband's extended conjugal family. Meena had now taken another course of TB medication, and the hospital discharged her with instructions to complete the course of medications. She was required to go to the hospital outpatient department to receive medication, but her husband managed to get her name transferred to a DOTS (Directly Observed Therapy, Short Term) center nearer their home. Meena completed the remaining course of medications from the DOTS center. For the next three months, she was free of symptoms and put on some weight. One can detect the altered affect even in the small entries in the diary of Purshottam, who was then covering her household for the survey.

> Today looking at Meena ji's [*ji* is an honorific in Hindi used for all elders] face, one felt that she was a little better. I asked Meena ji, "how are you?" She smiled and said, "Now I am better. I went to get medicine for Rahul [her younger son]." She showed me the medicine—ampicillin with cloxacillin. On the label was printed "MCD—Not for Sale."[26] I

said, "But this medicine is not for sale." She said, "Brother, I don't
know—this is the medicine Titu [name of practitioner] gave me, and
with this, Rahul is absolutely fine."[27]

A few days later, Purshottam recorded in the diary that while he was visiting the household, Meena's husband came from the market with a bag of
pomegranates and handed them to Meena to eat. (Pomegranates and grapes
are among the most expensive fruits and often denote the showering of
extra care on a sick person.)

In the third year of the ISERDD survey, Meena's symptoms reappeared.
The diary entries record that she lay in bed coughing. At one point, she said
to the field researcher, Purshottam, "Brother, I feel broken from inside." On
her husband's request, two members of ISERDD (the research organization)
took her for a consultation to a referral hospital in Kingsway Camp, where
the attending physician was prepared to admit her as an inpatient, though
no one was willing to explore why her symptoms kept recurring. Off the
record, one physician told one of us (Veena) that conducting diagnostic tests
for multidrug-resistant TB would be futile because the hospital did not have
the resources to provide treatment. Meena's husband did not want her admitted to a hospital so far from home, so they went to another DOTS center and provided a false address. Here again, she received the anti-TB regimen under the DOTS protocol but reported serious side effects such as
continuous nausea. Her condition continued to worsen, so she stopped taking medications. She died in a private nursing home in December 2003 after
being rushed there two days earlier. At the end of her life, the family was
several thousand rupees in debt.

Given the weight of the literature on TB and stigma, one might have expected that stigma would play a major role in this illness trajectory.[28] However, the theme that seems to emerge from Meena's story is consistent institutional neglect and incoherence. This neglect existed in conjunction with
the care and neglect built into Meena's domestic relations. In each episode
of the disease, she completed the course of medications given by the DOTS
center and was declared to be sputum negative and thus "cured." In addition to taking the prescribed first-order drugs in the TB regime, she consulted a private practitioner between treatments and received medicines to
address specific symptoms such as fever, pain, and cough. She did not conceal her illness from anyone. The private practitioner she consulted in the
locality was well aware that she had consulted various practitioners about
her disease and that she had been on medication for TB. Though she had the
treatment cards that she had collected from the DOTS centers as well as

those from the hospital, she did not carry her medical records from one government institution to another. Nor did any practitioner try to get a detailed medical history from her. This disinterest in patients' medical histories is consistent with the common practice in the area among practitioners trained in all streams (biomedicine, ayurveda, homeopathy, *unani*) to assert that "residual" effects of TB include weakened respiratory functions and to treat coughs and fevers with analgesics and inappropriate antibiotics, even after the patient has been declared cured by the DOTS center.

Meena's death cannot be attributed to a simple notion of stigma that prevented her from going to a DOTS center for treatment. Her family made no effort to conceal her disease.[29] Paradoxically, the notion of stigma operates more in patients' alliances with the medical system: Meena's family members had to move her from one DOTS center to another because they feared that she would be held responsible for her failure to be cured. As a result of these treatment strategies by patients and their families, we have no way of knowing whether Meena was repeatedly reinfected because of compromised immunity, environmental factors, or concomitant HIV infection or whether she was infected by an acquired or transmitted drug-resistant strain. Meanwhile, the records of each DOTS center classify her as a cured case. We might note that if HIV were to become endemic in such areas, classifying cases of repeat infections would be even more difficult.[30]

Meena was completely bewildered about the fact that her symptoms kept recurring when she was pronounced cured at the end of each treatment cycle. Throughout her treatment, she ricocheted between despair and hope. If her symptoms improved, she became active in making little improvements in the house, such as paving a little space in front of her *jhuggi* with cement so that she could wash it and keep the entrance clean. When the symptoms recurred, she lay inside the *jhuggi* and said, "Now I must prepare for going to Jamna ji (the river near the cremation ground). Yet she hoped to survive, and even in the last month of her life, her husband tried to take her back to the DOTS center from which she had received the last course of treatment. The nurse in attendance there was not willing to register her case again; she told her that they had done all they could and that their records showed that she had been cured of her TB. In the last week of Meena's life, when she was coughing incessantly, her husband took her again to a private nursing home, which admitted her, albeit at enormous cost, and she finally died there.

In telling this story, we do not seek to pit heroic patients against heartless doctors; we are struggling to understand how the "letting die" happens even as international agencies and the government participate in the global

Stop TB program. In Foucault's rendering, this "letting die" is an aspect of biopower in which a cut is made that separates those whose lives are to be enhanced from those whose lives are not worth preserving. In his famous formulation, "Sovereignty took life and let live. And we have the emergence of a power of regularization, and it, in contrast, consists in making live and letting die" (Foucault 2003: 247). We hope to show that the way in which the family lets a relation die has a different texture of feeling than the way in which the state does so. Thus, terms such as *abandonment* or *triage* cannot be deployed in a seamless manner as we traverse the milieu of the family and the state, even as we track the manner in which the state's signature can be read in the lives of families and local communities.

The micropolitics of families and communities have qualitative differences and variations that are internal to the family. Thus, we do not seek to paint a stark contrast between the "care" provided by families and the "neglect" of the state. In Meena's life, she faced periods of neglect, when her husband probably just wanted to get rid of her. She also had periods of care, when he would make the long journey to the hospital whenever he could get leave from his work or come home in the afternoon during his lunch break and cook food for her and the children.

The family tried to devise strategies of treatment within the institutions of their local ecology. The inability to acknowledge treatment failures seems to be an unintended consequence of the planning to equip DOTS centers to treat easily identifiable and easily treatable patients in the first phase of the Stop TB program (see Blower and Daly 2002). This strategy has led to practices built on the assumption that patients who do not recover are noncompliant whereas treatments are always efficacious. Though many conditions might arise that prevent patients from complying, treatment failures, repeated reinfections, and the unresponsiveness of multidrug-resistant TB also make "therapeutic fidelity" impossible to maintain.

In the literature on the economic consequences of diseases such as TB and AIDS, one sometimes finds calculations of the impact of deaths on particular populations (the young versus the old, heads of households versus dependents, and so on). The consequences of the death of a young mother for the life of the family, however, cannot be computed in strictly economic terms. During her illness, Meena ceased being an earning member of the family, and paying for her treatments deepened her husband's debt. In this sense, she was an economic liability while she was alive; thus, deaths of unproductive members of the family might be seen as less grievous for the family from a strictly economic point of view. Yet, however much Meena's illness drained the family's resources, her husband and children mourned for her. Less tangible effects of her death on the family exist that will become manifest only over time. Her elder son, for instance, who had passed sixth grade with excellent marks because, as he told one of us, he wanted to please his mother, is now studying in middle school. Will he lose his motivation for studying hard? Will his father continue to give him money for schoolbooks and school uniforms, or will the absence of the mother affect relations between them? Finding the answers to such questions requires long-term observation. Meena's younger son already refuses to go to school regularly, and because the father is away at work during the day, no one is at home to see that he goes to school in a timely manner. The child refuses to acknowledge that his mother is dead, insisting that she has gone to the village and will return later. Meena's two sisters live in the neighborhood, but relations between the families are full of conflicts; thus, responsibility falls on the neighbors and the elder son to provide some supervision to the younger son. The impact of the mother's death on the children, and thus the social and emotional costs of institutional incoherence in the treatment of TB, cannot be computed in strict economic terms. But more importantly, we should ask what the loss of a mother might mean to the children: how do they learn to read their social environment or to trust institutions that seem to have failed them so dismally?

DEADLY INTIMACY

While walking through the streets of the neighborhoods that were part of this study, one sometimes comes across billboards that assure a cure of *uppari chakkar*, along with advertisements for various diagnostic tests and treatments for varied conditions. *Uppari chakkar* has a complex semantic range: Muslims use it to refer to a *jinn* (a being of smokeless fire) passing above who sometimes becomes enamored of a beautiful child or a woman and thus might come to possess him or her. Among the Hindus, this term simply refers to mechanisms through which the ill will of a neighbor or a jealous relative subjects a family to repeated illnesses and misfortunes. The following story of K illustrates this notion.

K traced the beginning of his misfortunes to his daughter's paralysis, which occurred after she received a vaccine from a practitioner in the area who was also a good friend of the family. The girl developed paralysis of the limb probably because the injection was wrongly administered. After some years, K had an accident, and though he was not badly hurt, his vehicle was damaged and he lost his job as a taxi driver. A series of other illnesses followed. Business ventures failed. Though the family has regularly accessed both private practitioners in the area and the public hospital, they attribute the series of misfortunes to the magic done by a jealous neighbor. At the time of the first survey, they told Komila (a field-worker) that the Hindu diviner *(jhad phook wala baba)* they consulted had not been very successful in warding off their misfortunes, because he had not been able to do any real harm to the neighbor. They had therefore shifted to a Muslim diviner *(maulavi)* who could use the verses of the Qu'ran in a clandestine way, trapping anger in its verses and directing the verses toward harming their neighbor. In a discussion with them, I asked why a Muslim diviner would be better. Because a Hindu, I was told, cannot bring enough anger against another Hindu. A Muslim has a reservoir of hate against Hindus, so they hoped he could make that hate into a powerful spell against the neighbor. The social practices of blaming here do not take the usual fault lines of sectarian conflict, in that the neighbor whom K's family blames for its misfortune is not Muslim. Yet K has created a collective subject and seeks to harness the diffused hate and anger that Muslims supposedly harbor against Hindus and use it against his Hindu neighbor. This situation give us insight into how particular Hindus and Muslims are able to inhabit the same local world in ordinary circumstances but can call on anger and hate residing in imagined collectivities.[31] A crisis can draw upon these common reservoirs of hate, which are a potentiality waiting on the door of reality.

In other instances, people in the neighborhoods placated goddesses with offerings of liquor or performed pig sacrifices to channel the energies of angry gods and goddesses against someone they wanted to punish. There is a widespread notion that illness persists because the social world is fraught with danger: "someone has done something." Thus, the experience of the neighborhood and of kinship is a profoundly ambivalent one. Support can be found in the local moral world, but it can overwhelm people and force them to act in confused ways. This phenomenon explains why people sometimes make successful therapeutic choices in *defiance* of the voices in their local world. At other times, as they come to believe that their illnesses are beyond the capacities of the practitioners and the medicines, they may resort to the clandestine sacred world of gods who require bloody sacrifices and goddesses who ask for offerings of liquor and meat. Depending upon the experience of the social world, one person may dismiss a symptom as a harmless part of the change of seasons, and another may read the same symptom as evidence of the power of those who seek to inflict harm. Though the narrative flow in any telling might render these events in linear terms—with the teller offering increasingly complicated explanations as symptoms and complaints become more recalcitrant—in the course of a person's life, these explanations are present as possibilities, located in simultaneity and interpreted within the dense web of socialities in urban life.

TOWARD SOME CONCLUSIONS

We have used illness experience as a lens for understanding the lives of the urban poor in Delhi. Unfortunately, a split has occurred in the field of medical anthropology, with some framing issues of health and disease in terms of political economy and others being more inclined to interpret the experience of illness in terms of meaning. This conflict is presented as one between political economy and culture. Although we need to critique the use of the concept of culture in medical discourse to assign blame for failures of treatment to patients and their beliefs rather than to the failures of the health-delivery system (Farmer 2003), we must also acknowledge the complexity of the social and cultural environment in which the poor live. We should not have to make patients into heroic fighters with a purity of consciousness akin to that of the proletariat in the Marxist imagination of history to make critical claims on their behalf. Illness narratives, when one reads them along with the data on morbidity burden and household patterns of treatment and health expenditure, provide insights into the way that people try to authorize the real within the precariousness of their everyday life, engaging explanations from both political economy and culture.

In describing illness experiences, people in our study used a wide range of possibilities. Just as therapies could be picked and discarded, so too could narratives of illness. The blind complexity of the present, in Byron Good's (1994) terms, left narratives unfinished. People did not move through illness experiences with ready-made "beliefs" about the causes of their illnesses. The mutations of biomedicine in the economy of low-income neighborhoods shaped the languages they deployed as much as the languages of magic and sorcery. The case of the family who moved from a Hindu diviner to a Muslim one to harness the potential of hate shows that notions of community and religion were themselves shaped in the course of illnesses and misfortunes; they were not ready-made pegs on which people could hang their illness experiences.

On the theme of the interconnectedness of political economy and culture, we offer two further observations. First, one can read the story of mistrust and anger that circulates among kin and neighbors as a way to displace the "real" causes of illness (such as the failure of the health-delivery system) to relationships in a world that is closer and hence easier to comprehend. This phenomenon is not the "bad faith" on which Bourdieu (1990) believed the politics of kinship to be based but rather a way of domesticating forces of work, money, and medical treatment that seem to be simultaneously within reach and outside it. If one can misread hate, however, one can also misread love. In Nancy Scheper-Hughes's (1992) powerful ethnography of child survival in Brazil, one of her informants says that she feels alive only when she can feel herself moving under a man. Yet another says about the death of her newborn baby that "he [the father] can make me pregnant but he cannot make me mourn for his child." In both cases, the women moved from one relationship to another, even jeopardizing more stable and caring relationships. Though Scheper-Hughes is inclined to interpret this movement as the women's exercise of freedom, one might say instead that defining self-worth only within a sexual relationship indicates the women's misrecognition of the nature of sociality into which they are tied. Thus, we cannot easily place judgment on the aporia we encountered in the narratives of women whose children had died in the course of their illnesses. The women could render the experience of their social relationships on so many different registers, whether in the positive affect because social relationships remained intact despite serious illness or in sorrow and anger in young women's narratives of their powerlessness within the family, which put their lives and those of their children in peril.

Second, we have tried to contest any generic notion of "the poor," and in this objective, our attempt is similar to Appadurai's. Appadurai offers notions of spectrality as a way of moving beyond the empirics of inequality into the experience of shortage, speculations, crowding, and public improvisation in coping with housing shortage in Bombay (2000: 628): "the absent, the ghostly, the speculative, the fantastic, all have their part to play in the simultaneous excesses and lacks of Bombay's housing scene. It is these experienced absurdities that warrant my use of the term spectral in a setting where housing and its lack are grossly real." Though we can empathize with the sense of dissonance in his vision of transforming slum dwellers into well-dressed nurses, bank tellers, or teachers in their commute to their respective places of work, what is at stake in considering this scene one of spectral housing? Does it reveal the subjects' insufficient hold over the real or the observer's sense of dissonance? By using the generic categories of "dwellers of shanty towns" and "vast army of the middle and working class," Appadurai comes to render the lives of the poor from the resolute perspective of an observer of social traffic rather than from the perspective of someone trying to document how the people themselves render these experiences. The absence of proper nouns in Appadurai's description seems like a well-thought-out ethnographic device to confront the global and avoid drowning the argument in a plethora of detail. One worries, though, that while creating a place for the specificity of Bombay's housing scene, thus contesting a global description of the poor, one might end up rendering experience in terms of Mauss's (1979) "average person."

We offer a final comment on the narrative thrust of this paper. If we look at Davis's rich accounts of the personal transformations and weaving of illness in local histories, we find that the overall story moves toward the act of divination. This movement occurs not because of the definitive authority of divination, as Davis is at pains to point out; the diviner plays with various possibilities. Explanations stick only if they make aesthetic and moral sense to the people seeking divination. People in the Congo village she studied were also inclined to visit the local dispensary, buy drugs at exorbitant prices from traveling traders, and try to visit the mission hospital in the course of an illness. Davis's narrative strategy, however, does not allow her to think that these events need the dense description of sociality that she accords to the other possibilities—leading to divination and diagnosis of the wrongs in the social relations. Our narrative strategy has been to think of the encounters within and outside the local as standing in need of ethnographic description. The traces of sociality when a woman in a low-income neighborhood says that she has low BP embody the history of global and national policies that seek to get rid of the diseases of the poor at a low cost. These explanations of their illnesses are as important as those that direct us toward people's resort to divination when intimacy fails. We recognize the great pull of the linear in making such contradictions intelligible, but we hope we have shown the complicated ways in which notions of the normal and the pathological play out in the context of health and illness in the lives of the urban poor. Technologies of the self intersect with objective points of power and constraint as the poor deal with illness: they engage their illnesses neither as heroic fighters nor as pure actors of cultural scripts. Such is the texture of the ordinary.

NOTES

This paper is part of a larger project on urban health. We gratefully acknowledge the financial support of Johns Hopkins University and the Center for Livable Futures. We are indebted to the team of researchers at the Institute of Socio-Economic Research on Development and Democracy (Delhi) for their participation in the project. We especially thank Charu, Rajan, Purshottam, Simi, Geeta, Poonam, Runa, and Ranjit for their long-term association. We thank Jishnu Das and Carolina Sanchez for their help throughout the data collection and writing.

1. Because forms of storytelling play a significant role in the therapeutic context of psychoanalysis, we do not suggest that storytelling and therapy are completely unrelated. The problem has other aspects relating to political economy, therapeutic failures, and (from the biomedical perspective) inappropriate use of drugs. These factors contribute to tension between symptoms, signs, and diagnosis to a greater degree than this literature acknowledges.

2. The number of households fluctuated during the survey period, because some households moved out or were temporarily unavailable due to visits to the village. However, at no time did the number fall below 285.

3. For a detailed anlaysis of the medical environment, see Das and Hammer 2004.

4. We developed the survey instruments during a one-year pilot phase. Forty households participated in the survey, helping us modify and translate the questions. The morbidity questionnaires were jointly developed by Renu Addlakha, Jishnu Das, Saumya Das, Veena Das, Charu Kumar and Carolina Sanchez. See Addlakha et al. 2000.

5. By this time, the households had completely assimilated the idea of research. Respondents often introduced us as: "Those with the form have come," or "they have come to fill forms." The sociality generated by the research procedures was fascinating. Younger field-workers were assimilated into various kinship positions, and joking relationships developed to bridge the class differences between the field-workers and the respondents, given that the field-workers' forms of language placed them in a different class position.

6. Each field-worker was trained to fill out questionnaires and to conduct ethnographic interviews, and each was responsible for twenty-five households. A field-worker surveyed five households on every working day. Field-workers maintained constancy of contact with households in most cases.

7. The distinction between a sick week and an episode is not useful for chronic diseases. The prevalence of chronic disease, biomedically defined, was much lower among low-income households, but many acute diseases were experienced as following the temporality of chronic diseases.

8. The impact of seasonality on the morbidity burden has been analyzed elsewhere. Here, we note only that the method we used was not only labor intensive but was also prone to interruptions caused by political or other disturbances. For example, we had to increase the number of survey weeks to eighteen in the first round because of protests against the closure of polluting industries (because the closure had a negative impact on the livelihood of the poor) in one of the localities, which impeded our access to households for one week in November.

9. *Jhuggi* and *jhompari* are impermanent houses, typically on the peripheries of the city, that are usually occupied by groups of migrants. Known in official parlance as JJ *(jhuggi-jhopdi)* colonies, these places lack civic amenities such as running water and sewage-disposal systems. Though settled on public land and thus strictly unauthorized, the inhabitants form vote banks and hence command some political leverage. Their position is often suspended between the legal and the illegal. In discussing the *jhuggi* cluster of our study, we are aware of the notorious difficulties of relying on reported income. We have collected data on household consumption and assets to arrive at a more informed way of classifying households as low income, middle income, and upper income.

10. Our use of the notion of primary term is different from Arthur Kleinman's (1980) use. In Kleinman's formulations, "although it would be analytically desirable

to distinguish between symptoms of disease and those of illness (e.g. calling them 'primary' or 'secondary' symptomatic manifestations respectively) this distinction is not easily sustained" (75).

11. David Locker's (1981) analysis of symptoms and illness distinguishes between definitions of disorder and definitions of illness. In his formulation, "The former definition is applied when the problematic experience involved does not result in a concerted change in activity" (101). Thus, in his examples, disorder is not converted into the category of illness if it does not impede normal activities. This perspective assumes that the concerted change in activity results from a purely cognitive organization of disorder. In our examples, the sick role was not defined by a change in activity because many individuals who defined themselves as sick could not be absent from work or from the responsibilities of domestic work.

12. The original entries are in Hindi and have been translated by Veena Das.

13. Integrated medicine refers to the curricula for alternative medicine in state-certified institutions, in which students learn the principles of ayurveda or *unani* as well as some elements of biomedicine.

14. Most men in Noida drink every day. Though we were originally hesitant to approach this issue, over the years, the fact that drinking is ubiquitous, and sometimes leads to wife beating, became common shared knowledge. Thus, I felt authorized to ask this question.

15. We note that the magnitude and pattern of visits stand in sharp contrast to the findings in the literature that suggest that the number of doctor visits increases with the household income (Peabody 1999).

16. In terms of sick weeks, of the 389 cases of self-medication in Bhagwanpur Kheda, 187 cases involved use of a previous prescription and 77 cases involved medicine that the patient claimed he or she had taken earlier and gotten better. In other cases, either a family member or other person suggested the medicine. These figures need to be coded as illness episodes, not sick weeks, because in many illnesses of longer duration, especially TB, patients used a prescription to buy medicines in small quantities rather than a full course at one time. We are currently analyzing these components in terms of illness episodes.

17. The general picture of the relation between social class and access to health care appears to need considerable modification for the urban setting. Writing on family-based popular health care in 1980, Kleinman reported that in the two districts in Taipei that he studied, "families who belonged to lower class treated all sickness episodes at home without resorting to professional or folk healers" (1981: 183). The magnitude and pattern of visits to practitioners by the low-income households in our sample stand in sharp contrast to this and similar findings, which suggest that the number of doctor visits increases with household income (Peabody 1999). Most likely, significant changes in the urban landscape over the past decade have altered the health-seeking practices of the poor in significant ways. Moreover, our weekly morbidity survey, as distinct from the single-interview technique used in most surveys, probably resulted in higher reporting of both nonsevere morbidities and visits to the local practitioners. For an analysis of the implications of these methodological differences, see Das and Sanchez 2002.

18. On the failure of regulation of pharmacies and medical practice, see Das 1999, Dua et al. 1994, Jesani et al. 1997, and Kamat and Nichter 1998.

19. Consider the following statement from the Alta Alma-Ata declaration: "It is now becoming clear that the ultimate solution to the health problems of develop-

ing nations is a fully integrated type of training embracing the essential principles of infectious systems of medicine and modern medical science so that practitioners can serve rural populations understandingly and at relatively low cost." Our findings suggest that such low-cost solutions have themselves become a major risk to the health of the poor.

20. We found households in upper-income groups engaging in such discussions, but the poor did not think of therapeutic choices in this way.

21. Based on an interview conducted by Rajan Singh. The translation is by Veena Das.

22. For a detailed discussion of the medical environment in this area, see Das and Hammer 2004 and Das and Das 2006. Other researchers have reported that practitioners in private clinics tend to use a range of treatments for patients reporting with symptoms of TB. Thus, Uplekar et al. (1998) reported that 79 different TB-treatment regimes were prescribed by 105 reporting private practitioners in a study in Maharashtra.

23. This interview was conducted in Hindi and has been translated by Bhrigupati Singh.

24. The relative advised them to admit Meena under the name of his wife; otherwise, she would have had to wait for a bed. As an employee of the hospital, the ward boy could get preference over others. At least, this was the reason her husband gave. We discovered this ploy quite accidentally when one of us went to visit Meena and could not find her name among the registered patients.

25. This conversation was originally in Hindi and has been translated by Veena Das.

26. MCD refers to Municipal Corporation of Delhi. Allegations abound that medicines in government dispensaries are illegally sold off by the attendant physicians or pharmacists. This practice is one instance of this kind of corruption in the area.

27. These entries were originally in Hindi and have been translated by Veena Das.

28. For instance, Rajeswari and colleagues (1999) reported that 15 percent of infected women in their sample were rejected by their families. One of the difficulties of interpreting these results is that a woman who is sent to her natal family is often reported by researchers as "abandoned" or "rejected" by the family. However, in our field sites, we found that women interpret the move to the natal family for treatment as part of their entitlement in the natal home and see their reception in the natal family as an opportunity to be free of domestic responsibilities in their conjugal families. Cases in which a woman is not allowed to come back to the conjugal home or a husband takes on another wife might indeed be cases of abandonment, but the fact of being sent to the natal home cannot, in itself, be interpreted as rejection. On the impact of tuberculosis on women, see also Connoly and Nunn 1996. Some of the literature completely confuses material and efficient causes in analyzing the factors that people cite as causes of TB.

29. We do not suggest that the notion of stigma is never evoked. However, in the kinds of shanty clusters under consideration here, people live their lives more in the street than in their houses. The material conditions for concealment are simply not available. Moreover, in an arms-length, one-shot survey in which researchers have one point of contact with subjects, respondents are more likely to try to conceal certain illnesses. We have cases in localities with built houses in which families conceal

illnesses, especially of unmarried daughters, for fear that public knowledge would affect the daughters' marriage prospects.

30. Some studies have estimated that 21 percent to 40 percent of cases among smear-positive patients in Maharashtra and Gujarat are retreatment cases (Lambregts-van Weezenbeek 2004).

31. For an analysis of how such diffused notions come to the surface in ethnic or sectarian riots see especially Das 2000; Mehta 2000; Mehta and Chatterji 2001.

SOURCES

Addlakha, R., J. Das, S. Das, V. Das, D. Kumar, and C. Sanchez. 2000. *Weekly Morbidity Survey Documentation.* Delhi: Institute for Socio-Economic Research on Development and Democracy.

Appadurai, Arjun. 2000. "Spectral Housing and Urban Cleansing: Notes on Millennial Mumbai." *Public Culture* 12(3): 627–51.

Blower, S. M., and Daley, C. L. 2002. "Problems and Solutions for the Stop TB Partnership." *Lancet* 2: 374–76.

Bourdieu, Pierre. 1990. *The Logic of Practice.* London: Polity Press.

Connolly, N., and P. Nunn. 1996. "Women and Tuberculosis." *World Health Statistics Quarterly* 49 (2): 115–19.

Das, Jishnu, and Jeffrey Hammer. 2004. "Strained Mercy: Quality of Medical Care in Delhi." *Economic and Political Weekly,* February, 951–61.

Das, Jishnu, and Carolina Sanchez. 2002. Short but Not Sweet; New Evidence on Short Duration Morbidity from India. Paper presented to All Bank Conference on Development Economics. March 11–17, Washington, D.C.

Das, Veena. 1999. "Public Good, Ethics, and Everyday Life: Beyond the Boundaries of Bioethics." *Daedalus* 128 (4): 99–133.

———. 2004. "The Signature of the State." In *Anthropology at the Margins of the State,* ed. V. Das and D. Poole (Santa Fe, NM: SAR Press).

Das, Veena, and Ranendra K. Das. 2006. "Pharmaceuticals in Urban Ecologies: The Register of the Local." In *Global Pharmaceuticals,* ed. Adriana Petryna, Andrew Lakoff, and Arthur Kleinman (Durham, NC: Duke University Press).

Davis, Christopher. 2000. *Death in Abeyance.* Edinburgh: Edinburgh University Press.

Dua, V., C. V. Kunin, and L. V. White. 1994. "The Use of Antimicrobial Drugs in Nagpur, India: A Window on Medical Care in a Developing County." *Social Science and Medicine* 38 (5): 717–24.

Farmer, Paul. 2003. *Pathologies of Power: Health, Human Rights, and the New War on the Poor.* Berkeley: University of California Press.

Foucault, Michel. 1977. *Discipline and Punish: The Birth of the Prison,* trans. Alan Sheridan. New York: Vintage.

———. 1991. "Governmentality." In *The Foucault Effect: Studies in Governmentality,* ed. Graham Burchell, Colin Gordon, and Peter Miller (Chicago: University of Chicago Press).

———. 2003. *Society Must Be Defended: Lectures at the College de France, 1975–1976.* London: Picador.

Frank, Artur W. 1995. *The Wounded Storyteller: Body, Illness and Ethics.* Chicago: University of Chicago Press.

Good, Byron J. 1994. *Medicine, Rationality and Experience: An Anthropological Perspective.* Cambridge: Cambridge University Press.

Jesani, A., et al., eds. 1997. *Market Medicine and Malpractice*. Mumbai: Center for Enquiry into Health and Allied Themes and Society for Public Health Awareness and Action.

Johansson, S. Ryan. 1991. "The Health Transition: The Cultural Inflation of Morbidity during the Decline of Mortality." *Health Transition Review* 1 (1): 39–68.

Kamat, V., and M. Nichter. 1998. "Pharmacies, Self-Medication and Pharmaceutical Marketing in Bombay, India." *Social Science and Medicine* 47 (6): 779–94.

Kleinman, Arthur. 1980. *Patients and Healers in the Context of Culture: An Exploration of the Borderland between Anthropology, Medicine, and Psychiatry*. Berkeley: University of California Press.

———. 1989. *The Illness Narratives: Suffering, Healing, and the Human Condition*. New York: Basic Books.

Lambregts-van Weezenbeek, Catharina. 2004. Multidrug Resistant Tuberculosis: Prevention or Cure? Presentation in Oslo, Norway, October 8, under the auspices of WHO HQ/STOP TB/THD.

Langford, Jean M. 2002. *Fluent Bodies: Ayurvedic Remedies for Postcolonial Imbalance*. Durham, NC: Duke University Press.

Locker, David. 1981. *Symptoms and Illness*. London: Tavistock Publications.

Marx, Karl. 1887. *Capital. Vol.1*, ed. Friedrich Engels. Moscow: Progressive Publishers.

Mauss, Marcel. 1979. "A Category of the Human Mind: The Notion of Person, the Notion of 'Self.' " In *Sociology and Psychology*, trans. Ben Brewster (London: Routledge).

Mehta, Deepak. 2000. "Circumcision, Body, Masculinity: The Ritual Wound and Collective Violence." In *Violence and Subjectivity*, ed. Veena Das, Arthur Kleinman, Margaret Lock, Mamphela Ramphele, and Pamela Reynolds (Berkeley: University of California Press), 79–102.

Mehta Deepak, and Roma Chatterji. 2001. "Boundaries, Names, Alterities." In *Remaking a World: Violence, Social Suffering, and Recovery*, ed. Veena Das, Arthur Kleinman, Margaret Lock, Mamphela Ramphele, and Pamela Reynolds (Berkeley: University of California Press), 201–25.

Morris, David B. 1998. *Illness and Culture*. Berkeley: University of California Press.

Peabody, John W., M. Omar Rahman, Paul J. Gertler, Joyce Mann, Donna O. Farley, Jeff Luck, Jr., and Charles Wolf. 1999. *Policy and Health: Implications for Development in Asia*. Cambridge: Cambridge University Press.

Rajeswari, R., V. Chandrasekaran, M. Suhadev, S. Sivasubramaniam, G. Sudha, and G. Renu. 2002. "Factors Associated with Patients and Health System Delays in the Diagnosis of Tuberculosis in South India." *The International Journal of Tuberculosis and Lung Disease* 6 (9): 789–95.

Scheper-Hughes, Nancy. 1992. *Death Without Weeping: The Violence of Everyday Life in Brazil*. Berkeley: University of California Press.

Singh, V., A. Jaiswal, J. D. H. Porter, J. A. Ogden, R. Sarin, P. P. Sharma, V. K. Arora, and R. C. Jam. 2002. "TB Control, Poverty, and Vulnerability in Delhi, India." *International Journal of Tuberculosis and Lung Diseases* 7 (8): 693–700.

Uplekar, M., S. Juvelkar, S. Morankar, S. Rangan, and P. Nunn. 1998. "Tuberculosis Patients, and Practitioners in Private Clinics in India." *International Journal of Tuberculosis and Lung Disease* 2 (4) 324–29.

4 Anthropological Observation and Self-Formation

PAUL RABINOW

The recent past has seen a number of relatively new forms of anthropological practice emerging; others most certainly will be invented in the near future. Among the current approaches is one that I have been experimenting with, an approach that privileges extensive interviewing with a distinctive group of actors, within a restricted field setting. The challenge of this undertaking is to determine what form to give the material that results. As a form of inquiry that is site restricted and dependent on directed interviews and problematized narratives, the approach can be contrasted to the more traditional ethnographic practice of broad-ranging observation that embraces multiple contexts and actors, aiming for a comprehensive understanding of a group's social relations, cultural symbols, psychological patterns, and the like. In this standard form, the ethnographer is physically present but despite all the prescriptions to participate, would be just as happy not to do so. Should it ever prove possible to be the proverbial "fly on the wall," then the job of observing, documenting, and interpreting multiple situations, ongoing interactions, and actor networks without disturbing them could satisfy the panoptic desire embedded in that mode of work. This desire, of course, differs from Foucault's Panopticism, which sought to develop and perfect observational technology as a means of producing disciplined and productive bodies. In contrast, the standard participant observing ethnographer wants, above all, not to change anything the natives are busy doing, thinking, and feeling. A third position is that of writing a genealogy of the Panopticon (or other arts and techniques) with the goal neither to discipline nor to oversee but to render things visible and vulnerable. Rendering things visible and vulnerable, we often forget, is not the same as denunciation. My current experimentation with form and mode requires me to bypass all three of the above alternatives.

From its inception, the traditional ethnographic approach has run into a core set of limitations, all connected to its initial privileging of the distinction between objectivity and subjectivity. One reaction to this dilemma has been to privilege a norm of objectivity—social facts are things—and to introduce a therapeutics of the observer as a means of overcoming subjective bias. The use of a range of technologies to purify the subject has been prominent in American anthropology at least since Margaret Mead and her generation, which had a pervasive interest in psychoanalysis as a method to reveal the deepest secrets of a culture as well as the projections of the anthropologist's own culture onto the object of study. In that form of analysis, subjectifying techniques became hygienics for identifying symptomatic patterns and objectifying them to make them available, eventually, for better scientific observation. This goal was shared by those who counseled psychotherapy for fledgling anthropologists so that they could ablate themselves from their own cultural prejudices and by adherents of more sophisticated psychoanalytic approaches that brought transference and countertransference into account to overcome the analytic noise in the observational system. Later, in the last several decades of the twentieth century, strategies for coping with the subject/object distinction shifted; subjectifying practices moved from being sites of preliminary purification to sui generis objects of inquiry. Confessional discourses and deployed voices gained prominence within certain sectors of American anthropology (although they were never dominant). Although providing a salutary counterweight to some of the epistemologically exhausted forms of objectivism (which had become increasingly obsessed with method), this subjectifying countermove has itself proved to be more reactive to than creative of new modes of inquiry or forms of writing. Now, at the beginning of the twenty-first century, the charm of this method is on the wane.

HOW TO OBSERVE OBSERVERS OBSERVING WITHIN A MODERN ECOLOGY OF IGNORANCE

In a perspicacious collection of Niklas Luhmann's essays entitled *Observations on Modernity*, we find reflections on a number of themes; of these themes, none is more acutely presented than that of the place of the future in modernity (and its various presents).[1] For Luhmann, the key question is how the future appears. (What is its modality?) And how should a social analyst observe this process? The basic answers are: (1) the future appears as a contingent set of possibilities that demand decisions, because the future appears as an eventuality about which we must do something (remembering that nonaction is an action, and not choosing is a choice); (2) social analysis consists in observing observers observing.

In his essay "Describing the Future," Luhmann explores the form that people are giving the future today as well as the nature of predictions about it, in this society that understands itself to be ever accelerating. Luhmann consistently speaks of "society" as a dynamic cybernetic system with no outside. Although our times abound in futurologists, prophets, and prognosticators, Luhmann observes, with some sarcasm, that we have difficulty taking these seers seriously because we actually have very little sense of what the future will look like in any detail. Two of my favorite confirmatory examples are: the world-historical failure of the experts to predict how the Soviet Empire would end (although a multitude of volumes now show how it was inevitable); and, more pertinently, the fact that for a couple of years, Bill Gates missed the import of the Internet. Luhmann argues that posing the question of the future in terms of form rather than content will produce sociologically more powerful insights.[2] He suggests that the only genre of answer to this question that we should take seriously is one that considers the future to be contingent, thereby compelling incessant decisions.

Of course, descriptions of the future are hardly an invention of modern times. Luhmann presents a standard perspective on the history of ideas, maintaining that until far into the eighteenth century, social life was experienced within a cosmos of essences that guaranteed the constancy of forms of being as well as their constituent elements. The *harmonia mundi* was beyond question. Within such a frame, what was at issue was not the appearance of any startling new things but concern about what would happen. Variation took place on the level of events. Fortune telling as well as expert prognostication turned on specification and hope (and, obviously, fear). Following various eighteenth-century trends, and taking form around the time of the French Revolution, a newly conceived trust in the future appeared: "Perfection was followed by perfectibility."[3] Improvement was possible. New things could come into being, and new types of things could happen. Such perfectibility and its associated optimism took shape in the diverse notions of progress and utility that proliferated throughout the late Enlightenment and permeated the rationality of modernity.[4] Luhmann's "Humankind" (an element we might more accurately analyze as a certain assemblage of discursive and nondiscursive technologies, a series of Deleuzian machines) moved beyond a self-understanding that assumed a pregiven form of perfection into uncharted spaces that allowed individuals a great deal more latitude (to make the world and themselves) and similarly envisioned a population that could improve itself by selection on an individual level. Although Luhmann does not mention Foucault, this political rationality that links individuals to populations in a field of living beings is equivalent to Foucault's biopower. "All in all," Luhmann observes, "we have the impression that around 1800 the impossibility of describing the new structures of modern society would be compensated for with projections of the future."[5] Both in the technological and in the humanistic spheres, society described itself in the projection of its future. This moment is, of course, also the moment in which a new understanding of the past, as history, was being articulated throughout the European elite, as Reinhart Koselleck has documented.[6] The answer to the challenge of how to incorporate finitude was to engage in the infinite task of seeking norms and forms adequate to it. The methodical way of life came of age—with its multiple modes of subjectivation and temporality.

In our time, as never before, the continuity between past and future is broken. However, the one thing we know is that much of what will be true in future presents will depend on current decisions. Decide now! To complicate the picture, we don't have anyone who can decide. We live in a time in which the social authority of experts has been undermined by their oft-proven inability either to forecast the future or to make it happen as envisioned. Dryly and without pathos or nostalgia, Luhmann calls that which has taken the place of authority "the politics of understanding." Understandings are negotiated provisos that can be relied upon for a given time. Such understandings do not imply consensus, nor do they represent reasonable or even correct solutions to problems. Instead, they attempt to fix reference points, those things that are removed from the argument to seed further controversies in which coalitions and oppositions can form anew. Understandings have one big advantage over the claims of authority: they cannot be discredited but can only be constantly renegotiated. Finally, their value does not increase but only decreases with age. Luhmann's point helps explain why we continue to turn to experts whose predictions of twenty years ago now look ridiculous; they may have been wrong, but at least they helped frame a discussion. For example, following the media whirlwind about cloning, everyone agreed that cloning is vitally important: President Clinton wants a position soon. Hurry, let's have a weighty discussion about its future impact, round up the usual spokespeople, and be sure to include a broad spectrum of views. Express concern! Issue a report![7]

A key diacritic of contemporary modernity is the form taken by the temporality of the future. For us, the present refers to a future that exists only as probable or improbable events. In other words, the form of the future is the form of probability that defines a two-sided observation, designating events as more or less probable or more or less improbable, and distributes these modalities across everything that is possible. The present calculates a future that can always turn out otherwise. Thus, the present can always assure itself that it calculated correctly, even if future events do not bear out predictions. This view does not rule out prognoses. In fact, it incessantly demands them; however, their only worth lies in the quickness with which they can be corrected or, more commonly, simply forgotten. Therefore, only a "provisional" foresight is possible whose function resides in the form it provides for a quick adjustment to an unexpected reality.

In such a situation, one finds the modern type of expert, someone who, when asked questions he cannot answer, responds in a mode that provides respectable uncertainty. With a little distance, experts and counterexperts appear to be equally convincing and equally plausible—that is, their assertions about the future are equally unconvincing and equally implausible. We want experts to have transparent interests and values. Their opinions count because we know what they represent. Negotiations then become attempts to increase uncertainty to the point that the only remaining reasonable option is to communicate with one another. However, because we do not have the unlimited time necessary to reach nondistorted agreement, we find ourselves in a quandary.

RESPONSIBILITY TO IGNORANCE

In an essay strikingly entitled "The Ecology of Ignorance," Luhmann further describes the place in which we reflexive moderns find ourselves and that we must take account of if we are to understand the contemporary world. We live amid systemic ignorance. Some of this ignorance is intentional, but some is not. Precisely because of the form we have given the future, we find ourselves within an ecology of ignorance. This fact does not mean that we need a better map of the unknown so that we can go about acquiring the requisite knowledge in an ever-more-comprehensive manner. That task would still fall somewhere between the encyclopedic projects of the Enlightenment (and their nineteenth-century humanistic descendants such as the *Encyclopedia Britannica*) and modernist projects with their Habermasian "universal norms."[8] Rather, it means that the world has inherently volatile, temporally unfolding spaces of ignorance that do not require filling in (because they were not always there and they will continue to multiply). These spaces are differentially distributed and are, of course, saturated by partially volatile and partially frozen sets of power relations.

The appropriate response is to reflexively acknowledge that an ecology of (partial and permanent) ignorance is the social and political ecology in which we live, labor, and discourse. Such an acknowledgment would have dramatic consequences. First, it would further deflate the authority of people making futuristic pronouncements.(Less than a decade ago, debate about mapping the genome turned on two alternatives: the genome as Holy Grail, leading to everlasting health; and genomic mapping as an ominous back door to eugenics. The people making such assertions had no possible knowledge on which to base their claims. Such claims fluctuate between tautologies—the rich will profit from this (whatever the "this" is)—to hype—a new age of medicine will dawn "within a decade." But why do people debate so passionately about things they cannot know—now? To pose the question is to answer it. The platitudes and clichés of these arguments are attempts to fix reference points for debate and communication. They are part of a sociologically essential form of hype that prognosticative observers of science and society cannot do without. Luhmann puts this insight bluntly: "[T]he intensity of ecological communication is based on ignorance. That the future is unknowable is expressed in the present as communication. Society is irritated but has only one way to react to its irritation, in its own manner of operation: communication." Let's hold a conference, set up a commission, have a lively debate, write editorials, take a stance, position ourselves. We often describe these activities as political, or, at times, ethical.

We have a responsibility to our ignorance.[9] Given the expansive normative nature of communication and given the imperative to make decisions in the face of a contingent but onrushing future, we should not be surprised that the term *ethics* appears promiscuously in the most surprising couplings—business ethics, baseball ethics, bioethics. Although at first blush these pairings seem to be oxymoronic, Luhmann's conceptual apparatus provides insights into the form these ethical discourses take.

We all know that our bureaucratically driven welfare states are permeated with and regulated by procedures. Luhmann observes, "If we do not know what good reasons are, then we at least want to be able to say how we can test whether good reasons are good reasons, namely in communication itself."[10] That communication is about values. Luhmann adds a significant insight: "A normative understanding of values serves to allow an ethics to formulate moral demands for the behavior of others, demands that can be maintained despite constant disappointments." Thus, stable reference points are impervious to the fact that people do not live up to them. No one can instantiate the value of autonomy. We have ethical experts whose work is to constantly reassert the importance of autonomy or dignity. Empirical failure in no way deflects or deflates their position. However, such value experts can explain themselves only in value terms. The power relations upon which and through which they construct, maintain, and expand their positions fall outside this discourse. When one group of ethicists ousts another, the only language available to explain the victory is one of better ethics.

Luhmann points to the philosophy of Hans Jonas as the most sustained attempt to develop an ethics (of procedure and value) in a technological age. Jonas argued that the heart of ethics lies in taking responsibility for the (future) consequences of our actions. This position has two major limitations. First, because we live in a modernity in which the future appears as contingent, the ethical actor cannot know the future chain of consequences of his actions. This situation leads to a dilemma: Either we do not act (but then who takes responsibility for the consequences of inaction?), or we act responsibly, knowing that we cannot know the stochastic results of our actions. Today, we are conscious of accepting risk, and ethics, at least until now, has not been able to provide any criteria for this situation. It has provided only procedures and values. Hence, the cost of a responsibility-based ethics may be its impossibility. If we are to be responsible to our ignorance, we have to think differently. If we do so, we face enormous problems in translating such structural ignorance—and a principled responsibility to it—into the kind of technical rationality and obligation to communicate that our bureaucracies and philosophers demand of us.

OBSERVING OBSERVERS OBSERVING

Luhmann's description of modernity is paradoxical. It is both a description of an epoch—modernity as a period of contingency, functional differentiation, and self-reflective individualism—and one of the most systematic critiques of epochal thinking as realism in the history of the social sciences. Luhmann's position is both close to and far from the position of Hans Blumenberg, who argues that in the early nineteenth century, the meaning of the term *epoch* shifted from its older meaning of a "point of view" (originally from astronomy) to that of a totalizing view of the world as historically organized into periods. Reinhart Koselleck shares this view, arguing that our contemporary sense of historicity emerged precisely at the moment Blumenberg indicates.[11] Blumenberg advocates a return to understanding the epoch as a place from which one looks out at things rather than continued pursuit of realist claims to identify periods that, he argues, can never be empirically justified and produce an infinite regress of detail and thus futile polemic over boundaries and definitions. Boldly, Luhmann wants to keep both uses of the term *epoch;* he fully accepts that his position is paradoxical. In fact, he has interesting things to say about paradox, to which we will return after elaborating on Luhmann's thoughts on observation.

In his essay "Modernity as Contemporary Society," Luhmann indicates that the best diacritic for distinguishing modernity, as an epoch, is one that marks a temporal break with the past.[12] The distinctive epochal marker is a historical one. Making a distinction identifies a rupture: it shows us where to look to see the crucial dimension of the world, which, as long as one accepts this distinction, has changed forever. Among the crucial distinctions in this view are the birth of historical consciousness, the actualization of freedom, the emergence of a self-reflective subject, the self-understanding of society as risk, the disenchantment of the world, and the triumph of alienation. Each of these claimants marks modernity differently, although, as Luhmann points out, each turns on a form of experience associated with a specific understanding of temporality.

Luhmann, as we have just seen, has his own candidate for characterizing this form: modernity as contingency. Again, however, Luhmann's entire work is at pains to show that the founding distinction of a system is by definition arbitrary—in the mathematical sense of the term. This fact does not mean that the distinction is false, only that once a distinction is drawn, it carries with it exclusions and blind spots. One of the most common blind spots is the inability to see the necessity of drawing distinctions and the fact that any clearly drawn distinctions exclude others. Once one sees and accepts this analytic arbitrariness as the condition of analytic rigor, then systems theory can move in good faith from that arbitrariness to a kind of realism. Luhmann gives us an epochal description of modernity as contingency, knowing full well that it is arbitrary. Such a description could be done otherwise, and Luhmann himself has marked other defining distinctions of modernity (functional differentiation, double reentry, and so on). Yet Luhmann's claim has one more level of paradox. The demand to live in a reflexive and contingent state can itself become a realist diacritic of the epoch; Anthony Giddens and Scott Lash coherently argue for this interpretation of modernity in their book *Reflexive Modernity*. Indeed, Luhmann claims, "[A]n individual in the modern sense is someone who can observe his or her own observing."[13] The difference between Luhmann and Giddens is that Luhmann must insist that this stance is only one way to cut up the pie. He must be able to make such a claim while saying with equal confidence that the claim is both incisive and arbitrary. Thus, Luhmann, unlike Giddens or Habermas or Beck or Koselleck, is crystal clear that he wants his construct both ways. He wants to have his cake and eat it too. To which we can only say, "bon appétit!"

OBSERVATION

What is observation? "Observation," Luhmann writes, "is any kind of operation that makes a distinction so as to designate one (but not the other) side. Such a definition is itself contingent, since what is defined would have another meaning given another distinction."[14] Luhmann's definition of *observation* is idiosyncratic; he simply sees it as the starting distinction that organizes and begins an inquiry. The starting distinction situates the observer and identifies that which is to be observed. Only then can inquiry proceed. First-order observations thus are ordinary realist attempts to grasp a referent. Most social scientists and most actors in the social world are content to do this type of observation. It establishes an environment, a point of observation, and a referent.

First-order observations work within limits that a fuller human scientific inquiry, or an inquiry about science qua inquiry, might well strive to take into account. Luhmann thus draws a distinction between first-order observations and second-order observations. "Observations of the first order (reference) use distinction as a schema but do not yet create a contingency for the observer himself."[15] Second-order observations are observations of first-order observations; they take the system (observer-environment) established by the first-order observations as their referent. By so doing, they are able to take up the blind spots created by the perfectly legitimate arbitrariness established by the first-order observations. Of course, a second-order observation has no absolute privilege, because it too calls for making a distinction. However, unlike first-order observations, second-order observations are, by definition, self-referential.

"Second order observations offer a choice . . . whether certain designations are to be attributed to the observed observer, thereby characterizing him, or seen as characteristics of what he observes. Both attributions, observer attribution and object attribution, are possible; the results can be considered contingent. They can be combined, for example, when an observation is believed to be factually correct but the question remains why the observed observer happens to be interested in this instead of something else."[16]

Thus, by definition and with complete legitimacy, first-order observations center on one context, situation, or environment. Second-order observations, also by definition and with complete legitimacy, focus on more than one context, situation, or environment; they include the observation of observers observing a context and the fact that they are observing them.

"Observations of the second order are observations of observations. This can include observations of other observers or observations of the same or different observers at different points in time. Depending on these variants, social and temporal dimensions can be distinguished in the production of meaning. This makes it possible to state that contingency is a form that takes on the factual dimension of the medium of meaning, whereas the social dimension and the temporal dimension pull observation apart. Or to put it another way: everything becomes contingent whenever what is observed depends on who is being observed."[17] Thus, one could well observe modernity as an epoch as long as one is aware that a second-order observer observes that starting point as a first-order observation.

CONTEMPORARY ANTHROPOLOGICAL OBSERVATION

In light of our preceding discussion, we can say that contemporary anthropologists whose object of study is modern (that is, self-reflexive and contingent) first-order observers must engage in second-order observation. Thus, they must set up a frame of inquiry that allows for this double reflexivity and contingency (of the first-order modern observer and the second-order observer). This demand, though complex, is self-evident once one accepts Luhmann's distinctions. Further, Luhmann has much to say about how one should conduct such an inquiry. A less self-evident but equally logical requirement is that anthropologists engaged in second-order observations of self-reflective first-order observers must find a way to take into account their own observation practice, however self-reflective it may be. As we have seen, the traditional approach to this task was to introduce a range of analytic practices that aimed to identify and neutralize factors that distorted the observational powers of the observer.

Luhmann's analytic helps us see another way to proceed: "One thing the observer must avoid is wanting to see himself and the world. Only the unity of the distinguished can be observed."[18] In accord with this maxim, anthropologists of the contemporary will find it helpful, perhaps even essential, to include a second (second-order) observer in the practice of anthropological inquiry. Such an observer would observe the (second-order) observer observing the (first-order) modern observers. This observer would be better than technical devices such as video cameras to record interview sessions and the like precisely because the second, second-order observer would know that she should not attempt to see herself and the world.

Although an infinite regress of higher levels of observers is logically possible, initial experience with the technique indicates that two observers with clearly defined functions offer a sufficiently powerful apparatus for the purposes at hand. This apparatus safeguards against blatant use of unintentional epideictic rhetoric or a belief in the transparency of immediate history. It also takes a major step beyond modernist irony, but that topic requires another paper.

INTERVIEWS

Ethnographers have used the technique of extended interviews for generations, with the aim of gathering data to improve their understanding of a culture or of a "life history" that itself cast light on a culture. The term *Bildung* in its nineteenth-century German sense of cultural self-formation is at least a partially appropriate descriptor of this process. It is only partially appropriate because the German use of the term privileged works of elite culture, and American anthropology has popularized the term *culture* and its terrain of application. Like observation, the interview process invites a dream of transparency at work; if an informant could speak into a tape recorder (or point the camera lens) without the anthropologist saying anything, then full transparency would be achieved. As graduate students have been gravely reminded for generations, the point of our profession is not "you"; it is the "other." If only one could disappear entirely and let the other speak, our science would be mature. In a different way, even Spivak's plaintive query about whether the subaltern could ever speak reflected a normative goal of transparency: if only power relations were different, then . . .

Thus, the interview starts with the distinctions that culture has a unity; the encultured or socialized individual has a self that is infused with the culture; and the anthropologist herself is a bearer of a self and a culture that only adequate scientific treatment can induce to recede asymptotically. Then, and only then, would the immediacy of the other—appropriated and appreciated—be available. The moral imperative driving these distinctions was a perfectly admirable attempt to valorize cultural difference. These distinctions and their associated operations have yielded much of value.

Once one recognizes that ethnographic practice can proceed from other distinctions, however, the previous form loses, at a minimum, if not its entire authority, at least its sense of self-evidence. Exploration of other possibilities has been ardently resisted mainly because people have heavily invested the previous form with moral assumptions and affects that they believed cohered in an essential manner with scientific principles. Sundering these connections, or making them available for questioning and inquiry, has proved a painful prospect for many, but in reality it in no way forecloses the practice of anthropology. On the contrary, problematizing assemblages reveals that other modes and forms are logically possible and at least imaginatively feasible. Actualizing them, however, requires not so much thinking as a sustained corrosion of the power relations embedded in the habitus of a generation. For better or worse, the human sciences change very slowly.

What if we did not begin with the distinction of subject and object and its secondary assumption that it is the culture that is enunciated through speaking subjects? What if we did not begin with the distinction between a whole to be captured and an inquiring subject to be rendered transparent? What if we did not assume that our task is to write culture? And what if the search for another form of anthropological inquiry proceeded from a different set of distinctions precisely because its object of inquiry appeared to be composed of forces driving and articulating assemblages defined by accelerated creation, efficiency, and associated stress of and for subjects, objects, and the elements that mediate them? What, then, would observation consist in? And what operations would assist that new form of observation?

IMMEDIATE HISTORY

Georg Wilhelm Friederich Hegel (1780–1831), at the beginning of his posthumously published lectures *Introduction to the Philosophy of History*, distinguishes three types of historical writing: original history, reflective history, and philosophic history. Although Hegel is known for the third kind of historical writing, unexpectedly, his presentation of the first type—"original history" *(ursprungliche Geschichte)*—is today the most vivid and relevant type for scholars seeking to carry out and to write about the practice we might call the anthropology of the actual.[19] Hegel is respectful of this genre, devoting several pages to it, but thinks it is not an adequate genre to portray modern times: "Our culture is essentially intellectual, and it immediately converts events into reports for intellectual representation."[20] Modern times are fundamentally mediated by concepts, and the immediacy of war and politics has given way to a more removed and divided situation. This claim is dubious, and we will return to it below.

Hegel says the following about original history:

> Herodotus, Thucydides, and other such historians primarily describe the actions, events, and situations they themselves have witnessed, and whose spirit they shared in. They translate what is externally present into the realm of mental representation. . . . Of course, such original

historians rely on reports and accounts of others, since it is not possible for one person to have seen everything. But they use these sources as ingredients only. . . . Legends, folksongs, traditions—these are to be excluded from original history, because they are obscure modes of memory, proper to the mentality of pre-literate peoples. On the contrary, in original history, we are concerned with peoples who knew what they were and what they wanted. . . . These original historians, then, transform the events, actions and situations present to them into works of representation. . . . Their essential material is what is present and alive in their surrounding world. . . . Short spans of time, the individual patterns of men and events—these are the singular, unreflected features out of which he composes his portrait of the time, in order to bring that picture to posterity with as much clarity as it had in his own direct observation or in the accounts of other direct witnesses. He is not concerned with offering reflections on these events, for he lives within the spirit of the times and cannot as yet transcend them.

We say that such a historian is not reflective but that persons and nations are directly present in history. Yet against this assumption are the speeches, which we can read, for example, in Thucydides; these orations were surely not spoken as they appear but were worked up by the writer of the history. Speeches, however, are actions among men, and indeed they are effective action in their essence. "If, in the Middle Ages, it was the bishops who were at the center of political activity, it was the monks who wrote history (in the form of naïve chronicles), and who were as isolated from events as the men of antiquity were involved in them."[21]

The point of presenting Hegel's claims is not to provide an opening to resurrect other parts of his philosophy. That being said, Hegel's claims resonate strongly with the project of problematizing and transforming the practice of ethnography announced, among other places, in the watershed 1986 collection *Writing Culture: The Politics and Poetics of Ethnography*. Of the many topics presented for further inquiry in this heteroclite collection of essays were whether the temporality of the ethnographic present can legitimately be deployed, whether distinct cultures (or *ethne*) can legitimately remain the object of anthropological inquiry, and whether narrative forms developed to present culture in an ethnographic present ("Balinese culture") can legitimately be deployed. Each of these questions could be answered definitively in the affirmative or negative or, in a more critical manner, could be posed to provoke thought about the issue of limits. Although *Writing Culture* presented varied positions on how to pose and answer these questions, all writers agreed, at least tacitly, that if anthropology was to move beyond its founding contextualization in twentieth-century social science as well as beyond colonialisms, then each of these topics—what temporality? what object? what form?—required imaginative invention and discovery.

If, as the majority of the authors in the volume held, the traditional form of ethnographic authority was in crisis, then practitioners in the field needed to revisit the question of what form of inquiry is appropriate for studying practices in their immediacy rather than cultures in their atemporality (or even their historicity). Once again, Hegel's claims have an uncanny ring of actuality. "What the original historian lets speak is not a borrowed consciousness but the speaker's own self-formation *[Bildung]*." The last term, which I translate as "self-formation," is translated in the text as "culture." To write this immediate history well, authors should not speak for those they aim to present but should seek a mode through which interviewees could speak for themselves.

We find a partial correspondence with the touchstone of symbolic anthropology—from the native's point of view. The correspondence is partial in that symbolic anthropologists tended to analyze cultures as they existed in the ethnographic present. As we have seen, both of these terms—*culture* and *present*—were under critical scrutiny. Hence, we opt to translate *"Bildung"* not as "culture" but as "self-formation." This choice is not mere pedantry, because not only does it help the reader avoid totalizing and self-standing objects such as "culture," but it provides an alternative that embodies the idea of process. It also implies, however, the attempt to achieve a unified self. Whether these associations are still desirable is a topic to which we return below. Finally, when Hegel identifies the subject as the "speaker," he enters the realm of discourse and *logos*. Savvy dialectician that he was, Hegel made distinctions that were equally applicable to subjects, objects, and the elements that mediate them through time.

Hegel's distinctions help us obtain some conceptual distance from the present; for precisely this reason, I need to indicate a few of the ways in which my position differs from Hegel's. First, his entire philosophy of the unfolding of Spirit in History is a dead letter. Hegel's assurance that Thucydides lived in a unified epoch, in which all free citizens moved in the culture of Greece like the proverbial fish in water, and that we can therefore take Thucydides as a spokesman for this epoch and this culture, is highly dubious. By doubting this claim, we in no way diminish the interest of Thucydides' work; quite the contrary, this stance enables us to find fascination in other aspects of his writing.

WRITING THINGS: DEICTIC, NOT EPIDEICTIC

Previous generations would not have been surprised by Hegel's attention to Thucydides, whose *On The Peloponnesian War* has for centuries occupied an important place in the canon of Greek thought. Today, Thucydides is unfortunately unknown to most American students, and my discussion of his work in part—but only in part—seeks to pique the interest of those who might be curious about such matters. Surprisingly little is known about this Athenian admiral, who was a member of a noble family. He was probably born around 460 B.C. and probably died in the mid-390s B.C., although both dates are uncertain. However, we do know from the famous opening sentences of the *On The War* that

> Thucydides, an Athenian, wrote the war between the Peloponnesians and the Athenians, beginning at the moment that it broke out, and believing that it would be a great war, and more worthy of relation than any that had preceded it. This belief was not without its grounds. (1.1)[22]

The war broke out at the end of the summer in 431 and Thucydides' chronicle finishes at the end of the summer 411 in the war's twenty-first year. I turn to Thucydides to indicate the existence of a genealogy of writing and thinking about events and their narration, so careful attention to the terms he used to discuss these issues is appropriate; this discussion is possible because of the invaluable aid of Professor James Faubion. Thus, for example, although the standard translation of the first line of Thucydides' text includes the term *history*, the word is not present in the Greek. Thucydides says literally that he "wrote the war."[23] We should not forget that the contrastive cases of "writing things" for Thucydides would have been Homer and Herodotus; in response to their "romance" or "fabulation," Thucydides proposed a sober accuracy.

The other significant fact that we know about Thucydides is that in 424, the rulers of Athens sent him to the northern city of Amphipolis to defend it against Spartan attack. He failed.

> It was also my fate to be an exile from my country for twenty years after my command at Amphipolis; and being present with both parties, and more especially with the Peloponnesians by reason of my exile, I had leisure to observe affairs more closely. (1.5.26.5)

Thucydides' simple declarative statement is moving in its assertion of enduring loyalty—"my country"—and unselfconscious in its linkage of the terms *leisure, observe, affairs,* and *closely.* Again, the translation of these terms is comprehensible but misleading: "leisure" is not the Greek "*skholè,*" which Pierre Bourdieu has analyzed in detail, but rather "calm;" "to observe" is a poor translation of the Greek *aesthesis*, for which a better translation is "to be acquainted with (through the senses);" "affairs" is simply "things," and "more closely" is "better." Hence, Thucydides says, "I had the calm to acquaint myself better with things." Although these changes do not change the fact that Thucydides' "immediate history" is closely tied to the author's own situation, they do introduce nuance and tone that indicate topics about which debate has flourished for millennia. Thus, to take only Bourdieu's attention to *scolè*—noting that Thucydides was of a class that depended on the labor of others and was in a position that allowed him the comfort to reflect, even in disgrace—is essential, but that he chose to do so in a state of calm is of equal interest.

Thucydides wrote throughout the two-decade-long war; his account has occasioned scholarly interest, factual correction, and debate for centuries. For example, Thomas Hobbes wrote a provocative, even polemic, translation that is still read today because Hobbes was able to give this rather dry chronicle of battles, tactics, and public speeches a keen sense of pertinence; that Hobbes's translation, which he wrote to move the audiences of the seventeenth century, still affects twenty-first-century readers is remarkable and indicative of the text's depth and/or its capacity to sustain multiple, and often incompatible, readings. Among the reasons for the long-lived readability and seeming accessibility of *On the War* are the famous speeches (some twenty-seven in all) that Thucydides groups at crucial junctures in his narrative. Although scholars have spilled much over the speeches' authenticity and veracity, less incisive reflection has focused on why Thucydides might have included them in his account in the first place. Hegel assumes that the speeches of Thucydides are present simply as part of "the spirit of his time." Thus, Hegel can take them not as examples of reflective or critical history but merely as instances of "representation." Today, Hegel's interpretation appears quaint; one can easily glide over the claim as merely another example of the early nineteenth-century Romantic German obsession with Athens that has been so well documented and dissected. Whatever the truth may be, an appeal to epochs would be incongruent with the spirit of my own text; hence, I will simply register my disagreement with this aspect of Hegel's interpretation of Thucydides while acknowledging and retaining his other valuable insights about the text. The status of the speeches' purpose remains open.

Here is Thucydides' explanation of why he included the speeches and where they fit in his manner of writing things:

Now, what was said in speeches by either side, as it was about to go to war or when it was already in it, has been difficult for me to remember exactly in terms of what precisely was spoken (both of what I heard myself or of what was reported to me by others). But as every individual would seem to have said pretty much what he had to concerning the circumstances at hand, so have I written it, staying as close as possible to the entire sense of what was actually spoken. And as far as the facts of what was done in the war are concerned, I do not think it fit to write what I learned from anyone who merely happened to be on the spot, nor merely what I thought seemed right. But both about those events I was witness to and to those I learned of from others, as much as possible I scrutinized everyone [and his account] with a view to accuracy. Even so it was a difficult task to discover [a true account] because participants in events do not agree with each other in their statements, but differed because of their memories [being faulty] or because of their interests in events. (1.22.1–3)[24]

We find a perspicacious account of the speeches in *On The War* in Marc Cogan's *The Human Thing: The Speeches and Principles of Thucydides' History*.[25] Cogan's thesis is that Thucydides included the many speeches, grouping them at turning points in the long war, because he sought to identify and make visible the elements and functioning of deliberation, showing the use of rhetoric to make prudential decisions, in this case political decisions, during a time of war between city-states, when confederations were shifting and the fate of a form of life was at stake. Cogan argues cogently that most interpretations of the speeches' function in Thucydides are misguided.

Cogan points out that most criticisms of Thucydides—as well as many of the interpretations of those who praise him—are misleading when they offer *On The War* as an example of epideictic rhetoric: a rhetoric of display and embellishment. They have taken the speeches to be mere devices through which Thucydides can present his own views, making the marionette characters speak. Commentators have chosen to see the speeches as examples of epideictic rhetoric because the speeches could not possibly be verbatim accounts, on the one hand, and, on the other hand, Thucydides explicitly does not present them as fictions. Cogan vigorously contests this view, arguing that interpreting the speeches as examples of epideictic rhetoric leads to a number of hermeneutic wrong turns. Rather, he urges us to take Thucydides literally when he argues that he has done his utmost to establish the speeches' accuracy. That accuracy turns not on the representation of a type of speech, but—in Cogan's thesis—precisely on the particularity of the given speech; albeit with a tacit understanding that all such speeches followed the established styles of rhetoric and logic. Cogan insists on particularity because it makes clear the real challenge: how to seize the situations in their particularity and thereby make available their generality. This approach is the exact inversion of an epideictic rhetoric that would use particulars as an element in the demonstration or elaboration of an established general thesis. One could call this reversal of emphasis a methodological caution, or even principle, if these modern terms were not so dissonant with the powerful immediacy of the speeches within Thucydides' text.

Moreover, Thucydides obviously could have made up or chosen to present literally thousands of the speeches made during the decades of the war. Thus, his selectivity reveals the significance of the drive for particularity. "Nowhere," Cogan writes, "is Thucydides' selectivity more accessible to us than in the speeches he records, and for this reason they provide the direct route to the understanding of his interpretation of the war."[26] Cogan's thesis is that these speeches vividly make available the processes and forces—including, above all else, the process of deliberation itself—that shaped political deliberation at the crucial turning points of the war; either when events could have gone in a different direction or when significant strategic decisions were taken through public deliberation, either by statesmen addressing the assembled citizenry (as in the famous speeches of Pericles in Athens during the plague) or in dialogues between city representatives (as in the famous Melian dialogue). Through the particularity of those discursive moments, significance is made performative, made public, debated, demonstrated, shown, enacted. Discourse in such settings was political action; it was an instantiation of itself, not a representation of something else. Thus, the vital point is that Thucydides adopted a reflective and reflexive stance toward discursive action and recognized its dependent but decisive function in the unfolding of events.

This claim leads us to another distinctive trait of Thucydides' practice: "his presentation of the speeches not as excerpts but as whole (if abridged) speeches. The practice is, of course, foreign to contemporary historical practice, but we must recognize, novel in Thucydides' time as well. In understanding his purposes in attempting to replicate the complex experience of political oratory on particular occasions, we can discover Thucydides' conceptions of the nature of action that required this form of presentation of the moments of deliberation."[27] Not only is this practice foreign to contemporary historical practice, but it is foreign to contemporary journalism and to contemporary science studies. Each of these forms of inquiry (and of narration) retains a type of authorial control that does not make the extended process of deliberation available for others to ponder and evaluate for themselves. In that sense, these other genres are all epideictic; they use quotation and empirical material only to illustrate, reinforce, or embellish a point or to bolster an interpretation or instantiate a theoretical claim. In journalism, the genre constraints are such that extended quotation is simply not allowed; journalists are paid to tell the audience what things mean, and editors are paid to police them, to improve their prose so that it fulfills this function. In science studies, the primacy of "theory" over "cases" means that the examples are almost exclusively deployed to strengthen and to (appear to) demonstrate a theoretical point. Even in the natural sciences, where papers must include a methods section, deliberative process is absent.

Of course, myriad excellent reasons exist to proceed in an epideictic fashion. Hence, I am certainly not arguing for the abandonment of other genres. I am, however, suggesting that we give due consideration to these genres' strengths and weakness and recognize that such an evaluation of genre and rhetoric will help us conduct more powerful and richer inquiries; and hence to know things in a more refined and appropriate manner. In other words, one of the diacritics that distinguishes an anthropology of the actual from its sisters in writing the present is its attempt to find conceptually mediated deictic forms—forms that would once again make immediate history a tool for bringing particularity and generality into more fruitful, mutually informing relationships, obliging the reader to take up an active and prudential stance toward the issues under deliberation. Thus, one version or another of such a form would allow us to introduce an ethical attitude into anthropological inquiry.

Finally, Thucydides sought to understand what happened in the long war (that he justly considered of prime significance for the fate of the Greek people), in part to establish what general lessons one could learn from thinking about it. While writing his history, Thucydides was no longer an actor in these events; he was in exile but immediately adjacent to things. Thus, we can fairly conclude that he was not writing solely in an "immediate" mode, as Hegel suggests, but rather in a mediated mode, one that was unquestionably reflective while remaining contemporary to the events themselves. No longer a citizen of Athens but still attached to it by myriad ties and affects (of kinship, style of thought, or attachment to place), Thucydides' presentation of the materials on the war sought to serve deliberation not just then—after all, the war had already taken place—but, in his famous phrase, "for all time." He took as his object public deliberation and made it available as an object to ponder, consider, debate; his chronicle is itself an object of deliberation. He argued that because other events would certainly occur in a form resembling the one he described, deliberators in the future would be well advised to take into account the things he had written about. The opening passage I cited earlier continues:

> The absence of romance in my ["writing of these things"] will, I fear, detract somewhat from its interest; but if it be judged useful by those inquirers who desire an exact knowledge of the past as an aid to the understanding of the future, which in the course of human things must resemble it if it does not reflect it, I shall be content. In fine, I have written, not to win the applause of the moment, but as a possession for all time. (1.22–3)[28]

Thucydides' meaning in this passage has been the subject of scholarly dispute. We can abstain from entering that fray. For our purposes, Thucydides' claim that bringing long-term material conditions of geography, culture, political alliance, style, and forms of life into a relationship with men's thoughts and deeds within those constraints and looking at how their deliberations effected change in those constraining forces are plausible starting points for understanding, especially if one is interested in the singularity of events. Whether this undertaking tells us anything "for all time" is for others to worry about.[29] Yet we are wise to ponder how a text written twenty-five hundred years ago remains such a keen deictic tool.

NOTES

1. We can compare Luhmann's work with Reinhart Koselleck's *Futures Past, On the Semantics of Historical Time* (trans. Keith Tribe; Cambridge, MA: MIT Press, 1985 [orig. 1979]), which analyzes how the past appears in modernity, and Michel Foucault's "What Is Enlightenment?" which queries the way the present appears in different historicities. Foucault shows how these questions lead to a problematization of modes of subjectivation, an issue that centrally concerns Luhmann, although he does not pose the question in these terms.

2. Niklas Luhmann, *Observations on Modernity* (Stanford, CA: Stanford University Press, 1998 [orig. 1992]), 63.

3. Ibid. 65.

4. One can relate Luhmann's ideas to Beck's two stages of modernity. See Ulrich Beck, *Risk Society: Towards a New Modernity*, translated by Mark Ritter (London: Sage, 1992).

5. Luhmann, *Observations on Modernity*, 66.

6. Koselleck, *Futures Past*.

7. Gregory Pence, *Who's Afraid of Human Cloning?* (Lanham, MD: Rowman and Littlefield, 1998).

8. See Alasdair MacIntyre, *Three Rival Versions of Moral Enquiry: Encyclopaedia, Genealogy, and Tradition* (South Bend, IN: Notre Dame University Press, 1990).

9. My thanks go to James Faubion for this phrase.

10. Niklas Luhmann, *Ecological Communication*, trans. John Bednarz Jr. (Chicago: University of Chicago Press, 1989), p. 93.

11. See Paul Rabinow, *Anthropos Today, Reflections on Modern Equipment* (Princeton, NJ: Princeton University Press, 2003).

12. Niklas Luhmann, "Modernity as Contemporary Society," in *Observations on Modernity*, 3.

13. Ibid, 7.

14. Niklas Luhmann, "Contingency as Modern Society's Defining Attribute," in *Observations on Modernity*, 47.

15. Ibid.

16. Ibid, 48.

17. Ibid., 47–48.

18. Niklas Luhmann, "The Ecology of Ignorance," in *Observations on Modernity*, 111.

19. Rabinow, *Anthropos Today*.

20. G. W. F. Hegel, *Introduction to the Philosophy of History*, trans. Leo Rauch (Indianapolis: Hackett Publishing Company, 1988), 5.

21. Hegel, *Introduction*, 3–5.

22. Robert B. Strassler, ed., *The Landmark Thucydides, A Comprehensive Guide to the Peloponnesian War* (New York: The Free Press, 1996). This edition of *The Pelopennesian War* is a revision of the Richard Crawley translation.

23. James Faubion has been generous in providing help with the Greek text as well as its meaning.

24. Cogan's translation.

25. Marc Cogan, *The Human Thing: The Speeches and Principles of Thucydides' History* (Chicago: University of Chicago Press, 1981).

26. Cogan, "Introduction," *The Human Thing*, xv.

27. Ibid., xvii.

28. Crawley's translation, altered.

29. Richard McKeon, *Freedom and History: The Semantics of Philosophical Controversies and Ideological Conflict* (New York: Noonday Press, 1952), 52. "Logistic history is not universal. It begins with particular data—the forces relevant to a great event, the occurrences of a particular period, the accomplishments and sufferings of a particular group, people, or nation—and with the lines of causal relations or with the probabilities of consequences—the evolution of political forms and political power, the development of military instruments and tactics, the influence of geographic environment, the elaboration and extension of tools and industry, the alteration of economic conditions, moral influences, and social forms and customs."

PART II

Political Subjects

In "Hamlet in Purgatory," literary scholar Stephen Greenblatt challenges Freud's privileging of Oedipus as the modern representative of psychological interiority. Greenblatt maintains that Shakespeare's Hamlet is the one who does this work (chapter 5 in this volume). "Remember me" is the haunting demand of the dead father to Prince Hamlet. Following Goethe's lead in seeing the prince as more of a neurotic than a hero, Greenblatt tests Jacques Lacan's idea that the subject is the doing of the phantasm (1979) by actually traversing Hamlet's ghost in history, so to speak. "Something have you heard of Hamlet's transformation: so I call it, since not the exterior, nor the inward man resembles that it was" (Shakespeare, *Hamlet* 2.2.5).

As Greenblatt unveils the materiality, politics, and aesthetics of this figure who haunts and transforms subjectivity, he inventively finds that Hamlet's way of measuring himself in pathos ("this corrosive inwardness") is not necessarily the outcome of a repression which has been miscarried (as Freud would have it) but the recycling of an elaborate social experiment around the cult of the dead. In Greenblatt's work, moderns are also the subjects of cultural cataclysm.

Greenblatt shows that while rewriting the original story of Hamlet as it appeared in a Danish chronicle, Shakespeare replaced the motif of revenge with that of remembrance, and the issue of remembrance was at the center of the sixteenth-century political debate in England about purgatory and the ontological status of the dead: how much of a claim can the dead make on the living? Greenblatt tracks the ways in which arguments about the existence of purgatory and institutional interventions have brought together and recast concepts of family, guilt, social responsibility, the location and source of power, and representation. He begins with an anticlerical book, *A Supplicacyon for the Beggers*, written in the early sixteenth century by a

London lawyer, Simon Fish. The book denounces purgatory not only as a false doctrine but as a cunningly designed imaginary space. Fish speaks in the name of the poor as he indicts Catholic representatives' practice of commodifying fiction and using purgatory for social domination and economic gain, and thus neglecting the kingdom's commonwealth. Fish was protected by King Henry VIII, who, for his own well-known reasons, supported a reformed religion.

Sir Thomas More, however, on the verge of becoming the king's lord chancellor, further complicated the political use of purgatory because he was an apologist for the ongoing Catholic order. In a public reply to Fish's heresies, More wrote that the miseries of the poor were vastly exceeded by the cries of dead ones who feared they had been forgotten. More counterposed the dead not to the beggars, as Fish did, but to the living. By not addressing the dead's claim to be remembered, the living doomed themselves to go straight to hell. Moving beyond the murky and vulnerable doctrine of the middle state and place of the souls, More's *The Supplication of Souls* enlisted public discussions about ghosts and made the case that no absolute line exists between the living and the dead because of the feelings one has toward the memories of loved kin. In the end, More urged people to give more money to the church—as a sign of remembrance. In fact, by 1563, purgatory had been shut down. The Church of England had rejected the doctrine of purgatory, and the whole intercessory system—the institutions and methods of dealing with the dead—had officially ended. The enforced Protestant cultural change, however, could not destroy the longings and fears that the Catholic Church had exploited.

Shakespeare understood that the representational contradictions lurking in debunked theological principles and in both damaged and new institutional structures could intensify his play's uncanny power. The ideological struggle that turned negotiations with the dead from an institutional process governed by the church into a subjective process governed by guilt, projection, and imagination finally found a place in theater. The force or energy that keeps Hamlet a seminal modern form of art in which people can see themselves and their inner conflicts and struggle of consciousness is directly tied, argues Greenblatt, to Shakespeare's ability to capitalize on the cult of the dead as it had evolved in the generations before he wrote.

In *Hamlet*, certain materials moved from a so-called real place to a place that now appeared to be imaginary or theatrical. Through Hamlet's relationship to his father's ghost, Shakespeare brought purgatory into the realm of personal reflection, and in so doing, he replaced its institutional bases with guilt, responsibility, conviction, and doubt. People now paid to see the ghost staged. New laws of perception and action were established, along with a distinct sense of self: a lack, a yearning, this very modern thing emerging in the subject as he was acted out.

In Greenblatt's archaeology, the malaise of modern man and woman emerges not just in relation to a new reality but also in relation to an engineered loss; that is, people can no longer deal symbolically with the dead in a familiar way. Moving from political subjection to imaginary servitude, the modern self enters the stage of history.

> We can become images and images become us. How is this transformation, by which a piece of fantasy or imaginary-perceptual construct acquires a part of me, taking place? Where does the imaginary gain its power so that it could mold the self? Where does the self attain its plasticity by which it can assume forms of the imaginary?

These questions, raised by Gabor Katona, a young historian of science who took his life in January 2003, convey the potentialities of images—the overwhelming sense of being overtaken by cultural representations—to remake the self into something unique yet shared.

Ethnographic studies of subjectivity must find ways to address the artifices and constructs that transform body and voice. In the workings of politically and monetarily infused assemblages, we can witness both the loss of human experience and novel becomings (Deleuze 1997). These movements from public spaces and meanings into intimate sensibility—movements at once constraining and enabling, repetitive and inventive—make history happen. They place us in time. They are the means to think through the materials of the times and the mediations through which lives are made real and death faced.

Ludwik Fleck, in his prescient book *Genesis and Development of a Scientific Fact* (1979), emphasizes the specific historical development of thinking, looking at how the making of scientific facts relates to reigning "thought-styles" and how social relations and experience are shaped by new conventions. He shows, for example, that in order for syphilis to appear as an empirical-therapeutic disease entity—that is, as an undoubtedly real fact—medical practitioners had to disregard other important facts, such as the ethical-mystical notion of syphilis as a "carnal scourge" and the sense that "the new conventions were not felt to be of equal value as the discharged ones." While exposing the workings of medical science in general, Fleck argues that it defines the morbid as an entity by rejecting some of the observed data and by guessing about nonobserved relations. In this way, the irrational becomes rational in its details, he says, but this approach also allows other things to be unaccounted for and remain unexplained (Fleck 1986: 39–40). The suggestion is that the sense of subjectivity becomes caught up in struggles over truth and efforts to learn how to forget or how much to remember (Prager 1998, 2002).

How are political formations and the public sphere tied to the dead and the work of memory today? How does the collective regulation of death influence individual attitudes and a sense of social anticipation?

In "Violence and the Politics of Remorse" (chapter 7), Nancy Scheper-Hughes explores the working ethics created around the dead bodies of apartheid in the new South Africa. Here, hope comes not out of principles generated in the privileged contexts of Western countries but from "cultures of terror" (Taussig 1986). The work of the Truth and Reconciliation Commission is meant to become the fabric of a new social contract and the foundation for building a new citizen.

Both victim and perpetrator suffer from a symbiotic and unworkable identity. The work of the Truth and Reconciliation Commission, in Scheper-Hughes's reading, is fraught with the difficulties of producing truth as a means of recovery, such as attempting to shift from a fact-finding, logical, or experiential truth to a negotiated, dramaturgical, "good enough" truth. In this process, temporality and emotions figure centrally: Whose pain is privileged? Whose suffering is ignored? What should be remembered? What forgotten? The possibilities and impossibilities for moving forward and the use of grief in judgment and truth are sites of powerful contestation. The embodied and the imaginary interact through the symbolic power of wounds, disputes about repatriation, and the shift from licensed forgetfulness to authorized knowledge and finally to the justice of acknowledgment. The model of a new nation and citizenry's identity is created for political value. Yet what power does this model of collective identity have to facilitate the social mobility that people so desperately need?

Scheper-Hughes significantly integrates affect at a deep level of analysis: in interpretations of truth, in contestations about recovery, and in her own engagements. The political economy of emotions is a key site of governance and ethnographic writing. Exploring complex struggles to bring meaning to the arbitrariness of suffering, Scheper-Hughes locates a truth intentionally produced at the intersection of moral, affective, symbolic, and therapeutic practices; this truth emerges through individual and collective attempts at recovery and hope. The anthropologist participates in a deeply affecting example of such an attempt, arranging a face-to-face encounter between Peter Biehl and "Easy" Nofemela and Ntbeko Peni, two of the killers of his daughter, Amy, well after the case had been addressed by the Truth and Reconciliation Commission. The meeting—initially painful and tense—ends with an extraordinary sense of weight lifted. The burden of remorse carried by Amy's killers and the angry grief borne by her father are lightened by the exchange, and by the end of the meeting, Peter has invited the two teenagers to work for the foundation established in memory of his daughter. "World repair," as Scheper-Hughes suggests, "cannot be accomplished through the application of reason and the rule of law alone."

Trauma and the biology of fear are at the core of the quintessential mental illness of today, post-traumatic stress disorder (PTSD), which diminishes, or even destroys, the power of "dead voices" to take hold of and mold a person's condition. New taxonomies of mental disorders and the scientific and clinical apparatuses in which they are imbricated are attempting to delete the term *neurosis* altogether from research and practice, "dropping it in the waste-bin of psychiatric history," according to Allan Young (2000). Experts are "passionately interested in discovering biological features particular to the disorder and its defining process," such as hypocortisolism (5, 14)—and this experimental "remnant" or "epistemic thing" (Rheinberger 1997) is to become a measure against which these subjects can define their "true" pathological status. Classificatory institutions, politics of disability and imaginary redemptions, biological measures, and pharmaceutical practices come together in PTSD, absorbing all symptoms of neurosis and making up new populations of mass symptoms and moral claims. Traumatology, adds Ian Hacking, "has become the science of the troubled soul, with victimology one of its bitter fruits" (2002: 18).[1]

In his essay for this collection, Allan Young works through Ian Hacking's concept of "transient mental illness" and traces the specific constellation of political, psychiatric, and social processes that are leading to a new category of mental illness: the self-traumatized perpetrator. Like Greenblatt, Young explores how the recycling of knowledge, institutions, and claims produces new social phenomena and affect, creating distinct possibilities for human choice and action. Young elaborates on the person who is traumatized by the effects of his own violence—by the pain, loss, and death caused to his victims. The self-traumatized perpetrator is, so to speak, his own victim. But, as Young points out, he is not only a victim and a perpetrator. He is also the patient of a specific medical-science and technological establishment *and* a regional phenomenon, an American psychological character.

This new medical-moral identity of the self-traumatized perpetrator came into being at the intersection of post–Vietnam War politics, diagnostic shifts brought up by the *Diagnostic and Statistical Manual of Mental Disorders (III)*, and an emergent concept of countertransference neurosis that recasts Freud's idea of the relationship between therapist and patient. This perpetrator-victim-patient subject position is contingent on the tailor-made space of post-traumatic stress disorder and on the cultural possibility of making another person's traumatic story a part of one's own memories, thus becoming this other person (Prager 1998, 2002). PTSD, argues Young, threatens to take away from the person his or her reliance on memory.

In Young's analysis, symptom, diagnosis, and treatment interpenetrate and influence each other. This mutual absorption challenges our traditional notions of mental pathology and its moral valence. Rather than existing as an isolated medical fact or a "mere" social construction, mental illness actually unites the social and biological streams of experience into a new subjectivity: the thoroughly modern traumatized self; the embodied icon of a century of genocide; ongoing medical and legal disputes about human nature and agency; and more war.

NOTE

1. Foucault's vision of an experimental mode of subjectivity at the end of "What Is an Author?" seems to be well on its way to realization: "I think that, as our society changes, the author function will disappear, and in such a manner that fiction and its polysemous texts will once again function according to another mode, but still with a system of constraint—one that will no longer be the author but will have to be determined or, perhaps, experimented with" (1998: 222, our emphasis).

REFERENCES

Deleuze, Gilles. 1997. *Essays: Critical and Clinical.* Minneapolis: University of Minnesota Press.

Fleck, Ludwik. 1979. "How the Modern Concept of Syphilis Originated." In *Genesis and Development of a Scientific Fact* (Chicago: University of Chicago Press), 1–19.

———. 1986. *Cognition and Fact.* Dordrecht: Kluwer Academic.

Freud, Sigmund. 1963. *An Autobiographical Study.* New York: W. W. Norton.

———. 1965. *The Interpretation of Dreams.* New York: Avon Books.

Hacking, Ian. 1998. *Mad Travelers: Reflections on the Reality of Transient Mental Illness.* Charlottesville: University of Virginia Press.

———. 2002. *Historical Ontology.* Cambridge, MA: Harvard University Press.

Lacan, Jacques. 1978. *The Four Fundamental Concepts of Psychoanalysis.* New York: W. W. Norton.

———. 1979. "The Neurotic's Individual Myth." *Psychoanalytic Quarterly* 48 (3): 386–425.

Prager, Jeffrey. 1998. *Presenting the Past: Psychoanalysis and the Sociology of Misremembering.* Cambridge, MA: Harvard University Press.

———. 2006. The Healing of History: Governments and Social Cure, a Psychoanalytic Inquiry. Paper presented at the Psychoanalysis and Governance Conference, St. Hugh's College, Oxford, March 24–26, 2006.

Rheinberger, Hans-Jörg. 1997. *Toward a History of Epistemic Things: Synthesizing Proteins in the Test Tube*. Stanford, CA: Stanford University Press.

Rivers, W. H. R. 1923. "Affect in the Dream." In *Conflict and Dream* (London: Kegan Paul, 1923), 65–82.

Taussig, Michael. 1986. *Shamanism, Colonialism, and the Wild Man*. Chicago: University of Chicago Press.

Young, Allan. 2000. "Our Traumatic Neurosis and Its Brain." Manuscript.

5 Hamlet in Purgatory

STEPHEN GREENBLATT

Early in 1529 a London lawyer, Simon Fish anonymously published a tract addressed to Henry VIII called *A Supplicacyon for the Beggers*. The tract was modest in length but explosive in content: Fish wrote on behalf of the homeless, desperate English men and women, "nedy, impotent, blinde, lame and sike," who pleaded for spare change on the streets of every city and town in the realm. These wretches, "on whome scarcely for horror any yie dare loke," have become so numerous that private charity can no longer sustain them, and they are dying of hunger.[1] Their plight, in Fish's account, is directly linked to the pestiferous proliferation throughout the realm of beggars of a different kind: bishops, abbots, priors, deacons, archdeacons, suffragans, priests, monks, canons, friars, pardoners, and summoners.

Simon Fish had already given a foretaste of his anticlerical sentiments and his satirical gifts. In his first year as a law student at Gray's Inn, according to John Foxe, one of Fish's mates, a certain Mr. Roo, had written a play holding Cardinal Wolsey up to ridicule. No one dared to take on the part of Wolsey until Simon Fish came forward and offered to do so. The performance so enraged the powerful cardinal that Fish was forced "the same night that this Tragedie was playd" to flee to the Low Countries to escape arrest.[2] There, he evidently met the exile William Tyndale, whose new English translation of the bible he subsequently helped to circulate.

At the time he wrote *A Supplicacyon for the Beggers*, Fish had probably returned to London but was in hiding. He was thus a man associated with Protestant beliefs, determined to risk his life to save the soul of his country and endowed, as were many religious revolutionaries in the 1520s and 1530s, with a kind of theatrical gift.[3] In *A Supplicacyon for the Beggers*, he not only speaks on behalf of the poor but also speaks in their voice, crying out to the king against those who have greedily taken for themselves the wealth that should otherwise have made England prosperous to the benefit of all its people. If his gracious majesty would only look around, he would see "a thing farre out of ioynt" (413). The ravenous monkish idlers "haue begged so importunatly that they haue gotten ynto theyre hondes more then the therd part of all youre Realme." No great people, not the Greeks nor the Romans nor the Turks, and no ruler, not King Arthur himself, could flourish with such parasites sucking at their lifeblood. Not only do monks and priests destroy the economy, interfere with royal prerogative and undermine the laws of the commonwealth, but, because they seduce "euery mannes wife, euery mannes doughter and euery mannes mayde," they subvert the nation's moral order as well. Boasting among themselves about the number of women they have slept with, the clerical drones carry contagion—syphilis and leprosy—through the whole realm. "Who is she that wil set her hondes to worke to get .iij. d. a day," the beggers ask, "and may haue at lest .xx.d. a day to slepe an houre with a frere, a monke, or a prest?" (417). With a politician's flair for shocking (and unverifiable) statistics, Fish estimates that one hundred thousand Englishwomen have been corrupted by monks. No man can be sure, he writes, that the child poised to inherit his estate is his own and not a priest's bastard.

Why have these diseased "bloudsuppers" succeeded in amassing so much wealth and power? Why would otherwise sensible, decent people, alert to threats to their property, their health, and their liberties, allow themselves to be ruthlessly exploited by a pack of "sturdy idell holy theues" (415)? The question would be relatively easy to answer were these acts cunningly concealed crimes or assaults on the powerless, but in Fish's account, virtually the entire society, from the king and the nobility to the poor housewife who has to give the priests every tenth egg her hen lays, has been openly victimized. How can one explain the dismaying spectacle that Montaigne's friend, Etienne de la Boétie, called "voluntary servitude?"[4] For la Boétie, the answer lies in networks of dependency that lock people into submission to their social superiors. Fish's answer centers not on social structure but on belief. The vast system of pillaging and sexual corruption relies, in his account, on the exploitation of a single core conviction: purgatory.

Not everyone is taken in by the clerical extortion racket. "Many men of great litterature and iudgement" dare to point out that purgatory does not exist and that "there is not one word spoken of hit in al holy scripture." Others observe that if a purgatory exists and if the pardons that the pope sells for money can in fact deliver souls from its pains, as the Catholic Church claims, then giving those same pardons freely, without charge would surely be equally effective. Moreover, if the pope can deliver one soul from torment, he can presumably deliver a thousand, and if he can deliver a thousand, he can presumably deliver everyone, "and so destroy purgatory." If he possesses such power and does not use it, if he leaves souls to languish in prison unless he is given money, then the pope is nothing but "a cruell tyrant without all charite." Indeed, if all priests and friars—"the hole sort of the spiritueltie"—will allow souls to be punished for want of prayers and will "pray for no man but for theim that gyue theim money" (419), then they are all tyrants.

Anyone who publicly says such things takes a serious risk, Fish acknowledges, for the priests are quick to accuse their critics of heresy. In fact, even those who have a clear cause of action against a cleric—for murder, "rauisshement of his wyfe, of his doughter, robbery, trespas, maiheme, dette, or eny other offence" (417)—are afraid to seek legal remedy for fear of excommunication.[5] Moreover, those who are wronged have no recourse to Parliament. If the king himself thought to make laws against the priests, Fish writes, "I am yn doubt whether ye be able: Are they not stronger in your owne parliament house then your silfe?" (417). But, if he acts on his own authority, the king has enough power to save his realm and succor his poor starving beadsmen. He can do so at a stroke by seizing the wealth that the wolfish priests have stolen from the people and using that wealth to relieve the needy. As for the thousands of lazy monks and friars, Fish urges the king to put an end to their racket once and for all: "Tye these holy idell theues to the cartes to be whipped naked about euery market towne til they will fall to laboure that they by theyre importunate begging take not awey the almesse that the good christen people wolde giue vnto vs sore impotent miserable people" (34).

A Supplicacyon for the Beggers is careful not to state flatly and on its own account that purgatory does not exist, though it rehearses sympathetically the opinion of "many men" that the fuel driving the whole monstrous juggernaut of the Catholic Church is a fantasy of purchased salvation from a fantasy of temporary postmortem punishment in a fantasy of a prison house for souls.[6] The faithful have been led to believe, without any scriptural authority, in the existence of a realm between heaven and hell and then, still more fantastically, led to believe that the pope has the power to mitigate the torments of souls imprisoned in this realm and will do so for a price. All one has to do is purchase the right prayers. "How ran we from post to pillar, from stock to stone, from idol to idol, from place to place," wrote the Protestant polemicist Thomas Becon, recalling the days of Catholic superstition; "What confidence we had to be delivered out of the pope's pinfold after our departure, though we lived never so ungodly, through the popish prattling of monstrous monks and the mumbling masses of those lazy soul-carriers."[7]

"The pope's pinfold": purgatory is not only a false doctrine, it is an imaginary space. Early sixteenth-century Reformers did not necessarily rule out the existence of some state in the afterlife between death and judgment, but they rejected the Catholic conception of a special, demarcated space. "Though it seem not impossible haply, that there might be a place where the souls might be kept for a space, to be taught and instructed," Tyndale writes in *The Exposition of Tracy's Testament*, "yet that there should be such a jail as they jangle, and such fashions as they feign, is plainly impossible, and repugnant to the scripture." But if no such jail exists, what does exist after death? Speaking of himself in the third person, Tyndale professes himself willing to wait and "to take it as he findeth it": "He intendeth to purge here, unto the uttermost of his power; and hopeth that death will end and finish his purgation. And if there be any other purging, he will commit it to God, and take it as he findeth it, when he cometh at it; and in the meantime take no thought therefore, but for this that is present, wherewith all saints were purged, and were taught so to be. And Tyndale marvelleth what secret pills they take to purge themselves, which not only will not purge here with the cross of Christ, but also buy out their purgatory there of the pope, for a groat or sixpence."[8]

The pope's purgatory, in this account, is a fantastic kingdom cunningly designed to extract wealth. The Catholics have "reigned [in] . . . this horrible bog of purgatory," writes Miles Coverdale, "to the intent that we, despairing in the assured and infinite mercy of God which cometh through Jesus Christ, might run to their churches, yea, to their chests, to be free from our sins with unreasonable money."[9] In their insatiable craving for riches, the clerical drones also resort to physical intimidation and coercion—the reformers dwell on the figure of Richard Hunne, arrested for heresy and then found hanging in his cell—but the priests' principal power derives from their hold upon the imagination of their flock, their ability to commodify a fiction. "This purgatory and the Popes pardons," Fish writes to the king, "is all the cause of the translacion of your kingdome so fast into their hondes" (419–20). For the wealth that is extracted by the pope's imaginary kingdom, Fish emphasizes, is wealth that should by rights go to the king's realm. Or, as Latimer puts it wittily, giving money for chantries, trentals, and pardons is rendering to God that which is Caesar's.[10]

According to Foxe, *A Supplicacyon for the Beggers* was sent to Anne Boleyn, who brought a copy to the king.[11] After Henry "kept the booke in his bosome" three or four days, the story goes, he contacted Fish's wife and, promising safe conduct, told her he wished to see her husband. Trusting one of Henry's promises was probably the rashest thing Fish ever did, but his book's suggestion that the crown seize monastic wealth had obviously delighted the king, who "embraced him with louing countenaunce," talked with him for three or four hours, and even took him hunting. For once, the king was as good as his word, giving Fish his signet ring as a token of his protection and instructing his lord chancellor, Sir Thomas More, not to touch the fugitive. The king, however, had neglected to say anything about Fish's wife, whom More promptly moved to interrogate.[12]

More had known about Fish and his dangerous book for some time. Only a few months after *A Supplicacyon for the Beggers* appeared, though More was busy with high affairs of state and on the brink of his elevation to the lord chancellorship, he wrote a substantial reply, divided into two long books, *The Supplication of Souls*. The length is characteristic of More's polemical writings, most of them disastrously misconceived as rhetorical performances, but it may also reflect a personal stake: in *Utopia* (1516), More had slyly satirized the idleness of friars, and he had imagined radical measures to solve the problems of poverty, homelessness, and hunger in England. In *Utopia*, More's imaginary traveler pointedly observes, everyone works, none more so than the members of the religious orders, who "allow themselves no leisure" but devote their full time to good works *(boniis officiis)*.

Lest the reader think that these good works are sacramental, More spells out in detail the tasks undertaken by the Utopian equivalent of monks and friars: "Some tend the sick. Others repair roads, clean out ditches, rebuild bridges, dig turf and sand and stone, fell and cut up trees, and transport wood, grain, and other things into the cities in carts."[13] The consequence of this universal work ethic is in startling contrast to the miseries so widespread at home: "In Utopia there is no poor man and no beggar" (239). Years after writing these words, when he encountered Fish's vision of an England in which "idell people be set to worke" and even the poorest wretches "haue ynough and more then shall suffice vs" (422), More must have glimpsed a crudely distorted reflection of his own earlier self.

If *A Supplicacyon for the Beggers* speaks in the voice of the poor, *The Supplication of Souls* speaks in the voice of the dead.[14] The reader encounters a desperate appeal for help, comfort, and pity from "your late acquayntaunce/kindred/spouses/companions/play felowes/& frendes" (111). These former intimates are crying out not because they are dead, not even because they are abiding the "greuouse paynys & hote clensynge fyre" of purgatory, but because they have become "humble & vnacquayted & halfe forgoten supplyauntys." They had once been able to count on relief and comfort from the private prayers of virtuous people and, still more, from "the dayly Masses & other gostely suffrages of prestys/relygyouse/and folke of holy churche." More's own father, notably, had in his last will and testament arranged, at considerable expense, for these suffrages, not only for himself but also for his three wives, the former husbands of his second and third wife, his parents, and other named dead people, including King Edward IV, as well as "all cristen soules."[15] Now those who had made comparably careful arrangements for the alleviation of their agonies fear that this consolation and help will vanish, for "certayne sedytyouse persones" have spread pestilent doubts about the very existence of purgatory and the efficacy of the Holy Church's good works on behalf of the dead.

The Supplication of Souls begins with the dead crying out in fear that they are being forgotten. The suffering souls know that their loud lamentings will be disturbing to the living, who desire understandably to take their ease and who have buried the dead precisely so that the dead will remain buried. But the dead now have no choice: though they have been good souls who have "longe layen and cryed so farre frome you that we seldome brake your slepe," they must now make their existence and their agonies known. They do so in order to counteract the pernicious influence of A Supplicacyon for the Beggers, which threatens not only the souls of the dead but the souls of the living. Indeed, after initially speaking for their own plight, the dead in More's book affirm that they, after all, are not the real victims of the anonymous author's venom, for when their purgatorial punishment has ceased, they will be "translated" to heavenly bliss. The living run the real risk, for they will find, "for lakke of belefe of purgatory / the very strayght way to hell" (113). To lure unsuspecting readers down this path is indeed the whole purpose of the wicked anonymous author whose identity, More's dead souls declare, is not unknown to them, both because certain of his associates before their deaths repented their heresies, returned to the true faith, and are now companions in purgatory and because "owre and your gostely enemy the deuyll" has visited purgatory in person to brag about his agent on earth. With his "enmyouse & enuyouse laughter gnasshyng the teeth and grynnynge" (114), the devil delights in the venomous power of the book that will deceive many simple readers.

In order to combat this satanic adversary, book 2 of The Supplication of Souls launches into an extended defense of the doctrine of purgatory, an odd enterprise perhaps for souls who profess to be suffering from its tormenting fires but one presumably justified both by their concern for misguided mortals and by their fear of being forgotten. Though reason alone, they claim, would lead inevitably to the idea of a process of purgation after death, much of this defense consists of rather strained interpretation of key biblical citations, such as 2 Maccabees 12:39–42 and 1 Corinthians 3:12–15.[16]

The problem, as More understood quite well, is that none of the scriptural passages comes very close to the Catholic Church's doctrine of purgatory, a doctrine not fully elaborated until the late twelfth century.[17] To be sure, 2 Maccabees speaks reasonably plainly about prayers for the dead (though not about a place called purgatory), but none of the Maccabean books were a part of the Hebrew canon, and many Christians, including the Reformers, relegated them to the Apocrypha. Paul's first epistle to the Corinthians was certainly canonical, but it said nothing about prayers for the dead, and its words of warning—about a fire that would test the worth of each man's work, whether built of gold, silver, and fine stone or of wood, hay, and stubble—do not in any obvious way refer to purgatory or assert the existence of a real fire, as distinct from a metaphorical one.

From time to time, when the strain of attempting to prove the existence of purgatory by natural reason or scriptural interpretation becomes too great, More's souls appeal to the witness of "the olde holy doctours" (194) and to the dogmatic authority of the Holy Church. Heretics claim that the book of Maccabees is apocryphal, but "syth the church of Cryste accounteth yt for holy scrypture: there can no man doubt thereof," for everyone who affirms himself to be a Christian, from "the noble doctour and gloryouse confessour" St. Augustine to the archheretic Luther, must necessarily believe that "the church cannot fayle surely and certeynly to discerne betwene the wordys of god and the wordys of men" (182). Without such an absolute assurance, "then stode all crystendome in dout and vnsurety /· whether saynt Iohans gospell were holy scripture or not / and so forth of all the new testament" (183). Of course, as More concedes, including the book of Maccabees in the canon will not settle the issue once and for all, because even that book does not mention purgatory, but there are other ancient tenets of the Christian faith, such as the Virgin Birth, that are not "playne proued" by the holy scriptures and yet cannot and must not be doubted. One fact alone should be enough "to stoppe the mowthys of all the prowde hygh harted malycyouse heretykes": "The catholyque churche of cryste hath allwaye byleued purgatory" (195).

The heretics challenged precisely this flat claim, as More himself knew, just as they challenged his scriptural readings. On a few occasions in the long treatise, More's souls reach beyond textual arguments and dogmatic pronouncements to appeal to the experience of the living. Nothing can enable you to "conceyue a very ryght imagynacyon of these thyngys whych ye neuer felte," they concede, but you may be able to grasp the nature of purgatorial suffering if you consider a ship wallowing about in high seas. A small number of passengers are so well "attempred of thym selfe" that they feel "as lusty and as iocunde" as if they were on land. Others are anything but jocund:

> But then shall ye sometyme se there some other whose body ys so / incurably corrupted / that they shall walter & tolter / and wryng theyre handys / and gnash the teeth / and theyr eyen water / theyr hed ake / theyre body frete / theyr stomake wamble / and all theyre body shyuer for payne / and yet shall neuer vomete at all: or yf they vomete / yet shall they vomyte styll and neuer fynde ease thereof. (189)

If the former group comprises the saved in heaven and the latter one represents the damned in hell, how shall we imagine the souls in purgatory? They are the passengers who feel horrible at first and yet who are, after a vomit or two, "so clene rydde of theyre gryefe / that they neuer fele dyspleasure of yt after." Such is the middle state, the betwixt-and-between condition of More's speakers.

But the problem remains of convincing readers who have been poisoned by *A Supplicacyon for the Beggers* that purgatory actually exists, for dogmatic appeals to the authority of the church, strained textual interpretation, and metaphors masquerading as realities are precisely the strategies that Fish's book attacked as mainstays of Roman Catholic hypocrisy. As a last resort, the souls in More's text can point to the testimony of ghosts. "For there hath in euery contrey and euery age apparycyons bene had," they say, "and well knowen and testyfyed / by whyche men haue had suffycyent reuelacyon and profe of purgatory / excepte suche as lyste not to byleue theym: & they be such as wolde be neuer the better yf they saw theym" (196). To be sure, one would be impious to demand to see such apparitions for oneself; they are rare precisely so that people can believe by faith. People who are stubborn enough to reject the well-authenticated stories of such apparitions and to demand further proof deserve the punishment they will undoubtedly receive after death, when they will "to theyr payne se such a grysly syght as shall so greue theyr hartys to loke theron" (197).

But how could apparitions leave the prison house of purgatory at all to appear on earth, if they are meant to be burning in fires? The souls explain that "we cary our payne wyth vs" (221); indeed their pain is intensified by witnessing the ongoing life of the living. The guardian devils whom God commands to accompany the souls back to the earth compel their miserable prisoners to look at the gold they have left behind and contemplate "our late

wyuys so sone waxen wanton / & forgetyng vs theyre old husbandys that
haue loued theym so tendrely and lefte theym so ryche / sytte and lawgh
& make mery and more to sumtyme / wyth theyr new woars / whyle our
kepers in dyspyte kepe vs there in payne to stande styll / & loke on" (222).
More characteristically does not imagine dead wives looking on at their
husbands' carousals, only dead husbands forced to witness the pleasures, including sexual pleasures, of their wives. The scene, more than any other he
invokes in his long work, seems to conjure up a passionate spectral outburst:

> Many tymes wold we then speke yf we coulde be suffred / & sore we
> long to say to her: Ah wyfe wyfe ywysse this was not couenaunt wyfe /
> when ye wepte and tolde me that yf I lefte you to lyue by / ye wold
> neuer wedde agayne. We se there our chyldren to / whom we loued so
> well / pype syng and dawnce / & no more thynke on theyre fathers
> soulys then on theyre olde shone: sauyng that sometyme cummeth owt
> god haue mercy on all crysten sowlys. But yt cummeth owt so coldely
> and wyth so dull affeccyon / that yt lyeth but in the lyppys and neuer
> cam nere the harte. (222)[18]

Vows are broken, mourning is forgotten, life resumes its round of heed-
less pleasures, and even piety takes the form of cold lip service. The dead—
in their individuality, their intense suffering, their urgent claims on personal remembrance—are consigned to oblivion or become at best an
anonymous, generalized category, the "all Christian souls" casually invoked
in a ritual phrase by thoughtless children.

Against this terrible indifference, the suffering souls in More's text cry
out, passionately claiming the rites of memory. They claim something more
tangible as well: the alms that will relieve some of their pains. Here, More
imagines dead wives speaking out, not to lament their surviving husbands'
pleasures but to regret their own past delight in gorgeous clothing, jewels,
and cosmetics. This "gay gere" is now burning hot upon their tormented
bodies, so that, looking back on their lives, they wish that their husbands
"never had folowed our fantasyes / nor neuer had so kokered vs nor made
vs so wanton / nor had geuen vs other ouchys [brooches] than ynions or
gret garlyk heddys" (224). For them, of course, such thoughts come too late,
but they have a generous desire to save others as well as to help themselves.
"We besech you," they cry out from beyond the grave to their living husbands, "syth ye gaue them vs let vs haue them still let them hurt none other
woman but help to do vs good: sell them for our sakys to set in sayntys
copys / and send the money hether by masse pennys & by pore men that
may pray for our soulys" (224).

How can you show that you remember the dead, that you care for your departed wives and husbands and children, that you are not cruelly indifferent to their sufferings? Give money to the church. Because masses for the dead were closely linked to alms giving, in principle, More could have rejected Fish's premise entirely and claimed that the doctrine of purgatory was in fact a strong incentive to charity; instead, he chose to set the dead against the living.[19] More's poor souls understand themselves to be in direct competition with Fish's beggars:

> If ye pyte the pore / there ys none so pore as we / yt haue not a bratte [rag] to put on our bakkys. If ye pyte the blynde / there ys none so blynd as we whych ar here in the dark sauyng for syghtis vnplesaunt and lothesum tyll sum comfort cum. If ye pyte the lame / there is none so lame as we / that nether can crepe one fote out of the fyre / nor haue one hand at lyberte to defend our face fro the flame. Fynally yf ye pyte any man in payn / neuer knew ye payn comparable to ours: whose fyre as farre passeth in hete all the firys that euer burned vppon erth / as the hotest of all those passeth a feynyd fyre payntyd on a wall. (225)

The miseries of the poor are vastly exceeded by the unspeakable miseries of souls in purgatory, and the good that alms can do for the living is vastly exceeded by the good that the same alms can do for the dead. Give more money to the church. Moreover, the money that is donated for the relief of souls is proof that the giver is not a heretic who dismisses the flames of purgatory as mere "feynyd fire" and "taketh in hys harte that story told by god for a very fantastyke fable" (227). Consequently, the souls declare, as if their supplication were an investment prospectus, whatever you give "shall also rebownd vppon your self an inestymable profyte" (227). Just give money to the church.

But, though the text reiterates the appeal for money, we should not conclude that More's principal aim was to augment the church's revenues. His concern was to counteract a serious and potentially damaging attack upon the church, against a doctrine that the scholarly humanist More knew perfectly well was one of its most vulnerable. Fish spoke in the name of the poor and dispossessed, but in his writing, he does not seem a tender-hearted philanthropist, and his concern most likely did not lay with their plight.[20] His book takes the form of a petition to the king, to whom it offers in effect a convenient, morally upright political cover for a cynical course of action Henry had probably already been contemplating, just as Henry was loudly professing that his moral scruples were the only reason he sought a divorce from Catharine of Aragon. Fish's own motives were almost certainly not mercenary; rather he sought to offer the king and the nation a kind of bait to embark on a path that would lead to a reformed religion.

More understood the bait and struggled to avert the danger by recalling his readers to their deep and ancient religious loyalty. Money is important, to be sure, as Fish and More agree, but for More, it is a sign of remembrance. "Let neuer eny slouthfull oblyvyon race vs out of your remembraunce," the souls cry; "remember what kyn ye and we be to gether"; "remember how nature & crystendom byndeth you to remember vs"; "remember our thurst whyle ye syt & drink: our honger whyle ye be festing: our restlesse wach whyle ye be slepyng: our sore and greuouse payn whyle ye be playing: our hote burnyng fyre whyle ye be in plesure & sportyng: so mote god make your ofsprynge after remember you" (227–28).

"Adieu, adieu, Hamlet. Remember me" (*Hamlet*, 1.5.91). If Thomas Lodge's recollection in *Wit's Misery and the World's Madness* (1596) is to be credited, an earlier Elizabethan play about Hamlet—the so-called *UrHamlet*—featured a pale ghost that cried "like an oyster-wife, 'Hamlet, revenge.'" Shakespeare's Ghost too cries out for vengeance: "If thou didst ever thy dear father love," he tells his groaning son, "Revenge his foul and most unnatural murder" (1.5.23–25). But the injunction upon which young Hamlet dwells obsessively is that he *remember:*

> Remember thee?
> Ay, thou poor ghost, while memory holds a seat
> In this distracted globe. Remember thee?
> Yea, from the table of my memory
> I'll wipe away all trivial fond records,
> All saws of books, all forms, all pressures past,
> That youth and observation copied there,
> And thy commandment all alone shall live
> Within the book and volume of my brain
> Unmixed with baser matter. (1.5.95–104)

Does the emphasis in the spectral command fall on "remember" or on "me"? Hamlet's response to the "poor ghost" teases out both terms, with his first repetition emphasizing the memory that holds a seat in his brain and the second insisting that all the contents of that memory, save one, will be wiped away. Contemplating Hamlet's wild and whirling words in the wake of the Ghost's departure, Coleridge remarked that "the terrible, by a law of the human mind, always touches on the verge of the ludicrous." Perhaps the law extends to this anxious insistence on remembrance, because the idea that Hamlet would or could ever forget the Ghost seems faintly ludicrous. Or rather, Hamlet's reiterated question precisely picks up on the seeming absurdity of the Ghost's injunction: "Remember thee?"

What is at stake in the shift of spectral obligation from vengeance to remembrance? In terms of plot, very little. When Hamlet first adjures the Ghost to speak—"Speak, I am bound to hear"—the Ghost's response, implicitly strengthening the force of the word *bound*, is a call for action: "So art thou to revenge when thou shalt hear" (1.5.6–7).[21] Hamlet hears this call and urgently demands the information that will enable him immediately to heed it:

> Haste, haste me to know it, that with wings as swift
> As meditation or the thoughts of love
> May sweep to my revenge. (1.5.29–31)

Meditation and love figure the spectacular rapidity of thought—not only the virtually instantaneous leap of the mind from here, say, to China but that leap *intensified* by the soul's passionate longing for God or for the beloved. Yet the metaphors Hamlet uses here have the strange effect of inadvertently introducing some resistance into the desired immediacy, because meditation and love are experiences that are inward, extended, and prolonged, and they lie at a far remove from the sudden, decisive, murderous action that he wishes to invoke. Later in the play, Hamlet famously complains that conscience—here consciousness itself—"doth make cowards of us all," that the "native hue of resolution / Is sicklied o'er with the pale cast of thought," and that "enterprises of great pith and moment . . . lose the name of action" (3.1.85–90). This corrosive inwardness—the hallmark of the entire play and the principal cause of its astonishing, worldwide renown—is glimpsed even in his first frantic response to the Ghost, and it is reinforced by the Ghost's command, "Remember me." What is at stake in the shift of emphasis from vengeance to remembrance is nothing less than the whole play.

Hamlet has made the Ghost's command his watchword:

> Now to my word:
> It is "Adieu, adieu, remember me."
> I have sworn it. (1.5.12–14)

The commandment, he proclaims, will live all alone in his brain; everything else will be erased. He has made it an oath upon which he can swear and a watchword that he will daily reiterate. But his actual experience is one of fading remembrance, a softening into what the play (like More's *Supplication*) repeatedly characterizes as dullness. When Hamlet speaks of sweeping to his revenge, the Ghost commends him in terms that bespeak his own fear of oblivion:

I find thee apt,
And duller shouldst thou be than the fat weed
That rots itself in ease on Lethe wharf
Wouldst thou not stir in this. (1.5.31–34)

With this forgetfulness, Hamlet comes to charge himself "a dull and muddy-mettled rascal" (3.1.569). "Do not forget," the Ghost reminds him in the scene in Gertrude's closet, "This visitation / Is but to whet thy almost blunted purpose" (3.4.100–101). "How all occasions do inform against me," Hamlet berates himself in a soliloquy dropped from the folio text, "And spur my dull revenge!" (Q2:4.4). Remembering the dead proves vastly more difficult than he had first thought it would be.

"When the ghost has vanished," says Goethe's Wilhelm Meister, in probably the most influential of all readings of *Hamlet*, "what do we see standing before us? A young hero thirsting for revenge? A prince by birth, happy to be charged with unseating the usurper of his throne? Not at all!" The tragedy is more inward: "A fine, pure, noble and highly moral person, but devoid of that emotional strength that characterizes a hero, goes to pieces beneath a burden that it can neither support nor cast off."[22] Generations of critics have agreed with Goethe, responding in effect to the Shakespearean shift from vengeance to remembrance. But we need to recognize that the psychological here is conditioned by the theological, specifically by the issue of remembrance that, as we have seen, lay at the heart of the crucial early sixteenth-century debate about purgatory. More's souls are in a panic that they will be forgotten, erased by "slothful oblivion." They are heartsick that they will fade from the minds of the living, that their wives will remarry, that their children will mention them only, if at all, "so coldly and with so dull affection that it lies but in the lips, and comes not near the heart" (149). They are harrowed above all by the fear that the living will cease to credit their sufferings, dismiss their prison house as a "fantastic fable," and doubt their very existence, in its horrible, prolonged pain. This fear seems to shape Shakespeare's depiction of the Ghost and of Hamlet's response.

The Ghost makes clear to Hamlet that he is in a state that Thomas White's early seventeenth-century text called "the middle state of souls," not damned for eternity but forced to suffer torments in a "prison-house" designed to purge him of the crimes he had committed in his life:

I am thy father's spirit,
Doomed for a certain term to walk the night,
And for the day confined to fast in fires,
Till the foul crimes done in my days of nature
Are burnt and purged away. (1.5.9–13)

The bland "for a certain term"— which appears merely to fill out the syllables of a line of blank verse, is in fact significant, because it helps set up the theological claim of the word *purged*.[23] "In purgatory my soule hath bene / a Thousand yeare in woe and teene," the Imperator Salvatus says in the Chester mystery play *The Last Judgment* (c. 1475).[24]

The excruciating pains of purgatory and of hell were, in church teachings, identical; the only difference was that the former were only "for a certain term." That one difference, of course, was crucial, but the Catholic Church—especially, it seems, the English Catholic Church—laid a heavy emphasis on the horrors of purgatorial torments, so that the faithful would be as anxious as possible to reduce the term they would have to endure. The intensity of the anguish is brilliantly represented in the greatest of English morality plays, *Everyman* (ca. 1495), in which God sends his agent Death to demand of the hero "a sure rekeninge / Without delay or ony taryenge" (70–71). Everyman frantically begs for time, for his "boke of rekeninge" is not ready, but Death grants him only the briefest of respites. Still, the interval is enough for the penitent to begin to scourge himself: "Take this, body, for the sinne of the flesshe!" (613). The grotesque spectacle of a dying man scourging himself makes sense only as a desperate, last-minute attempt to alter the "reckoning" by substituting penitential pain in this life for the far more terrible pain that lies ahead. "Now of penaunce I will wade the water clere," declares Everyman, intensifying his blows, "To save me from purgatory, that sharpe fire" (618–19).

Everyman thus narrowly escapes one of the worst medieval nightmares, a sudden and painless death. This nightmare, of course, is the fate that befalls Hamlet's father: the horror is not only the fact of his murder, at the hands of his treacherous brother, but also the precise circumstances of that murder—in his sleep, comfortable and secure. Old Hamlet's ghostly state is a grievous one—the term of his sufferings or their intensity vastly increased—because of the way he was dispatched, unprepared for death:

Cut off even in the blossoms of my sin,
Unhouseled, dis-appointed, unaneled,
No reck'ning made, but sent to my account
With all my imperfections on my head.
O horrible, O horrible, most horrible! (1.5.76–80)

That the father can speak of "imperfections" presumably means that his sins were not mortal; after all, he will eventually burn and purge away his crimes. But his inability to make a proper reckoning weighs heavily against him.

When he first encounters the apparition, Hamlet envisages only two possibilities for the ghost's origin:

> Be thou a spirit of health or goblin damned,
> Bring with thee airs from heaven or blasts from hell,
> Be thy intents wicked or charitable,
> Thou com'st in such a questionable shape
> That I will speak to thee. (1.4.19–23)

Nothing Hamlet says in the wake of his fateful exchange with his father's spirit explicitly acknowledges a third possibility, a middle state between heaven and hell. But, as scholars have observed, something is strange about the terms of Hamlet's response to Horatio's remark, "There's no offense, my lord":

> Yes, by Saint Patrick, but there is, Horatio,
> And much offence too. Touching this vision here—
> It is an honest ghost, that let me tell you. (1.5.140–43)

The assertion that the ghost is "honest" seems to mark Hamlet's acceptance of its claim that it has come from a place of purgation, and that acceptance may in turn be marked by the invocation—unique in Shakespeare's works—of Saint Patrick, the patron saint of purgatory.[25]

To this possible allusion we can add another, a few lines further on, that has not, to my knowledge, been noted. When Hamlet adjures his friends to take an oath that they will not reveal what they have seen, the ghost, from under the stage, cries "Swear." When they shift ground to a new position, the ghost once again cries out beneath them, and Hamlet asks, "*Hic et ubique?*" (1.5.162). The Latin tag here has never been adequately explained. The words obviously refer to restless movement, a certain placelessness, which is comparable to Roderigo's description of Othello as "an extravagant and wheeling stranger / Of here and everywhere" (1.1.137–38). The use of Latin—besides suggesting that Hamlet is, like his friend Horatio, something of a scholar—may also convey a theological resonance, one evidently in Shakespeare's mind at the time that he wrote *Hamlet*. In *Twelfth Night*, a play of the same year, Sebastian, baffled by the appearance of his double, declares that there cannot be "that deity in my nature / Of here and everywhere" (5.1.220–21). The words refer in jest to the divine power to violate the laws of physics, a power that became an issue in the Reformation in a dispute about the Lutheran doctrine of Christ's ubiquity. If this resonance is present in *Hamlet,* as it well may be, the prince's jest is deepened by a disquieting association of his father's ghost with the omnipresence of God.

But I believe that these words have further theological resonance that is specifically relevant to purgatory. Traditional Catholic ritual in England included a prayer to be recited for the dead who were laid to rest in the churchyard:

> Pro quiescentibus in cimiterio.
>
> Oratio Deus, in cijus miseratione animae fidelium requiescunt; animabus famulorum famularumque tuarum omnium, hic et ubique in Christo quiescentium, da propitius veniam peccatorum, ut a cunctis reatibus absoluti, tecum sine fine laetentur. Per Dominum.[26]

The point is not only that such prayers for the dead include the key phrase *hic et ubique* but also that they are specifically connected to a belief in purgatory. In *The Catholic Doctrine of the Church of England* (1607), the Protestant Thomas Rogers, ridiculing this connection, quotes the papal indulgence from the Sarum *Horae Beatissimae Virginis Mariae*: "Pope John the Twelfth hath granted to all persons, which, going through the churchyard, do say the prayer following, so many years of pardons as there have been bodies buried since it was a churchyard." The prayer begins *"Avete, omnes animae fideles, quarum corpora hic et ubique requiescunt in pulvere"* ("Hail all faithful souls, whose bodies here and everywhere do rest in the dust"). In the context of the Ghost's claim that he is being purged, and in the context of Hamlet's invocation of Saint Patrick, the words *hic et ubique*, addressed to the spirit who seems to be moving beneath the earth, seem to acknowledge the place where his father's spirit is imprisoned.

The famous problem, of course, is that by 1563, the Church of England had explicitly rejected the doctrine of purgatory. The twenty-second article in the *The Thirty-Nine Articles of the Church of England* declares that "The Romish doctrine concerning Purgatory, Pardons, Worshipping, and Adoration, as well of Images as of Reliques, and also invocation of Saints, is a fond thing, vainly invented, and grounded upon no warranty of Scripture, but rather repugnant to the word of God."[27] Thus, at least an implicit censorship is built into the theatrical representation of the afterlife. One could ridicule purgatory, as Marlowe does in *Doctor Faustus:* when the invisible Faustus snatches food and drink away from the pope, the baffled cardinal of Lorraine speculates that "it may be some ghost newly crept out of Purgatory to begge a pardon of your holinesse."[28] As this and many similar moments in Tudor and Stuart drama bear witness, belief in purgatory could be represented as a fantasy or a lie. But it could not be represented as a frightening reality. *Hamlet* comes closer to doing so than any other play of this period, but

Shakespeare still uses only a network of allusions: "for a certain term," "burned and purged away," "Yes, by St. Patrick," "*hic et ubique.*" Moreover, even were these allusions less cautious and equivocal, a second famous problem would remain: souls in purgatory received salvation. "The fact that old Hamlet died suddenly, without time for last rites—"unhouseled, disappointed, unaneled"—left him with a heavy burden of earthly sins that had painfully to be burned away after death, but he could not possibly commit new sins. The trouble is that purgatory, along with theological language of communion ("houseling"), death-bed confession ("appointment"), and anointing ("aneling"), while compatible with a Christian call for remembrance, is utterly incompatible with a Senecan call for vengeance.

I will not now rehearse the long series of debates by Eleanor Prosser, Christopher Devlin, Miriam Joseph, Peter Milward, Roy Battenhouse, and others, whose intricate arguments, for me at least, are not evacuated by the fact that they are doomed to inconclusiveness. Here, I am more concerned with the particular uses that Shakespeare made of the struggle between Simon Fish and Thomas More and its aftermath. Those uses are not necessarily direct. Two chantry acts—1545 (Henry VIII's last Parliament) and 1547 (Edward VI's first Parliament)—resolved that struggle by abolishing the elaborate Catholic intercessory system—with its chantries, lights, obits, anniversaries, confraternities, and stipendiary priests—with which English men and women had done suffrages for the sake of the dead in purgatory and in anticipation of their own future condition as dead people.[29] The brief reign of the Catholic Mary Tudor evidently did little to revive this system, and gauging the extent of residual belief in purgatory among the great mass of English men and women at the century's end is extremely difficult.[30]

The funeral service in the first Edwardian prayer book (1549) still addressed the dead person directly: the priest is instructed to cast earth upon the corpse and say, "I commende thy soule to God the father almyghty, and thy bodye to the grounde, earth to earth, asshes to asshes, dust to dust." In the 1552 revision, which was later confirmed by Queen Elizabeth and used throughout Shakespeare's lifetime, the words changed decisively. The dead person could no longer be addressed. Instead, the priest says to the bystanders around the grave, "We therfore committe his body to the ground, earth to earth, asshes to asshes, dust to dust."[31] These words would have been familiar to anyone in late sixteenth- and seventeenth-century England. Yet the continued outpouring of polemical literature, reviving the old arguments of Fish and More and rehearsing them again and again throughout the reigns of Elizabeth and James, suggests that the boundary between the living and the dead was not so decisively closed.

Shakespeare's sensitivity to the status of the dead may have intensified upon the death in 1596 of his son Hamnet (a name virtually interchangeable with Hamlet in the period's public records) and still more perhaps upon the death of his father, John, in 1601, the most likely year in which the playwright created *Hamlet*. When in April 1757, the owner of Shakespeare's birthplace in Stratford-upon-Avon decided to retile the roof, one of the workmen, described as of "very honest, sober, and industrious character," found an old document between the rafters and the tiling. The document, six leaves stitched together, was a profession of faith in fourteen articles, conspicuously Catholic in form; it was, if genuine (for the original has disappeared), by John Shakespeare. The clear implication of this find, that the playwright was probably brought up in a Roman Catholic household in a time of official suspicion and persecution of recusancy, has found support in a recent biographical study by E. A. J. Honigmann. Honigmann has turned up a network of interlinked Catholic families in Lancashire with whom one "William Shakeshafte," possibly a young schoolmaster or player, was connected in the late 1570s or early 1580s.

Shakespeare, in any case, is likely to have encountered *A Supplicacyon for the Beggers*, because it was reprinted in Foxe's *Actes and Monuments* (1546), a copy of which was placed, by government order, in every church in the realm. Shakespeare also may well have read More's *The Supplication of Souls*. Like the Ghost of old Hamlet, More's poor souls cry out to be remembered, fear the dull forgetfulness of the living, disrupt the corrupt ease of the world with horrifying tales of their sufferings, and lament the remarriage of their wives. But all of these ideas and more Shakespeare could have gotten from texts other than More's or from his own not inconsiderable imagination. Rather, these works are sources for Shakespeare's play in a different sense: they stage an ontological argument about spectrality and remembrance, a momentous public debate, that unsettled the institutional moorings of a crucial body of imaginative materials and therefore made them available for theatrical appropriation.

To grasp the significance of this unsettling, let us return to Fish's pamphlet. Like Tyndale's New Testament, *A Supplicacyon for the Beggers* was first printed on the Continent and smuggled into England. Probably as a tribute to government persecution during the chancellorship of Thomas More, only one copy of this edition is known to survive, but inclusion in *Actes and Monuments* assured the widest circulation. Foxe provides a brief account of Fish's life, conveniently omitting More's claim that before his death, Fish "repented himself, and came into the church again, and forswore and forsook all the whole hill of those heresies out of which the fountain of that same good zele sprang."[32] In *Actes and Monuments,* after he reprints Fish's *Supplicacyon,* Foxe glances briefly at More's answer "under the name and title of the poore sely soules pewlyng out of Purgatory."[33] Foxe does not undertake in this place to refute More's theology; instead he ridicules his art.

More makes the dead men's souls, Foxe writes, "by a Rhetoricall *Prosopopoea* to speake out of Purgatory pynfolde, sometymes lamentably complaynyng, sometymes pleasauntly dalying and scoffing, at the authour of the Beggers booke, sometymes scoldyng and raylyng at hym, callyng him foole, witlesse, frantike, an asse, a goose, a madde dogge, an hereticke, and all that naught is" (viii). Foxe wryly speculates that so much testiness must be the result of the heat in purgatory, and he professes concern that the souls' lack of charity may bring them to hell rather than to heaven. He confesses, however, that he is not after all terribly concerned, for he does not credit the existence of "Purgatory at all (vnlesse it be in M. Mores Vtopia) as Maister Mores Poeticall vayne doth imagine" (ix). "Unless it be in M. More's Utopia": purgatory, as Hugh Latimer had sardonically remarked in a sermon in 1536, is a "pleasant fiction."[34] More precisely, it is, in Foxe's account, a no-place, a piece of poetry with no more claim to reality than More's famous imaginary commonwealth. Elsewhere, Foxe will speak of the pope's conspiracies and cunning frauds, but not here. The passionate claims to remembrance, the institutional structures, the dogmatic elaborations by sophisticated theologians, the popular superstitions, the charges of heresy, the indulgences, the confraternities and masses and chantries, the tales of ghostly apparitions: all are, for a moment at least, deposited not in the realm of lies but in the realm of poetry.

The rhetorical advantage of this polemical game is that Foxe can proceed to play not the committed ideologue but the judicious critic. Quintilian had written of the figure *propopoeia* that "gives both variety and animation to eloquence in a wonderful degree," so that it is "allowable even to bring down the gods from heaven and evoke the dead." But, he warned, "our inventions of that sort will meet with credit only so far as we represent people saying what it is not unreasonable to suppose that they may have meditated."[35] Hence, in Foxe's account of *The Supplication of Souls,* More, "the authour and contriuer of this Poeticall booke," should be censured "for not kepyng *Decorum Personae,* as a perfect Poet should haue done." "They that geue preceptes of Arte," Foxe explains, "do note thys in all Poeticall fictions, as a speciall obseruation, to foresee and expresse what is conuenient for euery person, accordyng to hys degree and condition, to speake and vtter" (ix). Therefore, he continues, if by More's own account, the souls in purgatory are made clean and wholesome by their sufferings, then he should not have depicted them railing "so fumishly" against their enemies. They should, after all, be on their way to becoming more charitable, not less so.

The point here is not to make a serious argument against purgatory—many others have done so, he notes, including John Frith—but to make fun of it, to expose it to ridicule. More had tried to exploit horror, fear, and guilt; Foxe tries to blow away this morbid perspective with laughter. Indeed, he proposes treating *The Supplication of Souls* as a comedy. "It maketh me to laugh," he writes, "to see ye mery Antiques of M. More," whose devil arrives in purgatory "laughyng, grynnyng, and gnashyng his teeth." But then he begins to worry about those teeth: how could the evil angel, "beyng a spirituall and no corporall substance" have "teeth to gnashe & a mouthe to grynne?" And where exactly, he wonders, was More standing to see the devil open his mouth so wide that the souls of purgatory all saw his teeth? He decides that More must have been in Utopia, "where M. Mores Purgatorye is founded."

This polemical performance seems very far indeed from Shakespeare's *Hamlet*, which probes precisely the fears, longings, and confusions that Foxe attempts to ridicule. The Ghost comes from purgatory bewailing his failure to receive full Christian last rites but then demands that his son avenge his death, thereby initiating a nightmare that will eventually destroy not only his usurping brother but also Polonius, Ophelia, Laertes, Rosencrantz, Guildenstern, Gertrude, and his own son. He tells Hamlet not to let "the royal bed of Denmark be / A couch for luxury and damned incest" (1.5.82–83) but then warns his son not to taint his mind or let his soul contrive anything against his mother. Hamlet receives the most vivid confirmation of the nature of the afterlife, with its "sulph'rous and tormenting flames" (1.5.3), but then, in a spectacular and mysterious act of forgetting, he speaks of death as the "undiscovered country from whose bourn / No traveller returns" (3.1.81–82). Foxe mercilessly mocks such representational contradictions. To notice, publish, and circulate them throughout the realm is to declare that key theological principles and emotional experiences cannot hold together and that the institution that generated them is bankrupt, worthy only of contempt and laughter.

But in *Hamlet*, the very contradictions that should lead to derision actually intensify the play's uncanny power. And Foxe's comedy helped make Shakespeare's tragedy possible. It did so by participating in a violent ideological struggle that turned negotiations with the dead from an institutional process governed by the church to a poetic process governed by guilt, projection, and imagination. Purgatory exists in the imaginary universe of

Hamlet, but only in a form that the suffering prince, in a different context, calls "a dream of passion" (2.2.554). Indeed, a striking link exists between Hamlet's description of the player who

> in a fiction, in a dream of passion,
> Could force his soul so to his whole conceit
> That from her working all his visage wanned,
> Tears in his eyes, distraction in's aspect,
> A broken voice, and his whole function suiting
> With forms to his conceit. (2.2.554–559)

and the Ghost's description of the effect that his tale of torment would have on Hamlet:

> I could a tale unfold whose lightest word
> Would harrow up thy soul, freeze thy young blood,
> Make thy two eyes like stars start from their spheres,
> Thy knotty and combined locks to part,
> And each particular hair to stand on end
> Like quills upon the fretful porcupine. (1.5.15–20)

The link is the astonishingly palpable physiological effect of spectral fiction, dream, tale: "And all for nothing" (2.2.559).

Of course, within the play's fiction, Hamlet does not know that purgatory is a fiction, as the state-sanctioned church of Shakespeare's time had declared it to be. On the contrary, he is desperate to establish the veracity of the Ghost's tale—"I'll take the Ghost's word for a thousand pound" (3.2.274–75), he exults after the play within the play—and hence to establish that the Ghost is in reality his father's spirit and not the devil. But this reality is theatrical rather than theological; it can accommodate elements, such as a Senecan call for revenge, that would radically undermine church doctrine. At the same time, it can offer the viewer, in an unforgettably vivid dream of passion, many of the deep imaginative experiences, the tangled longing, guilt, pity, and rage, evoked by More.

Not all forms of energy in Shakespeare's theater, of course, have been transferred, openly or covertly, from the zone of the real to the zone of the imaginary. Plays can borrow, imitate, and reflect many elements that pass for everyday reality without necessarily evacuating this reality or exposing it as made up. But the power of Shakespeare's theater is here, as elsewhere, linked to its appropriation of weakened or damaged institutional structures.

And at a deep level, we can see something magnificently opportunistic, appropriative, absorptive, even cannibalistic about Shakespeare's art, as if poor, envious Robert Greene had sensed something more important than he knew when he attacked the "upstart crow, beautified with our feathers." In the case of purgatory, important forces had been busily struggling for decades to prepare the playwright's feast. And the struggle did not end with the performance of the play or with the playwright's death.

In 1624, a year after the publication of the First Folio, John Gee, a staunch Protestant who confessed that he had once himself been tangled in the Jesuits' subtle nets, published *New Shreds of the Old Snare.*[36] In the book, Gee relates a series of incidents during the past three years in which Jesuits had tried to convert young women to Catholicism, induce them to flee to the Continent and join nunneries, and lure them to give their money to the Catholic Church. To achieve their cynical ends, "the thrice honourable Company of Iesuites, Players to the Popes Holiness" (10), turn "heaven and holy things" into "Theatrical and fabulous tricks" (16). Their principal device is to stage mysterious apparitions: with a burst of light, "a woman all in white, with countenance pale and wanne, with long tresses of haire hanging downe to her middle" (3) appears before an impressionable young woman and declares that she has come from the torments of purgatory. The young woman is told that she can avert these same torments after death if she is "Nunnified" (7). In a related trick, the apparition—"a shape like vnto a woman all in white: from her face seemed to come little streames of fire, or glittering light" (12)—declares that she is St. Lucy, urging a wealthy woman to whom she appears to follow her holy example by giving away her worldly wealth to the priests and joining a convent.

Gee undertakes to dispel the illusion, which is not, as some think, the result of witchcraft but rather of theater. The mysterious light, he explains, can be produced by "Paper Lanthornes or transparent Glasses" enhanced by the "artificiall directing of refractions." The acting can be done "by some nimble handed and footed *Nouice Iesuitable Boy,* that can as easily put on the person of *St. Lucy* or *The virgin Mary,* as a Play-boy can act winged *Mercury,* or Eagle mounted *Ganimedes.*" The key thing is to understand that the Jesuits are a gifted troupe of actors. "I see no reason," Gee writes, "but that they should set up a company for themselues, which surely will put down *The Fortune, Red-Bull, Cock-pit, & Globe*" (17).

But then, as if he has had second thoughts about the actors' chances for success in the competitive world of London theater, Gee considers three problems with their performances. First, he observes, "the plots of their

Comedies twang all vpon one string" (18). The effect is as if they own a single costume and can imagine only one character: "none comes in Acting but *A Woman, A Woman, A Woman,* arrayed in *white, white, white.*" In a repertory company performing daily, the device will quickly lose its force. Still, if you are seeing a performance for the first time, it is, Gee concedes, an impressive show.

The second problem is the more serious one of a failure to observe decorum, the logical and representational contradictions that Foxe had enjoyed observing in More. The Poet, Gee observes, makes an obvious blunder by sending a ghost in a white robe "from the smoakie burning Kitchen of *Purgatory*" (19). Surely that robe should have been scorched. But Gee counters this and similar incongruities with mock generosity, noting that, after all, "the *Poet* kept within his Circle. For he well knew that deepe passions, especially affright and astonishing admiration, doe for the time bereaue and suspend exact inquiring discourse" (19). Once you regard the apparition as performance and not as truth, you can dispense with anxiety about incoherence and admire the calculation of a powerful psychic and somatic effect.

The third problem is the most serious: quite simply, "*they make their spectators pay to[o] deare*" (20). Gee had explained how the Jesuits managed to get the astronomical sum of two hundred pounds from just one of their victims; that amount is, he soberly observes, a very dear market price for the product people are actually purchasing: "Representations and Apparitions from the dead might be seene farre cheaper at other Play-houses. As for example, the *Ghost in Hamblet, Don Andreas Ghost in Hieronimo.* As for flashes of light, we might see very cheape in the Comedie of *Piramus and Thisbe,* where one comes in with a Lanthorne and Acts *Mooneshine*" (20).

"As for example, the *Ghost in Hamblet*": this extraordinary remark goes to the heart of the process I have been describing. With the doctrine of purgatory and the elaborate practices that grew up around it, the church provided a powerful method of negotiating with the dead, or rather with those who were at once dead and yet—because they could still speak, appeal, and appall—not completely dead. The Protestant attack on the "middle state of souls" and the middle place those souls inhabited destroyed this method for most people in England, but it did not destroy the longings and fears that Catholic doctrine had focused and exploited. Instead, as Gee perceives, the space of purgatory became the space of the stage where old Hamlet's Ghost is doomed for a certain term to walk the night. That term has lasted for more than four hundred years, and it has brought with it a cult of the dead that we continue to serve today.

NOTES

A version of this chapter appeared as chapter 5 of my book *Hamlet in Purgatory,* published by Princeton University Press in 2001.

1. *A Supplicacyon for the Beggers,* appendix B, in *Yale Edition of the Complete Works of St. Thomas More,* vol. 7, *Letter to Bugenhagen, Supplication of Souls, Letter Against Frith,* ed. Frank Manley, Germain Marc'hardour, Richard Marius, and Clarence H. Miller (New Haven, CT: Yale University Press, 1990), 412. In *Poverty and Policy in Tudor and Stuart England* (London: Longman, 1988), Paul Slack notes that grain was scarce in some localities in 1527–28, possibility causing cases of starvation, though, like most social historians, he emphasize that the figures are extremely unreliable.

2. John Foxe, "The Story of M. Symon Fishe," in *Actes and Monumentes,* quoted in Frederick J. Furnivall, ed., *A Supplication for the Beggers* (London: EETS, 1871), vi.

3. On Fish and the early Protestant agitators, see W. A. Clebsch, *England's Earliest Protestants* (New Haven: Yale University Press, 1964); Susan Brigden, *London and the Reformation* (Oxford: Clarendon, 1989); and A. G. Dickens, *The English Reformation,* 2nd ed. (London: Batsford, 1989).

4. La Boétie's answer was a structural one: a chain of clientage and dependency extended geometrically from the small number of exploiters at the top to the great mass of the exploited below. The analysis is secular, but it was quickly adopted by the Huguenots.

5. Fish refers to the notorious case of Richard Hunne, who refused to pay the customary gift known as a "mortuary"—the priest's claim for a deceased parishioner—for his dead infant son. Hunne was accused of heresy and was found hanging in his cell on December 4, 1514. Catholics (including Thomas More) argued that he had committed suicide; Protestants argued that he was murdered by thugs in the employ of the bishop of London and his chancellor, William Horsey. In February 1515, a London coroner's jury found that Hunne had been murdered and named Horsey and the two jailors as the killers. The case figures prominently in Foxe's writing.

6. "But there be many men of greate litterature and iudgement that . . . have not feared . . . yn perill of deth to declare theyre oppinnion in this matter, which is that there is no purgatory but that it is a thing inuented by the couitousnesse of the spiritualtie onlely to translate all kingdomes from other princes vnto theim" (Fish, *Supplicacyon,* 419).

7. Thomas Becon, *Jewel of Joy* (addressed to Elizabeth I), in *Prayers and Other Pieces,* ed. John Ayre, Parker Society vol. 13 (Cambridge: Cambridge University Press, 1844), 413–14.

8. Tyndale, *An Answer to Sir Thomas More's Dialogue . . . and Wm. Tracy's Testament Expounded,* ed. Henry Walter, Parker Society vol. 44 (Cambridge: Cambridge University Press, 1850), 214. For a similar expression of uncertainty, see Hugh Latimer, *Sermons and Remains,* ed. George Elwes Corrie (Cambridge: Cambridge University Press, 1845). In "Articles Untruly, Unjustly, Falsely, Uncharitably Imputed to Me"(probably 1533, reprinted in Foxe), Latimer seems to believe that a middle state exists but that the souls in it are not suffering: "They need to cry loud to God: they be in Christ and Christ in them" (236). They might do something for the living, but the living can do (and need do) nothing for them. See also the ex-

pression of uncertainty in Hugh Latimer, *Works*, vol. 1 (Cambridge: Cambridge University Press, 1844): "Now my answer is this: 'I cannot tell' " (550).

9. Miles Coverdale, *Remains*, ed. George Pearson (Cambridge: Cambridge University Press, 1846), 475.

10. Latimer, *Works*, 305.

11. This account is one of two that Foxe gives of the book's transmission. The other account says that the book was brought to the king by two London merchants, who read it aloud. The king reportedly remarked, "If a man should pull down an old stone wall, and begin at the lower part, the upper part thereof might chance to fall upon his head." The apparent meaning of this gnomic comment is that Henry foresaw that he would have to establish the principle of royal supremacy before he could safely meddle with the wealth of the monks and friars. The king in this account put the book away and told the merchants to keep their interview with him a secret.

12. In the event, the interrogation, according to Foxe, did not take place because Fish's young daughter was ill with plague. Fish himself died of the disease within the year. His wife survived and went on to marry James Bainham, another Protestant, who was arrested by More a few years later and burned at the stake.

13. Thomas More, *Utopia*, eds. Edward Surtz, S. J. Hexter, and J. H. Hexter. In *The Complete Works of St. Thomas More*, vol. 4 (New Haven: Yale University Press, 1965), 225. "How great and how lazy is the crowd of priests and so-called religious!" (131), More's traveler had earlier exclaimed, in accounting for the grinding poverty in Europe.

14. More follows Jean Gerson's *Querela defunctorum in igne purgatorio detentorum ad superstites in terra amicos* (1427). See Germain Marc'hadour's introduction to *The Supplication of Souls* in *Yale Edition*, vol. 7, xcvi–ciii.

15. John More's will, signed February 26, 1527, "bestows more money on masses to be said for his soul than on any other purpose: œ5 (or more) per year for seven years for two priests studying divinity, one at Oxford the other at Cambridge; an annual obit at St. Lawrence Jewry for ten years; and a trental of masses (in addition to a dirge and requiem) to be said by each of the four orders of friars" (Germain Marc'hadour, "Popular Devotions Concerning Purgatory," in *Supplication of Souls*, *Yale Edition*, appendix E, 452–53).

16. For More's use of Scripture, see Germain Marc'hadour's introduction to the Yale edition of *The Supplication of Souls*, lxxiv–lxxxvii. An attempt to justify the doctrine of puratory only "by natural reason & good phylosophye" (Aiiv) was made by More's brother-in-law, John Rastell, in *A new boke of purgatory which is a dyaloge & disputacyon betwene one Comyngo an Almayne a Christen man & one Gyngemyn a turke of Machometts law* . . . (London, 1530). The Turk persuades the German, who is rehearsing Protestant objections to purgatory, that purgatory must exist.

17. "Purgatory," writes Jacques Le Goff, "did not exist before 1170 at the earliest." *The Birth of Purgatory*, trans. Arthur Goldhammer (Chicago: University of Chicago Press, 1981), 135.

18. The passage concludes with a conventional misogynistic joke of a type that More enjoyed: "Yet hear we sometimes our wives pray for us most warmly. For in chyding with her second husband to spight him withal, God have mercy says she on my first husband's soul, for he was y-wisse an honest man far unlike you. And then marvel we much when we hear they say so well by us. For they were wont to tell us far otherwise" (*Supplication*, 149).

19. On the close relation between purgatory and charity, see, for example, Clive Burgess, "By Quick and by Dead: Wills and Pious Provision in Late Medieval Bristol," *English Historical Review* 305 (1987), 837–58. Because the prayers of the virtuous poor were thought to be particularly efficacious, the rich in effect purchased them through charitable donations. Doles of bread or money, Burgess points out, invariably accompanied funerals, and the wills of the wealthy often established long-term alms giving, in the hope and expectation of the beneficiaries' prayers.

20. On poor relief in Tudor England, see Paul Slack, *Poverty and Policy in Tudor and Stuart England* (London: Longman, 1988).

21. Delius makes the interesting observation that Hamlet uses the word *bound* in the sense of "ready addressed," whereas the Ghost uses it as the past participle of the verb *to bind*. The shift then is from preparation or expectation to obligation.

22. Johann Wolfgang von Goethe, *Wilhelm Meister's Apprenticeship*, trans. Eric Blackall (Princeton: Princeton University Press, 1989), 146.

23. "Claim" rather than "meaning" because the Ghost may only by lying lure Hamlet into a belief that Purgatory actually exists and then lure him further toward damnation by inducing him to commit an act of vengeance.

24. *The Last Judgment*, in *The Chester Plays*, ed. Dr. Matthews, Early English Text Society, Extra Series 115, pt. 2 (London: Kegan, Paul, Trench Trübner, & Co., 1916 [1914], 430). See, similarly, "A lyttel boke . . . of Purgatorye" (London, [1534]):

Betwene the payne of hell / certaynly
And betwene the payne / of Purgatorye
Is no dyfference / but certes that one
Shall haue an ende / and that other none.

(Quoted in Marc'hadour, "Popular Devotions," 447.)

25. See Thomas Dekker, *2 Honest Whore*: "S. Patricke you know keepest Purgatory"; and Dekker's *Old Fortunatus* (1600): "here end my torments in Saint Patrickes Purgatorie." See, likewise, John Grange's *The Golden Aphroditis* (1577): "I come not from Trophonius care [sic], for then I should be lothde: / Nor from S. Patrickes purgatorie"; and Ralph Knevet's short poem "Securitye":

Yet Hee [man] lives, as if Hell,
Were but a fable, or a storye,
A place of fancye, that might paralell
The old St Patrickes Purgatory.
Hee mirth recrutes with cup's, and seldome thinkes
Of Death, untill into the grave Hee sinkes.

26. *Missale Ad Usum Insignis et Praeclarae Ecclesiae Sarum [Missale Sarum]*, ed. Francis Dickinson (Oxford: J. Parker, 1861–83), 878. The phrase *hic et ubique* is repeated in the *Secreta and Postcommunio* as well.

27. Edgar C. S Gibson, *The Thirty-Nine Articles of the Church of England*, 2 vols. (London: Methuen & Co. 1897), 2:37.

28. *Doctor Faustus*, ll. 876–77, in *The Works of Christopher Marlowe*, ed. C. F. Tucker Brooke (Oxford: Clarendon, 1910).

29. See Alan Kreider, *English Chantries: The Road to Dissolution* (Cambridge, MA: Harvard University Press, 1979).

30. See Robert Whiting, *The Blind Devotion of the People: Popular Religion and the English Reformation* (Cambridge: Cambridge University Press, 1989); Christopher Haigh, *Reformation and Resistance in Tudor Lancashire* (Cambridge: Cam-

bridge University Press, 1975); and J. J. Scarisbrick, *The Reformation and the English People* (Oxford: Blackwell, 1984).

31. F. E. Brightman, ed. *The English Rite*, 2 vols., 2nd ed. revised (London: Rivingtons, 1921), 2: 858. See the remarks in Eamon Duffy, *The Stripping of the Altars: Traditional Religion in England, c.1400–c.1580* (New Haven: Yale University Press, 1992), 475.

32. More, *Works*, 1557, 881.

33. All citations of Foxe's account are to the introduction of Frederick J. Furnivall's edition of Fish's *A Supplication for the Beggers* (London: EETS, 1871). Foxe took his mock title from More's dead, who characterize themselves as "we sely poore pewlyng sowles" (136).

34. Hugh Latimer, "Sermon Preached Before the Convocation of the Clergy," in *The Works of Hugh Latimer*, 1:50.

35. *Quintilian's Institutes of Oratory, or Education of an Orator*, 2 vols., trans. John Selby Watson (London: George Bell, 1902), 2:161. See the similar warning in Puttenham's account of "Hypotiposis, or the counterfeit representation: The matter and occasion leadeth vs many times to describe and set foorth many things, in such sort as it should appeare they were truly before our eyes though they were not present, which to do it requireth cunning: for nothing can be kindly counterfait or represented in his absence, but by great discretion in the doer. And if the things we couet to describe be not naturall or not veritable, than yet the same axeth more cunning to do it, because to faine a thing that neuer was nor is like to be, proceedeth of a great wit and sharper inuention than to describe things that be true." Puttenham goes on to distinguish between Prosopographia, which includes the feigning of "the visage, speach and countenance of any person absent or dead" and " Prosopeia, or the Counterfait in personation *[sic]*," which includes giving "reason or speech to dombe creatures or other insensible things." Glady Doidge Willcock and Alice Walker, eds. *The Arte of English Poesie* (Cambridge: Cambridge University Press, 1936), 238–39.

36. John Gee, *New Shreds of the Old Snare* (London: Robert Mylbourne, 1624).

6 America's Transient Mental Illness

A Brief History of the
Self-Traumatized Perpetrator

ALLAN YOUNG

PSEUDOLOGIA FANTASTICA

In May 2000, the *New York Times* carried a story headlined "G.I.'s Tell of a US Massacre in Korean War." It described an event kept secret from the American public for half a century. The journalists who uncovered the story were assisted by an army veteran named Edward Daily, who provided an eyewitness account and the names of other participants. Daily confessed that he himself had shot many of the Korean refugees and now, decades later, was still haunted by the sound of "little kids screaming." Six months later, he made another confession, revealing that he had *not* participated in the massacre nor in any other military operation in Korea (Barringer 2000a, 2000b; Moss 2000).

In 1998, the Cable News Network (CNN) had broadcast a similar story about the Vietnam War. The account originated with a veteran, Robert Van Buskirk, who described a top-secret mission in Laos in which he had participated. His unit's job had been to either capture or kill a band of renegade American soldiers. In the course of the operation, Van Buskirk told reporters, he had sprayed the nerve gas sarin from his helicopter onto the Americans and the Vietnamese who accompanied them. The use of nerve gas is prohibited by international law, and Van Buskirk sorrowfully acknowledged that he had committed a war crime. Shortly after the CNN broadcast, Van Buskirk retracted his story, claiming that he suffered from "repressed memory syndrome," which explained his false account (Pogrebin and Barringer 1998; Sharkey 1998).

In 1988, CBS television had broadcast a documentary, "The Wall Within," that featured interviews with five Vietnam War veterans diagnosed with post-traumatic stress disorder (PTSD). Three of the men confessed to participating in atrocities during the war. One veteran described how he had flayed scores of live people, including children, and how he held eviscerated human hearts in his hand. In the 1990s, an investigator, a veteran named B. G. Burkett, obtained the military records of the men who appeared in this documentary. Burkett discovered that, despite their passionate confessions, the veterans had not participated in either atrocities or (with one exception) combat operations (Burkett and Whitley 1998: ch. 5).

Each of these episodes begins with a self-incriminating confession, and each confession mentions the perpetrator's feelings of guilt, disturbing and intrusive memories, the responsibility of the American government for putting soldiers in atrocity-producing situations, and the conspiracy of silence that keeps the American public in the dark. Although these men have fabricated their pasts, they are not "simple liars" who set out to deceive people. They may have ulterior motives—perhaps to grab five minutes of fame, gratify sadistic impulses, punish themselves, or make fools of superior people. But they also have a strong psychological identification with their assumed identities and their victims. In their own eyes, their pain is real and is an extension of the victims' suffering. For some, the fabricated past is the product of *cryptoamnesia* (or so it seems). They have forgotten or suppressed the actual sources of these "memories," which most likely are news stories and tales told by other veterans.

If we were to describe these false confessions and memories as a disorder, we could call this disorder *pseudologia fantastica,* or "factitious disorder with psychological symptoms" (Newmark, Adiytanjee, and Kay 1999). Freud wrote about a similar phenomenon, the "family romance," in which an individual invents a new family for himself and weaves a new life narrative. The person imagines that he was not born to his real parents and is really the child of someone grander. Through his fantasy, he exalts himself and exacts symbolic revenge and retaliation on his biological family (Freud 1959, orig. 1909). At its most extreme, the imaginary past is manifested as a paranoid delusion. The fraudulent perpetrator engages in a similar project, in which paranoid or conspiratorial elements are often conspicuous. He departs from Freud's model of the family romance mainly in identifying himself with an infamous event rather than an important individual, and with a stock figure, or topos, rather than a real person.

TRANSIENT MENTAL ILLNESSES

This topos is a creation of American psychiatry. He is the person who has been traumatized by the effects of his own violence—the pain, loss, and death caused to his victims. He is unlike the figure who is familiar to practitioners of forensic psychiatry, the victim whose traumatic past has transformed him into a victimizer, such as the abused child who grows up to be a child abuser. The self-traumatized perpetrator is unlike this figure because he is his own victim. Thus, he becomes a victim as a consequence of being a perpetrator, rather than the other way round. He is likewise different from that other familiar figure, the individual who, like Lady Macbeth, suffers guilt, remorse, and horror in reaction to something awful that she has done. If Lady Macbeth is a kind of victim by our standards, she is a victim in a single sense—namely, that she suffers. Unlike Lady Macbeth, the self-traumatized perpetrator is a victim in a double sense: he not only suffers, but his suffering is somehow unjust. And he is not only a victim and a perpetrator, but he is also a patient (a medical case). Finally, the self-traumatized perpetrator is exceptional in that he is a regional phenomenon, limited mainly to the United States. Some mental health workers have occasionally suggested that this medical-moral identity be extended to other countries—notably to include child soldiers who have participated in grisly atrocities in Angola, Mozambique, and Sierra Leone (Goleman 1987; Boothby Upton, and Sultan 1992; Cohn and Goodwin-Gill 1994; Shaw and Harris 1994). However, in these cases, the identity has failed to find a place or a reality either in African medical institutions or in popular consciousness.

In other words, the self-traumatized perpetrator (and therefore the spurious perpetrator) represents a psychiatric disorder that has emerged at a particular time in a particular place. Although the characterization may be adopted elsewhere, it has not yet found traction. In the following pages, I describe the disorder's historical origins and explain why it is likely to fade away within a few decades. In *Mad Travelers* (1998), Ian Hacking coined the term *transient mental illnesses* as a label for such disorders. The book is about hysterical fugue in late nineteenth-century France and Germany. This disorder is unrelated to my subject: Hacking's concept rather than his history interests me here. Every transient mental illness, he writes, comes to life within an "ecological niche" formed by four (possibly more) historical conditions.

The first condition is a contemporary diagnostic framework within which the emergent mental illness has a place. The third edition of the official nosology of the American Psychiatric Association, the *Diagnostic and Statistical Manual of Mental Disorders* (DSM-III, 1980), opened a taxonomic box called "post-traumatic stress disorder," inside which self-traumatized perpetrators have a place as a distinctive "patient population."

Diagnosticians, psychotherapists, and psychiatric researchers also consider this group to be a special class of patients. The spurious perpetrator fits into another taxonomic box, among the "factitious disorders."

Hacking's second condition is visibility: the disorder must possess features that make it strange, disturbing, and noticed. In a moment, I will describe in some detail how the two disorders acquired these qualities. Visibility likewise entails a system of detection, within which the patients come to the attention of experts. In our case, two systems performed this task. In the decade leading to the adoption of *DSM-III*, patients were identified through a network of psychiatrists and antiwar activists. Following the publication of *DSM-III*, the job of identification became the responsibility of specialized diagnostic and therapeutic facilities operated by the U.S. Veterans Administration (VA) Medical System.

Hacking's third condition is that the illness must provide dysfunctional individuals with a psychological release that would be difficult, perhaps impossible, to find elsewhere in their culture.

The final condition consists of a "cultural polarity": the illness takes shape between historically contingent and morally opposed elements of contemporary culture. This element is the least transparent of Hacking's four conditions. In the case of hysterical fugue, one pole is virtuous, and the other is vicious and criminal. The fuguer's compulsive travels imitate emergent forms of mass tourism. This pole is the virtuous one, because of its association with self-education and the like. The fuguer also resembles the vagabonds and wandering felons who are targets of the police. This element is the criminal pole. The fuguer sits between the poles: too poor to be a true tourist, too faithful to social convention to become a criminal. These "poles" are aspects of institutions and forensic and clinical practices. Clinical narratives, authored by nineteenth-century French physicians, tell a typical story. A fuguer crosses the German border and is arrested by the police. He is sent to jail as a suspected felon, but an investigation and exchange of telegrams with France establish that he is an innocent amnesic.

Hacking does not explain why he believes that cultural polarity is a necessary feature of transient mental disorders. Nevertheless, he is correct about the situation of self-traumatized and fraudulent perpetrators. An obvious polarity arises here—victim versus perpetrator—and it surfaces whenever clinicians and Vietnam War veterans engage in diagnosing and treating PTSD. The poles do not coincide entirely with Hacking's virtue-versus-vice model. The perpetrator fits Hacking's model: he is vicious and criminal. But the victim of violence is not a perfect match, because victimhood is not intrinsically virtuous, at least not in any currently accepted sense.

A second difference applies as well. The opposites that define the fuguer are juxtaposed but never intersect. The patient is neither a criminal nor a tourist but mimics them both. This phenomenon marks him as strange and visible. In contrast, the self-traumatized perpetrator makes an appearance at the intersection of opposites. What is a victim? Someone who suffers pain or loss without deserving it. What is a perpetrator? Someone who inflicts pain or loss and who must accept responsibility. Victim and perpetrator are poles apart so long as the perpetrator is a morally autonomous agent, in complete control of his actions. What about situations in which a perpetrator is not an autonomous agent but is compelled to accept responsibility anyway? He suffers pain and loss without (entirely) deserving the suffering. The opposites intersect: he is both perpetrator and victim.

Moral autonomy is a recurrent theme in psychiatric accounts of atrocities committed in Vietnam. One argument suggests that the psychological conditioning during military training reduced soldiers' capacity for critical thinking (Shatan 1973: 646–47). This capacity was further weakened during moments of extreme physiological arousal and fatigue, common events in the combat zone (Shay 1994: ch. 4). Soldiers had to choose between contradictory moral principles—between traditional, universalistic codes acquired in childhood and the moral code of men at arms, which gives highest priority to group loyalty and submission to authority (Bourne 1971). The traditional morality categorically forbids doing certain things to other people; the morality of men at arms is more pragmatic. Is torturing prisoners morally wrong if one obtains information that might prevent the death or injury of one's comrades? Is a policy of political terror morally wrong if killing or maiming a small number of innocent people serves to intimidate a large number of potential troublemakers (Nagel 1972: 123–24)? Group pressures, including the realistic fear of violent retribution from fellow soldiers, further reduce a man's options and moral autonomy (Bilton and Sim 1992: 123; Lang 1970).

The cultural polarity that defined hysterical fugue was a product of historical developments: cheap railway travel, telegraphy, the invention of the passport, a period of peaceful relations among the European states, and so on. Of course, the emergence of self-traumatized and fraudulent perpetrators a century later grew out of a very different set of developments. But another, less obvious difference exists. In the case of hysterical fugue, the opposites—tourism, vagabondage—aligned themselves spontaneously. No one *intended* to create the symbolic space within which the fuguer gestated. As we shall see, the perpetrators' illness is different, for it emerged within a tailor-made space.

ORIGINS OF THE SELF-TRAUMATIZED PERPETRATOR

Psychiatric casualty rates during the Vietnam War were initially low, only 6 percent of total medical casualties (versus 23 percent in World War II) (Bloch 1969). Military psychiatrists attributed the low figures to the environment: intense but sporadic combat, short tours of duty, high morale and esprit de corps (Tiffany 1967). Toward the end of the war, a different view took hold: psychiatric problems were common and a consequence of fighting a guerrilla war that entailed atrocities and civilian casualties (Gault 1971; Shatan 1973; Laufer, Gallops, and Frey-Wouters 1985). In reality, the Vietnam War was less exceptional than either account suggested. It was not America's first guerrilla war, nor was it the first conflict in which American atrocities were common. Operations against Filipino insurgents early in the century had been very brutal (Wulff 1961: 252–54, 304–307, 318; Asprey 1975: 207–208, 211–12), and many atrocities were committed by American forces in the Pacific Theater during World War II (Jones 1946: 49–50; Dower 1991; also Bourke 1999: ch. 6).

A niche favorable to the emergence of the self-traumatized perpetrator failed to develop on these occasions. This fact can be explained partly by the spirit of the times. American soldiers tended to think of atrocities against the Japanese as acts of retribution rather than crimes. Nearly all of the atrocities were inflicted on soldiers and not civilians. American soldiers were welcomed home as heroes, and their war work was uncritically celebrated. In these conditions, neither perpetrators nor anyone else had a psychological or social need to focus on atrocities. No one was likely to call them to account, and, in some social circles, a perpetrator could be proud of his actions. Substantial numbers of returning soldiers were diagnosed with war neurosis, a syndrome that combined guilt, depression, anxiety, and disturbing memories. No doubt some patients were troubled by memories of atrocities, but they were treated no differently from other traumatized veterans. Symptoms were generally explained in developmental and characterological terms. Treatment favored the abreaction of repressed emotions (using hypnosis and drugs such as sodium pentothal), not the investigation of traumatic experiences (Watkins 2000). When clinicians did explore mental content, their investigations led them away from the battlefield, toward the discovery of the patient's "consecutive depressions—the depression of leaving his family, friends, and the life he would have had if not for military service; and finally the depression caused by separating from his fellow soldiers either by their deaths or his discharge" (Haley 1974: 92). This strategy persisted long after the end of World War II and was still common during the Vietnam War (Goldsmith and Cretekos 1969; Strange and Brown 1970).

The situation began to change in the 1970s. The defining event was the decision, in 1980, to include PTSD in the official psychiatric nosology (*DSM-III*). Not everyone welcomed the decision. A segment of the psychiatric community believed that PTSD was not a valid classification but merely a syndrome that combined depression, generalized anxiety, and panic disorder. The only feature that made PTSD distinctive was its unscientific etiology. The U.S. Department of Veterans Affairs was also unhappy with the classification, because PTSD would now qualify as a "service-connected disability." The VA would now be obligated to develop specialized diagnostic and treatment units, establish a process for assessing claims and dispersing compensation, and obtain the staff and other resources required for this major undertaking. The prevailing opinion in the VA was that insufficient psychiatric evidence existed to justify this effort.

Like other *DSM-III* classifications, PTSD was the work of a committee (Scott 1993: ch. 3). This eight-member Committee on Reactive Disorders had included Robert Jay Lifton, a professor of psychiatry at Yale University, and Chaim Shatan, a psychoanalyst. During the 1970s, the two psychiatrists had collaborated in a weekly discussion group with troubled veterans (Lifton 1973: 75–80). Another member, Jack Smith, had been nominated by Lifton and Shatan. He had been a Marine Corps sergeant in Vietnam and was now an activist for veterans' rights. The committee also included Mardi Horowitz, the author of a widely consulted monograph on stress-response syndromes (Horowitz 1976). A majority of the committee wanted to define the disorder in a way that would facilitate eligibility for service-connected status and reduce the possibility of "false negatives," patients who fail to get the diagnosis they deserve. PTSD's defining feature is its etiological event and traumatic memory, the motor that drives the other symptoms—flashbacks, phobias, and so on. The committee did not specify the content of these events and said nothing about the source or direction of etiological violence. In this way, the definition they adopted opened the diagnostic door to self-traumatizing acts (Young 1995: chs. 3 and 4).

The new classification included cases in which the syndrome emerges months or even years after the etiological event ("delayed-onset PTSD"). This scheme admitted cases for whom the etiological events, notably atrocities, were not unpleasant. How is this situation possible, given that trau-

matic events are defined as "distressful"? If one assumes that distress is always conscious and that patients invariably recall their actual emotional
states, then the idea of a pleasurable traumatic experience is absurd. The
psychiatry of trauma does not make this assumption, though. Emotions can
be dissociated (split off from awareness), and a patient may be unaware of
the emotional meaning of his experience. Doctors who treated shell-shocked
soldiers during World War I believed that they had observed this phenomenon (Leys 1994), and the mechanism is frequently mentioned in traumatology today (van der Kolk, van der Hart, and Marmar 1996; van der Kolk
1996). When the committee defined traumatic events as intrinsically distressful, they did not bar self-traumatized perpetrators.

I am not suggesting that the PTSD committee tailored the diagnostic criteria to fit self-traumatized perpetrators. Rather, *DSM-III* created a taxonomic space within which self-traumatized perpetrators could emerge.

ORDINARY MEN

The Committee on Reactive Disorders understood the implications of its
definition of PTSD. Lifton was an opponent of American military involvement in Vietnam, as were Shatan and Smith. During the late 1960s, the
three men had ties to the Vietnam Veterans Against the War (VVAW; Scott
1993: chs. 1–3). The organization had two goals: end American intervention
in Vietnam, and end the victimization of Vietnam War veterans. The VVAW
claimed that many veterans were psychologically damaged by their experiences in Vietnam and their homecoming reception in the United States. The
public treated them with contempt, the press called them "baby killers" and
"walking time bombs," the VA was unable or unwilling to provide necessary services, and the Department of Defense inserted secret codes in their
discharge papers, warning prospective employers about their supposed
mental problems (Lifton 1973: 75; Helmer 1974: 91, 94–5; Swiers 1984; Meshad 1984). These circumstances had kindled an epidemic of self-destructive
behavior that could be seen in the veterans' high rates of suicide, parasui-
cide, alcohol and drug abuse, domestic violence, divorce, nomadism, unemployment, poverty, and criminal behavior. (This view is that of the VVAW;
for systematic critiques, see Dean 1997: ch. 1; Lembcke 1998; Burkett and
Whitley 1998: chs. 1–4.)

The VVAW was initially more of a social network than a movement. It
lacked an effective strategy and the resources necessary to publicize its
grievances (Scott 1993: chs. 6–7). The situation changed in October 1969,
with news of a massacre that had occurred during the previous year, when

American troops had murdered five hundred unarmed civilians—mainly children, infants, women, and old people—in the hamlet of My Lai. An army photographer had been present, and his pictures appeared in *Life* magazine in November. In the same month, one of the soldiers was interviewed on television. Following the interview was a highly publicized series of trials, appeals, petitions, and an intervention by President Nixon on behalf of the most notorious perpetrator, Lieutenant "Rusty" Calley.

American public opinion was deeply divided by the war, and no consensus emerged about the meaning of the incident (see the results of newspaper polls in Hersh 1970: 151, 155, 161). The one point on which everyone seemed to agree was that the massacre had been carried out by perfectly *ordinary* American soldiers. The perpetrators' ordinariness, not just the scale of their atrocities, was the aspect that Americans found disquieting. E. M. Opton, a psychologist who had visited Vietnam, informed a congressional commission on the massacre that

> No one has reported behavior of the officers or enlisted men before or after My Lai that smacks of abnormality. Parents of the [My Lai] men have rarely complained that their sons returned from Vietnam in any abnormal state. The men are reported to have gone about their gruesome work for the most part with cool efficiency and tragic effectiveness. The fact that the accused officers and men did nothing to draw attention to themselves in the months before or after the massacre indicates that they were not remarkably different from the run-of-the-mill soldier. (quoted in Knoll and McFadden 1970: 112)

Lieutenant Calley had described himself as a "run-of-the-mill-guy," and a psychiatric examination conducted prior to his trial found no evidence of "disease, defect, derangement or impairment or anything we could observe that would make us feel his mental functioning was disturbed" (Everett, Johnson, and Rosenthal 1971: 190–91, 221; Sack 1971: 103).

The perpetrators' ordinariness also attracted the attention of Lifton and the VVAW. In comments to the National Veterans' Inquiry tribunal in 1970, Lifton observed that

> it does not require an abnormal person to commit atrocities. Atrocities are . . . the well adjusted form of behavior in Vietnam. . . . It takes the unusual man—someone who is in some way idiosyncratic or not too well adjusted—to avoid atrocities. . . . I had occasion to talk to a man who had been at My Lai, who had not shot at all, and sure enough it turned out that he was not too well adjusted in many ways. He was a kind of a loner. He was not in with his group. (Quoted in Kunen 1971: 273–74, 281)

The same year, the VVAW organized a tribunal, modeled on highly publicized European tribunals held prior to My Lai (Jackson 1971; Russell 1967;
Limqueco and Weiss 1971; Sartre 1968). Veterans gave eyewitness accounts
of atrocities committed by American units throughout Vietnam, and the
point was repeatedly made that these war crimes were routine and not isolated acts of out-of-control berserkers (Hubbard 1972: xiii; see Shay 1994:
87). The tribunal sought to track responsibility for the war and its atrocities
up the military chain of command and into the White House.

The atrocity strategy was initially effective. In 1968, the VVAW consisted of six hundred veterans, and its fortunes were in decline; by 1971,
membership had increased to twenty thousand, and the organization had
acquired the support of members of Congress (Helmer 1974: 93). (Some
members of the VVAW were concerned that the plan might further stig-
matize veterans, notwithstanding its exculpatory "ordinary man" clause.
See Scott 1993: 12, 19, on Lifton's advocacy.) But events soon overtook the
plan. Large-scale troop reductions began in 1970; by 1973, relatively few
American combat troops remained in Vietnam, and the war ended two years
later. The VVAW's reason for existing disappeared, and the organization
dissolved. Militant veterans now focused on obtaining government programs to improve their life conditions. Psychiatric problems remained a priority.

The atrocity strategy had produced two versions of the American perpetrator. Version number one was *the unwilling executioner,* the ordinary
man who had been victimized by politicians and military careerists and
whose atrocities symbolized the moral bankruptcy of American intervention in Vietnam. By 1975, the war was over, and this version of the perpetrator had faded from collective memory. Version number two was the
psychiatric counterpart of the unwilling executioner. He was *the self-
traumatized perpetrator,* the ordinary man who was not merely a victim
but also a patient. The unwilling executioner was gone, but the self-
traumatized perpetrator survived.

A COUNTERTRANSFERENCE NEUROSIS

Sarah Haley, a VA social worker, was one of the first writers to describe the
problems of providing psychotherapy for Vietnam War perpetrators. She
wrote the following in the *American Journal of Psychiatry* about one of her
patients, a veteran who participated in the My Lai massacre:

When a patient reports atrocities, where does the therapist begin? . . .
The first task . . . is for the therapist to confront his/her own sadistic
feelings, not only in response to the patient, but in terms of his/her
own potential as well. The therapist must be able to envision the possibility that under extreme physical and psychic stress, or in an atmosphere of overt license and encouragement, he/she might very well murder. (Haley 1974: 194–95)

Haley's approach to the patient was psychodynamic, and her comments
are to be understood in relation to Freud's ideas about "transference." During the clinical encounter, Freud wrote, the patient transfers to the analyst
unconscious wishes and fantasies that he or she originally attached to the
love objects and authority figures of childhood. Freud called this clinical
phenomenon an "artificial neurosis" and described it as a medium in which
a patient acts out unconscious desires and conflicts. These unconscious elements are now accessible to analyst and patient and help to advance the analytic process. Freud likewise cautioned against dangers inherent in the
transference relationship. The therapist must refuse to be seduced into a
reenactment of the patient's imagined past; the patient's psychoneurosis
cannot be permitted to displace the artificial neurosis. And the therapist
must control "countertransference" of the sort that Haley described. The
therapist must avoid situations in which she displaces her own libidinal or
aggressive desires onto the patient.[1]

Some writers "take the counter-transference to include everything in the
analyst's personality liable to affect the treatment, while others restrict it to
those unconscious processes which are brought about in the analyst by the
[patient's] transference" (Laplanche and Pontalis 1973: 92–93; also Blum
and Goodman 1995). Haley had the second meaning in mind when she
mentioned the therapist's sadistic feelings. Therapists treating PTSD are
still concerned with problems of countertransference, especially with patients who are the victims of violence. Haley warned clinicians about feelings of guilt, anger, and fascination that might distort the therapeutic process (Kinzie 1993; Simpson 1993: 681; Weiss 1998) and about the mental
"contagion" that induces therapists to overidentify with their patients'
traumas to the point that they develop similar symptoms, in a subclinical
syndrome called "vicarious PTSD" (Braun 1993: 44; Agger and Jensen
1993: 689, 690). The patient who is a perpetrator creates a special problem
in this regard, and his illness can undermine the solidarity of the therapeutic regime by splitting the staff into conflicting factions: one side identifies
with the patient's victim and longs to punish the patient, whereas the other

side identifies vicariously with the patient's violent acts and aggressive urges (Herman 1992: 598–99).

In Haley's account of her relations with the My Lai soldier, the engagement takes a form that we might call a *countertransference neurosis*—a newly invented piece of psychiatric theater that parallels Freud's conception of the transference neurosis. In the countertransference neurosis, however, the moral hierarchy of the clinic is challenged rather than confirmed; the therapist acts out unconscious conflicts and drives in a way that demands attention and remediation.

PARANOIA

Haley introduced her My Lai veteran to Lifton, who fully explored the possibilities of a countertransference neurosis in his books, articles, and talks. Lifton's interest in the victims and perpetrators of traumatic violence began with *Death in Life: Survivors in Hiroshima*, published a year before the My Lai massacre. Lifton writes in the book that Japanese A-bomb survivors experienced "a permanent encounter *with death;* the fear of annihilation of self and of individual identity, along with a *sense of having virtually experienced that annihilation.*" Survivors are overcome with guilt (believing that survival was purchased at the price of their relatives' death), paranoia, and "rage over having been rendered so thoroughly helpless and inactivated" (Lifton 1967: 30, 35, 36; 1973: 513). Lifton's literary point of reference is *Crowds and Power,* in which Elias Canetti examines the case of Paul Daniel Schreber, author of *Memoirs of My Nervous Disease* (1903) and the subject of Freud's paper on paranoia. Schreber believed that a plague had killed everyone on earth but that he was immortal. Canetti described Schreber's delusion as a defense against overwhelming fear.

> He wants to be the only man left alive, standing in an immense field of corpses. . . . It is not only as a paranoic that he reveals himself here. To be the last man to remain alive is the deepest urge of every real seeker after power. Such a man sends others to their death; he diverts death on to them in order to be spared it himself. . . . Once he feels himself threatened his passionate desire to see *everyone* lying dead before him can scarcely be mastered by his reason. (Canetti 1973: 443)

His delusion is the purest expression of survivor paranoia, and it is also the mental state of extreme despots. Schreber, Hitler, and Stalin are peas in one paranoid pod—the great difference being that the despots possessed the means to enact their destructive impulses.

In 1973, Lifton published his widely read book on Vietnam, *Home From the War*, which drew on interviews with veterans, including participants in the My Lai massacre. Like his Hiroshima book, this volume is about death immersion, feelings of helplessness, and fears of annihilation. Lifton discusses the efficacy of atrocities, but the paranoid despot is gone. To be more precise, the despot is democratized, replaced by ordinary men who are marooned in a state that Lifton calls "the atrocity-producing situation." This state is the moral equivalent of Hiroshima ground zero, a place where men are overwhelmed by unbearable fear and guilt (for their atrocities and survival). Back home, they protect themselves from their painful feelings through a "psychic closing-off." The end state of this process is a form of "symbolic death," a refuge from madness (Lifton 1967: 34, 35, 500).

At this point, Lifton considers the possibilities of countertransference. He writes that all psychiatrists fear the "psychic death" that they associate with mental illness (Lifton 1973: 520). They protect themselves by closing themselves off to their patients' suffering, which is a source of "contamination." The easiest way to do so in cases involving atrocities is to demedicalize the patient's condition—define him as morally perverse. Alternatively, a psychiatrist can limit himself to treating the patient's symptoms (depression, anxiety) and refuse to engage the source of his despair. The therapist who responds in these ways commits a grave act, because he revictimizes the victim. He reenacts his patient's etiological aggression, *mutatis mutandis*, and enters the circle of perpetrators and victims (Lifton 1973: 519; also, see Mason 1998 on therapists who are fascinated rather than repelled by perpetrators' accounts). But the clinician has another option. He can bear witness to the patient's condition, listen to his privileged knowledge of the world, and grasp the "image beyond the atrocity," the point at which perpetrators become victims and doctors can become perpetrators (Lifton in Lifton et al. 1972: 517; 1973: 127, 129n). The act of acceptance is simultaneously an act of healing. This phenomenon is also what Haley meant when she wrote that "Establishment of a therapeutic alliance for this group of patients is the treatment rather than facilitator of treatment" (1974: 195).

Lifton believed that German psychiatrists faced and failed a similar test following World War II, when their patients included people "who had experienced the most extreme forms of death immersion and brutalization." The doctors responded to this terrible suffering by numbing themselves. Patients were "refused compensation on the grounds . . . that such symptoms were due to 'constitutional impairment' or to previously existing [constitutional] tendencies . . . [or because] the specific relationship of these symptoms to persecution could not be proven" (Lifton 1973: 519). The doctors were shielded from their patients' traumatic knowledge by the biological orientation of German psychiatry, which allowed them to ignore the psychological and existential dimensions of illness. A parallel situation seemed to be developing in the United States at this point, circa 1973, in the opposition to a PTSD classification and the movement of neo-Kraepelinian positivists into positions of influence in the American Psychiatric Association.

WHOSE HISTORY?

The countertransference neurosis is powered by the therapist's fear of contagion. He defends himself against his patient's traumatic memory. The more frightening the events in this memory, the more desperate is the defense. The more desperate the defense, the greater is the moral danger to the therapist—the risk that he will be drawn into the patient's disorder. The calculus of countertransference and contagion extends beyond clinical work with Vietnam War veterans. Therapists treating civilians frequently experience "disgust, revulsion, despair, terror, and helplessness" (Miller 1998: 253):

> The affront to the sense of self . . . can be so overwhelming that . . . [therapists] exhibit the same characteristics as their patients . . . [and] experience a change in their interactions with the world, themselves, and their families. They may begin to have intrusive thoughts, nightmares, and generalized anxiety. At this point, therapists themselves clearly need supervision and assistance in coping with *their trauma.* (Cerney 1995: 13, my emphasis; also Catherall 1991 and 1995; Figley 1995; Munroe, Shay, Fisher, Makary, Rapperport, and Zimering 1995; Valent 1995)

> Countertransference feelings can lead [the therapist], under the guise of giving comfort, to repeat the trauma of the previous experience . . . [by] taking an overly rigid or punitive stance or tone. . . . The patient experiences feelings of being persecuted by the therapist. When these persecutory feelings become unbearable, the patient tends to project them outward, often with such intensity that the therapist internalizes the feelings to the point of identifying with them, and then acts accordingly, as a persecutor. (Miller 1998: 253–54)

The most repellent traumatic memories are atrocity memories, which are highly contagious and therefore dangerous (Newberry 1985: 155). In principle, all atrocity confessions should work in this way. In practice, a complication exists, which we can trace back to the VVAW's atrocity strategy. The perpetrator must be a victim in a double sense: he must suffer as a result of his atrocity (like Lady Macbeth) and he must have diminished moral responsibility for his atrocity (unlike Lady Macbeth). Lifton sought to make this point when he coined the term *atrocity-producing situation*—a place where soldiers are overwhelmed by "a combination of fear, confusion, rage, and frustration, and . . . a desperate need for an enemy" (quoted in Kunen 1971: 273–74).

The My Lai massacre typifies the atrocity-producing situation for Lifton. He interviewed My Lai soldiers for his book on Vietnam veterans, and he seems to be familiar with the documentary evidence that has accumulated over the past thirty years (Lifton 1998). Other commentators have questioned whether My Lai actually was a product of this kind of "atrocity-producing situation." For example, according to Christopher Hitchens,

> [My Lai] was not some panicky "collateral damage" firefight: the men of Charlie Company took a long time to dishonour and dismember the women, round up and despatch the children and make the rest of the villagers lie down in ditches while they walked up and down shooting them. Not one of the allegedly 'searing' films about the war . . . has dared show anything remotely like the truth of this and many other similar episodes, more evocative of Poland or the Ukraine in 1941. (Hitchens 1998: 14)

Lieutenant Calley, testifying at his own court martial, gave no grounds for supposing that he had been a victim of "fear, confusion, rage" when entering My Lai:

> Well I was ordered to go in and destroy the enemy. That was my job that day. . . . I did not sit down and think in terms of men, women and children. . . . I acted as I was directed, and I carried out the orders that I was given, and I do not feel wrong in doing so, sir. . . . We weren't in My Lai to kill human beings, really. We were there to kill ideology that is carried by . . . Pawns. Blobs. Pieces of flesh. (Calley, quoted in Everett, Johnson, and Rosenthal 1971: 190–91, 221; also Sack 1971: 103)

Everything that we have learned about the massacre since the Calley court-martial seems to confirm Hitchens's judgment. For example, the meticulously detailed book by Michael Bilton and Kevin Sim (1992) includes an interview with My Lai veteran Michael Bernhardt. Lifton had also interviewed Bernhardt for his Vietnam book and believed that he vindicated "the ordinary man thesis" of the massacre. Bernhardt had refused to kill villagers (see above). According to Lifton, he was the odd man who did not fit into his primary group because of his "loner" personality (Lifton 1979: 140–42). Bilton and Sim reached a different conclusion—namely, that Bernhardt's sense of isolation had nothing to do with his personality. He became a loner after the massacre, as a consequence of his refusal to murder civilians:

> It occurred to me [following the massacre] I might get killed by my own people. [Captain] Medina called me to the command post bunker; there were the platoon leaders, my platoon sergeant, and some others there. Medina asked me some questions about what I thought happened. Was I thinking of writing to my Congressman or was I going to tell anybody back home? . . . I had to spend the rest of the tour . . . with a company of men just about all of whom would be considered culpable and they knew it. I knew I had nobody else to rely on [and that] . . . the men I was with probably would not be too unhappy if I didn't make it back. (Bilton and Sim 1992: 180; see also Lang 1970)

These reports notwithstanding, Lifton's position has remained unchanged: "[In] all psychological judgement there has to be ethical judgement. There is no separation in an absolute way of ethical and psychological judgement . . . Killing on a large scale is always an attempt at affirming the life-power of one's own" (in an interview, Caruth 1991: 168). One would think that the unhurried and pleasure-taking elements of massacre—rape, infanticide, mutilation, and mass murder punctuated by a lunch break—are symptomatic of a deeper truth, to which we gain access by *going beyond our spontaneous moral response to the events*. Lifton does not ask his audience to suspend moral judgment. To the contrary, he believes that judgment in such cases is inevitable but that it should be within the moral calculus of the countertransference neurosis (see O'Brien 1998 for an opposing view).

THE MISSING LINK

I have described the genesis of two, relatively recent transient mental illnesses: the illness of the fraudulent perpetrator and the illness it mimics. These two illnesses emerged from a shared ecological niche and a new piece of psychiatric theater, the countertransference neurosis. But there is a missing link. I have said nothing about the medium on which the theater is performed. This medium is Freud's concept of neurosis. The neurosis concept is alive and well in American psychiatry. How can it persist when everyone knows that mainstream psychiatry has seen the last of Freud and his neuroses?

Let us go back to 1980 and the adoption of *DSM-III*. The editorial board made two claims about its diagnostic classifications in the manual: the classifications are symptom based and empirical, and they are compatible with all the major clinical orientations. The psychoanalytical community rejected the compatibility claim. The proposed symptom-based diagnostic system would be antithetical to psychoanalysis, in both principle and practice. Psychiatric problems are expressed in polymorphous symptoms, and disorders cannot be reduced to unvarying diagnostic criteria, said the psychoanalysts. The American Psychiatric Association adopted the *DSM-III* system nevertheless. The new system became the standard for record keeping, training, insurance and billing, and the preparation of manuscripts for publication in mainstream psychiatric journals. Psychoanalysts complained that adoption of the *DSM-III* system was a coup d'état to unseat them. If so, the revolution's most visible victim was to be their concept of neurosis.

DSM-III gave two pages to explain why the neurosis concept had to be purged. Its reference point was Sigmund Freud. According to the editors, Freud used the term *neurosis* in two ways: descriptively, to contrast neurosis with psychosis and organic brain disorders; and etiologically, to identify disorders that originate in anxiety-producing mental conflicts that elicit defensive reactions. To preserve the new manual's symptom-based nosology, the editors wrote, *DSM-III* would use *neurosis* only in the descriptive sense (in parentheses following the names of approved disorders). The current edition, *DSM-IV* (1994), dropped the term *neurosis* altogether, casting it into the waste bin of history along with disorders like "monomania" and "psychasthenia."

Or so one might think. Let us return to the editorial reference point, Sigmund Freud. Over the years, Freud referred to several kinds of neurosis. His main interest was in *psychoneurosis*, disorders traced to psychosexual conflicts. But he also had much to say about *traumatic* neuroses, the subject of his earliest clinical writing, *Studies on Hysteria* (1893–95) and a topic that continued to attract his interest, from *Totem and Taboo* (1913), *Beyond the Pleasure Principle* (1920), *Group Psychology and the Analysis of the Ego* (1921), and *Inhibitions, Symptoms and Anxiety* (1926) to the time of his final monograph, *Moses and Monotheism* (1938). But *DSM-III* mentions only psychoneurosis. Why no reference to the traumatic type? The two kinds of neuroses are quite similar. Their polymorphous symptoms represent the patient's efforts to cope with anxiety. The present is a symbolic continuation of the past. And the phenomenon of clinical transference emerges from this past-present connection.

Why does the introduction to the *DSM-III* make no reference to the traumatic type of neurosis? The manual fails to mention traumatic neurosis because the editors had no need to explain its disappearance. The name *traumatic neurosis* is absent, but the neurosis is there with the new name of "post-traumatic stress disorder." The committee that produced PTSD relied on two canonic sources, Abram Kardiner's *Traumatic Neuroses of War* (1941) and Mardi Horowitz's *Stress Response Syndromes* (1976). And both books relied on Freud's post-1920 theory of traumatic neurosis as their source.

Freud did not invent the term *neurosis*. William Cullen coined it in 1769 as a tag for nervous disease, and it soon became associated with a ragbag of symptoms and "functional" conditions. By the 1870s, physicians had adopted the distinction between neuroses and psychoses (Beer 1996; Laplanche and Pontalis 1974: 266–69). The *DSM-III* "descriptive" definition of neurosis was an effort to freeze the "neurosis" at this point, circa 1870. This plan did not succeed, however. The real victim of *DSM-III* was the psychosexual version of neurosis.

The traumatic version survived because it served the interests of its target population: American veterans of the Vietnam War. Freud's repetition compulsion is a causal and exogenic explanation. Its disorder originates in conditions that are outside the patient's body and mind—life in the combat zone, for instance. This quality gives PTSD its "service-connected" designation and explains away the disorder's otherwise embarrassing resemblance to depression and generalized anxiety disorder—psychiatric conditions that are ineligible for compensation by the VA. The newly coined syndrome needed a proper etiology to work. The PTSD committee reached for the most credible candidate.

HAS THIS TRANSIENT MENTAL ILLNESS A FUTURE?

If we take Hacking's notion seriously, we can expect every transient mental illness to disappear within a reasonable span of time. True, the self-traumatized perpetrator is still with us, but his ecological niche seems to be drying up. The political conditions and cultural polarities that made him possible and useful are gone, at least for the present. In the United States, an aging cohort of self-traumatized perpetrators lingers on. Perhaps a future minipopulation will emerge from psychiatric clinics in the Balkans: the region is saturated with perpetrators, visiting traumatologists, and homegrown PTSD counselors. So far, this group has failed to find mention in any mainstream psychiatric journal.

Also uncertain is whether the Freudian concept of neurosis has much of a future. Will research on PTSD (its current home) continue in its present direction, exploring the anatomy and physiology of trauma? Will the hypothalamic-pituitary-adrenal axis and hippocampus replace mind and memory in efforts to explain the pathogenesis of this syndrome? Without a clinical commitment to the concept of neurosis according to Freud, the theater of countertransference will close. Once this concept is gone, the self-traumatized perpetrator—victim *and* patient—will no longer be tenable, only hateful.

We have reasons to suppose that the fraudulent perpetrator may outlive the authentic article. In 1994, Helen Demidenko, a young Australian of Ukrainian descent, published *The Hand That Signed the Paper*. The novel won the Australian equivalent of the Booker Prize, notwithstanding the fact that it was a sympathetic account of the Ukrainian auxiliaries who collaborated with the Nazis in the mass murder of Jews during World War II. Demidenko said that the novel's events are grounded in the experiences of her own family. Part of her message is that the Jews had brought Ukrainian vengeance on their own heads through their murderous association with the Bolsheviks. "Most of my father's family, including my grandfather, were killed by Jewish Communist Party officials," she wrote. A reviewer for the Australian Broadcasting System described the novel as a "work of extraordinary redemptive power" and commended her for confessing that her own family included war criminals.

In August 1995, an Australian newspaper revealed that the autobiography was a fabrication. The author is really an Anglo-Saxon named Helen Darville. Darville admitted her true identity but told reporters that an anonymous young Ukrainian neighbor had been her actual source and that her book's details are accurate. This statement was followed by a second discovery, involving plagiarism. Large parts of Darville's prize novel had been lifted from other works, including an obscure pseudohistory called *The Black Deeds of the Kremlin*. Helen confessed to this deed also. Her confession included a fascinating bit of self-diagnosis, recalling the cases of cryptomnesia and family romance with which I began. Helen claimed that she is neither a self-conscious plagiarist nor a poseur. She believes that she is the victim of an uncontrollable photographic memory—an example of hypermnesia that parallels or imitates the intrusive "flashbulb memories" sometimes attributed to PTSD. Helen's self-analysis was that she had appropriated the narratives that she read and heard (from her spectral friend) and with which she felt a powerful psychological identification. Other people's stories became a part of her own memories, transforming her into this other person. Or so she was able to say, thanks to the developments I've described here. (See Craven 1995 and Daniels 1999 for accounts of the Demidenko case.)

NOTE

A version of this chapter appeared as "The Self-Traumatized Perpetrator as a 'Transient Mental Illness'" in *Evolution Psychiatrique* 67 (2002).

1. Compare Haley's reaction to her My Lai veteran with a report from Denmark. The patient was a refugee, a veteran of a Middle Eastern army, trained to torture prisoners. He reported that he initially enjoyed his work but, in time, experienced nightmares and somatic symptoms. He deserted, was captured, and was sent to prison, where he was tortured. He was released and sent into combat, where he was wounded. He escaped from hospital, made his way to Denmark, and was now requesting refugee status. He continued to suffer psychological and somatic symptoms, and a Danish doctor referred him to a unit specializing in post-traumatic stress disorder. His psychotherapist at the unit was sympathetic, but the therapist's attitude changed when he saw the patient, while in a dissociative state, assume the role of a torturer. The therapist, untroubled by thoughts of countertransference, now regarded the patient "with a feeling of discomfort and disgust rather than 'empathy' . . . feeling anger toward a [refugee] system which grants quick asylum to murderers while many victims of torture have to wait in insecurity for long periods of time" (Agger and Jensen 1993: 695, 696).

SOURCES

Agger, Inger, and Søren Jensen. 1993. "Psychosexual Sequelae of Torture." In *International Handbook of Traumatic Stress Syndromes*, ed. John P. Wilson and Beverley Raphael (New York: Plenum), 685–702.

Asprey, R. B. 1975. *War in the Shadows: The Guerilla in History*, Vol. I. Garden City, NY: Doubleday.

Barringer, Felicity. 2000a. "A Press Divided: Disputed Accounts of a Korean War Massacre." *New York Times*, May 22, 2000.

———. 2000b. "Ex-G.I. in A.P. Account Concedes He Didn't See Korea Massacre." *New York Times*, May 26, 2000.

Beer, M. Dominic. 1996. "The Dichotomies: Psychosis/Neurosis and Functional/Organic: A Historical Perspective." *History of Psychiatry* 7: 231–55.

Bilton, Michael, and Kevin Sim. 1992. *Four Hours in My Lai*. New York: Penguin.

Bloch, H. S. 1969. "Army Clinical Psychiatry in the Combat Zone—1967–1968." *American Journal of Psychiatry* 126: 289–98.

Blum, Harold P., and Warren H. Goodman. 1995. "Countertransference." In *Psychoanalysis: The Major Concepts*, ed. Burness E. Moore and Bernard D. Fine (New Haven: Yale University Press), 121–29.

Boothby, Neil, Peter Upton, and Abucar Sultan. 1992. *Boy Soldiers of Mozambique*. Oxford: Refugee Studies Programme.

Bourke, Joanna. 1999. *An Intimate History of Killing: Face to Face Killing in Twentieth-Century Warfare*. London: Granta.

Bourne, Peter. 1971. "From Boot Camp to My Lai." In *Crimes of War: A Legal, Political-Documentary, and Psychological Inquiry into the Responsibility of Leaders, Citizens, and Soldiers for Criminal Acts in Wars*, ed. R. A. Falk, G. Kolko, and R. J. Lifton (New York: Random House).

Braun, Bennett G. 1993. "Multiple Personality Disorder and Posttraumatic Stress Disorder: Similarities and Differences." In *International Handbook of Traumatic Stress Syndromes*, ed. John P. Wilson and Beverley Raphael (New York: Plenum), 35–48.

Burkett, B. G., and Glenna Whitley. 1998. *Stolen Valor: How the Vietnam Generation Was Robbed of Its Heroes and Its History.* Dallas, TX: Verity Press.

Canetti, Elias. 1973. *Crowds and Power.* New York: Continuum.

Caruth, Cathy. 1991. "Interview with Robert Jay Lifton." *American Imago* 48: 153–75.

Catherall, D. R. 1991. "Aggression and Projective Identification in the Treatment of Victims." *Psychotherapy* 28: 145–49.

———.1995. "Preventing Institutional Secondary Traumatic Stress Disorder." In *Compassion Fatigue: Coping with SecondaryTtraumatic Stress Disorder in Those Who Treat the Traumatized*, ed. C. R. Figley (New York: Brunner/Mazel), 232–47.

Cerney, Mary S. 1995. Treating the "Heroic Healers." In *Compassion Fatigue: Coping with Secondary Traumatic Stress Disorder in Those Who Treat the Traumatized*, ed. C. R. Figley (New York: Brunner/Mazel), 131–49.

Cohn, Ilene, and Guy S. Goodwin-Gill. 1994. *Child Soldiers: The Role of Children in Armed Conflict.* Oxford: Clarendon Press.

Craven, Peter. 1995. "Diary." *London Review of Books*, November 16, 25.

Daniels, Anthony. 1999. "Literary Victimhood." *The New Criterion*, September.

Dean, Eric T. 1997. *Shook-Over Hell: Post-Traumatic Stress, Vietnam, and the Civil War.* Cambridge, MA: Harvard University Press.

Dower, J. 1991. *War without Mercy: Race and Power in the Pacific War.* New York: Pantheon.

Everett, A., K. Johnson, and H. F. Rosenthal. 1971. *Calley.* New York: Dell.

Figley, Charles R. 1995. "Compassion Fatigue as Secondary Traumatic Stress Disorder." In *Compassion Fatigue: Coping with SecondaryTtraumatic Stress Disorder in Those Who Treat the Traumatized*, ed. C. R. Figley (New York: Brunner/Mazel), 1–20.

Freud, Sigmund. 1959 [orig. 1909]. "Family Romances." In *Sigmund Freud: Collected Papers*, Volume 5, ed. James Strachey (New York: Basic Books), 74–78.

Gault, William Barry. 1971. "Some Remarks on Slaughter." *American Journal of Psychiatry* 128: 450–54.

Goldsmith, W., and C. Cretekos. 1969. "Unhappy Odysseys: Psychiatric Hospitalizations among Vietnam Returnees." *Archives of General Psychiatry* 20: 78–83.

Goleman Daniel. 1987. "Terror's Children: Mending Mental Wounds." *New York Times*, February 24, 1987.

Hacking, Ian. 1998. *Mad Travelers: Reflections on the Reality of Transient Mental Illness.* Charlottesville: University of Virginia Press.

Haley, Sarah. 1974. "When the Patient Reports Atrocities: Specific Treatment Considerations of the Vietnam Veteran." *American Journal of Psychiatry* 30: 191–96.

Helmer, John. 1974. *Bringing the War Home: The American Soldier in Vietnam and After.* New York: Free Press.

Herman, Judith Lewis. 1992. *Trauma and Recovery.* New York: Basic Books.

Hersh, Seymour. 1970. *My Lai 4: A Report on the Massacre and Its Aftermath.* New York: Random House.

Hitchens, Christopher. 1998. "Acts of Violence in Grovesnor Square." *London Review of Books*, June 4, 14–15.

Horowitz, Mardi. 1976. *Stress Response Syndromes*. New York: Aronson.

Hubbard, A. 1972. Preface. *The Winter Soldier Investigation: An Inquiry into American War Crimes*. Boston: Beacon Press.

Jackson, D. 1971. "Confessions of 'The Winter Soldiers.' " *Life*, July 9, 71: 23–27.

Jones, E. L. 1946. "One War Is Enough: A Veteran Talks Back." *Atlantic*, February, 48–52.

Kinzie, J. David. 1993. "Posttraumatic Effects and Their Treatment among Southeast Asian Refugees." In *International Handbook of Traumatic Stress Syndromes*, ed. John P. Wilson and Beverley Raphael (New York: Plenum), 311–20.

Knoll, E., and J. N. McFadden, eds. 1970. *War Crimes and the American Conscience* New York: Holt, Rinehart and Winston.

Kunen, J. S. 1971. *Standard Operating Procedure: Notes of a Draft-Age American*. New York: Avon.

Lang, D. 1970. *Incident on Hill 192*. London: Secker and Warburg.

Laplanche, J., and J.-B. Pontalis. 1974. *The Language of Psycho-Analysis*. London: Hogarth Press.

Laufer, R. S., M. S. Gallops, and E. Frey-Wouters. 1985. "Stress and Trauma: The Vietnam Veteran Experience." *Journal of Health and Social Behavior* 25: 65–85.

Lembcke, Jerry. 1998. *The Spitting Image: Myth, Memory, and the Legacy of Vietnam*. New York: New York University Press.

Leys, Ruth. 1994. "Traumatic Cures: Shell Shock, Janet, and the Question of Memory." *Critical Inquiry* 20: 623–62.

Lifton, Robert Jay. 1967. *Death in Life: Survivors of Hiroshima*. New York: Random House.

———. 1971. "Victims and Executioners." In *Crimes of War: A Legal, Political-Documentary, and Psychological Inquiry into the Responsibility of Leaders, Citizens, and Soldiers for Criminal Acts in Wars*, ed. R. A. Falk, G. Kolko, and R. J. Lifton (New York: Random House), 419–29.

———. 1973. *Home from the War: Vietnam Veterans, Neither Victims Nor Executioners*. New York: Simon and Schuster.

———. 1979. *The Broken Connection: On Death and the Continuity of Life*. New York: Simon and Schuster.

———. 1987. *The Future of Immortality and Other Essays for a Nuclear Age*. New York: Basic Books.

———. 1986. *The Nazi Doctors: Medical Killing and the Psychology of Genocide*. New York: Basic Books.

———. 1998. "Looking into the Abyss: Bearing Witness to My Lai and Vietnam." In *Facing My Lai: Moving beyond the Massacre*, ed. David L. Anderson (Lawrence: University Press of Kansas), 19–25, 151.

Lifton, Robert Jay, Leslie Farber, William Phillips, Richard Sennett, Irving Kovel, Arthur Egendorf, Marshall Berman, Peter Brooks, Morris Dickstein, and Norman Birnbaum. 1972. "Questions of Guilt." *Partisan Review* 34: 514–30.

Limqueco, Peter, and Peter Weiss, eds. 1971. *Prevent the Crime of Silence: Reports for the Sessions of the International War Crimes Tribunal Founded by Bertrand Russell*. London: Allen Lane/Penguin.

Mason, Henry. 1998. "Military Lessons Learned." In *Facing My Lai: Moving beyond the Massacre*, ed. David L. Anderson (Lawrence: University Press of Kansas), 165–70.

Meshad, S. 1984. "The Treatment of Vietnam Veterans: From Rap Groups to Counseling Centers." In *Vietnam Reconsidered: Lessons from a War*, ed. H. Salisbury (New York: Harper and Row).

Miller, Laurence. 1998. *Shocks to the System: Psychotherapy of Traumatic Disability Syndromes*. New York: W. W. Norton.

Moss, Michael. 2000. "The Story behind a Soldier's Story." *New York Times*, May 31.

Munroe, James F., Jonathan Shay, Lisa Fisher, Christine Makary, Kathryn Rapperport, and Rose Zimering. 1995. "Preventing Compassion Fatigue: A Team Treatment Model." In *Compassion Fatigue: Coping with Secondary Traumatic Stress Disorder in Those Who Treat the Traumatized*, ed. C. R. Figley (New York: Brunner/Mazel), 209–31.

Nagel, Thomas. 1972. "War and Massacre." *Philosophy and Public Affairs* 1: 123–44.

Newberry, Thomas B. 1985. "Levels of Countertransference toward Vietnam Veterans with Posttraumatic Stress Disorder." *Bulletin of the Menninger Clinic* 49: 151–60.

Newmark, Noreen, Adiytanjee, and Jerald Kay. 1999. "Pseudologia Fantastica and Factitious Disorder: Review of the Literature and a Case Report." *Comprehensive Psychiatry* 40: 89–95.

O'Brien, Tim. 1998. "The Mystery of My Lai." In *Facing My Lai: Moving beyond the Massacre*, ed. David L. Anderson (Lawrence: University Press of Kansas), 171–78.

Pogrebin, Robin, and Felicity Barringer. 1998. "CNN Retracts Report that U.S. Used Nerve Gas." *New York Times*, July 3.

Russell, Bertrand. 1967. *War Crimes in Vietnam*. New York: Monthly Review Press.

Sack, John. 1971. *Lieutenant Calley's Story as Told to John Sack*. London: Hutchison.

Sartre, Jean Paul. 1968. *On Genocide*. Boston: Beacon Press.

Scott, W. J. 1993. *The Politics of Readjustment: Vietnam Veterans since the War*. New York: Aldine de Gruyter.

Sharkey, Joe. 1998. "Memories of Wars Never Fought." *New York Times*, Week in Review section, June 28, 6.

Shatan, Chaim F. 1973. "The Grief of Soldiers: Vietnam Combat Veterans' Self-Help Movement." *American Journal of Orthopsychiatry* 43: 640–53.

Shaw, Jon A., and Jesse J. Harris. 1994. "Children of War and Children at War: Child Victims of Terrorism in Mozambique." In *Individual and Community Responses to Trauma and Disaster: The Structure of Human Chaos*, ed. Robert Ursano, Brian McCaughey, and Carol Fullerton (Cambridge: Cambridge University Press), 287–305.

Shay, Jonathan. 1994. *Achilles in Vietnam: Combat Trauma and the Undoing of Character*. New York: Simon and Schuster.

Simpson, Michael A. 1993. "Bitter Waters: Effects on Children of the Stresses of Unrest and Oppression." In *International Handbook of Traumatic Stress Syndromes*, ed. John P. Wilson and Beverley Raphael (New York: Plenum), 601–24.

Stone, Leo. 1995. "Transference." In *Psychoanalysis: The Major Concepts*, ed. Burness E. Moore and Bernard D. Fine (New Haven, CT: Yale University Press), 110–20.

Strange, R. E., and D. E. Brown, Jr. 1970. "Home from the War: A Study of Psychiatric Problems in Vietnam Returnees." *American Journal of Psychiatry* 127: 488–92.

Swiers, G. 1984. "Demented Vets and Other Myths: The Moral Obligation of Veterans." In *Vietnam Reconsidered: Lessons from a War,* ed. H. Salisbury (New York: Harper and Row).

Tiffany, W. J. 1967. "The Mental Health of Army Troops in Viet Nam." *American Journal of Psychiatry* 123: 1585–86.

Valent, Paul. 1995. "Survival Strategies: A Framework for Understanding Secondary Traumatic Stress Disorders." In *Compassion Fatigue: Coping with Secondary Traumatic Stress Disorder in Those Who Treat the Traumatized,* ed. C. R. Figley (New York: Brunner/Mazel), 21–50.

van der Kolk, Bessel. 1996. "The Body Keeps the Score: Approaches to the Psychobiology of Posttraumatic Stess Disorder." In *Traumatic Stress: The Effects of Overwhelming Experience on Mind, Body, and Society,* ed. Bessel van der Kolk, Alexander McFarlane, and Lars Weisath (New York: Guilford Press), 214–41.

van der Kolk, Bessel, Onno van der Hart, and Charles Marmar. 1996. "Dissociation and Information Processing in Posttraumatic Stress Disorder." In *Traumatic Stress: The Effects of Overwhelming Experience on Mind, Body, and Society,* ed. Bessel van der Kolk, Alexander McFarlane, and Lars Weisath (New York: Guilford Press), 303–27.

Vines, Alex. 1991. *RENAMO: Terrorism in Mozambique.* Bloomington: Indiana University Press.

Watkins, John G. 2000. "The Psychodynamic Treatment of Combat Neurosis (PTSD) with Hypnosis during World War II." *International Journal of Clinical and Experimental Hypnosis* 48: 324–35.

Weiss, Joshua M. 1998. "Some Reflections on Countertransference in the Treatment of Criminals." *Psychiatry* 61: 173–77.

Wulff, L. 1961. *Little Brown Brother: How the United States Purchased and Pacified the Philippine Islands at the Century's Turn.* Garden City, NY: Doubleday.

Young, Allan. 1995. *The Harmony of Illusions: Inventing Posttraumatic Stress Disorder.* Princeton, NJ: Princeton University Press.

7 Violence and the Politics of Remorse

Lessons from South Africa

NANCY SCHEPER-HUGHES

"Brother, Brother, what are you saying? I mean you have blood on
your hands!" Dunya cried in despair.
—Fyodor Dostoyevsky

There is therefore a poetics of blood. It is a poetics of tragedy and
pain, for blood is never happy.
—Gaston Bachelard

PROLOGUE

This chapter does not pretend to offer an anthropological theory of remorse,
a field that does not exist and that I have no intention of inventing here.[1]
Anthropologists' lack of attention to remorse either suggests an appalling
oversight or alerts us to the Western and modernist nature of concepts. Although anthropological references to vengeance, blood feuds, countersor-
cery, and witch hunts are many, ethnographic descriptions of individual or
collective rituals of remorse and reparation are few indeed.

At the heart of this lacuna are the culturally specific meanings and experiences of human emotions—like sorrow, grief, rage, regret, and remorse—often thought (by nonanthropologists) to be universally shared.
Earlier generations of psychological anthropologists invoked a rickety dichotomy between *guilt-* and *shame*-oriented societies (Benedict 1946; Lebra
1971; Doi 1973). The experience of deeply personal and internalized feelings
of responsibility, guilt, and remorse[2]—as distinguished from public specta-
cles of confession that stem more from externalized social sentiments of
blaming and shaming—were assumed to be weakly developed or absent in
many non-Western societies. Remorse presupposes the existence of a certain kind of Western-"civilized" or "cultivated" self (Elias 1978; Foucault
1986), a culturally produced "self" that is acutely self-conscious, highly individuated, autonomous, reflexive, and brooding—a prototypical Hamlet
figure, if you will, overly preoccupied by a guilty, confessional conscience.

The overly scrupulous Irish Catholic conscience that James Joyce captured in his *Portrait of the Artist as a Young Man* is a good example of this phenomenon. The almost gleefully, shamelessly, unrepentant, head-hunting Ilongot warriors of northern Luzon, Philippines—studied by Michelle Rosaldo (1980, 1983) and Renato Rosaldo (1980, 1983)—exemplify something very different.

An older Ilongot man explained to Renato Rosaldo that the practice of severing and "tossing away" a victim's head allowed Ilongot males to "toss away" their anger following the death of a loved one. Instead of centering around depression, immobilization, guilt, anger, and remorse, the Ilongot ethnopsychiatry of mourning was built around excitement, exhilaration, hyperactivity, and murderous, even gleeful rage. The Ilongot "self" was a social self, relatively undifferentiated, nonautonomous, and embedded within an alternative moral/ethical system.

Rosaldo's Ilongot informants denied any "rational" explanation for their head-hunting practices. Their actions were not motivated, they said, by ideas about social interchangeability, such that one death (or one head) might cancel the death of another. Head-hunting, they insisted, was for pleasure and a sense of well-being. Taking a stranger's head "lightened" a personal loss, and the singing of head-hunting war chants made Ilongot informants feel happy, calm, and at one with the world.[3] Only upon the tragic experience of his wife's death in the field was Renato Rosaldo able to overcome his cultural resistance to the Ilongot ethnopsychology of emotions. Following Shelly Rosaldo's fall to her death, Ilongot emotions finally made sense to Rosaldo, not because they conformed to a universal script of mourning, but because the anthropologist had learned Ilongot ways of experiencing emotions and the self. The Ilongots' unforgiving—we could almost say remorseless—way of grieving suddenly became tragically available to the anthropologist. He *knew* how they felt.

Like Rosaldo, I resisted accepting at face value what impoverished Northeast Brazilian women told me about their lack of grief, regret, or remorse upon the deaths of their infants—deaths they sometimes facilitated by reducing or withdrawing food and liquids from babies they saw as "doomed." "Infants are like birds," women of Alto do Cruzeiro said. "Here today, gone tomorrow. It is all the same to them." "They die," mothers explained, "because they *want* to die, because they have no 'taste' or 'knack' for life." Eventually, I interpreted the lack of grief and maternal remorse for their "angel babies" in terms of a political economy of emotions in which mothers responded to the culture of scarcity and lived in a constant state of anticipation and psychological mobilization for loss (Scheper-Hughes 1993: ch. 9).

Some isolated ethnographic accounts of remorse stand out. One is Colin Turnbull's (1962) account of the remorse of an Mbuti Pygmy hunter, Cephu, who violated the social mores for communal hunting and redistribution of game. Cephu cheated by running ahead of his band and capturing some of the game for himself just before the animals ran into the communal nets. Caught cooking the purloined game alone in his hut, Cephu was banished to the forest. Before two nights passed, however, the selfish hunter crawled back to the base camp, shamefaced, remorseful, and repentant. He confessed his guilt, begged forgiveness, and promised to observe Mbuti mores. Consequently, Cephu was allowed to rejoin the small group.

Anthropologist Jean Briggs (1970) wrote a moving account of her experience of transgression and social ostracism by her Netsilik Eskimo "family" after her culturally inappropriate outburst of anger in a society in which group survival demanded rigorous repression of dangerously negative emotions. The modern North American value of honest and direct emotional expression was perceived as antisocial and immature in this small-scale society. Like Cephu, Jean Briggs was made to apologize for her childlike and unruly outburst before her family would readopt her and feed her from the communal store of scarce winter-camp rations.

In this chapter, I focus on a single ethnographic instance—an account of political violence and remorse during the transition to the new South Africa. I am assuming the politically and morally ambiguous task of telling the story of political violence, remorse, and reconciliation largely through the experiences, narratives, and points of view of a small number of white South Africans, drawn from the full spectrum of social class and political affiliation. This account seeks to provide a psychological, anthropologically informed reflection on the experiences of white South Africans (who along with black and brown compatriots) were historically and "existentially thrown" into a nightmarish political scenario in which they were cast, willingly or coercively, into the roles of active collaborators, passive beneficiaries, bystanders, victims, and/or revolutionary and (if white) "race traitors" vis-à-vis the apartheid state. Today, these same South Africans (who in the illustrative cases I describe below share little more than the color of their skin) are also trying to make sense of their country's violent past and of their roles in that history. Most white South Africans are merely trying to preserve their social and economic privileges and to resume interrupted lives. Some are also trying to undo past wrongs. A much smaller number of white South Africans have wholeheartedly cast their lots with the new political dispensation and have gracefully accepted a reduced realm of political (if not economic) influence. In a distressing number of cases, however, white South Africans remain mired in a bitter and disgruntled refusal of the new order. For these hard-core "refusenik" individuals (as well as for the thousands of previously unacknowledged victims of apartheid's violent madness), the Truth and Reconciliation Commission (TRC) was established (Boraine, Levy, and Scheffer 1994).[4]

Given the long history of apartheid, "Black," "Colored," and "White" South Africans still inhabit vastly different spatial, social, psychological, moral, and lived worlds. They have developed elaborate protocols and defenses for dealing with each other across the vast class, ethnic, and cultural divides. Humor (including gallows humor) is rarely used as a survival tactic.[5] If one may dare to speak at all of a South African "ethos" or "national culture," one might note that both black and white South Africans are markedly decorous, reserved, guarded, and sensitive (if not brittle) in their *public* presentations of self (this stance, however, may be an artifact of late apartheid and the bitter contestations around it). And because of their extraordinary experience of social and geographical segregation, white and black South Africans have obviously experienced the transition and the formal processes of social healing and new nation building with a very different range of emotions, meanings, expectations, and consequences.[6]

STILL WAITING

I went to the Cape of Good Hope in 1993 in a fit of postpartum depression following the publication of *Death without Weeping* (1992), which concluded more than twenty years of intermittent research on hunger and death among impoverished sugar-plantation workers and their families in Northeast Brazil. I went to lose my self in a new "field site." This time, I wanted to be in a place where something good, beautiful, and hopeful was about to happen. The first-ever democratic elections in South Africa were surely a beacon in an otherwise increasingly dark and chaotic world. Temporarily assuming a senior position at the University of Cape Town, I hoped that during my tenure I could document some aspect of the radical changes that were occurring and to be something of an ethnographer of the (democratic) transition.

I had intended to revisit the small and "picturesque" Western Cape fruit- and wine-producing village of "Wyndal" [Franschhoek], which was the ethnographic setting for Vincent Crapanzano's (1985) brilliant and controversial book *Waiting: The Whites of South Africa*. Out of his conversations with some forty white villagers, Crapanzano produced a devastating portrait of South African whites. As a skillful pathologist of the South African con-

1. Franschhoek, White Farmhouse. (Nancy Scheper-Hughes)

dition, he deftly exposed the soft underbelly of race apartheid in the dark, airless, occasionally soulless narratives of affluent white farmers during the early 1980s. His study took place when the antiapartheid struggle was gathering its greatest momentum, strength, and moral conviction amid heightened police and state repression.

According to Crapanzano, the response of the white villagers of Wyndal/Franschhoek to the political storm clouds gathering over their heads was to retreat all the deeper into a kind of paranoid, isolated domesticity. Some sought redemption through participation in a charismatic, Evangelical Christian Renewal movement that was sweeping white rural villages and towns in the Western Cape, even reaching cosmopolitan Cape Town. He portrayed the whites of Wyndal as comfortable, self-absorbed racists trapped in a passive mode, a "dead time" of suspended animation, waiting in fear and dread for the inevitable future to somehow miraculously pass over them and leave them alone to pursue life as they always had. Because the protagonists lacked any critical self-awareness, a situation that could have been tragic was simply pathetic, little more than a story of self-indulgence, cowardice, and bad faith. The root metaphor Crapanzano evoked, "waiting," implied a bunker or citadel mentality, a stubborn, head-in-sand, waiting it out.

Waiting was heatedly contested by white South African anthropologists and intellectuals, who saw in the portraits a caricature of South Africa's far more complex white spectrum. The book was unfair and "biased," local critics charged, a blow beneath the belt. Above all, they felt that it was self-serving, projecting an image of white South African racists to ease the guilt of American whites, who would at last find a population even more despicable than they in the politics of race. According to his South African critics, Crapanzano had betrayed his hosts at the university and in the gracious farm homes of Wyndal/Franschhoek where he had been kindly received. "Don't *Crapanzano* us!" white South Africans often warned me during the early months of my fieldwork. Had they known more about my own complex relations with those whom I have studied (Scheper-Hughes 2000), they might just as easily have said, "Don't Scheper-Hughes us!" Indeed, the problems of subject/object relations in the field do not disappear when anthropologists study people who are very much like themselves.

Of course, whites were not the only South Africans who were "waiting." Black South Africans were also waiting, but their waiting was illuminated by hope and poised for decisive action. Theirs was the waiting of angry young lions, the image and metaphor that young militants adopted for themselves. ("Wake up and roar, young lions, *roar!*" was how Winnie Mandela opened one of her political rallies in 1993 in the Western Cape. And roar they did!) The large Colored population, caught in between, were also waiting, of course, though given their liminal social and political position— caught halfway between white and black worlds, theirs was a cautious *watchful waiting,* in which hope for the future was seasoned with fear that things might not work out so well for them (Scheper-Hughes in press).

I wondered what I could learn by revisiting the Wyndal/Franschhoek farm community more than a decade after Crapanzano's fieldwork and just as the nation was on the cusp of its democratic revolution. By the time I arrived in Cape Town in July 1993, official apartheid was over. The ban on radical movements and oppositional political parties had been lifted, and Nelson Mandela had been released from his final prison, a kind of "halfway house," where he was held under a complicated form of house arrest. A kindly prison guard took me to see the pleasant suburban California-style stucco ranch house on the grounds of Victor Verster prison, just a few miles from the village of Franschhoek, where Mandela was being carefully prepared for release—to assume his destiny, which, by then, even his Afrikaner jailers saw as inevitable.

I went to Franschhoek for four successive periods of intensive fieldwork (each lasting a few months) between 1993 and 1999, during which time I moved freely among the older (Afrikaner) and more recently arrived

English-speaking whites, the larger population of Coloreds (with whom I lived for most of the time I spent in Franschhoek), and the new black "settlers" in Chris Hani squatter camp (Scheper-Hughes 1995a).[7] From the outset, however, the intense political events of the period interrupted my original research plans.

The elections that would eventually sweep Mr. Mandela and the ANC (African National Congress) into power in a glorious display of popular victory in April 1994 were preceded by a final, desperate attempt of the National Party government's internal security forces to disrupt the transition. Meanwhile, the PAC (Pan Africanist Congress) and its military wing, Azanian Peoples Liberation Army, and other radical factions on the extreme right and left of South African politics were dissatisfied with the direction of the negotiated settlement being hammered out in Kempton Park, and they were stepping up the militant struggle.

The assassination of Chris Hani, hero and intellectual mentor to the politicized youth of the townships, in the spring of 1993 spurred riots and other acts of township resistance. The leaders of PASO, the Pan African Student Association, launched Operation Vala (close down) and then Operation Barcelona, a campaign of antigovernment burnings and stonings by township youths. The latter campaign took its name from the Olympic Games in Barcelona and took its symbolism from the torches carried by lead athletes and runners. But the PASO torches would be used to clear out all suspected government agents and to prevent white motorists from entering the townships, which were declared "no go" zones for all white outsiders during this period. The violence peaked in a government-orchestrated "Third Force" attack of bombs, bullets, stones, and sticks designed to block the coming elections. Thus, 1993 was the most violent year in more than a decade of undeclared civil war in South Africa: 3,794 people died in political violence that year, the first year of my field research.

BLOOD IN THE GARDEN

The day after my family and I arrived in Cape Town on July 25, 1993, three young men dressed in overalls and head scarves burst into the evening service of the St. James Evangelical Christian Church in the white suburb of Kenilworth, which bordered the University of Cape Town (UCT) community where we had just settled into a faculty-student dorm on Main Road. The young men—one was a boy of seventeen years—opened several rounds of ammunition and tossed nail-spiked hand grenades into the congregation of more than six hundred worshippers as they sang the opening hymn, "Come to the Garden." In seconds—for an attack of this sort happens that quickly—eleven people were dead and more than fifty others were seriously wounded and maimed. Some would lose their arms and legs; others lost their voices from the shock. Hundreds lost friends and loved ones. Thousands lost their faith, at least temporarily. Even more might have died in the St. James Church Massacre, as it came to be called, had not a young white parishioner pulled out a gun and fired back at the assailants, who turned and fled from the church auditorium. The attackers escaped in a getaway car they had stolen earlier that day in Khayalitsha, a sprawling black township containing nearly a million refugees from former apartheid-designated homelands.

Less than a month later, during Operation Barcelona, American Fulbright student Amy Biehl was dragged from her car as it approached the entrance to Guguletu township in Cape Town, and she was stoned and stabbed to death by a few PAC ringleaders, who were egged on by a cheering crowd of "toyi-toying" high school students. The driver of the car was identified as a "white," "a settler" (a non-African), and therefore, an enemy of the people of Guguletu. The murder of Amy Biehl was a watershed in the final months of the antiapartheid struggle; her death was invoked to explain, depending on the speaker's political views, why the elections *must* go forward or why the elections must *never* go forward.

Then, on New Year's Day 1994, a nondescript tavern in the student "bohemian" quarter of Observatory in Cape Town was attacked by PAC revolutionaries. Four people were killed, two of them University of Cape Town students, one white and one brown. A third victim was an acquaintance of ours, the owner of a Portuguese seafood restaurant, Machados, where we often went to *matar saudades* (kill our homesickness) for Brazil. The fourth victim was a young, mixed-race ("Colored") woman, a grade-school teacher. Two of our own UCT student children were down the street at another student hangout when the Heidelberg Pub Massacre took place. Indeed, everyone—black, white, and Colored—was suspect of harboring some sort of violent sentiments during the final phase of the antiapartheid struggle. The Heidelberg tavern massacre, though modest in its carnage, stayed with me the longest—along with the images of the frozen, startled faces of the four victims—for I accompanied a state pathologist, Len Lehrer, to the Salt River Mortuary for the autopsies and identifications (Scheper-Hughes 1994a)—and their "random" deaths determined the focus of my research on democracy and violence.

But, of course, these much-publicized incidents of "black-on-white" violence were exceptions to the general rule of official, institutionalized, and

2. Aerial view of Khayelitsha township, Cape Town, an apartheid-invented South African ghetto with more than one million inhabitants. (Nancy Scheper-Hughes)

3. Heidelberg Pub massacre, December 31, 1993. (Courtesy of *The Argus* newspaper)

sanctioned "white-on-black" violence, some of which was promulgated by paid or intimidated black collaborators. So overwhelming were the daily "stats" on township deaths that year (1993–94) that both black and white newspapers recorded them only as body counts: "Another 40 Bodies Found on the East Rand"; "Dozen Bodies Removed from Guguletu in Weekend Casualties"; "Nine Bodies Found in Two Shacks Gutted by Fires in Khayelitsha," and so on. Violent and premature deaths were, and remain today, the legacy of black South Africans.

Still, the democratic elections prevailed, and a celebratory mood bathed all South Africans momentarily in a luxurious sea of goodwill. A sense of humor and vitality appeared, and the intensely private, claustrophobic worlds of long-hibernating white Capetonians opened up to a newly fashioned public space. Indeed, people had much to celebrate in this land of terrible beauty. But the legacy of the violence remains. The scars are deep—etched into the gutted and destroyed landscapes left by the apartheid state, in the empty spaces left by those who died in the political violence, and in the wounded bodies of those who survived the violence and chaos, but just barely. The following entry from my field notes in February 1994 illustrates the situation:

> You cannot avoid them for they are present at every political event. Father Michael Lapsley with the startling metal hooks where his hands should be. . . . There he is mischievously lighting a young woman's cigarette (a magician's trick!) or, over there, skillfully holding the stem of a wine glass raised in a defiant toast. . . . Once the shock leaves one wants to caress his gentle hook-hand, to stroke the ruptured, discolored skin where his unwounded eye once was, and to toast him, noble wounded warrior, with goblets raised high, clinking glass with metal, champagne with tears. And over there, with his back carelessly turned to the door, stands Albie Sachs with his handsomely lined face and his resonant soothing voice, the agnostics' theologian, dressed in his priestly robes, his bright and bold dashiki . . . with its freely waving sleeve, Albie's sweet banner of liberty. . . . Of thee, I sing, Albie.

My new research questions were ready-made. What narratives of self, suffering, and reconciliation were South Africans telling? How did people emerging from a past characterized by competing and contradictory histories begin to build a new sense of individual, social, and national identity? What role did South Africa's Truth and Reconciliation Commission play in personal, collective, and national reconstruction given the Commission's uncompromising demands for "truth," reconciliation, and forgiveness?

In focusing here primarily on the experiences of "white" South Africans, I am walking on thin ice. I run the risk of highlighting the "suffering" of one

4. Father Michael Lapsey, African National Congress warrior, displaying his wounds under the icons of Christ and Che Guevara. (Nancy Scheper-Hughes)

5. South African Constitutional Court Justice Albie Sachs demonstrating his "soft vengeance" against the apartheid murderers who put a bomb inside the boot of his car. (Courtesy of Albie Sachs)

social group, indeed, those generally identified as either the perpetrators or the passive beneficiaries of race apartheid, at the expense of other social groups—namely, black and Colored South Africans, who are the primary victims of that same genocidal-like system. In mixing and combining the narratives of white South Africans who suffered violence and death as the anonymous "soft targets" of end-stage PAC terrorist attacks with those of whites who suffered *strategic* attacks on their lives as the targets and known political enemies of the apartheid government (interspersed with the testimonies of white South African operatives of apartheid's death machine), I risk perpetuating a category fallacy. For the only things that this small assemblage of "white" South Africans have in common is the color of their skin and the accident of their birth in a nation obsessed with race and ancestry.

The old apartheid state constructed and enforced, often with violence, a set of arbitrary racial categories and group identities (Boonzaier and Sharp 1989).[8] Over time, the state revised and modernized the official system of classification and its discourses. Ethnicity, culture, and tribe became the softer proxies for race and racism. The language of development and urban renewal replaced the cruder apartheid language of eradicating "black spots" and racial containment. "Public security" was the covert language used by the police state to control political dissent and to eradicate so-called enemies of that state (Gordin 1998). Consequently, one of the deepest collective scars left by the old apartheid state is the legacy of spoiled identities. Erving Goffman (1963) identified the social dynamics of "spoiled identity" resulting from the stigmas of physical difference, ethnicity, and tribe, to which I would add the stigmas of history and place. But if the history of apartheid spoiled all cultural and racial identities, some are more spoiled than others: Zulu identity, because of its identification with the right-wing Inkatha Freedom Party and that party's collusions with the apartheid government; "Colored" identity, because it was a fictive category, an invention of apartheid; Black "youth," once the courageous "young lions" of the antiapartheid struggle, relabeled a lost generation once the official struggle was over.

A strong counterculture of political resistance has sought to free South Africans from the legacy of racist thinking by constructing alternative identities in terms of political commitment to the antiapartheid struggle and to the creation of a democratic and pluralistic state. Most South Africans are keenly aware of the uses and abuses of the socially invented categories of "race," "color," "tribe," "ethnicity," and "culture" in service of apartheid.[9] Thus, South Africans from all communities now have their hands raised and fingers flexed, ready to supply the necessary "air quotes" that question and destabilize the race terms and the social fictions that the old state wanted South Africans to accept as plain facts and as part of the natural, given world (Sharp 1994).[10]

THE UNBEARABLE WHITENESS OF BEING

> And that, my friend, is why I ran away. I ran away because I was scared of the coming changes, and scared of the consequences of not changing. I ran because I wouldn't carry a gun for apartheid, and because I wouldn't carry a gun against it. I ran away because I hated Afrikaners [white Afrikaans-speakers] and loved blacks. I ran away because I was an Afrikaner and feared blacks. You could say, I suppose, that I ran away from the paradox.
> —Rian Malan, *My Traitor's Heart*

To be "white" in South Africa was and remains a heavy and fraught condition (De Villiers 1987; Giliomee 1994; Goodwin and Schiff 1995). Of course, no easy way exists to be "White" in South Africa, even in the "new" non-racial South Africa (Malan 1990; Gordimer 1998; Krog 1998; Coetzee 1999). During apartheid, whites of good conscience faced a double bind: If they left the country, they were deserters and cowards. (Where were you during the antiapartheid struggle? How did your life, your family, your home, your choices, your work, your profession figure into the struggle?) If they stayed behind (unless engaged in the armed struggle), they were suspected of complicity and of enjoying white privilege and riding on the coattails of apartheid. All white South Africans—English or Afrikaans speaking, Jewish, gay, or Marxist—at times had to prove their political credentials to the outside world (and to themselves as well), graphically on the canvas of their own wounded bodies (Worsnip 1996; Sachs 2000).

   During a visit to the University of California, Berkeley, campus in the late 1990s, Judge Richard Goldstone, who headed the Standing Commission of Inquiry into Violence and Intimidation (the so-called Goldstone Commission) and who was one of the few judges who used his power during apartheid to assist political detainees (becoming known among Transvaal political prisoners as the "comrade judge") remarked on the difference between his reception in 1997 and his reception during his first visit to Berkeley in 1991, when anyone associated with the South African justice system was suspected of evil complicity.

   Rian Malan, the author of the problematic and politically incorrect but powerful testimonial *My Traitor's Heart,* traces his family roots through colonialism and apartheid, going back to Jacques Malan, who had fled religious oppression in France to arrive as a "settler" to the Western Cape. Before fleeing into exile himself, the younger Malan struggled with his inherited history and imposed race identity. He asked himself the question raised by a hybrid "Boer reggae" song: "How do I live in this strange place?" Initially, he tried to escape his whiteness by becoming a communist, experimenting with drugs, taking a black lover, espousing violence, espousing nonviolence, smoking *daccha* (dope), growing his hair long, cutting it short, spray painting American Black Power slogans on the walls of white monuments in the white suburbs of Johannesburg: "I'm Black and I'm Proud." And then, in confusion, he simply ran away. Malan returned for the transition to African rule, but still he is "caught."

   What, in short, does "whiteness" (Lipsitz 1998) mean today for the descendants of Afrikaner "settlers" and farmers? Afrikaner whites cannot leave the land, because, unlike English-speaking South Africans, they have no other option. Neither can they freely inherit or inhabit comfortably the land of their settler ancestors (Gordimer 1998). Can the South African "Boer" identity (which once meant simply Dutch/Huguenot "farmer") be reclaimed and reconstituted today?

Michael Lapsley, a naturalized South African from New Zealand and a chaplain to the ANC, reflected on his "whiteness" for the first time when he arrived as a young Anglican priest in South Africa and experienced his white skin as a mark of Cain, a stigma. He said, "Whiteness became for me like leprosy, something that wouldn't wash off. Although I knew a lot about apartheid before I came, I never understood what it would mean, really, to be seen as an oppressor. . . . So my decision to join the struggle for liberation was actually a struggle for the recovery of my own humanity." I knew exactly what he meant.[11]

GETTING OVER VERSUS UNDOING

In contrast to John Borneman's (1997) notion of "settling accounts" (in his book of the same name), with its obvious subtexts of getting even and of harboring barely submerged rage and vengeance, Lawrence Weschler (1990, 1993) settled on a more pragmatic metaphor for the processes of personal and national recovery: "getting over" (see also Ignatieff 1997). "Getting over" evokes biblical images of river crossings, safe passage, and overcoming, the key symbol of the American civil-rights movement. I have chosen, however, Hannah Arendt's metaphor, "undoing," despite its utopian premise. Although individuals can eventually "get over" a personal and collective history of violence, undoing demands a more Herculean task of mending, healing, repairing, remaking, even rebirthing the world. If the term carries a touch of the sorcerer's magic, we can excuse it. World repair cannot be accomplished through the applications of reason and the rule of law alone.

In *The Human Condition*, written barely a decade after the Holocaust, Arendt (1969) grappled with the terrible "burden of irreversibility," with deeds that can never be undone because the process that any single human act sets into play "is never fully consummated."[12] For Arendt, the only escape from the "predicament of irreversibility" comes unbidden, in the form of grace expressed in unconditional forgiveness (an act that Derrida [2001] calls "forgiving the unforgivable") accompanied by the ability to make and keep new promises. *Nunca Mas!* Forgiveness *and* forging a new social contract seem to offer the only possibility for overcoming past horrors.

But is this kind of forgiveness and reconciliation possible without the mediating presence of a powerful, transcendental, or political faith? Joe Slovo (1996; and Scheper-Hughes 1995b), the "believing atheist" (as he once called himself) offered one model of secular faith and a refusal to dwell on his past suffering at the hands of apartheid murderers. Ginn Fourie, the still-grieving mother of Lindy-Anne, one of the four victims of the 1994 Heidelberg Pub massacre in Cape Town, expressed her doubts to me during a meeting in 1999:

> How can we possibly get over and *re*-concile what was never *conciled* in the first place? We are starting from ground zero, less than zero, for we [affluent whites] must try to overcome hatreds and angers we never even recognized as existing in our lives. It was as if we were anesthetized and emotionally eviscerated.

Meanwhile, many Black victims and survivors of South Africa's violent history are wary of premature calls for national reconciliation, recognizing in them coded language for a return to the "quiet life," to life as usual, which is the last thing they want. Their resistance to the rhetoric of reconciliation—though by no means universal in a larger population that has proven itself to be extraordinarily generous, at times almost unbelievably so, toward their former white oppressors—bears some resemblance to Laura Nader's cogent critique of the "controlling processes" (1997) that are silently, sometimes lethally, at work in all "harmony ideologies" (Nader 1990).

For most victims and survivors, however, a first step in the process of "getting over" a collective trauma is knowledge seeking, learning exactly what happened to whom, who did it, and why. Here, the work of a truth commission, with all its built-in limitations and failures, is absolutely indispensable.

"I sometimes wonder," Father Michael Lapsley said to me in 1995, "just who that man or woman was who carefully typed my name on the manila envelope that was meant to kill me. I wonder what did they tell their spouses or children that night at supper about what they did in the office that day? Either they are so dehumanized that they don't care or else they have learned to live comfortably with their guilt. . . . I don't so much want vengeance, but I think that the names and faces of these people should be made known."

The official vehicle to facilitate individual and collective "getting over" so as to liberate South Africa from the ghosts of its past was the Truth and Reconciliation Commission (Krog 1998; Minnow 1998; Scheper-Hughes 1998; Gobodo-Sachs 2000; Wilson 2000, 2001; Ross 2001; Hamber and Wilson 2002; Madikizela 2003; Colvin 2005). In hundreds of hearings around the country, more than two thousand victims of apartheid-era brutality told their stories to the TRC's committee on human-rights violations. A smaller number of perpetrators of the violence have come forward to confess the details of their attacks on civilians in exchange for political amnesty.

Many scholars and ordinary South Africans have criticized the TRC process. Some have objected to the focus on the "exceptional," "extreme," and "gross" human-rights violations, which they believe has obscured the damage caused by the more ordinary and pervasive routines of apartheid violence: the legal, medical, economic, bureaucratic acts of violence against Black South Africans. Residential and economic apartheid remains largely unchanged, and accusations of betrayal of the struggle are rife among aging young lions and marginalized youth. But one could not expect a single institution like the TRC, with its limited brief, to remedy the effects of apartheid itself. Other critics have expressed worry about the "numbing" of South Africans by the constant barrage of media images and televised segments, which threatened to routinize the atrocities and trivialize the suffering of survivors. Meanwhile, the very structure of the TRC pits victims and perpetrators against one another in a battle over memory and truth. Richard Wilson (2001) argues that the South African TRC was designed primarily to legitimize the postapartheid state by promulgating the image of the new South Africa as a world leader and defender of human rights and liberal democracy. Popular support for the process was generated by the crafty blend of Western human-rights talk and "traditional" African humanism expressed by Bishop Tutu's marshaling of *ubuntu* (the idea that no man or woman is an island) and "African" notions of justice. Although "confession" and "forgiveness" are important elements of South African popular justice, the TRC did not recognize popular calls and demands for vengeance and revenge or for material (over symbolic) restitution.

Prior to the South African TRC, many other countries, mainly in Latin America, had tried to establish official or independent, church-run truth commissions to clean up after military states and dirty wars. Not all were successful at producing either truths or justice. Michael Taussig told me about a chilling scene he observed some years ago in the capital of a South American country during a period of official truth and soul searching. In a local municipal building in a rural town, people who had been tortured during the previous regime sought to file documents with bureaucrats seated at a long table. In front of each official stood a long line of ordinary people (some of them poor and barefoot), each in turn testifying to the suffering he or she had endured. Each had already had to complete an official protocol and was now allowed a few minutes at best to answer the questions: When were you abducted? Where were you taken? Were you beaten? tortured? On which parts of your body? What instruments were used? What questions were you asked? How did you reply? The government agents might have been tax collectors. Taussig suggested that this (indifferent) state interrogation mimetically reproduced the original torture.

MAKING SENSE OF SUFFERING

In recent years, an anthropology of suffering has emerged as a new kind of theodicy, a cultural inquiry into the ways that people attempt to explain the presence of pain, affliction, and evil in the world (Kleinman, Das, and Lock 1997; Das, Kleinman, Ramphele, and Reynolds 2000; Das, Kleinman, Lock, Ramphele, and Reynolds 2001). At times of crisis and moments of intense suffering, people everywhere demand an answer to the existential questions "Why me (of all people), oh God? Why now?" The quest for meaning may seek to vindicate an indifferent God, quell one's self-doubt, or restore one's faith in an orderly and righteous world. The one notion that humans seem unable to accept is the idea that the world is deficient in meaning.

Accounting for one's own suffering is one thing. Making sense of the suffering of the other is quite another and is fraught with ethical quandaries (Levinas 1986). This distinction is explicit following any collective tragedy, whether it is a natural one or a political one. "Why me?" becomes "Why *not* me? Why was *I* spared?" as survivors try to account for their exemption, their saving grace.

Although members of the St. James Church congregation are extremely faithful in their attendance, some regular worshippers did, of course, miss the Sunday service on the rainy evening in late July 1993 when the massacre occurred. A clerical worker had car trouble; a teacher was down with the flu; a university student grew impatient waiting in the rain for a friend to arrive, and she went home rather than disrupt the Sunday evening service after it had begun. Several people shared their thoughts with me about why God had chosen to spare them on that night, along with their doubts about whether being spared was a good or a bad thing. "You see," said Nadja, "God was speaking very directly to us at that moment." And for those present during the ninety-second attack that changed their lives and transformed their understanding of the world forever, the challenge was to make sense of the checkerboard pattern that killed some, injured so many others, and left the others physically unscathed.

Dawie Ackerman, who lost his wife in the massacre, has played over and over in his mind the moment that he walked into the church a few minutes after his wife and, rather than disrupt Marita and the woman with whom she was sitting and chatting in the front left pew, quietly took his place several pews behind her. During a painful interview in February 1998, he said:

Now why didn't I take my seat next to my wife? Why didn't I interrupt the conversation and smiling take her by the arm to sit beside me where she might have been safe? But I left her, instead, in the front line of the attack, surely one of the first to be killed. . . . My nature is to act quickly, so that when the attack happened I would have thought that I would have been one of the first up there to try and stop it. But, obviously, I had no gun . . . and . . . and well, I just fell down and hid like everyone else. Which I don't have a problem with . . . but I wonder what if I had sat next to my wife? Knowing myself I think I would have jumped up and wrestled with the attackers or tried to take their gun or something. But I didn't, I didn't . . . and those are the sorts of things that were always going through my mind at first. You would try to sleep and it would get to you. . . . But I realize now, afterwards, that there was a reason why I did not die. I was protected through God's intervention. The two hand grenades that were thrown into the congregation just missed me. One exploded only three meters away and the other was about six meters from me. That is very close. People all around me were hurt, hit by shrapnel, some were sprayed with rifle bullets, some people sitting just behind me were killed by stray bullets. A man sitting on one side of me lost both his arms and his legs. I had to walk over several dead and wounded bodies to get to my wife. But neither the grenades nor the bullets caused me any damage. Not a bit of the shrapnel hit me. I was spared.

Why?

I believe I had been spared to take care of my three children. In the grand scheme of things, I had to ask why it was *me*, a leader and Elder of the Church, who was spared. Later on I had to accept that God had both chosen our Church [for the attack] and He had chosen those who survived to give testimony that would bring honor to His name. And, since the first moment of the attack that has been the desire of my heart, to do that. That became my purpose in life.

Two weeks after the massacre, I joined a few dozen church members at the large tearoom above the auditorium following Sunday evening service. The massacre was still, of course, uppermost in everyone's mind. Their pastor, Bishop Reteif, had been leading them through a series of theological reflections on the meaning of suffering. But their own independent interpretations were, paradoxically, both more mystical and more embodied than the smart and intellectualized sermon "Where was God?" they had just heard their pastor deliver. Instead, they spoke intensely among themselves about a "secret message" encoded in the attack. If only they knew what it was. "We *know* God was trying to tell us something," said Marlene Sidreic. "Only, the true meaning hasn't been revealed to us yet." Most agreed, citing the inscrutability of God's ways, but Cynthia had a more direct interpretation: "I believe God's message to us was that life is given, life is taken away. Live life fully, day to day. Be kind to those you love, cherish them now, for you never know if they will all be wiped out tomorrow."

Barely a week after the Heidelberg tavern massacre, I attended two post-trauma therapy and healing sessions for several survivors at the Anglican Church–sponsored Center for Victims of Torture and Political Violence in Cape Town. All the survivors were preoccupied with having so narrowly escaped death. "I was in Cape Town," said an older woman, "to celebrate my daughter's wedding. I almost celebrated her funeral instead." But despite the heavy media coverage and the informed commentary about this attack on "innocent" soft targets during the late and extremely optimistic stages of political negotiations, all these survivors understood the attack as strategically and politically motivated. "This is South Africa," said a white former soldier. "We knew something like this was going to happen sooner or later."

Another survivor, a young mixed-race "Colored" man said, "I live in a township and I understand the rage that lies behind this attack, and the feelings some young people have that the negotiations aren't going right, that things are not going to change their lives for the better." A local hospital worker who lost a friend in the attack agreed. "Every day I see the wounds of the townships that come into the emergency room. And I think to myself, 'how long can things go on like this?' " While attributing a larger political meaning and purpose to the attack, all saw themselves as misplaced, misidentified targets. "Why did they go for us? We are not the enemy. People of all colors come to this pub." And they doubted, even as they hung onto the hope, that—as one participant said—"some good might come out of this in the end."

The ability to transform evil into good requires either a strong religious faith or powerful political convictions. In South Africa, both are often called into play simultaneously. Father Michael Lapsley, the victim of a 1990 deadly letter bomb sent him by some still-unknown officials of the apartheid government, reframes his experience by insisting that he is a *victor* and not a *victim* of the state that tried to kill him. Each day that he lives and participates in the construction of the new South Africa, he defeats evil and death. Like some of the St. James Church survivors (albeit survivors of a different sort of violence), Lapsley believes he was never closer to God than in the transcendent moment of the bomb explosion that took away an eye and both of his hands: "I sensed the presence of the Holy Sprit accompanying me and sustaining me," he said to me in 1994. During a visit to Harlem's Caanan Baptist Church of Christ on 116th Street in Harlem less than three years after the bomb, he addressed the congregation:

> I stand before you as a sign of what apartheid has done, of the physical ruptures it has caused. . . . But I also stand before you as a sign of the power of God to heal, the power of love, of gentleness, of compassion. The power of light is stronger than the power of darkness, and in the power of God we shall be victorious.

SACRED WOUNDS

The wounded body often becomes a template of individual and collective memory, both a map and a moral charter. In the St. James Church tea room, Mrs. K, one of the wounded, rolled back her turtleneck to reveal a large and inflamed wound covering her neck and shoulder where shrapnel had been removed: "Do you know what this means? she asked me. I shook my head dumbly. "This means I belong to Jesus. I am His. This wound is precious to me. It has removed all my fears. Nothing can ever hurt me again. Let them return. I am ready for them for His mark is upon me. He owns me and what is left of my life is in His hands." The woman's intensity frightened me. Suddenly I wanted to change the subject, even though, presumably, this *was* my subject.

The quest to make sense of suffering and premature, chaotic death is as old as Job, and as fraught with moral ambiguity. This quest is as important to the anthropologist/witness as to the companions of Job. It is so for whoever demands a reason, an explanation, for suffering—usually one that is compatible with one's religious or political convictions. Just as the companions of Job taunt him to elicit an explanation for his suffering ("You must have sinned against God"), the friends and relatives of the blameless people kidnapped and tortured during the Argentine "dirty war" insisted, "You must have been into *something*." Similarly, at the memorial service at the University of the Western Cape the day after the stoning of Amy Biehl, her grieving friends and colleagues whispered conspiratorially among themselves, "We don't want to blame her, but Amy of all people should have known better!" What was she doing driving her comrades home to Guguletu, a no-go zone, a war zone, during those tense days?

But Job righteously and steadfastly refuses the temptation to self-blame, insisting that he is a just man. Albie Sachs, who lost an arm to the anti-apartheid struggle, insists that he and his ANC comrades suffered and died "because we were good, not because we were bad." So, too, Amy Biehl refused the judgment of her attackers. She approached their raised arms (smiling, even, I was told) saying, "No, stop. You are mistaken. I am not a settler. I'm Amy, a comrade." Amy's naive and possibly even presumptuous claim—her large, white smiling face—may have enraged the angry young men further. But, later, her words came back to haunt the young men who were ultimately convicted of her death. (Indeed, at his TRC amnesty hearing, Ntobeko Peni ended his painful testimony with the following ambivalent statement of remorse: "I feel sorry and very downhearted, especially today [when I see that] I took part in a killing of someone who was on our side, someone we could have used to achieve our aims. Amy was one of those people who, in an international sense, could have worked for the country." Thus, Ntobeko came to accept that Amy was a comrade, as she had said.)

The danger, Immanuel Levinas notes, of all theodicies, of all attempts to make meaningful the suffering of others, is the risk of normalizing and accepting the suffering and death of the other. In all theodicies—theological, philosophical, psychological, political, and anthropological—the arbitrary nature of suffering and death is hidden. The companions of Job return to goad the hurt, the disappeared, the maimed, the dying: "You must have been into something"; "You must have neglected your religious [or political] obligations"; "You yourself must have really wanted to suffer or die"; "Your death will serve as a lesson for the living"; "Your wounds will serve as a sign, a beacon." Levinas says that the endless search for meaning, the attempt to make sense of suffering, has allowed people to blame sufferers for their own pain and to value suffering as penance for past sins or as a means to an end or as the price of sensitivity and consciousness or, especially within the Christian tradition, as the path of saints and martyrs.

The grieving mother of Amy Biehl, for example, whispered to me during a break in the trial of Amy's alleged killers in Cape Town: "Don't you think there was something *destined* about Amy's death? Don't you think that for some reason, perhaps not known to us here and now, Amy *had* to die?" Later during a break in the trial, I asked Linda Biehl to elaborate on her comment. She replied over a cup of Roibos tea,

> There is something you need to know about Amy. She was so dedicated, an incredible high achiever, but in the end something always happened to check her, to trip her up. Perhaps she was ambivalent about her success. So I wasn't really surprised when I heard that she was murdered on the day before she was to leave South Africa. . . . In a way I was even prepared for it. . . . Amy was very competitive, a high diver and a marathon runner. The very last photo I have of her is a newspaper clip-

6. Accused killers of Amy Biehl, hiding their faces on the steps of the Municipal Supreme Court in Cape Town, 1994. (Nancy Scheper-Hughes)

7. Linda Biehl, courageous mother of Amy Biehl, at the trial of her daughter's killers, Municipal Court House, Cape Town, 1994. (Nancy Scheper-Hughes)

ping showing Amy just as she came through the finish line in a [Cape Town] marathon. Her face is full of ecstasy, pain, exhaustion, and relief. I like to think that this is how Amy looked when she died in Guguletu—as if she was just breaking through another, her most difficult, finish line.

Mrs. Jeanette Fourie, who lost her daughter in the Heidelberg Pub massacre, said that she thought—though her husband, Johan (she cautioned me) must never know her thoughts—that Lindy-Anne would have been proud and even willing to have given her life for the new South Africa. "Even," I asked, "in such an absurd and meaningless attack?" Yes, she replied calmly, "I really do believe this."

One can readily sympathize with Linda Biehl's desire to substitute an image of beauty and light for the brutal photos in Amy's autopsy reports. And she must have had to summon all her faith to refer to Amy as a "martyr" in the tradition of Saint Stephen, whose life was also taken in a battery of stones. This painful sort of accommodationist "maternal thinking" allows a mother—Linda Biehl or Jeanette Fourie—to accept the suffering and death of her child as meaningful and even necessary.[13] But these sentiments are redeemed, as it were, by the mothers' lifesaving refusal to condemn their children's youthful killers, opting to see them, as one survivor said, "as children just like our own, children who under normal circumstances would have led ordinary lives."

Linda Biehl's faith in the idea of meaningful suffering allowed her to approach and to embrace the mother of one of her daughter's killers and, at the TRC hearings, to publicly forgive the young men who murdered her daughter and to refuse to stand in the way of their receiving political amnesty. Linda Biehl—along with a multitude of mothers, sisters, and wives in South Africa who are being called on to do the same—summoned her family's tragedy to serve the larger cause of national reconciliation and healing. Of course, these individuals are exemplary figures.

The majority of whites in South Africa have yet to acknowledge their passive complicity with the apartheid state. Most have failed to get the point of the TRC. A great many ordinary South African whites I spoke with in malls and shopping centers, in tearooms and in public gardens, in office buildings and in hospitals, in private homes and large farm estates throughout the Western Cape described the TRC as witch-hunting, scapegoating, and a persecution of whites. If General Malan ordered massacres and if Eugene de Kock (Gobodo-Madikizela 2002) administered barbaric tortures on dissidents, they *had* to do so for the sake of national security. Those who were detained, "disappeared," and killed were "terrorists" and "communists" who were part of an international conspiracy to take over all of Southern Africa. Such statements were heard through the end of the 1990s.

SPEAKING TRUTH TO POWER

From the start, the TRC had to grapple with how to define truth during its work. Justice Albie Sachs (personal communication, 1999 and 2000) identified four levels of truth: *legal truth*, which can be verified only through hypothesis testing and hard evidence; *logical truth*, which is deduced from logical propositions; *experiential truth*, which is phenomenologically, subjectively, and personally experienced as "true" while not necessarily being historically or verifiably true; and *dialogical truth*, which is "negotiated" out of a vibrant cacophony of voices contesting, combating, sharing, and sometimes drowning each other out. Sachs concluded that the TRC was most able to produce the fourth form, dialogical truth.

Although these heuristic distinctions are useful, many ordinary people who came to the TRC seeking "truth" or some version of redemption left disappointed. Instead of finding the single, objective, sweet truth of the moralist, they had to make do with, as Sachs suggests, a compromise, settling for a crazy quilt of competing narratives, losses, sorrows, halting and incomplete confessions, and contested truths. The victims of gross human-rights abuses, in particular, did not want to be served anything resembling the partial, fragmented, indeterminate, shifting "truths" of the postmodernist, which so resembled the dissembling political realities circulated by the old apartheid state. Victims came to the TRC looking for an objective truth and with it, a partially restored sense of wholeness and a taste of justice. They had to settle, instead, for a "good enough" truth—an agreed-upon negotiated national narrative, but one that will at least place Black and White South Africans; Afrikaners and English speakers; Xhosas and Zulus; ANC and PAC members on the same map rather than in different "countries" across the road from each other.

FAILURES OF REMORSE

> Reconciliation does not come cheaply.
> —Archbishop Desmond Tutu

Archbishop Tutu, the administrative and moral leader of the TRC, was constantly challenged and disappointed by the refusal of so many white South African apartheid operatives to come to terms with their perverse actions. Justice Albie Sachs confided (personal communication) that he, too, wished that the perpetrators of political violence had offered more expressions of remorse. For Sachs, the expression of remorse was essential not because of a sentimental fantasy of individual rebirth or psychological conversion but for the sake of the nation. An expression of remorse represented a public and personal *acknowledgment* of what had actually transpired during apartheid. Failing such expressions, the narratives of suffering so painfully wrought from the victims of the political terror could be easily dissembled by future historical revisionists of the era.

Justice Sachs's disappointment centered on people like P. W. Botha, Winnie Mandela, death-squad commander Dirk Coetzee, and F. W. de Klerk, who refused to acknowledge their roles in the pointless suffering of innocent victims and who thereby rejected the new history and remained frozen in the past. Indeed, few of those who played a central role in apartheid's dirty wars have acknowledged the evil actions, let alone accepted responsibility for them or expressed remorse for their actions using the TRC's idealized script for national reconciliation. To the contrary, the chief architects of and operatives behind the kidnapping, torture, and extrajudicial executions of political suspects defended their innocence to the bitter end, leaving the amnesty commissioners frustrated and the victims and survivors deeply disappointed.

The security police who kidnapped, tortured, and murdered the Black Consciousness leader Steven Biko told the TRC that they were not responsible for Steven's death in their custody. If so, why did they bother appearing at the amnesty hearings? If they had *no* gross human-rights violations to confess, then they had no crimes to be pardoned. At times, the "petitioners" seemed to be manipulating the amnesty hearings to affirm before TV cameras their unreconstituted political positions and to further humiliate the victims of their crimes, normally by asserting how "quickly" ANC activists could be turned into police informers.

"We discovered in the course of the [Amnesty] Commission's investigations," Archbishop Tutu sadly observed "that the supporters of apartheid were willing to lie at the drop of a hat. . . . They lied as if it were going out of fashion, brazenly, and with considerable conviction."

To what extent did perpetrators' lack of cooperation cast doubt on the entire TRC mission and process?

F. W. de Klerk, for example, refused to cooperate with the TRC. He refused to acknowledge his role in the operation of Vlakplas, the state-supported death-squad camp outside Pretoria, the state capital. When confronted with accusations by former National Party security police that they

8.   Archbishop Tutu, on election day, April 1994. (Courtesy of *The Argus* newspaper)

were acting on orders from above, de Klerk angrily replied, "My hands are clean."

In March 1996, I was granted an hour-long, open-ended interview with then Deputy President F. W. de Klerk at his parliamentary offices in Cape Town. The interview took place a few days before de Klerk stepped down from the Government of National Unity. Toward the end of the taped interview (Nancy Scheper-Hughes 1996), I broached the delicate question of the TRC and the role of the National Party (and of the former state president himself) in gross human-rights violations. Ex-President de Klerk replied:

"Political violence from the side of government forces is wrong. But political violence from the side of the so-called "liberation forces" where innocent civilians have been killed is equally wrong. There must be even-handed treatment of this violence by the TRC. I fought for that essential principle."

In response to my objections that *revolutionary* and *state-level* violence could not be morally equated, "F. W." replied:

"It is a fallacy that the National Party state behaved as it did just to suppress people. It is also a fallacy that everything was done just to promote apartheid. . . . I'm not saying that when security force people went beyond

9.   Frederik Willem de Klerk, former President of
South Africa; vice president under Nelson Mandela at the time this photo was taken, in his chamber a few days before he resigned from office,
April 1996. (Nancy Scheper-Hughes)

what is internationally acceptable in fighting terrorism in our country that
it was right. I don't want to whitewash it at all. . . . There are international
norms. But what do you do when you are fighting revolutionary forces aiming to overthrow the state in an unlawful manner when that state is internationally recognized, as ours was?"

"Do you have regrets about *anything?*" I asked.

"If I with all the advantage of hindsight, had to do everything all over
again, *none* of my major decisions would have been taken any differently."

"How would you like to be remembered?"

"As someone who made a positive difference, who had the guts to take
very fundamental decisions when the time was ripe."

When during the TRC hearings de Klerk was confronted with evidence that he personally and his National Party government had ordered death-squad killings, de Klerk, the Nobel Peace Prize winner, responded by slapping a lawsuit against the TRC and having his testimony (and the testimony against him and the National Party) deleted from the published transactions of the TRC hearings.

Two years later, in 1998, I interviewed Wynand Breytenbach, a former deputy defense minister who served in the Ministry of Defense under both Presidents Botha and de Klerk. Today, Breytanbach is comfortably retired on a government pension and living out the remainder of his days as a recovering heart-transplant patient in a luxurious and securely "gated" community in Sun Valley, outside Cape Town. I asked him his opinion of the TRC and of the amnesty hearings in particular. Like most of his colleagues in the Defense Forces, Breytanbach had not applied for amnesty. He explained to me:

"I just don't think this TRC is the right thing to do. Instead of reconciling us, it is making the divisions even larger. It is becoming a witch-hunt. What we must be doing now is to join people together. Most people—even I, as an official in the Secretary of Defense—were completely unaware of what was going on. I was shocked out of my mind to hear of the . . . Well, let's just call them atrocities and that sort of thing. It positively gives me goose bumps. I just can't believe it. Some of those people standing up there before the TRC, I know them well. You would never have thought that such things were going on. What is coming out there, well, it just shakes me out of my mind."

"Do you watch the weekly televised summaries of the TRC?"

"Yah, I watch it, I watch it with disgust. But I can tell you that I sat in at all the top executive meetings where all these decisions were taken. There was [General] Magnus Malan, myself, the whole Defense Council, all the generals and so on and I swear to you *never* were these sorts of things discussed. O.K., we said that we must experiment with some things in this area [i.e., torture; dirty tricks] to try to get stability for the country. But some of these characters went out and slaughtered people like cattle. . . . It was like . . . well, if you ever read the *Sword and the Swastika* you can see what the Germans did to the Jews in the past war. It was sickening, I walked around the house for days after I read it. It left such an impression. You just can't believe it. Even there in Germany, in Europe, you can find the same things as happened here. It all boils down to a few bad individuals, a few rotten apples, small people sitting in big jobs who think that they can play God.

Chaps thinking that they can just 'remove' certain people. But nowhere and at no time were these things ever discussed during our executive meetings."

"So communication had broken down and de Klerk and Botha had no idea of what was happening within their own forces?" (I asked incredulously).

"No, they must have known *something* because when I was a member of the Security Committee we kept asking for money for arms and such to take care of the problems. It was a case of people looking you in the eye and saying one thing while doing another. Now some of these chaps are in for the high jump, and as far as I am concerned, let them go. I don't care."

"You are opposed to amnesty then?"

"No, amnesty is a good thing. If a man has something on his chest, he should come out and confess it and get amnesty for it."

"Has anything really shocked you coming out of the TRC hearings?"

[Deep sigh!] "Ach! So many things. That [Eugene] de Kock fellow . . . now *he's* a real monster.[14] That shocked me. And the Biko thing. And this Kondile case that is going on now [at the Cape Town TRC amnesty hearings]. The burnings of the bodies and all that. It is just terrible. But, again, I go back to the Nazi era when pretty much the same thing happened. People lost all sense of humanity. If you really want to talk about atrocities, when I was stationed in Kenya during the Mau Mau massacres I used to fly and do observations from the air. I saw farmers, cattle, and small babies— all of them slaughtered. You can't sleep for months after seeing something like that. And, even today into KwaZulu–Natal you will find massacres still going on. Blacks killing the Blacks. So, this whole business is not so clear-cut. *All* the races are to blame, and there is a lot more to this than just apartheid politics."

"What else is at stake?"

"What really concerns me now is that there is no more law and order in the country. When my four grown sons see these so-called disadvantaged people marching in the streets, breaking things, and stealing whatever they want, they become very negative and cynical. They think that there is no good policing any more. And they think that if *these people* can get away with this, whites can too. But I tell them never to lower their standards, not to become like the bad eggs who are destroying what is left of our poor country."

In this extraordinary interview, the former deputy minister of defense managed to both deny and assert his role in police atrocities, to attribute blame to those both above and below him, to reassure himself that the atrocities committed by the apartheid state were not unique to his country and that similar events had taken place in a "civilized" place like Germany, not to mention in Kenya during the Mau Mau era. In the end, Breytanbach identified those responsible as a "few bad apples," the almost laughable defense used by most of the former National Party leaders. And he identified the present-day "spoilers" as poor and black South Africans who have "no respect" for law and order and who are corrupting the morals of good young white people, including his own sons.

Like a great many South African whites I have met and interviewed since 1993, General Breytanbach failed to see the enormous grace by which he, his sons, and all white South Africans have been miraculously spared. Breytenbach never gave serious thought to applying for amnesty under the TRC for any human-rights violations in which his own ministry had a role. Most amnesty petitions came not from the higher ranks of apartheid leadership but from their small-fry operatives, including many black police collaborators whose public admissions of guilt and complicity with the white state often provoked rage and hate among their victims and former neighbors and kin.[15] Amnesty petitions also came from PAC militants, like the Biehl killers and those convicted in the tavern and church massacres, who were already in jail and had the most to gain (and nothing to lose) from a public confession.

One spectacular amnesty plea from a leading white police security officer and particularly hated interrogator, police Sergeant Jeffrey Benzien, captured international attention. During his halting testimony at the TRC, Sergeant Benzien, a large beefy white man with a blunt nose and bulging eyes, got out of his seat and bent down before live TV cameras to demonstrate on the floor his special "wet-bag" torture. This technique took police detainees to the edge of death and back, and it usually got them to talk. In all the apartheid state trials of Black activists from the Eastern Cape who were sentenced to long prison terms, most were convicted solely on "confessions" and other information that Benzien extracted during his infamous torture sessions.

While observing Benzien expertly pin a man's arms behind his back and putting the wet sack over his head, one of his former victims present at the amnesty hearing could not refrain from asking Benzien the question "Tell me, what kind of man uses a method like that on other human beings?" Benzien replied that he had actually asked himself the same question. This question was why he decided to come before the TRC: "It is something I have to sort out with myself." When asked by Tony Yengeni, an ANC militant and youth leader, how it felt to put the bag around Yengeni's head, causing him to suffocate and wish that he were dead, Benzien briefly lost his composure. But all he would concede was that the methods he used followed a "Draconian law instituted by the Nationalist Government."

Pressed for details on his various rampages, Benzien, like many of his colleagues in the security forces, claimed to be confused, anxious, sleepless, and forgetful, amnesiac even. When confronted with his victims' accusations, Benzien would say only that he "might" have done something like that: "If I said that I put electrodes in his nose I could be wrong. If I said that I attached electrodes to his genitals, I may be wrong. If I said that I put a probe into his rectum, I might be wrong. The specific methods . . . I can't say. I could have used any of those."

When Benzien's victims expressed their profound skepticism that he could "forget" the beatings, tortures, and humiliations he had visited upon them in detention, Benzien pointed out that, naturally, these memories would matter much more to the survivor than to the security officer: "I am willing to concede that your memory will be better than mine on these details." Like Adolf Eichmann (Arendt 1963), Jeffrey Benzien appeared to be a shallow and hollow human being, a career police officer who followed orders and was proud of the trust his superiors put in him. He expressed no (and was perhaps incapable of) remorse. His only regret was that his former superiors were not present at the TRC to back him up: "What I find in the absence of those in the Security Branch who could possibly help this [TRC] commission is that I have been left out on a limb." He implied, too, that he was being scapegoated and publicly humiliated (before his wife and children) for actions that were thoroughly acceptable to the state and to his superiors.

Ashly Forbes, another of Benzien's victims who was present for his testimony, expressed empathy for the murderer: "At first I felt a bit sorry for him when I heard him speak because he had a lot on his shoulders, a lot of things to get off his chest . . . and he seemed like such a lonely figure up there." But then a glimmer of the evil one reappeared. When Forbes's turn came, he asked Benzien this question: "Why do you think that after three months in your hands I had tried to commit suicide. Could you perhaps from your perspective try to explain to the Commission how I could have come to that point? That I tried to escape you by trying to commit suicide?"

Benzien resisted Forbes's description of their relationship, and he reminded him that on the day after he assaulted Forbes, they went out to eat together: "To refresh your memory—and I'm not saying it flippantly—didn't you say that it was the most Kentucky Fry [sic] Chicken you had ever eaten? And on the way to the Eastern Transvaal where you were going to do some 'pointing out' [playing the role of police informer] can you remember that you saw snow for the first time? Do you remember that a husband and wife and their two children took pictures of you playing in the snow?"

In this wily counterattack, Benzien stripped his victim of his honor and his credibility, showing how easily the famous ANC militant was turned into an informer. All he needed to turn on his compatriots were a short reprieve from torture, a bucket of "Kentucky Fry Chicken," and a frolic in the snow. Yet, though Benzien could recall these details, he could not remember throwing Forbes on the ground and inserting an electric rod into his anus. "I deny!" he said. "And if I deny this, than one of the two of us is lying." In the end, the absent-minded torturer was rescued by the clinical defense by Benzien's personal therapist, Ria Kotze, a young Afrikaner psychologist who said that her patient had suffered a nervous breakdown and showed classic symptoms of post-traumatic stress disorder (Herman 1994). Benzien, she said, suffered from auditory hallucinations, was insomniac, and was emotionally labile, having on at least one occasion burst into tears, without explanation, in front of his wife. In short, Benzien, too, Ria Kotze argued, was also a victim of apartheid.

Benzien ultimately received political amnesty, and he is still working for the South African police, though he has been reduced to a low-profile job at the Cape Town airport. Benzien's torture victim, Ashly Forbes, did not contest the amnesty, and he (for one) accepted Benzien's medicalized dispensation.

> After he had put electrodes on me and knock me out and after that he would change his clothes and he would come over all fresh like and say, "Everything is OK. You have done very well, lets go out shopping or something." Then afterwards he would take you back to the cell again and he would start the torture all over again. And so, I tried to block it out of my memory. I didn't want to think about it. And I guess the same goes for him, maybe a defense mechanism takes over so that he forgets what it was he did to us. I can believe that.

Still, as Allan Young (1997) has noted about the American soldiers who participated in the My Lai massacre, the ability to apply a medical diagnosis and exemption just as easily to the perpetrator as to the victim is deeply morally troubling.

An attempt to interview Benzien led me to a rundown, working-class bungalow in a white suburb of Cape Town. Weeds had overtaken an area that was once a garden. The drapes were tightly drawn. Several loud raps brought a timid, pale-faced little girl of perhaps nine or ten years to the front door. On encountering a stranger with a foreign accent, she shook her head and quickly closed the door, bolting it from inside. Her distress and shame were palpable. "Daddy, is it true what they say about you at my school?"

FORGIVENESS AND THE MADNESS OF THE POSSIBLE

> Must one not maintain that an act of forgiveness, if there is such a thing, must forgive the unforgivable, and without condition?
> . . . Even if this radical purity can seem excessive, hyperbolic? Because if I say (as I think) forgiveness is mad, and that it must remain a madness of the impossible, this is certainly not to exclude or disqualify it. It is even, perhaps, the only thing that arrives, that surprises, like a revolution, the ordinary course of history, politics, and law.
> —Jacques Derrida

Of all the mandates of the South African TRC, the strong institutional support (via the presence of "briefers" and "comforters") to encourage—though not demand—victims to "forgive" those who maimed, tortured, and humiliated them or murdered their loved ones has been the most widely criticized and contested aspect of the Commission, both within and outside South Africa (see especially Wilson 2000, 2001; Hamber and Wilson 2002). Sally Engle Merry (2001) notes that the strongly Christian conception of forgiveness that infuses TRC proceedings is oddly lacking in the equally Christian obligation to repent and to do penance for evil acts.[16] Nader (1995) worries, with reason, about the fusing of the globalization of Western Christian morality with a transnational human-rights discourse that produces unstable truces that are vulnerable to outbreaks of collective retaliatory rage toward unpunished aggressors, as the history of the Balkans and Central Africa indicate.

Father Michael Lapsley, an Anglican priest, criticized the TRC on these grounds, accusing it of imposing a "cheap theology" of forgiveness. Although he accepted the conditional amnesty process of the TRC "on principle and for the sake of the greater good of South Africa," Lapsley expressed resentment toward those who expected him to show a spirit of uncomplicated, unconditional, "Christian" forgiveness. Father Lapsley said that his speeches and homilies were often misheard by white South Africans and by Americans, who would come up to thank him for being "so forgiving" toward the apartheid operatives who had tried to kill him, when he never once mentioned forgiveness.

Albie Sachs (personal communication, 1998; see also Sachs 2000) told me about a situation in which he refused to embrace the national ethos of unconditional forgiveness, which had become a kind of civic duty. Soon after returning from exile in Mozambique, Albie was enjoying an evening out at a jazz bar, Rosie's and All That Jazz, on Cape Town's beautiful waterfront. He was approached by a heavyset white man, who asked in thickly Afrikaner-accented English: "Are you Albie Sachs?" "I am," Albie replied brusquely, and tried to move past him. But the large man blocked his way in the crowded room. "*Verskoon my*" ("Forgive me"), he said huskily in Afrikaans, staring at Albie's empty sleeve. His voice was almost drowned out by the drummers. Sachs said nothing. The man repeated more loudly, "Forgive me." Albie brushed him aside, saying in a broken Afrikaans mixed with English and Portuguese, "This lovely club is your forgiveness." And they parted company, both dissatisfied. Later, Albie thought of the things he might have said: "Don't ask *me* for forgiveness. I was a volunteer in the struggle. I chose my fate. What about the millions of Black South Africans who had no choice but to suffer and die under apartheid? Why not ask *them* for forgiveness?" Still later, when I met with Albie in 1998, he conceded: "What I probably *should* have done was to put my one good arm around the man, give him a half bear hug, and accept his forgiveness. But I just wasn't ready to do that."

Failures to forgive are easy to understand. The remorselessness of so many deeply implicated perpetrators is more difficult to accept. In observing the amnesty proceedings in Cape Town between January and March in 1998, I was struck by the dry, banal, legalistic questioning and the emotionally and morally stunted testimonies given by tanned, relaxed, legally protected South African security police officers, such as the four officers who were implicated in the kidnapping, torture, murder, and burning of comrade Sizwe Kondile in 1981. Kondile's case involved some of the top brass of the old Police Security Forces.

The four former Eastern Security Cape security police who applied for amnesty for crimes, including thirteen counts of murder, admitted that they had met to compare notes and refresh each others' memories. Still, their recitations of the "facts" diverged in many ways. Kondile had been severely tortured at Jeffreys Bay police station, where he was held incommunicado under the state's Terrorism Act. Police officer Raath had bragged to another operative that they had really taught Kondile a lesson: "his brain was splattered." When the policemen were done with him, they carried Kondile's semiconscious body to a secluded spot in the country where the officers held a *braii*—an Afrikaner family-style picnic. They purchased *vous* (sausages) and other meats, cold beer, brandy, and sodas. They built a bonfire and cooked the meats, offering some to Kondile, who was tied up nearby. At some point during the *braii*, the police shot and dragged Kondile's body to the fire, where he was burned, while the picnickers passed around drinks (and jokes).

The amnesty applications disagreed on many details, such as who was present at the *braii* murder of comrade Kondile. Police officer Raath startled the commissioners at one point by saying, "I don't know these other people, but Dirk Coetzee and I were clearly at the same *party*." Asked to repeat his answer, an uncomfortable and embarrassed Raath tried to recover: "I mean, we were not at the same *place*." However, all four amnesty petitioners agreed on the motive for the execution: Kondile was a dangerous and untrustworthy double agent. After the police discovered a letter revealing that Kondile was clearly double-crossing them by passing on privileged information to ANC comrades across the border, they decided that they had to execute him. They faked his release from jail and abducted him to the border town of Kmonatipoort, where they murdered him and burned his body to hide the evidence. Adding insult to injury, the four colluding police officers described the victim in the presence of Kondile's grieving family members, as a despicable *askary*, a police informer: "At first he resisted, but then Kondile gave us a lot of useful information."

At some moments during these painful amnesty hearings, the bloodless recitation of the tortures and defamation of character seemed only to rub salt in the wounds of the survivors who sat in front-row seats marked "Family Members." As the police began to describe the *braii* burning of her son, Charity Kondile had to be borne up on either side by her surviving adult children. As she walked unsteadily out of the room, she stated, "I will *never* forgive them."

BYSTANDERS: APATHY AND INDIFFERENCE

An intriguing moment took place during the TRC process when an unnamed Indian–South African woman applied for amnesty for "apathy." She noted that all individuals "should be held accountable by history for our lack of necessary action in times of crisis. . . . In exercising apathy rather than commitment we allowed others to sacrifice their lives for the sake of our freedom and an increase in our standard of living." Unfortunately, though perhaps necessarily, the petition was rejected by the TRC as falling outside its brief. Apathy was not a punishable crime and had no clear political intent. Therefore, it could not be considered for official pardon. As Jackie Rose (2002) noted in her discussion of this case, the TRC lost a crucial opportunity to explore the real extent of social and self-transformation in the new South Africa.

The TRC will apparently stand or fall on the extent to which it has been able to touch the lives of ordinary South Africans, forcing them to reconsider their roles during the apartheid years. Obviously, apartheid could not have survived without the consent of a large number of ordinary bystanders: English-speaking whites, as well as Afrikaners, Jews, Hindus, Moslems, and Christians—all those who were enriched and enabled by the systematic violence against the majority population of black South Africans. Daniel Goldhagen (1996) called these ordinary South African beneficiaries of apartheid the necessary passive executioners: they were good enough within the context of their contained and constricted lives.

Among these bystanders was Jack Swart, the rather soft-spoken, gentle Afrikaner man who was Nelson Mandela's guard, personal assistant, cook, and bottle washer at Victor Verster in Paarl, Mr. Madiba's (the Mandela clan name) last prison, where he was kept under a kind of house arrest. A career prison police officer who enjoyed cooking, Swart's duties included preparing the future president of South Africa for his anticipated release. Swart instructed Mandela in how to dress, how to swim a dog paddle in the small private pool attached to the ranch house in a secluded part of the prison grounds, and how to use such innovations as the computer, the remote control, and the microwave oven. During my two visits with him, the stiff but amiable prison guard reminisced about Victor Verster's most celebrated prisoner and about Nelson Mandela's enjoyment of brown rice and lasagna, which were novelties to him.

Swart said he was amazed to find that Mandela was such an easy inmate and that the prisoner didn't have the look or demeanor of a terrorist. But the guard never once questioned the absolute right of the apartheid state to deny Mandela his freedom for twenty-seven years. Life had its little ironies, he seemed to suggest. Moreover, Jack Swart clearly had an agenda in meeting with me. Toward the end of my first visit to his neat little stucco home on the grounds of Victor Verster prison, during which I had jotted down a few of Madiba's favorite recipes, including one for a creamy chicken and mushroom pasta, Jack asked if I might want to work as his literary agent. He hoped that a market might exist—and some royalties—in peddling a

10.   Captain Jack Swart, Nelson Mandela's cook, at his
home on the grounds of Victor Verster Prison, 1996.
(Nancy Scheper-Hughes)

collection of recipes under the title, proposed without a hit of irony: *The
Nelson Mandela Prison Cook Book.*

When I confronted Albie Sachs with this story, his reply was "even Jack
Swart, in his own little way, is part of the transformation of South Africa.
Can't you see that he is recognizing that the tables have been changed and
he is hoping that he can benefit from his 'accidental' proximity to his former prisoner? That strikes me as quite wonderful!"

Similarly, when Larry King (*Larry King Live*, CNN, May 16, 2000) asked
Mandela whether he hated his former prison captors, the president answered, "No, because you must take into account that all promotions were
dependent on pretending a show of support for apartheid, and many times
this was a false front. I know from my own experiences with prison wardens

that many good people put on a false attitude to get a promotion, not because they believed in it. Some of the wardens became our friends, and they would never make us do anything that was beneath our dignity."

In their statements, both Albie Sachs and Nelson Mandela (who suffered atrociously under apartheid) come close to exonerating the complicit bystander or the obedient civil servant who was "just" carrying out state's orders (*Eichmann in Jerusalem*, for example) on the same grounds that Hannah Arendt (and others) have used to condemn them—that the operatives were small and limited human beings, lacking moral vision, who were concerned only with their own and their family's well-being. Mandela accepts this argument as reason enough for his prison warders to follow state's orders, an amazing position for him to take. His position is a dramatic embodiment of the African value of *umbuntu* (we are who we are by virtue of a shared humanity, with all the limitations as well as the transcendent capabilities). In other words, Mandela was able to empathize with his jailers.

THE SPIRIT MOVES

I once reminded Albie Sachs of his own "failure" to accept the remorse of the Afrikaner stranger who appeared unbidden at Rosie's café. Sachs smiled ruefully. But Albie's own day of final reckoning, brought about by the machinations of the TRC, did finally come about. He told me the following story:

> In February 1999 I received a call in my chambers in Johannesburg. "Judge Sachs, a man named Henry is here to see you. He says he was involved in an assassination attempt and would you be willing to see him?" So, I went out to the reception area and standing next to my secretary was Henry, a little man, shorter than myself. Younger, leaner. I looked at him; he looked at me. We walked together down the hall to my chambers—he with a tight, military gait, me with my looser judicial ambulatory style. Henry told me that he had come from a very decent family, God-fearing. He joined the army at a young age and had advanced thorough the ranks rapidly. He was quite proud of that. He was chosen for an elite corps involved with planning the logistics for commando-like attacks on enemy targets, of which I had been one. He had photographed my car, planned where the bomb should be placed. Then the plan was postponed and he had a falling out with his superior about it. Finally, he read about the attack on my life he had planned in the newspapers. By then he was involved in many other "operations" in Mozambique that were designed to create mayhem. President Botha fi-

nally called it off. I was curious to know more, but on the other hand I wanted to leave all the detailed questioning to the TRC.

We talked and talked. Henry told me about his life since leaving the army. He was full of grievances and complaints. He had been asked to leave the army and was given a "golden handshake" of 150,000 rand (then about $30,000) which he considered grossly inadequate and which he had invested in some murky arms importation deal that had gone bankrupt. He said that he, too, had been injured during duty in his foot (suggesting, perhaps, that we were both victims of physical injury). Finally, Henry remarked at how unfair the world was. Here I was now ["the terrorist"] sitting in [the high] Court, honored and respected, paid a handsome salary, and here was he, after being so faithful to the old government, he who had fought so hard to preserve what he was told was justice and civilized values, now discarded, unemployed, and out in the cold. He was now angry at the generals and the other higher ups who had used him. Unbelievably, he was looking to *me* for sympathy and validation of his view that life was terribly unfair. Meanwhile, I looked at him wondering just who this man was who had tried to kill me. He didn't know me. He didn't seem to hate me, then or now. At the time of the bombing the one thing I could not stand was the idea that someone who did not know me at all was willing to extinguish me. And here it was confirmed. There was no personal connection, no relation. I was simply in the way of the old state. Perhaps he was thinking along similar lines about me.

We were both reluctant to end the conversation. But when the time came I took the initiative. "Henry," I said. "Normally when people leave my chambers I shake hands with them." I resisted making a cheap joke [waving his empty shirt sleeve]: "But you *know* why I can't shake hands with you." Instead I said: "I can't shake hands with you *now*, but if you go to the TRC and tell them everything that you know, then afterwards I will shake your hand." Henry walked away, but this time, he didn't have that smart soldier stride, instead he looked like a soldier in retreat, his shoulders were hunched over, he had a defeated, downhearted, disconsolate air.

About a year later, at a party given by the producer of a new South African soap opera, Sachs heard his name being called: "Albie!" Then louder: "Albie." Sachs said that he turned to see a familiar face: "Henry! It's you!" "Yes." So the two men went to a corner of the room, where Henry started talking very rapidly. "I wrote to the TRC and I told them everything I knew. And then Bobby, Sue, and Farouk came to question me." "These were *my* ANC friends," said Albie. "I was in exile with them, and now suddenly Henry was their friend, on a first-name basis with them. I could tell that he had told the truth. So I repeated to him my promise, and I shook his hand, and Henry went away bouncy and elated. But I nearly fainted."

Like Albie Sachs, Dawie Ackerman also had to confront the people who had done him harm. Ackerman faced the young men who killed his wife in the St. James Church massacre when he appeared at the TRC, intending initially to contest their petition for amnesty. But toward the end of the amnesty proceedings Dawie was transformed. In making a final statement before the amnesty panel, Dawie directly confronted the young men who killed his wife. He told the four young men how he had had to step over dead bodies to get to Marita, his wife of more than twenty years, who was still sitting upright in her front-row pew. He told them that he was hoping against hope that Marita might just be shell-shocked but still alive, until he finally crossed that endless expanse of space and reached for her, but just as he touched her back, her body rolled over and fell with a dull thud to the floor, her special Sunday clothes splattered with blood. Dawie continued, his composure broken, his voice cracking with the tears that, he said, had been a very long time—five years—in coming:

> I never cried since I lost my wife other than to have silent cries. I've never had an emotional outburst till now. When . . . when Mr. Makoma here [the young man who was seventeen at the time he took part in the church attack] was testifying, he talked about his own tortures in prison, and that he was suicidal at times, but that he never once cried. I thought to myself—and I passed you [a TRC counselor] a note, asking you to please bring your cross-examination to an end. Because . . . what are we doing here? The truth . . . the truth . . . yes. But when I looked at the way Mr. Makoma answered and saw all his anger . . . I thought, what on earth are we doing? *He* cannot be reconciled.

At this point in his statement, weeping and emotionally overwrought, Dawie Ackerman asked the three young amnesty applicants to turn their heads and face him directly. Amazingly, their heads (which had been bowed to the floor) snapped up to attention, and they looked directly at Dawie, who said, "This is the first opportunity we have had to look each other in the eye while talking. I want to ask Mr. Makoma, who actually entered the Church, a question. . . . My . . . my wife was sitting at the door when you came in. [Dawie weeps, and the words seem to be dragged from the roots of his shaking body]. She was wearing a long blue coat. *Please, can you remember if you shot her?*"

Makoma looked up at Dawie terrified, as though seeing Hamlet's father's ghost. He bit his lower lip and slowly shook his head. No, he could not remember—not Marita nor her long, blue coat. But all three young men apologized to Dawie. Makoma, the most affected, said, "We are truly sorry for what we have done. But it was not intentional. Although people died we did not do that out of our own will. It was the situation in South Africa we were living under. And now we are asking you please, do forgive us."

Dawie Ackerman did so by withdrawing his carefully prepared legal objections to the amnesty process. Immediately after the hearing, Dawie and several other survivors, including Bishop Reteif, withdrew to a smaller room that the TRC arranged for them, where, in private, they met with the young militants, each of whom walked around the table addressing each survivor in turn, shaking hands, and expressing messages of condolence. Brian Smart, a survivor of St. James, was impressed by the ages of the young militants: "They were only seventeen years old, and I could relate to that. When I was eighteen I was in the South Africa Air Force and sent out in defense of the realm, if you like. The only difference between myself and them was that I was operating under controlled military orders. So a massacre like this one would not have happened. In their case the command structure was very weak and, unfortunately, they had the normal soldier's ability to kill, just as I had."

Bishop Reteif, who was not in the church until moments after the massacre took place, and who suffered a great deal of pastoral survivor guilt, originally opposed amnesty for the PAC "terrorists." His initial response to the massacre was to heroize the South African police and to demonize the PAC youth as the "instruments" of evil forces. After the TRC hearings, the bishop was contrite and conscious of the "blindness" of his evangelical church to the suffering caused by apartheid and to the ways that his congregation had benefited from the suffering of the majority population. He told me, "Finally, I understood why it [the TRC] was necessary."

As for Linda and Peter Biehl, their extraordinary faith in their daughter's "meaningful death" allowed them to "move forward," as Peter said in his down-to-earth Midwestern style. For them, moving forward meant not only facing, but embracing, their daughter's killers and devoting the remainder of their lives to human-rights and community-development work in the townships surrounding Cape Town, especially Guguletu, where Amy was killed and where three of the young men convicted in her death—Easy Nofemela, Mangesi, and Ntobeko Peni—have returned to live since they were granted amnesty by the TRC.

In accepting amnesty for the killers of their loved ones, Albie Sachs, the Biehls, Jeanette Fourie, and Dawie Ackerman—along with a multitude of black South Africans who have done the same—have allowed their own per-

11. Easy Nofemela, one of the killers of Amy
Biehl, at home in Guguletu township, Cape Town,
1999, after release from prison following the Truth
and Reconciliation Commission. (Nancy Scheper-
Hughes)

sonal tragedies to serve the process of national healing and reconciliation. This transcendent goal has allowed them to find some meaning, some peace, some beauty even, in the original tragedy and the mayhem it created. To be sure, however, some, like young Makoma, remain bitter and unreconciled, feeling abandoned by their command structure and humiliated before their comrades or peers. The very structure of the TRC pathologized and individualized the political struggle, turning all those who participated in the proceedings into either victims or perpetrators. Political resistance was a residual category.

After his TRC amnesty hearing, Makoma, then serving a twenty-year sentence for his part in the St. James Church massacre, returned to Polsmor prison to await the result of his amnesty petition, which was eventually accepted. But though Dawie Ackerman, Bishop Reteif, and other church members seem to have experienced a personal and collective catharsis through the TRC process, Makoma did not find any such relief. During a prison visit that was arranged between Makoma and Leisel, Dawie Ackerman's daughter, she asked Makoma how he *felt* during his amnesty hearings when he was shown the graphic police photos "of all the bodies of the people and all the blood" of those he had killed. Makoma replied to the young woman whose mother he had killed:

> Yah, I remember seeing that and I had bad feelings then. It *was* bad. But, no matter how I feel now, at this time, or at this moment, about what I did then was bad, there is nothing which I can do. Those people are dead. Why ask me how I feel about that? How I feel cannot change anything, cannot bring them back to life.

As a disciplined revolutionary, Makoma felt that these questions (about his "feelings") were unseemly and beside the point. Dead is dead; what happened cannot be undone.

But Ntobeko Peni and Easy Nofemela, who petitioned for and received amnesty for their role in the killing of Amy Biehl, felt differently about the TRC. With great difficulty, I arranged to meet with the young men in their shacks in a muddy section of Guguletu in July 1999.

At first, I faced a wall of seething silence. Finally, Ntobeko explained that he did not believe in or trust the TRC, which he described as "an arm of the ANC" and no friend of their organization, the PAC. But, he said, he decided to "confess" anyway because of the "heaviness" in his heart. Yet, the confession had not helped, and since he had received amnesty and returned home to live in Guguletu, his days had been very dark. Ntobeko said that he could not sleep. He could not romance his girlfriend. He could not work. He could not study. He hid from people. He was angry and full of shame. Then he said, "I thought to myself that there might be one thing that could make me better. I wanted to tell that Mr. Biehl one to his face that I did not take the death of his daughter lightly. That this thing has weighed heavily on me. And I wanted him to know that he is a hero father to me. So I thought that I would ask you to help me, to get that Peter Biehl to listen to me and to really forgive me. That would be good, as good as bread."

I arranged for Peter Biehl to come to the home of Ntobeko Peni and accompanied him to the meeting. Initially, Peter responded with anger at my

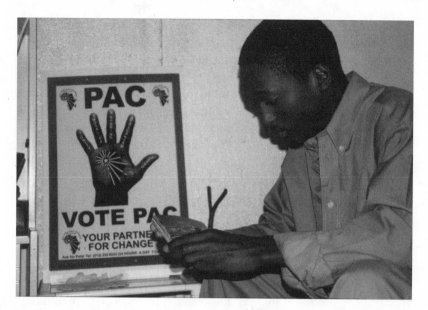

12.   Ntobeko Peni, one of Amy Biehl's killers, in his shack in Guguletu township, Cape Town, 1999. (Nancy Scheper-Hughes)

suggestion. Hadn't he suffered enough? Then he called Linda Biehl, who was back at their home in Southern California, and she urged Peter to meet with the boys because maybe (she said) Amy was wanting this meeting to happen. After an initially painful standoff between Peter Biehl and Ntobeko, Easy Nofemela, and several of their comrades, the boys tried to explain their political position to Peter along with their sense of sadness over a death, they now said, should never have happened. They told Peter about the youth group they had started in Gugs, and they showed us photos of the hikes they took with the young people up and around Table Mountain. Peter began to listen attentively, and before the meeting had ended, he had invited the two boys to work for the Amy Biehl Foundation. After shaking their heads in disbelief, they accepted.

The boys were apprenticed as welders and helped Peter Biehl (who died in 2001) organize the distribution and sale of "Amy's Bread" out of the large communal bakery the Biehls helped establish in the community. Linda Biehl told me that she is proud that Easy and Ntobeko shyly call her "Mama," a term of respect that Xhosa youth use for all mature women. "It may sound strange," she once said, "but I feel so close to Amy when I am holding the hand of the young man who killed her." Not only Ntobeko, but

13.   Hope and optimism despite present difficulties: the late Peter Biehl with Easy Nofemela and Ntobeko Peni, two of his daughter's killers, Guguletu township, Cape Town, 1999. (Nancy Scheper-Hughes)

Linda, too, refers to the "great weight" that has been lifted from her, even if her forgiveness will never fill her permanent void and sadness.

HOPE AND OPTIMISM DESPITE PRESENT DIFFICULTIES

The TRC process opened up new social spaces in which conversations and interactions that were once unthinkable could take place. The unlikely encounters between perpetrators and victims who find that they are able to empathize with each other's situation are one wholly unanticipated effect of the TRC, and they appear to be unique in the history of such formal approaches to reconciliation. Pumla Gobodo-Madikizela (2003), whom I interviewed at her TRC office in downtown Cape Town in 2001, was surprised by the empathy she was able to feel (and express) toward Eugene de Kock, the merciless apartheid killer known to South Africans as "Prime Evil." Once she addressed de Kock by his Christian name, Eugene, she realized that even this serial killer was a human being who suffered and repented and who accepted his life sentence in prison, asking only that he be transferred to a cell closer to "common" Black prisoners, because he could no longer tolerate the inane racist talk of the die-hard Afrikaners with whom he was imprisoned.

LESSONS AND LEGACY OF THE TRC

The South African TRC was a hybrid institution; it was neither a court of law nor guerrilla theater but shared aspects of both. It was like no other truth commission. It was videotaped and televised, and its proceedings had almost complete transparency. The TRC tried experiments and innovations. For example, the Commission offered witnesses and survivors of human-rights atrocities the support of "comforters," people who were comparable to the traditional "doulas" who serve laboring mothers. Unlike regular court hearings, the TRC hearings encouraged the expression of strong emotions, led by Archbishop Tutu, who set an example to a country that thought it had lost the ability to feel anything. The TRC provided a national theater on a large stage where dialogue, difference, and dignity were displayed and celebrated. Consequently, the moral as well as the political climate of South Africa has changed. The transformation of knowledge into personal acknowledgment has reintegrated the aberrant actions inside a moral universe.

The idea of a truth commission provoked a national soul-searching that sometimes turned up in the oddest places. For example, an elderly Afrikaner couple with concerned looks on their faces approached me one day on the steps of St. George's Cathedral in Cape Town (the Anglican church of Archbishop Tutu). Where could they find "the Bishop," they asked me. When I said he was away, they looked crestfallen. I asked why they wanted to see him. "To confess to the Truth Commission," they said. "You see, we realize now that we did not treat Black people very well, and now we want to make a fresh start." I explained that the TRC was a very formal process "with lawyers and official documents" and that it was meant for murderers and torturers, not for ordinary people like them who could have behaved better.

The real effects of the TRC are and will continue to be felt in such small ripples, in community and church meetings where people can now talk about what happened to them, how they behaved, and how they might begin to set the record straight. Long after the formal TRC has disbanded and all the grief counselors have returned to business as usual, a multitude of little TRCs will still be needed to help ordinary people deal with the many perversions and horrors of apartheid.

I will end with the story of Hennie's redemption. Hennie was, at the time I first knew him, an Afrikaner security guard for the University of Cape

Town. He frequently dropped by our home in 1993 and 1994 and I feared at the time that either he was a spy or he had a special fondness for one of our adult daughters. But he seemed genuinely curious and well-intentioned. I ran into Hennie again in Cape Town in 1996 during the spontaneous celebration of South Africa's winning the All-Africa Soccer Cup that year. Hennie was simply beside himself with excitement. He tried to whirl me around in the street as he struggled in his limited English to find just the right words to express the magnitude of the moment. "Did you see the game?" he asked. I did, I said, and on a big screen at the new and decidedly integrated Manneberg Pub in downtown Cape Town . "*Both* goals?" he probed. "I did," I replied.

"And did you see our President [Mandela] right there out on the field? Do you know what this means for us?" And without waiting for an answer, Hennie continued: "It means we white people are not all, one hundred percent bad. And God is willing to forgive us. Imagine—that He would give *us*, of all people, such great heroes! It is a sign that we are going in a good way now. We are not hated any more. Before, in the old South Africa, it was like we were Fat Elvis—sick, disgusting, bloated, ugly. And now, in the new, we are like skinny Elvis—young, handsome, strong. In the new South Africa, we have all been reborn."

In his awkward way, Hennie invoked the "miracle of rebirth that saves the world," to which Hannah Arendt referred in *The Human Condition*. Even in Hennie the Boer, we can see the emergence of new men and women made possible through hope and optimism. Collectively, the narratives of TRC participants and others illustrate history's working itself out as grace, not divine grace but the human grace of those white South Africans who have not turned their backs and those millions of black South Africans who have not raised their hands in righteous anger and vengeance and who are both willing to take a chance on the birth of a new nation, a new covenant.

NOTES

This chapter was completed while I was a 2003 summer fellow at the School of American Research in Santa Fe. Grants from the Harry Frank Guggenheim Foundation and the Open Society Foundation made possible return field trips to South Africa in 1997, 1998, and 2000. I dedicate this chapter to the late Peter Biehl, whose extraordinary grace and compassion toward his daughter's township killers moved a divided nation closer to peacemaking and to social justice.

1. Despite the absence of an anthropological theory of remorse, a large and substantial literature is available on the theology (see, for example, Thomas Aquinas [1932] on conscientia), the psychology/psychoanalysis (see Freud's "Mourning and

Melancholia" [1917] and "Ego and the Id" [1923]), and the moral philosophy (see Kierkegaard 1980a and 1980b) of remorse. *Remorse and Reparation*, edited by Murray Cox (1999), is a good place to begin.

2. Remorse is a concept that is part of a larger semantic network that includes guilt, shame, regret, repentance, reparation, and more distantly, (self-)accusation, culpability, punishment, and justice. Collectively, the terms refer to the aftermaths of one human being's intentional (or not) grievous harm to another. The etymology of *remorse* (Latin, *re-* and *morde*) includes the meanings "to bite," "to sting," "to attack again." Perhaps a good vernacular translation is "what goes around comes around." One is attacked, bitten by the sting of one's own aggression. In this context, I think of the story of Eugene de Kock, South Africa's notorious organizer of death squads at Vlakplas, the apartheid government's killing farm. In a private interview in his prison, de Kock told Pumla Gobodo-Madikizela (2003), a member of the Truth and Reconciliation Commission, that following one killing spree in particular. he could not remove the stink from his body despite several showers. The taint of death also remained on his laundered clothing. All he could do was discard his clothing and try to mask the stench of his own flesh. De Kock was suffering from unconscious *re-morde*, stung by as-yet-unacknowledged remorse.

3. In his anthropological study of serial killers, *Hunting Humans*, the Canadian anthropologist Elliot Leyton describes a complex of psychopathological emotions that are not far from those in Renato Rosaldo's depiction of Ilongot headhunters. This observation returns psychological anthropology to a very uncomfortable space, the early anthropological notion that behavior that may be considered mentally deranged behavior in one society (our own, say) may be expected and rewarded behavior in another (the Ilongot, say).

4. At the closed conference "Dealing with the Past" in the Western Cape in early 1994, which I was privileged to attend and from which emerged the shape that the South African truth commission would take, attendees expressed concern about the problem of white South African "denial" and the need to make explicit, transparent, and public the atrocities committed by apartheid in their name.

5. Satire was once described as tragedy plus time. In an interview with the South African playwright and humorist Pieter-Dirk Uys, he said that apartheid's culture of death didn't allow South Africans the luxury of satire: "We just had to show the way it was, the blood still fresh and slippery on our hands. . . . For so many years I was blessed with a government that had absolutely no sense of humor. . . . It didn't take much to make them madder. All one had to do was to repeat what they had said. The South African government wrote my script and that is why I resented paying taxes; I called it royalties. . . . How can you take seriously a person who won't sit next to another person because of their race, creed, or color? Racism is absurd. Absurdity can kill when it loses its label and becomes a way of life. Laughter controls the madness of humans and makes them human again."

6. This degree of social alienation did not exist between white and mixed-race ("Colored") Capetonians, insofar as this part of Africa, especially the Boland (farm) region, was a special labor reserve for colored workers during the apartheid years. I treat the special dilemma of the mixed-race population elsewhere (Scheper-Hughes 2006).

7. In the fertile valley of Franschhoek, the small population of white farmers had forced Colored residents out of the spectacularly beautiful central village under the Group Areas Act in the late 1960s. More than a hundred Colored farmers and home-

owners were forced to sell their sturdy Cape Dutch homes and some of the country's most valuable real estate to white Afrikaners for a pittance. The Group Areas Act was nothing more than a huge real-estate swindle. To date, only seventeen of these households have been able to locate clear titles to their original properties, and even for these people, restitution is uncertain. Achieving restitution is certain to take a very long time and will entail protracted legal struggles, for which most white families in central Franschhoek are preparing themselves.

8. Any social scientist working in South Africa has to confront the ambiguities and legacies of European colonial and Afrikaner apartheid classifications of race and culture. Under apartheid (1948–94), racial classifications were used to separate people into absolute categories of difference. The apartheid state constructed and enforced—with violence—a cockamamie system of group identities. Over time, the state revised its official categories and modernized its arguments to marshal national and international support for its racist policies. The Population Registration Act of 1950, which was the backbone of the apartheid system, was amended fifteen times between 1956 and 1986 (West 1988: 102). Section 1 of the act established three basic racial classifications: Black, Colored, and White. A Black (previously "Native" or Bantu) was defined as a person "who is, or who is generally accepted as, a member of any aboriginal race or tribe of Africa." A White person was defined (in extremely hedged-in language) as "a person who is (a) in appearance obviously a White person, and who is *not* generally accepted as a Coloured person; or (b) is generally accepted as a White person and is not in appearance obviously not a White person" (101). Later clauses deleted those formerly classified as White who by their "habits, education, speech, deportment, and demeanor" or by their residence or their employment or by virtue of their social mixing were recognized and accepted by another racial group. This clause referred to "race traitors" who married into another racial group and therefore had to live in non-White communities. It also covered South African entertainers like Johnny Clegg, the "White Zulu," who used Zulu dress, language, dance, and affect in his stage performances. Finally, the White category excluded "those who were once classified as White but who voluntarily confess that they are by descent a Black or a Coloured person, unless it is proven that this admission is patently false." Coloreds were defined under apartheid as the racial population formed by historical mixing of the indigenous Khoi-San peoples and the early European settlers: the Dutch, but also the English, Portuguese, and Germans. Later, Coloreds mixed with African Bantu groups and Malay peoples who were brought to the Cape Colony as slaves. But the official legal category of "Coloured" in the Population Registration Act was simply a residual one. A Colored person was a "person who is *not* a White person or a *Black*." These racial classifications, reinforced by neighborhood and residential apartheid, have not been destroyed by political democratization or by the new political ideology of the rainbow nation. Thus, the observer is left with the everyday reality of simultaneously contested and claimed deeply racialized social self-identities. Political correctness in South Africa demands that scare quotes be used to destabilize the races—so that "Black," "Bantu," "Colored," and "White" convey the social reality within the unfinished revolution.

9. By way of comparison with views of race in South Africa, see V. S. Naipaul (1989) for a searing and disturbing portrait of whites and white racism in the "new" American South.

10. South Africa today is something of a terminological land mine. One must be painfully conscious of the contested nature of almost every social category—from

Xhosa to gay to Zionist Christian to Cape Colored to Boer. One refers politely, for example, to "so-called" Coloreds or even more awkwardly to "those people who were formerly classified as Colored." Sometimes one offers a double qualifier, simultaneously making the sign for quotation marks and using "so-called"; for example, one might refer to an "Indian [supply air quotes] so-called Colored person." The indeterminacy of racial labels signifies both language and identity in motion and represents a fierce reaction against the ways that ethnicity and race have been frozen in an essentialist discourse. Still, some South African social identities are understood as "more real" (or less questionable) than others. Rarely does one hear reference to "so-called whites," for example. "White" remains an unmarked and uncontested category.

11. Raised in an immigrant Eastern European section of New York City, I never thought much about being "white" at all until, when I was a civil-rights worker in Selma, Alabama, in the late 1960s, several black Student Nonviolent Coordination Committee (SNCC) freedom workers "kidnapped" me and another "white" field worker for a night of interrogation and "clarification of thought." Our "captors" repeatedly asked us to look at our pale white faces in a hand mirror and to repeat "White is ugly, white is deadly." One black SNCC worker taunted, "Girl, you are so white you are whiter than the underbelly of a dead fish. Your white flesh makes my black skin crawl . . . " and so on. Although I later tried to politicize the trauma, I will probably, like a great many other white Euro-Americans, die a premature death from skin cancer due to the interminable quest for an acceptable degree of brownness. Today in the United States, "white" is an amorphous identity peg that allows for multiple exceptions: white but lesbian, white but Marxist, white but feminist; white but Latino, white but Jewish, and so on. Clearly, the way to soften and destigmatize "whiteness" in America is by way of disqualification and the addition of a mediating (and previously stigmatized) counteridentity. This approach allows a great many whites to join the more socially acceptable ranks of the formerly despised, victimized, and oppressed "communities of suffering" that include women, gays, and the disabled as well as the older racial/ethnic categories. Years after my SNCC experience, I had another reminder of my whiteness, this time in South Africa. While walking down a sun-splashed street in the mixed university student community of Mowbray on a brilliant Saturday morning in 1993, I smiled up at the pleasant face of a tall young black student. "Die, settler!" the young man whispered conspiratorially in my ear as he passed by. Crushed, I had to see myself as the young African must have: as a modern day Madam Von Trapp in a blowzy, flowered pink dress with a big "settler" lace collar, a style then in fashion among whites. I added coiled braids around my ears, reminiscent of Woody Allen's unforgettable film sequence in which he is transformed in his mind's eye into an orthodox Jew complete with earlocks at the dinner table of his WASP girlfriend's family.

12. This view of "irreversible" deeds calls to mind a personal anecdote. As a small girl in training for my first confession before Holy Communion, I was impressed by the following story a nun told to our catechism class: An old woman went to her priest to ask for forgiveness for a sin of gossip that had harmed the reputation of a neighbor. The priest accepted the woman's sincere expression of remorse, gave her conditional absolution, told her to mend her ways, and gave her the following penance. He ordered the old woman to climb the belfry of the parish church, where she was to cut a small hole in a pillow and shake the feathers loose onto the streets below. Then she was to go about the village collecting the feathers until she had enough to sew back into the pillow. "But Father," the woman protested, "that would

be impossible!" "And, so too," the good priest replied sadly, "is it impossible to undo the damage caused by malicious acts."

13. Perhaps my obvious anxiety about the all-too-human capacity for "making meaning" out of untold suffering has its origins in my long-term immersion in the sugar-plantation zone of Northeast Brazil, where mothers struggle daily to make sense of the useless suffering and unnecessary deaths of a multitude of angel babies, sacrificed to hunger and thirst, which medical people fancily call protein-calorie malnutrition and dehydration. I have long maintained that these deaths, too, are political deaths: brave little unknown Brazilian soldiers lying in their unmarked graves. The women of the hillside shantytown appropriately named O Cruzeiro, Crucifix Hill, explained their infants' deaths not only as meaningful but in many cases as necessary. "Why do so many infants die on the Alto do Cruzeiro?" Sister Juliana asked at a liberation-theology "base community" meeting, to which the women had a ready supply of answers: "God takes them to save their mothers from much pain and suffering"; "There is always a reason. If they lived, who knows, they might have grown up into thieves or murderers"; "They die because they themselves want to die"; "God takes them to punish us for the sins of the world"; "They fly up to heaven to decorate the throne of God and to entertain the Virgin Mother." I began to think of the little sacrificed angel babies, some of whom were said to have died "so that others—but especially their mothers—could live," in terms of Rene Giraud's notion of the ritual scapegoat, the one who dies (like Jesus) to relieve the community of unbearable tension and guilt.

14. See Jeremy Gordin, 1998, *A Long Night's Damage: Working for the Apartheid State* (Saxonwold: Contra Press).

15. The painful testimony of a Xhosa-speaking police collaborator, Ginotry Danaster, was a case in point. Danaster told the amnesty committee that he had helped interrogate and torture Sizwe Kondile, an ANC militant, during the period that Kondile was held in police cells at Jeffreys Bay. Although Danaster retired from the security police, he testified that on three occasions, he was picked up and taken, against his will, to the security-police offices to help with interrogations. Danaster gave the most graphic of all the descriptions of the torture and *braii* burning of Kondile, to the hisses and anger of the victim's family and neighbors.

16. Elsewhere (Scheper-Hughes 1995a, 1998), I have argued that the institutions of popular justice that the urban townships invented during the apartheid struggle as an alternative to the state relied heavily on public rituals of confession, repentance, formal apologies, and forgiveness (in addition to the rough justice of the lash and in extreme cases, the necklace). Whether these institutions were Christian, postcolonial, or indigenous, or, most likely, a blend of the three (see Jeffreys 1952; Ngubane 1977; Berglund 1989) is beside the point. They are certainly recognized, embraced, and "owned" by the black South African population. Confessions, apologies, and public acts of forgiveness are not alien, externally imposed, or in any sense "strange" behaviors to Xhosas and other recent arrivals to the city and the Western Cape from the so-called rural homelands.

SOURCES

Aquinas, Thomas. 1932. *The Summa Theologica of St. Thomas Aquinas.* London: Burns, Oates and Washburn.

Arendt, Hannah. 1958. *The Human Condition.* Chicago: University of Chicago Press.

Benedict, Ruth. 1946. *Chrysanthemum and the Sword: Patterns of Japanese Culture.* Boston: Houghton Mifflin.

Berglund, Axel-Ivar. 1989. "Confessions of Guilt and Restoration of Health. Some Illustrative Zulu Examples." In *Culture, Experience and Pluralism: Essays on African Ideas of Illness and Healing,* Department of Anthropology, University of Upsala (Sweden: Upsala Studies in Cultural Anthropology).

Boonzaier, Emile, and John Sharp, eds. 1989. *South African Keywords.* Cape Town: David Philip.

Boraine, Alex, Janet Levy, and Ronael Scheffer, eds. 1994. *Dealing with the Past: Truth and Reconciliation in South Africa.* Cape Town: Institute for Democratic Alternatives in South Africa.

Borneman, John. 1997. *Settling Accounts: Violence, Justice, and Accountability in Postsocialist Europe.* Princeton, NJ: Princeton University Press.

Briggs, Jean. 1970. *Never in Anger: Portrait of an Eskimo Family.* Cambridge, MA: Harvard University Press.

Coetzee, J. M. 1999. *Disgrace.* New York: Viking.

Colvin, Christopher. 2005. "Political Violence." In *A Companion to Psychological Anthropology,* ed. Conerly Casey and Robert B. Edgerton (Malden, MA; Oxford: Blackwell Publishing), 453–68.

Cox, Murray. 1999. *Remorse and Reparation.* London: Jessica Kingsley.

Crapanzano, Vincent. 1985. *Waiting: The Whites of South Africa.* New York: Vintage.

Das, Veena. 1997. "Language and the Body: Transactions in the Construction of Pain." In *Social Suffering,* ed. Arthur Kleinman, Veena Das, and Margaret Lock (Berkeley: University of California Press).

Das, Veena, Arthur Kleinman, Margaret Lock, Mamphela Ramphele, and Pamela Reynolds, eds. 2001. *Remaking a World: Violence, Social Suffering and Recovery.* Berkeley: University of California Press.

Das, Veena, Arthur Kleinman, Mamphela Ramphele, and Pamela Reynolds, eds. 2000. *Violence and Subjectivity.* Berkeley: University of California Press.

Demos, John. 1996. "Shame and Guilt in Early New England." In *The Emotions: Social, Cultural, and Biological Determinations,* ed. R. Hare and W. G. Parrott (London: Sage).

Derrida, Jacques. 2001. *On Cosmopolitanism and Forgiveness.* London and New York: Routledge.

De Villiers, Marq. 1987. *White Tribe Dreaming: Apartheid's Bitter Roots as Witnessed by Eight Generations of an Afrikaner Family.* New York: Penguin.

Doi, T. 1973. *The Anatomy of Dependence.* Tokyo: Kodansha.

Douglas, Mary, ed. 1970. *Witchcraft Confessions and Accusations.* ASA Monographs. No. 9. London: Tavistock.

Elias, Norbert. 1978. *The Civilizing Process. The History of Manners,* vol. 1. Trans. Edmund Jephcott. New York: Urizen Books. Originally published as *Über den Prozeß der Zivilisation. Soziogenetische und psychogenetische Untersuchungen* (Oxford: Blackwell, 1976).

Foucault, Michel. 1986. *The Care of the Self.* New York: Vintage.

Freud, Sigmund. 1917. "Mourning and Melancholia." In *Standard Edition of the*

Complete Psychological Works of Sigmund Freud, vol. XIV (London: Hogarth Press), 237–58.

———. 1923. "Ego and the Id." In *Standard Edition of the Complete Psychological Works of Sigmund Freud,* vol. XIX (London: Hogarth Press), 3–66.

Giliomee, Hermann. 1994. "Afrikaner Identity and Franchise Contraction and Expansion in South Africa." Paper presented at the international conference Democracy and Difference, University of Cape Town, May 5–7.

Girard, Rene. 1987. "Generative Scapegoating." In *Violent Origins: Ritual Killing and Cultural Formation,* ed. Robert G. Hamerton-Kelly (Stanford, CA: Stanford University Press).

Gobodo-Madikizela, Pumla. 2002. *A Human Being Died That Night: A South African Story of Forgiveness.* Boston: Houghton-Mifflin.

Goffman, Erving. 1963. *Stigma: Note on the Management of Spoiled Identity.* Englewood Cliffs, NJ: Prentice-Hall.

Goldhagen, Daniel. 1996. *Hitler's Willing Executioners: Ordinary Germans and the Holocaust.* New York: Knopf.

Goodwin, June, and Ben Schiff. 1995. *Heart of Whiteness: Afrikaners Face Black Rule in the New South Africa.* New York: Scribner.

Gordimer, Nadine. 1998. *The House Gun.* Cape Town: David Philip.

Gordin, Jeremy. 1998. *A Long Night's Damage: Working for the Apartheid State.* Saxonwold: Contra Press.

Hamber, Brandon, and Richard Wilson. 2002. "Symbolic Closure through Memory, Reparation and Revenge in Post-Conflict Societies." *Journal of Human Rights* 1(1): 35–53.

Herman, Judith. 1994. *Trauma and Recovery.* New York: Basic Books.

Ignatieff, Michael. 1997. "Digging up the Dead." *The New Yorker,* November 10, 85–93.

Jeffreys, M. D. W. 1952. "Confessions by Africans." *Eastern Anthropologist* 6: 42–57.

Kierkegaard, Søren. 1980a. *The Concept of Anxiety.* Princeton, NJ: Princeton University Press.

———. 1980b, *The Sickness Unto Death.* Princeton, NJ: Princeton University Press.

Kleinman, Arthur, Veena Das, and Margaret Lock, eds. 1997. *Social Suffering.* Berkeley: University of California Press.

Krog, Antjie. 1998. *Country of My Skull.* Cape Town: Random House.

Lebra, T. 1971. "The Social Mechanism of Guilt and Shame: The Japanese Case." *Anthropology Quarterly* 44: 241–55.

Leighton, Elliot. 1989. *Hunting Humans: The Rise of the Modern Multiple Murderer.* London: Penguin Books.

Lévinas, Immanuel. 1986. "Useless Suffering." In *Face to Face with Lévinas,* ed. Richard A. Cohen (Albany, NY: State University of New York Press).

Lipsitz, George. 1998. *The Possessive Investment in Whiteness: How White People Profit from Identity Politics.* Philadelphia: Temple University Press.

Lurie, David, and Rian Malan. 1994. *Life in the Liberated Zone.* Rivonia, South Africa: William Waterman Publications.

Malan, Rian. 1990. *My Traitor's Heart: A South African Exile Returns to Face His Country, His Tribe, and His Conscience.* New York: Atlantic Monthly Press.

Marx, Anthony W. 1998. *Making Race and Nation: A Comparison of the U.S., South Africa, and Brazil.* Cambridge: Cambridge University Press.

Merry, Sally Engle. 2001. "Rights, Religion, and Community: Approaches to Violence against Women in the Context of Globalization." *Law and Society Review* 35: 39–88.

Minnow, Martha. 1998. *Between Vengeance and Forgiveness*. Boston: Beacon Press.

Nader, Laura. 1990. *Harmony Ideology: Justice and Control in a Mountain Zapotec Village*. Stanford: Stanford University Press.

———. 1995. "Reply to N. Scheper-Hughes, 'Primacy of the Ethical.' " *Current Anthropology* 36 (3): 426–27.

———. 1997. "Controlling Processes: Tracing the Components of Power." *Current Anthropology* 38: 711–37.

Naipaul, V. S. 1998. *A Turn in the South*. New York: Vintage.

Ngubane, Harriet. 1977. *Body and Mind in Zulu Medicine*. London: Academic Press.

Rosaldo, Michelle. 1980. *Knowledge and Passion*. Cambridge, MA: Harvard University Press.

———. 1983. "The Shame of the Headhunters and the Autonomy of the Self." *Ethos* 11(3): 135–51.

Rosaldo, Renato. 1980. *Ilongot Headhunting, 1883–1974*. Stanford: Stanford University Press.

———. 1983. "Grief and a Headhunter's Rage: On the Cultural Construction of Emotions." In *Text, Play and Story*, ed. S. Plathner and E. Bruner (Washington, D.C.: American Ethnological Society), 78–195.

Rose, Jackie. 2002. "Apathy and Accountability: The Challenge of South Africa's Truth and Reconciliation Commission to Intellectuals in the Modern World." In *The Public Intellectual*, ed. Helen Small (Malden, MA: Blackwell), 159–70.

Ross, Fiona. 2001. "Speech and Silence: Women's Testimonies in the First Five Weeks of Public Hearings of the South African Truth and Reconciliation Commission." In *Remaking a World: Violence, Social Suffering, and Recovery*, ed. Veena Das, Arthur Kleinman, Margaret Lock, Mamphela Ramphele, and Pamela Reynolds (Berkeley: University of California Press).

Sachs, Albie. 2000. *Soft Vengeance of a Freedom Fighter* (new updated edition, with a preface by Desmund Tutu and an introduction by Nancy Scheper-Hughes). Berkeley: University of California Press.

Scheper-Hughes, Nancy. 1993. *Death without Weeping: The Violence of Everyday Life in Brazil*. Berkeley: University of California Press.

———. 1994a. "The Last White Christmas: The Heidelberg Pub Massacre (South Africa)." *American Anthropologist* (December) 96 (4): 1–28.

———. 1994b "Dangerous Young Lions." Editorial *The New York Times*, November 4, Op-Ed page.

———. 1995a. "Who's the Killer? Popular Justice and Human Rights in a South African Squatter Camp." *Social Justice* 32(3) (Issue 61, Fall): 143–64.

———. 1995b. "Joe Slovo: A Believing Atheist." Letters to the Editor, *The New York Times*, January 7, (with Nathanael E. Hughes).

———. 1996. "Positively FW: An Interview with Deputy President F. W. de Klerk." *Democracy in Action* (July). Cape Town, South Africa.

———. 1998. "Undoing: Social Suffering and the Politics of Remorse in the New South Africa." *Social Justice* 25(4): 114–42.

———. 2000. "Ire in Ireland." *Ethnography* 1(2): 117–40.

———. 2006. "Mixed Feelings: Spoiled Identities in the New South Africa." In *Eth-*

nic Identity: Problems and Prospects for the 21st Century, ed. George De Vos and Lola Romanucci-Ross (Walnut Creek, CA: AltaMira Press).

Sharp, John. 1994. "Should We Condemn All Primordial Discourses? A Comparative Perspective on a South African Dilemma." Colloquium lecture to the Department of Social Anthropology, University of Cape Town, December 3.

Slovo, Joe. 1996. *Slovo: The Unfinished Autobiography.* London: Hodder and Sloughton.

Turnbull, Colin M. 1962. *The Lonely African.* New York: Simon and Schuster.

Weschler, Lawrence. 1990. *A Miracle, a Universe: Settling Accounts with Torturers.* New York: Viking.

———. 1993. "Getting Over." *The New Yorker,* April 5: 5–6.

West, Martin. 1988. "Confusing Categories: Population Groups, National States and Citizenship." In *South African Keywords: The Uses and Abuses of Political Concepts,* ed. Emile Boonzaier and John Sharp (Cape Town: D. Philip, 1988), 100–110.

Wilson, Richard A. 2000. "Reconciliation and Revenge in Post-Apartheid South Africa." *Current Anthropology* 41(1) (February): 75–98.

———. 2001. *The Politics of Truth and Reconciliation in South Africa: Legitimizing the Post-Apartheid State.* Cambridge: Cambridge University Press.

Worsnip, Michael. 1996. *Michael Lapsley: Priest and Partisan.* Melbourne: Ocean Press.

Young, Alan. 1997. *The Harmony of Illusions: Inventing Post-Traumatic Stress Disorder.* Princeton: Princeton University Press.

PART III

Madness and Social Suffering

. . . . . .

Madness or psychotic illness fundamentally challenges local understandings of human nature, as well as the theorization of subjectivity. Societies and individuals understand madness in various ways: as possession by haunting spirits, a flight from reason, a regression to childlike or primitive states, an essential mode of being in the world and a distinctive form of human subjectivity, the entry into an alternative world, or a mode of deeply disturbed and pathological subjectivity reflecting disordered brain chemistry. Whatever the interpretation, the chaotic and disturbing qualities of psychosis are deeply threatening to those undergoing the experience as well as to their families and communities.

Those in the social environment of persons who are psychotic often feel threatened, fearing physical violence; feeling uneasy and anxious about the uncanny qualities or shocking behaviors of those who are psychotic, as well as their disregard for propriety and morally sanctioned order; or harboring a broader sense that madness represents a fundamental cosmological threat. These feelings lead to powerful social responses, often in the name of healing, restoration of order, or the protection of those who are ill. These responses in turn can redouble suffering, constituting madness as a social threat and redirecting violence to the vulnerable individual.

At the same time, the language of madness is widely used to represent and respond to everyday forms of impropriety—are you crazy?!—or to articulate and analyze larger modes of social action that suspend ordinary social or moral rules, or permit forms of mass consciousness or "mob behavior" to overtake everyday forms of rationality. These actions include the orgiastic or pleasurable, present in the liminal moments of ritual or celebration, but also mass violence, in which participants may commit unspeakable horrors. Such irruptions of violence or urges to act out the for-

bidden evoke questions about the part of subjectivity that is normally repressed, the "primitive" qualities of human nature, and ultimately the
essence of human nature. The fluid movement of references to madness
across these terrains—the disordered experience of individuals in psychotic
states or with major mental illnesses and the forms of violence (or pleasure)
that dislocate ordinary assumptions about the rational or moral bases of
human nature—make theorizing about madness or psychoses important to
our thinking about subjectivity. And the illusive, disorienting quality of
psychotic experience and utterances—at once fragmented and incoherent
but subject to moments of brilliant insight that reveal normally hidden aspects of the psyche and the social world—challenges theories of subjectivity that rest on everyday assumptions about normal psychology.

We should not be surprised that fundamental assumptions about human
nature, social order, and human diversity permeate, often surreptitiously,
medical theorizing about psychosis or psychotic experience. Emil Kraepelin,
who is often considered the founder of descriptive psychiatry, developed a
mode of psychiatric theorizing that he claimed was theoretically neutral.
However, Kraepelin's assumptions about the genetic and physiological
bases for mental diseases (plural) produced a deeply biological vision of the
subject and subjective experience—casting the mentally ill as a medicalized
subject—that remains powerful in much of psychiatry today. Hidden in
Kraepelin's work are assumptions about disorders of the will and basic assumptions about degeneracy that are less obvious (Barrett 1996; Good 2003;
Pick 1989). Kraepelin came to believe that dementia praecox, or schizophrenia, is a permanent, deteriorating condition, leaving the sufferer little
or no chance for recovery. This view, which turns out to be empirically
wrong, is rooted in an old understanding of schizophrenia as a disease of degeneracy, the end of a genetic decline causing "degenerate" families, ethnic
groups, and whole societies to have clusters of alcoholics, criminals, mentally retarded people—and persons with schizophrenia. This view, based in
colonial theorizing about human evolution, provided the rationale for notorious laws permitting sterilization of persons with schizophrenia or mental retardation and led to deep pessimism about schizophrenia among psychiatrists and the public alike, a view that persists to this day.

But not only among biological psychiatrists, of course, have social ideologies and medical theories commingled in the analysis of psychotic disorders. Psychoanalysis and neurobiology share a language of primitivism,
pointing on the one hand to forms of "regression" and the emergence of
"primitive" impulses or affects and, on the other, to "primitive" aspects of
the human brain (Lucas and Barrett 1995). Although offering data on

human biological evolution, on the one hand, and clinical observations, on the other, such theories also grow out of a colonial language of social evolution, in which images of "primitive" social organization and forms of psychological experience appear with little comment. Studies of psychosis are thus key sites for a continual reworking of assumptions about subjectivity and human nature.

In this section, chapters by Byron Good, Subandi, and Mary-Jo DelVecchio Good; by Ellen Corin; and by Anne Lovell explore issues of subjectivity through ethnographic investigations of psychotic experience in contemporary Indonesia, North America, and India. These papers consistently interpret the experience of psychosis as social experience, at once psychological, interpersonal, and institutional. Experiences of psychosis are mediated by life history and psychological development, by family complexes, by systems of power and institutional structures, by patterns of cultural interpretation, and by medical translations of and affective responses to persons suffering psychotic episodes (Corin and Lauzon 1992, 1994; Fabrega 1989; Jenkins 1997, 2004).

In "The Subject of Mental Illness," Good and his colleagues explore the relationship between the subjective experience of psychotic illness and political subjectivity, and between the madness of the psychotic and the madness of violent crowds in contemporary Indonesia. Their ethnographic approach to psychotic experience reveals profound fractures in the symbolic ordering of sufferers' relation to families, as well as to the world of commodity capitalism and the medicoscientific order of reality, both presented as the sites of desire. Here, the richness of the phenomenology of psychosis lies not just in language but in the sufferers' struggles to find a place in the world. In the story of Yani, for example, Good and his colleagues show that family complexes are the contexts for the experiences of psychosis: as the mother attempts to give medication to the young woman, the sufferer rejects the offer and focuses instead on prayers and on cleansing herself. As global pharmaceuticals find their way into households, medical and religious forms of subjectivity come into conflict, and efforts at integration meet with resistance, as people like Yani reject the biologized subject for a religious or spiritual one with a deeper grounding in experience.

While showing us how experiences of acute psychoses are entangled with Indonesia's current political and economic turmoil (a nation "run *amuk*"), the ghostliness of its postcolonial history, and an expanding global psychiatry, Good, Subandi, and M-J Good also emphasize the ambiguities, dissonances, and limitations of representing subjectivity in mental illness. They point out the incompleteness of representation: observations "out of the corner of our eye"; stories as part of the action; the interplay of imaginaries and experiences; narratives and practices as personal experience and as political, economic, and social commentary and consequences. The chapter sketches an anthropological sensibility that keeps at least three analytic moves simultaneously in focus: the first works inward through cultural phenomenology and cultural psychology to get at how a person's experience and construction of meaning are implicated in the domestic space and the forceful coherence of that space; the second is a critical reading of the political significance of representations of mental illness and subjectivity, both in the medicalization of psychopathology and in use of the figure of "madness" to pathologize social protest; and the third leads outward to reflections on the importance of sociality as a basic element in creating subjectivity. Good and his colleagues refuse easy juxtaposition or integration of these gazes and relentlessly pursue analysis that refuses closure, thus challenging anthropology to maintain an unfinished quality in any analysis of subjectivity and psychosis.

Psychotic illness produces dramatic episodes of strange, disorienting experiences that occur in the midst of everyday worlds and often lead to distinctive forms of withdrawal. The psychotic person's isolation is not merely a flight from reality, argues Ellen Corin in "The Other of Culture in Psychosis," but a tinkering with the cultural and social frameworks that make possible a sense of exclusion. Over the years, she and her colleagues have focused on distinctive modes of withdrawal among persons suffering psychotic illness—in Montreal and more recently, in India (Corin 1990, 1998; Corin and Lauzon 1992; Corin, Thara, and Padmavati 2004)—working to demystify the irrationality and sheer craziness of psychotic behavior. People with psychotic illness can use social isolation as a rational method to negotiate reality, explains Corin, a mode of "positive withdrawal." In some cases, they maintain such an attitude of withdrawal to help construct and protect frontiers and boundaries, to defend an inner space from the intrusion of the others as well as to limit their own tendency to become "diffuse" and lose themselves in the world.

In this sense, withdrawal seems to provide a kind of psychic skin that parallels the social skin: "I've never confided in anybody. You have to keep a secret side. You can't tell everything. You don't have to tell everything," a sufferer states. This protection of otherness is achieved by reworking and appropriating cultural signifiers, particularly religious and spiritual language, to tame the confusion while maintaining the strangeness. It also links directly with larger social and religious modes of withdrawal that are typical of particular societies or religious systems. Psychotic withdrawal in the context of Hinduism or North American sociality thus necessarily assumes different forms. Subjectivity itself is constructed in relation to this tinkering, a practice that dominant biopsychiatric categories and interventions ignore. Corin suggests that these relationships to withdrawal and to otherness, to that which is outside of language and symbols, expands the borders of psychology and anthropology as we attempt to understand personal and public experiences of meaning-making. While escaping coherence and meaning in the matrix of cultural signifiers, psychosis raises the ethical question of intelligibility within a given culture, and while exposing the plasticity of cultural signifiers, psychosis opens the possibility of rethinking reality from this lacuna. We are thus challenged to enlarge the possibilities of social intelligibility that psychotic patients struggle to resolve.

In "Hoarders and Scrappers," Anne Lovell inquires into how mentally ill homeless people in New York City rework psychiatric personhood and patienthood outside clinical networks. The uncertainty and interstitiality of their existence requires constant negotiation of identity as they endure a generalized lack of empathy. As if their conditions had been self-generated, the people around them see the homeless as beyond remedy and associate them with the disposability of garbage. Homeless subjectivities are constructed through identification and play with values of medicine and society (for example, through the use of discarded food to fulfill a social role or self-identification as an entrepreneur through collecting cans). This process produces affects (shame, pride), ethics (social hierarchies within homeless communities), and self-perceptions that constitute moral agency, as mentally ill and homeless men and women interact conceptually, physically, and interpersonally with mechanisms of exclusion.

The ethnographic studies in this section do not suggest that mental disorders are basically a matter of social construction, free of biological constraints, or that psychosis is merely a cultural judgment. Instead, these papers show that psychotic experience and subjectivity take form at the most personal juncture between the subject, his/her biology, and local regimes of normalcy and power. And they suggest why psychosis and its mysterious qualities will continue to challenge our understandings of subjectivity well into the future.

REFERENCES

Barrett, Rob. 1996. The Psychiatric Team and the Social Definition of Schizophrenia. Cambridge: Cambridge University Press.

Corin, Ellen. 1990. "Facts and Meaning in Psychiatry: An Anthropological Approach to the Lifeworld of Schizophrenics." *Culture, Medicine and Psychiatry* 14: 153–88.

———. 1998. "The Thickness of Being: Intentional Worlds, Strategies of Identify, and Experience among Schizophrenics." *Psychiatry* 61: 133–46.

Corin, Ellen, and Gilles Lauzon. 1992. "Positive Withdrawal and the Quest for Meaning: The Reconstruction of Experience among Schizophrenics." *Psychiatry* 55: 266–81.

———. 1994. "From Symptom to Phenomena: The Articulation of Experience in Schizophrenia." *Journal of Phenomenological Psychology* 25: 3–50.

Corin, Ellen, Rangaswami Thara, and Ramachandran Padmavati. 2004. In *Schizophrenia, Culture, and Subjectivity: The Edge of Experience*, ed. Robert Barrett and Janis Jenkins (Cambridge: Cambridge University Press).

Fabrega, Horacio. 1989. "On the Significance of an Anthropological Approach to Schizophrenia." *Psychiatry* 52: 45–65.

Good, Byron. 2003. "Emil Kraepelin on the Pathologies of the Will." Paper presented at the American Anthropological Association annual meeting, Chicago, November.

Jenkins, Janis. 1997. "Subjective Experience of Persistent Schizophrenia and Depression among U.S. Latinos and Euro-Americans." *British Journal of Psychiatry* 171: 20–25.

———. 2004. "Schizophrenia as a Paradigm Case for Understanding Fundamental Human Processes." In *Schizophrenia, Culture, and Subjectivity: The Edge of Experience*, ed. Robert Barrett and Janis Jenkins (Cambridge: Cambridge University Press).

Lucas, Rodney H., and Robert J. Barrett. 1995. "Interpreting Culture and Psychopathology: Primitivist Themes in Cross-Cultural Debate." *Culture, Medicine and Psychiatry* 19: 287–326.

Pick, Daniel. 1989. *Faces of Degeneration: A European Disorder, c. 1848–c. 1918.* Cambridge: Cambridge University Press.

8 The Subject of Mental Illness

Psychosis, Mad Violence, and Subjectivity in Indonesia

BYRON J. GOOD, SUBANDI, AND MARY-JO DELVECCHIO GOOD

Near noon on a hot, sunny day in August 1997, Subandi and I [BG[went to visit a woman we will call Yani, a thirty-six-year-old Javanese woman who was participating in our study of mental illness in the old city of Yogyakarta in central Java.[1] We had first met her for an interview two months earlier and were returning for a follow-up interview. We walked down a narrow alleyway that wanders through one of Yogya's poor *kampungs*, a crowded neighborhood that spills downward to one of the rivers running through the town, passing women, children and young people sitting in open doorways and little shops, chatting in the heat of the day. We found Yani and her mother in their small house. The sitting room was opened for us, and we were relieved to be greeted warmly, to find Yani in apparent good health, and to see that both she and her mother appeared happy to see us. We chatted with the two of them, took out our tape recorder and picked up our interview. Not until some time into our conversation did we learn that Yani had had another acute psychotic episode in the two-month interval since we had last seen her. Her mother said that she had just begun to recognize the signs that Yani was getting sick when we were last there, signs she knew well from previous episodes. Together, Yani and her mother told how she had become sick again and had decided not to return to the private psychiatric hospital where she had been taken for treatment on several previous occasions; instead, she had elected to rely on the prayers she had received from Pak Han, a *kiyai* or Islamic teacher whose group she had been attending for some time. Both Yani and her mother were delighted to tell us how they had recited the prayers and how quickly and completely she had recovered this time.

Subandi and I were startled to hear of Yani's illness, because she showed no apparent residual symptoms of the rather severe episode she described.

Hearing her story, however, reminded us of several other patients we had recently interviewed and crystallized our sense of a common phenomenological pattern. These persons had had relatively brief, acute psychoses, some of them suffering only one episode and some of them suffering regular recurrences. They experienced classic auditory hallucinations and confusion, and several of them also told stories of going off on a kind of trek—around the city, to a nearby town, along the river and into the countryside—remaining lost for some time before being returned home. The episodes tended to be rather short, not lasting long enough to meet the *Diagnostic and Statistical Manual of Mental Disorders* (*DSM-IV*) six-month-duration criterion for schizophrenia, and we met these patients when they were clearly intact—interestingly diverse people, both men and women, often young, who had no apparent residual symptoms of hallucinations or thought disorder. Some had enough depressive symptoms to further confuse the diagnostic picture. As we heard stories of the illnesses from these individuals and their families, classic themes from Javanese cultural psychology emerged, reflecting a broadly shared lifeworld in this highly diverse but predominantly Javanese and Islamic old city.

We begin this paper by telling stories that Yani and her mother told us about their efforts to come to terms with Yani's strange experiences. In the background are questions about the nature of this and similar illnesses, the cultural shaping of psychotic experience in Java, healing resources, and what these suggest about Javanese cultural psychology and subjectivity. Present also are questions about mental illness and biology and some thoughts on the "biologization" of those subjected to contemporary psychiatric practice in Indonesia. But these stories of mental illness lead to others, stories of madness and violence that erupted during our stay in Yogya and during the subsequent years of political turmoil in Indonesia—the tale of an old village man who goes crazy, runs *amuk*, and is tragically killed by a group of his fellow villagers; stories of violence during the 1997 political campaign, represented by Indonesian journalists as the masses going crazy or running *amuk*; older stories of Malay madness told by colonial psychiatrists, which seem to reverberate through contemporary analyses; and more recent stories of strange killings of Islamic clergymen by *ninja*s, persons with miraculous powers later chased down by villagers and killed, some of whom turned out to be wandering madmen.

In the lovely paper "The Spirit of the Story," Mary Steedly (1999) prefaces her recounting of a mythic tale from the Karo Batak highlands of Sumatra with a quote from Italo Calvino's novel, *If on a Winter's Night a Traveler*.

What I want is for you to feel, around the story, a saturation of other stories that I could tell and maybe will tell or who knows may already have told on some other occasion, a space full of stories that perhaps is simply my lifetime, where you can move in all directions, as in space, always finding stories that cannot be told until other stories are told first.

Perhaps it is a stretch to say that Yani's story cannot be told unless the stories of colonial psychiatrists and accounts of *ninja* killers be told. But her story is refracted in these tales, woven into a network of stories of Yogya's Islamic healers and paranormals, meditation groups and psychiatric hospitals. And not far off are other stories—rumors and hints of hidden plots, suspected conspiracies behind the current violence—stories in which the figure of madness appears over and again.

The "narrative function," Ricoeur (1981: 277) tells us, is a particular form of sense making. "To follow a story," he writes, "is to understand the successive actions, thoughts and feelings as displaying a particular *directedness*." He suggests that stories are actively emplotted by both storytellers and their audiences, writers and readers; stories allow both to " 'grasp together' successive events," "*to extract a configuration from a succession*" (278). But stories of madness and violence do both more and less than this. They do less, because they resist this form of sense making, this grasping together as a means of finding cognitive or moral coherence. They do more, because stories are part of the action, self-serving justifications for past or proposed actions, crafted tales disguising interests of the powerful, rumors inciting fear and vengeance, claims with powerful effects, and poetic resources for imaginative universes.

This essay suggests that ethnographic studies of mental illness not only take us deeply into the lives of individuals, families, and communities but constantly lead us outward, toward broader forms of social rupture, resisting closure and our efforts to control our data. We suggest that such studies are sites upon which analyses of meaning, on the one hand, and power and its effects, on the other, inevitably meet. And we raise questions about the figure of "the subject" that appears in these analyses—both meaning-centered analyses of culture-saturated subjectivity and psychological experience, and critical analyses of postcolonial subjectivity in settings of authoritarian rule punctuated by public violence.

Madness has long provided a site for theorization of the subject. Phenomenological and psychological studies of psychopathology place disordered subjectivity and the experiencing self at the center of their analyses. Psychiatry today too often displaces this psychological subject in favor of a biologized subject, reducing health, illness, and treatment ultimately to brain states and neurochemistry. In the social sciences, a quite different set of debates has framed understandings of mental illness and subjectivity. For example, Foucault's work is representative of a broad body of scholarship that interprets the subject in relation to "subjection" and the mad as those subjected—to confinement and to knowledge practices and discipline. Even more, many poststructuralist accounts juxtapose the subject who is constituted through processes of power, hierarchy, and subjection with the humanist self critiqued as a figure of Romantic theorizing.[2]

In the following pages, we examine madness and subjectivity in contemporary Java. We first describe in more detail Yani's experiences of psychotic illness, illustrating how interpretation of Yani's vivid stories requires an understanding of Javanese cultural psychology. We then describe how the figure of madness emerged in Indonesian public discourses on social and political violence in the late 1990s, providing a broader context for interpretations of madness in Javanese culture. Throughout, we attend explicitly to the theories of the subject assumed at each stage of the analysis. We conclude not with an argument for a single, coherent theory of the subject of madness but with recognition of the complementarity of these theoretical perspectives—and the limitations of each.

Our research is in Yogyakarta, a center of classic Javanese culture and the site of a still-functioning Javanese court. The city and the court have a special place in Javanese cosmology, mediating between the spiritually powerful Mount Merapi, an active volcano to the north of the city, and the Queen of the South Sea, a mighty spirit who inhabits the coastal waters to the south. The city, its sultan, and its population also have an important place in Indonesian nationalist history, having been active in the long independence struggle against the Dutch. The city was the site of Sukarno's first national assembly and more recently was the setting for massive demonstrations, led by the sultan himself, as part of the movement that gathered under the banner of *reformasi* and ultimately led to the ouster of President Suharto in 1998. Yogya is a city of universities and students; it is politically and intellectually progressive, an active center of modernist Islamic thought and political organization and a center of traditional arts and culture. It is religiously diverse, with a sizable Christian minority and numerous Islamic traditions and organizations. And it has a postmodern flavor, dotted with *warnet*, tiny *warungs*, or shops with computers linked into the World Wide Web; banners announcing lectures and seminars on diverse aspects of *globalizasi*, or globalization; and malls that were filled with international commodities before the disastrous *krismon*, or monetary crisis, began late in

1997. At the same time the city maintains a commitment to organized forms of Javanese spirituality, cultural performances, and aesthetic life.

In this context of Javanese modernity, Indonesians must craft and actively negotiate Subjectivity. And in this complex center of Javanese and Indonesian urban culture, along with its network of rural and periurban villages, we carry out our research. Our study of mental illness is classically anthropological; it is an attempt to explore dimensions of Indonesian and Javanese culture and society by focusing on the language and experience of illness, particularly forms of psychological distress and madness, and to gather data to test claims about the naturalness of categories of mental illness—such as schizophrenia—rooted in Euro-American cultural history and clinical experience. At the same time, our data include observations made "out of the corner of our eye" of events that thrust themselves upon us or that we stumble upon by accident. These observations allow us to extend our analysis of madness outward to that larger "space full of stories."

STORIES OF YANI

We first met Yani and her mother for an interview in June 1997.[3] Yani was born in 1961, the last of four siblings. Her father had been a tailor in the university hospital, working personally for the prominent physician who was the hospital's first director. When Yani was six years old, her father died, leaving her to be raised by her mother and her mother's mother, who relied on a small pension left from her father's death. The family was poor, and Yani is the only one of her siblings to have gone to the university. She entered the university in 1980 and graduated with a degree in agriculture in 1987. When we said to her mother that she must have been happy with her daughter's achievements, she replied, "Yes, very happy. But after she got sick, my feeling, I don't know . . . I don't know, it was like when you plant a tree and expect it to bear fruit, but in the end it does not bear fruit, like that." And thus we began to talk about Yani's illness, with her mother's open, poignant acknowledgment of her disappointment in Yani.[4]

Yani and her mother sat side by side, speaking in a kind of joint and overlapping voice, at times enacting an apparent long-standing conflict in a way that seemed unusually explicit for Javanese who were speaking with strangers; as a result, the conversation was sometimes uncomfortable for us as well as for them. They described how Yani had become ill as a student, had been treated and recovered so that she could complete her exams and graduate, but then had fallen ill and recovered over and over again, being hospitalized a number of times.

And how did she feel when she was sick? She would become irritated, *mangkel,* they said, using the Javanese term *kecewa,* frustrated or disappointed. And with whom was she irritated? It isn't necessary to say, because that was in the past. But yes, in the beginning she was irritated with one person, an acquaintance in the university, but as time went on and the situation at home became difficult, everything piled up. And so she would get sick, then get better, then get sick again.

SUBANDI: And when you were sick the first time, what did you feel?

YANI: The first time, it was because of being *jengkel,* but the cause of the following times, sometimes it was because the attitude of my mother was not *cocok,* not compatible with me.

SUBANDI: So what were you feeling and experiencing at that time?

YANI: Yes, at that time, the feeling of my heart was not at peace. I didn't have (enough) religious knowledge *(ilmu agama).* Then I learned how to read the Qur'an, then I studied religious knowledge, so that I was not so easily *jengkel,* irritated, by other people. But when I studied religious knowledge, what happened to me was that I sometimes couldn't understand clearly, so that [I questioned why what I saw another person doing didn't fit with the religious knowledge that I was learning].

SUBANDI: So what did you do?

YANI: What I wanted, I wanted to have religious teaching. I wanted to have an Islam that is pure, *murni,* original. Therefore, I wanted to go out of the house.

SUBANDI: Oh, to go? To go where?

YANI: I wanted to have a pure Islam, for example like that in Saudi Arabia.

YANI'S MOTHER: At that time, she left the house. She has already (run away from) the house two times. At that time, when she was in Yogya, she went and then returned home again; she turned herself in to the police, and asked the police to tell her mother, and then we picked her up in the police office. The second time, in Jakarta, at the place of her older sister, she also ran away. She was sick again at that time. She said that she was going to go to Saudi Arabia, but in reality, because she was sick, she was walking along the toll road. [When she was asked by the police where she was going, she said,] "I want to go home but I don't remember the way."

Her mother completed the story of the Jakarta episode by telling how the police sent her home by a motorcycle taxi, in the care of a driver who took her home even though she had no money.

And thus, with these brief vignettes, the initial outlines of Yani's life emerged. She hinted at a relationship with someone she had known as a student that had gone awry, leaving her disappointed, frustrated, and angry, but she refused to speak about it. Her mother later confirmed that he was a boyfriend, someone she had been close with. After graduating, she had gone to live and work in Jakarta. She had had difficulty making friends, had gotten sick, and after seven months, had returned home. She has continued to live at home since that time, remaining in the small home in which she grew up, locked into an intense relationship with her mother, who is primarily responsible for her whenever she is sick. She has been sick many times, and during one of her episodes, she left home, wandered off along a river, and did not return for many days. It was this brief outline of a story that we attempted to make sense of, to explore, during this visit.

We went to visit Yani again two months later. In the meantime, we had spent an afternoon with Pak Han, a *kiyai*, or Islamic teacher, whom Yani had been visiting for religious treatment. He knew Yani but knew little of her story; he was clearly not involved in a psychotherapeutic relationship with her, in the usual sense of that term. In addition, Subandi had stopped by to bring Yani an Indonesian translation of the Qur'an, as a gift, and had been told by Yani's mother that she was sick and could not see him at that time. We were thus concerned that Yani might be sick and feel that our discussion had been too stressful for her. We arrived, were relieved to find Yani well and both Yani and her mother happy to see us, and chatted comfortably with them for some time before moving more formally into an interview.

Yani seemed in good spirits, showing no appearance of illness, and she and her mother seemed more at ease than the last time we were together. Subandi and I were thus surprised when Yani launched into the story of her most recent illness.

> I've got the *doa* (an Islamic prayer), the *doa* which should be recited when I get sick. So I have recovered (become aware, conscious, *sadar*) from the illness, because every time after practicing *sholat* (the formal ritual prayer, done five times per day), I recited this *doa*. When I was sick, my hand was involuntarily pinching myself, twisting the skin, and pulling my hair, twisting, pulling my ears. It could not be controlled. I continued this, pulling my hair, pulling my hair, and it hurt. My mother also knew. She held my hand, trying to stop me. Then every time after practicing *sholat*, I said this *doa*. Then, I told Pak Han that the *doa* which was taught by the Prophet was already proven. The *doa* was accepted.

Yani's mother expanded on the story, from her perspective. "So right after you left the house, she became sick. Then when you came here to give her the Qur'an, she could only sleep. I asked her to do some things. She didn't want to do anything, she didn't even want to eat." "When my feet were cold," Yani broke in, "my feet were rubbed with kerosene, and then my mother *ndremimil* (mumbled a prayer or mantra to me)." "Her feet were so cold, I was so worried," her mother responded. "Mother recited a mantra," Yani continued. "Why did you recite mantras? It isn't proper *(cocok)* for me to be brought to a *dukun* (a traditional healer)." "It wasn't a mantra," her mother responded in good spirits. "It was a prayer from Islam. I recited whatever I could, like *'astagfirullah alhazim nggihlhailahhailaa-haa . . . ,'* whatever I could do. But Yani was angry. 'Why do you do that? Why do you like using mantras?' 'This isn't a mantra, this is a prayer from Islam,' I said like that. When she got sick, I became like her enemy, so I had to be really patient, *sabar*. She recovered after I recited *Sholawat nariah* every night forty-one times, for almost one hour."

Yani provided vivid descriptions of the experience she had just been through. Unlike our previous meeting, when she seemed to blame her mother for her difficulties, she seemed to have a relatively clear sense of her experience as illness.

"When I was sick, it seemed as though there was a whisper *(bisikan)* in my ear, my hand twisting my skin until I hurt—" "It was involuntary," her mother interjected. "What was the whispering like?" Bandi asked. "The whispering was continuous . . . 'You are still small [*cilik*, a word used commonly for a small child], but you have to be responsible'—many times, so my thought was pressed down, suppressed." She described how she avoided people, because her feelings would be hurt and she would get into quarrels. "That is why I stayed in my room. But when I didn't want to eat, my mother struggled to make me eat, so I have become small *(cilik)*," she said, suggesting an image of regression.

She returned several times to the strange changes in her thinking. "It seemed that there was something pressing down, so my thoughts were not my own, the thoughts were pressing down, being pressed down continuously, the whispering over-lapping, one coming before the other finished . . . It was not me. Why was I controlled by something bad? Even inside, there was a being inside me . . . Inside my body, there was a being that was not me myself, like that, like that." Or again, "the thought was suppressed *(pikiran itu ditekan)* from the inside of my thought, as if continuously, the ears were whispered (into), as if my life was not my own. So I was like a robot. Why was I like a robot? thoughts were not my own thoughts? whispering. Hands were controlled. . . . When I performed *sholat*, I had little consciousness. The rest, it was not my own consciousness *(kesadaran pribadi)."*

"According to Yani, who took control?" Bandi asked. "According to me, there was an attack from the outside. So there were other people who hate, then attacked, with *kejawen* (Javanese)," she said, using a term that implied Javanese magic. "So 'black magic' [said in English]—last time you asked me and I said there was no one who attacked, that the problem was in the house," she said, drawing our previous interview into her story. "After I became aware of this, there was this attack from other people." "By whom? Who might it be?" Bandi asked. "Yes, there was someone who was suspected," Yani replied. "My mother already knew . . . It was not his own hand," she said, suggesting that the perpetrator had hired a specialist to attack her.

Yani went on to tell a long story about the man she suspected. He was a friend of the man she had previously described as her *pacar*, the boyfriend she had had since returning to Yogya. She told a rather vague story about rooming in the same house with his sister when she worked in Jakarta, while he lived nearby. One night she woke to find him standing near her bed. Yani then returned to the present and told an elaborate story about finding a fishhook in her prayer gown, thinking her mother had done something to her, then remembering that this man often talked about fishing and that she had found *kejawen* books in his house. It is difficult to tell if this story represents paranoia and a fixed certainty or simply has a "subjunctive" quality (Good 1994: ch. 6), suggesting the indeterminate, mysterious, and potentially revealing dimensions of reality. Such stories are thoroughly reality based in the lifeworld of Yani and her mother, and this one provided a reasonable interpretation of her strange experiences as resulting from a kind of possession—by thoughts not her own and a power that was not herself.

Yani and her mother had noted that when Yani became sick, she would see her mother differently, as her "enemy." As we talked, she vividly described the perceptual changes that led her to suspect even those close to her. "It seemed that outside, there were different beings. It seemed if I met other people, I was not really a human being. For example," she told us, "if I met my neighbor, her voice was changed, her face was changed, so how could I interact with others?" "So how did you see them?" Bandi asked. "For example, I met Ningsih, like that, she changed and became Bu Min. Bu Min is the nurse at [the hospital]. The voice of Bu Min . . . the face changed to be like Bu Min, but only a little. Then, for example, there is someone who lives behind my house whose name is Aziz, his voice changed, became the voice of someone . . . it turned out like that. So it was as if someone frightened me or there were voices, like 'dug-dug-dug' . . . it seemed to frighten me. . . . People who usually help me became like my enemies when I was sick." She went on, "People seemed like different beings, because of changes in faces, in voices. I even asked my mother, are you a spirit, or are you a human being?" "When she got sick, she thought I was a *shetan*," her mother interjected, "so we were in conflict. She thought I was her enemy."

Finally, Yani returned to the story that she and her mother had mentioned earlier in the interview about how she had left the house, run away, gone off to the river again. She had been bothered by sounds, she told us, such as the noise of the small children playing outside her window, and she wanted to go someplace quiet. So she went to the river again, with a rice field beside it. A farmer found her lying beside the river, offered her lunch, and urged her to come to his house, to be with his wife, so that she would not be bothered by young people. And then suddenly her legs had begun carrying her home, beyond her control, simply moving as though they had their own will.

"I just wanted to find a quiet place. I told my mother, basically, I want to clean my body. . . . I just wanted to stay quietly in my room to clean my body. My body was a dirty thing. I told my mother I wanted to pray. Maybe it would take six months, but if I wasn't yet clean, I would not go out from the house. I ate, but I said if you disturb me, I will run away. So I cleaned myself by using prayers." "You cleaned yourself because—?" Bandi asked. "There was whispering, the feeling of pressing, automatically, because it was not my own self, it was hard. So when I got sick, I often fought with my mother. She offered me medicine, but I wanted prayers. The medicine made my *doa* weak. And then we argued until I cried." And thus she returned to tell us about how she had used prayers, rather than medicine, to achieve her recovery.

We returned a year later, in August 1998, to visit Yani again. This time, her mother greeted us, saying, "Oh, Yani remembered that you were supposed to return in June, and she was looking for you." She then went to call Yani. Though it was midday, we heard her asking Yani to get up and realized she must be sick again. Yani joined us, looking rather disheveled. Her hair was wet, from rinsing her face, and she wore an open dress, not appropriate for meeting guests. She spoke with us quite coherently but in very abstract terms. She refused to be tape-recorded, and her conversation was so abstract as to be difficult to reproduce: she talked about what life means,

Islam, her disappointment in her environment, her disappointment in Islamic values.

Yani left, and her mother returned to talk with us. Yani had become sick again in June, when the sister of the man she spends time with told Yani that she opposed their relationship and tried to stop them from seeing each other. This behavior hurt her feelings, made her feel *kagol*, and she became sick again. Yani's mother was in despair. She had had a nurse coming to give Yani injections, but the Indonesian economic crisis had left her without resources to buy any more medication. "We have nothing left but prayer," she told us. After giving her a gift, which she could use to buy medicines, we left, promising to see her after a year. Subandi returned to visit Yani six months later, in February 1999, and found her to be quite well again. She had been hospitalized for eighteen days in October, treated with neuroleptic medications, and had finally recovered and returned home. She was continuing to take her medications and had tried to make a small business selling fried food. She gave up this undertaking because the economic crisis continued to make any small-business activities difficult. However, she was active and talked about finding work.

Our last visits with Yani to date were in July and November of 1999. She was still quite healthy at this time, although she had decided to continue taking antipsychotic medication, while complaining about how much weight she had gained. She was open and reflective and told us several additional stories about her experiences.

Yani said that when she was sick, she felt the bed she was using was former president Sukarno's bed. Because she understood that Sukarno had been killed by his own assistants, persons she said were members of the Indonesian Communist Party, she did not want to remain in the bed. She also told how when sick she felt that one of her neighbors, a man who had once been jailed for being a member of the Communist Party, was able to divert to her the punishment that he should have received. For this reason, she would shout out her neighbor's name, calling him a "genius."

Yani also told us that when she was ill, she sometimes heard two groups of voices. One set of voices was bad voices, which she associated with the voice of one of her boyfriends. These voices sometimes urged her to kill herself. Another set of voices, good ones, she identified as those of Pak Han and another religious leader. These voices whispered prayers in her ears and told her that she should not kill herself, that she should die as a good Muslim. She described how these voices helped her respond to the voices urging her to kill herself.

Finally, we learned from Yani's mother that Yani's father had had an episode of paranoia not long before he died of a heart attack.[5] The father had secretly borrowed money and set up a small sewing business with another man in the neighborhood, refusing to tell his wife about the business. The two men were poor managers, and the business was failing. About this time, the father began acting strangely, staying awake at night and holding a weapon to protect himself. He began to feel that the Communists were threatening him or that he might be accused of being a Communist, though he was not. At the time, in 1967, many members of the Indonesian Communist Party were killed throughout Indonesia, including in Yogyakarta, so fears of this kind were potentially realistic. However, Yani's mother insisted that her husband had become sick and withdrawn, had dug a large hole in the ground in the neighborhood, which he said was for the Communists, had dropped out of work, and had finally been hospitalized. Unfortunately, while hospitalized for his psychiatric problems, he died quite suddenly of a heart attack.

REFLECTIONS ON YANI:
CULTURE, BIOLOGY, AND SUBJECTIVITY

We turn now to brief reflections on Yani—on the stories she tells, as well as the stories we might tell through retelling her story, and the nature of subjectivity assumed by these. Yani's experience might serve as an entrée to a cultural phenomenology of mental illness in Java. Javanese Islam and local debates about whether Islam should be purified of its *abangan,* or traditional Javanese elements, mediate her experience.[6] Yani's talk about Islam has an obsessive quality. She wants to practice only true, non-*abangan,* Islam. She talks about the rules for fasting and complains that her mother's wish that she fast on certain calendar days is not in keeping with true Islam. However, when asked if she has been praying regularly, she says no, she is too lazy, *malas,* or that she doesn't need to because she has been ill. When she becomes ill, she continues to talk about these themes, but now much more abstractly, in global terms, focusing on the lack of a true Islam in Indonesia.

Themes of Islamic purity and impurity, linked to a similar dichotomy in classic Javanese culture, are also important mediators of her experience.[7] She begins to feel that the house is *haram*—defiled, forbidden—that the food, her clothing, the neighborhood are all *haram.* Her body is a dirty thing. And so she goes on a quest for a place that is pure, holy, to find a spring. The category of purity is not a cognitive abstraction but an embodied sense. In cases of depression in Java, feelings that the body is impure often play powerfully along with feelings of being sinful and guilty and of having disappointed God and lost his favor—familiar patterns to those who treat Christian and Jewish patients in Europe and North America. Yani's discussion of the impure has a more obsessive, less depressive quality, and it provides a motive for her extraordinary periods of wandering.

Islam is also present in her discourse as a potent source of healing. The *doa* she recites, along with her mother, offer the possibility of recovery. They have power, and their power is threatened by pharmaceuticals, Yani feels. The ritual practices—daily prayers, repetition of *sura* from the Qur'an, recitation of *doa*—organize her behavior and mark both her illness and recovery, as she loses and regains her ability to concentrate.

Themes of black magic figure in her discourse and experience, and powerful spirits and experiences of sorcery are often present in psychotic experience. The Javanese lifeworld is deeply vitalistic; it is a world of powers and forces and of persons who have the ability to cause harm by destroying one's vitality; it is also a world of spiritual practices aimed at enhancing one's *tanaga dalam*, or inner powers. There is thus less of a disjuncture between the everyday world and that of those who are psychotic than some societies have. A sense of something being done to one, of harm sent one's way, is common in both worlds—for example, Yani's world and that of her mother. Spirits belong to both worlds. As some persons who are psychotic recover, they begin to doubt the veracity of experiences they have had—of hearing or seeing threatening spirits in their houses or their neighborhoods, for example—acknowledging that these encounters may have been part of their illness. But this world of spiritual forces is widely shared across all social classes and religious groups in Yogya and is the source of endless storytelling. *Kampung* families and university professors, Javanese and Islamic healers and physicians alike, all tell stories about their encounters with powerful persons, spirits, and powerful sites or objects. Particularly common are experiences at graveyards or sites associated with the old Mataram Javanese kingdom, with power objects such as *kris*, and in attacks by outside forces and their efforts to strengthen themselves. (There are many stories we would have to relate to make this generalization meaningful—stories of physicians who experiment with using spiritual powers to stop bleeding during surgery, a professor who asks for help in writing grant applications to test whether Islamic or Christian healers are more powerful, a village *kiyai* who reports spirits crying when they realize they will have to leave their homes as he begins to clear land for his Islamic school, and endless others.)

Finally, Yani's stories of wandering bring to mind not simply clinical examples of psychosis-related confusion but also tales in the classic Javanese Hindu literature—in the *Ramayana* and many other collections—of the heroes who go off wandering *(ngelelona)* in the forest and meet up with demonic ogres. The heroes confront the evil forces, enter into battle, and return transformed, bearing enhanced power and status.

Conveying the texture of this lifeworld is essential to understanding the subjectivity of those suffering mental illness in Java. This lifeworld is constituted as fields of force, which impinge on and threaten persons, especially the vulnerable. Persons are understood and experienced as more or less powerful, more or less vulnerable, and nearly all Javanese engage in practices to enhance their inner power and protect themselves from those who would harm them.[8] The terrors of psychosis are thus terrors specific to this lifeworld.

A more psychological story, rooted in Javanese cultural psychology, could also be told. Yani suffered the loss of her father at age six and grew up in an intense and conflicted relationship with her mother and grandmother. She seems quite sensitive to losses. For example, she uses the word *kagol*, which translates literally as "frustrated" but suggests the kind of feeling a child has when he or she does not receive something longed for and expected, to describe her feelings of loss when her relationship with the young man she hoped to marry was cut off. Her stories of her relationships with men since that time are colored by the fact that she has been ill, but they reveal ambivalence about how close to get to men, a longing for a relationship but a fear of relationships as dangerous. And ultimately, a man she once thought was a friend, who later appeared threateningly in her bedroom in Jakarta, she now suspects of causing her most recent illnesses by doing black magic against her.

These retellings assume a cultural and psychological subject, a person whose experience has depth and coherence lent by life history and culture and psychic structures. But biological versions of the retelling of this story also exist that are quite different from the cultural phenomenology I have briefly outlined. One of these retellings belongs to a conversation between medical anthropology or cultural psychiatry and more conventional biological psychiatry. The larger project in which we are involved is investigating the symptoms and course of the psychoses, exploring the adequacy of current diagnostic criteria (in manuals such as the *International Classification of Diseases* [ICD-10] and the American Psychiatric Association's DSM-IV) and the role of social factors in influencing the course and prognosis of psychotic illness. The details of this work—involving debates about the nature of brief psychotic disorders, particularly those with historical labels like *boufée délirante*, and the inadequacy of the Kraepelinian under-standing of schizophrenia as embedded in degeneracy, or the optimistic claims of the World Health Organization's International Pilot Study of Schizophrenia that prognosis for schizophrenia is far better in "developing" countries than in "developed" countries—is beyond the scope of this paper.[9] We can note, however, that such projects are framed in reaction to claims, implicit or explicit in much biological psychiatry, that the psychiatric sub-ject is essentially a biological subject and that illness experience is ulti-mately understandable only by knowledge of the neurobiological substrate, particularly in cases of severe mental illnesses such as schizophrenia.

For Indonesian psychiatrists, these assumptions are not philosophical but quite practical. The critical issue for psychiatrists who treat patients like Yani is the psychosis—indicated by hallucinations and grossly disorganized behavior. And whatever the cause of psychoses, they suggest to psychia-trists the need for organic treatments. Given the historical influences of Dutch neuropsychiatry in Indonesia, the primacy of hospital-based services, and worldwide trends in biological psychiatry, responses are almost always to prescribe neuroleptic medications, often (in Yogya, at least) in combina-tion with electroconvulsive therapies. Thus, we cannot be surprised that Yani was treated as she was.

But this observation leads immediately to consideration of psychiatry's transnational project of "biologization" and "medicalization"—and in In-donesia, to stories of the pharmaceutical industry and psychiatric education. For example, I [BG] jotted the following note to myself when I attended the session "Treatment Resistant Schizophrenia" at the Indonesian Psychiatric Association Congress in 1996 in Surabaya:

> No one is talking about the real world of psychiatric practice. This is a globalized language of neurotransmitters and drugs—and the implica-tions are extremely important. Yesterday [in a session entitled "Schizo-phrenia: Toward the 21st Century," sponsored by Jannssen Pharmaceu-tica, distributors of Risperdal], we heard about the benefits of risperidone used at low levels (2–4 mg/day) and the terrible dangers of clozapine, especially of sudden withdrawal from clozapine treatment. Today [in "Treatment Resistant Schizophrenia," sponsored by Novartis, distributors of Clozaril], only benefits of clozapine, and its usefulness for most patients, is discussed, arguing that risperidone produces EPS [extra-pyramidal symptoms]. . . . next panel, another drug, another set of claims.

After the panel, I asked a psychiatrist attending the session about these contradictory claims. "Oh," he said, "it isn't important. None of us here use either of these drugs. They are too expensive." (By 2003, however, both drugs were in much wider use.)

Although the sponsorship of academic sessions by pharmaceutical firms—a widespread practice in much of the world—may or may not succeed in selling new drugs for schizophrenia, it is part of a much larger project of transnational psychiatry. Massive technologies are employed in the search for biological essences of mental illness—seeking syntagmatic chains linking the genome to expression to protein synthesis to neurotransmission to neuroendocrines to madness. This truth quest belongs to a massive industry of knowledge production—but also one that seeks to further the production, marketing, and consumption of pharmaceutical agents. Settings such as Indonesia are peripheral sites—sites of incomplete but active penetration—for the marketing of drugs, teaching of diagnostic and therapeutic practices, and development of mental health institutions. Meetings such as the Indonesian Psychiatric Asssociation congress belong to this expanding "regime of truth." They produce fantasies even in the absence of real objects, and for the psychiatrists, they facilitate an experience of the scientific, a sense of belonging to the cosmopolitan world of medical psychiatry, even for a moment, and an opportunity to imagine a future. Such events are elementary sites of the production of modern biopractices of psychiatry.

Of course, a counternarrative—or perhaps a more dominant narrative—situates psychiatry amid an emergent modernity, which is experienced both as a gap between the present and the ideal and as a nostalgic loss of the essentially Javanese. Psychiatry as practiced by most Indonesian physicians is confounded by a lack of resources; it is experienced as a deeply inadequate medical practice, bedeviled by incompetence and limited by shortages of practitioners, new medications, laboratory facilities, and educated patients. Many Indonesian psychiatrists feel as if they are practicing in psychiatry's past, relying on drugs and procedures from the 1960s rather than those on psychiatry's cutting edge—prescribing haloparidol rather than the new antipsychotics discussed at the congress. This gap, produced by a progressive modernity, lends a sense of tragedy, a sense of tragic inability to help those in desperate need, simply because resources are lacking—a sense that we often share. It also produces feelings of inadequacy and shame among many physicians. Little wonder that participation in a scientific congress is a ready relief from the daily world of practice.

The other face of modernity is nostalgia—a nostalgia for the Javanese or Indonesian world that is giving way to industrialization and progressive rationalization and disenchantment. Some psychiatrists are deeply invested in an older form of enchanted healing, reporting that they can sense when an illness is biological and when it is caused by a spiritual force. Some of them even practice as healers outside their medical clinics. Others point to the breakdown of Indonesian values, particularly among the youth, as a source of rising social problems and increased psychopathology, evincing nostalgia for the cultural past.

Thus psychiatry's "biosociality," its reading of mental illnesses as biological and as calling for a set of medical responses, belongs to an expanding regime of biotechnical truths and pharmaceutical markets. But it also belongs to an emerging world of increasingly effective medications, to a cosmopolitan world of progressive medicine, and to one of Indonesia's primary modernity projects. In a low-income society like Indonesia, participating in this world, but doing so with deeply inadequate resources, creates for thoughtful practitioners a sense of inadequacy associated with postcolonial modernity. Medicine's making of the psychiatric subject into a biological or biosocial subject is thus a complex project, only partially achieved, and Yani's story belongs to this narrative as well.

MADNESS AND MAD VIOLENCE
IN PSYCHIATRIC AND POLITICAL DISCOURSE

We could reasonably stop at this point—to attempt to draw some conclusions from Yani's case study and the analyses we have outlined. However, at the risk of providing an incoherent narrative, we turn briefly to another set of stories about madness and violence, a network of stories that surround, undergird, and frame the more clinical discourses we have been describing. We do so in part to raise broader questions about the relation between notions of subjectivity in cultural phenomenology and in critical theory.

As we were carrying out our interviews with Yani and others who suffered mental illnesses, we were unable to ignore the political campaign that was under way. In April and May 1997, *konvois* of youth on motorcycles or in trucks and automobiles, elaborately decorated in party colors and carrying banners, took over the urban streets throughout Indonesia, as part of the *pemilu* process, the final election of Suharto's New Order. Although little real expression of opposition was allowed, the *konvois* of *kampung* youth represented a real form of protest and class resistance, and they occasionally turned violent. News reports of the campaign and of the rioting in several cities earlier in the year characterized the election as the most violent in Indonesian history.

Near the end of the campaign, an American reporter, a Fulbright scholar, was invited to Yogyakarta's Institute for Journalism to talk about news reporting in Indonesia. At the end of the talk, the journalists asked for my observations. I [BG] observed simply that I was surprised by the near-exclusive focus on campaign violence in the papers: I was surprised not that the violence was reported but that little was reported about the issues the candidates discussed and every event seemed to be judged solely on where it lay along a continuum from order to disorder. The reporters asked whether I thought this emphasis was a "cultural" matter. I replied that it might be, but that it also had a "hegemonic" element, a quality of naturalizing order and treating nearly all political action as disorder and thus disruptive of social and political order and potentially anarchic.

As I thought later about these comments, I began to reflect on the effects of characterizing political violence as a form of "madness"—and seeing its function as a means of pathologizing political protest. A tragedy involving a mentally ill man focused our attention on one aspect of this language.

We found a Javanese friend, a woman from a poor village outside Yogya who worked on the university staff, in tears one afternoon. The story was not yet clear, but a man from her village had gone mad, had been attacked by a group of village men who attempted to subdue him, and had been killed. The police had taken members of her family for questioning. Over the next several days, the story began to emerge, as she and others in our neighborhood traveled back and forth to the village some two hours outside of Yogya. The man who had been killed was a man we had seen and caught on video several months earlier when we had visited an annual *slametan* in our friend's village. He had inserted himself into the dances of the day in a way we later learned had been inappropriate. The whole village knew he had been mentally ill, though he was relatively well on that day.

The story emerged that he had been periodically mad since several years before, when he sold his house and land to the government as a site for a television relay station. As workers began preparing for the station, tearing his house down, he had begun to go crazy. People speculated about the cause. Perhaps the stress of selling his land and seeing his house torn down had been too much and he had become crazy. Perhaps the spirit of the land had been angered and had possessed him. Or perhaps the forty-five million rupiah he had received from selling his land had attracted jealousy and made him a target of black magic. Whatever the reason, this vigorous man in his fifties had begun, for the first time in his life, to suffer bouts of madness. He would become violent, threaten other villagers, chop down their trees and agricultural plants, and resist their efforts to stop him. His family had sent him to a mental hospital for treatment several times. Each time he would return, suffer relapses, and become violent again. Villagers were fed up; his family seemed helpless to control him, and the police had stopped responding to their complaints.

And then on a day in July he had become violent again, attacking a villager's crop with his scythe. When the owner tried to stop him, the old man threatened to hit him. The owner called a friend, but the two friends were unable to stop him. The two ran for help, found a group of forty village men working on a voluntary work project, repairing a road. The workers came running to stop him. When he threatened them, they picked up a stick and began beating him. When the incident was over, the old man was dead.

We were, of course, caught up in the affair, helping support our friends whose family members were being held for questioning. My attention was also drawn to the wording of the reports in the local newspapers. One report included the sentence, "At the culmination or peak of his emotional condition, Pawiro Rejo *ngamuk*—'ran *amuk*'—and threatened those who tried to approach him." (*"Dalam keadaan emosinya memuncak itu Pawiro Rejo ngamuk dan mengancam penduduk yang berusaha mendekat."*) Each report used the Javanese verbal form *ngamuk* or the Indonesian form *mengamuk*.

These terms, more commonly in the noun form *amuk* (or "amok"), are well-known to cultural psychiatrists (and have, of course, entered common parlance). *Amuk* is a classic in the literature on "culture-bound syndromes," denoting an individual—often from Malay culture—who suddenly goes berserk, becomes wild and dangerous, attacking others, until he is subdued or killed by those he is threatening. The psychiatric literature treats *amuk* as individual pathology, not as a form of mob violence by a group: the madness of the old man, not of the group who killed him. From this perspective, the case of this villager was interesting because it was an example of a much more chronic or persistent mental illness than this literature usually describes, for which the term *amuk* nonetheless was used.

However, when the case occurred, it also drew my attention to the use of the term *mengamuk* in the newspaper stories about campaign violence and riots that had been occurring earlier in 1997. *"Kenapa Massa Gampang Mengamuk?"* ("Why do the masses so easily run *amuk?*") reads the cover of a special issue of *Gatra* (May 31, 1997) devoted entirely to this topic. *"Massa Mengamuk di Pekalongan"*—"The Masses Run Amuk in Pekalongan"—reads a headline in *Kompas*. And so it goes: observers frame analyses of the violence as the masses running *amuk*, as *kerusuhan* or riots; as *anarkis* or *kebrutalan*, anarchy or brutality, of the masses. This conjunction set me to thinking and suggested the value of reading these two literatures—the historical writing on *amuk* (usually of individuals) and the news reports and analyses of mass political violence—against one another.

Here, we can provide only a few examples of the insights such a reading might yield. *Amuk*, in its restricted meaning as a psychiatric syndrome, was defined in 1951 by P. M. Yap as "an acute outburst of unrestrained violence, associated with homicidal attacks preceded by a period of brooding and ending with exhaustion and amnesia" (41). This view of *amuk* as a culture-bound syndrome was based on reports by travelers, colonial administrators, judges, and colonial psychiatrists, as well as more recent anthropologists and psychologists, dating in particular from the nineteenth century. Case reports—from Malaysia, Singapore, Java, and Sumatra—of persons who "ran *amuk*"—becoming depressed, brooding, and suddenly going on a homicidal rampage, which ended only when they were subdued or killed—have long fascinated observers and led to speculations that ranged from accounts of Malay culture and personality to studies of the effects of infectious disease or the use of opium and attempts to understand these cases as a form of mental illness or a distinctive form of suicide. For example, D. J. Galloway, a psychiatrist who read a paper at the Fifth Congress of the Far Eastern Association of Tropical Medicine in Singapore in 1923, distinguished cases representing known forms of insanity from those he termed "true *amuks*." These cases included individuals who were publicly shamed or humiliated, and after brooding, retaliated, until the incidents escalated to rampages that ended in the *pengamuks'* deaths.

"The impress of the primitive mind lies brood over the whole series of events; the inflated self-esteem, the proportionate resentment at the wounding of it, the tendency of the resentment to pass uninhibited into action against the offender, the necessity of re-establishing his prestige . . . , the appeal to arms . . . thus explains the action" (Galloway 1923: 168, quoted in Winzeler 1990: 109).

Or, in another example, Van Loon, a Dutch psychiatrist in charge of the Batavia Hospital, writing in the *British Journal of Medical Psychology* in 1928, combined a cultural and developmental view: "In the *malu* feeling (unbearable shame and embarrassment, especially when made ridiculous in public), in *mata gelap* (blind rage) and in the *binggung* reaction (losing one's head), etc., the Malay shows the same characteristic weakness, a *lack of resistance against sudden emotion*" (267).

Following this reading into the writing on political violence, we can find many similarities in the grammar of the discourse. *Amuk*, in colonial psychiatry, is pathological, impulsive or instinctual, and developmentally primitive, a form of wild, uncontrolled—and exotic—antisocial behavior. And psychiatrists tended to see it as an overwhelming emotional response to frustration and humiliation. Analysis of the sources of mass violence in the news at that time often drew on a similar logic. Mass violence indexes a lack of social, political, and intellectual development, suggesting that the masses are not yet ready for democracy. It represents pathological, impulsive reactions to emotionally frustrating social conditions. The presence of the term *amuk* or *mengamuk* in the popular press reports on the campaign-related violence thus served to naturalize a reading of mass violence as pathology.

But although sufficient examples exist to support our hypothesis about the function of the term *amuk* in such reports, we would be wrong to end the analysis at this point. Our reading of the historical works shows that colonial writing about *amuk* is a complex resource for interpreting views of political violence in Indonesia.

The term *amuk* in the colonial literature does not begin as a psychiatric term. It apparently entered European languages in the mid-sixteenth century, referring to "groups of exceptionally courageous men who had taken a vow to sacrifice themselves in battle against an enemy" (Murphy 1973:34). In the nineteenth century, use of the term *amuk* to refer to heroic acts of bravery on the part of warriors, *kris* (sacred dagger) in hand, was known but was said to be largely archaic; the term largely came to mean individual pathological violence. However, the attempt to define the "true *amuk*," such as that by Galloway, was not simply an attempt to distinguish heroic acts from pathology. It was rooted in a set of debates in colonial Malaysia and the Dutch Indies. First, it had roots in legal debates about whether a person who committed murder while "running *amuk*" should be held legally responsible for his acts. In a widely quoted ruling in 1846, Judge William Norris ruled that a man in Penang who was captured after killing eight persons was guilty, despite the defense that he had been grieving for his child, who had died recently, had killed indiscriminately, and claimed he had no memory of killing anyone. Judge Norris found him guilty, sentenced him to hanging and then ordered that his body be "cut into pieces and cast into the sea or into a ditch or scattered upon the ground" (Norris 1849:462–63; quoted in Winzeler 1990:101–102). This incident contrasted with the case of a Bugis sailor on board a ship in Singapore who had "suddenly picked up a dagger and slain a relative who was visiting him, then rushed on deck and began attacking and killing everyone in his vicinity," who was acquitted by reason of insanity (Earl 1837:377–78, quoted in

Winzeler 1990:101). Psychiatrists' efforts to describe *amuk* as a culture-bound psychiatric disorder thus aimed less to portray the exotic than to defend the *pengamuk* on grounds of madness.

This debate opened onto a more general question of how the *pengamuk*, the person who runs *amuk*, should be punished and onto associated speculation on the cause of the phenomenon. As early as the end of the eighteenth century, William Marsden, in *The History of Sumatra*, rejected the notion that opium caused the behavior, reporting that it was more likely caused by colonialists' mistreatment of slaves or servants (1811:279–80). He reported a case he had personally observed of a slave, who, "being treated by his mistress with extreme severity, for a trifling offence, vowed he would have revenge if she attempted to strike him again; and ran down the steps of the house, with a knife in each hand." When she cried out *"mengamok!"* the civil guard came and fired upon him. Marsden reports that in Batavia, where such persons "are broken on the wheel, with every aggravation of punishment that the most rigorous justice can inflict, the mucks happen in great frequency," proving the inefficacy of harsh punishment, in contrast to the "influence that mild government has upon the manners of people." Thus, Marsden contrasted detrimental responses to Dutch rule with the beneficial effects of English rule.

We can see, then, that though people speculated about the causes of *amuk*—whether it reflected Malay or Javanese character, stemmed from Islamic fanaticism, reflected a constitution weakened by disease or opium use, or represented a culturally distinctive form of suicide—these debates took place within larger discussions of native violence in response to colonial rule. As with the colonial responses to cases of worker violence on the plantations of Sumatra, which Ann Stoler (1985, 1992) analyzes, discussions of *amuk* reflected concerns about order and disorder under the colonial regime and included clear examples of resistance to harsh rule; some even saw the use of amuk as an "instrument of social protest by individuals against rulers who abused their power" (Carr 1985:202).

And so it is in the contemporary reflections on violence by Indonesian intellectuals. Writings on outbreaks of violence during the run-up to the 1997 election often describe the violence as a result of frustration *(frustrasi)*, "displaced aggression," "emotional illiteracy," "jealousy" associated with the gap between rich and poor, or the suggestibility of the masses. However, in an often remarkably open critique of the growing gap between rich and poor, the corruption of the elite, and the arrogance of government officials, writers in the Indonesian press of the mid-1990s, still under the censorship of the Suharto regime, carved out a space for social reflection and social critique. The special issue of *Gatra*, entitled *"Kenapa Massa Gampang Mengamuk,"* describes a poll they had undertaken of 787 university students and recent graduates; 57 percent of respondents agreed with the statement "riots can't be avoided in the process of democratization"; 49 percent agreed that "riots are important to stimulate change"; 93 percent agreed that violence reflects the growing social and economic gap; and 82 percent agreed that violence reflects the ineffectiveness of political channels.

Intellectuals were often asked to write commentaries on the sources of violence. Arief Budiman criticized the lack of a "culture of tolerance" and the increasing place of violence in the language of politics, particularly in response to the growing role of the military in politics. "People have learned that if you want to play politics," he wrote (*Jakarta Post*, May 15, 1997), "you have to use power and violence, not intellectual arguments." Berhanuddin, writing in *Kompas* (January 9, 1997), analyzed the growing differentiation of Indonesian society as a result of modernization, the loss of social and moral coherence, and the replacement of religious leaders with a background in the *pesantren* and a closeness to the people by *kiyai* who are part of the alienated political elite. Violence thus triggered a critical reading of Indonesian society and politics and became a site of at least covert contestation, and commentaries both ascribed rational motives to the actors and read violence as mad, mob action.

These reflections on the hegemonic uses of images of madness in public writings on violence and disorder share a markedly different understanding of the subject than writing within a cultural phenomenology of madness. The subject is decentered, the implied object of hegemonic discursive practices and of an oppressive social regime, as well as seen as the source of resistance to them. Subjection and resistance replace meaning and experience as central issues for analysis.

MAD VIOLENCE AND NINJA KILLERS

If the figure of madness—of the masses "running *amuk*" during the 1997 election campaign—moved from pathologizing political violence to opening a space for political critique, the figure of madness appeared in a more sinister way during the ethnic, religious, and political violence that erupted in various parts of Indonesia following the collapse of the economy and the fall of the Suharto regime. Many feared that the society was literally going mad and that ethnic/religious fighting in West Kalimantan and in previously peaceful Ambon was a sign of a general societal breakdown. In this setting, the mysterious and the mad emerged not as figures of language but as key actors. One final story illustrates this view: a journalist's report of *ninja* killers in East Java.[10]

> As the sun sets in the towns and villages of East Java, men hurry home quicker than usual from their evening prayers. In some areas, a bell tolls to empty the streets of women and children. Windows will be shut and the doors bolted till the next morning. In the darkness, wary men with swords or sickles patrol deserted roads. They are searching for the black-clad, masked men whom residents believe are responsible for the killings of over 150 locals. Since early August, the night here has been haunted by mysterious murders. The government cannot solve the slayings or put a stop to them. They have sent shivers of fear throughout the nation.

The article reports that Banuywangi in East Java has a history of lynchings of suspected sorcerers—*dukun santet,* or practitioners of black magic.

> But this season of bloodshed has been highly unusual, not only in the number of victims but in the apparently well-organized nature of the killings. Eyewitnesses report bands of well-trained and equipped killers, whom they call "ninjas." They commit the murders themselves or incite neighbors to violence. Noha, 59, was one victim. About a month before his murder, his widow, Sa'adah, recalls, rumors of his dark powers started swirling. One evening as he was watching TV, the electricity went out. Noha then heard a harsh knock on the door. He answered it— and quickly succumbed to blows and knife thrusts from masked marauders. They left in a minivan and cars. "They never said a word," says Sa'adah. "They did their job very quickly." Noha's throat was cut, his head nearly separated from his body.

News reported mobs gathering to kill suspected *dukun santhet* or ninjas, though who was killing whom remained vague. Leaders of the political opposition at that time—Amien Rais and Abdurrahman Wahid (by 2000, head of the Parliament and president of the Republic, respectively)—speculated that the killings were part of a paramilitary conspiracy of followers of former president Suharto who were seeking to provoke chaos and a return to military rule. A November 7, 1998, story in the *Sydney Morning*

Herald by Louise Williams ("Indonesia's Black Death") reported additional details.

> The Commission for Victims of Violence, a human rights organization, found signs of organization: the assassins were outsiders who came with maps and appeared to be trained. So terrified were the people of the rural areas that vigilante squads were formed and the lynchings began. But locals say the victims of the mobs are not real "ninjas," but lunatics mysteriously dumped on the streets. The man whose head was paraded through Malang was a drifter suffering from mental illness.

And so the circle closes. Madness is no longer a figure of speech but is embodied in lunatics, picked up and delivered mysteriously to rural areas, where they are suspected of being *dukun santhet* or ninjas—a term taken from Japanese movies, popularized on Indonesian television—and killed in a continued circle of violence.

CONCLUDING THOUGHTS

We began with a rather conventional (American) anthropological account of psychosis in Java, juxtaposing a cultural and psychological subject with the biological subject of contemporary psychiatry. However, we proceeded to suggest a more critical or liberatory psychology, which asks how hegemonic images of order and disorder become embedded in ordinary subjectivity—a view of the subject as both subjected and resisting those constituting linguistic practices. And we concluded with images of the subject facing the terrors of social breakdown, an image that reveals the dependency of the subject upon ordered, hierarchical social relationships.

We have tried to join these perspectives using a sleight of hand—suggesting that they are a set of stories, narratives that presume one another, perhaps like A. L. Becker's analysis of the classic Old Javanese collection of tales, the *Tantri Kamandaka*. Becker (1989: 290) writes, "Most of the stories have stories within them, and stories within the stories, each framing the other, so that the texture is thick and full of nice resonances, like *gamelan* music." But in the end, the theories we have produced are hardly *gamelan* music. They are not coherent in this way simply because the theories are disjunct rather than coherent or neatly complementary. In a special issue of the journal *Representations* dedicated to reflections on Geertz's concepts of culture, Sherry Ortner (1997) suggests that Geertz resurrected the centrality of meaning in an era of mechanistic functionalist analyses but did so by placing issues of power, domination, and social asymmetry on the side of mechanistic theorizing. She argues that the "Foucauldian/Saidian" shift in American anthropology, influenced by postcolonial and poststructural theorizing, has displaced meaning in the Geertzian sense, and along with it, the "subject" of interpretive anthropology. If Francois Dosse (in *L'empire du sens*, 1995) is correct, at the same moment many French culture theorists may be passing in the opposite direction, moving from poststructuralism to meaning-centered theories. Whatever valiant attempts Ortner and others may make to reconcile these competing views of subjectivity, we are far from a unified theory.

At the same time, our sleight of hand fails because of the nature of the object of study: madness and social violence. In his classic book *The Sense of the Ending*, Frank Kermode (1966: 129) quotes Ortega: "Reality has such a violent temper that it does not tolerate the ideal even when reality itself is idealized." He argues that the simplicity inherent in narrative order is always, at least partly, an illusion, reminding the reader of the hero of Robert Musil's *The Man Without Qualities*, who "lost this elementary narrative element" (127). We have tried here to "thicken the texture" and "highlight the resonances," in Becker's terms, rather than to create a single account. We have sought to acknowledge the resistances in the material, as well as our own inadequacies to theorize coherently. We are left with "plateaus," using the image of Deleuze and Guattari.

And so we close with a final reflection, based on Deleuze and Guattari on secrecy (1987: 286–90). For a long time, Indonesians have accepted a certain amnesia—not only of the primal events of 1965–66 but also of the corruption symptomatic of the ruling order—voicing the unspoken, unspeakable, and the repressed in a language of hierarchy and respect, discipline, order, and consensus. A terror, a modest anxiety seeps into awareness that there might be a secret, but the guardians of this secret, the censors, ensure that the secret not be noticed, acknowledged, made real. But the terror appears as a moment of irrationality, for the dislodging of the father looses all forms of terrifying and destructive forces: the ninja killers and their killers, the masses and the protectors of primal order, the vengeance turned on the foreign, the overlords, the Christian, the Muslim. And the mad. The mad emerge as ninjas, the spiritual forms who can appear and disappear, draw cosmic energy, destroy, and protect themselves. And the mad are exploited as ninjas as well—sacrificed, dropped into the path of the pack, severed heads lifted on bamboos. And this madness is supplemented by the paranoid, the hint of the completely ordered, the hidden hand. These are the phenomena we struggle to theorize.

NOTES

A version of this paper was published in French as "Le sujet de la maladie mentale: psychose, folie furieuse et subjectivité en Indonésie," in *La pathologie mentale en mutation: Psychiatrie et société*, ed. Alain Ehrenberg and Anne M. Lovell (Paris: Edition Odile Jacob, 2001), 163–95.

1. The first-person pronoun in this paper refers to the first author, Byron Good, who is responsible for the written text of this chapter. Subandi is a collaborator in this project, playing a major role in conducting interviews and participating in analysis of the data. Mary-Jo DelVecchio Good is a collaborator in the research in Indonesia, having a particular interest in representations of violence. This project was supported by Senior Fulbright Lectureships in 1996 and a National Science Foundation grant in 1997–98.

2. Judith Butler's book, *The Psychic Life of Power*, explores this understanding of subjectivity. She poses the problem as follows:

> We are used to thinking of power as what presses on the subject from the outside, . . . But if, following Foucault, we understand power as forming the subject as well, as providing the very condition of its existence and the trajectory of its desire, then power is not simply what we oppose but also, in a strong sense, what we depend on for our existence and what we harbor and preserve in the beings that we are. (Butler 1997: 2)

3. The name "Yani" is, of course, a pseudonym. Particular identifying features have been changed or omitted to hide her identity. A more detailed version of this case appears in Good and Subandi (2004).

4. For all interviews, Subandi, Byron Good, and Yani and/or her mother were present. Subandi led the interviews. When the interviews were in Indonesian, Good participated in the interviews. When the conversations shifted into Javanese, Subandi took over, translating occasionally for Good.

5. This story emerged in an interview we carried out jointly with Dr. Robert Barrett, who was visiting Yogyakarta and accompanied us on a visit to Yani and her mother.

6. The classic text outlining three streams of Javanese religion is Geertz's *The Religion of Java* (1960). Geertz distinguishes among *priyayi*, classic Javanese practices of spirituality associated with the Javanese courts; *abangan*, village practices associated with exchange and spirit offerings; and *santri*, modernist Islam associated with a class of merchants. Woodward (1989) places Islam at the center of Javanese religious life, and Hefner and Horvatich (1997) have collected essays on contemporary Islam in Indonesia. Bowen (1993), although he focuses on a Muslim society in Sumatra, provides the best ethnographic description of Islamic religious practice in Indonesia. See also Subandi (1993) for an analysis of one Sufi group.

7. In commenting on a draft of this paper, John Bowen pointed out the importance of the trope of purity not only in Yani's talk and experience but in social and political movements in Indonesia. The theme of "providing greater purity in

crowded and disorienting circumstances" is one that Islamic movements have played to the hilt, he notes. We appreciate his reflections.

8. See Anderson (1972) for the classic analysis of "power" in Javanese culture. Geertz (1960; in his chapters on priyayi spiritual practices), Errington (1984), and Keeler (1987) provide classic statements about the role of concepts of power in Javanese personhood. See Mulder (1978) and Stange (1984) on spiritual practices in recent Javanese *kebatinan* movements. See Good and Subandi (2004) for a fuller analysis of Yani's case in these terms.

9. Good and Subandi (2004) explore these issues in depth. The work referred to here addresses classic cross-cultural psychiatry questions about the influence of culture on the course and outcome of psychotic disorders (see Hopper 1991 and Good 1997 for reviews). It also examines nosological questions about the so-called atypical psychoses, which differ from both schizophrenia and manic-depressive disorder and have gone by such names as *boufée délirante*, cycloid psychoses, reactive psychoses, and acute and transient psychoses (Leonhard 1961; Manschreck and Petri 1978; Menuck, Legault, Schmidt, and Remington 1989; Pichot 1986). Classic work by Susser and his colleagues suggests that "nonaffective acute remitting psychosis" is a distinctive disorder and is far more common in "developing" countries than in North America and Europe (Susser, Finnerty, and Sohler 1996; Susser et al. 1995a, 1995b).

10. This from an *Asiaweek* version of the story, November 6, 1998, entitled "Death's Long Shadow."

REFERENCES

Anderson, Benedict R. 1972. "The Idea of Power in Javanese Culture." In *Culture and Politics in Indonesia*, ed. Claire Holt (Ithaca, NY: Cornell University Press), 1–69.
Becker, A. L. 1989. "Aridharma: Framing an Old Javanese Tale." In *Writing on the Tongue*. Michigan Papers on South and Southeast Asia.
Bowen, John R. 1993. *Muslims through Discourse: Religion and Ritual in Gayo Society*. Princeton, NJ: Princeton University Press.
Butler, Judith. 1997. *The Psychic Life of Power: Theories in Subjection*. Stanford, CA: Stanford University Press.
Carr, John E. 1985. "Ethno-Behaviorism and the Culture-Bound Syndromes: The Case of *Amok*." In *The Culture-Bound Syndromes: Folk Illnesses of Psychiatric and Anthropological Interest*, ed. Ronald C. Simons and Charles C. Hughes (Dordrecht: D. Reidel Publishing Co.).
Deleuze, Gilles, and Felix Guattari. 1987. *A Thousand Plateaus: Capitalism and Schizophrenia*. Minneapolis: University of Minnesota Press.
Dosse, Francois. 1999. *Empire of Meaning: The Humanization of the Social Sciences*. Minneapolis: University of Minnesota Press.
Earl, G. 1837 [1981]. *The Eastern Seas*. London: W. H. Allen and Co., reprinted Kuala Lampur: Oxford University Press.
Errington, J. Joseph. 1984. "Self and Self-Conduct among the Javanese *Priyayi* Elite." *American Ethnologist* 11: 275–90.
Galloway, D. J. 1923. "On Amok." *Transactions of the Fifth Congress of the Far-Eastern Association of Tropical Medicine*, Singapore, 162–71.

Geertz, Clifford. 1960. *The Religion of Java*. New York: Free Press.

Good, Byron. 1994. *Medicine, Rationality and Experience: An Anthropological Perspective*. Cambridge: Cambridge University Press.

———. 1997. "Studying Mental Illness in Context: Local, Global, or Universal?" *Ethos* 25: 230–48.

Good, Byron, and Subandi. 2004. "Experiences of Psychosis in Javanese Culture: Reflections on a Case of Acute, Recurrent Psychosis in Contemporary Yogyakarta, Indonesia." In *Culture and Schizophrenia*, ed. Janis Jenkins and Robert Barrett (New York: Russell Sage Foundation; Cambridge: Cambridge University Press), 167–95.

Hefner, Robert, and Patricia Horvatich. 1997. *Islam in an Era of Nation-States*. Honolulu: University of Hawaii Press.

Hopper, Kim. 1991. "Some Old Questions for the New Cross-Cultural Psychiatry." *Medical Anthropology Quarterly* 5: 299–330.

Keeler, Ward. 1987. *Javanese Shadow Plays, Javanese Selves*. Princeton, NJ: Princeton University Press.

Kermode, Frank. 1967. *The Sense of an Ending. Studies in the Theory of Fiction*. London: Oxford University Press.

Leonhard, K. 1961. "Cycloid Psychoses—Endogenous Psychoses which Are Neither Schizophrenic nor Manic-Depressive." *Journal of Mental Science* 197: 632–48.

Manschreck, Theo C., and Michelle Petri. 1978. "The Atypical Psychoses." *Culture, Medicine and Psychiatry* 2: 233–68.

Marsden, William. 1811. *The History of Sumatra*. London: Longman, Hurst, Rees, Orme, and Brown.

Menuck, Morton, S. Legault, P. Schmidt, and G. Remington. 1989. "The Nosologic Status of the Remitting Atypical Psychoses." *Comprehensive Psychiatry* 30: 53–73.

Mulder, Niels. 1978. *Mysticism and Everyday Life in Contemporary Java: Cultural Persistence and Change*. Singapore: Singapore University Press.

Murphy, H. B. M. 1973. "History and the Evolution of Syndromes: The Striking Case of Latah and Amok." In *Psychopathology: Contributions from the Social, Behavioral and Biological Sciences*, ed. Muriel Hammer, Kurt Salzinger, and Samuel Sutton (New York: Wiley and Sons).

Norris, W. 1849. "Malay Amoks Referred to Mahomedanism." *Journal of the Indian Archipelago and Eastern Asia* 3: 462–63.

Ortner, Sherry. 1997. "Thick Resistance: Death and the Cultural Construction of Agency in Himalayan Mountaineering." *Representations* 59.

Pichot, P. 1986. "The Concept of 'Bouffee delirante' with Special Reference to the Scandinavian Concept of Reactive Psychosis." *Psychopathology* 19: 35–43.

Ricoeur, Paul. 1981. *Hermeneutics and the Human Sciences*. Ed. John B. Thompson. Cambridge: Cambridge University Press.

Stange, Paul. 1984. "The Logic of *Rasa* in Java." *Indonesia* 38: 113–34.

Steedly, Mary. 1999. The Spirit of the Story. Inaugural Lecture, Dept. of Anthropology, Harvard University, May 11 (manuscript).

Stoler, Ann Laura. 1985. "Perceptions of Protest: Defining the Dangerous in Colonial Sumatra." *American Ethnologist* 12: 642–58.

———. 1992. " 'In Cold Blood' ": Hierarchies of Credibility and the Politics of Colonial Narratives." *Representations* 37: 151–89.

Subandi. 1993. A Psychological Study of Religious Transformation among Moslems

Who Practice *Dzikir Tawakkal*. M.A. Thesis, School of Social Sciences, Queensland University of Technology, Brisbane, Australia.

Susser, Ezra, Shmuel Fennig, Lina Jandorf, Xavier Amador, and Evelyn Bromet. 1995a. "Epidemiology, Diagnosis, and Course of Brief Psychoses." *American Journal of Psychiatry* 152: 1743–48.

Susser, Ezra, Molly T. Finnerty, and Nancy Sohler. 1996. "Acute Psychoses: A Proposed Diagnosis for ICD-11 and DSM-V." *Psychiatric Quarterly* 67: 165–76.

Susser, Ezra, Vijoy K. Varma, Savita Malhotra, Sarah Conover, and Xavier F. Amador. 1995b. "Delineation of Acute and Transient Psychotic Disorders in a Developing Country Setting." *British Journal of Psychiatry* 167: 216–19.

Van Loon, F. G. H. 1928. "Protopathic-Instinctive Phenomena in Normal and Pathological Malay Life." *British Journal of Psychology* 8: 264–76.

Winzeler, Robert. 1990. "Amok: Historical, Psychological, and Cultural Perspectives." In *Emotions of Culture: A Malay Perspective*, ed. Wazir Jahan Karim (Singapore: Oxford University Press).

Woodward, Mark R. 1989. *Islam in Java: Normative Piety and Mysticism in the Sultanate of Yogyakarta*. Tucson: University of Arizona Press.

Yap, P. M. 1951. "Mental Diseases Peculiar to Certain Cultures." *Journal of Mental Science* 97: 313–27.

9 The "Other" of Culture in Psychosis

The Ex-Centricity of the Subject

ELLEN CORIN

When asked to speak about their first psychotic experience, patients interviewed in Québec could hardly find the words to describe what had happened to them: "I was confused, I was losing memory, I was like in confusion." "I was completely down, I couldn't speak anymore, I was out of touch with reality, I was totally confused." "Ah! It's more than just sickness of the soul; it's a huge rent. It's . . . yes . . . it's hell" (Rodriguez, Corin, and Guay 2000). Narratives collected in southern India illustrate the depth of the alteration of patients' experiences: "I was frightened and did not understand what was happening . . . the confusion only increased and I couldn't control it . . . the fear, only this fear, not anxiety, only some kind of fear." "First, you are positive, you are confident, then suddenly some doubt comes into your mind, you can't do this, you can't do that, what is this, you get all confused, you are not sure about something and suddenly you feel you are not capable of doing things, feel afraid . . . so all these negative thoughts were coming and I had been imagining all sorts of things and I was not like a normal person." ". . . a kind of fear within myself, a kind of fear which could not be disclosed to others . . . a kind of fear without understanding" (Corin, Thara, and Padmavati, in press).

Whatever the context, narratives suggest that something rises from within the subject's experience and destabilizes it, shaking the lived world at its roots. Patients speak of a loss of vital energy that extends to the core of their being and attacks physiological functions; they say that this initial experience invades their entire lives, blocks their capacity to express emotions or relate to people, and leads progressively to isolation; it is a kind of "staggering" that undermines their ability to act and to relate to the world. Paradoxically, this "immobility" can manifest itself as jerky, excessive movement, as if the person were running on the spot. Wolfgang Blankenburg, a psychiatrist from the European philosophical phenomenological tradition, argues that the core alteration of the experience in schizophrenia is the "loss of the natural evidence," which he describes as a preintentional way of situating oneself in a world where things may be taken for granted—the world of the "common sense."[1]

In parallel, cross-cultural studies on schizophrenia and its evolution also strongly suggest that the course and outcome of psychotic problems differ from society to society, even if we still poorly understand the influential pathways of social and cultural factors. Researchers have attempted to identify the variables or conditions of context likely to play a role. However, most studies remain framed within an epidemiological paradigm that disregards the experiential dimension of schizophrenia for patients and family members. Knowledge produced in this way remains distant from the living reality of psychosis sufferers. One could hypothesize that this distance strongly limits the heuristic value of the research for understanding the stakes in the differential outcome of schizophrenia.

MEANING AS THE VANISHING POINT OF KNOWLEDGE

At the experiential level, no meaning or explanation appears able to account for how people experience schizophrenia. Although people diagnosed with schizophrenia often say little in response to explicit questions about causes or explanations, their narratives seem permeated by the question of meaning; they are filled with shifting, tentative hypotheses that attempt to anchor their experience in the events, incidents, or other aspects of their life paths (Corin 1998). The search for explanations appears to be absorbed into a larger quest for meaning—but no answers are available to stabilize this quest or bring it to a conclusion. Therefore, available cultural etiologies, so cherished by anthropologists, are unlikely to offer the best avenue for approaching the influence of culture on schizophrenia.

From a psychiatric standpoint, psychosis has been the locus of convergence for a number of studies that try to pin down its elusiveness and identify a concrete substratum: neurotransmitters, genes, and neuropsychological cognitive dysfunction, for example. These approaches served to expand and complete the movement toward the objectification of symptoms and the medicalization of psychiatric disorders that animated the redaction of the third edition of the *Diagnostic and Statistical Manual of Mental Disorders (DSM-III)* and its subsequent versions (Klerman 1984). They reinforce a position of exteriority toward symptoms and their significance: patients and their families are asked to adopt an analogous, external stance through sessions of psychoeducation in which they are informed of the "real" biomedical nature of the patient's problems and difficulties and are instructed how to deal with them.

One should not underestimate the fact that these approaches—which are ultimately reductionist—may provide reassuring landmarks for people overburdened by the feelings of emotional vertigo that often accompany psychosis. Family members, in particular, tend to welcome the idea that psychosis is like any other organic chronic disease and is rooted in neurotransmitters or genetic defects.[2] Some patients also appear to be reassured when a diagnosis puts a name to—and to a certain extent explains—their experiences.[3] Other patients recall that psychiatric diagnosis led some people to acknowledge the "reality" of their pain or suffering. However, patients may also receive the diagnosis and its implications as a verdict that threatens to engulf their lives (Rodriguez, Corin, and Guay 2000).

In itself, the logic of diagnosis supposes that within a range of symptoms and manifestations, one isolates and retains those that correspond to a preexisting grid and to a specific *savoir faire*—that of the clinician (Lanteri-Laura 1986). Diagnostic approaches are therefore deliberately partial and functional. However, the clinician faces the ever-present risk of losing sight of the bias inherent to diagnosis and of confusing the perception of a phenomenon with the reality of that phenomenon. Indeed, contemporary psychiatry and current approaches to psychosis may have a kind of hubris, believing that the perspective offered by empirical science could lead to a complete understanding of the phenomenon and to its mastery in a near future.

However, interaction with psychosis sufferers also shows that a large part of the psychotic experience remains at the fringe of biomedical discourse—a discourse that has great difficulty in completely explaining this experience. The narratives of psychosis sufferers suggest that scientific knowledge and rehabilitative practices cover the "public face" of mental health problems and difficulties—those that may be described objectively, glossed over, and integrated into a circuit of social exchange and communication. However, the fear and stigma remain intact and continue to be attached to psychosis in both Western and other social and cultural worlds. More profoundly, empirical science disregards the fact that for people suffering from it, psychosis remains a boundless experience—one that is beyond anything they can name and explain. Thus, one can easily get the impression that the gulf is widening between the uncertain, elusive psychotic experience and scientific knowledge, which is increasingly objective and objectifying and is rich with the flavor of certainty and the promise of control.

At stake is the relative weighting of the "natural" (read biological) and the "social" orders as criteria of truth and legitimacy in today's Western society. The anthropologist Françoise Héritier noted the preeminence given to biological truth in delineating descent in contemporary Western societies. Commenting on this notion, Serge Leclaire (1998), a French psychoanalyst, emphasized that every order consists of a symbolic organization—a system of laws. The opposition between "natural" and "social" orders should therefore be understood as a struggle between two kinds of symbolic orders. On the one hand, the "natural" order, which commands research and scientific production, seeks to discover and account for the order of things; it leads to a praxis or a use. Thus, technology and related practices engender an effect of truth in the strongest sense of the term; however, this truth deals with things, discarding the "truth" of the subject. On the other hand, the "social" order, which regulates all aspects of social praxis, considers the determining importance of the symbolic order in regulating human relationships. Its main substance is symbolic, and its reality depends uniquely on the representations a society builds. However, the fading power and credibility of major belief systems in contemporary societies render increasingly problematic the prospect of founding and legitimizing a symbolic order. When people face the ethical question "How do I live with the 'other'?" they tend to turn toward an order that has demonstrated coherence and effectiveness. But, then, they recast this basic human question as, "How do I live a healthy life?"

Schizophrenia resists incorporation into a social order, however. One might say that psychosis has an ambiguous relationship to culture. On one hand, it is a foreign body within a culture, arousing a variety of reactions such as fear, rejection, and fascination, which act like antibodies to encapsulate and eliminate noxious foreign elements. On the other hand, research suggests that psychosis is also permeated and modified by culture, and anthropology must do justice to this double dimension of psychosis. I suggest that rather than impose a cultural grid on the psychotic experience, we begin by listening to what those who are most closely concerned with psychosis have to say about psychotic alteration and by identifying the cultural signifiers that the patients and family members use.

This chapter aims to re-place within the social order a register of experience that contemporary ethos increasingly defines within a biomedical paradigm. It attempts to question psychosis from the perspective of the people who experience it; to explore how they trace pathways within society and culture and borrow cultural signifiers to articulate experience that essentially eludes communication and mastery. In the case of psychosis, such an exploration points up the limits of words and narratives and maximizes the unavoidable gap between "reality," experience, and its expression (Bruner 1986). One must pay attention to what emerges at the border of language and meaning and listen to silences and to the expression of things beyond language, those things expressed in an embodied way. David B. Morris speaks of the irreducible "otherness" of suffering. "The quality of such suffering remains as blank to thought as the void opened up by a scream" (Morris 1997: 27). Correlatively, one must examine the way in which patients borrow, displace, and transform cultural signifiers in their attempts to name and tame an elusive sense of themselves and the world. One must also examine whether cultures (and the approaches to culture) make allowances for experiences that escape coherence and meaning—the "Other" of culture.

We must approach the cultural articulation of psychosis indirectly, through successive approximations that do not obscure the uncanny and strange dimensions of the psychotic experience. In my reflections here, I draw on a personal journey that introduced me to various figures of "Otherness," first through studies of spirit-possession rituals and later through my psychoanalytical training and clinical practice. My exploration will proceed, therefore, under the aegis of Otherness, a floating signifier that tries to approach both culture and experience from their peripheries—from elements that escape full understanding and mastery. One could expect that societies differ in their sensitivity to Otherness and in the degree to which they elaborate it through representations and symbols.

To approach the place of Otherness in psychosis and its cultural elaboration, I will successively relate three scenes. By starting with a study in Montréal with people diagnosed as schizophrenic (Corin 1990, 1998), I can explore why I coined the expression "positive withdrawal" to attempt to convey how some patients elaborate their inner experience and form singular ways of living in the world. I suggest that, at least in part, positive withdrawal is a way to tame, contain, and articulate a sense of Otherness in psychosis. Next, I turn to research I conducted in India in collaboration with Indian colleagues to explore how culture helps shape psychotic experience, for both patients and family members. I argue that Indian society proposes and culturally elaborates stances of retreat and withdrawal that may act as "myth models" for articulating limit-experiences.[4] Cultural signifiers allow subjects to name and work out ideas of Otherness in socially (if ambiguously) valued ways. Finally, I briefly relate some reflections emerging from my clinical practice about specific manifestations of unbinding processes, through which a feeling of strangeness arises in the clinical session.

In order to discuss the heuristic value of this type of dynamic for understanding the contribution of culture to "the work of Otherness" in psychosis, I will build on the idea of the "work of the negative" both in the formation of representations and symbols and in certain forms of severe mental health problems. The "work of the negative" is a powerful heuristic device for approaching the complex interplay of the "binding" and "unbinding" processes in psychic life. The viewpoints in this chapter aim to contribute to current anthropological thinking about the treatment of Otherness.

These reflections grow out of the impressions that patients' narratives—their words and expressions—made on me. To transmit the texture of these narratives, I place a great deal of emphasis on narrative excerpts. I decided to juxtapose sentences from different patients (as indicated by the quotation marks) rather than simply to present case histories for three main reasons: a reluctance to appropriate patients' narratives and read them from a "privileged" point of view, and a corresponding desire to protect the privacy of their world; an interest in elements that escape "narrativity" and in a theory of interpretation and language influenced by my psychoanalytical work; and a desire to bring out the resonance, convergence, and dissonance of different narratives that point toward the "work of culture" in psychosis. My particular way of analyzing patient narratives also makes reference to a theory of psychosis influenced by the European phenomenological school that reads symptoms as "phenomena," expressing an alteration of the basic coordinates of the patient's "being-in-the-world."[5]

BEING ALONE IN A CULTURE:
SURVIVING PSYCHOSIS IN MONTRÉAL

The need to pay attention to what springs up at the borders of language, coherence, and meaning struck me in a study in Montréal in which I collaborated with Gilles Lauzon. The study looked at people who had been diagnosed as schizophrenic for five to fourteen years and who were differentiated according to their rate of hospitalization over the previous four years. We collected data through a set of open-ended questions that guided, but did not unduly constrain, the interview process. We met with most patients three or four times, either at their homes, in a restaurant, or in another place of their choosing. The analysis combined quantitative data that identified recurrent formal patterns of the patients' relationship to the world in a variety of areas and qualitative data that unlocked the subjective world of these people.

In its beginnings, the research focused on the meaning of "social integration" for people with schizophrenia. We approached the world as experienced by schizophrenic patients from a socio-anthropological standpoint, inspired by research on social networks and social roles.[6] With the study participants, we explored their subjective positions and practices in various categories of social relationships and social roles. We also examined their perceptions of their place in family dynamics and their circulation in time and space in their everyday lives. We asked patients to describe and characterize themselves and reconstructed the subjective network of meanings arising from the terms they used to describe themselves. We hypothesized that the capacity of patients to remain in the community without being rehospitalized depended on their ability to maintain, restore, or create significant social links and to resume a valued place within society. We suspected that social forces acting toward stigmatization and rejection were the main factors that pushed patients back into hospital.[7]

Our methodology was to code narrative data on behaviors, perceptions, and expectations. We qualified the analytical categories as a function of the orientation to society that they indicated: toward (+), away from (−), neutral (o). We grouped patients according to their rehospitalization history over the previous four years and did intergroup comparisons.[8] This analysis revealed that patients who were not rehospitalized differed from frequently rehospitalized patients in a few statistically significant features. In each group, we identified all other variables statistically correlated with these discriminant characteristics and examined how these correlated variables themselves associated with other variables. This procedure allowed us to locate discriminant features within larger associative chains and laid out the significant texture of indices within each group of patients.[9] Next, we returned to the individual data and examined the specific patterns that were indicative of individual patients' orientations to society (toward, away from, neutral); we explored the data's significance within individual life paths.[10] Finally, we did a qualitative analysis of the narratives to further clarify the meaning of the structural orientation abstracted through quantitative techniques and to examine how the narratives translated to everyday life. In keeping with Paul Ricoeur's approach to hermeneutics, we paid particular attention to recurrences, opposites, and combinations that provided access to the text structure and ways of "holding the text together" (Ricoeur 1986).

Statistical analyses revealed two main findings. First, the "objective" situation of the two groups of patients (frequently hospitalized and non-rehospitalized) did not greatly differ, with both groups having a relative paucity of interpersonal relationships with family members and the social network and an overall marginality in the area of normative social roles. Patients of both groups expressed a feeling of being outside society. If a difference existed, it was in the apparent disadvantage of non-rehospitalized patients, who said they received less social support and had fewer social contacts in their daily lives.

Second, though both groups expressed a sense of being outside society, the two groups embedded this feeling in contrasting frameworks of meaning. Hospitalized patients often perceived their marginality negatively—as being imposed on them by others. They expressed a feeling of exclusion and resentment mixed with a desire for more social contacts and social support, and they had a desire to perform and succeed in normal social roles. One could say that they continued to adhere to the values and ideals promoted by society as a whole but, at the same time, felt somehow rejected by society. In contrast, the non-rehospitalized patients tended to accept or even view positively this sense of being outside, an attitude that surfaced through perceptions, expectations, and values. This attitude pervaded most areas of their lives and tended to be described as an inner attitude rather than one that was imposed by external conditions. These people were well aware of their eccentricity with respect to normal societal rules and behaviors. A few of them claimed the right to contest the dominant order and to follow more singular pathways through life. Others attempted to temporize and gain time, postponing their full social reintegration indefinitely. One might say that the sort of recovery that allowed patients to remain out of hospital required them to distance themselves from the social world.

Thus, a patient's marginality in society appears to exist in two different semantic frameworks, depending on the group. We qualified this attitude of "distance" among non-rehospitalized patients as "positive withdrawal." Individual narratives confirmed and further pinpointed the importance of this stance for these people. Personal stories revealed the variety of ways that individuals could express this position. But at the same time, narratives showed that this dominant position was consistently compensated for by more tenuous ways of relating to the social and cultural milieu, along lines that differed from person to person. The expression "positive withdrawal" tries to express the copresence and relative weight of the "retreat" and "advance" that characterized non-rehospitalized patients' lived worlds.

These analyses led us to revise and shift our original position and our approach to the lived world of people with schizophrenia. In fact, we discovered that for patients, the ability to construct a personal protected space at the margins of the ordinary "normal" world was of central importance. Specifically, we modified the relative weight we gave, on one hand, to the external, social dimension of patients' situations within society, and on the other, to the internal, personal facets of their attitudes toward society. In parallel, our interest in the role of the central societal codes that govern participation in a shared milieu was replaced by an attention to solitary, singular ways of relating to the world. Cultural signifiers did not so much appear to impose their coherence on patients' discourse as to be borrowed, appropriated, and transformed in patients' attempts to tame their unusual experience.

In retrospect, the term "positive withdrawal" served to shift our attention from well-defined, substantial roles, norms, and values to ways of relating and gaining perspective—from content to style. It led us to take note of words and behaviors that patients mentioned only in passing but that added flesh and meaning to our understanding of the patients' worlds and their relationships to culture. I focus here on two main aspects of the personal and cultural development of positive withdrawal. The first gives it a pragmatic, embodied dimension; the second suggests its semantic depth.

SPATIOTEMPORAL EMBODIMENT OF
POSITIVE WITHDRAWAL

Reanalyzing patients' ethnographic reconstructions of their previous few days highlighted the importance of "empty time"—a time that, to the patient, appeared to expand indefinitely and give rise to feelings of vacuity and boredom. Patients described the hours spent resting on their beds, taking a bath, listening to the radio while walking back and forth in the apartment, smoking cigarettes, taking naps, not knowing what to do: "I go to bed early; nobody is there to keep me up." "I'm terribly bored; it's always the same thing." "I find my lifestyle 'flat.' I pace back and forth. I drink water, coffee. I listen to the radio and watch TV at the same time. I don't often go out. I drink juice, coffee. I smoke cigarettes. I look out the window. I feed the birds." Such feelings of emptiness are like icons of patients' eccentric situations vis-à-vis mainstream life.

However, most non-rehospitalized patients reshaped the void created by this empty time as a particular way of inhabiting the world and of moving about within the city. I have described elsewhere the important, almost ritualized function that sitting or walking in public places has for non-rehospitalized patients (Corin 1990): places where they can mix with people without interacting with them and places that allow them to insert their solitude into a social space—to be "with," but at a distance. The perceived anonymity of public places may differ from person to person. Some patients go regularly to the same restaurant or shop at certain hours of the day. Some integrate several places into their well-ordered daily circuit. Bartenders or restaurant personnel may provide an imaginary anchorage to patients' wanderings and even to their emotional lives. Some patients strike up superficial conversations with these people that are, at the same time, significant for them. Other patients prefer more anonymous settings such as shopping centers or busy downtown streets. Rhythm and routine appear to contribute to the significance of these activities. I have suggested that going to these kinds of places can add structure to patients' spatial and temporal worlds. It also offers a way for them to relate to others without having to commit themselves in personal interactions. One might say that this behavior provides patients with a kind of "social skin" that both contains and protects an inner space and mediates their relationships with the outside world.[11] We could see it as a concrete metaphor of a relationship with the world that weaves a dominant "distancing" stance with interrelated threads. Connecting with the world paradoxically appears to be secondary to the ability to remain separated from it—to stay at a distance and introduce a kind of "blank space" into the social fabric.

THE SIGNIFICANT TEXTURE OF WITHDRAWING

The non-rehospitalized patients in Montréal tended to perceive their relative isolation as a fact of life and, in some way, to accept it: "I don't go out much. I'd rather stay at home. I let time pass." "I have to stay quiet . . . just keep things the same . . . make it stay the way it is." "I was always in bars. I was looking for a companion. I developed a way of living that made me a loner." They may see solitude as an expression of the difficulty of finding a place in the outside world: "The most difficult thing is to reintegrate into the public, to mesh with people." More often, however, patients appeared to actively build such places at the margins of society. This activity took on a precious character that required care and attention. One patient, who created his own church and nominated himself its pope, said, "After dinner, I spent three hours cleaning pictures and mirrors. I was sleepless, I sat in my sanctuary for five hours. " On another day, he said, "I spent an hour painting my statues gold; then, I sat in the sanctuary, admiring them for another hour." Another patient said, "When I want peace, I go to my room and lay on my bed. I meditate. I listen to music. I listen to the vibration of the silence of the house. It is like a presence . . . I want calm, to be with myself and to evolve inwardly. I have a radio in my room, but I prefer silence."

In some cases, patients saw such an attitude of withdrawal as a way to help construct and protect frontiers and boundaries; to defend an inner space from the intrusion of the others as well as to limit their own tendency to become "diffuse" and lose themselves in the world. In this sense, withdrawal seems to provide a kind of psychic skin that parallels the social skin: "I've never confided in anybody. You have to keep a secret side. You can't tell everything. You don't have to tell everything." "I concentrate too much on the outside and not enough on my inner self and on being at peace with myself . . . I would like to find an inner peace that would give me confidence." "Everyone wants to talk to me. But I'm afraid to let myself go, to give too much advice. Sometimes, I forget myself, it's not good." The importance of keeping a secret space can lead people to react strongly against particular forms of therapy: "There were group meetings. I hate that. I asked them if we could keep our matters personal and private."

For others, solitude appeared to be a kind of textured environment in which they could rest and progress at their own pace: "I'm used to living alone. It's because I rest. I completely empty my body." "It's slow, I go quietly. I want to master things. I am used to living alone. It is better for reflecting, for praying." Another patient explained the complex balance he keeps between a very busy life and the perceived necessity of protecting a sense of solitude: "I am solitary. I don't communicate a lot. My time is well filled. I don't suffer from my solitude. I'm like that. I accept being alone. Once I was married, I was very active . . . but I need to withdraw and be alone occasionally." This patient, like others saw the ability to introduce a distance between oneself and the world as an important accomplishment associated with positive personal evolution: "Before I was ill, my life was very stressful. I never stopped. When I went to the hospital, I settled things with myself. . . . It has now been ten years since I left the rat race. Maybe if I went back today, it would be less bad. But I don't think I'll start working again. I accept myself as being calm and quiet." Building a space of solitude was sometimes seen as a first step toward a more complete social reintegration that would occur at some indefinite point in the future: "First, I have to rebuild calm within myself, through a reference to God. Then, I'll be able to have a more active life again and be more socially active." "I have projects, but they're for later. My head is not strong enough now. I am afraid I'll go into depression." However, the line between positive withdrawal and falling into a void is very thin: "I am calm, but sometimes, it's a bad thing because I become too calm and I don't have feelings anymore. It seems like depression. Good and bad. At times, I'm too calm. People tell me that . . . in normal life, you need a certain dose of stress."

Overall, one gets the impression that the ability to build a private, protected space creates the conditions from which patients can face the world again without the threat of being overwhelmed by it or becoming sick again. However, in our modern world, withdrawing from the social world remains culturally abnormal and tends to be negatively perceived. Most patients expressed a degree of awareness of the cultural marginality of their position. One person commented, "If I lived in the country, nobody would care about my solitude. But in the city, you can't afford to live like a hermit. I know that I'm more solitary than normal people and that it's a negative thing for other people."

We were struck by how creatively patients used and appropriated elements of the cultural framework to develop their position of distance. These elements sometimes became central organizers of their lives. For example, a man born in a remote area of Québec who moved to Montréal when in his twenties remembered how terrified he was when he arrived in the city; he was afraid of everything. He is now divorced and rarely sees his children: "I don't want to take up too much room. When someone offers you something, it is better not to take too much." Two sets of activities gave structure to his life. Every day, he went to two restaurants and interacted with waitresses, who occupied an important place in his imaginary world; and one of his preferred activities was to read an etymological dictionary while lying in his bed. He commented, "Without the dictionary, I would feel lonely." He explained that his father also used to read etymological dictionaries. For this person, the quest for the origins of words perhaps parallels and reiterates his own quest for an anchorage, especially because this quest also situates him within a paternal line of transmission.

Another young man, who lived in a very dark basement with the curtains closed all day, said he had always been marginalized. When he was young, his schoolmates called him a "fifi" (homosexual). He described having a bad relationship with his parents, whom he qualified as intrusive, miserly, and quick-tempered. He described himself as shy, and his network of contacts at the time appeared to be very limited: "Because people are nasty. People look at you, they stare at you . . . because they can tell I'm not somebody who works steady . . . the way you walk . . . you cross the street and people look at you." He said he often went to shopping centers. But the most striking and organizing feature of his life was listening to shortwave radio broadcasts and trying to identify the transmitters. He collected information on radio transmitters and wrote it in a meticulously kept register. He attempted to pick up signals and recalled listening to signals from South America, the United States, and Canada. For him, the radio was a technical device that let him actively insert himself into a virtual network of people, participate vicariously in a communications circuit, and expand the frontiers of his social world beyond geographical borders while remaining in his own space. This case and the other cases I've described here stand out as examples of the individual ways in which patients insert themselves into a culture and use its signifiers to transform a position of distance from the social world.

POLYSEMY OF RELIGIOUS REFERENCES IN PATIENTS' LIVES

At a symbolic level, the non-rehospitalized patients manifested a particular sensitivity to broadly defined religious signifiers, which seemed to help them transcend and relativize the pressures of everyday life. In a few cases, religious groups provided patients with a social web that allowed them to feel accepted and cared for—not by individuals but by a collective (which might be less threatening and can mediate interpersonal contacts). However, these patients also appear to appropriate the signifiers of the group in a personal way. In fact, only one person explicitly mentioned participation in a charismatic religious group that offered him a positive, supportive network as well as benchmarks of morality: "The Christians took me out of my misery and did the most good things in my life. I like honest people—people who say the truth, who have good intentions in their relationships. Now, I want to surround myself with such people . . . Where there are Christians and evangelization, there are good messages. We have respect for each other." He also commented, "I'm not very disciplined. I sometimes fall asleep reading the Bible. But once you understand, a great relief overcomes you. It is as though God's light is within you." This person added that group members gave him feedback that helped him tune his interpersonal contacts and not be too intrusive toward others. Another person, affiliated with a meditation group run by a guru in Florida, observed: "God's name is revealed to me. You have to repeat it, concentrate on it. Meditation is an individual thing. You have to find satisfaction in yourself . . . When you meditate, you think only a very little and you feel well. You don't think all sorts of foolish things. You concentrate on your inner being." His links to the group's milieu remained primarily virtual; the sense of group membership was relatively independent of actual involvement in the group's activities: "There are meetings in people's houses in the evening, but I don't go; there are too many people." However, for years, this person had had daily communication with a member of the group whom he called his "contact." The link was essentially maintained by telephone, and he did not know where his "contact" lived.

For other patients, God remained a floating signifier detached from any religion—a word that designated a virtual presence: "I am not a practicing religious person, I do not believe in religious practice. I often think about God. I don't ask him anything. I don't pray to him." "I'm not religious, but I'm not an atheist either. Religion . . . I could talk about it for hours. It's deep. But there are too many contradictions in the Bible . . . I pray. My prayer is for my life, and not to hurt my fellow men." In these cases, the term *spirituality* would be a better descriptor than *religion*.

The psychiatric literature reports the importance of religious themes among schizophrenic patients' delusional ideas. It limits itself, however, to compiling and classifying these themes as objective symptomatic data. Patients' narratives indicate that the content of these ideas is less important than the ways they are used and integrated within patients' life trajectories. Several patients associated the beginning of their problems with a religious experience of some sort or with a change in their religious attitude—as if religious referents pointed toward the virtual and enigmatic meaning of experiences that seemed to escape order and significance: "The church fucked me up . . . I was at St. Anthony's feast . . . I wasn't right . . . something wasn't working. My brain went wild. I fell on the ground outside the church. See, God wants me to do something, but I don't know what it is . . . When he tells me what it is, I'll do it." "I believe in God because one day, light had a different quality. I woke up and I believed in God."

In fact, several of the non-rehospitalized patients clearly distinguished this mode of relating to God, which they deemed excessive, from a more internal and peaceful relationship with God. They associated these contrasting religious attitudes with different periods of their lives. The first mode was associated with periods of crisis, during which religious elements seemed to be part of and to reinforce a general delirious quality to their lives: "If I don't take my medication, I turn into a religious fanatic and I fall into crisis . . . If I get hospitalized, it's because I wanted to understand a mystery and I went too far. I tried to visualize God, but it's not possible . . . When I went to the hospital, I found that many patients had a link with God. But they were mixing up God with their own beings." "When I was having schizophrenic and paranoid episodes, I spoke all the time of religion, spiritualism, and reincarnation. I felt a force directing me. I wasn't the one driving the car. There were spiritual forces . . . I felt the forces of the Evil. I became totally possessed. It was unbearable. I began to have fears about reincarnation, spiritualism, and evil forces . . . " In these cases, finding empathic listeners can be of great help: "I have let off steam in religion. Twice, I confided in Jesuits. They allowed me to confide in them. I opened myself to them. They reassured me. It worked."

The second attitude, which associates God with an inner peace and quietness, is consonant with a stance of positive withdrawal, which it helps construct and reinforce. Borrowing religious symbols and representations thus remains a creative enterprise, different from an orthodox allegiance to a specific organized belief system. Some people insist on the importance of picking and choosing the portions of a doctrine that they feel are most appropriate for them. They may also mix religious references with representations from different systems like Hindu philosophy or science fiction, or they may interpolate personal beliefs and images. This "collage," in which patients borrow and appropriate elements of beliefs and symbols, gives them a sense of freedom in this matter.

This distinction between two relationships with religious signifiers and their association with different moments in the evolution of patients' problems confirms that the availability of cultural symbols does not by itself impose order or meaning onto psychotic experience.[12] We need a more complex model of the interaction between personal experience and culture.

Patients' narratives also emphasize the need to consider culture as heterogeneous and polysemic and to examine the ways in which psychotic people navigate within culture's complex webs of signifiers. Religious references by the non-rehospitalized patients tended to be associated with marginal religious groups rather than with well-established, mainstream religions. One might wonder whether such appropriations of religious signifiers stem from (or are allowed by) the general noncentral position of religious symbols and beliefs in today's Western world. However, work in other cultural contexts indicates that people suffering from psychosis do not usually integrate easily into well-established, culturally central religious rituals and ceremonies.[13] Psychotic patients appropriate and modify collective representations, beliefs, and symbols in an idiosyncratic manner. This method of resorting to cultural signifiers echoes, on a semantic plane, the process of subjunctivization that Byron Good describes in his analysis of the narratives of epileptics in Turkey (Good 1994). I have described elsewhere how such a process also permeates self-perceptions and narratives of identity (Corin 1998). More generally, one might speculate that the healing potential of religious signifiers for psychosis sufferers assumes the possibility of desemanticizing signifiers to some degree; of unbinding or loosening their connection with a shared collective frame of reference and using these signifiers in a flexible, idiosyncratic way.

By framing and naming experiences as on the edges of normal life, broadly defined religious signifiers offer patients a way to explore and tame the feeling of strangeness that eludes description by any diagnostic system and that is radically alien to the societal order. At the beginning of this chapter, I showed how current psychiatric paradigms aim to absorb psychotic disorders into an all-encompassing scientific vision of the world. Western cultures do not offer many ways of addressing the alienating aspects of psychotic experience or of integrating it within self-experience. The fading symbolic power of cultural idioms that have traditionally dealt with the spiritual dimension of life could augment the sense of dismissal by society that people experience when they enter psychosis. I suggest that for psychosis sufferers, resorting to broadly defined religious signifiers is a way of introducing a sense of Otherness and strangeness into language and culture. It is a way to bind Otherness at a symbolic level without resolving or suppressing its alien character. However, this process remains a solitary one, and patients are largely left to themselves to invent ways of naming and elaborating spaces of positive withdrawal using available social and cultural signifiers. I hypothesize that the North American context encourages a bias toward the withdrawal component of positive withdrawal.

AT THE MARGINS OF CULTURE:
ARTICULATING PSYCHOTIC EXPERIENCE IN SOUTH INDIA

The research in Montréal focused on the relational and social dimension of schizophrenic patients' lives, even if we were led to progressively give more emphasis to patients' inner worlds. Because the research studied people who had been diagnosed for a number of years, their modes of being and their strategies were the products of a history that we knew little about. We decided to create an open-ended interview grid that focused more directly on the psychotic patient's inner world and to explore the alteration and reconstruction of this world over time. We focused on the onset of patients' problems and difficulties in order to better examine how people try to articulate an "unanchored," or drifting, experience and to pinpoint the cultural and social influences that shape their lived world. This research strategy plunged us into troubled lifetimes during which the articulation of a drifting experience remains unstable and fragile. It did not allow us to verify the long-term protective value of particular ways of relating to the social and cultural world. Nevertheless, it allowed us to observe these processes "in the making" and to examine their conditions of possibility. It settled the ground for further longitudinal research to deepen the understanding of the work of culture in psychosis, in an Indian setting.

To explore the influence of cultural context on how patients frame the experience of psychosis, we conducted an exploratory study in Chennai,

South India, focusing on people diagnosed with schizophrenia during the previous few years. This study is part of a larger collaboration with Dr. Rangaswami Thara, director of the Schizophrenia Research Foundation (SCARF) and Dr. Ramachandran Padmavati.[14] Both Thara and Padmavati are clinicians at SCARF. In addition to providing services for psychotic patients and playing a leadership role in public awareness campaigns, SCARF is participating in a series of national and international studies, including follow-up studies to investigate the claim of the International Pilot Study of Schizophrenia that the course and outcome of schizophrenia are more benign in that part of the world than in Western societies. I was particularly interested in the place and significance of withdrawal in the phenomenology and experience of schizophrenia in India and by the role of the cultural and social environment in shaping it. In India, more particularly, the question was whether the philosophy and religious system of Hinduism provide "myth models" of withdrawal for people going through "limit-experiences" such as psychosis. A complementary study we are currently undertaking in close collaboration with Professor Ravi Kapur of the National Institute of Advanced Studies in Bangalore will provide a broader interpretive context for understanding the narratives of psychotic patients and their families. This ongoing research aims to explore the lived universe of *sadhus*—people who have taken an ascetic spiritual path and have formally withdrawn from social obligations. It is exploring how individuals appropriate and transform aspects of the Hindu religious system and its significance in the context of their life trajectories.

We conducted our exploratory study with ten male patients diagnosed with schizophrenia in the previous few years as per *DSM-IV* criteria, along with one family member of each patient. All patients were in their twenties. Interviews took place in a clinical setting with practitioners familiar to the patients.

Interviewers collected narratives using an open-ended grid, the Turning Point/Period Interview (TPI),[15] developed by our research group in Montréal. Open questions reconstruct the key actors' perceptions of a patient's transformation from the onset of symptoms, including the perceived turning points of this process, particularly prior to a patient's first hospitalization. For each period, we explored behaviors and feelings, interpretations, and strategies for coping and seeking help, and changes in social relationships and activities. Narrative analysis explored two complementary vantage points. The first, which we'll call the centripetal vantage point, considered what the narratives revealed about the emotional and cognitive qualities of the experience. The second, the centrifugal vantage point, considered how cultural signifiers in the narratives connected to broader aspects of the cultural framework. A draft version of the interview was tested with a few patients in Toronto and Montréal under the supervision of Dr. Alain Lesage. For the sake of comparison, I will mention here some findings of this Canadian pilot study.

A DRIFTING WORLD

The manner in which patients and families in India described the transformation of the lived world in early schizophrenia, along with its dramatic alteration, is discussed elsewhere (Corin, Thara, and Padmavati 2004). Most narratives evoked a kind of creeping fear, vague but persistent, or they crystallized around concerns about an external or internal threatening reality. This fear radiated in three primary directions, which, together, made it tangible and illustrated the encompassing character of the alteration that patients experienced: a sense of being in a hostile environment, where the looks of other people seem inquisitive, mocking, or accusatory and where other people seem to have an enigmatic knowledge of the patient; a sense of the porosity and fragility of personal barriers and boundaries, and the perceived invasion of one's mind by insistent voices and messages that can take over the patient's thoughts and behaviors; and a feeling of confusion that becomes uncontrollable and may occupy all of the patient's attention and block his or her ability to think. Confusion and fear may also blur linguistic boundaries and cloud the patient's sense of judgment about the world, destabilizing the fundamental benchmarks of existence.

Family members recalled a vague sense that something was wrong—the feeling that a difficult-to-identify change was occurring. The relatives repeatedly mentioned four areas of life: a particular way of speaking and a lack of respect or deference for family members, an alteration of eating habits or a refusal to share meals with other people, a change in sleeping and waking patterns, and a lack of personal cleanliness—a refusal to bathe regularly and take care of oneself. These behaviors, mentioned by relatives, are key to framing a shared relational world; such behaviors structure everyday life and define the human quality of existence. Changes in them are signals that provoke intense concern, worry, and anxiety among close relatives.

In the early stages of psychosis, the enigmatic and threatening character of the experience seems to dominate patients' lived world. At this point, patients are still under the direct influence of the destructive forces that have caused their worlds to fall apart; relationships with themselves and their environments are permeated by feelings of strangeness and uncertainty. This subjective stance shapes and colors the forms and significance of withdrawal as well as the role of religious signifiers.

FIGURES OF WITHDRAWAL IN EARLY PSYCHOSIS

The narratives of both patients and relatives illustrate the extent to which patients in India tended to withdraw from society and the extreme forms this withdrawal could take. At this early stage of psychosis, pulling away from social contacts rarely seemed motivated by a desire for more deeply personal experiences, as was the case among the non-rehospitalized patients in Montréal.[16] In some cases, withdrawal was the internal side of actual solitude, of an absence of friends: "I began smoking because I was lonely; I started to be alone; I had no friends. Everybody ran away. Nobody came to help me." "I don't have any friends, except for the ones at SCARF; I am like a lonely tree." Running away was also experienced as an order or a constraint: "Suddenly, it happened again. I had to run away. I wandered to different places."

Most commonly, however, social withdrawal was a reaction to a world perceived as hostile, or at least uncertain and potentially threatening: "I started feeling shy; I thought people were looking at me. I was more sensitive and became more and more reserved . . . In my school, they used to say I was going into a shell . . . I keep silent and don't talk to anyone." "I don't have any friends . . . I feel detached from my father, mother, sister." "Because from that time onwards, I had a kind of fear. Some customers took it the wrong way: OK, this fellow should die." The actual or perceived hostility of the world could actually overwhelm the patients' lived world and accentuate a radical distancing vis-à-vis the social environment: "Because everyone was ragging, I would sit on the college ground. They would ask me why. I would yell back at them, but I would stay like that . . . So, I imagined that I was shouting back at them in my mind . . . I would keep quiet, even if I couldn't tolerate it. I kept it within myself. I used to yell at them in my mind. I used to imagine that they were falling down at my feet, asking for forgiveness." "I was not able to look anyone in the face. Initially, it was as if people were laughing at me. Then if they spit, I would have a kind of fear within myself. I felt like everyone was against me. I started feeling like being alone, I wouldn't say anything, I wouldn't say anything at all, so I lost contact." Thus, in most cases, patients' narratives suggest that withdrawal is reactive and has a protective function.

This general tendency to withdraw from "reality" may surface in a variety of ways. At the physical level, it can manifest itself as a desire to sleep, thereby suspending all links with the outside world: "I sleep as long as possible. I won't think of anything." "When I go home, I go to sleep right away." "I get up in the morning, and immediately I want to go back to sleep. I was escaping from the situation." "Somewhere in the house, I would sleep—cover myself and sleep. I didn't like to go out and all that. I would sit with my head bent down." Sleeping allows patients to distance themselves and forget about their situations. This behavior may also be compounded by medication, which then only reinforces the patient's withdrawal: "I was sleeping when I was adjusting to the medicine. I lost control of what was happening around myself."

Patients' efforts to keep their experiences secret may be another form of withdrawal that manifests itself in their interpersonal contacts. The Canadian pilot study to test the Turning Point/Period Interview revealed the care patients took to conceal the transformation of their lived world: "I didn't speak of it to anyone, I kept it inside myself." "Nobody noticed . . . and it was important that it didn't surface . . . I was smiling but in my head, everything became too, too confused." "I didn't want anybody to know; it was private . . . I wanted to run away and hide . . . " Patients justified this attitude as a response to a feeling of fear, a certainty that nobody could help or the idea that no one could understand anyway: "I told myself, it would just stir up trouble." Protecting a secret inner space may also be a concrete attempt to help restore personal boundaries that psychosis renders extremely porous and fragile.

The importance of preserving such "secret areas" also emerged from the Indian narratives: "I did not tell it to anyone. I was hiding it from them . . . I was experiencing within myself." "I felt a kind of fear which couldn't be disclosed to others . . . I had a feeling that everyone was against me. I started to like being alone . . . I would say to myself: Don't talk."

However, feelings of shame appeared more consistently in the Indian patients' narratives: "I haven't told anyone that I have an illness, I feel bad disclosing it." "I was not doing that well in my studies . . . but I never told this at home." Particularly striking was the extent to which this reserve corresponded to a desire to preserve one's image within the family: "See, I'm running the family and how can I tell to someone? If I tell them, what will happen?" "I felt that if I told my mother, it would be shameful, I didn't speak to anyone . . . I told her no one would respect me at home if I told them my problems." At this level, concealing one's illness must be seen against the backdrop of the enormous feelings of sorrow and grief expressed by both patients and relatives about the patients' failures to live up to the expectations attached to their status and position within the family: "Everybody has a degree and people respect them. But I don't have anything. Work is the essence of man, I should have the capacity to earn." "I should work and earn some money and take care of my father and mother." "If we do our duty, nothing happens. Looking at your duty, you will live till you grew old; after that it will go." For patients, doing one's duty served as a differential marker between "before" and "now." The prevalence of this complaint in the narratives of both patients and relatives is in line with the Hindu notion of dharma, the moral order of the universe, and the necessity to act in conformity with the behaviors associated with one's position within kinship and caste groups and with one's age and gender.[17]

The concern with keeping things secret also points to the great stigma attached to mental health disorders in India, not just for patients but for their entire families. In fact, some relatives appeared to collude with patients to isolate them from the outside world: "Mother said, 'We can stay here. We can live our life here and we don't need to go out.'. . . My mother asked me not to leave the house." "Always, they watch me and observe me: 'Don't go out often.' I would say, 'It's boring to stay at home. Let me come and go as I please.' " However, patients tended to oppose these sorts of restrictions when coming from family members, even if they themselves tended to retreat from society.

Most families were deeply affected by patients' tendency to withdraw from the world, which goes contrary to normal family life. Sadness and sorrow were among the frequently expressed sentiments. Nonetheless, general reactions tended to reflect tolerance and empathy. Relatives explained that they tried not to confront the patient and attempted to accompany him throughout his illness: "We used to go according to his will: 'You can study when you get better, so, don't worry.' If we do not understand him, who else will?" "We have to adjust to the problems and help him. We also do not look at him as if he was some strange creature. If he does not do anything, if it is fine with him, it is OK. We don't want to trouble him to do something." "We never used to force him. We felt a bit distressed. We also felt sympathy for him: 'look what has happened to him.' " A smaller number of relatives also expressed resentment or more confused attitudes and expectations.

THE "WORK OF RELIGION" IN PSYCHOSIS

In his work in Sri Lanka, Gananath Obeyesekere was struck by the analogy between characteristics described as symptoms of depression in the West and as aspects of a valued vision of life in Buddhism. He called the "work of culture" the process whereby painful motives and emotions are trans-

formed into publicly accepted sets of meanings and symbols. He acknowledged briefly, however, that the notion is broader and could be expanded to
larger areas of existence (Obeyesekere 1985). Obeyesekere later (1990) corrected the implicit directionality of his first definition and coined an expression, the "work of culture" to describe "the process whereby symbolic
forms existing on the cultural level get created and recreated through the
mind of the people." In Obeyesekere's terminology, personal symbols play
a crucial role in this articulation: symbols have a large cultural loading and,
at the same time, are tuned in to personal experience, requiring a "double
hermeneutics." At the personal level, these symbols provide a basis for self-
reflection and offer grounds for elaborating the experience; at a cultural
level, they allow communication with others. Obeyesekere indicates that
personal symbols may also help define the idiosyncratic nature of the experience; in this case, rather than contributing to the cultural articulation of
the experience, their regressive dynamics emphasize its "dark side."

At this point, I would like to focus on the role of religious references in
shaping the experiences of patients and relatives, both because of their significance in the Montréal study and, more importantly, because of their significant presence in the Indian narratives. In the Canadian pilot study to test
the TPI, most patients recalled that the onset of their problems coincided
with a deep quest for the meaning of life—as if the turmoil they were experiencing was part of a more general shaking of the commonsense world
where things are taken for granted: "I didn't know why I was alive, I asked
myself all sorts of questions: Why am I here?" "I choose that moment for
engaging in a broad reflection about life, death, love, everything; I like realized the importance of life." "I thought it was the end of the world. It was
better. I was going to go and see God." Most patients reported immersing
themselves in religious books, particularly the Bible: "I began reading the
Bible and isolating myself. I would talk about God because I was reading the
Bible. I was everything in the Bible. I tried to be perfect so that people would
accept me." Another person mentioned the Tibetan Book of Life and Death.
Religious books, however, may be carried along with the delirious experience and add to the enigmatic quality of the world rather than "fix" it: "I
asked my voices what these red balls I saw wandering in the house were. I
opened the Bible. At that very page, I saw 'Ba,' a divinity to whom children
were sacrificed. I began reading the Bible but I began to mix everything up."

Indian narratives confirmed the importance of religious signifiers for
psychotic patients. References to religion and spirituality were in fact more
developed in the Indian study than in the Montréal and Canadian studies,
and their significance expanded more broadly, for both patients and rela-

tives. Religious references in the Indian patients' narratives took three main directions.

In the first direction, religion provides a virtual framework of meaning that patients can lay out and mobilize. It places their experience within a larger, more meaningful design that integrates various cultural representations and images. For example, one patient's attempt to understand the significance of his experience was like a personal version of Karma theory and the value of equilibrium in Hindu philosophy: "I realized that I'm suffering now to live better in the future . . . I have shown how badly a man can suffer. I have shown it to God. I have maintained a contact with God . . . Loss here and loss there, gain here and loss in the other world. So I should live well and show it to the world and in the other world also I should live well." Building more specifically on religious representations, another patient hypothesized: "I'm a devotee of Lord Shiva. They say that if you are a devotee of Shiva, then you will be a mental. So, I think I have Shiva *dosham*."[18]

At this level, patients' references to religious or philosophical signifiers often retain an aura of strangeness and are framed within an idiosyncratic discourse, giving the impression that they are absorbed in a drifting perception of themselves and of the world. Religious signifiers thus echo the enigmatic quality of the experience and correspond to an attempt to name and interpret it without reducing its mysterious flavor. One patient recalled a vision that preceded the onset of his problems: "I saw a man. He was very beautiful, very powerful. He looked like Moses. He was filled with orange light . . . walking with a bird in his hand and saying, 'Yes, Yes,' something like that. That time, some strong force attacked me. A white light was inside my throat . . . From then on, everything started decreasing." One could interpret this vision as providing a visual icon to a diffuse sense of otherness and translating it into a religious calling with a positive, if uncertain, value: "I thought, I am going to be some spiritual person, some saint or something like that." The vision recurred at different moments in his life, each time in a mode that resonated with his current condition: "Once again that light spread in my heart. Then again an orange light came in my head. But both were rejected. When the light comes, the body never accepts light actually. Now, I feel I have lost everything. I have nothing. This kind of fear." The last time he saw the man, "he was very old and all. He said, 'Go, Go,' something like that. I gave him some money." In this case, the patient transformed religious signifiers and absorbed them into a destroying world: "Somebody is going to kill me. Some religious person."

In the second direction, religion provides guidance—a structure that helps patients find some moral certainty to offset the indecipherable character of their world. This function is particularly important because of the general confusion often described by patients: "I was only interested in joining an ashram because I never had a good idea of a good public life . . . I don't have any direction. So, it's a big problem." One patient's narrative poignantly illustrated this drifting quality of the lived world and its destructive impact on the sense of self: "I can't identify my normal self. I don't even know what my real self is like. Up till grade eight, I had a picture of myself. I knew 'this is me . . . ' I never had an overview of what was going on . . . I couldn't understand myself like another person could by looking at me from the outside . . . couldn't get a subjective view of myself . . . All people have a basic knowledge in their mind; they have a collection of knowledge in their mind. They can think about certain things. They read the paper. I don't think I have enough general knowledge to think about things." This patient's mother encouraged him to find religious benchmarks: "Mother told me to read prayers. She was making me more devotional, taking me to the temple every day . . . It was useful. I felt there was moralization there. I was getting moralized . . . " The patient also started reading religious books and books about psychology, despite his family's reluctance to see him so absorbed in this reading.

Another narrative illustrates an analogous "fixing" function of religious signifiers. The patient described the depth of his confusion: "The confusion only increased . . . I didn't know what to do . . . I thought, what is the problem I have got? I can't understand anything." In this case, ritual gestures of the Islamic faith contributed to his entry into a shared symbolic world: "I was frightened without my knowledge. What I did was according to Islamic law: I read the Qu'ran, I fasted, brushed my teeth with a mishura stick . . . " He also found a person at the mosque whom his father recommended to him and who gave him attention and advice: "I only had one friend. He was in the mosque conducting rituals. So I used to go and meet him, talk to him . . . I used to tell him my problems regularly."

In a third and related direction, religious signifiers provide shelter—a "container" for an elusive experience. At this level, religious signifiers can help the patient construct a space of withdrawal. As we have seen, religious signifiers can give a sort of regularity to existence: "Going to the mosque almost everyday." "When I feel I have not gone to the temple for quite some time, I go." "Only after I went to the temple did I feel better." But the spatial boundaries that religious places provide and the protected solitude they allow are also much valued by patients: "I stayed alone and read the Qu'ran." "I used to only sleep in the temple. Sometimes I went by myself to go and sleep, in a place where there is peace and silence." One mother recounted, "Just staying in the *pooja* [a broad term designating domestic and public rituals] room, staying alone, going inside the room and staying alone." For patients, absorbing themselves in religious books may well help to build a space of solitude and self-reflection. Generally, this activity was negatively perceived by the families, who disliked seeing their relatives so absorbed and isolated. Another patient projected the reassuring function of religious referents forward, guaranteeing a possible shelter in an uncertain future: "After my parents' death, I can beg at the temple." To what extent might the pursuit of solitary religious space translate into an embodied quest that is comparable to, or in contrast to, that of the wandering ascetics all over India? "I thought, What do I do? I'll join an ashram. I thought, I am a very special person. I thought, people will give me refuge . . . but it did not happen like that."

The "containing" function may also manifest itself at a cognitive level, providing the patient with values and principles to rationalize and justify transgressive or unusual behaviors. The patient who mentioned being immersed in religious visions commented, "I never changed my clothes, took a bath . . . I didn't notice my body smelling: it was pure only." Another patient said, "I didn't like anybody: only God is good enough. I started disliking family members." The mother of the patient who mentioned staying alone and reading the Qu'ran said that he increasingly isolated himself: "He used to take food on a plate and ask everyone to eat; to give a little bit of food to everyone . . . He is alone, doesn't eat with family members. He would simply sit silently or lie down somewhere." This attitude led him to an extreme form of isolation in which he enclosed himself in a room, eventually withdrawing completely from the human world. His mother described this isolation: "There is a room in our house and nobody sleeps there. He puts a mat down and sleeps there . . . among the insects and the lizards . . . only when he stays alone. I feel bad." The patient developed a vision of his mission that translated into a radical detachment and gave it a religious justification and value: "I felt that living in this world is a wash. So, I thought I should live a simple life. I thought, I don't want to study . . . share the money I have with some people . . . to buy something related to religion. And give to people, and live in a hut."

For another patient, the "containing" function of religious signifiers developed visually, through the creation of a space that protected him from a rampant fear, "a kind of fear as if all males would die . . . I used to always look at photographs of gods. They took me to a priest. He gave me a picture of a goddess . . . Again, I started looking at that." However, the contemplation of a deity image appeared to progressively loose its hold on the patient.

The image broke into disconnected parts, and the contemplation seemed to engulf the patient in a kind of accelerating spiral that absorbed his entire life: "After that again, I started to look at the photo for many days. I used to stick the photo in the shop, to look at it continuously . . . It grew and grew . . . Sometimes, I would be looking at the nose, suddenly, I looked at the eyes. Soon, my confusion started . . . as I should look at it repeatedly, again and again."

These excerpts illustrate the importance and the roles of religious signifiers in patients' narratives and their potential for articulation, even if that articulation often entails building a position at the margins of the normal world and retaining an aura of strangeness. Some excerpts also indicate the strength of the psychotic alteration that patients experience and its potential to absorb the significance of cultural signifiers. From the patients' standpoint, the significance of religious representations and symbols depended on the degree to which they converged with and were complementary to their experience. Patients reworked and transformed elements they borrowed from religion and integrated them into a kind of collage. Family members generally resisted patients' turn to religion and spirituality.

In parallel, relatives consulted temple priests, astrologists, and healers. In particular, women (mothers and sisters) regularly went to temples and performed *poojas* either at home or at the temple. Performing rituals is an important aspect of popular Hinduism and also plays an important function in the rhythm of family life. Family members seemed to want to build a "ritual web" to rescue their sons or brothers and to help ameliorate the patients' sense of confusion and despair as well as their own feelings of disarray and helplessness. Rituals created a protective net and reintegrated patients within the family and the social milieu. However, on the patients' side, even if some of them agreed to accompany their relatives to the temple, they tended to remain on the periphery of these sorts of celebrations. When they mentioned spending time in the *pooja* room at home, they characterized the time as a quest for peace and calm rather than an opportunity to perform rituals.

I will not expand here on the specific religious and philosophical signifiers that relatives used to explore the meaning of the patients' problems or to deal with their own anguish and anxiety. I will only mention that for families, reliance on and trust in God for the future played a vital role in that context, as did building an inner space of detachment. In a study we conducted in Montréal with immigrants from India, detachment was also an essential way of coping with external hazards and difficulties, and it gave people strength to face the world. This attitude is anchored in the Hindu philosophy of life and the notion of the person. It also resonates with the position of "positive withdrawal" that psychotic patients adopt, and one might wonder, over the long term, how far this analogy might go in supporting patients' ability to deal with the psychotic experience.

In general, patients and relatives did not resort to identical religious signifiers. When they did, they did not interpret or use the signifiers in similar ways. Patients and relatives were often in open conflict about religion and spirituality, even if the content of their respective positions varied from case to case. We have argued that this disagreement is not simply incidental and that it reflects a structural conflict associated with differences in participants' attitudes toward psychosis (Corin, Thara, and Padmavati 2004). Patients who used cultural signifiers were trying to name, tame, and in some way integrate a pervading feeling of strangeness; they left this strangeness intact—and possibly even protected it. In contrast, the relatives tried to erase and diminish the oddness of the patients' behavior and integrate them into a collective, culturally textured framework. Their frequent use of astrologers might have had a similarly integrative function, situating the patients' problems within the movement of the planets, which they considered to be responsible; astrologers also predicted how long the planets would take to move back into positions more favorable for patients' return to normalcy.

Discrepancies between the ways that patients and relatives used religion and spirituality draw attention to the heterogeneity of the cultural framework itself.[19] In the case of Hinduism, some authors have described a tension between ritual and worship, on one hand, and a more solitary path to spirituality, through ascetic practices and personal quests for enlightenment, on the other. The latter avenue is illustrated by *sadhus*, wandering ascetics who travel India and converge in places of pilgrimage. T. N. Madan (1987) argues that an implicit tension exists in Hindu society between the high value placed on renunciation, which is considered to be the apogee of life (ideally carried out in the last of the four stages of life), and the importance of fulfilling one's tasks in the world according to the notion of dharma. Madan argues that detachment is a compromise between the two positions, introducing the philosophy of renunciation into the life of the householder or, more broadly, life in the world.

Confronted with the task of articulating a painful and threatening experience, patients and relatives play with this cultural heterogeneity and trace their own pathways through it. Narratives thus suggest that at first sight, the availability of cultural signifiers does not automatically facilitate social communication. This fact does not, however, preclude the possibility that situating themselves in a world that remains intensely religious and animated by philosophical and spiritual questions may not only help some patients integrate their experience but also have an impact on their future clinical evolution. Cultural signifiers may allow patients more freedom to explore and tame the sense of strangeness in their lives, to articulate a space of Otherness rooted in their sense of self and of the world and, ultimately, to trace individual pathways through culture. Exploring this hypothesis further calls for following up patients for a longer period of their lives, along with documentation of their evolving relationships to cultural and religious signifiers.

I argue that we can consider Otherness a personal symbol, in Obeyesekere's sense. I have illustrated its centrality to the psychotic's personal sense of self and of the world. At the collective level, it may take on various forms, but traditionally it is developed primarily in the areas of religion and spirituality. Cultural systems tend to give shape to the Otherness of the sacred through a series of beliefs, rituals, and symbols. Societies differ, however, in the degree to which they acknowledge the irreducible presence of a radical strangeness that expands beyond the borders of philosophical and religious systems. They also show differing degrees of tolerance for people who explore these borders of culture. The level of tolerance could influence the latitude given to people engaged in limit-experiences (including psychosis) to explore marginal ways of life without radically marginalizing them (or "normalizing them," which might be the equivalent). Our current research with sadhus and renouncers aims to explore the broader significance of the figure of the ascetic as a kind of myth model allowing people, including patients, to integrate and culturally elaborate a range of personal and social limit-experiences.

THE OTHER OF CULTURE

Traditional anthropology is poorly equipped to deal with aspects of experience that go beyond words, representations, and symbols. In fact, in seeking to position cultural elements within integrated webs of meaning, interpretive anthropology might be said to accomplish a work of "binding." In this context, some authors have also described diverging, differentially weighted cultural codes that coexist in a paradoxical tension. This structural heterogeneity, internal to cultures, may serve to relax the constraints of cultural codes and make room for the expression of unconventional ways of being.[20] The varied religious pathways in Hinduism illustrate this phenomenon. I have suggested that psychotic people may slip into such a complex system in order to express and frame their sense of difference, even if their action does not normalize their behaviors and attitudes in the eyes of others.

Giving a shape to alien phenomena within the cultural framework is not exclusive to anthropologists. We can see the beliefs and rituals of spirit possession as cultural attempts to give shape to forces that lay at the periphery of culture or even beyond. At the same time, at least in Central Africa, people also acknowledge that this shaping is never complete. Spirits always retain something of their wild, radically unbound character, and this wildness is essential to their power.[21]

The participation of culture in this shaping process is under attack in contemporary anthropology. Anthropologists denounce the notion of culture itself as an artificial construct, ultimately based on a process of "othering" non-Western societies, that conceals power differentials both between and within societies. Well-bounded, cohesive cultures are seen as a deception constructed by anthropologists.[22] More importantly, this criticism of culture belongs to a broader movement led by poststructuralism and the postcolonial critique of Western hegemony. It supports a larger questioning of the regime of representation and obliges a fundamental reassessment of how knowledge is produced in a number of disciplines.[23] Paradoxically, however, this position might absorb the differences of "others" into "our" sameness, replacing culturally specific webs of meaning by a generalized web of significance. Overemphasizing globalization and crossbreeding could therefore support new forms of "scientific totalitarianism" and add to the spread and legitimization of the Western contemporary ethos as a blind spot in our participation in the process of globalization.

A few critical postcolonial writers also describe a radical form of "unshaped" Otherness that permeates hegemonic systems and destabilizes standard modes of thinking from the inside. This perspective views cultural differences as privileged markers of an irreducible difference operating within societies.[24] By their very existence, these differences reveal the contingency of social and cultural rules and challenge the evidence and legitimacy of the codes that articulate the representation of oneself and one's relationship with others. At the level of language, for example, the ultimate untranslatability of languages draws attention to the "shadow" or "darkness" that constitutes language itself and introduces a different way of inhabiting and decoding language. Thus, the limits of translation make all languages foreign to themselves. Homi Bhabha comments, "In the act of translation, the 'given' content becomes alien and estranged; and that, in turn, leaves the language of translation *Aufgabe*, always confronted by its

double, the untranslatable—alien and foreign" (1994: 164). Cultural difference becomes less a problem of foreign people than a question of Otherness
within the "people-as-one," to borrow Bhabha's expression. By definition,
this space of Otherness within cultures is not part of "all-encompassing"
cultural discourses. It may only emerge at a performative level.

This view echoes Jean-François Lyotard's criticism of liberal capitalism
and his description of "the System's" anxiety when it faces the threat of undifferentiated energies sweeping from the inner and outer margins in the
guise of "strangers, unknown persons, pariahs, anything that proliferates,
does not have place to live or a job" (1994: 13).[25] A measure of that anxiety
would be the strength of the barriers that the system puts up against these
figures. Lyotard illustrates his point using music: on one hand, the filters in
sound systems desensitize entire regions of sound and reject them as
"noise"; on the other hand, the forms of resistance against "the System,"
exemplified by dodecaphonic music, allow one to confront dissonance and
all its consequences.

Contrary to the Otherness of spirits in spirit-possession rituals, the kind
of radical Otherness in postcolonial and postmodern writings remains diffuse, beyond language and symbols and beyond culture. As a result, the fading of the ritual codes that lay out a space of Otherness internal to cultures
appears to open the way to its infinite dispersion and accentuate its elusive
character—to reverse the balance between the shaping and unshaping processes in favor of unshaping.

The consideration of contemporary cultures from this perspective could
offer a better stance from which to question the place of psychosis in culture and, in particular, its fate in Western societies. On one hand, the hegemonic tone of today's psychiatric- and psychosocial-rehabilitation discourses obliterates the disquieting potential of psychosis and its questioning
power. On the other hand, it is from the margins of society and culture that
people explore and attempt to tame the strangeness of their experience, in
a kind of solitary collage that remains at the fringe of the shared world. By
contrast, other societies may be more open to exploring the borders of culture and laying out cultural avenues that people can follow in individual,
idiosyncratic journeys.

FIGURES OF THE NEGATIVE IN THE CLINICAL SPACE

Psychotic patients' accounts of their experience speak to an excess of signifiers, sensations, and meanings that escape order and coherence, and to a
blurring of boundaries that creates a deep sense of confusion and uncer-

tainty. This quality of excess is reminiscent of the nightmare of Irénéo, the Jorge Luis Borges character who cannot forget and suffers from both total perception and absolute memory; he records the sum of all features that make up a perception, without synthesis, and he cannot erase his thoughts from his memory. Referring to this figure in the context of his thoughts on the negative, André Green comments, "And now, overwhelmed, he dies of it, because how may one live without generalizing and therefore without forgetting, suppressing and abstracting, all operations necessary for thinking?" (1995: 21). Erasing and distancing introduce blanks and negation, conditions of the thinking process.

In the case of psychosis, words and representations seem to escape and swirl around. In parallel, the enigmatic and uncertain quality of the experience may also open abyssal chasms that paralyze and freeze life. One might suspect that both excess and void hinder the formation of representations and ideas that can pin down the elusive character of the experience and risk engulfing thought itself. Withdrawal, in its multiple forms, might construct a distance or introduce a "blank" within this "too-full" space and allow the patient to think again. This process would amount to introducing into the lived world a physical space of negativity that is necessary to the formation and use of concepts and symbols.

This exploration of the work of culture in psychosis reminded me of parallel processes that I observed surfacing suddenly in some psychoanalytic sessions and making their mark on the clinical-transference space. The sudden appearance of a "void" can transform the atmosphere of a session and modify its perceptual and cognitive qualities. This phenomenon is not restricted to patients with a psychotic structure. It may also break through when persons confront an irrepresentable element in their origin or feel an urgency to disengage from capturing. Such fusional relationships invade and threaten the clinical relationship. Nathalie Zalztman, in her reflections on the notion of "healing" and the *Kulturarbeit* from a psychoanalytical perspective, evokes a particular form of mobilization of the death drive, and its effect of dissolving limits *(déliaison)* in "extreme situations." Such situations involve the seizure of a human being's mental and physical life and expose him to the constant possibility of death. The death drive then allows one to establish separating limits; it creates the possibility of absence. It has an individuating function and may help shift a deadly external reality into a reality of mental representations. In my clinical work, I now pay more attention to the occurrence of such "void spaces" and consider such moments to be essential stages in certain cures.

While I was attempting to understand what is at stake in these situations,

I looked into the writings on the work of the negative in psychic life and in the process of symbolization. In French psychoanalysis, the "negative" has been an important subject.[26] In keeping with Hegelian perspectives, the negative is considered a force or process that works through the psyche or, better yet, puts the psyche to work and acts as a source of creativity: "To deny what is given without ending up in nothingness is to produce something which does not yet exist." Or inversely: "One may really create only in negating the real as given."[27]

Words themselves build on a double negation: the absence of the concrete thing and the unavoidable discrepancy between the word, the thing, and its representation (as formalized by Charles S. Peirce's ternary distinction between sign, reality, and the interpretant); and its difference from other words within a particular language. Symbols and metaphors add to these primary negations at a more abstract level. Jacques Derrida's notion of *differance* (with an *a*), which implies that meaning is revealed only obliquely, in a deferred way, is another way of alluding to the discrepancy, or negation, inherent in language.[28]

In discussing the "work of the negative," André Green contends that in addition to an organizing negative associated with symbolization, a disorganizing negative exists that infiltrates psychic life; ruptures linkages and associations; and has a paralyzing, destructuring, and sterilizing tonality. The two forms of negative differ in the relative importance they give to the binding and unbinding processes.

By its very framework, the psychoanalytical setting liberates a process of unbinding *(déliaison)*. It undoes the narrative coherence of speech and releases the connection between words and meanings. On the patient's side, the rule of "free association" suspends rational judgment and gives priority to meaning; it allows words to make bonds independent of argumentative logic and liberates them from their intentional, conscious significance within a particular sentence; it frees the space for apparently random rebinding *(reliaison)*. Free association lets out the multiple associative chains that coalesce in a word or image for a particular person. On the psychoanalyst's side, the rule of "floating attention" does not *a priori* sort out the more important elements from the less important ones; it allows the listener to follow the movement of speech outside its explicit content, to notice its blanks and failures, and to be drawn by the texture of words and images behind coherent discourse.[29] Free association and floating attention are the two complementary forms of *déliaison* in psychoanalytic clinical work. In this context, interpretation is not a substitute for a latent, intelligible narrative content. Instead, it helps unveil the opaque, inaudible, and unknowable inherent in every narrative. It also modifies the patient's relationship to his or her own history. However, such a process of *déliaison* is not always benign and can help destabilize current defense mechanisms, opening a breach in the narratives that a patient builds for himself or herself or others.

For some people, this kind of setting may awaken or evoke the shadows of an initial void that can endanger their sense of identity and threaten their ability to think. This void may derive from an inability to represent their origins or to conceive of themselves as coming into the world by virtue of the hopes and wishes of loving parents (Aulagnier 1975). For others, the void may result, for example, from having had a mother who grieved over a dead loved one and who therefore lacked the strength to invest in and psychically carry the child (Green 1983). Personal circumstances may also converge with social and broadly historical forces to reinforce patients' difficulties in forming individual representations of their histories.[30] These various contexts may generate a sort of insurmountable gap between words and experience, or they may absorb representations and feelings and preclude any attempt to communicate and speak: "I can't seem to say what is inside me. As soon as it comes to the surface, it is as though it disintegrates, breaks up." "I get so I can't say things anymore, as if I can't find the words any longer, like I can't access the world of language anymore."

The sense of an abyssal void may arise abruptly in a particular session, through a certain quality of the atmosphere—as if both patient and analyst were overcome by a cold wind; as if something out of Julia Kristeva's (1980) "power of the horror" were invading the session. One of my patients, a young woman who normally speaks at length, sometimes stops talking in a silence that she detests: "*Nothing,*" "*It falls away.*" Once, this remark took a broader extension and appeared to invade the clinical space. She noticed the white color of my walls: "Each object evokes something. White walls, that's the only thing that you can't talk about. This very sentence, a sentence one could analyze. As if I was writing another sentence with 'white,' one could analyze it." For her, the experience was as though language were falling to pieces. She felt uncomfortable and wanted to leave.

With patients who are particularly fragile, I have been struck by the number of times "void" arises as the psychoanalytical work unfolds, particularly during the sessions. Patients convey a sense of being swallowed up and of fascination, as if an intuited hole were welling up, to be stamped on the realm of perception. This sense of void may attach to a particular sentence a patient heard in a banal life circumstance: "*Girls are like holes,*" for instance, which creates for one patient a physical panic, a perceived bleeding of life that clashes with other memories that have an analogous "swallowing" quality; the void "etches" on the body the icon of an origin that, for reasons I cannot explain here, are impossible to represent. For another person, this void may also be a sensorial image of intense anguish, such as the idea of vomiting on my office floor, of losing oneself—the impression that by vomiting, the patient would drain him- or herself. Or in another case, a sudden change in the sunlight that shines on my office wall, which in other sessions activated pleasurable memories, might now seem to have acquired a deeply threatening significance through association with childhood memories of fear of abandonment, the death of a sibling and the mother's glance that remains absorbed in the memory of her dead child; for the patient, this might have resonated with another type of abandonment: a trip that may necessitate my absence for a short period, with my impending departure raising questions about mysterious (for the patient) activities I may carry out and my voyage into an alien world. For yet another person, the void might manifest itself by casting a weekend interruption of sessions as an insufferable void that comes out in the person's voiceless presence—in a silence that goes on session after session, with the patient huddled in the chair, eyes looking away—and in the "no" shouted at the end of each session.

Images associate in my mind, all speaking of a suffering of the being itself that surfaces through embodied memories that have taken root even before memory itself. I am convinced that it is essential to allow these sensorial icons to take shape in the clinical psychoanalytical space, to endure their intolerable character and measure the weight of anxiety and terror attached to them; that it is important not to resort to interpretation too quickly to reduce their threatening quality. For the analyst, the diminishing utility of her common theoretical constructions and a sense of helplessness add to her discomfort and open the way to a vicarious experience of this unspeakable void.

I have come to believe that the apparition of these void images within the psychoanalytical setting corresponds to a perceptual embodiment of elements that memory and narration do not succeed in linking together. These images often coincide with a turning point in the analysis, even if it is reversible. They support a "work of the void," which can help transform a "yawning void" into an "absence void" that might aid in representation and thinking. They may participate in the creation of a protorepresentation of negation associated with the formation of symbols and of embodied "blanks" necessary to the thinking process. One patient mentioned that, in some circumstances, she felt like she had a hole, a void in her belly, partic-

ularly in situations in which she felt abandoned and surrounded by a
threatening world. This feeling was both agonizing and precious—"something belonging to her alone"—as if something lacking in her personal history was manifesting itself physically on her body. Such a void may also be
an initial representation of a "lack" in her history—of her unknown origin—seemingly allowing her to envision an enigmatic, potentially reassuring presence within the blank memory of her origins and to transform an
engulfing voice into mere absence.

I argue that these protorepresentations, when given room in the space of
transference, act as a third form of the negative, whose role is to mediate between its organizing and disorganizing forms and allow passage from one
to the other. Their clinical manifestation is essential to the psychoanalytic
process for patients whose access to speech and memories appears to be
blocked or frozen, as if their psychic life were captured by something impossible to articulate. Playing with these images of void, however, is a dangerous undertaking because of their closeness to the "yawning void," which
is always at risk of contaminating psychic life. These images can be dealt
with only with great sensitivity to the patient's individual rhythm and progression.

These protorepresentations transform over time, in a process that is
never purely unidirectional and that, at any moment, could turn into frag-
mentation and abyss. They may be close to inner forces that are alien to the
self. In a psychoanalytic context, they may be evoked only through words
that allude to images and sensations and that are understood in both their
sensorial texture and their semantically explicit content.

I suggest that positive withdrawal, with its embodied quality, indicates an
analogous "work of the void" that allows patients to build distance, introduce interstices, and tame a feeling of radical Otherness inhabiting the self;
it could be a pathway for forming protorepresentations and reestablishing
distinctions and caesurae in patients' representations of themselves and the
world.

THE EX-CENTRIC SUBJECT OF PSYCHOSIS

When Jacques Lacan (1966) initiated the "return to Freud" movement, he
proposed a renewed way of thinking about the foundations of psychoanalysis within language. Specifically, he argued that the speaking subject
both leans on the "field of language" and extricates himself from language
and the symbolic framework, to enounce essentially individual words. Well
before birth, symbols envelop human life in a web that defines basic collec-

tive benchmarks about gender and descent, death and the origin of life, and intergenerational relationships and inheritances. People domesticate and appropriate these words: they integrate, reject, forget, and transform words in individual ways. Piera Aulagnier (1975) argues that the mother acts as a spokesperson for culture in a child's universe and that becoming a "subject," or person, involves both an integration with and a freeing from the projects that others construct for one's future. From this perspective, the subject in him- or herself may be ex-centric to culture; his relationship to collective images and symbols is always tangential.

In the case of psychosis, however, the ex-centricity of this position becomes maximal. On one hand, patients do not find a "host" within the normal social and cultural world for the strange feelings that they experience and that permeates their lives. On the other hand, they often do not take for granted the basic certainties and conventions that organize the consensual vision of the world and define the meaning of life. I suggest that positive withdrawal offers a way to understand how patients try to tame a strange experience and redefine their place within the world.

This chapter has adopted a broad notion of Otherness as a guiding thread for commenting on what is at stake for psychotic people in positive withdrawal. I could have followed alternative interpretive threads in the narratives such as the protection of a "secret place," which could help patients value thinking in a context dominated by confusion and a lack of clear boundaries; or the construction of a second (social or psychic) skin, which allows patients to restore limits and boundaries; or the moral and anchoring aspect of religious signifiers, which can support patients' efforts to find stability in an unstable world. These threads would have led to dialogues with other authors working in related fields, such as the psychoanalysts Aulagnier (1991), in the case of the secret place; Didier Anzieu (1985), with his notion of the *moi-peau;* or Derrida (1967), with his work on the anxiety provoked by the "structurality of the structure"—its infinite drift and the cultural effort to invent anchorages that give this structure some stability. The notion of Otherness is rooted in the sense of alienation that patients experience in their encounters with the world and in the feeling of disarray that others experience when faced with psychosis.

I argue that we can consider Otherness a personal symbol loaded with a double significance—private and public. I have traced its images and shadows at the level of the psychotic experience and indicated the importance of its development for the patient. Culturally speaking, religion and spirituality constitute preferred methods of developing the notion of Otherness. In Indian society, one could say that withdrawal and detachment embody the alien character of Otherness and provide a kind of mythical model that can frame a variety of experiences.[31] I have also suggested that in the case of psychosis, such a development remains partial and that a risk always exists that feelings of radical strangeness and alienation will surface, drawing up emotions and thoughts in a psychotic swirl.

Anthropology and psychoanalysis both have a special relationship with particular forms of Otherness: in anthropology, the relationship is with foreign cultures or with phenomena that elude and transcend culture; in psychoanalysis, the relationship is with the unconscious. Both disciplines have developed particular ways of conceptualizing Otherness and dealing with it. But for both, psychosis remains an elusive reality, as does the idea of its cultural articulation.

By proposing a dialogue between these two disciplines, or between research and clinical work, I do not seek to import frames of reference from one perspective into the other or to "apply" one to the other. Rather, such a dialogue would try to expand the horizons of both approaches, explore the elusive elements at their margins, and enrich their reflections with new harmonics and a kind of resonance.

NOTES

I want to thank Dr Rangaswami Thara and Professors Ravi Kapur and Gilles Bibeau for their careful reading and their comments on prior versions of this paper. However, I am the only one responsible for the content of the paper. This work was made possible by grants from the Social Sciences and Humanities Research Council (Canada) and from the Fonds pour la Formation de Chercheurs et l'Aide à la Recherche (Québec).

1. W. Blankenburg (1991) explains and illustrates how the loss of the natural evidence radiates into and deeply transforms key aspects of human experience: the relationship to the world when the rules that govern everyday life are lost; the temporal dimension of existence when a perceived discontinuity with the past prevents an orientation toward the future; a sense of grounding and legitimacy that provides motivation, autonomy, and the power to act; the feeling of participating in an intersubjective world.

2. I vividly remember my shock when, as an anthropologist trying to reintroduce meaning and experience into the understanding of psychosis, I saw an entire audience applaud Fuller Torrey's explanation that schizophrenia is like the flu or diabetes.

3. Explanations of the neuropathological process of the disease can also help patients control their anxiety or recover some sense of mastery over what happens to them.

4. I borrow the term *myth model* from Gananath Obeyesekere, who states "I use 'myth model' in two ways: First, an important or paradigmatic myth may serve as a model for other kinds of myth construction. Second and more importantly, a 'myth

model' refers to an underlying set of ideas (a myth structure or cluster of mythemes) employed in a variety of narrative forms. These idea-sets are 'structures of the long run' that get attached to larger narrative forms such as fiction, history, or biography" (1992: 10).

5. In Corin 1998, I contrast the European phenomenological psychiatric approach to psychotic disorders with the current understanding of "phenomenology" in contemporary North American psychiatry.

6. The methods and postulates underlying this study have been described elsewhere. See in particular Corin 1990.

7. Broadening the notion of deinstitutionalization, we hypothesized that deinstitutionalization from psychiatric institutions is paralleled by a process of "social deinstitutionalization," through which patients are prevented from resuming normative social roles and are therefore pushed back toward psychiatric institutions and become at risk for readmission.

8. Statistical tests allowed us to verify the comparability of the three groups according to sociodemographic variables, age of first contact with psychiatry, stability of diagnosis, and initial symptomatic picture. Further comparisons of the three groups revealed that the number of hospitalizations during the previous four years (our initial selection criterion) was closely associated with widely different manners of relating to psychiatric services.

9. This process revealed that the significance of a particular feature, like minimal contact with siblings, may have a contrasting value according to groups (Corin 1990).

10. Corin and Lauzon 1992 presents a single case study that illustrates various figures of "positive withdrawal" in one person's life.

11. This expression builds on Didier Anzieu's (1985) notion of *moi-peau* (ego skin), which makes an analogy between the functions of the ego and the skin.

12. The dual significance of religious signifiers in people's lives is reminiscent of the bidirectional potential impact (regressive and progressive) of personal symbols that Gananath Obeyesekere (1990) describes. He says that personal symbols may help give structure and meaning to a problematic experience or be used in a regressive way and be absorbed into destructive processes.

13. Two recently completed PhD theses in anthropology vividly illustrate the extent to which people suffering from psychotic problems borrow and transform cultural referents. Based on fieldwork in the state of Bahia, in northeastern Brazil, Monica Nunes describes and comments on the specific ways in which psychotic people resort to and modify Candomblé cultural symbols and beliefs. Cristina Redko discusses the role played by a range of religious signifiers in the articulation of incipient psychosis and compares patients with family members in this regard. She based her analysis on ethnographic interviews with patients and families and observations conducted in São Paulo, Brazil.

14. The Schizophrenia Research Foundation in Chennai (formerly Madras) is a voluntary, nonprofit organization that formed in 1984 to address the needs of mentally ill patients. It has three main objectives: rehabilitation, research, and public awareness. It is a resource center for psychosocial rehabilitation in India and an internationally renowned center for research in liaison with several international agencies. SCARF is also a collaborating center of the World Mental Health Organization for Mental Health Research and Training.

15. We constructed this grid in collaboration with Alain Lesage. Ian Van Haaster,

Marina Bandeira, Tonya Dominique, and Amanda Hunt helped design and validate a systematic coding procedure. This paper, however, relies on a more open process of coding that takes into account recurrences and oppositions that occur within and across narratives.

16. However, one patient noted, "I didn't actually hate them, but I wanted to be left alone . . . I was experiencing within myself."

17. Charles Malamoud distinguishes two levels of meaning in the notion of dharma. "In the narrow sense, dharma is the system of rules thought by the Vedas and the texts deriving from the Vedas: the one who conforms gains merits for the other world. But in the larger sense, dharma is the order of the world and of society; concretely, it is a network of relations which links while keeping distinct the classes (varna) and the 'life stages' (asrama)" (1989 : 151). Family members' disappointment also stems from the fact that patients had been invested with significant roles affecting the family's future and destiny: "Not only we but the family expects great things of him because that is how he studied." "Oh, this boy has become like this. He is my only son. As my only son, we used to give him all respect . . . If he had been well, I would have been happy. He would have had a certain responsibility in the family." "Because we were not educated, we wanted our children to do well. Since we have no parents and we have to support him, I thought my son would make me happy . . . We sold some property and thought we could use it for his education." These comments also reflect the fact that much of the SCARF clientele is of a middle-class background.

18. Shiva is one of the major deities in the Hindu pantheon. With Vishnu, Shiva commands the universe and uses his vast power to sustain the sociocosmic order. Shiva also combines paradoxical elements. He is both the creator and the destroyer and is associated with both life and death; he is both the great ascetic and the deity of the phallus, embodied in the linga, an erected stone associated with the Shiva cult (Doniger O'Flaherty 1981).

19. On the basis of ethnographic and clinical work in western Africa, Edmond and Marie-Cécile Ortigues and Andras and Jacqueline Zempleni (1968) developed an approach to culture inspired by French structuralism and Lacanian psychoanalysis. This approach assumes that the apparent "unity" of cultural representations and symbols is deceptive; cultural symbols condense several chains of signifiers that intersect with other chains of meanings and representations and connect with the whole web of social and cultural life. Different chains of associations are evident in different cases. The ethnographer's task is therefore less to describe "the meaning" of cultural symbols than to study the range of intersecting associative chains converging in cultural representations and symbols and to examine which ones individual people use in specific circumstances. In our study, the use of religious references varies according to the patients' and family members' attitudes toward psychosis.

20. Processes of symbolic inversion modify the relative importance of these various levels of code, thus revealing the arbitrariness—and the limits—of dominant codes (see Babcock 1978 and Dumont 1983). I discuss the heuristic value of this perspective in kinship systems and spirit-possession rituals in Corin 1995.

21. This phenomenon is splendidly illustrated by Jean Rouch's movie *Horendi*, about the seven-day learning of a spirit-possession dance in western Africa. The time and space delineated by the dancers' circle is periodically pierced and ruptured by wild possession trances in which the women's bodies are shaken by the spirits.

The greater the mastery of the spirit-possession dance as the seven days proceed, the wilder the trance—as if cultural codes were delineating a space for the emergence of the unshaped.

22. However, in reviewing contemporary critics of culture, R. Brightman reproaches contemporary anthropologists for their rhetorical strategies that (re)construct an essentialized culture concept in the antipodes of contemporary theoretical orientations in order to justify its rejection. He argues that these images of culture are themselves inventions rather than representations but that we must take them seriously because of their efficacy: "These are invented images of culture, both arbitrary and partial with respect to a much more diverse and versatile field of definition and use. Such images, nonetheless, are rapidly acquiring more authoritative perlocutionary effects" (1995: 541).

23. See Padmini Mongia's introduction to *Contemporary Postcolonial Theory. A Reader*: "Moreover, these issues were addressed with a new interest in representation and discourse. In a whole host of academic disciplines, attention shifted towards the fluid, contested modes, whereby textual and disciplinary authority was constructed. This 'turn to language' problematized the nature of representation itself and of an assumed linguistic transparency that gave access to a 'reality' that lay outside" (1997: 4).

24. Homi Bhabha argues that the characteristic heterogeneity of contemporary societies is not pure diversity but opens a "liminal signifying space that is internally marked by discourses of minorities, the heterogeneous histories of contending people, antagonistic authorities and tense locations of cultural differences" (1994: 148).

25. One might hypothesize that psychotic people are just such alien figures and that the normalizing character of rehabilitative programs seeks to provide a barrier or filter against the deep anxiety and discomfort they evoke.

26. In an introduction to *Le Négatif*, Gilbert Diatkine (1995), one of three people who wrote introductions to the book, mentions three main implications of current thoughts about the negative: the development of a clinic of the negative, particularly with André Green's notion of the "work of the negative"; a technical reorientation that considers the place an "unrepresentable" in psychic life; and attention to "crypts" and phantoms in transgenerational transmission.

27. Alexandre Kojeve, interpreting Hegel, is quoted by Roger Dorey (1995: 12) in an introduction to *Le Négatif*.

28. Stuart Hall comments on the significance of this notion for a theory of representation: "This second sense of difference challenges the fixed boundaries which stabilize meaning and representation and shows how meaning is never finished or completed, but keeps moving to encompass other, additional or supplementary meanings. Without relations of difference, no representation could occur. But what is then constituted within representation is always open to being deferred, staggered, serialized" (1997: 115). Hall also quotes Christopher Norris: "Where Derrida breaks new grounds . . . is the extent to which 'differ' shades into 'defer' . . . the idea that meaning is always deferred, perhaps to this point of an endless supplementarity, by the play of signification" (115).

29. Gantheret (1996) illustrates how this kind of unbinding also unfolds at the level of words, through a double process of desemanticization and resemanticization.

30. The enigmatic character of the silent ghost from the past who "imprints" on

the present in Toni Morrison's *Beloved*. This novel provides an excellent illustration of this reduplication of personal and collective history.

31. Our current research with *sadhus* and *sanyasis* confirms the large range of life paths and experiences that can converge in an ascetic lifestyle.

REFERENCES

Anzieu, D. 1985. *Le Moi-peau*. Paris: Dunod.

Aulagnier, P. 1975. *La violence de l'interprétation. Du pictogramme à l'énoncé*. Paris: Presses Universitaires de France.

———. 1991. "Le droit au secret: condition pour pouvoir penser." In *Un interprète en quête de sens* (Paris: Payot), 219–38.

Babcock, B., ed. 1978. *The Reversible World*. London: Cornell University Press.

Bhabha, H. 1994. *The Location of Culture*. London: Routledge.

Blankenberg, W. 1991. *La perte de l'évidence naturelle. Une contribution à la psychopathologie des schizophrénies pauci-symptomatiques*. Paris: Presses Universitaires de France.

Brightman, R. 1995. "Forget Culture: Replacement, Transcendence, Relexification." *Cultural Anthropology* 10 (4): 509–46.

Bruner, E. M. 1986. Introduction. In *The Anthropology of Experience*, ed. V. W. Turner and E. M. Bruner (Urbana and Chicago: University of Illinois Press), 3–30.

Corin, E. 1990. "Facts and Meaning in Psychiatry: An Anthropological Approach to the Lived World of Schizophrenics." *Culture, Medicine and Psychiatry* 14: 153–88.

———. 1995. "Meaning Games at the Margins: The Cultural Centrality of Subordinated Structures." In *Beyond Textuality. Asceticism and Violence in Anthropological Interpretation*, ed. G. Bibeau and E. Corin (Berlin: Mouton de Gruyter), 173–92.

———. 1998. "The Thickness of Being: Intentional Worlds, Strategies of Identity, and Experience among Schizophrenics." *Psychiatry* 61: 133–46.

Corin, E., and G. Lauzon. 1992. "Positive Withdrawal and the Quest for Meaning: The Reconstruction of the Experience among Schizophrenics." *Psychiatry* 55 (3): 266–78.

Corin, E., R. Thara, and R. Padmavati. Forthcoming. "Living through a Staggering World. The Play of Signifiers in Early Psychosis in South India." In *Schizophrenia, Culture and Subjectivity: The Edge of Experience*, ed. J. Jenkins and R. Barrett (Cambridge: Cambridge University Press), 110–45.

Derrida, J. 1967. "La structure, le signe et le jeu dans le discours des sciences humaines." In *L'écriture et la différence* (Paris: Le Seuil), 409–28.

Diatkine, G. 1995. Introduction. In *Le Négatif*, ed. A. Green, B. Favarel-Garrigues, J. Guillaumin, P. Fedida, et al. (Paris: L'esprit du temps).

Doniger O'Flaherty, W. 1981. *Asceticism and Eroticism in the Mythology of Siva*. Oxford University Press.

Dorey, R. 1995. Introduction. In *Le Négatif*, ed. A. Green, B. Favarel-Garrigues, J. Guillaumin, P. Fedida, et al. (Paris: L'esprit du temps).

Dumont, L. 1983. *Essays on Individualism: Modern Ideology in Anthropological Perspective*. Chicago: University of Chicago Press.

Gantheret, F. 1996. *Moi, monde, mots*. Paris: Gallimard.

Good, B. 1994. *Medicine, Rationality and Experience: An Anthropological Perspective*. Cambridge: Cambridge University Press.

Green, A. 1983. *Narcissisme de vie, Narcissisme de mort*. Paris: Les Éditions de Minuit.

———. 1995. "Instances du négatif: Transfert, tiercéité, temps." In *Le Négatif*, ed. A. Green, B. Favarel-Garrigues, J. Guillaumin, P. Fedida, et al. (Paris: L'esprit du temps), 15–56.

Hall, S. 1997. "Cultural identity and diaspora." In *Contemporary Postcolonial Theory. A Reader*, ed. P. Mongia (Delhi: Oxford University Press).

Klerman, G. L. 1984. "The Advantages of DSM-III." *American Journal of Psychiatry* 14 (4): 539–42.

Kristeva, Julia. 1980. *Pouvoirs de l'horreur*. Paris: Le Seuil.

Lacan, Jacques. 1966. "Fonctions et champ de la parole et du langage en psychanalyse." In *Écrits* (Paris: Le Seuil), 237–322.

Lanteri-Laura, G. 1986. "Sémiologie et critique de la connaissance." *L'Évolution Psychiatrique* 51 (4): 825–33.

Leclaire, S. 1998. *Écrits pour la psychanalyse 1. Demeures de l'ailleurs*. Paris: Le Seuil/Éditions Arcanes.

Lyotard, J.-F. 1994. *Des dispositifs pulsionnels*. Paris: Galilée.

Madan, T. N. 1987. *Non-Renunciation. Themes and Interpretation of Hindu Culture*. Delhi: Oxford University Press.

Malamoud, C. 1989. *Cuire le monde. Rite et pensée dans l'Inde ancienne*. Paris: Éditions de la Découverte.

Mongia, P. 1997. Introduction. In *Contemporary Postcolonial Theory. A Reader*, ed. P. Mongia (Delhi: Oxford University Press).

Morris, D. B. 1997. "About Suffering: Voice, Genre, and Moral Community." In *Social Suffering*, ed. Arthur Kleinman, Veena Das, and Margaret Lock (Berkeley: University of California Press), 25–45.

Obeyesekere, G. 1985. "Depression, Buddhism and the Work of Culture in Sri Lanka." In *Culture and Depression: Studies in the Anthropology and Cross-Cultural Psychiatry of Affect and Disorder*, ed. Arthur Kleinman and Byron Good (Berkeley: University of California Press), 134–52.

———. 1990. *The Work of Culture: Transformation in Psychoanalysis and Anthropology*. Chicago: University of Chicago Press.

———. 1992. *The Apotheosis of Captain Cook: European Mythmaking in the Pacific*. Princeton, NJ: Princeton University Press.

Ortigues, E., M.-C. Ortigues, A. Zempleni, and J. Zempleni. 1968. "Psychologie clinique et ethnologie (Sénégal)." *Bulletin de Psychologie* 21 (15–19): 950–58.

Ricoeur, P. 1986. *Du texte à l'action. Essais d'herméneutique* (II). Paris: Le Seuil.

Rodriguez, L., E. Corin, and L. Guay. 2000. "La thérapie alternative: Se (re)mettre en mouvement." In *Les ressources alternatives de traitement*, ed. Santé Mentale au Québec and Regroupement des ressources alternatives en santé mentale du Québec (Montréal: Santé Mentale au Québec), 49–94.

Zaltzman, N. 1999. *De la guérison psychanalytique*. Paris: Presses Universitaires de France.

10   Hoarders and Scrappers

Madness and the Social Person
in the Interstices of the City

ANNE M. LOVELL

La rue est un chemin, ce n'est pas un asile; la rue appartient à ceux
qui passent, et non à ceux qui l'habitent. [The street is a walkway,
not an asylum; the streets belong to passersby, not to those who
live in them.]
—From a French news document, mid-1800s (Girardin and Vissière 1986)

My work is very simple. I have come to New York because it is the
most forlorn of places, the most abject. The brokenness is
everywhere, the disarray is universal. You have only to open your
eyes to see it. The broken people, the broken things, the broken
thoughts. The whole city is a junk heap. It suits my purposes
admirably. I find the streets an endless source of material, an
inexhaustible storehouse of shattered things. Each day I go out
with my bag and collect objects that seem worthy of investigation.
—Stillman, the philosopher-bagman, in *City of Glass*, by Paul Auster

Rubbish collectors are the unsung heroes of modernity. Day in
and day out, they refresh and make salient again the borderline
between normality and pathology, health and illness, the desirable
and the rejected, the *comme il faut* and *comme il ne faut pas*, the
inside and the outside of the human universe.
—Zygmunt Bauman, *Wasted Lives, Modernity and Its Outcasts*

As anthropologists rush to salvage culture in the wake of an increasingly
biologized and globally homogenized psychiatry, they are focusing anew
on phenomenology and the subjective experience of people afflicted with
the anomalous states, feelings, and cognition of madness. But recent studies suggest that, in the Western settings in which psychiatry evolved, the
cultural, macrosocial, and microsocial underpinnings of severe psychiatric
conditions cannot so easily be separated from psychiatric knowledge. The
comparative method of cross-cultural research, useful in uncovering the
cultural dimension of psychiatric conditions outside the realm of biomedicine and Western psychiatry, is less helpful for recognizing the work of

culture in psychiatric disorders in North America and Europe. This difficulty arises because disorders and their subjective and social representations are entangled in the interactive process of psychiatric knowledge production.

Robert Barrett, for example, has shown how the disease category of schizophrenia and its manifestation in people defined as "schizophrenic" are shaped by institutional and disciplinary discourses and frameworks hewn in the nineteenth-century asylum and still present in contemporary psychiatric institutions (Barrett 1996). Psychiatric ideologies and practices, and the web of institutions in which they are embedded (pharmaceutical companies, research centers, consumer and family groups, and so on) generate "the schizophrenic" as an anomalous and liminal category of the person (Barrett 1998). More recently, the philosopher Ian Hacking has used the notion of "classificatory looping" to describe how persons experiencing schizophrenia inevitably react to the way they are defined and treated. Their behavior feeds new psychiatric classifications and knowledge in a recursive process. Hence, anomalous experiences such as the category we call schizophrenia are socially constructed as the afflicted individuals interact with their diagnosis as well as with the practices, institutions, and so forth in which these psychiatric classifications thrive and evolve (Hacking 1999). Darin Weinberg's analysis of the occurrences at a substance-abuse program when diagnosis is ambiguous or when personal experience is incongruent with psychiatric explanations can be applied to psychiatric conditions in general. Behavior is often reinterpreted as a sign of another type of psychiatric disorder, another mental disorder, a biological or brain disorder, or "the effects of some human agent adept at reproducing the local appearance of mental disorder for his or her own private, but eminently discoverable, human purpose." Some staff and clients even suggest that medication, biological mechanisms, and other phenomena found in psychiatric explanations cause experiences, as if these phenomena were endowed with agency (Weinberg 1997). The psychiatric frame of reference dominates the semantic network of meanings to which both sufferers and observers of psychiatric conditions turn as they seek to make sense of their experiences.

Does this perspective hold true outside the clinic's reach? Can we envision a situation, in complex societies immersed in scientific and biomedical discourse, that gives precedence to the macrosocial and cultural shaping of experience while the clinical influences of diagnosis, medication, therapy, and even popular knowledge of psychiatric categories, causes, and treatment modalities recede? Can the typical rapid socialization into the patient role be avoided (Good 1992)?

In the past few decades, the phenomenon of individuals' experiencing madness in public space in the United States has opened up the possibility of examining psychiatric conditions outside of a psychiatric framework. In fact, public places provided a starting point for sociological and anthropological understanding of madness in the 1950s and 1960s.[1] But this focus soon gave way to the study of psychiatric institutions, socialization into the patient role, and family relations (Caudill 1958; Stanton and Schwartz 1954). By 1980, a convergence of forces, from the retrenchment of public psychiatry and the globalization of cities and the economy, had shifted the locus of suffering for many people afflicted with severe psychiatric symptoms. The deprivation of closed institutions so decried after World War II gave way to the social misery of those who found themselves in the streets or in precarious living situations.

This chapter examines the cultural shaping of identity through a particular aspect of homelessness and mental illness: that of street people who subjectively experience and traffic in the waste and the cast-off items of the privileged. I do not address homelessness generally, most of which does not concern mental illness (Tessler and Dennis 1989). Rather, I am concerned with those who suffer from severe psychiatric conditions while living in the interstices of the city. I address, first, how individuals cobble together personal and social identities, by necessity, in urban places of discard. I then shift the focus from intersubjectivity to the person, understood anthropologically. Waste and the trafficking practices around it expose not only tensions of exclusion and incorporation, but more specifically the type of incorporation toward which these subjects strive, in their imaginations or in practice.

THE DILEMMA OF IDENTITY IN INTERSTITIAL SPACES

This chapter draws on multisite ethnography, carried out mostly in the early 1990s, in transportation terminals, commercial areas, abandoned lots, and other interstitial spaces of Manhattan and Brooklyn (New York City). It draws on informal conversations, observations, and tape-recorded semi-directed interviews of street people who experienced severe psychiatric symptoms.[2] The sites at which we encountered these individuals are interstitial because they exist between other, more compact physical, social, and private spaces. They include passageways or anonymous waiting areas (stations, store entrances, subway platforms), spaces that simultaneously move through and dissolve urban territories (buses and subways), and areas for relaxation or pause before reentering other types of space (parks, atriums, sidewalk benches). Some interstitial spaces are private but involve little filtering or screening of their users (the area around a bank machine or fast-food joints); others are public or private places long abandoned (the no-man's-land between residential buildings or stores, boarded-up storefronts and condemned buildings, the areas under bridges and overpasses). Finally, some are unintended for human occupancy (subway gratings, vents, disused train tunnels, and so on). Much of the everyday interaction of the street people we encountered, including those who occasionally slept in shelters at night, took place in such interstitial spaces.[3]

The interstitiality of these spaces can be understood through two other aspects, institutional and social, both of which have consequences for the personal and social identities of street people who display signs of severe psychiatric conditions. First, mental health and social services that intervene in these places are themselves organizationally interstitial, located between or at the margins of major social, health, and charitable organizations. They map the spatial trajectories of their potential clients, grafting themselves onto the loosely bound terrain that these street people have temporarily appropriated. Thus, they intervene outside the walls of more conventional and visible psychiatric settings, such as mental health centers or supervised residences, and often without clear legal or administrative authority. They must work in the recesses of the city without clear notions of who is mentally ill and hence who their potential clients are. (This inarticulateness, or absence of criteria of similitude for conferring identity on the homeless mentally ill as a class, constitutes interstitiality in the sense that Mary Douglas [Douglas 1966, 1986] accords the expression.) And because mental health workers, wary of deterring potential clients, cannot display visible signs or "props" that indicate their psychiatric role, their legitimacy is questioned by homeless persons themselves and sometimes by passersby and others (see Lovell 1996 for an extended discussion of this dilemma). They operate outside a psychiatric frame.

Second, the public nature of these spaces constitutes a social interstitiality—that is, a social space between more stable domains, or networks, of social action. The spaces are liminal, characterized by the short-term copresence of, often, strangers; they serve temporally as moments of transition between the spaces of social action linked to longer-term ties, identities, and social worlds (Mische and White 1998).

In the large urban centers of modernity, the publicity of interstitial spaces generates a particular paradox.[4] Primarily anonymous, such spaces engender interactions between individuals who do not know each other. Typical of such interactions is the "polite inattention," or mutual engagement in unspoken conventions, between strangers or quasi strangers. Attention to the gestures and attitudes of the other minimizes the risk of encroaching on that other's personal territory, the *umwelt* (Goffman 1971b), or on the individual's moving world of normalcy, the protective cocoon placed between himself or herself and the risks and potentially fateful moments of each new situation (Giddens 1991). This necessity engendered by the copresence of strangers is the paradox of sociality in public space, in which avoidance of interaction is itself an interaction (Bordreuil 1990). Both Goffman-like attention to the detail of microsituations and the breaching experiments of ethnomethodology confirm the moral imperative of this mutual inattention. In other words, even strangers are held to the social expectation of reciprocity, silent or not.

In such public situations, social identity is emergent through the interaction at hand (Quéré and Brezger 1992). How strangers respond to one another depends on how they perceive one other. Yet imparting clues and signs of one's identity—or picking up these messages—is problematic. For street people—or those who might be taken as such—giving off clues to identity is a delicate balancing act.[5] Social identity is attributed or imputed to an individual. It emerges from the dialectic between the messages (appearance, words, and so on) that one gives off, given one's constraints, possibilities, and intention; and the meaning that others glean. In the contemporary United States, as in socially mobile societies in general (Duncan 1983), the totality of one's relationships and possessions go into the making of social identities: the inscription in a network of kin, one's car, electronics and appliances, job, diplomas, home page, health-club membership. Whereas identities shift in modernity, in urban space, this repertoire nevertheless comes into play in nonnegligible ways. Private spaces, such as homes, are particularly important for social identity in the United States, given the level to which they are commodified (Duncan 1983; Perrin 1977, 1988), but individuals tap some of the objects and relationships with which they surround themselves even in the transitory social situations of public space. They can also flaunt, mask, or play with other culturally evaluated and embodied characteristics (height, skin condition, involuntary hand movements, accent, and so on).

For street people in public space, the meager access to material and symbolic resources and the limited ability to control and manipulate embodied characteristics pose major problems for projecting the elements that others can use to attribute to them a social identity. Street people, in fact, tend to be defined in the negative, or by *absence*—the lack of most possessions, of a domicile, and, at least in the public eye, of relationships. They lack even simple props, such as the computer case that indicates where one is headed or bags full of groceries suggesting where one has come from or certain types of clothes. To be perceived as homeless is not only stigmatizing but can be highly dangerous, as when police round up loiterers to clean the city center before a major convention or when youth gangs physically assault isolated street people. Hence, bodily and verbal self-fashioning in (conscious or not) identity work, and skills in "passing" as other than who one "is," presents a constant challenge to social survival.[6]

For anyone constrained to living privately in public space, then, identity making is problematic (Snow and Anderson 1987). The stakes go up, however, when a street person in public space is perceived as "crazy." The commonsense term "craziness" applies to behavior in public that conveys some sort of challenge to the ongoing organization of social encounters. Following Goffman (Goffman 1963, 1967, 1971a) one can include among challenges the following examples (which I observed in the streets of New York, so they are context specific): nonauthorized initiatives (showing sudden familiarity with a stranger), situational inconveniences (disrobing in an ATM area, sitting on the ground in one's excrement), or inability to repair situational breaches in the immediate moment (not excusing oneself for walking too closely to a stranger, emitting strong body odor in a closed, crowded space, such as a subway train). In some cases, the inability to access resources, such as a place to clean up, may explain such behavior. In others, people with delusions or extremely withdrawn behavior may occupy public spaces unnoticed. But the unpredictability of "insults to interaction" and their repair in public situations become socially problematic. This lack of predictability parallels a more general anthropological definition of "craziness" as the inability to meet social obligations or the disruption of daily life in communities, for reasons unexplainable to most of the members of that community (Goddard 1998).

Identity work thus becomes a form of dual "damage control" in public space, as someone prone to disrupting ongoing interaction in the taken-for-granted world of everyday encounters attempts to moderate the perceptions of others. Individuals deemed "crazy" may engage in reciprocity, but in a way that is unanchored in the interaction at hand. The framing of this reciprocity, its reference to another place and time, even a private world, renders it inappropriate to the situation (Goffman 1974).

Damage control thus involves manipulating the dialectic between personal identity and the social identity that others attribute (Snow and Anderson 1987), as street people come to terms with the social relations in which they are caught, even if fleetingly. But it also involves the frame at hand: the materiality that the homeless individual constantly confronts. Others perceive this individual surrounded by cast-off things, garbage, refuse, all of which are highly charged symbolically. Elsewhere, I have described how some homeless people construct identities by cognitively distancing themselves from the situation at hand, through delusional misidentification (Lovell 2001). Here I turn to identity work that involves coming to terms with the discard and refuse.

GLEANERS, HOARDERS, SCRAPPERS, AND CANNERS

Survivors of the urban interstices invent ways of consuming and trafficking in resources at hand: that which has been cast off, discarded, given away, abandoned, or left in special places for garbage. This activity is not limited to homeless persons. Historically, ragpickers, soap-fat men, rubbish men, and other poor of New York City scrounged the streets and rubbish piles under bridges for discarded material and waste. Men, women, and sometimes children spent their lives picking and sorting through refuse, collecting anything that could be reused, repaired, recycled, or sold (Snyder 1885). Traditionally, gypsy communities weave symbiotic relationships with the better-off, through the collection, trade, or consumption of items the so-called host community has discarded—capitalizing on the surplus value (Gmelch 1986). Some of these items will be sold back to the discarders, in other forms, or through flea markets or *brocantes*. In low-income countries, garbage disposal can be a highly privatized function, and entire communities live off of and next to dumps. The Zabaline, a rural migrant community in Cairo, survives by recycling discarded consumer goods into glassware, pottery, metal objects, and other items, which they obtain from a second group, the Wâhiya, through informal but highly structured relationships (Assad 1988; Haynes and El-Hakim 1979). The fact that upwardly mobile rural migrants in many cities of Africa and Asia pick trash part-time or as their only means of livelihood, in giant garbage dumps inhabited by communities of thousands, was brought home by satellite to global viewers after the tragic landslide of the Promised Land dumpsite in Manila (Mydans 2000). And cast-off or "donated" clothes and other goods are now exported from wealthy countries to poorer ones, where they are resold in markets and warehouses.[7]

In New York City today, homeless and other economically precarious people make ends meet by living off of and exchanging cast-off goods. In the late 1980s and 1990s, hoarding, scrapping, and canning became viable means of surviving on the margins. Food, clothes, CDs, books, and crockery were gleaned from garbage cans, giant dumpsters, windowsills, piles in front of apartment buildings, and restaurants. These things were stored for later use, in shopping bags, shopping carts, milk crates, backpacks, and other containers, or they were discarded, traded, or sold.[8]

Makeshift shelters were bricolaged with cardboard boxes that once contained large appliances or from huge plastic sheets and tarmac left over from construction sites. Abandoned and boarded-up buildings, even disused train tunnels, were furnished with used mattresses, blankets, broken chairs, and TVs. Dumpsters, construction sites, buildings that had been recently renovated, and stores that had changed ownership or appearance provided a rich array of furnishings and industrial material from which copper, brass, and aluminum could be picked out or extracted. These materials were then sold to junkyards, scrap-metal places, or recycling centers. Abandoned television sets, air-conditioners, and other sophisticated consumer goods were also sources of scrap metal. Even thrown-out mattresses could be opened up for usable, sellable foam.

In the late 1980s, after the introduction of obligatory sorting of domestic garbage, and as New York's solid-waste disposal reached crisis proportions, can and bottle redemption became a major source of income for homeless and poor people in New York City. Canning ranged from taking a few bottles or cans to the corner supermarket or deli to careful and quick picking of huge quantities with gloved hands along recycling routes. Homeless and even service providers regarded canning as a sign of entrepreneurship and independence, distinct from living off of handouts from soup kitchens, mobile services, or commuters. One psychiatrically disabled woman created her own business, as a "middleman" between collectors and redeeming centers. Her example became the subject of a mental health training tape on success stories of psychiatrically disabled homeless.

Sometimes the line blurred between "stolen" and "found" or between "snatching" and "scrapping." At the time of my fieldwork, it was not unusual for residents of a neighborhood to find their clearly recognizable bedsheets or speakers displayed for sale on a nearby sidewalk. A telling joke at private homeless shelters was how fast clothes or other goods distributed by charities to the clients might appear on the sidewalk with a penciled price tag. Others complained that used-clothing stores, often catering to downtown "coolness," sold wares they picked up from charity intended for homeless people.

THE HIERARCHY OF DISCARD

The semantics of social identity in the interstices depends not only on a homeless person's control of the signs she emits but also on the types of objects and trafficking in which she engages. Turning now to specific encounters, I wish to consider two, parallel hierarchies of discard: that of the object and that of the homeless person's relationship to the object.

The French philosopher of "materiology" Francois Dagognet, in his critique of Western society's dualisms of ideal/material and mind/body, proposes a classification of material, a new *scala naturae*, based on two major groups: "objects for objects" (those which are used to produce, contain, or carry other objects or are exchanged with other objects—for clarity's sake, let's refer to them simply as "objects") and "meta-objects," the very things that Western cultures reject. This latter group, which he also terms *épaves*—unclaimed objects or wreckage—comprises five categories: fragments of formerly whole but still recognizable objects (the wheel from a toy, a used tire, a piece of pipeline); scraps and shreds (that which is left over when wood is sawed or cloth cut; all that resembles crumbs); scoria (the residues from refining metals or smelting ore, such as slag, cinders, and body dirt); detritus or rubbish (that which is no longer clearly recognizable because it is fermenting, inconsistent, amorphous—a category not only socially cumbersome but often dangerous); and the stercoral (feces, dung, that which is decomposed and rotten; see Dagognet 1997).

This categorization complexifies the analysis of things that are lumped together because they are found in the same place. Now a hierarchy appears: a broken radio, earphones without a Walkman, and broken furniture belong to Dagognet's fragments. Rags, bits of paper, but also leftover food wrappers, empty cans, and cardboard boxes, fall under "scraps." The leftover parts from construction sites constitute scoria. Rubbish and filth fill containers and dumps. And excrement, matter that is rotten or decomposed, is found in garbage and, in unfortunate cases, on people.

The amorphous, rotting matter at the bottom of Dagognet's hierarchy is the category that appears most problematic for street people. At the level of the social imaginary, homeless persons are associated with both the decomposing matter that is collected and the act of collecting it, as the terms "bagman" or "shopping-bag lady" suggest. Service providers and the media typically refer to gleaning as "foraging" or "scavenging" (a term that refers to lower forms of life, such as rodents and other animals that feed on dead or decaying matter) (Lovell 1996; Mossman 1997). I have observed a shopkeeper spray a homeless woman with insect repellant and then shoo her away, like a fly. The homeless mentally ill have been likened to vermin in the media, and their public handling of garbage has been deemed a public eyesore. The *New York Times* cited a city policy to spray the food supply [*sic*] of the homeless—beach-area garbage—with kerosene, to discourage "foraging" (Mossman 1997).

In our fieldwork, homeless street people classified each other according to a hierarchy of dignity, distinguishing those infested with lice and "vermin" or malodorous from those who use ingenious ways to keep clean; those who "cat" (sleep on the ground) or stoop down to eat out of garbage from those who manipulate their environment so as to sleep high off the ground or who take food only from on top of garbage (Lovell and Barrow 1990).

Thus, even those who failed to widen the gap between themselves and garbage went to great lengths, verbally, to distance themselves from the rotten, dirty, or decaying, oscillating between the first and third person, as these examples suggest:

> You be riding the subway system for so long, stay up there over a week, you get an odor on your body that's horrifying and they come in there and they say "Oh my god what is that." And I knew it was me. And it's a hurting thing, a hurtsome thing, unless you get so far gone 'til none of that don't bother you.

> You know [someone in the street] got more needs than just eating food now, he still want to feel like a man, like a human being, he don't want to feel like he's some kind of piece of dirt that you can just walk up and throw some crumbs at him.

> I couldn't adjust to that point and the way some people would just go into a public bathroom and stand there and pull their pants down and wash themselves. I mean, I still felt dirty, you know.

Some were indeed unaware of how their gleaning appeared to others— as scavenging. They could spend the better part of a day going from garbage can to garbage can, rifling through the containers, picking out a half-finished sandwich or soda, tasting it, discarding it, or carrying it with them as they moved along . Others, however, were careful about what they ate, using gloves as they adeptly handled the garbage. Some made distinctions of the sort expressed by a man who opposed "dumpster diving" to "dumpster dining":

> I believe in dumpster dining. I've become real good at it , self-
> sufficient. . . . I prefer gourmet restaurant dumpsters, Dean and Deluca,
> Graces Market, Balducci's and a couple of others. They have such great

stuff. The patés, the cheeses, roast beef, the cookies, strawberries. . . . Trash can dining is also something I practice: you walk past the trash can and there is this cute little package with a bow on it, inside you have filet mignon with a fork and spoon, tartar sauce and a bottle of Perrier water.[9]

Street people's relationship to higher-level meta-objects is more ambiguous. In fact, Dagognet's *scala natura* is missing a type of material that falls between the two classes: objects, still intact and unused, whose owners have lost them or cast them off. Here are found still-wrapped packaged food, new clothes that have never been worn, unwanted presents that have been thrown away. These objects evoke a relational rather than a material dimension. They have been transferred from individual sovereignty or ownership to a moral entity, public administration, or power that is allowed to dispose of them or recycle them into other objects. under legal jurisdiction. But the fact of having been cast off or donated, even if intact and unused, renders them "lesser" objects, closer to meta-objects than to owned objects. Some street people rejected food or clothes simply because they were offers—charity or gifts. Some delusions transformed discarded things or garbage into gifts left by a specific person (Lovell 1997a). However, others took pleasure in the amount of things they found on the street: brand-new socks, sweaters, shoes, CDs—items they could pick up, by chance, and use to distinguish themselves from the "mental" look or "institution" style of the items typically distributed through shelters and thrift programs.

This "higher-level," ambiguous trafficking also blurred the lines between the behavior of street people and efforts by artists and status-conscious consumers to value the cast-off as a way to differentiate themselves. Designers create furniture and sculptures from found objects and recycled industrial materials; architects built from them.[10] In the 1980s and 1990s, stylists launched all sorts of "street" fashions, including, at one point, tatters and raglike clothes that clearly evoked the stereotypical homeless person.

SOCIAL IMAGINARY AND SCHOLARLY CONSTRUCTS

Social representations of mentally ill homeless that view them as "close to" garbage and discard are evident in the discourse of psychiatrists and social scientists. Psychiatrists have long defined garbage collecting and hoarding as classical symptoms of mental illness. These activities are considered abnormal social behaviors typical of schizophrenia but also associated with obsessive-compulsive disorder, anorexia, Alzheimer's disease, and dementia. Psychoanalysts see hoarding in psychosis as regression to a childlike state (as is the fascination with excrement) or an attempt to stop time or bring up the past.

Neuroscientists have begun to look for brain anomalies and brain functions that might relate to this behavior. Hoarding is currently treated with medication and therapy. Hoarding and "scavenging" have also occurred in closed psychiatric institutions, and sociological analyses have suggested that these behaviors are the result of material deprivation and the lack of safe places for storing personal belongings (Goffman 1961). But even in institutional settings, hoarding items, especially "illogical" ones (other patients' toothbrushes, soiled tissue, and so on) in odd places, has been interpreted as a sign of psychosis (Chong, Tan, and Lee 1996). (Hoarding is also considered a nonclinical problem, as attested to by the self-help groups for hoarders and clutterers that are cropping up alongside the clinically identified groups across the United States today.)[11]

Several men and women I met kept wads of old newspapers, uneaten food, rags, wrappers, broken transistor radios, gum wrappers, and other discarded material in plastic or paper shopping bags (themselves discarded) or in shopping carts—which are iconic inversions of the consumption society and the normalcy of "compulsive" shopping and "bulimic" buying.[12] (Of course, not all bags contained rubbish, and in most cases, I was not shown and did not seek to look inside these highly private portable devices for safekeeping.) Others carried around single items, such as broken headphones without a Walkman, or attached layers of pins, feathers, and other odd accessories to their clothes. Thus, some street people clearly hoarded for purposes other than physical means of survival. But whether collecting garbage was a clinical symptom or was simply a means of survival shared with poor people who are not mentally disturbed could not always be determined. As a common phenomenon, or social fact, however, such behavior cannot be separated from either its cultural meaning or material foundation.

Garbage shows up as well when we move from individual-level to macrosocial analyses of the management of mental illness. Ethnopsychiatric anthropologist Roger Bastide, in his treatise on the sociology of mental illness, called for a "sociology of garbage," one that pays attention to activities in the streets of the city at the wee hours of the morning. Industrial society, he insisted, has to eject the superfluous and useless. But he was not writing about solid matter; he was referring to people who are mentally ill and to their place in the social world (Devereux 1969).

The social imaginary is thus doubled by scholarly uses of the metaphor of garbage and discard to refer to the management of persons who are mentally ill and of other "service-dependent" populations, such as homeless people. Comparisons of superfluous people to garbage surfaced in the 1950s, in a heated exchange between a rather provocative Erving Goffman and a somewhat appalled Margaret Mead (Goffman 1956). At a conference on group processes that brought together psychiatrists and anthropologists, Goffman was presenting the characteristics of total institutions based on his fieldwork at St. Elisabeth's psychiatric hospital in Washington, D.C., the foundation for the great sociology classic *Asylums* (Goffman 1961). His original intention was to borrow the term *metabolic cycle* to refer to the way in which psychiatric hospitals and other total institutions bring in, work over, and then disgorge [sic] human beings. He used this analogy to biology to show how the institution—unlike a biological organism, which rejects what it has swallowed in another, more amorphous form—actually modifies the people it "disgorges," so that they are fit for a socially necessary task. Perhaps Margaret Mead's strong reaction to the analogy between waste and mental patients and other inmates was the factor that led Goffman to change his mind.[13] Mead finally admitted that "[waste products] is not a very appropriate term for people who graduate from Harvard Law School perhaps, but it could possibly be appropriate for *some* of the people that come through our prisons and mental hospitals" (Goffman 1956: 136). In *Asylums*, however, the entire functional analysis of the institution as a processing machine disappears, along with the unfortunate figure of speech.

Fleeting as they might be, these elements of social analysis—and the outrage they provoke—reflect the moral position of a community or society toward groups that are excluded economically, politically, and socially as polluting—a point probably not lost on Goffman. Today, we might see such readings as the fruit of a naive critique of institutions, focused solely on the aspect of social control. Yet the metaphor returns outside the walls of the total institution, in the global city and postindustrial world. Contemporary scholarly accounts, however, have shifted from a concern with the process of handling surplus people to a focus on the *place* to which such people are relegated. Geographers and urban sociologists have mapped the topology of wastelands, or areas no longer deemed of use to dominant social groups, to which surplus people or "service-dependent populations" are sent or go to (Dear and Wolch 1987; Duncan 1983). These places have a negligible property value, sit on the edges of more valued neighborhoods, or, as in the special case of New York City, are pocketed between thriving residential or commercial areas. In a pictorial essay constructed over several years, Camilo Vergara demonstrates how many of the nursing homes, homeless shelters, supervised residences, and especially prisons (which house many of those

who years ago would have found themselves in psychiatric institutions) reside in these types of wasteland (Vergara 1995). Furthermore, not only psychiatric patients but those who might be considered "crazy" in commonsense terms or who have avoided psychiatric services so far—the "hard to
reach" to psychiatric workers and "hidden" populations to social scientists—are directed by services or by processes of discrimination, or direct
themselves toward, urban zones of discard (Dear and Wolch 1987). One
homeless person referred to the vast areas of no-man's-land stretching from
parts of lower Manhattan over to inner-city Brooklyn as a big "dustbin."

SALVAGING THE SOCIAL COORDINATES: FROM INTERSUBJECTIVITY TO THE PERSON

Until now, I have focused on the way in which homeless people must negotiate a social identity in relation to the cast-off materials, waste, or garbage
around them. Constrained by interstitiality and the publicness of the spaces
they inhabit, they engage in a representation of self that must account for
the materiality of garbage and the cast-off and for their proximity to it. This
materiality is doubled by the public imagination and sometimes implied in
scholarly discourse, whether or not it is a corporeality. In either case,
garbage and the cast-off become metaphors that affect those who live in the
street. These men and women oscillate between powerlessness and resistance, sometimes embracing or immerging in the negatively charged symbols that others associate with them and sometimes prevailing over them,
with or without grandeur.[14] In this process, the cultural dimension of hoarding, scavenging, and otherwise trafficking with garbage and the cast-off
often dominates the psychiatric picture to the point that individuating a biological or psychic dimension from a social one is difficult.

This intersubjective, interactionist perspective, however, limits the dimension of the social to a copresent or imagined Other. Epistemologically,
this stance is phenomenological, bracketing the particulars of the community of the society in which self and other are inscribed. This perspective
simply pushes larger processes and forms of sociality to the background to
better understand the microsocial or intersubjective processes. Such an ex-
pedient may carry the tacit acknowledgment of a nonspecified "social" or
"community" in the background. But the notion remains vague, meaningful only as an opposition (to an individual or to a self and others). It is similar to some social scientists' thoughts about mental illness when the
boundaries around its definition and management have been loosened. In
these cases, "community" is never specified; it is simply posited as an ideal

space, a topological opposition to the closed space of the asylum or institution (Gordon 1986), or a consensual space of language. A danger also exists of unveiling historical and larger social-cultural processes that are under way. Relegating to the background the question of which community or what type of society is at work also runs the risk of closing the door before acknowledging questions of moral agency.

Recent theories of justification, or the logics underlying the accounts people use to give good reason for their everyday actions to others, provide one way to link intersubjectivity and collective phenomena, but as tensions rather than as dichotomies. Luc Boltanski and Laurent Thévenot (1991) developed a major theoretical approach, which they and other sociologists have applied to a range of situations, such as medical labeling, environmental damage, and local politics. Using the style of the parable, the authors draw on classical texts to identify six logics, or "regimes" of justification: the market world of competition, the domestic world of tradition and hierarchy, the world of fame, and the civic, inspirational, and industrial worlds.[15] Each world (*cité*, or city) involves a specific type of social structure and set of rules and obligations. Individuals legitimize situations and viewpoints with references to competing *cités*, or moral worlds.

From an anthropological stance, the empirical, embodied individual justifying his or her action is also a person: a site of relations enacted by moral agents and thus expressive of the values and ethos of a society. The other persons in these relations, of course, may be human beings, supernatural entities, or, one could argue, an entity such as a state. The nature of those relations, the obligations they carry—whether they exist prior to the person or are integral to it—may differ culturally. But the category of the person populates most anthropological perspectives. And the anthropologist can grasp the nature of that person through the network of transactions in which the individual qua person engages.[16] Thus, an individual's personhood—a social or moral role—can be gleaned from the types of relationships he or she sustains with others.

Goffman's definition of *insanity* (his term) as the inability to make amends for or repair an insult to interaction can put such an individual outside the realm of personhood. Such a categorization fits with the historical treatment of the "schizophrenic," because the construction of that medical category, as a nonperson, is not understandable and hence is outside the realm of communication. It also accords with Barrett's alternative proposal of liminality or anomaly to categorize the "schizophrenic" (Barrett 1998). In either case, severe mental illness puts one outside the public space of conversation, off the coordinates, and beyond personhood.

Does this nonperson emerge in the ways that street people engage in discard and garbage? This figure of the isolate is very present in the examples at hand and provides grist for our analysis. Many street people perceive themselves as social outcasts in a complex urban structure. Some of them glean and/or hoard, either by compulsion, a psychological need to attach themselves to meta-objects, or for survival, to eat and live. The isolate is expressed in the prototypical shopping-bag lady muttering to herself as she picks over found objects or in the homeless man described above, who spent his day wandering from one garbage can to the other, oblivious to whether others saw him picking through half-eaten salad or sipping an abandoned cup of soda.

However, extremely isolated homeless people may also express an awareness of standards outside of themselves that belong to a larger social world. Sometimes the isolate gleaner is very aware of his fragile position; the larger world is peopled with dangerous agents. Ken, a highly educated West African man, evoked the widespread violence of the streets in the early 1990s. His needs were met outside of social obligations, through the serendipity of finding abandoned money, which he called "windfall money."[17]

> You pick up money easily in busy commercial areas with clients and customers streaming to and fro. Someone invariably drops money. Fifty dollars is possible. Homeless men drop money too, in the parks when it's windy. Some count money, and the wind blows it away . . . . [On pay day] you have twenty-dollar and ten-dollar and five-dollar and one-dollar bills flying about in the park. Others are drug dealers who sell crack, but they are so drug crazed that soon they go away forgetting the plastic bag of money. If someone sees you pick up money, you may be in a fist fight . . . Those who carry money in the park invariably carry a knife, and you can lose your heart for a little money.

In other cases, a profound sense of shame reflects the awareness of shared values. Does an isolate perceive herself as a nonperson, invisible, when she is constantly conscious of being seen? Shame, as Charles Taylor suggests, has significance for a person because it is not shared with nonpersonal agents. It shows "what the person is aware of: standards which only apply to a being who is self-aware, and who shares this awareness of his personhood with others" (Taylor 1985: 264). Such awareness is expressed in the helplessness and remorse of a man, who suffered from severe depression and spent years on the street.

> You can go to a lot of places and see some homeless people, that their minds are really deteriorated, they're wearing clothes from way back in

the sixties . . . stuff that's really old. But, they done deteriorated so bad that they don't really know this, they don't really see themselves. You can go, you get to a state of mind, you just don't even see yourself no more . . . you just surviving, they'll even go to the garbage can. And I hate to say it, I ate out of a garbage can one time . . . I did. I watched a person actually put the food in it, and I waited 'til night. I watched that garbage 'til night so no one would see me, and went and ate the food, that's how hungry I was.

Part of his shame is evident in the way he goes to great lengths to associate garbage with the lowliness of *other* homeless people, at the same time admitting that he himself succumbed to this activity of self-degradation. Thus, in Taylor's sense, this man is not a nonperson; rather, he speaks to an unnamed interlocutor, perhaps embodied in the anthropologist, but perhaps to the moral agency present in his earlier socialization or out there in a capitalist, achievement-oriented society that does not legitimize trafficking in the cast off.

This morality is evident in dumpster dining, which reveals still another relationship between isolation and the larger society. Lars Eighner, who wrote about his three years homeless and his much briefer period on a psychiatric ward (Eighner 1994), also produced an essay on this variant of gleaning as a modern form of self-reliance. (He also stated that he continues to "scavenge" although he is no longer homeless):

> Many times in my travels I have lost everything but the clothes I was wearing and [my dog]. The things I find in dumpsters, the love letters and rag dolls of so many lives, remind me of this lesson. Now I hardly pick up a thing without envisioning the time I will cast it away. This I think is a healthy state of mind. Almost everything I have now has been cast out at least once, proving that what I own is valueless to someone.
>
> Anyway, I find my desire to grab for the gaudy bubble has been largely sated. I think this is an attitude I share with the very wealthy— we both know there is plenty more where what we have came from. Between us are the rat-race millions who have confounded their selves with the objects they grasp and who nightly scavenge the cable channels for they know not what. (Eighner 1992: 94–95)

Although the isolate corresponds to the stereotype many Americans hold of homeless mentally ill people, the above accounts presented relate in a dynamic way to the larger consumerist society. Paradoxically, these homeless individuals are expressing their own moral agency, as members of the very community that treats them like moral exiles, beyond personhood.

A second figure is the person for whom discard represents an egalitarian ideal. Homeless people in this category see themselves as part of an implicit community that cares for everyone. This perception is the polar opposite of isolation and exclusion. Traffic in garbage is reinterpreted in dignified terms. For example, some street gleaners believe that the food, money, or other goods they find are purposely put out to be passed around. Gary expresses this ethos:

> In New York I can always find food. Someone might put down something they didn't want to eat. Or they'd put clothes or a book they didn't want, maybe on their window ledge. I put books out too, and bread for the birds, knowing I was impervious to the red death, black death, blue death. Once I found some clothes in the bushes—literally Christian Dior, the square kind of outfit to impress someone. I've also found a St. Laurent jacket, and one of these Western kinds of hats that look like caning on a chair. I once found about $300 worth of Gucci clothes too, right under my feet.

Gary's relationship to poverty seems almost "Christian" and "saintly" in the manner of the followers of Saint Francis: people put things out for others, just as the saint put crumbs out for the birds.[18] Gary was also involved with a local theater group in a communal-type relationship, sharing the basement space the group rented and sometimes lived in.

A similar ethos was expressed by a group of former homeless persons and psychiatric patients who handed out sandwiches they made from donations of packaged food that had gone beyond the expiration date. They spoke in the language of sharing—of bounty, harvest, and other quasi-biblical concepts. Another egalitarian vision was shared by employees in homeless programs who preferred to remain homeless despite the fact that they had salaries, because they wished to remain close to the deprivation their clients experienced. These people belong to a loosely bounded (envisioned) enclave within a larger, nonegalitarian society. The moral agency reflected in their personhood is that of the enclave, not the larger society that has rendered them homeless.

A more structured egalitarian utopia was envisioned by Harold, who constructed his social identity through a fantasy that intersected with that of domiciled artists and housing activists. "I have designed and built a bed called a 'life capsule' ," he announced on a flyer besieging homeless programs and all other interested parties to refer people to his community. "This enclosed bed has a mattress, heater, light, storage space and security curtain to insure a quiet, comfortable place to sleep." He said he was placing the life capsules in ten buildings on twenty-six acres of riverfront property in Brooklyn.[19] The area would eventually sport a mall, a Rollerblade area, good security service, and other attractions. In fact, his life capsules were those designed by a Japanese architect and found today in Japanese hotels for the presumably nonclaustrophobic. (Harold's flyer had photocopied designs of the capsules.) I last heard of him after I had left New York: a magazine article mentioned his attendance at a meeting with housing activists and artists who were planning to take over abandoned government property on the riverfront to build housing. The article gave no indication that Harold's project was a fantasy.

A third person inhabits the entrepreneurial ideal of the canners. Like some isolates, this type of entrepreneur is incorporated into the larger community, rather than excluded, through the conflict of competitive individualism—hence, the woman who founded her own canning-redemption business, buying a van with savings from entitlements so that she could take cans that others collected to the redemption center.

Another type of entrepreneurship, however, suggests at once the entrepreneurial ideal and a fourth type of person, one who is embedded in a nexus of strongly incorporated groups within a complex, hierarchical society. This ideal was mostly absent in the way people trafficked with garbage, given that some of their tactics aimed precisely to avoid the bureaucratic obstacles and multiple demands of social services. One man's vision reflected tension between the highly structured, highly incorporated social person and the egalitarianism of communal groups. Scott, a religious man ("JC is my Lord and savior"), amateur artist, and avid canner, denounced the way in which racism (he is African-American) and the "warlike" conditions of homelessness affected him and others. In a long taped conversation, he repeatedly brought up the theme of reclaiming garbage as a way of equalizing the distribution of resources:

> The city is always claiming they short of money, but why if they're short of money do they pay the Sanitation Department guys money to go by and pick up the same garbage can three or four times a day? And the garbage he's picking up, he's taking money out of the poor people's hands! . . . [Poor] people come through here to get the cans, they get twelve dollars for 240 cans. When [the Sanitation guys] dump the cans in that garbage truck, that's loss, you understand?

He then elaborates a plan for recycling garbage. Homeless people should have places to sleep, wash, keep their clothes clean, and recycle garbage: paper, aluminum, glass, copper. He sketches a project for the city to encourage homeless people to collect two million dollars' worth of cans, then put the money into a fund: a canning corp [corporation or co-op]: "Ten dollars is powerless in the hands of one homeless person. If it's put in the corporation, won't be smoked up [on crack] or spent on a shot of liquor." Whoever maintains the quota should be entitled to become part of the corp and should benefit from the housing that will be constructed or purchased with the money collected. People will then grow food, buy tanks, and turn minnows into big fish, like those in Central Park lake. He continues:

> [They should] take obsolete subways and stack them up, redesign the interior for 'em, where each one could house say four or five single guys, could put a restroom in there, a sink, a stove, a refrigerator. And boom, that's housing right there for poor people, man, and to keep 'em from taking up space like I say you could have 'em like set up one on top of another like maybe ten stories high. In the center you got an elevator would take 'em up and down and then you solving the homeless problem. It's temporary basically, but it's housing.

The city would have "a capital thing, with all these cans: after paying rents, homeless people could start little delis and restaurants all over the city. The city could take that food, [the homeless] could open up businesses, they could start schools and teach each other skills, then you would have more people would come to this city, you would have more tourists here, people wouldn't be afraid, you could cut the crime rate and everything."

He ends with an idea that others often put forth: to get a van. That way, he can hook up with a man he knows, whom he sees lugging cans around all day, a man with strong muscles (Scott is a small man), and turn his canning enterprise into a small business. His narrative comes full circle to the familiar entrepreneurial person.

Scott's account reflects his relationship to a larger, capitalist society (the city, the public services) that victimizes him and others like him by taking away their opportunities to survive. But the utopia he proposes is an egalitarian one, perhaps less an enclave than a community similar to those we described for cities of Africa and Asia. His is a total civic engagement.[20]

CONCLUSION

Those confined to trafficking in waste, as Zygmunt Bauman suggests in the quotation that opens this chapter, perform the daily border work that keeps them at bay, that "divines, literally conjures up . . . the difference between . . . the admitted and the rejected, the included and the excluded" (Bauman 2004: 28). This paper shifts our gaze from Bauman's stance—where we discern the mechanisms of the overconsuming fortress nations and gated communities that must continually expel industrial, household, and human waste to live at their chosen standards—to the ground level of those unsung heroes of modernity, the waste traffickers or "rubbish men" and women. My street-level gaze reveals how trafficking in garbage and discard reflects and enacts ways in which particular people—those doubly excluded because of their homelessness and because of severe psychic suffering and its stigma—link up with that "something larger" that we call society.

At the microsocial level of interaction in public space, such trafficking becomes an element in the construction of social identity. At another level, however, views of garbage and ways of trafficking reflect the strivings of these street people toward particular types of moral agency. These types of personhood are culturally constructed from notions of power, sociality, and exclusion, beyond the contours of the reduced psychiatric person or patienthood. In the figures of the homeless persons I've presented, even delusional discourse reveals itself to be profoundly political, not simply because it condemns or reflects existing inequalities and forms of domination and exclusion but because it projects possible moral worlds. We must contrast these visions with the reductionist view held by the domiciled, the professionals, and ourselves, social scientists, and note the practical consequences that follow.

NOTES

Sue Makiesky Barrow, Samuel Bordreuil, Alain Ehrenberg, and Peter Stastny provided critical readings of an earlier version of this paper, which takes its inspiration from Alain Epelboin and his work on the Dakar garbage dump. Some of the data collection was made possible by a National Institute for Mental Health Services grant to Dr. D. L. Shern. Thanks to the field-workers for their part in this coproduction.

1. The prototypical study is Goffman's description of the spiral of interactions between rule breakers and "collusive others" that lead to hospitalization (Goffman 1971a).

2. I describe the methodology in Lovell 1996 and 1997a. Mental health workers determined psychiatric status (primarily schizophrenia but also affective disorders) using standardized diagnostic criteria (the third edition of the *Diagnostic and Statistical Manual of Mental Disorders*), but only at the end of a long process of outreach and engagement, comprising numerous brief time frames, in which a potential client's behavior could appear to be highly contaminated by environment.

3. My conceptualization of interstitial space bears a family resemblance to the "non-places" described by Marc Augé (1992). For him, a nonplace lacks an identity, has no historical or collective memory, and is not relational. His metaphor is the

duty-free area in an airport, where everyone is free of social obligations, having given up their identity to get in. Once inside, they are reduced, like everyone else, to solitude and similitude. I take issue with this view, which ignores the double problem of civil inattention and emergent identity in public settings or zones of passage, which I discuss below.

4. In this discussion, the public nature, or publicity, of such spaces refers to the specific sites of my fieldwork. In other times and cultural settings, similar spaces may exhibit different degrees of publicity (Lovell 1995).

5. Emergent identities in public space may be especially problematic for other types of people, such as women (Lovell 1997b). But here I am concerned specifically with homelessness.

6. Jonathon Nossiter's 1996 film *Sunday* is an interesting case study of "passing" as an interactive process: an aging, melancholic actress misidentifies a homeless man as a famous film director, a role that the man proceeds to play to the hilt.

7. Agnès Varda's poetic film *Les glaneurs et la glaneuse* (2000) records the multiple modern forms of gleaning, relating them to urban forms (in French, *la récup*) and the rural forms, allowed by law. In biblical tradition, the fields are gleaned after the harvest; something must be left behind as a kind of tithe for use by the poor (Peyah). This "tithe" is symbolized by the edges of a man's hair—thus, locks left on the corners (Peter Stastny, personal communication).

8. See also Duneier's ethnography of street vendors in Greenwich Village (Duneier 2000).

9. A television ad at the time blurred the lines between begging and gestures of distinction through a homeless man on a street corner who produces a jar of Grey Poupon mustard.

10. Many artists create with cast-off materials. Marcel Duchamp, Joseph Beuys, and Christian Boltanski and more recently, El Anatsui, Romuald Hazoume, and Willie Bester are but a few artists whose work merits a discussion beyond the scope of this paper. More pertinent to this chapter are the marginal artists who construct worlds for themselves from discarded, undignified material. In Newark, across the river from the site of the World Trade Center towers, Kea Tawana, "a carpenter, electrical worker, and scavenger" with a sixth-grade education, created a remarkable ark on the edge of a church parking lot. "The dark four-by-sixes that once supported houses were the ribs that gave the boat its shape. Hundreds of books and magazines, heaps of hardware, building ornaments, theater seats, bicycle parts, electrical equipment, radiators, window frames, shards of colored glass, buckets full of nuts, pots and pans, and parts of five pipe organs" created the "mayhem" of her boat. Newark officials considered the boat an eyesore; after a three-year court battle, she was forced to take it down (Vergara 1995).

11. See www.alt.recovery.clutter for a list of groups and websites.

12. This phenomenon is brilliantly portrayed in Percy Adlon's 1989 film, *Rosalie Goes Shopping.*

13. Here is an excerpt from the exchange between Goffman and Mead (Goffman 1956: 119–21):

> *Goffman:* I should like to go on now to empirical speculation, and to describe the metabolic cycle with respect to mental hospitals. Does the word still bother you?
>
> *Mead:* Yes, it does. [. . .] Why don't you describe the process as it occurs in a total institution?

Goffman: I shall try, but I want to stress that these are processes oriented to the taking in and disgorgement of people. I want a word to cover that. I shall use metabolism in quotes from now on, if you wish.

Mead: Disgorgement usually means vomit. Is that what you mean?

Bateson: How about "processing of people"?

Goffman: Is processing of people acceptable to everyone? There are some moral feelings cropping up in this discussion that I hope will not arise too often.

14. This identity is surely gendered, as were polluting images in other contexts (Lovell and Cohn 1998). Unfortunately, the homeless women encountered in this study were fewer and more isolated than the men, which hampered detailed observation of interactions.

15. Mary Douglas and Steven Ney (1998) place this sociological essay in the tradition of parables in political philosophy.

16. In other words, the "free-standing, self-contained individual" in the West is an ideological construct; anthropology would uncover the social relations in which the person is embedded, even as she or he acts as if individual—as opposed to related and dividual or divisible and multiple (LiPuma 1998). Societies differ in the degree to which the dividual aspect is latent, not according to whether it is present or absent.

17. A windfall usually refers to an unexpected bit of good luck. Some homeless persons speak of windfalls when they receive large benefit or disability checks because of back pay or because of bureaucratic errors that temporarily halted monthly payments. In speaking of windfall money, Ken means money that literally falls from the sky or is carried by the wind. Another woman I met in Central Park used to stare at the sky waiting for money to drop from airplanes.

18. Gary is a Catholic Italian-American, but I do not know how this background affected his ethos of gleaning.

19. In describing the life capsules, Harold evoked the homeless vehicle built by public artist Kryztof Wodiczko and David Lurie a few years earlier. The vehicle, made from a grocery cart (itself commonly used by homeless people to transport their belongings), contained an armorlike snout for washing up and cooking. The overall effect, especially as the cart projected its shadows onto the walls of corporate buildings, was that of an armored vehicle moving through the city.

20. These four examples of personhood resemble the "social person" developed by Mary Douglas and Steven Ney, according to a grid/group schema or fourfold graph with social structure and social incorporation as the axes (Douglas and Ney 1998). For these authors, however, the isolate is outside the realm of moral agency, like, one might assume, the nonperson embodied in the "schizophrenic" in Barrett's analysis. In fact, such a culturalist view of the "social person" deflects our attention from the specific historical situation and the agent in the person. (For a critique that also accepts the usefulness of Douglas's schemas, see Strathern and Lambek 1998.)

SOURCES

Assad, Ragui. 1988. "L'informel structurel. Les zabbälin du Caire." *Peuples méditerranéens* 41–42 (October 1987–March 1988): 181–92.

Augé, Marc. 1992. *Non-lieux: Introduction à une anthropologie de la surmodernité.* Paris: Seuil.

Barrett, Robert J. 1996. *The Psychiatric Team and the Social Definition of Schizophrenia: An Anthropological Study of Person and Illness.* New York: Cambridge University Press.

———. 1998. "The 'schizophrenic' and the liminal persona in modern society." *Culture, Medicine and Psychiatry* 22: 465–94.

Bauman, Zygmunt. 2004. *Wasted Lives. Modernity and Its Outcasts.* Cambridge: Polity Press.

Boltanski, Luc, and Laurent Thévenot. 2006. *On Justification.* Princeton, NJ: Princeton University Press. Originally published as *De la justification: Les economies de grandeur* (Paris: Gallimard, 1991).

Bordreuil, Jean Samuel. 1990. "L'identité à l'épreuve de la ville. Eléments pour une géographie des (in)civilités." In *L'humanisme en géographie*, ed. A. Bailly and R. Scariati (Paris: Anthropos).

Caudill, William. 1958. *The Psychiatry Hospital as a Small Society.* Cambridge, MA: Harvard University Press.

Chong, Siow Ann, Chay Hoon Tan, and How Sung Lee. 1996. "Hoarding and Clozapine-Risperidone Combination." *Canadian Journal of Psychiatry* 41(5): 315–16.

Dagognet, François. 1997. *Des détritus, des déchets, de l'abject: Une philosophie écologique.* Le Plessis-Robinson: Institut Synthélabo.

Dear, Michael J., and Jennifer R. Wolch. 1987. *Landscapes of Despair: From Deinstitutionalization to Homelessness.* Princeton, NJ: Princeton University Press.

Devereux, Georges. 1969. *Sociologie de la maladie mentale.* Paris: Flammarion.

Douglas, Mary. 1966. *Purity and Danger.* London: Routledge and Kegan Paul.

———. 1986. *How Institutions Think.* Syracuse, NY: Syracuse University Press.

Douglas, Mary, and Steven Ney. 1998. *Missing Persons. A Critique of Personhood in the Social Sciences.* Berkeley: University of California Press.

Duncan, James S. 1983. "Men without Property. The Tramp's Classification and Use of Urban Space." In *Readings in Urban Analysis,* ed. R. Lake (New Brunswick, NJ: Rutgers University Press).

Duneier, Mitchell. 2000. *Sidewalk.* New York: Farrar, Straus and Giroux.

Eighner, Lars. 1992. "On Dumpster Diving." *New England Journal of Public Policy* 8(1): 87–95.

———. 1994. *Travels with Lisbeth.* New York: Fawcett Books.

Giddens, Anthony. 1991. *Modernity and Self-Identity. Self and Society in the Late Modern Age.* Cambridge: Polity Press.

Girardin, Delphine de, and Jean-Louis Vissière. 1986. *Chroniques parisiennes, 1836–1848.* Paris: Des Femmes.

Gmelch, Sharon Bohn. 1986. "Groups That Don't Want In: Gypsies, and Other Artisan, Trader, and Entertainment Minorities." *Annual Review of Anthropology* 15: 307–30.

Goddard, Michael. 1998. "What Makes Hari Run? The Social Construction of Madness in a Highland Papua New Guinea Society." *Critique of Anthropology* 18: 61–82.

Goffman, Erving. 1956. "Interpersonal Persuasion." In *Group Processes. Transactions of the Third Conference,* ed. B. Schaffner (New York: Josiah Macy Foundation), 117–38.

————. 1961. *Asylums: Essays on the Social Situation of Mental Patients and Other Inmates*. Garden City, NY: Anchor Books.

————. 1963. *Behavior in Public Places*. New York: The Free Press.

————. 1967. *Interaction Ritual: Essays on Face-to-Face Behavior*. New York: Pantheon Books.

————. 1971a. *The Insanity of Place*. New York: Harper and Row.

————. 1971b. *Relations in Public*. New York: Harper and Row.

————. 1974. *Frame Analysis. An Essay on the Organization of Experience*. Cambridge, MA: Harvard University Press.

Good, Byron J. 1992. "Culture and Psychopathology: Directions for Psychiatric Anthropology." In *New Directions in Psychological Anthropology*, ed. T. Schwartz, G. M. White, and C. A. Lutz (Cambridge: Cambridge University Press), 181–205.

Gordon, Colin. 1986. "Psychiatry as a Problem of Democracy." In *The Power of Psychiatry*, ed. P. Miller and N. Rose (Cambridge: Polity Press).

Hacking, Ian. 1999. *The Social Construction of What*. Cambridge, MA: Harvard University Press.

Haynes, Kingsley E., and Sherif M. El-Hakim. 1979. "Appropriate Technology and Public Policy: The Urban Waste Management System in Cairo." *The Geographical Review* 69: 101–108.

LiPuma, Edward. 1996. "Mobilité des cadres et psychiatrie 'hors les murs.' " *Raisons Pratiques* 16: 55–81.

————1998. "Modernity and Forms of Personhood in Melanesia." In *Bodies and Persons. Comparative Perspectives from Africa and Melanesia*, ed. M. Lambek and A. Strathern (New York and Melbourne: Cambridge University Press).

Lovell, Anne M. 1995. La construction des espaces sexués: le vécu des femmes dans les espaces publics de différents contextes culturels. Deuxième Forum des Femmes de la Méditéranné, Tunis, 1995.

————. 1996. "Mobilite des cadres et psychiatrie hors les murs." *Raisons Pratiques* 7: 59–85.

————. 1997a. " 'The City Is My Mother': Narratives of Homelessness and Schizophrenia." *American Anthropologist* 99(2): 355–68.

————. 1997b. "Les ruses de la rue. Légitimité des femmes dans l'espace sexué." In *Le forum et le harem. Femmes et hommes, pratiques et représentations* (Aix-en-Provence: Presses de l'Université de Provence).

————. 2001. "Les fictions de soi-même, ou les délires identificatoires: La maladie mentale en mutation." In *Psychiatrie et société*, ed. A. Ehrenberg and A. M. Lovell (Paris: Odile Jacob), 127–61.

Lovell, Anne M., and Susan Makiesky Barrow. 1990. "Portable Images: Post-Industrial Constructions of Home and Homelessness." Section on Anthropology, New York Academy of Sciences.

Lovell, Anne M., and Sandra Cohn. 1998. "The Elaboration of 'Choice' in a Program for Homeless Persons Labelled Psychiatrically Disabled." *Human Organization* 57: 8–20.

Mische, Ann, and Harrison White. 1998. "Between Conversation and Situation: Public Switching Dynamics across Network Domains." *Social Research* 65(3): 1–15.

Mossman, Douglas. 1997. "Deinstitutionalization, Homelessness, and the Myth of Psychiatric Abandonment: A Structural Anthropology Perspective." *Social Science and Medicine* 44(1): 71–83.

Mydans, Seth. 2000. "A World of Scavengers on the Fringe of Wealth," The Week in Review. *New York Times*, July 23, p. 16.

Perrin, Constance. 1977. *Everything in Its Place. Social Order and Land Use in America*. Princeton, NJ: Princeton University Press.

———. 1988. *Belonging in America. Reading Between the Lines*. Madison: University of Wisconsin Press.

Quéré, Louis, and Daniel Brezger. 1992. "L'étrangeté mutuelle des passants. Le mode de coexistence du public urbain." *Les Annales de la Recherche Urbaine* 57–58: 89–100.

Snow, David A., and Leon Anderson. 1987. "Identity Work among the Homeless: The Verbal Construction and Avowal of Personal Identities." *American Journal of Sociology* 92: 1336–71.

Snyder, W. P. 1885. "Life under the Dumps in New York City." *Harpers Weekly*, November 14.

Stanton, A. H., and M. S. Schwartz. 1954. *The Mental Hospital*. New York: Basic Books.

Strathern, Andrew, and Michael Lambek. 1998. "Embodying Sociality: African-Melanesianist Comparisons." In *Bodies and Persons. Comparative Perspectives from Africa and Melanesia*, ed. M. Lambek and A. Strathern (New York and Melbourne: Cambridge University Press), 1–25.

Taylor, Charles. 1985. "The Person." In *The Category of the Person: Anthropology, Philosophy, History*, ed. M. Carrithers, S. Collins, and S. Lukes (Cambridge: Cambridge University Press).

Tessler, Richard C., and Debbie L. Dennis. 1989. *A Synthesis of NIMH-funded Research Concerning Persons Who are Homeless and Mentally Ill*. Rockville, MD: Program for the Mentally Ill Homeless, National Institute of Mental Health.

Vergara, Camilo José. 1995. *The New American Ghetto*. New Brunswick, NJ: Rutgers University Press.

Weinberg, Darin. 1997. "The Social Construction of Non-human Agency: The Case of Mental Disorder." *Social Problems* 44(2): 217–34.

PART IV

Life Technologies

．　　．　　．　　．　　．

Science and technology are integral to the definition of reality and to the restructuring of power relations and bodily experience. In *The Human Condition*, Hannah Arendt argues that in the course of the twentieth century, political action has increasingly focused on the control of natural life and on the fabrication of automatons.[1] The *homo faber* gave way to the *homo laborans*—that is, people became ever more involved in mass production and were most concerned with physiological existence. Scientific practices have been central to this transformation. Arendt argues that the experimental process that came to define the natural sciences—"the attempt to imitate under artificial conditions the process of 'making' by which a natural thing came into existence"—has acquired such significance that it now serves "as well or even better as the principle for doing in the realm of human affairs" (299).

Michel Foucault pursued the historical complexities that emerged as science became a central component of the ways in which modern institutions and self-governance function. In his work on psychiatric power (1997), for example, he exposed the role of expertise in the constitution of mental illness, its spatialization and embodied forms, making it a phenomenon completely accessible to knowledge. Or, as Ian Hacking says, "Instead of knowledge being that which is true, the objects of knowledge become ourselves" (2002: 4). Jacques Lacan would also argue that we moderns are not without a relationship to changing forms of truth (1989: 13). Truth has become our labor. "The loss of human experience involved in this development is extraordinarily striking," writes Arendt (1958: 321).

New forms of knowledge are emerging around life itself, and complex technologies and regulations are being developed to put this knowledge into play. The essays in this section by Evelyn Fox Keller, Mary-Jo DelVecchio

Good, Eric Krakauer, and João Biehl explore the forms a technically medi-ated subjectivity is taking in the life sciences, in experimental medicine, and in domestic spaces.[2] The modernization of life, with its accompanying epis-temological, medical, and political implications, is being problematized. Which possibilities does the "biological body" carry to cultural critique and human experience? And in the world of high-technology medicine, one might ask, How are the rights of patients and families and the duties of physicians being negotiated vis-à-vis life-extending technologies? How do we understand ourselves as affected by these new forms of knowledge, com-merce, and care?

The issue is not one of relativizing the content of science but of explor-ing the practices and worldviews embedded in scientific research, as well as the contingent forms that science empirically takes (see the works of Dumit, Fischer, Franklin, Lock, Petryna, Rabinow, and Rapp). These are not straight-forward developments with predetermined outcomes. Life sciences and technologies are matters of intense negotiation; their local realizations are shaped by contingency, imagination, and uncertainty. Such realizations en-code diverse economic and political interests as well as group and individ-ual anxieties and desires; they also involve shifts from one form of bodily and medical knowledge to another. Pragmatic and embodied responses to science and technology shape concepts of personhood and degrees of polit-ical membership.

As scientific and medical technologies materialize, so do new ethical questions and analytical questions: What kind of scientific literacy do we, the general public, need to participate responsibly in emergent therapeutic cultures? What is the perceived value of health, and what price do people pay to extend life? Which forms of governance and ideas of the social good and public health are at stake in the global flows of medical technologies? How do we as social scientists situate ourselves to study these experimen-tal life regimes?

The engagement with new biological knowledge unsettles some of our most critical assumptions about cultural malleability and difference in human nature, argues Evelyn Fox Keller in her essay, "Whole Bodies, Whole Persons?" Genomics certifies a distinct diversity—that of the species—and this new knowledge gives us the possibility of relating biology and subjectivity in new terms. The natural sciences have never known what to do about the problem of subjectivity, and numerous authors in cultural studies have argued that subjective experience is no more than a composite of multiple discursive and social constructs. Recent work in cognitive neuroscience, however, has resurrected the concept of self in ways that suggest the usefulness of reexamining these arguments.

Fox Keller indicates that the view of subjectivity as open, multiple, fractured, and culturally contingent has left something behind: the biological body and its contribution to experiences of selfhood. Just as the concept of whole bodies continues to make referential sense for members of the human species, despite the manifest variability in individual and societal stances toward physical impairment, so too, Keller writes, the concept of whole persons, simultaneously embodied and interactive, might make a claim to cross-cultural translatability.

A biologically grounded concept of selfhood helps account for the agency, resistance, and involvement in meaning-making that are often absent in discussions of identities and bodies as culturally constructed entities. Keller further emphasizes the dialogic process of making and representing selves as a way to conflate the two without reifying or stabilizing either. She uses this formulation to analyze the influence of contemporary representations of personhood (in genetics, technology, or cultural studies) on the development of individual subjective experience. For example, Keller writes that genetic identity is "*in* us and *of* us" but "inaccessible *to* us; our sole access . . . is through the experts." Through the dialogic process of subjectivity, such a conception turns an "I" into an "It," simultaneously affecting both our representations of identity and our experience of selfhood. In deemphasizing the unilaterally pervasive influence of cultural values on the subject, Keller maintains the subject's own intentionality in translating not the influence but knowledge itself and managing subjectivity beyond the classic analytic terms of ambivalence.

For Mary-Jo DelVecchio Good, in turn, contested encounters in clinical settings make explicit the value assumptions of life technologies as therapeutics as well as commercial and social enterprise. Popular, technical, market, and cultural perceptions of biomedical developments are bound together in a "political economy of hope," she writes. "The Medical Imaginary and the Biotechnical Embrace: Subjective Experiences of Clinical Scientists and Patients" draws on her cross-cultural research on oncology to explore knowledge and technology in relation to affect. DelVecchio Good importantly shows that economic investments run parallel to the emotional and cultural investments of clinicians and patients and their families that inform the use or refusal of experimental techniques and machines.

Analyzing clinical narratives helps reveal the effects, affects, and production of biomedical hope. As such narratives plot the statistics, the therapeutic course, the desire for treatment, and expectations, they link the experimental and the therapeutic for the clinician and patient. This emphasis on the possible brings ambiguity strongly into the picture: bizarre imaginaries of the future, ironic humor, and acceptance of the unknown help patients understand and use new developments in biotechnology. DelVecchio Good thereby directs us to the complexities of the biotechnical embrace in bringing together imaginary and efficacious; venture capital, researcher, clinician, and patient; and hope, as a managed politics and an affect with its own momentum.

Inasmuch as these technologies occasion a time-specific clinical reality, they also mediate changes in the ways in which people value and perceive physical pain, argues Eric L. Krakauer, and they thus pioneer a new moral common sense in the interface of familial, professional, institutional, and economic pressures. In " 'To Be Freed From the Infirmity of (the) Age': Subjectivity, Life-Sustaining Treatment, and Palliative Medicine," Krakauer addresses the ways in which technology, as a mode of intervention and as a mode of analysis, operates in our conceptions and experience of death. He draws from his clinical work with terminal patients, their families, and a palliative-care team and ethics committee at the Massachusetts General Hospital.

The capacity to modify the experience of disease, to preside over the onset of dying and extension of life according to novel technological and social norms, requires explication of authority and ethical representation. For Krakauer, life-sustaining technologies such as the hemodialysis machine and mechanical ventilator create a force and momentum through their widespread use, enabling the production of ethical and emotional boundaries, hopes, and expectations. As a result of this momentum, the decision not to use such technologies is difficult: new regulations, policies, and legal codification are necessary to specify areas in which the lack of use is permissible. As these new technologies produce a new circle of exchanges, obligations, and expectations, people wager prior legal and ethical understandings. Family needs and wants, redefined by the availability of technology, run up against hospital policies and decisions are adjudicated by the state and managed care; medical ethics thus becomes a primary arbiter in decisions about the proper use of technologies, potentially eclipsing religious beliefs, experiences, and values.

Krakauer works through Descartes and Heidegger on Descartes to explore the philosophical roots of the conception of death as an object to be mastered. He suggests that such a view, prevalent in current biomedical institutions, elides the ways that technologies can extend and produce suffer-

ing. Palliative medicine, for Krakauer, addresses the aspects of suffering that
have been excluded or left behind: feelings of loss about the ability to function, feelings about loved ones and relationships, and the discovery of
meanings not restricted to physical pain. By attending to personal meanings
of suffering without an agenda of cure, palliative medicine allows the subject to emerge within his or her own context of meaning, cultural tradition,
and local world.³ Paradoxically, the process also gives rise to a medical science of human death. As medical technology and bioethics capture the familial tragic and matters historically reserved for the religious domain, the
understanding of how to suffer (Geertz)—the chance for something other
than a scientifically informed subjectivity—is lost from sight.

An immense parceling out of specific ways of assembling and valuing
communities, families, and personal lives and of embedding them in larger
institutional rearrangements comes with the on-the-ground study of a singular Other. João Biehl's essay "A Life" focuses on a young woman named
Catarina, who was deemed mad and left by her family in an asylum called
Vita in southern Brazil. Disabled and abandoned, Catarina began to compile
a "dictionary" of words that had meaning for her and gave form to her
being, both present and past. By tracing Catarina's words back to the people,
households, and medical institutions that she had once been a part of, Biehl
illuminates the complex circuits in which her abandonment and pathology
took form as well as the edges of human imagination that she keeps expanding.

Catarina's subjectivity is approached as a complex symbolic, social, and
medical artifact in the making. Biehl finds that in Catarina's case, scientific
assessments of reality (in the form of biological knowledge and psychiatric
diagnostics and treatments) were deeply embedded in changing households
and institutions, informing colloquial thoughts and actions that led to her
terminal exclusion. As Biehl opens up layers of subjectivity and reality, the
figure and thought of Catarina provide critical access to the value systems
and oft-invisible machineries of life and death that are indeed at work both
in the state and in the intimacy of the house. The essay thus also represents
the anthropologist's ethical journey—identifying some of the ordinary, violent, and inescapable limits of human inclusion and exclusion and learning to think with the inarticulate theories that people like Catarina have of
their condition and their hope.

The essay is a progressive unraveling of Catarina's story—misdiagnosis,
excessive medication, complicity among health professionals and family in
creating her status as psychotic—leading to the ultimate discovery of her
"real" illness, a genetic disorder, not a psychiatric one. As the medical

archival research and the ethnography of local health-care systems showed, Catarina's presumed psychosis was intimately related to changing political and labor regimes and to the pharmaceutical forms of knowledge and care embedded in nets of relatedness and betrayals. In this context, argues Biehl, the abandonment of unproductive family members is mediated and legitimated by psychiatric drugs, both through the scientific truth-value they bestow and the chemical alterations they produce.

Psychiatric drugs make the loss of social ties irreversible: they become moral technologies through which families and medical practitioners partake in the local triage work of the state. Catarina's is not just bare life, though. Marked off as mad and left to death, yet claiming understanding and desire, Catarina signifies the circuits in which her experience took form and suggests that life is potentially inexhaustible.

Indeed, Catarina constantly recalled the events leading to her abandonment. But she was not simply trying to make sense of them and to find a place for herself in history. She actually constructed her subjectivity in relation to this tinkering. By going through all the components and singularities of these events, she sought to resume her place in them "as in a becoming," in Gilles Deleuze's words, "to grow both young and old in [them] at once. Becoming isn't part of history; history amounts only to the set of preconditions, however recent, that one leaves behind in order to 'become,' that is to create something new" (1995: 170–71). As Catarina rethought the literalism that made possible a sense of exclusion, she demanded one more chance at life.

Overall, this set of essays conveys a sense that subjectivity is neither reducible to the idea the person has of himself or herself nor necessarily an individual confrontation with the powers that be. Subjectivity is rather the material and means of a continuous process of experimentation—inner, familial, medico-scientific, and political. Always social, subjectivity encompasses all the identifications that can be formed by, discovered in, or attributed to the person. Although identification-making mechanisms are quite difficult to detect, this process of subjective experimentation is the very fabric of novel infrastructures, value systems, and personal trajectories. Subjectivity is thus at once the tension and representation one has in one's body as the personal, the domestic, and the public fuse with measures of the "true" and the "normal."

Throughout the book, ethnographic studies have shown the many ways in which embattled geopolitics, as well as economic, technoscientific, and legal developments, shape the temporality and value of agency claims into the twenty-first century. Subjectivities are now "raucous *terrae incognitae*" for anthropological inquiry, writes Michael M. J. Fischer in his concluding remarks—"landscapes of explosions, noise, alienating silences, disconnects and dissociations, fears, terror machineries, pleasure principles, illusions, fantasies, displacements, and secondary revisions, mixed with reason, rationalizations, and paralogics—all of which have powerful sociopolitical dimensions and effects."

We need to attend to more than the "enunciative function" of the subject, Fischer argues: witnessing and testimony do "not do the job for either mental health or social governance." Subjectivity does not merely speak as resistance, nor is it simply spoken (or silenced) by power. It continually forms and returns in the complex play of bodily, linguistic, political, and psychological dimensions of human experience. "In highly charged arenas," Fischer suggests, "the feedback among the four registers of subjectivity . . . is an essential part of the struggle to 'authorize the real.' "

At the intersection of three emergent sites of "deep play"—the recovery of society in the wake of trauma, immersion in telemedia, and transformations in life technologies—multilayered forms of agency are crafted to reconstruct individual, social, and civic selves. Returns to subjectivity take shape within and against new infrastructures, value systems, and the transforming afflictions and injustices of modernity; they "come from the descent after Dante, Ovid, and Orpheus; the meditations of Buddha and the anger of the Bengali widow; and experiences of the ills of the world, misrecognitions, misdirections, and illusory identifications."

The anthropology of present workings of subjectivities—as individuals struggle to articulate desire, pain, and knowledge in novel constellations—can help us chart paths across larger structures and forces of repetition, technologies at play, and the slippery slopes of unforeseeable consequences of action. It can help us account for people, experiences, and voices that remain unaddressed and raise calls for new ethics and politics. Ethnography matters.

NOTES

1. In *Group Psychology,* Freud spoke of the weakening of religious ties in his day and the engineering of new ties between the individual and the collective via socialism, which showed a similar intolerance toward outsiders. He speculated about what would happen if scientific opinions were to attain a similar significance for groups (1959: 31). Adorno (1982) politicized Freud's model and took modern man and

woman's rational-technical formation as the starting point of his critical analysis of fascism (1959). Nazi science, notably biology, and propaganda created new mechanisms of identification that held German citizens together and turned them against outsiders, in a state of moral blindness. The peculiar aspect of modern authoritarian ties, says Adorno, is not simply the reoccurrence of the primitive and the past but "its reproduction in and by civilization itself" (1982: 122). See also Biehl 2001.

2. The social studies of science launched by Thomas Kuhn, Bruno Latour, Evelyn Fox Keller, Steve Shapin and Simon Schaefer, and Donna Haraway, among others, have predominantly investigated laboratory practices and showed that the great abstractions of science are also the product of these localized practices. Science is also culture: it does not exist outside of relations of knowledge and power, and as such, it is real. The authors in this volume are in dialogue with these works and reveal that the terrain is ready for reevaluation and new directions.

3. Other questions have emerged and demand further inquiry: How are the themes of salvation and sacrifice engaged today to justify biomedical triage by institutions and families? How is the taboo of killing reworked in the interaction of families, health professionals, and ethical experts? What conceptions of the value of life and bodily resurrection inform the uses of technologies? What becomes of the status of religious belief more generally in the bioethical settings that regulate these uses?

REFERENCES

Adorno, Theodor. 1982. "Freudian Theory and the Pattern of Fascist Propaganda." In *The Essential Frankfurt Schoold Reader*, ed. Andrew Arato and Eike Gebhart. New York: Continuum.

Arendt, Hannah. 1958. *The Human Condition*. Chicago: University of Chicago Press.

Biehl, João (with Denise Coutinho and Ana Luzia Outeiro). 2001. "Technology and Affect: HIV/AIDS Testing in Brazil." *Culture, Medicine and Psychiatry* 25: 87–129.

Deleuze, Gilles. 1995. *Negotiations, 1971–1990*. New York: Columbia University Press.

Dumit, Joseph. 2004. *Picturing Personhood: Brain Scans and Biomedical Identity*. Princeton, NJ: Princeton University Press.

Fischer, Michael M. J. 2003. *Emergent Forms of Life and the Anthropological Voice*. Durham, NC: Duke University Press.

Foucault, Michel. 1997. *Ethics: Subjectivity and Truth*. Ed. Paul Rabinow. New York: The New Press.

Franklin, Sarah. 1997. *Embodied Progress: A Cultural Account of Assisted Conception*. London; New York: Routledge.

Freud, Sigmund. 1959. *Group Psychology and the Analysis of the Ego*. New York: W. W. Norton.

Geertz, Clifford. 1973. "Religion as a Cultural System." In *The Interpretation of Cultures*. New York: Basic Books.

Hacking, Ian. 2002. *Historical Ontology*. Cambridge, MA: Harvard University Press.

Haraway, Donna. 1991. *Simians, Cyborgs, and Women: The Reinvention of Nature.* New York: Routledge.

Keller, Evelyn Fox. 1992. *Secrets of Life, Secrets of Death: Essays on Language, Gender and Science.* New York: Routledge.

Kuhn, Thomas S. 1962. *The Structure of Scientific Revolutions.* Chicago: University of Chicago Press.

Lacan, Jacques. 1989. "Science and Truth." *Newsletter of the Freudian Field* 3: 4–29.

Latour, Bruno. 1979. *Laboratory Life: The Social Construction of Scientific Facts.* Beverly Hills: Sage Publications.

———. 2004. *Politics of Nature: How to Bring the Sciences into Democracy.* Cambridge, MA: Harvard University Press.

Lock, Margaret. 2002. *Twice Dead: Organ Transplants and the Reinvention of Death.* Berkeley: University of California Press.

Petryna, Adriana. 2002. *Life Exposed: Biological Citizens after Chernobyl.* Princeton, NJ: Princeton University Press.

Rabinow, Paul. 1996. *Essays on the Anthropology of Reason.* Princeton, NJ: Princeton University Press.

———. 1999. *French DNA: Trouble in Purgatory.* Chicago: University of Chicago Press.

———. 2003. *Anthropos Today: Reflections on Modern Equipment.* Princeton, NJ: Princeton University Press.

Rabinow, Paul, and Talia Dan-Cohen. 2005. *A Machine to Make a Future: Biotech Chronicles.* Princeton, NJ: Princeton University Press.

Rapp, Rayna. 1999. *Testing Women, Testing the Fetus: The Social Impact of Amniocentesis in America.* New York: Routledge.

Shapin, Steven, and Simon Schaffer. 1985. *Leviathan and the Air-Pump: Hobbes, Boyle, and the Experimental Life.* Princeton, NJ: Princeton University Press.

11 Whole Bodies, Whole Persons?

Cultural Studies, Psychoanalysis, and Biology

EVELYN FOX KELLER

BY WAY OF THINKING ABOUT BODIES

If cultural studies have a core principle, it is a negative one: against universality, against any and all suppositions of a "human nature," physical or behavioral. From cultural studies, we learn both of the diversity of bodies and of their manifest cultural malleability. As Elizabeth Grosz says, bodies are "male or female, black, brown, white, large or small . . . not as entities in themselves or simply on a linear continuum with its polar extremes occupied by male and female bodies . . . but as a field, a 2-D continuum in which race (and possibly even class, caste or religion) form body specification . . . a defiant affirmation of a multiplicity, a field of differences" (quoted in Rose 1998: 7).

Biology, too, teaches us about diversity: In an important sense, one might say the genome project is a diversity project. But having as its subject a far broader range of bodies, the diversity with which biology—and even genetics—is concerned is not solely that which obtains among individual beings (human or otherwise): its subject is also the diversity of species. Thus, the Human Genome Project (HGP) is in fact misnamed, for it aims both to identify the genetic counterpart of individual phenotypic differences and to establish the genetic basis of a generic human nature—as in *the* human genome. What makes human bodies recognizable as human, and so clearly distinguishable from the bodies of other organisms? From a biological perspective, human bodies have a structural commonality transcending even differences of sex: they walk erect, they have a distinctive body plan, they are equipped with five senses, linguistic capacity, consciousness, and so on. These properties are human universals. To be sure, such "universals" are overlaid by differences of all sorts, not only of sex but

of eye color, hair texture and color, height, weight, handedness, physiog-
nomy, and a zillion other differences we usually think of as primarily, if not
entirely, biological. They are also overlaid by a vast number of other differences we generally think of as primarily, if not entirely, cultural. But none
of these variations compromise our ability to recognize a member of the
human species as such. In this sense, then, we might usefully speak of a universal human body.

Even so, what exactly do we mean by "universal"? Certainly we don't
mean that every biologically human organism must be so equipped, for we
know that some people cannot walk erect and some are blind, deaf, linguistically incompetent, or perhaps not even conscious. And though some people
might argue that consciousness (or the capacity for consciousness) is a prerequisite for legal (or moral) definitions of "human," virtually no one today
would want to suggest that blind or hearing-impaired people are in any sense
less than human. Clearly, we do not want to claim possession of a full set of
human universals as prerequisite to human rights. Yet we might want to
consider such universals as necessary to a notion of a "whole body"—that
is, as long as such a description does not compromise the claims of individuals with less than whole bodies to full membership in the social category of
"human." Or that, at least, is what I want to suggest. In other words, I want
to take the risk of political incorrectness and argue that people with special
needs are indeed handicapped—that they have less than whole bodies.[1]

Might we say something analogous about personhood or subjectivity?
Probably, no other concept has been under more sustained attack from cultural studies than that of the "self." As Clifford Geertz wrote, almost thirty
years ago:

> The Western conception of the person as a bounded, unique, more or
> less integrated motivational and cognitive universe, a dynamic center of
> awareness, emotion, judgement and action, organized into a distinctive
> whole and set contrastively against other such wholes and against a so-
> cial and natural background is, however incorrigible it may seem to us, a
> rather peculiar idea within the context of the world's cultures. (1979:
> 229)

At the time, his claim might have seemed radical. Today, at least in many academic circles, it has become a truism. Subjects are epiphenomena, constructed by culturally specific discursive regimes (marked by race, gender,
sexual orientation, and so on), and subjectivity itself is more properly
viewed as the consequence of actions, behavior, or "performativity" than as
their source. Similarly, selves are multiple and fractured rather than unitary,
mobile rather than stable, porous rather than enclosed, externally consti-

tuted rather than internal or "inner" natural essences. Indeed, for many writers, the very notion of an inner self is now nothing more than a Western cultural fantasy, elaborated and reified by the psychological disciplines.

Surely we have gone too far, or in any case, I believe so. In fact, I suggest that, in the rush to do justice to cultural diversity, we have made a rather serious error (akin to Ulrich Neisser's [1988, 1993] definition of the *conceptual* self)—namely, of conflating a particular (and perhaps exclusively Western) characterization (or ideal) of subjectivity with experiences of first personhood that may be as much a part of being human as having a certain kind of body—and I think the mistake is well illustrated in Geertz's statement. The problem lies neither in the description Geertz gives of "the Western conception" of self nor in his suggestion that such a conception is a "rather peculiar idea," but rather in his failure to distinguish what aspects of that conception might be peculiar. He thereby invites the careless reader to conclude that all the elements of that description are peculiarly Western, and equally so. Thus, the notion of a "more or less integrated motivational and cognitive universe, a dynamic center of awareness, emotion, judgement and action" is concatenated with (and effectively equated to) such recognizably particular and culturally distinctive assumptions as the one that the universe or center is "bounded," "unique," "organized into a distinctive whole and set contrastively against other such wholes and against a social and natural background." Just as with talk of bodies, I suggest that any meaningful discussion of subjectivity requires some separation of its generic from its specific dimensions, perhaps corresponding to different levels of subjective experience.

Indeed, I argue for the existence of an innate (and near-universal) capacity for self-reflection underlying experiences of first personhood—in Neisser's terms, the *perceived* self (1993)—that are so clearly indicated in common talk of "me, myself, and I" in virtually all human languages (Lakoff and Johnson 1999)—a capacity, in short, that is analogous to the basic body plan of nearly all human organisms. Identifying and characterizing such a capacity is obviously a far from simple matter, but I suggest that recent discussions of a near-universal and complementary capacity for mind reading—that is, for recognizing states of mind in other similarly endowed beings and for making affective contact with them—provides us with a place to start.[2] (The invocation of "mind" in this context may seem to imply an excessively cognitive bias, and for just this reason, it has been severely criticized by Peter Hobson [1993a: 207], among others. In my use of the term, however, *mind* refers to a composite that includes both cognitive and affective perceptual-relational capacities.) Much of the grounding for the supposition of an innate capacity for mind reading derives from studies of autism—a condition that has been characterized as a specific deficit in mind reading ability, or "mind-blindness" (Baron-Cohen 1990, 1995).

What exactly does not function in autism? Baron-Cohen (1995) posits four quasi-independent biological mechanisms as necessary for the normal capacity for mind reading: an Intentionality Detector enabling the subject to identify goal-directed or "agentlike" behavior; an Eye-Direction Detector enabling the subject to determine whether the eyes of another are directed at him or her or elsewhere and hence to distinguish "seeing" from "gazing"; a Shared-Attention Mechanism responsible for triadic representations; and finally, a Theory-of-Mind Mechanism for integrating the information obtained from the first three mechanisms into a coherent picture of how mental states and actions are related (that is, into a theory of mind). Autism, in this view, is the consequence of a defect in one or more of these biologically wired (or embodied) mechanisms.[3]

By now, my direction should be obvious. I want to suggest that the capacity for first personhood—an ability to read one's own mental states—is the flip side of the capacity for mind reading. However, Baron-Cohen's description of mind reading first needs modification: it presupposes the existence of already established concepts of self, other, and mental states, thereby inviting the assumption that a capacity for "inner mind reading" must precede the attribution of agency, first personhood, or mental states to others; before one can attribute anything to others, one would need a means of distinguishing those others from a perceived "self," from an entity identifiable as "me," and before one can attribute mental states to others, prior experience of a mental state of one's own would be necessary. But concepts of self, other, and mental state are not pregiven; rather they are themselves products of development. Thus, perhaps we need to consider that the capacity for mind reading might develop as part and parcel of a capacity for "inner mind reading" and even use the same mechanisms; similarly, we can view the development of a sense of self as occurring in tandem and in reciprocity with the development of a sense of other, and the recognition of both one's own and others' mental states as emerging from just such a dialogical process. Recent studies provide strong evidence for the appearance of an "interpersonal" sense of self in infants as young as six to eight weeks and for its dependence on just such dialogue.[4] This age may be earlier than Lacan anticipated in his discussion of the "mirror-stage," but the dynamics of his analysis, and perhaps even more so of Winnicott's discussion of the "mirror-role of the mother," are surely relevant here.[5]

I have no idea what kinds of mechanisms might be at work in "inner mind reading," but I think we can reasonably suppose that human bodies (or at least "whole" human bodies) come naturally equipped with whatever mechanisms might be required. To the extent that "inner mind reading" is involved in (or required for) the recognition of "me-ness," of a self with agency and mental states of one's own, it can be said to provide the biological basis of a core subjectivity—that is, of a set of experiences roughly corresponding to Geertz's description of a "more or less integrated motivational and cognitive universe, a dynamic center of awareness, emotion, judgement and action." Moreover, I submit that without such a core subjectivity, individuals of any culture whatsoever would simply not be able to function—or not, at least, as "whole persons."

. . .

The ways in which we represent that self, either to others or to ourselves, are, of course, variable—as much so as the ways in which we represent others. Equally variable is the importance we attach to subjective experience (experiences of selfhood) and the extent to which we employ it. We may or may not valorize the ideal of a fully integrated (unitary) subject, and we may or may not represent that subject as standing in opposition to other selves, society, or nature. Furthermore, though I may have sometimes referred to "experience" as if one could distinguish a phenomenon of that name that is not already mediated by representation, experience is never pristine. In fact, the thing we call "experience" is, in just the ways that perception of self and others is, a product of dynamic interactions between sensory input and biologically given mechanisms. Thus, our representations of self inevitably affect our subjective experience of selfhood, on every level at which that experience is constituted.

Some ways of representing selfhood, both to ourselves and to others, may be characteristic of particular cultural traditions (as the ideal of a unitary and autonomous self is said to be characteristically Western), but cultural traditions are not static, and one of the most striking features of our time is the radical upheavals under way in the ways in which we think and talk about, and in turn, come to experience, first personhood. Indeed, current trends calling subjectivity into question, stressing the lability, multiplicity, and constructed dimensions of selves and selfhood, are themselves both symptom and description of this upheaval. For its direct antecedents, however, I think we need to look elsewhere—for example, to the inspiration of recent technological developments. Of course, technological change is in the first instance a product of human agency, and hardly an agent of change in itself. (Technological innovation is the outcome of what human agents have in the first instance, as Elaine Scarry [1992] says, made up, and only after making something up did they succeed in making it real.) Nevertheless, these products of human desire, imagination, agency, and practical acumen inevitably have a profound impact on the possibilities, domain, and even meaning of human agency. In particular, they shape both our representations and our experiences of first personhood.

Consider computers, for example: Although computers were initially imagined, designed, and constructed in imitation (simulation) of certain aspects of our own mental processes, they have come to provide the principal models from which we draw our representations of human mentality. Notice, for example, the extent to which Baron-Cohen's description of the mechanisms of mind reading draws on the modular structures of computer architecture.[6]

The Prozac revolution offers another example. In the past decade, psychopharmaceuticals have taken the Western world by storm, and as Sherry Turkle has frequently commented, use of these mind-altering drugs has had a dramatic effect on our perception of ourselves as agentic subjects. Indeed, one might argue that psychopharmaceuticals have been more effective in persuading people of their essentially mechanistic and physical-chemical nature than all of modern science put together.

Like contemporary computers, genomics also issues from a long history of making up and making real. In the early part of the century, genes were imaginary entities, which scientists invoked to account for those properties of living beings that seemed otherwise unaccountable, especially the development and persistence of individual traits. As originally conceived, the gene was an entity that needed to do the seemingly impossible for any ordinary physical structure—namely, to commingle the properties of the physicist's atom with those of a prime mover. But over the course of the twentieth century, it acquired ever-greater reality, until finally, in midcentury, it was revealed as nothing more than a molecule—a molecule simple enough to understand in physicochemical terms yet complex enough to carry the secrets of life in its structure (that is, in its sequence). When the HGP was first proposed, it was seen as the natural and obvious dénouement of this history, the climax of the century-long search for identity in the genetic book of life. Spelling out his "Vision of the Grail," Walter Gilbert wrote, "Three billion bases of sequence can be put on a single compact disk (CD), and one will be able to pull a CD out of one's pocket and say, 'Here is a human being; it's me!' " (1992: 84–85). Today, we have the sequence of a composite (and presumably "generic") human genome in hand. What does it mean? We now realize that the answer to this question (perhaps not surprisingly) will depend critically on who is asking it and in what context. Thus, if one puts the question to molecular geneticists on their home turf, seeking to illuminate problems of biological development, they increasingly respond that sequence data, by themselves, mean far less than expected; indeed, their primary value may be in providing the tools for probing the ways in which cells use the primary sequences stored in DNA to construct biological meaning. If one asks molecular geneticists working in biotech companies (or seeking funding from such ventures), they are likely to speak of using sequence data in the synthesis of marketable products.

But readers of popular accounts—in other words, most of us—are likely to see the prospect of having access to sequences of individual genomes in the terms that Gilbert offered: as promising to tell us not only who we are but who we are destined to become. In other words, we see genomes as the grounding for a new kind of subject, formed not from cumulative processing of internal and interpersonal perceptual-relational experience but in effect given from without. What I mean by this is that, however deeply our genetic identities may be said to reside within us, however idiosyncratic they might be, they are utterly opaque to all internal or interpersonal processes. Though they are *in* us and *of* us, they are internally inaccessible *to* us; our sole access as subjects is external, through the experts who are equipped to read and interpret our genetic selves. Nevertheless, consumers/inhabitants of Western culture have increasingly come to embrace this account of identity; since the end of the twentieth century, we have come to believe that our genes determine—at least significantly, if not quite fully—our personalities, our behavior, our sexual orientation, our desires, the people we will love—in short, our futures (Hamer and Copeland 1998). As the saying goes, "Genes R Us."

The relevance of this view in thinking about subjectivity is not so much that it is bad biology (which of course it is), nor that biologists themselves have played so conspicuous a role in encouraging such misconceptions. To me, the immediate issues lie elsewhere: first, in the readiness with which we have accepted and absorbed such a representation of identity; and second, in the ways in which the resulting reification affects the experience of first personhood.

Our readiness to accept a gene-driven representation of identity seems to me part and parcel of our readiness to think of ourselves as bundles of chemical receptors or as networks of computational modules. Indeed, each of these pictures endows the others with greater plausibility and credence. And they all affect our experience of first personhood in similar ways. Lacan associated a decisive alienation between I and me with the mirror-stage, but here we see a more radical kind of alienation that affects both the *I* and the *me*. By internalizing representations that characterize selfhood as the product of genes, receptors, or computer modules, in which the ultimate referents of internal experience are simultaneously external and inert, are not all personal pronouns (I, me, you) at risk of merging into the single impersonal "it"?

. . .

Undoubtedly, people's experiences of first personhood vary even more than human bodies do. Some of the differences are clearly cultural; others are probably at least partly structural and, in certain cases, even genetic. Furthermore, just as with bodily differences, the significance of people's experiences of themselves in human culture depends entirely on the mores of that culture. So, too, even the magnitude of such differences might depend on cultural framework. Imagine, for example, a hypothetical society in which olfactory evidence counts for naught, and in which the expression of other priorities leads (inadvertently) to the systematic dulling of olfactory senses (our own society, for example). In such a world, people would have little occasion for using their biologically given olfactory abilities and would probably not even notice the progressive diminution of these capacities (either from atrophy or from externally inflicted damage). The net effect would not simply be that differences with a biological origin would have little social relevance; the actual magnitude of such differences would also diminish. Moreover, in a world in which no one had much of a sense of smell, the cause would hardly matter.

In a similar vein, I can imagine a world in which capacities for psychological perception of self and others (for reading one's own and others' mental states) counted for naught and in which persons with highly developed inner worlds became the exception rather than the rule we used to think them to be. In such a world, a condition such as autism might not even count as a failure of normal functioning, for the condition we would take as normal would become progressively more difficult to distinguish from that of autism. In other words, not just our representations of subjectivity would be culturally constructed but subjectivity itself. I admit to my biases—I am. after all, a product of a culture that places high value on self-reflection and the "inner life"—and I realize that many would argue that to impose these biases is to commit, once again, the sin of universalizing. Along with Oliver Sacks, they might simply conclude that, although the internalization of more reified conceptions of self would certainly make us different, we would be, as Sacks writes about autism, "no less human for being so, but, rather, human in another way" (1995: 16). Yet I am loath to abandon a meaning of "being human" that is so fundamental, and so unmistakably important to so many beyond my own Western heritage. My concerns are thus similar to those of Arthur Kleinman, who writes about the related "moral mutation of experience" that he sees in the power of contemporary global transformations to erode the capacity for empathy in people worldwide: "Like some universal solvent the disordering effects of advanced capitalism appear to be dissolving much that really matters to ordinary men and women globally." And along with Kleinman, I ask, "Is this merely an essentializing millenarian dismay? . . . Or is it . . . a self-reflexive sensibility that we are ourselves becoming alien?" (Kleinman 1999: 404).

NOTES

1. One way to avoid the political/moral problems that such a description might evoke is to emphasize the role that social conventions play in marking the limits of biology in all known human cultures. Thus, while such a biologically based assessment of whole-body-ness will almost surely be relevant to the individuals affected, in the end, the collective (ethical) judgment of the group rather than any biological judgment determines the prerequisites for membership in human society, and hence their moral and legal relevance.

2. Although most of the work on mind reading concerns humans, a growing literature documents a similar capacity in other primates as well (see, for example, Whiten 1993).

3. The centrality of vision in these accounts has obvious implications for the development of first personhood in congenitally blind children, and indeed, evidence exists of extensive overlap in symptoms exhibited in autism and congenital blindness (such as echolalia, difficulty with the use of personal pronouns, recognition of emotions). Hobson writes, "What congenitally blind and autistic children may have in common is difficulty in developing a full awareness of self and others as persons with subjective orientations" (1993b: 272–73). However, some evidence indicates that blind children eventually overcome many of these difficulties, presumably by relying on other sensory modalities.

4. Particularly impressive are the studies using closed-circuit television to observe infants in interaction with their mothers; dramatic contrasts occur in their responses when the possibility of direct interaction is removed (summarized in Neisser 1993a: 17). For a more extensive treatment of the role of affect in the "interpersonal world of the infant," see Stern 1985.

5. My guess is that all sensory modalities (not just vision) play a role in this process. Vision, however, is unique among the senses in being inherently "blind"—that is, in requiring an external "mirror" for its own reflection. Other senses are equipped with built-in capacities for reflection.

6. The reciprocity of the interaction between imagination and construction continues with Rodney Brooks's use of Baron-Cohen's hypothetical mechanisms in the construction of interactive robots—robots so responsive to human input that their trainers soon come to experience these robots as entities with minds like theirs, and hence, in some sense, as kindred beings. That such experiences eventually influence

the trainers' representations, and even experiences, of their own minds is only natural.

REFERENCES

Baron-Cohen, Simon. 1990. "Autism: A Specific Cognitive Disorder of 'Mind-Blindness.' " *International Review of Psychiatry* 2: 81–90.

————. 1995. *Mindblindness: An Essay on Autism and Theory of Mind.* Cambridge, MA: MIT Press.

Baron-Cohen, Simon, Helen Tager-Flusberg, and Donald J. Cohen, eds. 1993. *Understanding Other Minds: Perspectives from Autism.* Oxford: Oxford University Press.

Geertz, Clifford. 1979. "From the Native's Point of View: On the Nature of Anthropological Understanding." In *Interpretive Social Science*, ed. P. Rabinow and W. M. Sullivan (Berkeley: University of California Press), 225–42.

Gilbert, Walter. 1992. "Vision of the Grail." In *The Code of Codes*, ed. D. J. Kevles and L. Hood (Cambridge, MA: Harvard University Press), 83–97.

Hamer, Dean, and Peter Copeland. 1998. *Living with Our Genes.* New York: Basic Books.

Hobson, R. Peter. 1993a. "Understanding Persons: The Role of Affect." In *Understanding Other Minds*, ed. Baron-Cohen, Tager-Flusberg, and Cohen (Oxford: Oxford University Press), 204–27.

————. 1993b. "Through Feeling and Sight to Self and Symbol." In Neisser, ed., *The Perceived Self*, 254–79.

Kleinman, Arthur. 1999. "Experience and Its Moral Modes." In *The Tanner Lectures on Human Values*, ed. G. B. Peterson (Salt Lake City: University of Utah Press), 20: 357–420.

Lakoff, George, and Mark Johnson. 1999. *Philosophy in the Flesh: The Embodied Mind and Its Challenge to Western Thought.* New York: Basic Books.

Neisser, Ulric, 1993a. "The Self Perceived." In *The Perceived Self*, ed. Neisser, 3–21.

————, ed. 1993b. *The Perceived Self.* New York: Cambridge University Press.

Rose, Nikolas. 1998. *Inventing Our Selves: Psychology, Power, and Personhood.* Cambridge: Cambridge University Press.

Sacks, Oliver. 1995. Foreword. *Thinking in Pictures and Other Reports from My Life with Autism*, by Temple Grandin (New York: Vintage).

Scarry, Elaine. 1992. "The Made-Up and the Made-Real." *The Yale Journal of Criticism* 5(2): 239–49.

Stern, Daniel N. 1985. *The Interpersonal World of the Infant.* New York: Basic Books.

Whiten, Andrew. 1993. "Evolving a Theory of Mind: The Nature of Non-Verbal Mentalism in Other Primates." In Baron-Cohen, Tager-Flusberg, and Cohen, eds., *Understanding Other Minds*, 367–96.

12 The Medical Imaginary and the Biotechnical Embrace

Subjective Experiences of
Clinical Scientists and Patients

MARY-JO DELVECCHIO GOOD

Subjective experiences of clinical scientists who produce and deliver high-technology medicine and of patients who receive treatment via this technology are fundamental to understanding the political economy and culture of hope that underlie bioscience and biomedicine. In this essay, I examine interpretive concepts linking bioscience and biotechnology and their societal institutions to subjective experience. These concepts are the medical imaginary, the biotechnical embrace, the political economy of hope, and the clinical narrative. Drawing on research and observations of the culture and political economy of biomedicine in the United States and internationally, I illustrate these interpretive concepts with examples from studies of clinical scientists, oncologists and their patients, and venture capitalists, as well as observations of public actions and discourses.

Cultural and social studies of biomedicine and biotechnology lend themselves to examining a concept that anthropologists Fischer (1991) and Marcus (1998) call "multiple regimes of truth" through multisited and comparative ethnographic research in science and technology. Although acknowledging the importance of "cultural pasts" and "cultural differences," Fischer argues that "it is increasingly artificial to speak of local perspectives in isolation from the global system . . . the world historical political-ical economy" and "transnational cultural processes" (1991: 526). This formulation echoes recent trends in anthropological studies of biomedicine and biotechnology and of scientific research and clinical culture. Such studies highlight the dynamic relationship, tensions, and exchanges between local worlds in which medicine is taught, practiced, organized, and consumed and global worlds in which knowledge, technologies, markets, and clinical standards are produced. Although we may speak about a plurality of biomedicines that are socially and culturally situated rather than about a single unified body of knowledge and practice, such local worlds are never-theless "transnational" in character: they are neither cultural isolates nor biomedical versions of indigenous healing traditions. Rather, global stan-dards and technologies overlie local meanings and social arrangements in nearly all aspects of local biomedicine.

COMPARATIVE QUERIES

This perspective encourages comparative questions: How do local and in-ternational political economies of medical research and biotechnology shape medicine's scientific imaginary; its cultural, moral, and ethical worlds; and inequalities of use, access, and distribution of medicine's cultural and mate-rial "goods"? How do local and international ideologies, politics, and poli-cies influence professional and institutional responses to specific needs of particular societies—from the disease plague of HIV to scarcity and poverty, trauma and civil strife, and public health and profit-driven health-service markets? What form does the "political economy of hope" take? How do the culture of medicine and the production of bioscience and biotechnology "live" in respective societies?

J. Rouse, an American philosopher of science and society, speaks about American science, about the "openness" of science, arguing for acknowl-edgment that "the traffic across the boundaries erected between science and society is always two-way." Rouse discusses the idea of destabilizing "dis-tinctions between what is inside and outside of science, or between what is scientific and what is social" (1992: 13). Bruno Latour, the prominent French scholar of the biosciences, also contends that "scientific work continually draws upon and is influenced by the culture 'outside' science." (Rouse 1992: 13). Although these comments are part of a long-lived internal debate among scholars of science studies, the concept they propose of two-way traffic across science and society is perhaps even more striking in biomedi-cine. The flow of knowledge, scientific and medical cultural power, market wealth, products, and ideas is thus not only between local cultures and in-stitutions that create medical knowledge and organize practice, ethics, and the medical market but also between the culture and market of international and cosmopolitan biomedicine and its local variants.

The dynamics of the global-local exchange challenge our notions of "universalism" in clinical science and "local" knowledge in clinical practice, stimulating a rethinking of the boundaries not only between science and so-ciety but also between the local and the global. With this sense of the transnational fluidity of knowledge and practices, appropriated locally and regionally and integrated into local culture, I wish to turn to the interpretive concepts that link bioscience and biotechnology to society and that have grown out of comparative cross-cultural analyses and conversations with colleagues from Europe, Africa, and Asia, as well as emerged from my own research in the United States and Indonesia. These concepts are "the medical imaginary," "the political economy of hope," "the biotechnical embrace," and "the clinical narrative."

THE MEDICAL IMAGINARY AND
THE POLITICAL ECONOMY OF HOPE

An ethnographic slice through "multiple regimes of truth," narratives of patient experience and of clinical science, and documents on medicine's political economy suggests ways in which the affective and imaginative dimensions of biomedicine and biotechnology envelop physicians, patients, and the public in a "biotechnical embrace." The medical imaginary, that which energizes medicine and makes it a fun and intriguing enterprise, circulates through professional and popular culture. Clinicians and their patients are subject to "constantly emerging regimes of truth in medical science" (Cooke 2001; Marcus 1995:3), and those who suffer serious illness become particularly susceptible to hope engendered by the cultural power of the medical imagination. The connection between medical science and patient populations and the cultural and financial flow thus becomes deeply woven; we can measure the intensity of such connections in part through the flourishing of disease-specific philanthropies, through nongovernmental organizations (NGOs) and political health-action groups, and through the financial health of the National Institutes of Health ($20.5 billion in the 2001 budget, $23.3 billion in 2002, $27.1 billion in 2003, and $27.9 billion in 2004), even under a political regime that promotes tax cuts and small government.

Americans invest in the medical imaginary—the many-possibility enterprise—culturally and emotionally as well as financially (Freudeheim 2002). Enthusiasm for medicine's possibilities arises not necessarily from material products with therapeutic efficacy but through the production of ideas with potential but as-yet-unproven therapeutic efficacy. An officer of one of the most successful biotechnology firms in America has indicated that biotechnology enterprises are in the business of producing ideas about potential therapeutics, from designer anticancer therapies to the manipulation of damaged genes.

Think about a biotechnology company as a pharmaceutical company. . . . If you start with an idea and you are by definition working on something in the pharmaceutical industry that is likely to fail 90% of the time. . . . one of the myths of biotech. . . . you are proposing to start a company in which there is a 90% chance of failure, the cost of product development is $500–$900 million, and from idea to the time when you have a revenue stream from product development is twelve to fifteen years. So your question is really, against that fundamental absurdity, how do you build a business, right?

If you start at that purely abstract level, what do you have to sell? You don't have your product yet, so what do you have to sell to feed the beast that you are about to build? Well, there are only two things that you have to sell: . . . you can sell things that are or look or smell like equity. . . . What's the problem with that? At the end of the day, the pie is so split up, nobody makes any money on their equity, the dilution is intolerable. So what else do I have to sell? Well, instead of selling pieces of the company, an interest in the home, I can sell pieces of pieces, which I call rights—for example, in certain of my discoveries or products—and this is where the pharmaceutical companies come in . . . They say we will pay for you to do some research on our behalf; we will take the product that results from it; we, the pharmaceutical company, will commercialize it and pay you a royalty. So I withstand the dilution, I start generating revenues from collaboration, . . . and then I hand off the more expensive parts of forward integration of manufacturing and sales, I don't have to take on those burdens.

. . . So call those your children. Keep the family alive by selling your children. The question is "is the nature of your platform prolific enough that in having sold off some of your children, you haven't sold off all of your future?" Because if . . . at the end of the day, [you are only] getting some royalties, from the 10% of your efforts that didn't fail, you are never going to be a big company. (Holtzman 2001)

Such firms seek to make public the scientific imaginary; until very recently, they have been the darlings of venture capital and continue to attract considerable investment. (See the business sections of the *New York Times* and the *Wall Street Journal* for analyses of recent market trends and for documentation of volatility in the financial side of the medical imaginary.) However, companies whose fortunes appear bright because of the remarkable scientific promise of potential and authorized new pharmaceutical products may find that the questionable long-term efficacy of once-promising drugs, such as VIOXX or hormone-replacement therapy (HRT), can threaten financial futures and disrupt evolving clinical practices. One such example is Johnson and Johnson's Eprex, an innovative platelet enhancer for treating anemia in cancer patients. Red-cell aplasia, the inability to produce red blood cells, has been associated with this formerly billion-dollar product (Pollack 2002; also Tagliabue 2002; Varmus 2002; and on HRT, Kolata 2002).

At more mundane levels, Americans live in a world in which the medical imaginary has star billing in medical journalism, television advertisements, and globally popular television productions such as *ER*. (*ER* is among the most popular television programs in Indonesia and China; the medical imaginary is a global phenomenon.) The imminent discovery of cancer cure, effective genetic therapy, the manufacturing of new and better mechanical hearts, the engineering of tissue and the genetic alteration of pig cells to off-set organ shortages, the latest results of clinical trials on AIDS therapies and reports of their effectiveness, cost, and contested patents—all become part of the daily global circulation of popular, business, and medical knowledge. Our vast interests, financial and certainly emotional, in the political economy of hope are evident in daily market reports and public discourses. Recent stories on the Abiomed mechanical heart illustrate the more extreme version of the link between product development and the political economy of hope. (See Stolberg 2002 about a patient who lived for nine months with the heart.)

The circulation of knowledge and of the ethereal products of the medical imaginary is of course uneven. The robustness of local scientific and medical communities, NGOs, and political health activists influence how people share, access, and use this global knowledge. (See these recent studies: on Brazil, Bastos 1999; on American research oncology, Cooke 2001; on French science, Rabinow 1999; and on medical missions for high-technology treatment of multidrug-resistant tuberculosis [MDRTB] and HIV for the poor, Farmer 1999, 2004.) Alternative stories, misuses, and failures of medicine's cultural power and possibilities are also part of the traffic in the medical imaginary: failures (in genetic therapy leading to patient death); fraud (in clinical trials in oncology); discouragement (upon learning that promising therapeutics are ineffective); greed (physicians trafficking in organs or brokering transfers from the poor to the rich; Cohen 1999; Sanal 2004). Yet these tales are set in the larger optimistic story of the hope and the many-possibility science of medicine.

THE BIOTECHNICAL EMBRACE

The image of the biotechnical embrace emerged serendipitously out of studies of the culture of oncology during the past decade and conversations with my colleagues in medicine, ethics, and social science in the United States, Europe, Asia, and Africa. The concept of "embrace" conjured the subjective experiences and affective responses of many clinicians and their patients when using new biotechnologies, high-technology experimental treatments, and even salvage therapies. Among my American medical colleagues are those who acknowledge the phenomenon, are energized by enthusiasm albeit tempered with irony, and recognize when patients are embraced. (One pediatrician and ethicist has incorporated the term into lectures on the latest transplant therapeutics.) The specifics of popular and professional enthusiasm for biomedicine and nascent technologies may be characteristically American, as some of my European colleagues suggest, but "embracing and being embraced" fundamentally link contemporary high-technology medicine and bioscience to the wider society.

Whether this enthusiasm is for new reproductive technologies, effective therapies to treat HIV or MDRTB, innovative organ-transplantation procedures, progress in therapeutic gene manipulation, or efficacious treatments for common life-threatening diseases such as cancer and heart disease, it sparks the medical imagination and drives the political economy of hope, as well as our society's investment in medical adventures and misadventures.

CLINICAL NARRATIVES AND ETHNOGRAPHIC FRAMES

The two worlds of American academic clinical oncology—the therapeutic and the scientific—provide vivid examples of how patients and their clinicians embrace, even as they are embraced by, biotechnology and how American medical culture generates enthusiasm for experimental clinical science and "medicine on the edge." (The success of Jerome Groopman's [2000] essays on cancer patients and experimental treatments is evidence of strong interest among certain groups of Americans.) In my studies of the culture of clinical oncology, I developed the concept of the "clinical narrative" to capture the dynamics of clinical interactions between oncologists and their patients that evolve over time through arduous and often lengthy therapeutic journeys. (See our work on clinical narratives and oncology studies in the reference list; of particular relevance are M. Good 1995a, 1995b, and M. Good et al. 1990, 1994; see Mattingly 1994 and 1998 for her creative work on therapeutic emplotment and Mattingly and Garro 2000 for elaboration.)

NARRATIVE ANALYSIS

When literary concepts such as narrative are introduced into observations of everyday clinical life, new aspects of medical work and therapeutic processes become evident. Concepts drawn from narrative analysis—plot, emplotment, and narrative time—illuminate how affect and desire play out in clinical narratives, seducing patients and clinicians and enveloping both in a world of the medical imagination, with a many-possibility regime of truth and with fantastic but apparently purposeful technical acts. This analytic approach highlights not only how clinical stories arise and how oncologists develop narrative strategies, but it also identifies antinarrative clinical talk, in which events have no meaning, strategies of communication fail, and clinical plots fragment or fail to emerge. This type of talk is common to medicine globally. (See B. Good 1994, B. Good and M. Good 1994, 2000; M. Good and B. Good 2000; Mattingly and Garro 2000; Ricoeur 1981a, 1981b; Brooks 1984; Iser 1978; and Eco 1994 for references on narrative analysis.)

Narrative analysis enables disaggregation of specialty power and its economic underpinnings; it leads us to ask how the cultural power and scientific robustness of clinical medicine at the academic medical center where our projects took place come into play—in "plotting" a coherent therapeutic course, structuring clinical time, instilling desire for treatment, giving hope, and in the case of diseases resistant to standard treatment, inviting patients to open their bodies to experimental treatments that are often of questionable efficacy. In the American case, oncologists use clinical narratives to incorporate evidence-based medicine into clinical culture and to introduce therapeutic meaning through reliance on the findings of clinical trials and relevant research in the biosciences. And through the clinical narrative, the aesthetics of statistics—how one conveys the odds and chances of particular treatments to patients—emerge as culturally shaped and institutionally sanctioned, taking on a centrality in the narrative discourse, even as the narrative skirts ultimate questions of death, and addressing the immediacy of therapeutic activities.

Patients' ironic engagement with their clinicians, as they negotiate the meanings of these clinical narratives, the odds and statistics, and the fantastic and questionable, affords a glimpse into how the medical imaginary engenders a certain bravado, an experience with many possibilities, that supports and sustains the emotional, financial, and cultural investment in experimental procedures and treatments (Gould 1996).

WORLDS OF ONCOLOGY

Case examples from our oncology studies illustrate how clinical narratives connect the public, in particular patients, to high-technology medical science and how patients experience and discuss invitations into a biotechnical embrace. Complementing these clinical examples are illustrations from a forum created and dominated by patients, BMT-Talk, a cyberspace network connecting bone-marrow–transplant (BMT) patients, friends, kin, researchers, and curious clinicians, some of whom dispense second opinions from as far away as Brazil. The global connection is evident. In addition, public documents from insurance hearings open additional perspectives on oncology's multiple "regimes of truth."

In the American culture of high-technology medicine, oncologists are expected to invite patients to enter the world of experimental therapeutics when cancer is resistant to standard treatments. Through this invitation to "salvage therapy" (a clinician's term), a clinical narrative that weds the experimental to the therapeutic begins to unfold. Clinical narratives direct action and technological interventions. They inscribe treatment experiences on a patient's psyche and soma, under the guise of multiple plots and subplots that the professional subspecialties envision for patient and clinicians.

"RULES CHANGE":
ABMT AND HIGH-DOSE CHEMOTHERAPIES

The current controversy about autologous bone-marrow transplants (ABMTs) for metastatic breast cancer poses an ethical dilemma about societal and individual costs, both financial and personal. As a medical oncologist noted in conversation in 1993, this expensive "salvage therapy" had dubious therapeutic credentials; and in clinical trials to that date, patients who initially responded positively to transplants "were all relapsing at six or eight months after the transplant." Yet, in 1994, some patients sued their insurers who refused coverage for these treatments, and many more medical oncologists encouraged their use. (A now-infamous suit brought by a California Kaiser patient who was refused coverage in 1994 helped establish this "experimental treatment" as a standard of care by 1995–96. "No HMO [health maintenance organization] would be able to refuse coverage now because of that suit," claimed the chief of surgery at the Harvard teaching hospitals in 1996.)

By 1995, clinical studies indicated that mortality from the procedure decreased from 30 percent to 3 percent, as innovative posttreatment care was introduced and healthier patients were recruited. Although the cost of providing autologous stem-cell/bone-marrow transplants declined quickly and dramatically (from approximately $150,000 in 1993 to $60,000–$75,000 today), as the technological fix became "technically sweet," increasingly efficient and standardized, and as treatment locales shifted from lengthy hospitalizations to outpatient services, questions continued about long-term therapeutic efficacy. As the bioscience of the field alters and decisions to choose competing therapeutic options (such as platelet treatments with new pharmaceuticals) become ever more complicated, especially given the uncertain efficacy of many treatments and the potential for serious clinical errors, careful orchestration of the medical imaginary is necessary. Yet, even with questionable efficacy, we see patients and physicians captured by the biotechnical embrace, with enthusiasm about the possibilities of the experimental. ABMT for metastatic breast cancer is a prime example of enthusiasm based on questionable clinical science.

NORMALIZING THE EXPERIMENTAL

Clinician-scientists such as Dr. William Peters of Duke University Medical School were among the early public promoters of experimental therapeutics, normalizing the technologies and the apparent high-tech oddities, turning the unusual into an event no more odd than a coffee break and adopting the housekeeping metaphors of daily life. In his persuasive presentation at federal government hearings on whether Medicare/Medicaid would support coverage of ABMT for metastatic disease, Dr. Peters characterized the procedure as follows:

> As our famous philosopher once said: "the future just ain't what it used to be"—this is what most people think of bone marrow transplants as being—a high-technology facility with isolation procedures, use of high-tech equipment, multiple supportive care efforts and so on. What is really happening is that, in the last few years, this is occurring more frequently. Two women from our institution (post transplant day two and day six)—are waiting for coffee to be delivered to the hotel where they are staying during their bone marrow transplant. We now essentially do all our bone marrow transplants as outpatient procedures. If one looks at the 100-day mortality in patients undergoing transplants, you can see that, back in the mid-1980's, the therapy-related mortality in the first hundred days was at over 30%. Now, it is in the range of about 3%. In fact, if you look at the 30-day mortality [it has dropped] from 15% down to the 3% to 4% realm. This represents massive change in therapy-related mortality. (Peters 1994)

IRONIC HUMOR: THE TWILIGHT ZONE
AND THE MEDICAL IMAGINATION

Patients, like clinicians, play the numbers. Ironic humor and an edge of cynicism (hope against hope?) mix with the medical imagination and the slightly bizarre imaginary of what the future might hold. The following comments by patients about the clinical narrative created for them are illustrative.

Mrs. R, a witty fifty-four-year-old educator, suffers from metastatic disease and is a candidate for autologous bone-marrow transplant and high-dose chemotherapy (Cytoxan). She discusses therapeutic choices with her medical oncologist and the transplant surgeon. The excerpts I include here cover several meetings over a period of nine months. When we first met Mrs. R, she was with the medical oncologist, who had just informed her that she had metastatic disease secondary to breast cancer.

The first excerpt is from her third visit with the medical oncologist, with whom she discusses "choices" and recommendations from the transplant surgeons, in August. The patient's sense of humor is dry; her comments nevertheless capture the strangeness and uncertainties of experimental treatments and medicine on the edge.

> *Patient (Mrs. R) comments to the interviewer about ABMT:* I guess if I had a concern, my concern is—is it going to damage my immune system so that it's going to make things worse? It seems like a very archaic sort of technique. [Speaks about postponing a vacation]. I don't want to jeopardize this great 15 percent to 20 percent chance. I really don't have a choice, do I?
>
> *Medical oncologist:* Yes, you do have a choice. You don't have a choice if you're only focusing on the big picture and ten years down the road. Then you don't have a choice because these choices can give you a chance. But if you focus on the next five years——
>
> *Mrs. R:* Five years is nothing.
>
> *Medical oncologist:* So you don't have a choice. It's your choice.
>
> *Mrs. R:* He [the transplant specialist] said it is not a choice.

The second encounter, which took place the following February, begins with an interview between the patient and the researcher; it then focuses on the clinical encounter as the physician removes the stem cells.

> *Mrs. R:* This is supposed to stimulate the stem cells to grow . . . and then they harvest them in ten days. It's kind of like gardening.
>
> *Interviewer:* It's just a very short growing period. Like radishes.

Mrs. R: That's right. Like radishes. That's right. These little radishes.
That's right.

. . .

Interviewer: So, I have my usual question, how does all this feel at this
point?

Mrs. R: Like a giant mistake. The truth? Like I made a mistake. I
shouldn't be doing this. . . . I wasn't feeling sick. And, you know, right
now it's getting toward the big time, and I don't want to do it. I don't
want to be here. I want to be on with my life. This is inconveniencing
my life, and I don't like that. Does that sound adequate enough? So I am
saying why the hell did I decide to do this? This is stupid. Besides, the
whole thing is Twilight Zone.

. . .

Transplanter: Good, good, good. Okay. So the fun part starts.

Mrs. R (to interviewer): He's got this sadistic humor.

Interviewer: You know you're in trouble when he starts rubbing his
hands.

Mrs.R: Oh, that's a sign? Okay. He's kind of got that Frankenstein look.
What are we going to make today?

. . .

(After that day's procedures)

Mrs. R: You know what the hardest part—not even the hardest part,
but—I guess the irony of the whole thing is to go through all this and
have absolutely not only no guarantee at the end, but not even an indication. . . . No way to have any idea whether it worked or didn't work.
When you think about it, it seems like at the end they should be able to
say, "it looks good," or "it doesn't look good."

Interviewer: What did they say about that?

Mrs. R: If I'm alive and well in five years they'll call it a success, and I'll
follow the 20 percent success rate. It's a hindsight thing. And it's funny,
one of the things that we did do initially that we've gotten off that we
have to get back on, I think, was to go on a diet and become vegetarian
[referring to tamoxifen and the idea that soy is a natural tamoxifen]. . . .
You listen to the medical profession but you must do your own thing.
So I'll keep eating tofu. So, I'll keep eating tofu. So, I don't know. It's all
so interesting. The teachers gave me a huge party. Very nice, a surprise
party. And they sent out invitations and they called it a shower. They
had a shower for me, a shower of friendship, they called it.

Five weeks after this interview, the patient returned for a follow-up treatment just after news articles revealed that a competing institution, the es-
teemed Dana Farber Cancer Center, had inadvertently overdosed two
women during high-dose chemotherapy, leading to one patient's death

(*Boston Globe*, March 22, 23, 24, 1995). The Joint Commission on Accreditation of Hospitals placed the center on probation.

In April, Mrs. R evaluated for her oncology nurse her physicians' skill at extracting bone marrow (not only for therapeutic purposes but for a clinical observation study). She scored each of them: "a five, a seven, a three!"

Nurse: Not a ten?

Mrs. R: Ten does not exist, nobody can get a ten.

[Just as no ABMT patient can be assured of a cure.]

Mrs. R: I decided that [cancer] can be a chronic disease. It doesn't have to be a—I always believed it was a death sentence. . . . Now my next big decision is, they did the second bone marrow for their research . . . to see if there's any breast cancer cells in the bone marrow. So do I want to know the answer to that?

Nurse: I don't think they can tell you the answer to that.

Mrs. R: Yeah, he said he could.

Nurse: Right . . , and you don't know what to do with the information . . . he shouldn't have even told you there was an option.

Mrs. R: I'll have to think about that.

The oncology nurse and patient conclude with additional talk about the 15 percent to 20 percent cure rate and about the uncertainty and ambiguity of what the future holds.

Narrative strategies in this type of clinical encounter draw heavily on humor, and many patients in our study responded in kind. Humor lends irony to ambiguity. Nevertheless, the clinicians and patient fully experienced the experimental nature of the procedure. Notably, in May 1999, the American Society for Clinical Oncology released data from five clinical trials comparing ABMT with high-dose chemotherapy to standard treatment protocols. Four of the five studies detected no difference in longevity, although one study indicated a small difference in quality of life (www.ASCO). The single trial that reported greater effectiveness was discovered to be flawed by fraudulent research and science. The clinician investigator responsible, Dr. Werner Bezwoda, chair of the oncology and hematology department of the University of Witwatersrand Medical School in Johannesburg, South Africa, acknowledged he adjusted his data in order to gain fame (Waldholz 2000). Clinical narratives may inadvertently introduce fraudulent science and treatment of questionable efficacy and high toxicity, even as they offer the power of scientific discovery and biotechnical innovation.

WILE E. COYOTE: BMT-TALK IN CYBERSPACE

BMT-Talk is filled with the fantastic—with images of the archaic, the Frankenstein, the cyborg, and the bizarre aspects of treatment. Below, a young patient writing about a bone-marrow transplant for his/her multiple myeloma also draws on American metaphors of the flexible cartoonlike and regenerating body (the coyote appears in many forms and, like a cat, has multiple lives).

> The thing that is weird to me is that the transplant, unlike a liver or kidney or other organ transplant, isn't what's supposed to help against the disease [multiple myeloma]. What's supposed to do the damage to the cancer/tumor cells is the chemotherapy. The transplant is a rescue technique because without it the chemo would be fatal. Wow. It's a really bizarre idea—like if the water in your aquarium were tainted somehow, you'd put a ton of salt or other medicines in it, then pump it ALL out (leaving the fish inside the aquarium), waiting for it to dry out, and then pumping the water back in and hoping the fish could still swim (and not just float upside down!). Hmmm . . . well I just thought up that analogy, and it's not quite right, but it's kind of how I feel about it. We'll drop a 16-ton weight on you. That'll kill all the cancer. Then, you'll walk along like an accordion, as though you were Wile E. Coyote in a Road Runner cartoon, until you pump the air back into yourself. In fact, we'll pump it in for you! . . . I know it's the best chance I have, but I can't help feeling that it's going to seem awfully primitive in (hopefully) not many years. It feels like with all the technological and medical advances we've made, we're not that far removed from bloodletting!

Patients' subjective experiences with BMT procedures—from enthusiasm to disappointment and struggle—contrast with those of physicians who have cared for BMT patients for whom the procedure has failed.[1] In our recent study of internists' emotional responses to patient deaths (M. Good et al. 2004), we found an alternate and chilling version of the bizarre "BMT-Talk," as illustrated in the following interview excerpts, which I present by clinician rank—faculty physicians (attendings), second- to fourth-year residents, and interns.[2]

Attendings commenting on training in bone-marrow stem-cell transplant:

> The big hope—there are incredible highs and lows—the high is when you get the disease to go away with the transplant and you have done good.

Sometimes transplant units are like a morgue; the transplant people don't see it that way; house staff rotate through and comment about it all the time.

It's a big risk, an up-front risk, a 20 percent mortality rate from the procedure.

Intellectually, bone-marrow transplantation is a numbers game—I firmly believe in the ability to cure the other 60 percent.

We threw everything we could at her and she died anyway, which is unfortunate, but that was the standard of care with transplant.

It was the standard transplant story: go in, get chemotherapy, radiotherapy, get the transplant, get sick a couple of weeks later, get sicker, get sicker, get sicker, wind up in the ICU, died a week later.

I don't expect transplants to work.

Although you haven't killed them theoretically, you have at least contributed to their death prematurely.

Some comments from residents:

I finished off my responsibility, but the next year I did not want to go back to the bone-marrow–transplant unit

Bone-marrow transplant is such an odd realm of the medical world, and frankly other programs don't even see any of it.

And this 35-year-old woman, like all people who enter transplant, looked good, then died of it.

Being given high doses of chemotherapy and a bone-marrow transplant is not a natural event.

Sometimes oncology in general kind of bugs me, in that it seems—especially for bone-marrow–transplant patients . . . I was feeling, Why are we doing this?

And, finally, interns:

They come to the ICU and we have to tell them, to tell their families. It's just so frustrating that the people don't know [the high rate of failure of BMT procedures].

I'm on a bone-marrow–transplant team, so this is like the worst of . . . I don't know.

These excerpts exemplify physicians' internal critique of practices they regard as clinical irrationalities. Their experiences with patients' deaths rather than recovery convey the negative side of the medical imaginary and the biotechnical embrace.

METAPHORS OF ENTERING THE BIZARRE

Patients in our studies also used metaphors of the bizarre. Even standard chemotherapy feels like one is "off to see the wizard." A primary-school teacher, fifty-three years of age, sang us a little ditty to the tune of "I'm off to see the Wizard, the wonderful Wizard of Oz," a song she sings with her daughters as they drive to chemotherapy treatment: "I'm off to see the wizard, I'm off to chemotherapy."

Other patients, especially those who seek every possible treatment, articulate their ambivalence in succumbing to the embrace of oncology's power:

> It makes me wonder what people are willing to accept when they think of something, some institution or doctor as being the best. Is it how bad you feel? [laughs] Is it how absolutely miserable and sick you are made as a result of a treatment they are willing to invite you to have? Is that what being a good patient is all about? Not complaining . . . I wonder, when will it be enough?

Metaphors of living are, of course, equally central to the way patients address the medical imaginary and the seduction of the biotechnical embrace, the desire for hope. The aesthetics of science are wed to art in the poignant reconfiguration of Botticelli's *The Birth of Venus* in *Art.Rage.Us* (Tasch 1998). Venus is refigured with a subtle, surgically elegant mastectomy, still beautiful. Thus, as life continues, beauty too may endure despite the inscriptions on the body of consequences of clinical narratives, medicine's technically sweet fixes, and life's illness traumas.

CONCLUDING REFLECTIONS

As we deconstruct American clinical culture, particularly the worlds of oncology, we find a persistent rhetoric of humanism contrasted with that of technology. Such public and professional dichotomies may lead us astray, endorsing professional power over lay knowledge. And yet the metaphoric language of many patients is profoundly affective, expressing hope and interest in the possibilities of biotechnical innovations and therapeutics, whether in consultation with their clinicians or in the less structured interviews with researchers. In BMT-Talk, cyberspace connections often appear to heighten the emotionality of discourses and graphic debates with other patients about the limits of therapeutic options. The affective dimensions of high-technology medicine are clearly soteriological (B. Good 1994), reflecting a salvation ethos that is fundamental to bioscience and biomedicine and to the political economy and culture of hope. The biotechnical embrace creates a popular culture that is enamored with the biology of hope, attracting venture capital that continues even in the face of contemporary constraints to generate new treatment modalities.

I began this essay by considering the relationship between science and society and its connection to the relationship between the global and the local in biomedicine, particularly high-technology medicine. A global moral dilemma arises when the cultural traffic from the biosciences and its attendant marketing of biomedical products influence the practice of clinical medicine in societies of scarcity. Whereas the world's dominant economies invest private and public monies in the production of biotechnology and aggressively seek to integrate these advances into clinical practice—thereby reaping financial as well as scientific returns on capital investments—all societies confront difficult questions about rationing biomedical interventions that are assumed to be central to competent clinical medicine. Local clinicians are thus subject to constantly shifting and competing claims and regimes of truth from the worlds of scientific power and transnational biomedicine. (See Bastos 1999 for a discussion of similar issues in AIDS science.) As metaphors of science and society merge, ethical questions arise about how best to serve all patients. Integrating cultural, ethical, and political-economy analyses of contemporary popular and professional biomedical cultures is critical to unmasking links between interests, be they economic or cultural, and policies on "best medical practices" for the global medical commons. How medicine serves humanity in the third millennium may be at least marginally affected by the way in which anthropology tackles this interdisciplinary analytic project.

NOTES

I owe appreciation to the City of Bologna 2000, the organizing committee of the international symposium, and to Dr. Manfredo Pace, for whom I prepared the original version of this paper; Susann Wilkinson, for her assistance with the breast cancer research; and Charles Weiner at the Massachusetts Institute of Technology, for discussions on the meaning and historical roots of "technically sweet." I thank Martha MacLeish Fuller for her assistance and the preparation of the bibliography. This paper originally appeared in 2001 in a shorter form, as "The Biotechnical Embrace" in *Culture, Medicine and Psychiatry* 25: 395–410.

1. To illustrate, the following describes a bone-marrow transplant for acute lymphocytic leukemia: "Treatment begins with chemotherapy designed to kill as many cancer cells as possible. If the cells have spread to the brain, the patient will also undergo radiation therapy and chemotherapy injected directly into the spinal fluid.

Generally, 70 to 80 percent of the patients achieve remission after chemotherapy. To reduce the risk of relapse, the patient is given maintenance chemotherapy treatments. Sixty-five percent of the patients relapse after remission, and begin aggressive chemotherapy again. Bone Marrow Transplants are usually performed during the second remission. Studies have found 60 percent long term survival rates (survival beyond three years) for those patients who receive BMT in the first remission, and 40 percent long term survival rates for those who receive them in the second. (Many doctors prefer to wait to see if a patient relapses after the first round of chemotherapy before deciding to perform BMT)." (www.peds.umn.edu/centers/BMT/all.html).

2. The study, Physicians' Emotional Reactions to Their Patients' Deaths, was funded by the Nathan Cummings Foundation. The primary investigators are Susan D. Block, M.D., Dana Farber Cancer Institute and Department of Psychiatry, Brigham and Women's Hospital; and Robert M. Arnold, M.D., University of Pittsburgh Medical Center. Research took place between 1999 and 2001. In addition to myself, the Boston research team included Patricia Ruopp, EdD, Nina Gadmer, Matt Lakoma, and Amy Sullivan, PhD. (See Good et al. 2004, for a project description.)

REFERENCES

Bastos, Cristiana. 1999. *Global Responses to AIDS: Science in Emergency.* Bloomington: Indiana University Press.

Brooks, Peter. 1984. *Reading for the Plot: Design and Intention in Narrative.* New York: Vintage Books.

Cohen, Lawrence. 1999. "Where It Hurts: Indian Material for an Ethics of Organ Transplantation." Special issue, "Bioethics and Beyond." *Daedalus* 128(4): 135–65.

Cooke, Robert. 2001. *Dr. Folkman's War: Angiogenesis and the Struggle to Defeat Cancer.* New York: Random House.

Eco, Umberto. 1994. *Six Walks in the Fictional Woods.* Cambridge, MA: Harvard University Press.

Fairview-University Medical Center. 2000. "Acute Lymphocytic Leukemia." Blood and Marrow Transplant Program, Fairview-University Medical Center, University of Minnesota. www.peds.umn.edu/centers/BMT/all.html.

Farmer, Paul. 1999. *Infections and Inequalities: The Modern Plagues.* Berkeley: University of California Press.

———. 2004. *Pathologies of Power: Health, Human Rights, and the New War on the Poor.* Berkeley: University of California Press.

Fischer, Michael M. J. 1991. "Anthropology as Cultural Critique: Inserts for the 1990s Cultural Studies of Science, Visual-Virtual Realities, and Post-Trauma Polities." *Cultural Anthropology* 6: 525–37.

Freudeheim, Milt. 2002. "The Healthier Side of Health Care." *New York Times,* October 23.

Good, Byron. 1994. *Medicine, Rationality, and Experience.* Cambridge: Cambridge University Press.

Good, Byron, and Mary-Jo DelVecchio Good. 1994. "In the Subjunctive Mode: Epilepsy Narratives in Turkey." Social Science and Medicine 38(6): 835–42.

———. 2000. " 'Fiction' and 'Historicity' in Doctors' Stories: Social and Narrative Dimensions of Learning Medicine." In *Narrative and the Cultural Construction of Illness and Healing*, ed. Cheryl Mattingly and Linda Garro (Berkeley: University of California Press).

Good, Mary-Jo DelVecchio. 1995a. "Cultural Studies of Biomedicine: An Agenda for Research." *Social Science and Medicine* 41(4): 461–73.

———. 1995b. *American Medicine: The Quest for Competence.* Berkeley: University of California Press.

———. 2001. "The Biotechnical Embrace." *Culture, Medicine, and Psychiatry* 25: 395–410.

Good, Mary-Jo DelVecchio, Nina M. Gadmer, Patricia Ruopp, Matthew Lakoma, Amy M. Sullivan, Robert M. Arnold, Susan D. Block. 2004. "Narrative Nuances on Good and Bad Deaths: Internists' Tales from High-technology Work Places." *Social Science and Medicine* 58 (March): 939–53.

Good, Mary-Jo DelVecchio, and Byron Good. 2000. "Clinical Narratives and the Study of Contemporary Doctor-Patient Relationships." In *The Handbook of Social Studies in Health and Medicine*, ed. Gary L. Albrecht, Ray Fitzpatrick, and Susan C. Scrimshaw (London: Sage Publications Ltd.).

Good, Mary-Jo DelVecchio, Byron J. Good, Cynthia Schaffer, and Stuart E. Lind. 1990. "American Oncology and the Discourse on Hope." *Culture, Medicine and Psychiatry* 14: 59–79.

Good, Mary-Jo DelVecchio, Tsuenetsu Munakata, Yasuki Kobayashi, Cheryl Mattingly, Byron Good. 1994. "Oncology and Narrative Time." *Social Science and Medicine* 38(6): 855–62.

Gould, Stephen Jay. 1996. *Full House: The Spread of Excellence from Plato to Darwin.* New York: Harmony Books.

Groopman, Jerome. 2000. *Second Opinions: Stories of Intuition and Choice in the Changing World of Medicine.* New York: Viking.

Holtzman, Steven. 2001. Interview with Michael M. J. Fischer, Byron Good, and Mary-Jo DelVecchio Good. January 16.

Iser, Wolfgang. 1978. *The Act of Reading: A Theory of Aesthetic Response.* Baltimore: Johns Hopkins University Press.

Kolata, Gina. 2002. "Scientists Debating Future of Hormone Replacement." *New York Times*, October 23.

Marcus, George, ed. 1995. *Technoscientific Imaginaries: Conversations, Profiles and Memoirs.* Chicago: University of Chicago Press.

———. 1998. "Ethnography in/of the World System: The Emergence of Multi-sited Ethnography." In *Ethnography through Thick and Thin* (Princeton, NJ: Princeton University Press).

Mattingly, Cheryl. 1994. "The Concept of Therapeutic 'Emplotment.' " *Social Science and Medicine* 38(6): 811–22.

———. 1998. *Healing Dramas and Clinical Plots.* Cambridge: Cambridge University Press.

Mattingly, Cheryl, and Linda Garro, eds. 2000. *Narrative and the Cultural Construction of Illness and Healing.* Berkeley: University of California Press.

Peters, William. 1994. Presentation to federal government hearings on Medicare/Medicaid coverage of bone-marrow transplant.

Pollack, Andrew. 2002. "U.S. Inquiry and Lawsuit Draw Reaction of Drug Maker." *New York Times*, July 20.

Rabinow, Paul. 1999. *French DNA: Trouble in Purgatory.* Chicago: University of Chicago Press.

Ricoeur, Paul. 1981a. *Hermeneutics and the Human Sciences.* Ed. and trans. John B. Thompson. Cambridge: Cambridge University Press.

———. 1981b. "Narrative Time." In *On Narrative,* ed. W. J. T. Mitchell (Chicago: University of Chicago Press), 165–86.

Rouse, Joseph. 1992. "What Are Cultural Studies of Scientific Knowledge?" *Configurations* 1(1): 1–22.

Sanal, Aslihan. 2004. " 'Robin Hood' of Techno-Turkey or Organ Trafficking in the State of Ethical Beings." *Culture, Medicine and Psychiatry* 28(3): 281–309.

Stolberg, Sheryl Gay. 2002. "On Medicine's Frontier: The Last Journey of James Quinn." *New York Times,* October 8.

Tagliabue, John. 2002. "Mystery Effect in Biotech Drug Puts Its Maker on Defensive." *New York Times* Business section, October 2.

Tasch, Jacqueline A., ed. 1998. *Art.Rage.Us: Art and Writing by Women with Breast Cancer.* San Francisco: Chronicle Books.

Varmus, Harold. 2002. "The DNA of a New Industry." *New York Times* Opinion page, September 24.

Waldholz, Michael. 2000. "South African Doctor Admits Falsifying Data on Treatments for Breast Cancer." *Wall Street Journal,* February 7.

13 "To Be Freed from the Infirmity of (the) Age"

Subjectivity, Life-Sustaining Treatment, and Palliative Medicine

ERIC L. KRAKAUER

INTRODUCTION:
THE GIFT OF LIFE-SUSTAINING TREATMENT

Ms. A is a seventy-five-year-old woman with multiple chronic medical problems related to her long history of diabetes mellitus, hypertension, and smoking. She had two myocardial infarctions that resulted in congestive heart failure. She also has a history of chronic renal failure, emphysema, chronic foot pain, and mild dementia that probably was the result of several small strokes. A working class, Protestant widow, Ms. A had lived in a retirement home for the past few years, where she required some assistance with her activities of daily living. She had worked intermittently at part-time jobs as a housekeeper and waitress, had not consistently had health insurance, and had received medical care irregularly in the emergency room and in the clinic staffed by medical residents of a university hospital. Her children and grandchildren do not live close by and had visited her at the retirement home only occasionally.

Ms. A was admitted to the hospital with pneumonia and a severe infection in her blood. Although her infections were controlled with antibiotics, her kidneys failed completely, and the doctors began hemodialysis. Shortly thereafter, she suffered a cardiac arrest and received cardiopulmonary resuscitation. Although she gradually awakened over the following few weeks, her doctors discovered that she had had another stroke during her cardiac arrest. Now, one month later, she remains confused and sometimes seems not to recognize her family members. She also remains dependent on mechanical ventilation and has undergone a tracheostomy. Thus, she is unable to speak or eat. A permanent feeding tube has been surgically inserted in her stomach to provide artificial nutrition. Her family continues to insist on full life-sustaining treatment.

381

Ms. A has required several types of life-sustaining technologies to re-main alive. Most of these technologies have become widely available only in the past several decades. One type is organ-replacement technology. When her kidneys failed, they were replaced with a hemodialysis machine, to which she is bound thrice weekly for a few hours. When her lungs and respiratory system no longer could function well enough to sustain life, she became bound to a mechanical ventilator. A second type of life-sustaining technology that Ms. A received was cardiopulmonary resuscitation (CPR). Finally, unable to eat, she now receives artificial nutrition and hydration.

Two important common phenomena appear in the brief histories of these life-sustaining technologies. First, once they became generally available, *not* using them became difficult. In each case, withholding treatment, and par-ticularly withdrawing treatment once started, was deemed unethical. Courts in the United States found legal grounds for disallowing the foregoing of life-sustaining treatments for patients unable to speak for themselves, and occasionally legislators drafted new laws with similar provisions. Second, experience showed that life-sustaining technologies not only had obvious potential benefits for patients but could also be very burdensome. The great gift of this technology brought with it the unforeseen danger of exacerbat-ing suffering. The medicine also could be poison. Increasingly in recent years, patients, surrogates, and physicians have agreed that sometimes withholding or withdrawing life-sustaining treatments is best (Prendergast and Luce 1997: 15–20). At the same time, courts have found legal grounds for allowing life-sustaining technologies to be withheld or withdrawn under certain circumstances.

Let us take a closer look at these technologies. Hemodialysis was in-vented in the 1940s but did not enter common use for chronic renal failure until the 1960s (Porter 1998: 620). In the 1970s, it became the standard of care for patients with end-stage renal disease if renal transplantation was not available or appropriate. In Massachusetts in 1979, the wife, son, and physician of a severely demented man receiving hemodialysis, Earle Spring, agreed that, for humanitarian reasons, this life-sustaining treatment should be stopped and Mr. Spring be allowed to die. However, owing to a decision by the Massachusetts Supreme Judicial Court earlier that year in the mat-ter of *Superintendent of Belchertown v. Saikewicz,* only the courts could make such a decision about withholding or withdrawal of life-sustaining treatment. Hemodialysis was continued for fourteen months against the wishes of the patient's family and physician while the case was debated in the courts. Mr. Spring finally died of complications of pneumonia (Beauchamp and Childress 1994: 515–17).

The first mechanical ventilators for prolonged respiratory failure were unwieldy negative-pressure ventilators, or "iron lungs," for polio victims in the 1920s (Paul 1971: 324–34). However, positive-pressure mechanical ventilation for respiratory failure, delivered via intubation of the trachea, did not enter common use until the 1950s and 1960s (Wackers 1994: 420–31; Pontoppidan, Wilson, Rie, and Schneider 1977: 96–116). It soon became the standard of care for patients with respiratory failure of many etiologies. Once a patient with little or no hope of recovering the ability to breathe independently began mechanical ventilation, discontinuation by a physician was deemed unethical and possibly felonious. In the celebrated case of Karen Ann Quinlan, a young woman in a permanent vegetative state with virtually no hope of regaining the ability to interact with her environment, both her physicians and the hospital where she was receiving life-sustaining treatment refused her family's request to withdraw mechanical ventilation until the New Jersey Supreme Court ordered them to do so in 1976.

CPR was introduced by Kouwenhoven, Jude, and Knickerbocker in 1960. They suggested that "anyone, anywhere" might apply CPR and that "anyone, anytime, anywhere" with sudden death might be resuscitated with this technique (Kouwenhoven, Jude, and Knickerbocker 1960: 1064–67; Jude, Kouwenhoven, and Knickerbocker 1961: 1063–70). By 1973, the National Conference on Standards for CPR and Emergency Cardiac Care recommended universal use of CPR for everyone who suffered sudden death (Timmermans 1999: 66). This violent technique of revival or "reanimation"—involving chest compressions forceful enough to fracture ribs, the application of electric shocks, and intubation of the trachea—became the standard of care for hospitalized patients who suffered cardiac arrest and standard practice for paramedics who encountered people in cardiac arrest outside the hospital. By 1976, hospitals had begun developing guidelines to justify *not* providing CPR in certain cases (Rabkin, Gillerman, and Rice 1976: 364–66; Rothman 1991: 230).

Artificial nutrition via surgically placed tube gastrostomy for patients chronically unable to eat entered common practice in 1975 (Torosian and Rombeau 1980: 919–27). In 1980, the introduction of a less invasive, endoscopic technique for tube gastrostomy greatly facilitated chronic artificial enteral nutrition (Gauderer, Ponsky, and Izant 1980: 872–75). As with other life-sustaining technologies, some soon deemed artificial nutrition to be universally beneficial. Even more believed that discontinuing it once it was started was morally unacceptable. In 1983, two California physicians were indicted for murder for removing artificial intravenous nutrition and hydration from a neurologically devastated man at the request of his family

(Paris and Reardon 1985: 2243–45). In 1985, the physicians and hospital administrators involved in the case of Paul Brophy, a retired firefighter in a persistent vegetative state for two years due to a ruptured brain artery, refused the unanimous request of his large family to discontinue artificial nutrition via gastrostomy. The family said that the patient had stated numerous times that he would not want to be kept alive on life support in a severely compromised condition. A probate court agreed with the physicians and hospital. The Massachusetts Supreme Judicial Court finally approved the family's request in a split decision, and artificial feeding was finally stopped nearly two years after the family's initial request (Beauchamp and Childress 1994: 522–24). In the same year, the Connecticut state legislature passed An Act Concerning Death with Dignity that permitted withdrawal of "life-support systems" from terminally ill patients but required provision of nutrition and hydration as comfort care (Winter 2000: 723–26; Connecticut General Statutes 1985). In 1990, the parents of Nancy Cruzan, a young woman in a permanent vegetative state for seven years due to a severe car accident, requested that artificial nutrition be discontinued. The hospital refused. A year-long court battle ensued that led to the U.S. Supreme Court. Finally, withdrawal of this life-sustaining technology was permitted (Pence 1995: 17–20).

The recourse to courts and legislatures indicates the depth of uncertainty that existed, and persists, about proper use of life-sustaining technology. This uncertainty, along with outrage at the discovery of widespread abuse of human research subjects, has provided much of the motivation for the rapid development of biomedical ethics as an academic discipline in the past four decades (Rothman 1991: 1–14). The work of biomedical ethics has commonly been to identify, elaborate, and iterate the dominant culture's ethical norms, the principles and rules that customarily guide moral action. Biomedical ethics also prescribes specific policies or actions in particular situations or cases reflecting such ethical norms. Biomedical ethics thereby plays a crucial role in maximizing the benefits and minimizing the burdens of life-sustaining technology, and of medical technology in general, for individual patients, within hospitals and within larger societies. Efforts to make biomedical ethics more sensitive to cultural difference increase its potential to minimize harm. Yet, for reasons that will become apparent, biomedical ethics does not address the fundamental danger of life-sustaining technology that has provoked widespread discomfort with this technology. Delineation of this danger requires attention to the foundation of technological thinking and of the technological age.

In this chapter, I describe a founding gesture of this age, the Cartesian *ego cogitans.* I show that Descartes' establishment of the ground of all things in the thinking subject radically changed the world by putting the world at the disposition of subjective technological thinking. I point out the privileged position of *medical* technology in Descartes' work and explain the danger of the Cartesian quest to technologically master death. Finally, I propose a palliative medicine that responds to this danger by seeking to attend to suffering in nontechnological ways. In closing, I show how such a palliative medicine might respond to Ms. A.

TECHNOLOGIES OF THE CARTESIAN SUBJECT

In the *Meditations on First Philosophy,* Descartes proposed to discover what, if anything, could be known indubitably. When the ontological legitimacy of all things and all thoughts was questioned, the thinking subject alone remained indubitable. For Descartes, the thinking subject alone *is* with perfect certainty. With Descartes' gesture, the thinking subject replaced God as the center and ground of all things (Heidegger 1979: 88 [128]). The *ego cogitans,* the thinking I or subject, is the *terra firma* or ontological foundation discovered by Cartesian radical doubt. Thus, as Heidegger emphasizes in his essay "The Age of the World Picture," the Cartesian *cogito* at the beginning of the *Meditations* was a founding gesture of the modern age. And Western philosophy since Descartes has not questioned the ontologically fundamental position of the thinking subject.

Once the ontological certainty of the subject was established, the subject provided a basis for sense certainty as well. The subject became what Heidegger calls, citing Descartes, a *"fundamentum absolutum inconcussum veritatis":* an absolute, unshakable foundation of truth as certainty (Heidegger 1979: 106–7; Descartes 1978: 24–28 [16]). On the basis of its self-certainty, the thinking subject could proceed to master the "chaos" of the world. In any age, it could master whatever is not yet known with certainty, not yet mastered. In the technological age, this includes death.

How does the Cartesian thinking subject master the world? In Descartes' work, the subject distinguishes itself from all objects of thought or perception. The subject posits all beings, whatever is, as standing opposite to it and in relation to it. The positing of the Cartesian subject thereby determines the meaning of being as being posed *(gestellt)* in this way by and before the subject. To be is to be present to the subject as a thought or "re-presentation" in subjective thinking. In the modern, technological age, says Heidegger, only that which is posed before and present to the subject in this way *is,* counts as being. In other words, all beings are now objects for the

thinking subject. Heidegger calls this subjective posing before and representing *Vorstellen*. Thinking which has become *Vorstellen* and which poses
beings as objects in this way thereby makes them measurable, calculable,
predictable, and manageable. It can be counted on "in advance and firmly"
that objects and only objects will be encountered. Thinking as subjective
"proposing *[Vorstellen]*," says Heidegger, is "mastering objectification
[meisternde Vergegenständlichung]" a violent "grasping, capturing and
conceiving *[das Ergreifen und Begreifen von]*" (Heidegger 1979: 108 [149]).
The thinking subject assumes a dominant position over all objects, actual or
potential. For Heidegger, this Cartesian subjective thinking that mathema-
tizes and masters the world is technology in the most fundamental sense.

Descartes' establishment of the thinking subject, and of all beings as objects at the disposition of the thinking subject, was both the most fundamental technological invention and, in a sense, the invention of modern
technology. The establishment of the thinking subject also prepared the way
for modern science. Science presupposes a world of objects that are susceptible to measurement, experiment, calculation, exposure, comprehension,
and mastery. Science, says Heidegger, is always already concerned with objects, always already because objectivity itself, the exposure of beings as objects, is the condition of the possibility of science. Whereas we usually understand technology to be based on science, as an application of science,
technology in this fundamental sense of subjective thinking that objectifies
and masters is rather the basis of science (Heidegger 1978: 27 [23]). It is the
basis of all modern sciences, including medical science.

CARTESIAN MEDICAL MASTERY

Because subjective, technological thinking posits all beings as objects that,
as objects, are knowable and masterable, it presupposes that all that is can
be known and mastered. Thinking masters objects by elucidating the forces
of nature, which generate, alter, and destroy all objects and determine their
every interaction. Thus, subjective, technological thinking clarifies cause
and effect. In principle, nothing can resist subjective clarification and mastery. Descartes states this explicitly in the *Discourse on Method:* "we could
know the force and actions of fire, water, air, the stars, the heavens and all
the other bodies in our environment, as distinctly as we know the various
crafts of our artisans; and we could use this knowledge—as artisans use
theirs—for all the purposes for which it is appropriate, and thus make ourselves like masters and possessors of nature" (Descartes 1979: 128
[142–43]). According to Descartes, religious revelation is not needed to ex-

plain the mysteries of nature, allay humankind's fear of the unknown and untamed, and assign humankind a dominant place in the universe. Technological thinking does this better.

Toward what purposes is subjective mastery most appropriate? Descartes writes, "This is desirable not only for the invention of an infinity of technologies *[artifices]* which would facilitate our enjoyment without pain of the fruits of the earth and all the commodities we find there, but also, and most importantly, for the maintenance of health, which is undoubtedly the chief good and the foundation of all the other goods in this life." Among the sciences, the objective domains of technological mastery, medicine is preeminent. Although all technological mastery facilitates the pursuit of happiness by securing goods for humankind, the greatest good is health. Medicine secures and maintains the preeminent good of health by mastering the body and its diseases.

Medicine, like any other science, can discern only objects. Whatever about health, disease, and human being that does not appear or "expose itself" to medicine as objective simply is not. Medicine does not ignore subjective data, however. Rather, subjective data are always data about an object and are therefore just other aspects of modern objective thinking. Medicine masters its object, the human body, by elucidating its function and the causes of its dysfunction or disease. Medicine seeks knowledge of, and thus power over, both normal physiology and pathophysiology. It seeks knowledge of how disease occurs and how health can be restored and maintained. Although medicine had much to learn in Descartes' time (as it does today), in principle, nothing can resist medical clarification and mastery. "All that we know in medicine is almost nothing in comparison with what remains to be known, and . . . we might be freed from innumerable diseases, both of the body and of the mind, and perhaps even from the infirmity of age, if we had sufficient knowledge of their causes and of all the remedies that nature has provided." Descartes asserts that medicine can master body, and to a certain extent mind as well, so as to maintain health indefinitely.

Both in the *Discourse on the Method* and *Meditations on the First Philosophy*, Descartes writes of the human body as a machine: "*machinamentum humani corporis*" (Descartes 1978: 12 [195]; cf. 1979: 20 [116]). It is a complex machine of many parts, "nerves, muscles, veins, blood, skin," and other "organs" that can malfunction like "a badly made clock." The result is disease. Subjective, objectifying medical thinking can, in principle, correct any such malfunction by clarifying its cause and inventing a remedy. The remedy for some malfunctions may be a medication. But because the body is a complex machine that God has made with myriad parts, the problem may be one or more faulty parts. Medicine can, in principle, repair or replace any such part. In other words, the body is composed of disposable and potentially replaceable parts. At the beginning of the technological era, Descartes prescribed organ replacement and life-sustaining technologies as means to maintain health and suggested that such interventions could sustain life and maintain health indefinitely.

Following Descartes, medicine can do God one better. Whereas God's machine, the human body, wears out and breaks down like an old clock, medicine, when it obtains enough knowledge and mastery of its objects, can free humankind from "the infirmity of age." By curing diseases and repairing or replacing faulty parts, medicine can defer death longer and longer. When it has enough knowledge and mastery, it will conquer death itself. Like any other natural phenomenon, death is an object that admits of clarification and mastery.

The Cartesian dream of mastering death—based ultimately on the thinking subject as the unshakable ground of all beings (as masterable objects)—largely determines contemporary medical education, research, and practice. It has resulted in the medicalization of death, the making of death into a medical-technological problem that requires primarily medical intervention (Timmermans 1999: 112–13). Thus, in the second half of the twentieth century, the site of death in Western culture shifted from the home to the hospital (Ariès 1974: 87–88). The Cartesian dream is manifested in the organ-replacement and life-sustaining technologies applied to gravely ill people with little prospect for improvement, such as Ms. A. In the past few centuries, Western medicine has indeed been able to defer death by several decades. Yet in the past few decades, unease and uncertainty about life-sustaining and death-deferring technologies have grown rapidly.

Unease about many technologies is growing. It has become increasingly clear that products of the project to master nature and assure our safety—toxic chemicals and weapons of mass destruction, for example—instead threaten our safety and lives. In medicine, life-sustaining/death-deferring technologies often prolong or intensify pain and other physical symptoms as well as psychological sources of suffering such as depression, dementia, and anxiety. They create painful choices and impossible dilemmas for patients and their loved ones, who must decide how to use or not use them. The project of conquering death has instead prolonged and complicated dying and propagated suffering. The project of freeing humankind from the infirmity of age has exacerbated this infirmity and thus revealed an infirmity of *the* age: of the technological age determined by thinking become "mastering objectification." The infirmity of the technological age is not that age continues to bring infirmity. Rather, it is perplexity about how to address the counterproductivity of the age's own fundamental project (Illich 1976: 207ff). It is that the endeavor to technologically master infirmity and death has led into what Illich calls an "iatrogenic loop" that reproduces infirmity and suffering while death remains inevitable (Illich 1976: 25). This is the fundamental danger of life-sustaining technology. The danger is that medicine has itself become thoroughly technological. Technological medicine knows how to address infirmity, suffering, and death—even that which medicine itself reproduces by its attempts at mastery—only with recurrent attempts at mastery. As a result, the complication of dying and the reproduction of infirmity and suffering continue.

Descartes' establishment of the thinking subject transformed thinking. Thinking has itself become technological. That does not mean simply that thinking is an instrument or a means to an end. Technology, says Heidegger, is most fundamentally a "way of disclosing" (Heidegger 1978: 16 [12]). Every act of thought reconceives the world as objective and thus masterable by the thinking subject (Krakauer 1996: 22, 29–30). Many scholars have asserted that Descartes' positing of the thinking subject is incorrect and has been superseded. Recently, for example, Damasio has claimed that Descartes' distinction between *res cogitans* and *res extensa*—the fundamental thinking subject or mind and its objective body—is "erroneous" because body in fact precedes and is closely "related to" mind (Damasio 2000; cf. Descartes 1969: 51–52, 120–121 [341, 375–76]). Yet this claim inadvertently reaffirms precisely the Cartesian, subjective, technological thinking it purports to overcome. Similarly, attempts such as those of biomedical ethics to resolve dilemmas over what Descartes called "appropriate" use of technology virtually inevitably reassert the Cartesian thinking subject and think technologically, thus perpetuating the same type of dilemmas that they resolve (Krakauer 1998a: 525–45). Technology has revealed itself to be dangerous. Although it is supposed to help, it also harms, and yet it admits of no alternative. The age is not only infirm but also "needy." It needs a way to confront the danger of technology that does not simply reproduce the danger.

PALLIATIVE MEDICINE: RESPONDING TO SUFFERING

In the 1960s and 1970s, as death became increasingly "medicalized" and powerful new life-sustaining technologies emerged, the search grew for a guide to the "proper" use of the new technologies. Attentive physicians and biomedical ethicists sought to understand what meaning an individual patient might find in a technologically sustained life of severe infirmity or whether the same patient would find the quality of such a life unacceptably low. However, technology's transformation of meanings and qualities into quantities has complicated this task. Physicians, ethicists, and policy makers alike look for objective indices of life no longer worthy of being technologically sustained: APACHE score, prognosis-based futility guidelines, performance status scales, quality of life indices, severe neurologic impairment such as permanent vegetative state (Knaus et al. 1991: 1619–36; Teno et al. 1994: 1202–7; Karnofsky and Burchenal 1949: 191–205; Zubrod 1960: 7–33; Spitzer et al. 1981: 585–97; American Academy of Neurology Quality Standards Committee 1995: 1015–18). Here again, the search is for purely technological solutions to a technological dilemma. Increasingly, yet often imperceptibly, the fundamental technological goal of mastery displaces traditional cultural and religious values, meanings, and goals. The end of technological thinking is always only greater mastery, which is to say, more technology. The means toward the ends of health and happiness—quantification, life-sustaining technologies—become ends in themselves (Krakauer 1998b: 21–23).

Adorno and Horkheimer call this displacement of (nontechnological) ends and tendency of technological means to become ends in themselves the fetishism of technology (Adorno and Horkheimer 1980: 8 [4]). Simply receiving CPR, mechanical ventilation, or hemodialysis becomes paramount. Deferring death becomes more important than attending to the soul or preparation for the afterlife or the next life; it becomes more important than being with or saying farewell to loved ones, reconciling with estranged loved ones, or being home; it becomes more important even than a patient's inability to do any of these tasks. Now that thinking has become technological, the technological age does not know how *not* to use life-sustaining technologies. Yet this not knowing—this need for a way out of the specific counterproductivity, the iatrogenic loop, the danger of life-sustaining treatment—has provoked a response.

Palliative medicine responds to this need and danger by responding to suffering. Palliative medicine was provoked or called into being by the suffering that the Cartesian medical project ignored, produced, and reproduced. It attends to the suffering of those facing life-threatening illness and recognizes the possibility that this suffering might be exacerbated by life-sustaining treatments.

Palliative medicine is a medical discipline. It locates itself within medicine and affirms the Hippocratic tradition insofar as it endeavors to help the sick and do no harm. It also has a long tradition of its own. Places of refuge for the poor, the sick, and the dying have existed in Western culture since antiquity. In the seventeenth century, a Catholic priest and contemporary of Descartes, Vincent de Paul, established the Sisters of Charity, an order of nuns devoted to nursing the indigent sick and dying. In the nineteenth century, the term *hospice* was first used to denote institutions devoted entirely to caring for the dying in France, Ireland, England, and New York. Based on her experiences in two such hospices in London, Dr. Cicely Saunders developed the first modern or "scientific" hospice in the 1960s. St. Christopher's Hospice was scientific because of its close medical attention to symptom assessment and control and its use of research to design and improve its interventions (Saunders 1998: v–ix). Yet contemporary palliative medicine also recognizes the reduction of medical thinking to "mastering objectification"—to a science whose exclusive goal is to technologically maintain health and master death.

Palliative medicine does not eschew medical technology. It makes no Luddite or nostalgic call for a return to supposedly more humane nontechnological care. Because it is a response to suffering, palliative medicine endeavors to use technology responsibly. This does not mean primarily that it seeks ethical deliberation about proper use of life-sustaining treatment or other medical technologies. Rather, palliative medicine decides on use of technologies by hearkening to the voice of suffering and by responding to its call. In doing so, palliative medicine frees itself from the technological imperative of mastery that determines medical thinking virtually completely.

When called for, palliative medicine uses medical technologies, including life-sustaining technologies, to respond to suffering. But when dictated by the response, palliative medicine also can leave life-sustaining technologies alone at any time (Heidegger 1979: 22–26 [54–57]). For palliative medicine, neither medical technology nor technological mastery is what matters most, what calls for a response. What calls is suffering, and attention to suffering reveals that life-sustaining technology is not always called for. Thus, palliative medicine is not determined entirely by technology. It is able to let technology be. More importantly, it *lets dying be*. It does not do so by ignoring dying patients or grieving loved ones, nor does it let patients die who could be saved and recover to an extent acceptable to them. Rather, palliative medicine does not approach dying exclusively with the goal of mastery. It strives to approach each sufferer with no particular agenda at all. This putting aside of agendas allows it to listen. Though palliative medicine responds quickly and with state-of-the-art technologies to pain and other uncomfortable symptoms, it simultaneously seeks to attend to calls of suffering that are less obvious—those that may be drowned out by the cacophony of subspecialized, highly rationalized disease management. These less audible calls may emanate less from physical distress than from feelings of loss: loss of health, of the ability to function, of loved ones, of relationships, of meaning, of the impending loss of self in the face of death. Perhaps most importantly, palliative medicine strives to recognize its own limits, the limits of all technological mastery. It acknowledges the inevitability of death and strives with each patient to find a way and a time to let dying happen, to let dying be.

As we have seen, technology is most fundamentally a mode of thinking, the subjective thinking that seeks to reveal and clarify all. It is "a way of disclosing," a way of revealing all that is as masterable. Subjective technological thinking recognizes no limits to its ability to clarify and master. It fails to recognize that all revealing also conceals and that all clarification also obscures. Technological thinking, like a speculum, looks into what is hidden, clarifies, and enlightens. Yet a speculum is also a mirror. The thinking subject perceives only objects, the objects that thinking itself constitutes. In an important sense, it sees only itself, what it itself puts there. It forgets that what it perceives, its very way of perceiving, may mask something radically different. Palliative medicine recognizes the specular character of medical thinking. It recognizes that medical technology can reveal, clarify, and master much. But it recognizes too that this revealing and clarifying also covers and conceals, that all mastery displaces and thereby conceals the unmasterable. The verb *to palliate* comes from the Latin *pallium* meaning "cloak." Palliative medicine seeks not to mask or hide anything, but instead to make explicit this concealing. It recognizes the importance of trying to clarify a diagnosis and to master a symptom or disease. But it also recognizes that all such clarification risks obscuring the singular suffering of the other and that all such mastery risks forgetting the ultimate unmasterability of death. Palliative medicine lets the unmasterable be by recognizing it as unmasterable.

By attending to suffering, palliative medicine thinks otherwise than subjectively and technologically. It encounters the sufferer, the other, in a way that cannot be characterized merely as objectification by a thinking subject. This may make palliative medicine necessarily remain a marginal discipline within medicine. Palliative medicine lets the other be such that the other can be more than just an object of medical mastery. It begins by letting the other be enmeshed in a context of meaning, a network of relationships, a cultural tradition, a local world, none of which can be exhaustively or definitively clarified. More importantly, palliative medicine lets the other be in its irreducible otherness.

Let us return to the case with which we began. Ms. A is now bedridden. Her life is sustained by a mechanical ventilator, a hemodialysis machine, and artificial nutrition and hydration. In the event of another cardiac arrest, she will again undergo CPR. She is bound permanently and at all times to the ventilator by a tube emanating from her throat. Three times per week, she must be attached to the dialysis machine for a few hours via a catheter in her arm. A feeding tube protrudes from her belly. She can neither speak nor eat. Bathing, sheet changing, and turning to prevent bedsores cause her to grimace in apparent pain. At times she seems to recognize family members, and at other times she does not. She sleeps most of the day and does not seem to watch TV when it is on. A trial of psychostimulants and antidepressants has had no effect.

Many would deem Ms. A's quality of life unacceptably poor and judge continued use of life-sustaining technologies to be more burdensome than beneficial. Why might her family continue to insist that all such technologies be used? Might their insistence stem from familial concerns such as wanting Ms. A to see an as-yet-unborn great-grandchild or to be present for a grandchild's graduation or marriage? Might it stem from family members' feelings of guilt about an actual or perceived insult or injury to Ms. A? Or from family members' inability to accept the imminence of her death? Might they believe that their religion forbids any forgoing of life-sustaining treatment? Might their insistence be motivated by cultural factors such as a belief in the preeminent value of any life over death shared by a historically persecuted population? Or by a belief in the preeminent value of medical care shared by a population that historically has been denied access to medical care? Or by mistrust among the same population of physicians whom they suspect might recommend against continued use of life-sustaining treatments because of racial prejudice? Might personality disorders or other psychiatric conditions sometimes inform family members' requests?

Regardless of the ostensible reason for the family's insistence, can the use of life-sustaining treatments such as CPR ever not be determined by the subjective will to master, by Cartesian techno-logic? Can a local world absorb technologies like CPR into itself without itself becoming determined by techno-logic (cf. Lantos 1995: 22–23)? Might life-sustaining technologies respond to Ms. A's suffering and that of her family? Or does their use indicate the dominance of technological thinking and a failure to palliate, to respond to suffering?

There can be no objective measure of suffering, nor of responding to it. There can be no basic algorithm for palliation. Palliation must be determined by attention to the singular suffering of each sufferer. This attending and responding is what matters, not whether or not life-sustaining technologies are employed in the response.

REFERENCES

All translations from the original German of Heidegger and Adorno and the original French of Descartes in this chapter are my own. The works cited below are among the best published English translations of the German, French, and Latin originals.
Adorno, T. W., and M. Horkheimer. 1980. *Dialektik der Aufklärung*. Frankfurt am Main: Fischer. Translated by T. W. Adorno and M. Horkheimer as *Dialectic of Enlightenment* (New York: Continuum, 1982).
American Academy of Neurology Quality Standards Committee. 1995. "Practice Parameters: Assessment and Management of Patients in the Persistent Vegetative State." *Neurology* 45: 1015–18.
Ariès, P. 1974. *Western Attitudes toward Death from the Middle Ages to the Present*. Baltimore: Johns Hopkins University Press.
Beauchamp, T. L., and J. F. Childress. 1994. *Principles of Biomedical Ethics*, 4th ed. New York: Oxford University Press.
Connecticut General Statutes. 1985. Section 19a-570, "An Act Concerning Death with Dignity, Removal of Life Support Systems."
Damasio, A. 2000. *Descartes' Error: Emotion, Reason, and the Human Brain*. New York: Harper Collins.
Descartes, R. 1969. *Les Passions de l'Âme*. Paris: Gallimard. Translation: "The Passions of the Soul." In *The Philosophical Writings of Descartes* (Cambridge: Cambridge University Press, 1985), 325–404.
———. 1978. *Meditationes de Prima Philosophia*. Paris: Vrin. Translation: *Meditations on First Philosophy* (Cambridge: Cambridge University Press, 1996).
———. 1979. *Discours de la Méthode*. Paris: Vrin. Translation: "Discourse on the Method." In *The Philosophical Writings of Descartes* (Cambridge: Cambridge University Press, 1985), 109–51.
Gauderer, M. W. L., J. L. Ponsky, and R. J. Izant. 1980. "Gastrostomy without Laparotomy: A Percutaneous Endoscopic Technique." *Journal of Pediatric Surgery* 15: 872–75.
Heidegger, M. 1959. *Gelassenheit*. Pfullingen: Neske. Translation: *Discourse on Thinking* (New York: Harper & Row, 1966).
———. 1971. "Hölderlin und das Wesen der Dichtung." In *Erläuterungen zu Hölderlins Dichtung* (Frankfurt am Main: Klostermann), 33–48. Translation: "Hölderlin and the Essence of Poetry." In *Existence and Being* (South Bend, IN: Regnery, 1979), 270–91.
———. 1978. "Die Frage nach der Technik." In *Vorträge und Aufsätze* (Pfullingen: Neske), 9–40. Translation: "The Question Concerning Technology." In *The Question Concerning Technology and Other Essays* (New York: Harper & Row, 1977), 3–35.

————. 1979. "Die Zeit des Weltbildes." In *Holzwege* (Frankfurt am Main: Klostermann), 73–110. Translation: "The Age of the World Picture." In *The Question Concerning Technology and Other Essays* (New York: Harper & Row, 1977), 115–54.

Illich, I. 1976. *Medical Nemesis*. New York: Bantam.

Jude, J. R., W. B. Kouwenhoven, and G. G. Knickerbocker. 1961. "Cardiac Arrest: Report of Application of External Cardiac Massage on 118 Patients." *Journal of the American Medical Association* 178: 1063–70.

Karnofsky, D. A., and J. H. Burchenal. 1949. "The Clinical Evaluation of Chemotherapeutic Agents in Cancer." In *Evaluation of Chemotherapeutic Agents*, ed. C. M. Macleod (New York: Columbia University Press), 191–205.

Knaus, W. A., D. P. Wagner, E. A. Drapner et al. 1991. "The APACHE III Prognostic System: Risk Prediction of Hospital Mortality for Critically Ill Hospitalized Adults." *Chest* 100: 1619–36.

Kouwenhoven, W. B., J. R. Jude, and G. G. Knickerbocker. 1960. "Closed Chest Cardiac Massage." *Journal of the American Medical Association* 173: 1064–67.

Krakauer, E. 1996. "Attending to Dying: Limitations of Medical Technology (A Resident's Perspective)." In *Facing Death: Where Culture, Religion, and Medicine Meet*, ed. H. M. Spiro, M. G. M. Curnen, and L. P. Wandel (New Haven, CT: Yale University Press), 22–32.

————. 1998a. *The Disposition of the Subject: Reading Adorno's Dialectic of Technology*. Evanston, IL: Northwestern University Press.

————. 1998b. "Prescriptions: Autonomy, Humanism, and the Purpose of Health Technology." *Theoretical Medicine and Bioethics* 19: 525–45.

Lantos, J. D. 1995. "Bethann's Death." *Hastings Center Report* 25: 22–23.

Paris, J. J., and F. E. Reardon. 1985. "Court Responses to Withholding or Withdrawing Artificial Nutrition and Fluids." *Journal of the American Medical Association* 253: 2243–45.

Paul, J. R. 1971. *A History of Poliomyelitis*. New Haven, CT: Yale University Press.

Pence, G. E. 1995. *Classic Cases in Medical Ethics*. New York: McGraw-Hill.

Pontoppidan, H., R. S. Wilson, M. A. Rie, and R. C. Schneider. 1977. "Respiratory Intensive Care." *Anesthesiology* 47: 96–116.

Porter, R. 1998. *The Greatest Benefit to Mankind: A Medical History of Humanity*. New York: Norton.

Prendergast, T. J., and J. M. Luce. 1997. "Increasing Incidence of Withholding and Withdrawal of Life Support from the Critically Ill." *American Journal of Respiratory and Critical Care Medicine* 155: 15–20.

Rabkin, M. T., G. Gillerman, and N. R. Rice. 1976. "Orders Not To Resuscitate." *New England Journal of Medicine* 295: 364–66.

Rothman, D. J. 1991. *Strangers at the Bedside*. New York: Basic Books.

Saunders, C. 1998. "Forward." In *Oxford Textbook of Palliative Medicine*, 2nd ed., ed. D. Doyle, G. W. C. Hanks, and N. MacDonald (New York: Oxford University Press), v–ix.

Spitzer, W. O., A. J. Dobson, J. Hall et al. 1981. "Measuring the Quality of Life of Cancer Patients: A Concise QL-index for Use by Physicians." *Journal of Chronic Diseases* 34: 585–97.

Teno, J. M., D. Murphy, J. Lynn et al. 1994. "Prognosis-Based Futility Guidelines: Does Anyone Win?" *Journal of the American Geriatrics Society* 42: 1202–7.

Timmermans, S. 1999. *Sudden Death and the Myth of CPR*. Philadelphia: Temple University Press.

Torosian, M. H., and J. L. Rombeau. 1980. "Feeding by Tube Enterostomy." *Surgery, Gynecology & Obstetrics* 150: 919–27.

Wackers, G. L. 1994. "Modern Anaesthesiological Principles for Bulbar Polio: Manual IRRP in the 1952 Polio Epidemic in Copenhagen." *Acta Anaesthesiologica Scandinavica* 38: 420–31.

Winter, S. M. 2000. "Terminal Nutrition: Framing the Debate for the Withdrawal of Nutritional Support in Terminally Ill Patients." *American Journal of Medicine* 109: 723–26.

Zubrod, C. G. 1960. "Appraisal of Methods for the Study of Chemotherapy in Cancer in Man." *Journal of Chronic Diseases* 11: 7–33.

14 A Life

*Between Psychiatric Drugs
and Social Abandonment*

JOÃO BIEHL

VITA

"In my thinking, I see that people forgot me," Catarina said to me as she pedaled an old exercise bicycle while holding a doll. This woman of kind manners and a piercing gaze was in her early thirties; her speech was lightly slurred. I first met Catarina in March 1997 in southern Brazil at an asylum called Vita. I remember asking myself, Where on earth does she think she is going on this bicycle? Vita is the end point. Like many others, Catarina had been left there to die.

Vita, which means "life" in Latin, was founded in 1987 by Zé das Drogas, a former street kid and drug dealer in Porto Alegre, a comparatively well-off city of some two million people. After his conversion to Pentecostalism, Zé had a vision in which the Holy Spirit told him to open an institution in which people like him could find God and regenerate. Zé and his religious friends squatted on private property near the downtown, where they founded a precarious rehabilitation center for drug addicts and alcoholics. Soon Vita's mission expanded. An increasing number of people who had been cut off from social life—the mentally ill and the sick, the unemployed and the homeless—were left at the center by relatives, neighbors, hospitals, and the police. Vita's team then opened an infirmary where the abandoned waited *with* death.[1]

I had traveled through and worked in several poor neighborhoods in the north and south of Brazil (Biehl 2001, 2005, 2006). I thought I knew the country. But nothing I had seen before prepared me for the desolation of Vita when I first visited it in 1995. A local human-rights activist had told me to go there if I really wanted to understand "what people do to people and what it means to be human these days."

14.   Vita, 2001. (Courtesy of Torben Eskerod)

Vita was indeed the end station on the road of poverty. Beyond any kind of accountability, most of the two hundred people in Vita's infirmary had no formal identification and lived in abject abandonment and a haunting stillness. For the most part, Vita's staff consisted of residents who had improved their mental well-being enough to administer care to newcomers and to those considered absolutely hopeless. Lacking funds, training, and proper equipment and medication, these volunteers were as ill equipped to deal with Vita's more debilitated residents as the people who ran the establishment. Though Vita's existence was acknowledged by officials and the public at large, it was not the object of any remedial policy.

Some fifty million Brazilians (more than a quarter of the population) live far below the poverty line; twenty-five million people are considered indigent. Although Vita was in many ways a microcosm of such misery, it was distinctive in some respects. A number of its residents came from working and middle-class families and once had been workers with families of their own. Others had previously lived in medical or state institutions, from which they had been evicted, thrown onto the streets, or sent directly to Vita.

Despite appearing to be a no-man's-land cut adrift, Vita was in fact entangled with several public institutions in its history and maintenance. Porto Alegre contained more than two hundred such institutions, most of which were euphemistically called "geriatric houses." Some 70 percent of them operated as clandestine businesses. These precarious places housed the unwanted in exchange for their welfare pensions; a good number of them also received state funds or philanthropic donations. In Brazil, these zones of social abandonment are symbiotic with changing households and public services: they absorb individuals who have no ties or resources left to sustain themselves, and they actually make residents' regeneration impossible and their dying imminent.

HUMAN-ANIMAL FORMS

Literally left to wither away, many in the infirmary had open wounds filled with maggots and lice. One fifty-year-old man had the maggots drawn from his eyes by an application of Pine Sol and bleach. The inhabitants of the infirmary were treated as nonhuman beings, argued Oscar, the resident-volunteer who guided my initial visits there: "Hospitals think that our patients are animals. Doctors see them as indigents and pretend that there is no cure. The other day we had to rush old Lucas to the emergency room. They cut him open and left surgical materials in him. He died from infections."

The factor that makes these humans-turned-animals unworthy of affection and care is their inability to pay, added Luciano, another volunteer: "The hospital's intervention is to throw the patient away. If they had sentiment, they would do more for them . . . so that there would not be such a waste of souls. Lack of love leaves these people abandoned. If you have money, then you have treatment; if not, you fall into Vita. *O Vita da vida* (the Vita of life)."

Oscar and Luciano used the term *human* to represent something other than the notion of shared corporeality or shared reason that dominates human-rights discourses (Ignatieff 2001). But they did not oppose *human* to *animal* either. Rather than referring to the animal nature of humans, they spoke of the animal nature of medical and social practices and of the values that shape the ways in which supposedly superior human forms treat the abandoned.

"There was no family, we ourselves buried old Lucas. A lone human

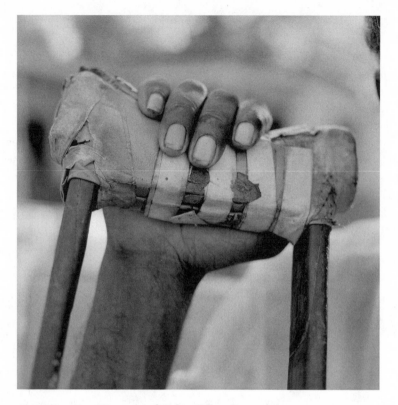

15. Vita, 1995. (Courtesy of Torben Eskerod)

being is the saddest thing, worse than being an animal." In emphasizing the "animalization" of people in Vita, Oscar and Luciano also conveyed a critical understanding of the relation of the terms *human* and *animal*. The negotiation of these relations, particularly in the medical realm, allows some human-animal forms to be considered inappropriate for life.[2]

In this essay, I chart Catarina's pathways into Vita, and explore the thinking and hope that exist in this zone of social abandonment. I trace the complex network of family, medicine, state, and economy in which Catarina's abandonment and pathology took form. I show how family members use psychiatric diagnostics and treatments to assess human value and to mediate the disposal of persons considered unproductive or unsound. Throughout this narrative, Catarina's life tells a larger story about the integral roles that places like Vita play in poor households and city life and about the ways in which novel sociomedical processes affect the course of biology and of dying.[3]

Following the plot of a single person can help us identify the many juxtaposed contexts and interactions—the "in-betweenness"—through which medical science and social life are empirically worked out. It also illuminates the subjective process by which the abandoned person, against all odds, keeps anticipating another chance at life. How can the anthropological artifact keep the story moving and unfinished?

THE ORIGINS OF PEOPLE

Catarina stood out from the others in Vita, many of whom lay on the ground or crouched in corners, simply because she was in motion. She wanted to communicate. Here is the story she told me when we first met in 1997:

> I have a daughter called Ana; she is eight years old. My ex-husband gave her to Urbano, his boss. I am here because I have problems in my legs.
>
> To be able to return home, I must go to a hospital first. It is very complicated for me to get to a hospital, and if I were to go, I would worsen. I will not like it because I am already used to being here.
>
> My brothers and my brother-in-law brought me here. Ademar, Armando . . .
>
> I exercise . . . so that I might walk. No. Now I can no longer leave. I must wait for some time. I consulted a private doctor, two or three times. When it is needed, they also give us medication here. So, one is always dependent. One becomes dependent.
>
> Then many times one does not want to return home. It is not that one does not want to . . . In my thinking, I see that people forgot me.

Later, I asked the volunteers whether they knew anything about Catarina. They knew nothing about her life outside Vita. I repeated some of the names and events Catarina had mentioned, but they said that she spoke nonsense, that she was *louca* (mad). She was a person apparently lacking common sense; her voice was annulled by psychiatric diagnosis.

Catarina's exercise and her recollections, in the context of Vita's stillness, stayed in the back of my mind. I was intrigued by the ways her story commingled elements of her previous life, the ways in which medicine had worsened her condition, her present abandonment in Vita, and her desire for a homecoming. I tried to think of her not as a mentally ill person but as an abandoned person who was claiming experience on her own terms. She knew what had made her so, but how was I to verify her account? As Catarina reflected on the events that had foreclosed her life, the degree of unintelligibility in her thinking and voice was not determined solely by her expression: we, the volunteers and the anthropologist, lacked the means to understand them.

As I kept returning to Vita, more and more people said that they wanted to tell me *minha vida* (my life). I was struck by the similarity of the accounts. Most of the residents said that they had no formal identification, and while recalling a home, a family, a childhood, or simply freedom in the streets, they described the specific events that led to their abandonment. As I listened, I was challenged to treat these condensed accounts as evidence of the reality that has been put off limits to the abandoned and of their failed attempts to reenter it. In this sense, these pieces ultimately gave language to the exclusion they embodied. Moreover, for the abandoned themselves, these accounts were spaces in which to rethink their destinies and reframe their desires.

EXPERIMENTAL REGIMES OF HEALTH

"These people in the infirmary represent the putrefaction of the street. They don't exist as a juridical fact. They have AIDS, tuberculosis, all these things that don't exist in statistics," explained Captain Osvaldo. Since 1997, Vita has been administered by Captain Osvaldo, a civilian policeman working for the state of Rio Grande do Sul. Zé das Drogas was evicted from the establishment by a philanthropic coalition called Friends of Vita, headed by Jandir Luchesi, the region's most famous radio-talk-show host and a state representative. During Zé das Drogas's administration, daily life in the rehabilitation area had been structured around worship and Bible studies; now, the emphasis is on personal hygiene, civic values, healthy eating, total abstinence from smoking and drinking, work therapy, and group self-reflection. As for the residents abandoned in the infirmary, the captain was straightforward: "We cannot bring them back to society. As horrible as it is, here one sees a truth."

As I talked to city administrators, public health officers, and human-rights activists, I was able to identify some of the institutional networks through which Vita emerged and has been integrated into local forms of governance, as well as some of the everyday practices that constitute the residents' nonexistence.

With the adoption of Brazil's democratic constitution in 1988, health care had become a public right, and many of the country's discourses and practices of citizenship in the 1990s sought to guarantee this right as the economy and the state underwent a major restructuring. The activism of mental health workers was exemplary. They worked hard to bring about laws that shaped the progressive closure of psychiatric institutions and their replacement by local networks of community- and family-based psychosocial care. This deinstitutionalization of the mentally ill was pioneered in the state of Rio Grande do Sul (Porto Alegre is its capital), where it was well under way by the early 1990s. In reality, however, the demands and strategies of the mental health movement became entangled in and even facilitated local government's neoliberalizing moves in public health: the mad were literally expelled from overcrowded and inefficient institutions, and the government allocated little new funding for the alternative services that had been proposed.

On the one hand, this local psychiatric reform confirmed the role of the Partido dos Trabalhadores (PT), the Worker's Party, as a representative of a novel politics of social inclusion; PT was already in power in the capital. It also occasioned a few exemplary services that treated "citizens burdened by mental suffering" and realized, if all too partially, a socialized form of self-governance. As I later learned, Catarina received treatment in one of these model services in the nearby city of Novo Hamburgo. On the other hand, this psychosocial politics shifted the burden of care from state institutions back to the family and communities, which failed to live up to their idealized representations in the reform movement's discourse. People had to learn new techniques to qualify for services and had to learn to live with the limitations of the new ideologies and institutions. An increasing number of mentally ill people began to live in the streets, along with the other leftovers of the country's unequal and exclusionary social project. Many ended up in places like Vita.

Everyday life in the 1980s and 1990s in that region was marked by high rates of migration and unemployment, the rise of a drug economy in the poorest outlying areas, and generalized violence. As police forces increasingly sought to erase from the city signs of misery, begging, and informal economies, philanthropic institutions took up the role of caregiver, albeit selectively. Simultaneously, families frequently responded to the growing burdens of their new responsibilities for care and narrowing options for employment by redefining their functional scope and value systems. In practice, the experimental mental health plan has also faced the widespread availability of new biochemical treatments. Free drug distribution (including psychopharmaceuticals) is a central component of Brazil's search for a cost-effective universal health-care system. Given the country's neoliberal reforms, drug imports increased substantially in the mid-1990s, and Brazil is now one of the world's ten largest pharmaceutical markets. The pharmaceuticalization of public health has run parallel with governmental decentralization and the overall demise of clinical infrastructures (Biehl 2006).

In engaging with these new regimes of public health and in allocating their own overstretched and meager resources, families have learned to act as *proxy psychiatrists*. Illness has become the ground on which experimentation and breaks in intimate household relations can occur. Families can dispose of their unwanted and unproductive members, sometimes without sanction, simply for failing to comply with their treatment protocols. This domestic activity of valuing and deciding which lives are worth living runs parallel with gender discrimination, market exploitation, and a managerial-style state that is increasingly distant from the people it governs.

"I WRITE ALL THE ILLNESSES I HAVE NOW"

When I visited Vita in December 1999, Catarina was still there. Now, however, she was seated on a wheelchair and writing.

Catarina looked dazed, and she spoke slowly and with much difficulty. Her health had deteriorated considerably; she insisted that she was suffering from rheumatism. Like most of the other residents, Catarina was taking antidepressants at the whim of the volunteers.

"What are you writing?" I asked.

"This is my dictionary," she said. "I write so that I don't forget the words. I write all the illnesses I have now, and the illnesses I had as a child." Her handwriting was uneven. The words were in block letters, with no cursive writing, and she wrote few verbs or full sentences.

I was amazed by the force of her words:

Divorce
Dictionary
Discipline
Diagnostics
Marriage for free
Paid marriage

Operation
Reality
To give an injection
To get a spasm
In the body
A cerebral spasm

"Why do you call it a dictionary?" I asked.

16.   Catarina, 2001. (Courtesy of Torben Eskerod)

"Because it does not require anything from me, nothing. If it were mathematics, I would have to find a solution, an answer. Here, there is only one subject matter, from beginning till the end . . . I write it and read it."

Catarina let me peruse the dictionary.

"I offer you my life." "In the womb of pain." "The present meaning."

Amid the continuous references to consultations, hospitals, and documents, she wrote of "the division of bodies" and of things being "out of justice."

"Who contradicts is convicted."

"Dead alive, dead outside, alive inside."

And she wrote expressions of longing:

"Recovery of my lost movements."

"A cure that finds the soul."

"With 'L' I write Love, with 'R' I write Remembrance."

MICROPOLITICS

I returned to talk to Catarina several times during that visit. She engaged in long recollections of life outside Vita, always adding more details to the story she had told me in our first meeting in 1997. The story thickened as she elaborated on her origin in a rural area and her migration to Novo Hamburgo to work in the city's shoe factories. She mentioned, in bits and pieces,

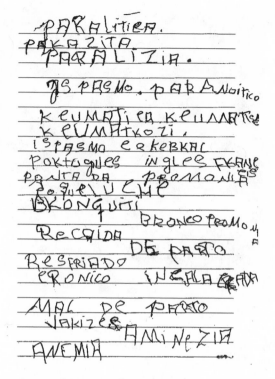

17. A page of Catarina's dictionary

having more children, fighting with her ex-husband, staying in mental wards. Catarina insisted that her abandonment had a history and a logic:

> When my thoughts corresponded with those of my ex-husband and his family everything was fine. But when they disagreed with me, I was mad. It was like a side of me had to be forgotten. The side of wisdom. My brothers want to see production and progress. They wouldn't dialogue and the science of the illness was forgotten. My legs weren't functioning or working well.

The forceful erasure of "a side of me" had prevented Catarina from finding a place in the changing family configuration, I thought.

"Did the doctors ever tell you what you had?" I asked.

"No, they said nothing . . . I am allergic to doctors. Doctors want to be knowledgeable, but they don't know what suffering is. They don't touch you there where it hurts. They only medicate."

Her affections seemed intimately connected to new domestic arrangements: "My brothers brought me to Vita. For some time I lived with my brothers . . . but I didn't want to take medication when I was there. Why was it only me who had to be medicated?"

"Why," I asked her, "do you think families, neighbors, and hospitals send people to Vita?"

"They say that it is better to place us here so that we don't have to be left alone at home, in solitude . . . that there are more people like us here. And all of us together, we form a society, a society of bodies."

Catarina had to think of herself and her history alongside the fact of her absence from the things she remembered: "Maybe my family still remembers me, but they don't miss me."

How to enlarge the possibilities of social intelligibility that Catarina had been left to resolve alone? What are the limits of human thought that she keeps expanding?

In posing these questions, I am not concerned with finding a psychological origin (I do not think one exists) for Catarina's condition or with simply tracking down the discursive templates of her experience. I understand the sense of psychological interiority as ethnological, as the whole of the individual's behavior in relation to her environment and to the measures that define boundaries, be they legal, medical, relational, or affective. Through family complexes and in technical and political domains, as they determine life possibilities and the conditions of representation, human behavior and its paradoxes belong to a certain order of being in the world.

How does one become another person today? What is the price one pays for doing so? How does this change in personal life become part of individual and collective memory? What methodologies can effectively address this agonistic openness of lived experience? How can one incorporate this openness into the analysis of a person's estrangement from reality?

I visited Catarina many times in the following years. I listened intently as she carried her story forward and backward. I also read the volumes of the dictionary she continued to write—a total of twenty-one—and discussed them with her. Taking Catarina's spoken and written words at face value took me on a detective-like journey into the various medical institutions, communities, and households to which she continuously alluded. With her consent, I retrieved her records from psychiatric hospitals and local branches of the universal health-care system. I was also able to locate her family members—her brothers, ex-husband, in-laws, and children—in Novo Hamburgo. Everything she had told me about the familial and medical pathways that led her into Vita matched the information I found in the archives and in the field.

Had I focused only on Catarina's utterances within Vita, a whole field of tensions and associations that existed between her family and medical and state institutions, a field that shaped her existence, would have remained invisible. Catarina didn't simply fall through the cracks of these domestic and public systems. Her abandonment was dramatized and realized in the novel interactions and juxtapositions of several social contexts. Scientific assessments of reality (in the form of biological knowledge and psychiatric diagnostics and treatments) were deeply embedded in households and institutions in flux, informing the colloquial thoughts and actions that led to her terminal exclusion. In the story that follows, I want to give you a sense of this powerful, noninstitutionalized ethnographic space in which the family gets rid of its undesirable members.

EX-FAMILY

Catarina was born in 1966 and grew up in a very poor place, in the western region of the Rio Grande do Sul province. In fourth grade, she was taken out of school. Her father abandoned the family, and she became the housekeeper as her youngest siblings aided their mother in agricultural work. In the mid-1980s, two of her brothers migrated and found jobs in the booming shoe industry in Novo Hamburgo. At the age of eighteen, Catarina married Nilson Moraes, and a year later, she gave birth to her son, Anderson.

A semblance. That was the first thing I heard about Catarina as I entered her former house, now occupied by Nilson's sister and her husband and two children.

"When Nilson first brought her photo home," stated Sirlei, "I said, 'Father and mother, look, what a beautiful girl he got for himself.' Everybody agreed."

Today's paralysis was not foreshadowed in the past: "She was then a perfect person, like us," said Sirlei. "She helped with everything." No longer in that family's image, Catarina was now past. She was associated with another disintegrating body: "Her mother also lost the legs and the hands."

Later, Catarina's brothers told me that they, too, were beginning to have problems walking, but they didn't know what the disease was: "It's a mystery." As Ademar, the oldest sibling said, "When we were kids, Catarina was normal." His wife again referred to Catarina's appearance: "She was very normal. I remember the wedding photos." I wondered about this gradation of normality and what elements in one's life or interests determined its application to another family member.

Shady deals, persistent bad harvests, and indebtedness to local vendors

18. Catarina at seventeen, with her future husband. (Courtesy of Torben Eskerod)

forced Nilson and Catarina to sell the land they had inherited to take care
of Catarina's ailing mother, and in the mid-1980s, the young couple decided
to migrate to Novo Hamburgo and join her brothers in the shoe industry.

Novo Hamburgo had become an El Dorado of sorts, attracting many
people in search of work and social mobility. City officials went to the
province's western region to recruit a semiliterate and cheap labor force.
Statistics show that at the end of the 1980s, the city actually had one of the
highest per capita income rates in the state, but at least one-fourth of its
growing population lived as squatters. This situation worsened in the early
1990s, when the city experienced an abrupt economic decline and acute im-
poverishment, mainly because of the country's inability to articulate a more
lucrative export policy and because of growing competition from China in
the global shoe market.

19.   Catarina's wedding party. (Courtesy of Torben Eskerod)

Catarina recalls enjoying her work in the factory. "I had my worker's ID and made my money." Her husband found a job as a security guard in the city hall. Soon the couple had a second child, Alessandra.

Catarina also took care of her mother, who had moved in with the couple. At that time, Catarina began having difficulties walking. "They fired her at the factory, because she began to fall there," said her sister-in-law. At the same time that she lost her value as a worker, she discovered that Nilson was seeing another woman, and her mother passed away. Overwhelmed, at times she left the house and wandered through the city. Her husband deployed his contacts at city hall and made sure that the police went after her: "They had to handcuff her . . . in the emergency ward they gave her shots and she calmed down," he told me. After a few of these episodes, Nilson began confining her in psychiatric units in Porto Alegre.

In the turbulent year of 1992, Catarina gave birth prematurely to her third child, a girl named Ana. Most of her hospitalizations took place between 1992 and 1994, when she and Nilson were no longer living together. "They gave her the best medication," said Nilson. "But she threw it into the toilet and flushed it down. At home, she didn't continue the treatment. She didn't help herself." Nilson now works in a shoe factory and has a new family. Like others, he spoke openly about Catarina. "It's all past," he said. "It is not even in my mind."

BODY AS MEDICATION

Notes on medical treatment and family discussions allow us to retrieve the patient's voice and, more importantly, the narrative of its alteration and the conditions of the patient's supposed intractability. At the Caridade and São Paulo Hospitals, the diagnoses of Catarina's condition varied from "schizophrenia" to "postpartum psychosis," "unspecified psychosis," "mood disorder," and "anorexia and anemia."

In tracing Catarina's passage through these medical institutions, I saw her not as an exception but as a patterned entity. Caught in struggles for deinstitutionalization, lack of public funding, and the proliferation of new classifications and treatments, the local psychiatry didn't account for her particularity or social condition. Thus, she was subjected to the typically uncertain and dangerous mental health treatment reserved for the urban working poor. Clinicians applied medical technologies blindly, with little calibration to her distinct condition. Like many patients, Catarina was assumed to be aggressive and thus was overly sedated so that the institution could continue to function without providing adequate care.[4]

Although Catarina's diagnosis softened over the years (mimicking psychiatric trends), she continued to be overmedicated with powerful antipsychotics and all kinds of drugs to treat neurological side effects. On several occasions, nurses reported hypotension, a clear indicator of drug overdose. For Catarina, as for others, treatment began with a drug surplus and was then scaled down, or not, through trial and error. As I read her files, I could not separate the symptoms of the psychiatric illness from the effects of the medication, and I was struck that doctors did not bother to differentiate between the two in Catarina.

To say that this approach is "just malpractice," as a local psychiatrist says, misses the productive quality of this unregulated medical automatism and experimentalism: *Pharmaceuticals are literally the body that is being treated.* And the process of overmedicating Catarina caused many of the symptoms that she called "rheumatism." As doctors remained fixated on her supposed hallucinations, the etiology of her walking difficulties, which nurses actually reported, remained medically unaddressed. The medical records also show that her husband and family were difficult to contact, that they left wrong telephone numbers and addresses, and that on several occasions, they left Catarina in the hospital beyond her designated stay.

Catarina's dictionary is filled with references to deficient movement, pain in her arms and legs, and muscular contractions. In writing, as in speech, Catarina refers to her condition, by and large, as "rheumatism." I followed the word *rheumatism* as it appeared throughout the dictionary, paying close attention to the words and expressions clustered around it.

At times, Catarina's writings relate her growing paralysis to a kind of biological marker, alluding to a certain "blood type becoming a physical deficiency," "a cerebral forgetfulness," and an "expired brain and aged cranium" that "impede change." Most of the time, however, Catarina writes of the man-made character of her bodily affections. In the following inscription, for example, she depicts rheumatism as a mangling of the threads that people tinker with:

> People think that they have the right to put their hands
> In the mangled threads and to mess with it
> Rheumatism
> They use my name for good and for evil
> They use it because of the rheumatism

Her rheumatism ties various life threads together. It is an untidy knot, a real matter that makes social exchange possible. It gives the body its stature and is the conduit of a morality. Catarina's bodily affection, not her name, is exchanged in that world: "What I was in the past does not matter."

In another fragment, she writes:

> Acute spasm
> Secret spasm
> Rheumatic woman
> The word of the rheumatic is of no value.

In my view, the "secret" of Catarina's condition stemmed from an unknown biology and the unconsidered experience of how people had defined it over time. We must consider side by side the acute pain that Catarina described and the authoritative story she became in medicine and in common sense—as being mad and ultimately having no value. The antipsychotic drugs Haldol (haloperidol) and Neozine (levomepromazine) are also words in Catarina's dictionary. In a fragment, she defiantly writes that her pain reveals the experimental ways of science:

> The dance of science
> Pain broadcasts sick science, the sick study
> Brain, illness
> Buscopan, Haldol, Neozine
> Invoked spirit

The goods of psychiatric science, such as Haldol and Neozine, have become as ordinary as Buscopan (an over-the-counter antispasmodic medication) and have become a part of familial practices. As Catarina's experience shows, the use of such drugs produces mental and physical effects apart from those related to her illness. These pharmaceutical goods—working, at times, like rituals—realize an imaginary spirit, rather than the material truth they supposedly stand for: *medical commodities become supposed subjects.* A moneymaking science plays a role in Catarina's afflictions. As transmitters of this science, her symptoms are typical.

"I need to change my blood with a tonic. Medication from the pharmacy costs money. To live is expensive," she wrote.

"Did Catarina tell you what happened in the hospital?" I asked her ex-husband.

"No, she didn't remember."

"MY DESIRE IS OF NO VALUE"

A complex plot had developed. After talking to all parties, I understood that, given certain physical signs, Catarina's husband, her brothers and their respective families believed that she would become an invalid as her mother had been. They had no interest in being part of that genetic script. Catarina's "defective" body then became a kind of battlefield in which decisions were made within local family/neighborhood/medical networks about her sanity and ultimately about whether "she could or not behave like a human being," as her mother-in-law said. With Catarina depersonalized and over-medicated, something stuck to her skin—the life determinants she could no longer shed.

As Catarina's situation worsened, Nilson found another woman, with whom he had a child, and had a judge grant him legal separation from Catarina. Catarina never signed the divorce papers herself. Her ex-husband also signed over his youngest daughter, Ana, to his boss in the city hall, but he insists that Catarina "gave her away." Nilson and his mother each kept one of Catarina's other two children, who still help in their respective domestic economies. At the height of Catarina's despair, her brother-in-law made her accept a deal in which he took her house and moved her into his shack, deeper into the slum.

Given that Catarina had been given away to Nilson and that the young couple squandered the family's land, Catarina's brothers felt no obligation to her. This attitude expressed the economic and gendered fabric of their moral thinking, beyond the domain of the blood tie. In more than one way, Catarina was repeating the script of her mother's illness experience: For both women, the development of the disease was entangled with spousal separation, abandonment, and predatory claims to available goods.

To Catarina's complete devastation, at the end of December 1994, her shack burned down and she was hospitalized again. This time, a Dr. Viola wrote, "I am against admission; patient should have a neurological evaluation." Nevertheless, Catarina was locked up and treated, as I learned, with haphazardly combined antipsychotic medications. On discharge, she wandered from one relative's house to another. Backed by a private psychiatrist, family members and neighbors experimented with many drugs and dosages.

"Bottom line, the ethics the family installs around mental suffering guarantees their own physical existence," I was told by Simone Laux, the director of the Novo Hamburgo psychosocial service where Catarina went before and between hospitalizations. One of her colleagues agreed that "the family quite often replaces a state that does not care." The family is thus a state within the state. In this bureaucratically and relationally sanctioned register of social death, the human, the mental, and the chemical are complicit. Finally, in 1996, after hearing about Vita from a Pentecostal pastor who knew of the place from a radio program, the brothers left her there.

In this dire context and in the face of disease, how does one speak of the evil that is done and the good one must do? For Ademar and other family members, the question was a rhetorical one to which the unspoken answer was "nothing": "It's tough, but what to do?" In the end, Catarina represented a failed medication regime that, paradoxically, allowed the lives, sentiments, and values of others to continue in a constantly changing social field marked by economic pressure and violence.

I do not mean to suggest that mental disorders are basically a matter of social construction, but rather that such disorders take form at the most personal juncture between the subject, her biology, and the technical and intersubjective recoding of "normal" ways of being in local worlds. Hence, mental disorders also implicate people who claim to represent common sense and reason, and these people have the responsibility to address their embroilment in the unfolding of disorders.

> Catarina cries and wants to leave
> Desire
> Watered, prayed, wept
> Tearful feeling, fearful, diabolic, betrayed
> My desire is of no value
> Desire is pharmaceutical
> It is not good for the circus

We can now more fully understand what Catarina meant when she said that she was writing a dictionary so as "not to forget the words, all the illness I had as a child and that I have now." The illnesses she now experienced were the outcome of events and practices that altered the person she had learned to become.

The drug Akineton, which aims to control the side effects of antipsychotics, was embedded in the new name Catarina gave herself in the dictionary: "CATKINE."

THE WORK OF TIME

I was able to get the genetics service of the Hospital das Clínicas, one of the ten best in the country, to see Catarina. Fourteen years after Catarina entered the maddening psychiatric world, molecular testing revealed that she suffered from the genetic disorder Machado-Joseph Disease, which causes degeneration of the central nervous system (Coutinho 1996; Jardim et al. 2001b). The disorder is inherited as an autosomal dominant disease (Jardim et al. 2001a) and was first reported in North American families of Portuguese-Azorean ancestry (Boutté 1990; Sequeiros 1996). The disease is characterized by a progressive cerebellar ataxia affecting gait, limb movements, speech articulation, and deglutition. Catarina's brothers had the same diagnostics and were able to use it to obtain disability benefits.

I was happy to hear that the geneticists who saw Catarina reported that "she knew of her condition, past and present, and presented no pathology." Dr. Laura Jardim was adamant that "there is no mental illness, psychosis or dementia linked to this genetic disorder. In Machado-Joseph your intelligence will be preserved, clean, and crystalline." Of course, biopsychiatrists could argue that Catarina was affected by two concomitant biological processes, but for me, the discovery of Machado-Joseph was a landmark in its overwhelming disqualification of her as mad and its ability to shed light on how her condition had evolved.

While reviewing the records of the one hundred families under the care of Dr. Jardim's team, I found that spousal abandonment and early onset of the disease were quite common among women, just as Catarina, her mother, her younger aunt, and a cousin had experienced. Affective, relational, and economic arrangements take shape around the visible carriers of the disease, and these gendered practices ultimately affect the course of dying. I also learned that after disease onset, Machado-Joseph patients survive on average fifteen to twenty years, most dying from pneumonia in wheelchairs or bedridden. Scientists have firmly established that the graver the gene mutation, the more it anticipates disease. And though the gravity of the gene mutation can account for 60 percent of the probability of earlier onset, the unknown 40 percent remains. Among siblings, Dr. Jardim told me, "the age of onset is almost always the same." How then can one explain Catarina's early onset, in her late teens, and her brothers' onset in their mid- to late twenties?

The various sociocultural and medical processes in which Catarina's biology resided, I thought, pointed to the materiality and morality of this "unknown 40 percent"—in other words: the social science of the biological mutation. To this notion, Dr. Jardim responded, "At the peak of her suffering, they were dismembering her . . . this dying flesh is all that remained." Rather than being the residue of obscure and undeveloped times, Catarina's condition was part of a regularity, forged in all the public spaces and hazy interactions in which a rapidly changing country, family, and medicine met.

The ethnography of Vita makes it painfully clear that there are places in the present, even in a state founded on the premise of inviolable human rights, where these rights no longer exist, where the living subjects of marginal institutions are constituted as something other, beings between life and death. Such places demonstrate that notions of universal human rights are socially and materially conditioned by medical and economic imperatives. Vita also reveals the extent to which a certain kind of human-rights discourse—the sort that generates "model programs" in restructuring states and economies—in practice works by a logic of exclusions; and it confirms that public death remains at the center of various social structures, animating and legitimating charity, political actors, medical ethics, and various domestic strategies.

In her thinking and writing, Catarina reworks this literality that creates her sense of exclusion. She discovers her subjectivity in relation to this tinkering and by making herself heard in a place where silence is the rule.

"I am not a pharmacist," Catarina once told me. "I cannot say which medication heals an illness, I cannot say the name of the pharmakon, but the name of my illness I know . . . How to say it?"

Silence.

She then said: "Mine is an illness of time."

"What do you mean?"

"Time has no cure."

NOTES

I want to express my deepest gratitude to the people of Vita, especially Catarina, for allowing me to spend time with them. I also want to thank Adriana Petryna, Laura B. Jardim, Torben Eskerod, and Robert Kimball for their support and Princeton University's Committee on Research in the Humanities and Social Sciences for funding part of this study. I have changed the names of people and institutions to protect their anonymity (unless requested otherwise).

1. Scholars of contemporary Brazil argue that the dramatic rise in urban violence and the partial privatization of security and health care have deepened divisions between the marketable and the socially excluded (Caldeira 2000; Escorel 1999; Fonseca 2002; Goldstein 2003; Hecht 1998; Ribeiro 2000). All the while, newly mobilized patient groups continue to demand that the state fulfill its biopolitical obligations (Biehl 2006). As economic indebtedness, ever present, transforms communities and revives paternalistic politics (Raffles 2002), larger segments of the population articulate citizenship in the sphere of consumer culture (Edmonds 2002; O'Dougherty 2002). Overburdened families are suffused with the materials, patterns, and paradoxes of these processes, which they by and large, must negotiate on their own.

See Nancy Scheper-Hughes's (2001) study of how shifting domestic economies affected family ties and mental illness in rural Ireland in the 1970s. See Luiz Fernando Dias Duarte 1986 for an analysis of "nervousness" among the urban poor in Brazil.

For a critical review of current social policies developed by the Brazilian state, see Fiori 2001 and Lamounier and Figueiredo 2002. Also see Hoffman and Centeno's (2003) review of persistent inequality in Latin America.

2. In the early 1990s, anthropologists began to follow the production of new bioscientific knowledge and the making of biotechnologies, inquiring into their multiple deployments and their interactions with old and new forms of power relations and ethical models (Rabinow 1999; Rapp 1999; Strathern 1992). Paul Rabinow (1996), for example, notes a dissolution of the traditional social domain and the emergence of new forms of identity and moral reasoning in light of the technical possibility of literally remodeling life (a phenomenon he calls "biosociality"). The recent work of anthropologists Veena Das (1997, 2000), Arthur Kleinman (1999), Allan Young (1995), Nancy Scheper-Hughes (2000), Margaret Lock (2002), Lawrence Cohen (1998), and Adriana Petryna (2002), among others, shows how medical and technical interventions affect—sometimes for better, sometimes for worse—the etiology, experience, and course of disease. The appearance and distribution of disorders such as drug-resistant tuberculosis and AIDS also correlate closely with poverty and social and technological inequality. These disorders are "pathologies of power" (Farmer 2003) mediated by biological, social, and technical and political-economic mechanisms. Concrete biological phenomena are thus intertwined with environmental conditions that are part of a larger context. On disability and citizenship, see Das and Addlakha 2001.

3. As George Marcus points out, "Life histories reveal juxtapositions of social contexts through a succession of narrated individual experiences that may be obscured in the structural study of processes as such" (1998: 94; see also Fischer 1991,

2003; Mattingly 1998). See Behar 1993; Crapanzano 1980; Das 2000; Desjarlais 2003; Goldstein 2003; Pandolfo 1998; Panourgiá 1995; and Shostak 1981.

Ochs and Capps (1996) review the expansive literature relating notions of the self to practices of narration, and Good (1994), Desjarlais (1994), and Chatterji (1998) discuss how far such ideas can go in interpreting the lives and words of the mentally ill; Scheper-Hughes and Lock (1987) expand on the "mindful body." On embodiment, see Csordas 1994, and on care and belonging, see Borneman 2001.

4. In dealing with psychosis, Jacques Lacan (1977: 216) urged psychiatrists and psychoanalysts to halt diagnosis and question their own trust in an order of reality; he also let patients define their own terms. See also Corin 1998; Corin and Padmavati 2003.

Ian Hacking has identified scientific and technical dynamics that mediate among processes by which "people are made up" (1990: 3; see also Hacking 1999).

For the broader literature on antipsychiatry debates and movements, see Laing 1967 and Scheper-Hughes and Lovell 1987. For interpretations of psychiatry and psychology in the United States and Western Europe, see Goffman 1961, Luhrman 2000, and Rose 1998, 2001; and for interpretations in Brazil, see Costa 1976. On new taxonomies of mental illness and psychopharmaceuticals and their clinical and politicoeconomic imbrications, see Young 1995, Cohen 1998, and Healy 1999. On the braiding of imaging technologies with new regimes of personhood, see Dumit 2004.

SOURCES

Behar, Ruth. 1993. Translated Woman: Crossing the Border with Esperanza's Story. Boston: Beacon Press.

Biehl, João. 2001. "Vita: Life in a Zone of Social Abandonment." *Social Text* 19 (3): 131–49.

———. 2005. *Vita: Life in a Zone of Social Abandonment.* Berkeley: University of California Press.

———. 2006. Pharmaceutical Governance. In *Global Pharmaceuticals: Ethics, Markets, Practices,* ed. Adriana Petryna, Andrew Lakoff, and Arthur Kleinman (Durham, NC: Duke University Press).

Borneman, John. 2001. "Caring and Being Cared For: Displacing Marriage, Kinship, Gender, and Sexuality." In *The Ethics of Kinship: Ethnographic Inquiries,* ed. James Faubion (New York: Rowman and Littlefield), 29–45.

Boutté, Marie I. 1990. "Waiting for the Family Legacy: The Experience of Being at Risk for Machado-Joseph Disease." *Social Science and Medicine* 30 (8): 839–47.

Caldeira, Teresa. 2000. *City of Walls: Crime, Segregation, and Citizenship in São Paulo.* Berkeley: University of California Press.

Chatterji, Roma. 1998. "An Ethnography of Dementia: A Case Study of an Alzheimer's Disease Patient in the Netherlands." *Culture, Medicine and Psychiatry* 22 (3): 355–82.

Cohen, Lawrence. 1998. *No Aging in India: Alzheimer's, the Bad Family, and Other Modern Things.* Berkeley: University of California Press.

Corin, Ellen. 1998. "The Thickness of Being: Intentional Worlds, Strategies of Identity, and Experience among Schizophrenics." *Psychiatry* 61 (2): 133–46.

Corin, Ellen, R. Thara, and R. Padmavati. 2003. "Living through a Staggering World: The Play of Signifiers in Early Psychosis in South India." In *Schizophrenia, Cul-*

ture, and Subjectivity: The Edge of Experience, ed. Janis Hunter Jenkins and Robert John Barrett (Cambridge: Cambridge University Press), 110–44.

Costa, Jurandir Freire. 1976. *História da psiquiatria no Brasil: Um corte ideológico.* Rio de Janeiro: Editora Documentário.

Coutinho, Paula. 1996. "Aspectos clínicos, história natural e epidemiologia na doença de Machado-Joseph." In *O teste preditivo da doença de Machado-Joseph*, ed. Jorge Sequeiros (Porto: UnIGene), 15–22.

Crapanzano, Vincent. 1980. *Tuhami: Portrait of a Moroccan.* Chicago: University of Chicago Press.

Csordas, Thomas. 1994. *Embodiment and Experience.* London: Cambridge University Press.

Das, Veena. 1997. "Language and Body: Transactions in the Construction of Pain." In *Social Suffering*, ed. Arthur Kleinman, Veena Das, and Margaret Lock (Berkeley: University of California Press), 67–91.

———. 2000. "The Act of Witnessing: Violence, Poisonous Knowledge, and Subjectivity." In *Violence and Subjectivity*, ed. Veena Das, Arthur Kleinman, Mamphela Ramphele, and Pamela Reynolds (Berkeley: University of California Press), 205–55.

Das, Veena, and Renu Addlakha. 2001. "Disability and Domestic Citizenship: Voice, Gender, and the Making of the Subject." *Public Culture* 13 (13): 511–31.

Das, Veena, and Arthur Kleinman. 2001. Introduction. In *Remaking a World: Violence, Social Suffering, and Recovery*, ed. Veena Das, Arthur Kleinman, Margaret Lock, Mamphela Ramphele, and Pamela Reynolds (Berkeley: University of California Press), 1–30.

Desjarlais, Robert. 1994. "Struggling Along: The Possibilities for Experience among the Homeless Mentally Ill." *American Anthropologist* 96 (4): 886–901.

———. 2003. *Sensory Biographies: Lives and Deaths among Nepal's Yolmo Buddhists.* Berkeley: University of California Press.

Duarte, Luiz Fernando Dias. 1986. *Da vida nervosa nas classes trabalhadoras urbanas.* Rio de Janeiro: Jorge Zahar.

Dumit, Joseph. 2004. *Picturing Personhood: Brain Scans and Biomedical Identity.* Princeton: Princeton University Press.

Edmonds, Alexander. 2002. "New Bodies, New Markets: An Ethnography of Brazil's Beauty Industry." PhD diss., Department of Anthropology, Princeton University.

Escorel, Sarah. 1999. *Vidas ao léu: Trajetórias de exclusão social.* Rio de Janeiro: Editora da Fiocruz.

Farmer, Paul. 2003. *Pathologies of Power: Health, Human Rights, and the War on the Poor.* Berkeley: University of California Press.

Fiori, José Luís. 2001. *O Brasil no espaço.* Petrópolis: Editora Vozes.

Fischer, Michael M. J. 1991. "The Uses of Life Histories." *Anthropology and Humanism Quarterly* 16 (1): 24–27.

———. 2003. *Emergent Forms of Life and the Anthropological Voice.* Durham, NC: Duke University Press.

Fonseca, Claudia. 2002. "Anthropological Perspectives on Problematic Youth." *Reviews in Anthropology* 31(4): 351–68.

Goffman, Erving. 1961. *Asylums: Essays on the Social Situation of Mental Patients and Other Inmates.* Garden City, NY: Doubleday.

Goldstein, Donna M. 2003. *Laughter Out of Place: Race, Class, Violence, and Sexuality in a Rio Shantytown.* Berkeley: University of California Press.

Good, Byron. 1994. *Medicine, Rationality, and Experience*. Cambridge: Cambridge University Press.

———. 2001. "Le sujet de la maladie mentale: Psychose, folie furieuse et subjectivite en Indonesia." In *La pathologie mentale en mutation: Psychiatrie et société*, ed. Alain Ehrenberg and Anne M. Lovell (Paris: Edition Odile Jacob), 163–95.

Hacking, Ian. 1990. *The Taming of Chance*. Cambridge: Cambridge University Press.

———. 1999. "Making Up People." In *The Science Studies Reader*, ed. Mario Biagioli (New York: Routledge), 160–75.

Healy, David. 1999. *The Antidepressant Era*. Cambridge, MA: Harvard University Press.

Hecht, Tobias. 1998. *At Home in the Street: Street Children of Northeast Brazil*. Cambridge: Cambridge University Press.

Hoffman, Kelly, and Miguel Angel Centeno. 2003. "The Lopsided Continent: Inequality in Latin America." *Annual Review of Sociology* 29: 363–90.

Ignatieff, Michael. 2001. *Human Rights as Politics and Idolatry*. Princeton: Princeton University Press.

Jardim, Laura B. 2000. "Aspectos clínicos e moleculares da doença de Machado-Joseph no Rio Grande do Sul: Sua relação com as outras ataxias espinocerebelares autossômicas dominantes e uma hipótese sobre seus fatores modificadores." PhD diss., Programa de Pós-Graduação em Medicina: Clínica Médica, Universidade Federal do Rio Grande do Sul.

Jardim, L. B., M. L. Pereira, I. Silviera, A. Ferro, J. Sequeiros, and R. Giugliani. 2001a. "Machado-Joseph Disease in South Brazil: Clinical and Molecular Characterizations of Kindreds." *Acta Neurologica Scandinavica* 104 (4): 224–31.

———. 2001b. "Neurological Findings in Machado-Joseph." *Archives of Neurology* 58 (6): 899–904.

Jenkins, Janis Hunter, and Robert John Barrett, eds. 2003. *Schizophrenia, Culture, and Subjectivity: The Edge of Experience*. Cambridge: Cambridge University Press.

Kleinman, Arthur. 1988. *The Illness Narratives: Suffering, Healing and the Human Condition*. New York: Basic Books.

———. 1999. *Experience and Its Moral Modes: Culture, Human Conditions, and Disorder*. The Tanner Lectures on Human Values. Salt Lake City: University of Utah Press.

Lacan, Jacques. 1977. "On a Question Preliminary to Any Possible Treatment of Psychosis." In *Écrits: A Selection* (New York: W. W. Norton), 179–225.

Laing, R. D. 1967. *The Politics of Experience*. New York: Ballantine Books.

Lamounier, Bolívar, and Rubens Figueiredo, eds. 2000. *A era FHC: Um balanço*. São Paulo: Cultura Editora Associados.

Luhrman, Tanya. 2000. *Of Two Minds: The Growing Disorder in American Psychiatry*. New York: Alfred A. Knopf.

Marcus, George E. 1998. *Ethnography through Thick and Thin*. Princeton, NJ: Princeton University Press.

Mattingly, Cheryl. 1998. *Healing Dramas and Clinical Plots: The Narrative Structure of Experience*. Cambridge: Cambridge University Press.

Ochs, Elinor, and Lisa Capps. 1996. "Narrating the Self." *Annual Review of Anthropology* 25: 19–43.

O'Dougherty, Maureen. 2002. *Consumption Intensified: The Politics of Middle-Class Daily Life in Brazil.* Durham, NC: Duke University Press.

Paley, Julia. 2001. *Marketing Democracy: Power and Social Movements in Post-Dictatorship Chile.* Berkeley: University of California Press.

Pandolfo, Stefania. 1998. *Impasse of the Angels: Scenes from a Moroccan Space of Memory.* Chicago: University of Chicago Press.

Panourgiá, Neni. 1995. *Fragments of Death, Fables of Identity: An Athenian Anthropography.* Madison: University of Wisconsin Press.

Petryna, Adriana. 2002. *Life Exposed: Biological Citizens after Chernobyl.* Princeton, NJ: Princeton University Press.

Rabinow, Paul. 1996. *Essays on the Anthropology of Reason.* Princeton, NJ: Princeton University Press.

———. 1999. *French DNA: Trouble in Purgatory.* Chicago: University of Chicago Press.

———. 2003. *Anthropos Today: Reflections on Modern Equipment.* Princeton, NJ: Princeton University Press.

Raffles, Hugh. 2002. *In Amazonia: A Natural History.* Princeton, NJ: Princeton University Press.

Rapp, Rayna. 1999. *Testing Women, Testing the Fetus: The Social Impact of Amniocentesis in America.* New York: Routledge.

Ribeiro, Renato Janine. 2000. *A sociedade contra o social: O alto custo da vida pública no Brasil.* São Paulo: Companhia das Letras.

Rose, Nikolas. 1998. *Inventing Ourselves: Psychology, Power and Personhood.* Cambridge: Cambridge University Press.

———. 2001 "Society, Madness and Control." In *The Care of the Mentally Disordered Offender in the Community,* ed. Alec Buchanan (Oxford: Oxford University Press), 3–25.

Scheper-Hughes, Nancy. 1992. *Death without Weeping: The Violence of Everyday Life in Brazil.* Berkeley: University of California Press.

———. 2000. "The Global Traffic in Human Organs." *Current Anthropology* 41 (2): 191–211.

———. 2001. *Saints, Scholars, and Schizophrenics: Mental Illness in Rural Ireland.* Berkeley: University of California Press.

Scheper-Hughes, Nancy, and Margaret Lock. 1987. "The Mindful Body: A Prolegomenon to Future Work in Medical Anthropology." *Medical Anthropology Quarterly* 1(1): 6–41.

Scheper-Hughes, Nancy, and Anne M. Lovell, eds. 1987. *Psychiatry Inside Out: Selected Writings of Franco Basaglia.* New York: Columbia University Press.

Sequeiros, Jorge, ed. 1996. *O teste preditivo da doença de Machado-Joseph.* Porto: UnIGene.

Shostak, Marjorie. 1981. *Nisa: The Life and Words of a !Kung Woman.* Cambridge, MA: Harvard University Press.

Strathern, Marilyn. 1992. *Reproducing the Future: Anthropology, Kinship, and the New Reproductive Technologies.* New York: Routledge.

Young, Allan. 1995. *The Harmony of Illusions: Inventing Post-Traumatic Stress Disorder.* Princeton, NJ: Princeton University Press.

Epilogue:
To Live with What Would
Otherwise Be Unendurable

Return(s) to Subjectivities

MICHAEL M. J. FISCHER

We have to manage to fold the line and establish an endurable
zone in which to install ourselves, confront things, take hold,
breathe—in short, think . . . to live with what would otherwise be
unendurable.
—Gilles Deleuze (1990/1995: 111, 113).

INTRODUCTION:
FORGET DESCARTES, WATCH MAKHMALBAF

What are the returns to subjectivities today—the interest payments in subjectivity; the stocks and bonds (and modalities or paths) of returns to constructions of, or subjectivations of, the feeling or cognitive self or plural
selves; the payoffs and paybacks for excavating or reconstructing painful illusions, the occulted or hidden injuries of fantasy, the erotic charges and
their penal codes (or intensities of identification and their prosecutory/per-
secutory charges), the centaurian or chimera terrors of war and politics?[1]

The implications, exchanges, and transductions of these returns play out
in four registers:

The *political subject* of moral sentiment or public solidarity:
Durkheim's conscience collective, Weber's legitimate domination,
Gramsci's hegemonic order, Marx's universalization of a ruling frac-
tion's or a state's ideology, or most generally, the subject position of
citizenship (moving from subject of a feudal lord to assertion of personal responsibility and agency in a political community).

Psychological subjectivity (self, selves) and private ethics: family-peer
self-constructions (distorted by conditions of insecurity and violence
or by security and cluelessness about the insecurity of others whose

423

lives condition one's own); selves constructed as continuous, coherent, and whole; or selves experienced as fractured shards, either in pain or in pleasure because they need not be maintained as sutured wholes.

The *linguistic subject:* the split enunciative and grammatical functions—that is, most simply and obviously, the differences between the subject of enunciation (the I who speaks), the grammatical subject of a statement or sentence, and the deictic physical body of a speaker. In Lacanian-Freudian notation, the subject, S (homophone of Freud's *das Es* and the shape of a Möbius strip), is a split or barred S ($\mathcal{S}\frac{s}{s}$), the splits being between the symbolic order (the subject is a subject only by virtue of subjection to the linguistic-symbolic order, Freud's *das Uber-Ich*, or superego), the imaginary-enunciative order of the ego (Freud's *das Ich*), and the order of the real, with its fleshy substrate and independent order of memory and response.[2]

And thus the tremulous *biological subject*, the body's organism; the carnal, nervous, vascular, mucal, and immunological substrate with its reflexes, responses, cascades of chain reactions, transmissions, parasites, symbiants, sensate folds where the body feels itself (the "reversible flesh of Merleau-Ponty); expressions of the body's training and injuries as well as its genetic, cellular, and muscle memories and mutations; "orchestration" of Lyotard's (1993 [1974]: 73) "semiotic of intensities," which "always involve an amnesia."[3]

In our high-velocity age of circulating media images, phrases, sentiments—outrage, calls to action, laments, catalogues and archives that place suffering elsewhere—suffering, witnessing, and testimonies are increasingly split modalities within each of these registers. Suffering is discounted (revalued) by political geopolitics, indirect chains of agency, and emotive enunciation that has subjective, but little objective (predicate, judicial, evidentiary), weight. Subjectivities, thus, for the anthropologist, are raucous *terrae incognitae*, landscapes of explosions, noise, alienating silences, disconnects and dissociations, fears, terror machineries, pleasure principles, illusions, fantasies, displacements, and secondary revisions, mixed with reason, rationalizations, and paralogics—all of which have powerful sociopolitical dimensions and effects. This feedback between the linguistic, personal, sociopolitical, and biological—which allows nothing to be taken at face value or at first sight—is becoming a foregrounded anthropological terrain. Moreover, this terrain is no longer on the margins of civilization: in the realm of the wild man and the shaman (Taussig 1986), the medusa's hair of ecstatic priests (Obeyesekere 1981), the healing *zar* cults of the Persian Gulf for hysterical conversion reactions brought on sometimes by the terrors of deep pearl diving (Sa'edi 1966), and the singularities of those who escaped the ethnic cleansing of Armenians (Archile Gorky) or the extermination camps of the Nazis (Primo Levi). Today, with sadness and confusion, we can add to the list the widening circles of the disappeared in Argentina and Central America; the holocausts of Cambodia, Rwanda, and the former Yugoslavia; the Palestine-Israel feud; and the AIDS epidemics around the world, each with its distinctive nightmare reality and its oft-historical ghosts, such as the Black Plague (Camus 1947/1948), preventable famines in India (Davis 2001), and ethnicized conflicts such as partition and communal riots of the Indian subcontinent and Africa (Das 2000, 2001; Werbner 1991).

Our high-technology age, however, is not just one of circulating media, but also one of turning the body—that other, fleshy substrate of subjectivity—into data, so that identity becomes deconstructed bits, pointers to databases, and parts of multiple modules with independent functions and purposes. With subjectivity as a (re)constructed platform for individual, social, and civic selves, the returns to subjectivity might be guarantors of privacy, ethical and social responsibility, and monitoring of integrity (of the body, accountability, civic community). These returns will not require subjectivity to be located only within the body, but it must be there in some degree. Anthropology has long recognized changing historical and cultural subjectivities, so we might conceive of today's continuing changes under conditions of technological doubles, prostheses, and proxies as simply one more set of changes, not fundamental changes in kind, though they might be changes in the quality of social solidarity, allowing (in Durkheimian language) increasing organic solidarity, increasing individuation, and yet a means of countering the alienations of nineteenth- and twentieth-century industrial societies. As Marx long ago recognized, this transformation, with its psychological rewards, cannot happen as a technological fix but must happen as a change in political consciousness, social organizations, and (to use Sartre's language) ongoing, continually self-renewing *projects*. Such visions become urgent in the early twenty-first-century redefinition of world geopolitics, in the aftermath of September 11, 2001, with the Bush administration's violent responses to nonstate terrorism and the institution of new domestic monitoring and disciplining technologies (thereby also recontextualizing the correlates around the world in societies that are more—and less—used to both terrorism and monitoring).[4]

What, then, are the returns to subjectivities at work today? How can the construction of new subjects, subjectivities, and communities of enunciation (Fortun 2001) contribute to the calls for new ethics and politics and allow us to chart paths across the slippery slopes of unforeseeable consequences of action?

We begin with dreamwork, mirror stage, *infans,* prespeech, preanalysis. In the middle passages, we find cracks in the mirror, intensities of reversible flesh, where "figure dwells in discourse like a phantasm while discourse dwells in the figure like a dream" (Lyotard 1989: 33). The descent ends in a *retournement,* a looking back and return to the topic of death and life, deep play, ethical plateaus in technological worlds, emergent forms of life, and the voice of an anthropology to come.

SUFFERING AS *ENFANS*, MIRROR STAGE, AND MUTE DREAMS

To take some patients/patience—both people and the care they call forth derive from the Latin "to suffer"—let us begin with two "mute dreams" that are diagnostic of the contemporary condition, engaging the puzzles of emerging forms of life in the twenty-first century, lifeworlds and their deep plays, and crossed technosciences and their ethical plateaus. The idiom in Persian for the state of awakening after a dream, when one is still bewildered but beginning to decipher the images, is *gonge xab dideh.* It is an idiom used explicitly by Mohsen Makhmalbaf, one of Iran's leading film directors—and indirectly by Abbas Kiarostami, another of Iran's major film directors—in describing how his films should work. The idiom also has an older prophetic resonance: *man gonge khab dide o alam tamam kat. Man ajez-am ze goftan-o khalq shenidanash* ("I saw a dream, a vision; I was struck mute, and the world was deaf; I am incapable of saying fully what I saw, and the world is incapable of hearing [the divine message]").

The first of these two mute dreams, *Gav ("The Cow"),* was the first New Wave Iranian film made before the Islamic revolution of 1977–79. Made by Dariush Mehrjui and Gholam Hossein Sa'edi, the film may stand for the traditional networks of subjectivities, projections, and fears. The second film, *Arusi Khuban ("Blessed Marriage"),* made after the revolution by Mohsen Makhmalbaf, may stand for the contemporary entry into photographic, cinematic, and successor mediations of distributed knowledges, emergent cyborgian subjectivities, and above all, traumas—which we already know to be repetitions and which therefore call for more than simple direct response to individual instances of suffering, requiring an intervention to break out of the larger structures and forces of repetition.

Mute Dream 1: Gav, *Grief and Mourning under Conditions of Political Repression*

Awaiting the revolution in 1969, an archetypal village, filmed in black and white, struggles to figure out how to deal with the bereavement of Mashd Hassan. Whether the death of his cow is due to the evil eye (something social and internal to the village), a snake (external natural causes), or to outsiders (external social causes) is unclear. Many clues exist, but all are ambiguous. The surreal oneiric-filmic images mimic the logic of emotion, turning Mashd Hassan into his cow. Overprotective of his cow, to the amusement of his fellow villagers, Mashd Hassan returns from an errand one day to find the cow dead. He goes into denial and then begins to bellow and rush about like a cow, eat at the fodder stall, and insist that he is the cow of Mashd Hassan. Such is the stuff of possession and insanity. Mashd Hassan becomes a cow—not one with four feet and a tail but one whose visage, behavior, and articulation take on bovine features; he is a portrait of grief gone awry. The loss of a cow is a serious matter in a poor village, and one can understand on the most literal level the obsession of Mashd Hassan: the cow is his existence, his essence. The outside threatening figures represent real danger but also the shadows of paranoia, the excessive fears that build up and help trigger his displaced grief. Around his grief, the village rhythm alternates with funerals and weddings, suggesting not only that life goes on but that healthy life has ways of dealing with tragedy, death, and sadness. The villagers attempt to channel Mashd Hassan's grief and hope at the end that the town doctor can help transform his denial and displacement into mature, realistic sadness. Sadness is not merely an appropriate feeling of loss but a central philosophical attitude, instilled through childhood teasing, cultivated through poetry as a companion to the soul, and elaborated in religion through *hadith* prayer and *rawza* (sermons and mourning ceremonies). Sadness is associated with depth of understanding, thoughtfulness, awareness of the nature of reality, and the cultivation of stoicism, patience, and inner strength; this strength can also translate into political determination and a willingness to sacrifice against the forces of social injustice.

Where is subjectivity in this dream world? Is it in Mashd Hasan's visceral identifications? In the viewers' commentaries (the villagers in the film or the urban viewers of the film)? In a phenomenological suspension of disbelief *(epoche)* in order to tease out the cultural values (stoicism, patience, gravitas)? In the filmmakers' "conscious intentional objects" (their *eidos*, or "essence")? In the cultural logic, the *langue* of the images? In, as Byron Good says in chapter 8 of this volume, the "unspoken, unspeakable, and the repressed, in a language of hierarchy and respect, discipline, order, and consensus . . . a terror, a modest anxiety seeping into awareness that there might be a secret, but the guardians of these secrets, the censors, have ensured that the secret not be noticed, acknowledged, made real"? What is the relation between political or structural violence and psychic running *amuk* (a precolonial martial term and a colonial psychiatric one)? What is the role of circulations of ninja killers (silent blows and knife thrusts), and other fantastic codings of real-world events, structures, and effects (see also Aretxaga 1997; Rouch 1957; Siegel 1997, 1998; Werbner 1991; White 2000)?

Fear of the father, the political allegory, was inescapable in 1969 Iran as the country awaited the revolution. The psychiatrist and story and scriptwriter, Gholam Hossein Sa'edi, was also an ethnographer of the *zar* possession cults of the Persian Gulf, a healing ritual that could deal with hysterical conversion reactions that paralyze parts of the body, grounded in and displaced by the traumas of pearl diving. The *zar* procedures appeal to the "people of the air" and deploy Islamically transgressive (blood-drinking), sensation-altering (percussive drumming, hyperventilation), and socially transformative ritual processes (isolation, insertion into new dietary and social-support networks). Trauma, fear, occupational stress, political and psychosocial repression, counter forces that favor the cultivation of social bonds, psychophilosophical mental states, religious and life-cycle rituals, care of the self and other—all these parts of the network remain knotted (and full of holes); we remain as mystified as the villagers. This mute dream has an economy not unlike that in the repetition dreams that Žižek (1991) analyzes as displayed in Zeno's paradoxes. (See also chapter 10 in this volume for a parallel conundrum that explains hoarding and scavenging variously as symptoms of mental illness, psychological responses to deprivation, neurological conditions to be treated with medication, and survival skills, mutual aid, and reconstructed morality.)

The network remains knotted and full of holes: the nets here are still those of fishermen, a mechanical model, not yet the electromagnetic one of copper, fiber optic, or wireless Net, icons of distributed knowledges and information, and of emergent cyborgian subjectivities. Do they differ, these two notions of network, do they support different ranges of subjectivities? Is cinema, as Virilio (1984/1989) once argued, a technology of mass derangement, marking populations for war and dislocation?

Mute Dream 2: Arusi Khuban, *Shell Shock and the Effects of Revolution and War*

1988, Khuzistan, a mental ward for the shell-shocked. A war photographer, Haji, is having flashbacks. His eyes open and shutter like a camera; images jump-cut between battlefront and ward, past and present, aspiration and corruption, photo and film, flux and iconic afterimage. Physically, the doctor says, nothing is wrong with Haji, a simple leg injury. The problems are psychosomatic. Medicine can do nothing: best to put him back to work, get him married and involved with family and community. Iatrogenic common sense: the photographer's work and the home front, not just the battlefront, are the causes of the photographer's problems. Many viewers received the documentation of urban social problems by the photographer and his fiancée as a courageous protest against the failures of the revolution to solve social inequities. Even more boldly, the film was seen as a protest against Ayatollah Ruhullah Khomeini's cease-fire with Iraq, which, people said, made a mockery of the idealistic sacrifice of a generation of youths. The cease-fire confirmed the young men's status as both disposable on the front and unassimilable in the cities at home. Makhmalbaf dedicated the film to the Baseej, the cannon-fodder troops of village boys indoctrinated into becoming martyrs and used to cross minefields and overrun mortar positions, resulting in the kinds of casualties not seen since World War I.

Are the subjectivities of this film deranged by the technologies at play? Does the film capture the temporalities of Iran in the 1980s as out of joint, caught between the technologies of World War I and those of the Gulf, Afghan, and Iraq wars to come? Operating palimpsest fashion with a cinematic mystic writing pad, thematizing photography that does not allow us to forget, the filmmaker delivers derangement as shell shock, not as the more recent post-traumatic stress disorder that Americans began to use as an elastic and omnipresent category after the Vietnam War (see chapter 6, by Allan Young, in this volume). The tactics of the Iran-Iraq war have often been compared to those of World War I, and the pressure explosions of the shells created the disorientation that Makhmalbaf, in interviews, has explicitly named.

In the hospital, in a locked ward with a bedlam of patients, technologies clash. One man wears a round tin on his head and calls in air support: "Send angels!" Screaming patients are injected with sedatives. Tanks and infantry appear along a ridge, and airplanes appear overhead. The tiny figure of the photographer points his camera upward at the planes as bombs drop. The picture is knocked askew. We see, on an angle, tanks, wounded bodies, a man stumbling and falling. A hand is on the photographer's face; he caresses it as comfort, then sees it is a severed hand. An armless man writhes nearby. Repeat; shutter clicks; open and shut, open and shut.

This scene is, of course, also a Freudian image from World War I, and one of his examples of the uncanny: encounters with "dismembered limbs, a severed head, a hand cut off at the wrist" (Freud 1925). Nightmares repeat. Early twentieth-century scenes repeat in the late twentieth century. Modernities jostle to catch up, mutate, and find alternative intensities and channels. Time's out of joint. Haji and his fiancée do their urban photography from the back of a motorcycle, undertaking an exercise in exposé: comparing past and present to counter the claims of progress and exposing poverty, inequality, and injustice as processes of demodernization.

As Haji points the camera, he often sees pictures of the past. As he takes a picture of two Baseej, one now crippled, the shutter clicks; we see the two men as healthy and young on the front. As the soundtrack slows (past tense), the photographer sees demonstrators with posters of Dr. Ali Shariati and Mortaza Motahheri; when he looks again through the viewfinder in the present, the same streets are empty of political activism. Taking a picture of his father-in-law-to-be and his business partner holding tea glasses, he sees them through the viewfinder before the revolution, drinking *arak*. The bourgeois father-in-law hopes that giving a daughter to a revolutionary idealist will curry favor with the new regime, and he worries that she is marrying someone who will not be able to support her as she has been raised; however, he soon learns that his son-in-law's sanity might be the more important issue. Or rather, determining what is sane, moral, just, or right is the larger issue.

The photographer's fiancée takes him into the darkroom to help him therapeutically "review our memories." She removes his war photos from the walls and directs his attention to pictures of their childhood to encourage him to forget the war. But when he sees a photograph of his mother, he says, "Did you have to remind me that my mother is a laundress?" She tries to get him to think about their marriage: "When did you ask for my hand?" He replies defensively, "My memory is all right, are you testing it?" She turns on a film projector: a scene of chadored women in a classroom studying. She reminds him that he had brought the film to her as a gift, then tries to turn off the projector just as it begins to show starving children in Ethiopia. He turns it back on: the films are ones he did of drought in Africa, the massacre of Palestinians at Shatilla, the Iranian revolution. The images trigger war memories, and he faints. (See Val Daniel [1996] on loss of consciousness when trauma victims in Sri Lanka attempt to provide witness accounts.) He has no escape from memories and associations. She pleads, "Why must you take on the burdens of the world?" Cinema, photography, won't let us forget.

Haji relapses, is back in the mental ward. The man in the tin hat still calls in the angels for air cover, and others engage in cacophonies of mock *sineh-zani* (the ritual rhythmic chest beating to mourn the martyrdom of Imam Husain, used also to accompany chanting for the liberation of Karbala in Iraq during the war); still others hold their hands in the air in surrender. Haji escapes into the city. He sleeps like a homeless person in a vacant lot, and when a photographer snaps his picture, he sits up to shout, "Don't take my picture!" No longer a revolutionary, a photographer, or a person with identity, he is now a vagrant *(velgard)*, a spectacle observer *(tamasha-gari)*, and himself an object of photography (see also chapter 10, by Anne Lovell, in this volume).

Final shots: the sharp rat-a-tat-tat of a typewriter against a battlefield. Has the recording machine of the war correspondent turned into a machine gun that causes friendly-fire damage to fellow Iranians? The image represents the feelings of betrayal that many Baseej reported when they heard about the cease-fire. It represents the corruption of the home front, which corroded spirit and commitment on the war front. The image juxtaposes two powerful historical and ethnographic writing machines: typewriter and camera, discourse and figure. And it speaks of the photographer's delirium: the sound of the typewriters in his editor's office causing battlefield flashbacks. Aerial views appear—not the shot–reverse shot of the plane that dropped the shells that concussed our photographer on the battlefront, but a view across the domestic battlefront, across working-class south Tehran, looking up, not at the warplane, but at the wealthy high-rises of north Tehran. Here is the battlefield of the Iranian revolution, the ethical plateaus of the unevenly distributed technosciences and teletechnologies of the twenty-first century.

Cinema, like Lacan's mirror stage, provides a device for observing, feeling, or retrospectively understanding the splits of each register of subjectivity: at the end of each narrative fantasy of a coherent whole, another register appears to undo the first; the sutures that bound together the point of view of the characters, the filmmakers (cinematographers, composers, scriptwriters, directors, actors), and the viewers are pulled out. Whose "voice" is enunciating what? And what contending models of ideology, subjecthood, and citizenship are at (dis)play? Reruns, like Freud's *fort-da*, occur not only of the same film but of one film restaging, commenting upon, or arguing with another. Nor is the rationale, the dialogue, or the story necessarily the dominant force; like the body for Freud, Lacan, Lyotard, Kristeva, and Cixous, sound reminds that the images one sees are not all that is happening; sound provides, says Iranian filmmaker Kiarostami, four-fifths of the cube of sensation.

CRACKS IN THE MIRROR, REVERSALS OF AGE, PASSAGES OF GOVERNANCE

> Open the so-called body and spread out all its surfaces.
>
> Let me be your surface and your tissues, you may be my orifices and my palms and my membranes.
>
> But what does she want . . . the woman-orchestra? . . . that she and he, different people, be identical in the insane connections of every tissue. . . . This will that everything flare up and catch fire is called the death drive by the thinkers, of course(!), those who think only, in the name of life, of collecting, uniting, capitalizing, conquering, extending, closing up and dominating.
>
> The semiotic of intensities . . . always involves an amnesia.
> —Jean-François Lyotard (1993 [1974]: 1, 65, 66, 73)

We began with cinematic screenings, which we might characterize as "figure-images" after Lyotard. In this section, we *descend* to Lyotard's figure-form, the usually unnoticed regulating line, the *Gestalt* of shifting figure-ground—the architecture of a painting, the scenography of cinema, the underlying schemas. Philosophers lose themselves in this labyrinth, disappearing down into Descartes' pineal gland. Lyotard suggests the descent be instead to Hades, following Virgil and Dante or better yet, Orpheus, especially upon his return. Suffering, not reason, allows perspective, a point that the princely Gautama, the Buddha, made iconic (after contemplating the infirmities of age) or that the old widow in Bengali literature later dragged into view (Cohen 1998: chs. 4 and 5; also, the interlude on the Aitasa Pralapa in the *Atharva Veda*). At issue here is a reverse transcription of the pediatricentric and pedocentric versions of psychoanalysis (Freud, Lacan, Kristeva, Klein), beginning with the adult's decay, the going down, the desire for eternal return, the parental desire for care, Kristeva's hormonal maternity as much as any patriarchal order, and Lyotard's sense of a descent from phenomenology to psychoanalysis, before the returns of wisdom, sensitivity, and perspective.

One of the great terrors of old age—for those who remain "intact," as medical professionals say—is the loss of subjectivity, the awareness of the loss of memory, cognitive function, embodied capacities, places and contexts, and time and geography; in turn, one loses the ability to communicate all one would like and becomes angry about being infantilized by caretakers and family. Unlike memoryless senility or Alzheimer's, this condition is akin to various forms of displacements, aphasias, paranoias, intermittent psychoses (as Ellen Corin describes in chapter 9 in this volume), disablements due to total institutionalization, and other ills that are cracked mirrors of social disabilities in the wider world.[5] "What is illness and what is treatment" under conditions of old age—to extend Veena and Ranendra Das's discussion of conditions of poverty and labor regimes (in chapter 3 of this volume)—is a matter of ecology of care.

Aging is an asymmetric invert to *infans* (infancy, the inability to speak) that is far more complex than the crisis decision-making dilemmas of end of life (technological medicine versus palliative care). In Edmund Husserl's late work, from *The Crisis of European Sciences* (1936/1970) onward, he contrasts the concept of *Lebenswelt* with Descartes' concept that identifies the ego with disembodied soul or intellect.[6] For Husserl, the whole person engages with the biological and social world. For this reason, Merleau-Ponty turned to Husserl (and drew upon neurological and psychiatric research) rather than to Heidegger, who substituted for the subject yet another philosophical abstraction, *Dasein* (see Eric L. Krakauer's different reading of Heidegger in chapter 13 of this volume, but see Matthews [2002] on Merleau-Ponty). As we grow and age, we repeatedly learn a new body and a new nervous system, made up of both body and social-support systems and of both capacities and compensation skills.

One of the key supports of personhood and subjectivity is a community of memory, which regrounds the self and mirrors it back to itself in an individual and social refractive process. Such memory can be a psychopolitical resource for healthy survival through trauma, including the reorienting public sentiments of shame (Scheper-Hughes in chapter 7 of this volume; Malkki 1995; Warren 1993). If post-traumatic stress disorder (see Allan Young in chapter 6 of this volume) is in part a derangement of the memory systems—which is somatic, intellectual, affect-laden, ideological, and the like—how do strong survivors manage? Selective repression and a refusal to relive the past are often part of the answer, but even so, whence come the values by which survivors chart the future course?

CAN CRACKS IN THE MIRROR BE REPAIRED?
GAZA AND FAMILY THERAPY

At a conference at Tel Aviv University on June 18, 2003, Gaza psychiatrist Dr. Eyad el-Sarraj spoke of the Palestinian-Israeli struggles (reconstructed from notes taken during the talk):

> Both sides are so exhausted and frightened that it seems maybe the talks this time will hold. We don't trust [Israeli Prime Minister Ariel] Sharon or Hamas. We in Gaza are in prison. The last two and a half years, each side has seen the ugliest side of the other. Neither side recognizes that the other can live with them peacefully. Israelis just want the Palestinian problem to go away. The occupation has lasted thirty-seven years but has never been so ugly as it has been in the past two and a half years. Twenty-four percent of children under twelve dream of becoming martyrs: stone-throwing kids of the first intifada have become the suicide bombers of the second intifada. There is radicalization of women, more so than of men, and women are the carriers and motivators of the culture of a society. In the first intifada, Israelis practiced systematic humiliation of fathers: 55 percent of children witnessed the beating of their father. The identification of a boy is with the power of the father. If the power of the father is not what he can identify with, he will switch to another source of power: in games, we see boys identifying with and playing the roles of Jewish soldiers. They also show increasingly violent behavior toward other children. As they grow up, Hamas takes the role of the father. I believe in every case of a suicide bomber there is a traumatic experience that has transformed them.
>
> In the first intifada, the individual was traumatized: thrown stones were responded to with rubber bullets and the breaking of bones. In the second intifada, the community was traumatized: the noise of fighter planes, helicopters, drones, loudspeakers, breaking of the sound barrier put the population into a state of chronic panic. Any sound is first thought to be maybe an F-16, even if it turns out to be only a washing machine. I myself have to shut off my refrigerator at night in order to get some sleep. After the attempt to assassinate [Hamas leader, Dr. Abdel Aziz] Rantisi, we saw some fifteen F-16s high in the sky—but it turned out to be only a cloud moving, and then we saw stars behind. Many children do not want to go to school for fear that when they return, there will be no home or parents, especially in Rafah where there have been many house demolitions. It is the psychopathology of Israelis to be so short-sighted, a form of paranoia, and a tribal psychology of revenge, especially among women. The level of aggression and violence among Palestinians increases: many are accused of being spies for Israel, which means also that their daughters cannot marry.

The celebration of martyrs is a form of denial: we have not had any opportunity to grieve for those who died, or for loss of land. Israelis need to go through a grieving process too. The only way to build a peace movement is to have such self-insight. Why do families beat children? It is a habit, a routine, but it creates a culture of fear. The first intifada was also a situation of children's rebelling against their fathers and against all authority.

People are ready to die for country and keep their homes clean, but the streets are dirty: the streets don't belong to them, they belong to the outside (to the Israelis, before them to Jordanians, to the Greeks, to the Romans). The feeling is that public institutions do not belong to us, so it is OK to steal from the government. We are tribal: the state is always foreign and alien (including Arafat); the new jeeps and Mercedes cars of the elite are exactly like those of the Israelis. I myself was arrested three times by Arafat. The question of revenge is decided by the community: an honorable family will pursue revenge unless there is public apology and public taking of responsibility; the only honorable response then is to say yes. Public apology and public taking of responsibility would be good for Israelis, because they too would become whole and reconciled with themselves. During the first intifada, a mayor in the north of Israel said we don't want Palestinians here, and if they are to be here, they should be tattooed on the shoulder—the reaction reminds one of the Nazis. When I was in Palestinian prison, I overheard a prison interrogation: the Palestinian interrogator started screaming, and then he started screaming in Hebrew, identifying with the aggression of the oppressor. I believe in one state, all equal before the law; I believe in the right of return of Jews, who have biblical roots to the land, but I too have a right of return.

Salim Tamari, professor at Bir Zeit University and New York University, used his prerogative as chair of the session to respond, clarify, and focus some of the rough edges: "Sarraj is a mesmerizing speaker, but he essentializes as if Palestinians were all one community. Regarding public space: where civil society is strong, and where there is a tax base, the streets have become cleaner. In times of disorder, people turn inwards and protect themselves and their family. We need to rethink the concept of the state as based on territory and sovereignty. I don't think a one-state solution is the answer because it would extend the Israeli state, and mean giving up independence for Palestinians. I think we need to find a hybrid constitutional arrangement: if we guarantee mobility for Palestinians, and restitution or compensation, return will be filtered."

I offer this example not to enter into the political debate about the Palestinian-Israeli struggles but to illustrate the mobilization of psychoanalytic and psychotherapeutic discourses. El-Sarraj says that his tasks at the Gaza Community Mental Health Program—established in 1990 to treat traumatized children, battered women, and adult (male) torture victims—are to treat mental illness not as a solitary event affecting an individual but as an element within family dynamics, and to make the therapeutic setting a pedagogical site for democracy. Therapeutic sessions are, he points out, sometimes the first time that fathers learn to listen to their children. People have to be taught democracy in a context where none has existed. "Our mental health problems are the result of the political and economic situation. Our society has been dominated by extremism . . . violence has become endemic in our culture, anything else is seen as surrender. I oppose this both as an activist and a psychiatrist. [Moving away from violence] is very hard to implement because it threatens the establishment on both sides. There are many examples around the world where non-violence has been successful, like India and South Africa. We have a just cause, and I believe we can win our struggle through taking the moral high ground" (el-Sarraj 2002).

Many of the same nightmares (of schools being bombed or parents being killed while one is away at school) that afflict Palestinian children—leading to refusals to go to school and psychosomatic fevers and distress—happen also to Israeli children, a fact that el-Sarraj and his international colleagues understand. Indeed, in an unusual project to train psychotherapists for Gaza and the West Bank, el-Sarraj has helped convene a consortium with members of the Psychology Department of Tel Aviv University as well as seven other universities around the world (Tunisia, Australia, the United States, and the United Kingdom); he is also collaborating with the Department of Social Medicine at Harvard University on a study of children and violence. Joint projects between Palestinians and Israelis at the moment are fraught, sometimes amusingly, but not trivially, so.[7]

The structural, psychotherapeutic, affect-attentive approach of these psychiatrists seems more promising than short, direct, first-person testimonials, the technique of choice for so many journalists, ideologues, and propagandists on all sides. Subjectivity, perhaps, is not usefully located merely in the enunciative function, particularly where traumatized subjects can mainly articulate laments. A minor test case is to read two accounts of the April 2002 invasion of Jenin, one a collection of mainly bewildered accounts edited by Ramzy Baroud (2003), the other an account of interviews with mainly reservists who were called up from their lives, wives, and small children to perform the operation with as little loss of life to themselves and to civilians as possible (Goldberg 2003). The two accounts are hard to reconcile, except in recognizing that almost half the people on Baroud's list of the dead are acknowledged members of the armed factions of Hamas, Islamic Jihad (including its local twenty-four-year-old leader Mahmud Tawalbe), the Al-Aqsa Brigade, and the Palestinian Security Forces.[8] Readers will believe one account, not the other; neither will persuade or elicit much more than exasperation from the other side.

Documentary film has similar problems (the Palestinian *Jenin, Jenin;* the Israeli *Jenin, Massacring Truth):* editing procedures are so well recognized that few viewers who are not predisposed to the message of the filmmakers take these works at face value. The films are good for footage (though people understand that even footage can be edited and manipulated), but footage is only one informational input amid many that any researcher or seriously interested party must consider. (On one-eyed, two-eyed, and triangulated narratives in conflict situations, see Fischer 2006.)

Interestingly, in highly charged arenas, the feedback among the four registers of subjectivity—citizen subjecthood or political agency, self or personhood and subjectivity, discursive/enunciative position, and somaticized responses (each with its split or doubled nature)—is an essential part of the struggle "to authorize the real" that Veena Das recounts in chapter 3 and in Biehl's efforts to track the ethnographic sites of Catarina's poetic "dictionary" codes of her life in chapter 14. Testimony—first-person witnessing, subjective-emotional certitude—is a sine qua non but does not do the job for either mental health or social governance.[9] Indeed as Scheper-Hughes reminds us in chapter 7, many of the most politically conscious people in South Africa refused to participate in the Truth and Reconciliation Commission hearings because they refused to be considered victims. This choice does not necessarily privilege them but reminds us that more forms of agency exist than witnessing and testifying and that witnessing and testifying are themselves genre forms within hierarchies of power and adjudication. (On the indirection of ethnic-identity formation, often against the will of the speaking subject and articulated through various tactics of talk story, transference, bilingualism, ironic humor, and trying on of other identities, see Fischer 1986.)

RETOURNEMENT, DEEP PLAY, ETHICAL PLATEAUS IN A TECHNOLOGICAL WORLD, EMERGENT FORMS OF LIFE, AND THE VOICE OF AN ANTHROPOLOGY TO COME

The subject does not vanish, but returns. It returns bodily (psychosomatically) in el-Sarraj's sleep-depriving refrigerators and F-16 clouds, in Haji's grenade-exploding pomegranates and camera that cannot forget, but also through soccer and restorative *jouissance*.[10] It returns socially through Kristeva's maternal hormones, el-Sarraj's (and Barbara Harlow's [1987]) identification of women as crucial transistors of radicalization, but it also returns through self-critical communities of affiliative anecdotes and creative projects and in women's narratives of everyday life that counterpoint young men's narratives of heroic intervention (and even for some, spaces of alternative listening [Pandolfo 1997]).[11] It returns linguistically and culturally through enunciative and grammatical speech acts, not just of one-sided recognition or inclusion but also of active listening, participation, dialogue, and coproduction.

We live (again) in an era in which practitioners assert a pervasive claim, or native model, in many contemporary arenas of life (law, sciences, political economy, education, security) that traditional concepts and ways of doing things no longer work, that life is outrunning the pedagogies in which we were trained, and that we are experiencing emergent new forms of life—in cyborgian, hybrid, cross-species biotechnological forms of life; in data-bank–networked and new materials infrastructures; in environmental and ecological changes; and in the legal, economic, psychological, and social-institutional innovations that these changes require. Call this claim an ethnographic datum. None of these shifts mean that our fleshy, vascular, nervous, immunological, and psychosocial bodies have ceased playing their vital regulative, subject, subjective, and enunciative roles.

We do, however, live (again) in an era that throws up new ethical and political spaces that require action and that can have quite serious consequences, but for which the possibilities for giving grounds quickly run out. Traditional ethical and moral guides seem not always helpful, and we must often negotiate interests and trade-offs over time in legal or other decision-making tournaments and across terrains configured with multiply interacting new technologies—regions that I call ethical plateaus with due deference to Gilles Deleuze, Gregory Bateson, and the Balinese. We can call this perspective a philosophical stance toward ethics and politics, one that Ludwig Wittgenstein formulated when he said that giving grounds comes to an end somewhere and that "the end is not an ungrounded presupposition; it is an ungrounded way of acting" or a "form of life," a sociality of action that always already contains within it ethical dilemmas, or, in the idiom of Emmanuel Levinas, "the face of the other." The "face of the other" is of particular concern in the peopling of new technologies and technosciences.

We operate today under the sign of the film *Safar-e Qandahar* by the Iranian director Mohsen Makhmalbaf, and its image of Red Cross helicopters parachuting prostheses to Afghan men running on crutches to catch them. Under this sign, at least three sites of deep play intersect (deep play of overinvestments of money, power, fantasy, hope, and fear that put our existential, ethical, and social stakes at risk): the reconstruction of society in the wake of, and often under continuing conditions of, social trauma and structural violence—a move from cockfight to buzkashi, one might say; immersion in the telemedia—subjecting ourselves to the autoimmune cultural toxicities of CNN and al-Jazeera—which affects access to information, formation of public sentiments, and manipulation of the public sphere, governance, and personal subjectivities; changes in life-science institutions between the 1960s and the 1990s, which involved both profound commercialization of biological research and efforts of patient groups using the Internet and other new information-technology tools to force accountability on the scientific institutions holding the powers of what is made to live and who is let die (see also Fischer 2001a, 2001b).

Deep Play 1: From cockfight to buzkashi.[12] On September 31, 2001, General Amin Said Tariq of the Northern Alliance in Afghanistan was quoted in a *Boston Globe* headline: "It is time for the Americans to join the game." He referred to the great game of and for Central Asia, the game of buzkashi. American special forces were folkloristically photographed astride Afghan steeds playing the game. Quite apart from one's political stand on just wars or the effectiveness of global interventions, one wonders how the United States will play the buzkashi game (in Afghanistan, in Iraq, and wars to come) with smart bombs, psychopharmacological uppers for long-range flights, nanotechnologies for smart protective uniforms, smart mobile surgical rooms. More importantly, how good are the game plans for picking up the land mines and repairing destroyed schools, water systems, and battered bodies and minds. Like the cockfight in an earlier era of violence, this buzkashi focuses our attention today again on violence, bare life, and states of exception. Buzkashi is an icon for the shift from disciplinary societies to societies of control (those that depend less on territorial integrity than on statistics, flows, codes, networks, and standards, and that, when attacked, create new zones of indistinction). The disconnect between the game on horseback (dragging a carcass) and the temporary separation of the rider from his airplane cover, tanks, night-vision scopes, global positioning system, and electronic screens and audio networks is as iconic as is the parachuting of prostheses for the nongovernmental organizations and armies attempting to parachute in humanitarian band aids for political disruption and "democracy" in local struggles for power.[13] The AIDS statistics in Brazil (who is counted and who is not), repetitive AIDS testing as a psychological substrate for displaced anxieties, and the abandonment of the socially unuseful are part of this ongoing shift, in which individual testimonies can provide powerful feedback not by themselves but only in their reconnection to the structures of governance, citizenship, and social personhood (see Biehl 1999 and chapter 14 in this volume; see also Petryna [2002] on biological citizenship).

Deep Play 2: War again and the autoimmune cultural toxicities of CNN and al-Jazeera, sermons, and government double-talk. No consideration of the current condition can avoid the new fabric of interacting media, which has changed the calculus of, and conditions of possibility for, governance and legitimacy, raising questions about what democracy could possibly mean in the future and who speaks for whom in which loci or settings. In this era, all must play through the media—scientists and physicians, religious leaders and politicians—yet anthropologists, for better and worse, are far behind (running after the fact). The use of telemedia both extends and undoes the messages, propaganda, persuasions, or pedagogies that their senders or patrons intend, and the truth is not so much hidden as partially revealed in measured and calculated unveilings that blur truth and falsity—as Hannah Arendt once said, hiding truth in the open where it can be assumed to be false, contaminated, or doctored, and is so by its nature, without being any less the truth. Such is the context in which the subjectivities of enunciation (as well as reception) form in the current age.

Deep Play 3: The biopolitics of globalization. Biopolitics are again at center stage, and at the center of the new ethical and political vortices are battles over the technosciences and biotechnologies themselves. Given pharmacists' and doctors' capture by the market and advertising, with pharmaceutical companies and health insurers monitoring their prescriptions and sales reps offering them emoluments for steady or increasing prescriptions, patient support groups are having to find ways to access information, provide counterforces, and pursue therapeutic settings beyond Valium, Prozac, and lithium, often drawing upon the expertise of insiders with personal and family experiences that make them allies of other patients/sufferers. Such doublings of expertise (life and work), hauntings and hopes, and tools of poesis, praxis, and gesture mark out an anthropology to come, a justice to come, a community to come. The sport of science often has a richness, a *jouissance*, a gamble with passion, and also metaphysical depth, an agon with the mysteries of the universe and life, not just aesthetic harmony or pleasure in technical skill. Above all, the search for accountability has transformed the ways in which the institutions of science and technoscience operate. We can see this transformation as a move from big science and the national-security state to science that is accountable to multiple constituents lest the complexity of the infrastructure become brittle and break down. The ethics of science—and the representations of science in both the epistemological (accuracy, reference, completeness) and political or stakeholders' senses—are no longer marginal issues that are left to the sensibility of the researcher or expert. Across the sciences, issues of ethics are becoming matters for institutional review and are triggering efforts at transparency and negotiations between publics and researchers over the propriety of research that involves people and publics. As the world becomes more integrated and interactive, questions of how information is collected, packaged, and made available through social institutions of reflexive or second-order modernization (to use Ulrich Beck's terms) become more important and insistent. And detouring through media circuits of advertising, advocacy, and persuasion only make these issues more suspect and subject to insistent questioning.

Does a local population always have to benefit from the collection of biological data, or does room exist to presume consent to the collection of certain types of data (blood, feces, cheek swabs, genetic test results, epidemiological data, pathology samples, medical records) and to its conversion, only after considerable processing, to statistical and "evidence-based" knowledge and pharmacological and medical products? The answers to these questions are not in, but today they are central questions of public debate and political negotiation—whether they focus on Iceland's experiment to allow deCode Corporation to link data banks of medical records, genealogies, and DNA samples or the Harvard-Millennium Pharmaceuticals project in China to collect DNA samples from populations in Anhui Province—and are not easily swept under the carpet. The biosciences directly pose questions of who shall live and who shall die. Moreover, as an area of deep play, they exert pressure toward new institutions of reflexive modernization or deliberative democracy in some of the most difficult areas of human experimental trials, informed consent, privacy and surveillance, patents and ownership of biological information, and power—not just the power of money and influence but also the power of ideology and fantasy.

Mirror sites of these deep plays exist in individual decision making, often highlighting the iatrogenic counterproductivity of high-tech medicine when it attempts to replace body parts and free us from the infirmities of age beyond considerations of the good death (see chapter 13, by Eric

Krakauer, in this volume) and beyond the use of statistics to construct narratives of hope for patients and doctors, both of whom are caught in "the biomedical embrace," as Mary-Jo DelVecchio Good terms the experience in chapter 12).

These struggles require feedback between the experiential and the systematic and between civic-subject, subjectivity, and enunciatory communities. The returns to the subject cannot come through the pure will or artistic endeavor of the individual (or the semantic clarification of the philosopher). The returns to the subject come from the descent after Dante, Ovid, and Orpheus; the meditations of Buddha and the anger of the Bengali widow; and experiences of the ills of the world, misrecognitions, misdirections, and illusory identifications. The returns to the subject in the twenty-first century still map out dangerous anthropological terrain—raucous *terrae incognitae* and landscapes of explosions, noise, alienating silences, disconnects and dissociations, fears, terror machineries, pleasure principles, illusions, fantasies, displacements, and secondary revisions, mixed in with reason, rationalizations, and paralogics—all of which have powerful sociopolitical dimensions and effects. As Amélie O. Rorty acknowledges in her essay in this volume (chapter 1), and as modern anthropology has been exploring these past two decades, the subject is made through dialogue and shared expertise; it does not preexist, or as Rabinow quotes Foucault (in chapter 4 of this volume), "the we remains incessantly to be invented." The subject does not vanish, it returns; and it repays its investments in unpredictable, shifting, and slippery-slope ways, not as a homeostatic feedback system as a constellation of complexities, emergences, and surprises.

NOTES

1. On this image of the centaur, see Lyotard 1993 [1974]: 81. An interesting image of American politics at the time of the (first) Gulf War is Eric Avery's multicolor silkscreen linocut print, *Chimera, Our Father of War* (1991), in Harvard's Fogg Museum Print Collection. Modeling his print on Jean Louis Desprez's eighteenth-century etching of the multiheaded man- and animal-eating monster born in the Sahara, Avery gave his chimera or centaur of war the multiple heads of President George H. W. Bush, General Schwarzkopf, and Secretary of State James Baker. He removed the breasts and added testicles, a misslelike phallus, and the American colors on its armored back (Fischer 2000: 76).

2. On the topologies into which this first schema can unfold, ranging from entwined real-world geometries like the Möbius strip to Borromean and other forms of knot theory and Klein bottles and other forms of three-dimensional geometries that can be formally constructed in thought but not in the physical world, see Ragland and Milovanovic 2004.

3. The "feedback" among these registers tends toward a temporary and unstable, growing and decaying homeostatic system but it is perhaps more productively conceived as a complex system full of emergences, and surprises.

4. Among the newer technologies are body-temperature thermal scanners (for identifying travelers with fever that might indicate contagious disease or new virus carriers); biometric identification technologies that recognize an individual's iris, fingerprint, walking gait, or facial pattern (at Superbowl 35 in Tampa, Florida, an overhead blimp scanned faces in the crowd); DNA dragnets (in a Gainesville, Florida, murder case, authorities asked hundreds of people to donate samples and for those who refused, took surreptitious samples from fast-food cups and other utensils); radio-frequency identification chips (for tracking pets and eventually for marking every manufactured object as unique, improving on today's bar-code system); and improved technologies for linking data sets. (Biehl 1999 discusses Brazil's use of epidemiological data to support decisions about which AIDS patients would live and which ones would be allowed to die.)

5. The opening quotes that Corin cites could come just as easily from elders who complain of intermittent confusion, disorientation, inability to tell dream from reality or time of day (despite such indices as bright sunshine or darkness), a sense of panic, and so on. As Byron Good points out in chapter 8 of this volume, psychotic events can be short or long, and persons can be quite normal at other times. Often, as Veena Das (chapter 3) also points out, notions of normality and pathology are affected by, and deployed within, family dynamics. Ambiguities of labeling are critical. Corin's schizophrenics and psychotics are doubtless not normal, but how their behaviors differ from the intermittent disorientations of age and the degree to which they are affected by medications and targeted social interactions— involving memory, language, and affective cues—remains underspecified.

6. In the fifth part of his *Meditations,* Descartes advises the reader to first dissect an animal's heart and circulatory system (see the delightful reading of this notion by Barker 1995: 86–90). But as both Barker and Krakauer (in this volume) note, despite his inquiries into the physical body, Descartes subordinated it to reason and soul.

7. The psychotherapy certificate program which operated from 1993 to 1996 grew out of a symposium in Lisbon convened by the psychotherapist Maria Belo. Ten Palestinian Israeli students and ten Jewish Israeli students were selected from the West Bank and Gaza. The Palestinians from the West Bank and Gaza complained that they had only ten people in their group, whereas the Israelis had twenty; the Jewish Israelis complained they had only ten members and the Palestinians had twenty. More trenchant was the shock of the Jewish Israelis when two ten-year-old boys ("children of the stones") who had been injured by Israeli bullets were brought in and expressed hatred and defiance. The Israeli Palestinians helped defuse the tension. The project experienced difficulties when the board of the Gaza clinic proved to be troublesome, being political rather than professional.

8. Perhaps, with much work, one could make the accounts appear to describe the same event. Of course, one can get a much better understanding of the battle from the better-armed and -prepared attackers than from the defenders. According to the Baroud accounts, the defenders who died did so primarily while trying to help the injured, rather than while fighting. This version seems unlikely, and the accounts given to Goldberg describe a good deal of cross fire. With Goldberg's accounts in mind, many of the actions that seem unfathomable (in these accounts) to Palestin-

ian ambulance drivers and men asked to strip to their shorts take on rationales. That many were killed and injured, and from the Palestinian side, that many remain unaccounted for—perhaps dead, perhaps in prison—is no light matter. From the Israeli side, the admitted bomb-making efforts of Mahmud Tawalbe all over the West Bank is also no light matter. War and armed resistance are not civilized.

9. Insofar as one can believe that the Goldberg book is an honest account of how reservists and soldiers think, it reveals the still-vital core of a citizen-soldier republic that constantly debates its own actions. My own interviews with a few reservists fit this pattern, including a group interview in which the June 2003 Faculty for Israel-Palestine Peace delegation spoke with five of the five hundred refusenik reservist combat officers who are willing to serve and fight anywhere but in the Occupied Territories. In the Baroud interviews, one does not get a similar sense of the organization of Jenin or the Jenin refugee camp or of the interviewees' relations to the several armed factions, the Palestinian Authority, or their own life trajectories. Perhaps this difference simply illustrates the point, by providing a portrait of the registers of subjectivities.

10. On the edge of the village of Ara, we met with a young groom-to-be and his friends at his lovely, newly constructed house. The house is under demolition orders, and the case in court has gone through appeal and been remanded back to the local court under a different judge. The young men wanted to talk more about soccer as a means of building peace between Israeli Arabs and Jews than about their struggles over demolition and village land rights (a previous Israeli government had officially returned once-confiscated land on which the house is built, but the army and courts have so far refused to recognize this fact).

11. At a much earlier stage of the Palestinian struggle, Barbara Harlow pointed out not only that with the incarceration of so many Palestinian men, their wives were forced into the public arena as heads of households, a development that could prove to be quite revolutionary for gender roles and politics. El-Sarraj's account points not only to the radicalization of Palestinian women (mothers, wives, sisters) but also to the radicalization of Israeli women on the hard nationalist-fundamentalist right. Later in this paragraph, I take the phrase "affiliative anecdote" from Homi Bhabha (1998), meaning storytelling that uses personal enunciative positioning not to self-contain accounts but to elicit and open them to other stories from other perspectives to illuminate larger historical events, and especially to build inclusive critical communities of commentary and civil political communities. On women's counterpoint narratives, see especially Miriam Cooke (1987) on women's "decentrist" poetry and stories from the Beirut civil war.

12. On buzkashi, see Azoy 1982 for the 1980s and the second edition (2003) for the more recent period. On the cockfight, see Geertz 1972.

13. The wonderful satirical film *Secret Ballot*, written by Makhmalbaf and directed by Babak Payami, begins with the image of a ballot box dropping by parachute onto an island in the Persian Gulf. The island's illiterate, often non-Persian speakers pay as little attention as possible to Tehran and its political campaigns.

SOURCES

Aretxaga, Begoña. 1997. *Shattering Silence: Women, Nationalism, and Political Subjectivity in Northern Ireland.* Princeton, NJ: Princeton University Press.

Azoy, Whitney. 1982. *Buzkashi: Game and Power in Afghanistan.* Philadelphia: University of Pennsylvania Press. [2nd edition, 2003, Prospects Heights, IL: Waveland Press.]

Barker, Francis. 1995. *The Tremulous Private Body.* Ann Arbor: University of Michigan Press.

Baroud, Ramzy. 2003. *Searching Jenin.* Seattle: Cune Press.

Beck, Ulrich. 1992. *Risk Society: Towards a New Modernity.* London: Sage.

Bhabha, Homi. 1998. "Joking Aside: The Idea of a Self-Critical Community." In *Modernity, Culture and "the Jew,"* ed. B. Cheyette and L. Marcus (Stanford, CA: Stanford University Press).

Biehl, João. 1999. "Other Life: AIDS, Biopolitics and Subjectivity in Brazil's Zones of Social Abandonment." PhD diss., University of California, Berkeley.

Camus, Albert. 1947/1948. *The Plague.* New York: Alfred A. Knopf.

Cohen, Lawrence. 1998. *No Aging in India.* Berkeley: University of California Press.

Cooke, Miriam. 1987. *War's Other Voices: Women Writers on the Lebanese Civil War.* Cambridge: Cambridge University Press.

Daniel, E. Valentine. 1996. *Charred Lullabies: Chapters in an Anthropology of Violence.* Princeton, NJ: Princeton University Press.

Das, Veena, ed. 2000. *Violence and Subjectivity.* Berkeley: University of California Press.

———. 2001. *Remaking a World: Violence, Social Suffering, and Recovery.* Berkeley: University of California Press.

Davis, Mike. 2001. *Late Victorian Holocausts.* New York: Verso.

Deleuze, Gilles. 1990/1995. *Negotiations.* New York: Columbia University Press.

Deleuze, Gilles, and Felix Guattari. 1987. *A Thousand Plateaus: Capitalism and Schizophrenia.* Minneapolis: University of Minnesota Press.

Derrida, Jacques. 1998. "Faith and Knowledge: The Two Sources of 'Religion' at the Limits of Reason Alone." In *Religion,* ed. J. Derrida and G. Vattimo (Stanford: Stanford University Press).

Fischer, Michael M. J. 1986. "Ethnicity and the Postmodern Arts of Memory." In *Writing Culture,* ed. J. Clifford and G. Marcus (Berkeley: University of Chicago Press).

———. 2000. " 'With a Hammer, a Gouge, and a Woodblock': The Work of Art and Medicine in the Age of Social Retraumatization—the Texas Woodcut Art of Dr. Eric Avery." In *Late Editions 7: Para-Sites, a Casebook Against Cynical Reason,* ed. G. Marcus (Chicago: University of Chicago Press).

———. 2001a. "In the Science Zone: The Yanamamo and the Fight for Representation." *Anthropology Today* 17 (4): 9–14; 17 (5): 10–13.

———. 2001b. "Ethnographic Critique and Technoscientific Narratives: The Old Mole, Ethical Plateaux, and the Governance of Emergent Biosocial Polities." *Culture, Medicine and Psychiatry* 25(4): 355–93.

———. 2006. "Changing Palestine-Israel Ecologies: Narratives of Water, Land, Conflict, and Political Economy, Then, Now, and Life to Come." *Cultural Politics* 2(2): 159–92.

Fortun, Kim. 2001. *Advocacy after Bhopal: Environmentalism, Disaster, New Global Orders.* Chicago: University of Chicago Press.

Freud, Sigmund. 1925. "The Uncanny." In *The Standard Edition of the Complete Psychological Works of Sigmund Freud,* vol. 17, *An Infantile Neurosis and Other Works,* ed. and trans. James Strachey (London: Hogarth, 1953), 219–52.

Geertz, Clifford. 1972. "Deep Play: Notes on the Balinese Cockfight." *Daedalus* 101: 1–37.

Goldberg, Brett. 2003. *A Psalm in Jenin*. Tel Aviv: Modan Publishing House.

Harlow, Barbara. 1987. *Resistance Literature*. New York: Methuen.

Husserl, Edmund. 1936/1970. *The Crisis of the European Sciences and Transcendental Phenomenology*. Evanston, IL: Northwestern University Press.

Lyotard, Jean-François. 1974/1993. *Libidinal Economy*. London: Athlone.

———. 1989. "The Dream Work Does Not Think." In *The Lyotard Reader*, ed. Andrew Benjamin (Cambridge, MA: Basil Blackwell).

Malkki, Liisa H. 1995. *Purity and Exile: Violence, Memory, and National Cosmology among Hutu Refugees in Tanzania*. Chicago: University of Chicago Press.

Matthews, Eric. 2002. *The Philosophy of Merleau-Ponty*. Montreal: McGill-Queens University Press.

Obeyesekere, Gananath. 1981. *Medusa's Hair*. Chicago: University of Chicago Press.

Pandolfo, Stefania. 1997. *Impasse of the Angels: Scenes from a Moroccan Space of Memory*. Chicago: University of Chicago Press.

Petryna, Adriana. 2002. *Life Exposed: Biological Citizens after Chernobyl*. Princeton, NJ: Princeton University Press.

Ragland, Ellie, and Dragan Milovanovic, eds. 2004. *Lacan: Topologically Speaking*. New York: Other Press

Rouch, Jean, dir. 1957. *Les Maitres Fou* [videorecording]. Watertown, MA: Documentary Educational Resources.

Sa'edi, Gholam-Hossein. 1966. *Ahl-e Hava*. Tehran: Chapkhaneh-i Danishgah [1345].

———. 1973. *Gav*. (2nd printing). Tehran: Agah [1352].

Sarraj, Eyad el-. 2002. "Why We Blow Ourselves Up." *Time*, April 8, 35–42.

———. 2002. "Dignity, Despair, and the Need for Hope." *Journal of Palestine Studies* 31(4).

Siegel, James T. 1997. *Fetish, Recognition, Revolution*. Princeton: Princeton University Press.

———. 1998. *A New Criminal Type in Jakarta: Counter-Revolution Today*. Durham, NC: Duke University Press.

Taussig, Michael T. 1986. *Shamanism, Colonialism, and the Wild Man: A Study in Terror and Healing*. Chicago: University of Chicago Press.

Virilio, Paul. 1984/1989. *War and Cinema: The Logistics of Perception*. New York: Verso.

Warren, Kay. 1993. The Violence Within: Cultural and Political Opposition in Divided Nations. Boulder, CO: Westview Press.

Werbner, Richard P. 1991. *Tears of the Dead*. Washington, D.C.: Smithsonian Press.

White, Luise. 2000. *Speaking with Vampires*. Berkeley: University of California Press.

Žižek, Slavoj. 1991. *Looking Awry: An Introduction to Jacques Lacan through Popular Culture*. Cambridge, MA: MIT Press.

Index

Abu Ghraib prison, torture in, 4
Ackerman, Dawie, 195–96, 218–19
Actes and Monuments (Foxe), 145, 146
action, social, 7, 32, 104, 237, 318
Adorno, Theodor, 349–50n1, 390
advertising, 440, 441
aesthetics, 15
affect, 1, 10, 15, 29; cross-cultural differences and, 3; experience and, 52; individual experience and, 5–6; as internal and external experience, 64; social changes in China and, 54
Afghanistan, 429, 439
Africa, 301, 311n21, 321, 334, 364, 367; Belgian colonialism in, 57, 58; child soldiers in, 157; communal riots in, 425. *See also* South Africa
Afrikaans language, 190, 191, 212
Agamben, Giorgio, 11
agency, 1, 6, 10, 17, 126, 316; community and, 329; homeless persons and, 331, 335; imagination and, 42; "inner mind reading" and, 355, 356; suffering and, 424; technological change and, 356–57
"Age of the World Picture, The" (Heidegger), 385
aging process, 75, 76, 432–33, 441
Ahmad, Shoyab, 76
AIDS (Acquired Immune Deficiency Syndrome), 3, 366, 402, 425; in

Brazil, 439–40, 443n4; economic consequences of, 87; as pathology of power, 417n2
Al-Aqsa Brigade, 437
alienation, 11, 105, 226n6, 265, 358, 359
Alzheimer's disease, 325, 433
American Psychiatric Association, 64, 157, 171, 256
amnesia, 262, 268, 424, 432
amuk, running, 239, 244, 261–64
Amy Biehl Foundation, 222
ANC (African National Congress), 185, 192, 198, 202; militants tortured by security forces, 212–13, 229n15; Truth and Reconciliation Commission and, 221
Anglican Church (Church of England), 122, 143, 192, 197, 224
Angola, 157
anorexia, 325, 411
anthropology, 1, 9, 12, 425; biology and, 52–53; corporeal self and, 8–9; cultural anthropology, 45–47; culture viewed by, 7, 301; ethics of methodology and, 45–47; first- and second-order observations in, 107–8; interview process and, 108; ironists and purists, 45–46, 50n36; lived experience and, 14; media and, 440; medical, 12, 27, 66, 90, 256; memory and, 11; Otherness and,

447

Text: 10/13 Aldus
Display: Aldus
Compositor: Binghamton Valley Composition, LLC
Indexer: Alexander Trotter
Printer and binder: Thomson-Shore, Inc.